Principles of Biomedical Ethics

Principles of Biomedical Ethics

SEVENTH EDITION

Tom L. Beauchamp
Georgetown University

James F. Childress
University of Virginia

New York   Oxford

Oxford University Press

Oxford University Press is a department of the University of Oxford.
It furthers the University's objective of excellence in research,
scholarship, and education by publishing worldwide.

Oxford   New York
Auckland   Cape Town   Dar es Salaam   Hong Kong   Karachi
Kuala Lumpur   Madrid   Melbourne   Mexico City   Nairobi
New Delhi   Shanghai   Taipei   Toronto

With offices in
Argentina   Austria   Brazil   Chile   Czech Republic   France   Greece
Guatemala   Hungary   Italy   Japan   Poland   Portugal   Singapore
South Korea   Switzerland   Thailand   Turkey   Ukraine   Vietnam

For titles covered by Section 112 of the US Higher Education Opportunity
Act, please visit www.oup.com/us/he for the latest information about
pricing and alternate formats.

Published by Oxford University Press
198 Madison Avenue, New York, New York 10016
www.oup.com

Oxford is a registered trademark of Oxford University Press.

Library of Congress Cataloging-in-Publication Data

Beauchamp, Tom L.
Principles of biomedical ethics / Tom L. Beauchamp, James F. Childress.—7th ed.
  p. cm.
 Includes bibliographical references and index.
 ISBN 978-0-19-992458-5
1. Medical ethics.   I. Childress, James F.   II. Title.
 R724.B36 2013
 174.2—dc23   2012029349

Printing number: 9 8 7 6 5 4 3 2 1

Printed in the United States of America
on acid-free paper

To

Georgia, Ruth, and Don

I can no other answer make but thanks,
And thanks, and ever thanks.

Twelfth Night

PREFACE TO THE SEVENTH EDITION

Biomedical ethics, or bioethics, was a youthful field when the first edition of this book went to press in late 1977, now thirty-five years ago. Immense changes have occurred in the field over these years. When we began to write this book, the word *bioethics* was a newly coined term, and the field—if it was a field—had virtually no literature and certainly no systematic work and no meta-reflection. Now the literature is so extensive that it is hard to keep in stride with new developments. For all who have been with us through successive editions of *Principles of Biomedical Ethics,* we express our thanks for your critical and constructive suggestions—a constant source of inspiration to us.

Major changes have appeared in all editions after the first, and this seventh edition is no exception. There are no changes in the book's basic structure, but the revisions are thoroughgoing. We have attempted to sharpen our analyses, strengthen our arguments, address issues raised by critics, and both reference (in notes) and take account of newly published material on the topics we cover. We have made changes in virtually every section and subsection of the book's ten chapters. The following are the most significant additions, expansions, and responses to critics:

Part I, Moral Foundations: In Chapter 1, "Moral Norms," we have clarified and tightened our account of the common morality and how it differs from particular moralities as well as the broad descriptive meaning of the term *morality.* We have moved a significant body of material on virtue ethics from Chapter 2, "Moral Character," to Chapter 9, where we have created a new section on virtue theory. We have had a major commitment to virtue theory and moral character since our first edition, and over the years we have expanded our discussion of these topics. This seventh edition contains deeper treatments of the concept of a moral virtue, moral ideals, and moral excellence. In Chapter 3, "Moral Status," we have added a new section on "Degrees of Moral Status," and we have modified the material in the section "Guidelines Governing Moral Status: Putting

Specification to Work." We have also added a new section entitled "The Moral
Significance of Moral Status."

   Part II, Moral Principles: In Chapter 4, "Respect for Autonomy," we
have expanded the section on theories of autonomy, revised the section on
"Therapeutic Use of Placebos," and enlarged the section on "Problems of
Information Processing." In Chapter 5, "Nonmaleficence," we have added new
sections on "Historical Problems of Underprotection" and "Recent Problems of
Overprotection" in human subjects research. We have also developed the idea
of reciprocity-based justifications and added a new section on group harm, with
examples drawn from recent literature on biobanking and broad consent; we
here feature the case of diabetes research on the Havasupai Indians of the Grand
Canyon. In Chapter 6, "Beneficence," we have expanded the sections on "A
Reciprocity-Based Justification of Obligations of Beneficence" and "Obligatory
Beneficence and Ideal Beneficence." We introduce in this chapter a treatment
of "Expanded Access and Continued Access in Research" and include a relo-
cated and integrated discussion of "Surrogate Decision Making for Incompetent
Patients." In Chapter 7, "Justice," we have enlarged the treatment of theories
of justice. This chapter now distinguishes "Traditional Theories of Justice,"
including utilitarian, libertarian, egalitarian, and communitarian theories, from
"Recent Theories of Justice," including both capabilities theories and well-being theories. We now examine each type of theory in closer detail than in previous editions. Our section on "Global Health Policy and the Right to Health"
distinguishes statist theories and global theories; almost all of the material in
this section is new to this edition. Finally, in Chapter 8, "Professional–Patient
Relationships," we have expanded our views in the section on "Arguments for
Noncommunication and Limited or Staged Communication of Bad News" and
other areas of the disclosure of information, as well as in our new discussion of
how to specify and balance rules of privacy with the need for public health surveillance. We have added a new section to this chapter on "Clinical Ethics and
Research Ethics." Here we critically investigate the ways in which biomedical
research and clinical medicine have been distinguished and how this distinction
has affected thinking—sometimes in questionable ways—about professional
ethics and research ethics.

   Part III, Theory and Method: Chapter 9, "Moral Theories," now incorporates a large new section on "Virtue Theory" that expands the account of the virtues that was in Chapter 2 in the sixth edition. We have also added a new section
on "Rights Theory" that presents a theory of rights as justified claims that are
uniformly correlative to obligations. Finally, in Chapter 10, "Method and Moral
Justification," we have extended and deepened our theory of method and justification in bioethics in the two major constructive sections of the chapter—namely,
the sections on "Reflective Equilibrium" and "Common-Morality Theory." We
here address criticisms of our account raised in the bioethics literature and

provide explanations of what we do and do not attempt. Changes are especially important in the subsection entitled "Three Types of Justification of Claims about a Universal Common Morality," which has been heavily rewritten to state more clearly our views and modest goals. These changes reflect ongoing discussions with critics and with colleagues at our institutions who have convinced us of the need for further qualification of the claims made in this part of the book.

To assist teachers who use our book in courses, we are arranging for the creation of a website that, based on classroom experiences, will contain suggestions for effectively using the book in the classroom, possible syllabi and examination questions, additional readings, useful exercises, and cases for discussion.

We again need to correct a misinterpretation of our overall theory that has persisted over the past thirty-five years. Many have suggested, especially our critics, that, in line with what they perceive as an American individualist orientation, the principle of respect for autonomy dominates and overrides all other moral principles and considerations in our work. This interpretation of our book is profoundly mistaken. In a properly structured account of biomedical ethics, respect for autonomy is not distinctly American and is not individualistic or overriding. We also do not emphasize individual rights to the neglect or exclusion of social responsibilities and communal goals. We do not now, and have never, treated the principle of respect for autonomy in the ways some of our critics allege. We have always argued that many kinds of competing moral considerations validly override this principle under certain conditions. Examples include the following: If our choices endanger public health, potentially harm innocent others, or require a scarce and unfunded resource, others can justifiably restrict our exercises of autonomy. The principle of respect for autonomy does not by itself determine what, on balance, a person ought to be free to do or what counts as a valid justification for constraining autonomy.

It is a mistake in biomedical ethics to assign priority to any basic principle over other basic principles—as if morality must be hierarchically structured or as if we must cherish one moral norm over another without consideration of particular circumstances. The better strategy is to appreciate both the contributions and the limits of various principles, virtues, and rights, which is the strategy we adopt throughout this book. While we have retained the basic framework of principles, we have continued to develop, refine, and modify our views as a result of many conversations with readers—some oral, some written; some informal, some published; some friendly, some adversarial.

To our abiding critics—conspicuously, John Arras, Edmund Pellegrino, Franklin Miller, David DeGrazia, Ronald Lindsay, Carson Strong, John-Stewart Gordon, Oliver Rauprich, Jochen Vollmann, Rebecca Kukla, Henry Richardson, Peter Herissone-Kelly, Robert Baker, and Tris Engelhardt—we express our appreciation for the civil and illuminating discourse that has improved our work. We also again wish to remember the late Dan Clouser, a wise man who seems to have been our first—and certainly one of our sternest—critics, and his friend and ours, the late Bernard Gert, whose trenchant criticisms time and again showed us the need for modifications in our views.

We have continued to receive many helpful suggestions for improvements in our work from students, colleagues, health professionals, and teachers who use the book. Jim is particularly grateful to his University of Virginia colleagues John Arras, already mentioned; Ruth Gaare Bernheim; Richard Bonnie; and the late John Fletcher for many illuminating discussions in team-taught courses and in other contexts. In addition, he thanks the faculty and graduate students of the Centre for the Advanced Study of Bioethics at the University of Münster for gracious hospitality and vigorous and valuable conversation and debate, particularly about paternalism and autonomy, in May and June 2011—Bettina Schöne-Seifert, Thomas Gutmann, and Michael Quante deserve special thanks. Jim also expresses his deep gratitude to Marcia Day Childress, his wife of fifteen years, for many valuable suggestions and unstinting support throughout this revision.

Tom likewise wishes to thank his many colleagues at Georgetown's Philosophy Department and the Kennedy Institute of Ethics as well as his colleagues at the Berman Institute of Bioethics at Johns Hopkins University. Henry Richardson and Rebecca Kukla have been penetrating, as well as constructive, critics from whom this work has greatly benefited. Between the sixth and seventh editions, Tom has benefited hugely from his colleagues in Baltimore on an NIH grant to study the need to revise our understanding of the research–practice distinction: Ruth Faden, Nancy Kass, Peter Pronovost, Steven Goodman, and Sean Tunis. When one has colleagues this talented and well informed, multidisciplinary work is as fun as it is instructive.

Tom also wishes to express appreciation to five undergraduate research assistants: Patrick Connolly, Stacylyn Dewey, Traviss Cassidy, Kekenus Sidik, and Patrick Gordon. Their research in the literature, their editing of copy, and their help with the index have made this book more comprehensive and readable. Likewise, Jim Childress wishes to thank three superb research assistants, Matt Puffer, Travis Pickell, and Laura Alexander, who have been particularly helpful in creating associated teaching materials for the website. We also acknowledge with due appreciation the support provided by the Kennedy Institute's library and information retrieval systems, which kept us in touch with new literature and reduced the burdens of library research; here we owe a special debt of gratitude to Martina Darragh for her help when we thought no help was to be found.

We also again express our gratitude to Jeffrey House, our editor at Oxford for thirty years, for believing in this book and seeing it through its formative editions.

We dedicate this edition, just as we have dedicated each of the previous six editions, to Georgia, Ruth, and Don. Georgia, Jim's wife of thirty-five years, died in 1994, just after the fourth edition appeared. Our dedication honors her wonderful memory and pays tribute to the enormous influence and devotion of Ruth Faden, Tom's wife, and Donald Seldin, an abiding inspiration in biomedical ethics since the early years of the field.

Washington, D.C. and *Chilmark, Massachussets*   T.L.B.
Charlottesville, Virginia   J.F.C.
April 2012

CONTENTS

PART I

MORAL FOUNDATIONS

1
Moral Norms

In the last third of the twentieth century, developments in the biological and health sciences and in biomedical technology presented a number of challenges to traditional professional ethics in medicine and in nursing.[1] Despite a remarkable continuity in medical ethics across millennia, the Hippocratic tradition was not well equipped to address problems such as informed consent, privacy, access to health care, communal and public health responsibilities, and research involving human subjects as these appeared in the modern context, and its paternalistic orientation provoked resistance from advocates of patients' rights. Professional ethics was also unable to provide an adequate framework to address emerging problems of public policy in a pluralistic society. We will not here ignore traditional professional ethics, but we will draw heavily on philosophical reflection on morality, which will allow us to examine and, where appropriate, depart from certain traditional assumptions in the biomedical sciences, health care, and public health.

NORMATIVE AND NONNORMATIVE ETHICS

The term *ethics* needs attention before we turn to the meanings of *morality* and *professional ethics*. *Ethics* is a generic term covering several different ways of understanding and examining the moral life. Some approaches to ethics are normative, others nonnormative.

Normative Ethics

General normative ethics addresses the question, "Which general moral norms for the guidance and evaluation of conduct should we accept, and why?" Ethical theories attempt to identify and justify these norms, which are often referred to as principles. In Chapter 9 we examine several types of normative ethical theory and offer criteria for assessing them.

1

Many practical questions would remain unanswered even if a fully satis-factory general ethical theory were available. *Practical ethics*—used here as synonymous with *applied ethics,* and by contrast to *theoretical ethics*—employs general concepts and norms to address particular problems. The term *practical* refers to the use of norms and other moral resources in deliberating about prob-lems, practices, and policies in professions, institutions, and public policy. Often no straightforward movement from general norms, principles, precedents, or the-ories to particular judgments is possible. General norms are usually only starting points for the development of norms of conduct suitable for specific contexts.

Nonnormative Ethics

Two types of nonnormative ethics are distinguishable. The first is *descriptive ethics,* which is the factual investigation of moral beliefs and conduct. It uses scientific techniques to study how people reason and act. For example, anthro-pologists, sociologists, psychologists, and historians determine which moral norms and attitudes are expressed in professional practice, in professional codes, in institutional mission statements and rules, and in public policies. They study phenomena such as surrogate decision making, treatment of the dying, and the nature of consent obtained from patients.

The second type is *metaethics,* which involves analysis of the language, concepts, and methods of reasoning in normative ethics. For example, metaeth-ics addresses the meanings of terms such as *right, obligation, virtue, justifica-tion, morality,* and *responsibility.* It is also concerned with moral epistemology (the theory of moral knowledge), the logic and patterns of moral reasoning and justification, and the possibility and nature of moral truth. Whether morality is objective or subjective, relative or nonrelative, and rational or nonrational are prominent questions in metaethics.

Descriptive ethics and metaethics are nonnormative because their objective is to establish what factually or conceptually *is* the case, not what ethically *ought to be* the case or what is ethically *valuable.* Often in this book we rely on reports in descriptive ethics, for example, when discussing the nature of professional codes of ethics, current forms of access to health care, and physician attitudes toward assisting patients in dying. However, our underlying interest is usually in how such information enables us to determine which practices are justifiable, which is a normative issue.[2]

THE COMMON MORALITY AS UNIVERSAL MORALITY

In its most familiar sense, the word *morality* (a much broader term than *common morality,* which is discussed immediately below in the next section, "The Nature of the Common Morality," and in more detail in Chapter 10) refers to norms about right and wrong human conduct that are so widely shared that they form a stable social compact. As a social institution, morality encompasses many standards of conduct, including moral principles, rules, ideals, rights, and virtues. We learn about morality as we grow up, and we learn to distinguish the part of morality that holds for everyone from moral norms that bind only members of specific communities or special groups such as physicians, nurses, or public health officials.

The Nature of the Common Morality

There are core tenets in every acceptable particular morality that are not relative to cultures, groups, or individuals. All persons living a moral life know several rules that are usually binding: not to lie, not to steal others' property, to keep promises, to respect the rights of others, and not to kill or cause harm to others. All persons committed to morality do not doubt the relevance and importance of these universally valid rules. Violation of these norms is unethical and will both generate feelings of remorse and provoke the moral censure of others. The literature of biomedical ethics virtually never debates the merit or acceptability of these central moral norms, though debates do occur about their precise meaning, scope, weight, and strength, often in regard to hard moral cases or current practices that merit careful scrutiny.

We will call the set of universal norms shared by all persons committed to morality *the common morality.* It is not merely *a* morality, in contrast to other moralities.[3] The common morality is applicable to all persons in all places, and we rightly judge all human conduct by its standards. The following norms are examples (far from a complete list) of generally binding *standards of action* (rules of obligation) found in the common morality: (1) Do not kill, (2) Do not cause pain or suffering to others, (3) Prevent evil or harm from occurring, (4) Rescue persons in danger, (5) Tell the truth, (6) Nurture the young and dependent, (7) Keep your promises, (8) Do not steal, (9) Do not punish the innocent, and (10) Obey just laws.

The common morality contains, in addition, standards other than rules of obligation. Here are ten examples of *moral character traits,* or virtues, recognized in the common morality (again, not a complete list): (1) nonmalevolence, (2) honesty, (3) integrity, (4) conscientiousness, (5) trustworthiness, (6) fidelity, (7) gratitude, (8) truthfulness, (9) lovingness, and (10) kindness. These virtues are universally admired traits of character.[4] A person is deficient in moral character if he or she lacks such traits. Negative traits that are the opposite of these virtues are *vices* (malevolence, dishonesty, lack of integrity, cruelty, etc.). They are universally recognized as substantial moral defects. In this chapter we will say no more about character and the virtues and vices, reserving this area of investigation for Chapter 2.

In addition to the vital obligations and virtues just mentioned, the common morality supports human rights and endorses many moral ideals such as charity and generosity. Philosophers debate whether one of these regions of the moral life—obligations, rights, or virtues—is more basic or more valuable than another, but in the common morality there is no reason to give primacy to any one area or type of norm. For example, human rights should not be considered more basic than moral virtues in universal morality, and moral ideals should not be less esteemed merely because people are not obligated to conform to them. An undue emphasis on any one of these areas disregards the full scope of the common morality.[5]

Our account of universal morality in this chapter and Chapter 10 does not conceive of the common morality as ahistorical or a priori.[6] This problem in moral theory cannot be adequately engaged until our discussions in Chapter 10, and we offer now only four simple clarifications of our position: First, the common morality is a product of human experience and history and is a universally shared product. The origin of the norms of the common morality is no different in principle from the origin of the norms of a particular morality for a profession. Both are learned and transmitted in communities. The primary difference is that the common morality has authority in all communities,[7] whereas particular moralities are authoritative only for specific groups. Second, we accept moral pluralism in *particular* moralities, as discussed later in this chapter, but we reject moral pluralism (or relativism) in the *common* morality. No particular way of life qualifies as morally acceptable unless it conforms to the standards in the common morality. Third, the common morality comprises moral *beliefs* (what all morally committed persons believe), not standards that exist prior to moral belief. Fourth, explications of the common morality—in books such as this one—are historical products, and every *theory* of the common morality has a history of development by the author(s) of the theory.

Ways of Examining the Common Morality

Various statements about or references to the common morality might be understood as normative, nonnormative, or possibly both. If the appeals are normative, the claim is that the common morality has normative force: It establishes moral standards for everyone, and violating these standards is unethical. If the references are nonnormative, the claim is that we can empirically study whether the common morality is present in all cultures. We accept both the normative force of the common morality and the objective of studying it empirically.

Some critics of our theory of the common morality have asserted that scant anthropological or historical evidence supports the empirical hypothesis that a universal common morality exists.[8] Accordingly, we need to consider how good the evidence is both for and against the existence of a universal common morality. This problem is difficult to address, but in principle, scientific research could either confirm or falsify the hypothesis of a universal morality. Our hypothesis is that all persons committed to morality accept the standards found in what we are calling the common morality. It would be absurd to assert that all persons do, in fact, accept the norms of the common morality, because many amoral, immoral, or selectively moral persons do not care about or identify with moral demands.

We explore this hypothesis about the empirical study of the common morality in Chapter 10. Here we note only that when we claim that the normative judgments found in many parts of this book are derived from the common morality, we are not asserting that our theory of the common morality gets it perfectly right or that it interprets or extends the common morality in just the right ways. No doubt there are dimensions of the common morality that we do not correctly capture or depict; and there are many parts of the common morality that we do not discuss at all. When we attempt to build on the common morality in this book by using it as a basis for critically examining problems of biomedical ethics, we do not mean to imply that our extensions can validly claim the authority of the common morality at every level of our account.

PARTICULAR MORALITIES AS NONUNIVERSAL

We shift now from universal morality (the common morality) to particular moralities, which contain moral norms that are not shared by all cultures, groups, and individuals.

The Nature of Particular Moralities

Whereas the common morality (insofar as we treat its content for our purposes in this book) contains moral norms that are abstract, universal, and content-thin (such as "Tell the truth"), particular moralities present concrete, nonuniversal, and content-rich norms (such as "Make conscientious oral disclosures to and obtain a written informed consent from all human research subjects"). Particular moralities are distinguished by the specificity of their norms, but these norms are not morally justified if they violate norms in the common morality. These specific moralities include the many responsibilities, aspirations, ideals, sentiments, attitudes, and sensitivities found in diverse cultural traditions, religious traditions, professional practice standards, and institutional guides. In some cases explication of the values in these moralities requires a special knowledge and may involve refinement by experts or scholars—as, for example, in the body of Jewish religious, legal, and moral norms in the Talmudic tradition. There may also be well-structured moral systems to adjudicate conflicts and provide methods for judgments in borderline cases—as, for example, the norms and methods in Roman Catholic casuistry.

Professional moralities, which include moral codes and standards of practice, are one form of particular morality. These moralities may legitimately
vary from other moralities in the way in which they handle certain conflicts of
interest, protocol reviews, advance directives, and similar matters. (See the next
section on "Professional and Public Moralities.") *Moral ideals* such as charitable
goals and aspirations to rescue suffering persons provide a second instructive
example of what may be parts of particular moralities. By definition, moral ideals such as charitable beneficence are not required of all persons; indeed, they
are not required of any person.[9] Persons who fail to fulfill their ideals cannot
be blamed or criticized by others. These ideals may nonetheless be critically
important parts of personal or communal moralities. Examples are found in physicians' individual commitments or physician codes that require assumption of a
significant level of risk in circumstances of communicable disease. It is reasonable to presume that all morally committed persons share an admiration of and
endorsement of many moral ideals of generosity and service, and in this respect
these ideals are part of shared moral beliefs in the common morality; they are
universally *praiseworthy* even though not universally required or universally
practiced. When such ideals are regarded by those who embrace them as obligations (as they are, for example, in some monastic traditions), the obligations
have been made parts of a particular morality, not universal morality.

Persons who accept a particular morality sometimes presume that they can
use this morality to speak with an authoritative moral voice for all persons. They
operate under the false belief that their particular convictions have the authority
of the common morality. These persons may have morally acceptable and even
praiseworthy beliefs, but their particular beliefs do not bind other persons or
communities. For example, persons who believe that scarce medical resources,
such as transplantable organs, should be distributed by lottery rather than by
medical need may have good moral reasons for their views, but they cannot
claim that their views are supported by the common morality.

Professional and Public Moralities

Just as the common morality is accepted by all morally committed persons, most
professions have, at least implicitly, a professional morality with standards of
conduct that are generally acknowledged and encouraged by those in the profession who are serious about their moral responsibilities. In medicine, professional
morality specifies general moral norms for the institutions and practices of medicine. Special roles and relationships in medicine require rules that other professions may not need. As we argue in Chapters 4 and 8, rules of informed consent
and medical confidentiality may not be serviceable or appropriate outside of
medicine and research, but they may be justified by general moral requirements
of respecting the autonomy of persons and protecting them from harm.

Members of professions often informally adhere to moral guidelines, such as rules prohibiting discrimination against colleagues on the basis of gender, race, religion, or national origin. In recent years formal codifications of and instruction in professional morality have increased through codes of medical and nursing ethics, codes of research ethics, corporate policies of bioethics, institutional guidelines governing conflict of interest, and the reports and recommendations of public commissions. Before we assess these guidelines, the nature of professions in general needs brief discussion.

Talcott Parsons defines a profession as "a cluster of occupational roles, that is, roles in which the incumbents perform certain functions valued in the society in general, and, by these activities, typically earn a living at a full-time job."[10] Under this definition, circus performers, exterminators, and garbage collectors are professionals. It is not surprising to find all such activities characterized as professions, inasmuch as the word *profession* has come, in common use, to mean almost any occupation by which a person earns a living. The once honorific sense of *profession* is now better reflected in the term *learned profession,* which assumes an extensive education in the arts, humanities, law, sciences, or technologies.

Professionals are usually distinguished by their specialized knowledge and training as well as by their commitment to provide important services or information to patients, clients, students, or consumers. Professions maintain self-regulating organizations that control entry into occupational roles by formally certifying that candidates have acquired the necessary knowledge and skills. In learned professions such as medicine, nursing, and public health, the professional's background knowledge is partly acquired through closely supervised training, and the professional is committed to providing a service to others.

Health care professions specify and enforce obligations for their members, thereby seeking to ensure that persons who enter into relationships with these professionals will find them competent and trustworthy. The obligations that professions attempt to enforce are determined by an accepted role. These obligations comprise the "ethics" of the profession, although there may also be role-specific rules or ideals such as self-effacement that are not obligatory. Problems of professional ethics usually arise either from conflicts over appropriate professional standards or conflicts between professional commitments and the commitments professionals have outside the profession.

Because the traditional standards of professional morality are often vague, some professions codify their standards in detailed statements aimed at reducing the vagueness. Their codes sometimes specify rules of etiquette in addition to rules of ethics. For example, a historically significant version of the code of the American Medical Association (AMA) dating from 1847 instructed physicians not to criticize fellow physicians who had previously been in charge of a case.[11] Such professional codes tend to foster and reinforce member identification with the prevailing values of the profession. These codes are beneficial when they effectively incorporate defensible moral norms, but some codes oversimplify moral requirements, make them indefensibly rigid, or make excessive and unwarranted claims about their completeness and authoritativeness. As a consequence, professionals may mistakenly suppose that they are satisfying all relevant moral requirements by strictly following the rules of the code, just as many people believe that they fully discharge their moral obligations when they meet all relevant legal requirements.

We can and should ask whether the codes specific to areas of science, medicine, nursing, health care, and public health are coherent, defensible, and comprehensive within their domain. Historically, few codes had much to say about the implications of several moral principles and rules such as veracity, respect for autonomy, and social justice that have been the subjects of intense discussion in recent biomedical ethics. From ancient medicine to the present, physicians have often generated codes for themselves without subjecting them to the scrutiny or acceptance of patients and the public. These codes have rarely appealed to general ethical standards or to a source of moral authority beyond the traditions and judgments of physicians themselves. Accordingly, the articulation of professional norms in these circumstances has often served to protect the profession's interests more than to offer a broad and impartial moral viewpoint or to address issues of importance to patients and society.[12]

Psychiatrist Jay Katz once poignantly expressed reservations about traditional principles and codes of medical ethics. Initially inspired by his outrage over the fate of Holocaust victims at the hands of German physicians, Katz became convinced that a professional ethics that reaches beyond traditional codes is indispensable:

> As I became increasingly involved in the world of law, I learned much that was new to me from my colleagues and students about such complex issues as the right to self-determination and privacy and the extent of the authority of governmental, professional, and other institutions to intrude into private life.... These issues ... had rarely been discussed in my medical education. Instead it had been all too uncritically assumed that they could be resolved by fidelity to such undefined principles as *primum non nocere* ["First, do no harm"] or to visionary codes of ethics.[13]

The Regulation and Oversight of Professional Conduct

Additional moral direction for health professionals and scientists comes through the public policy process, which includes regulations and guidelines promulgated by governmental bodies. The term *public policy* refers to a set of normative, enforceable guidelines accepted by an official public body, such as an agency of government or a legislature, to govern a particular area of conduct. The policies of corporations, hospitals, trade groups, and professional societies sometimes have a deep impact on public policy, but these policies are private, not public—even if these bodies are regulated to some degree by public policies.

A close connection exists between law and public policy: All laws constitute public policies, but not all public policies are, in the conventional sense, laws. In contrast to laws, public policies need not be explicitly formulated or codified. For example, an official who decides not to fund a newly recommended government program with no prior history of funding is formulating a public policy. Decisions not to act, as well as decisions to act, can constitute policies.

Policies such as those that fund health care for the indigent or those that protect subjects of biomedical research usually incorporate moral considerations. Moral analysis is part of good policy formation, not merely a method for evaluating existing policy. Efforts to protect the rights of patients and research subjects are instructive examples. Over the past few decades the U.S. government has created several national commissions, advisory committees, and councils to formulate guidelines for research involving human subjects, for the distribution of health care, and for addressing moral mistakes made in the health professions. Morally informed policies have guided decision making about other areas of practice as well. For example, the U.S. Congress passed the Patient Self-Determination Act (PSDA) as the first federal legislation to ensure that health care institutions inform patients about institutional policies that allow them to accept or refuse medical treatment and about their rights under state law, including a right to formulate advance directives.[14] The relevance of bioethics to public policy is now recognized in most developed countries, several of which have influential national bioethics committees.

Many courts have developed case law that sets standards for science, medicine, and health care. Legal decisions often express communal moral norms and stimulate ethical reflection that over time alters those norms. For example, the line of court decisions in the United States starting with the Karen Ann Quinlan case in the mid-1970s has constituted a nascent tradition of moral reflection that has been influenced by, and in turn has influenced, literature in biomedical ethics on topics such as whether medically administered nutrition and hydration should be viewed as a medical treatment that is subject to the same standards of decision making as other forms of treatment.

Policy formation and criticism generally involve more condensed moral judgments than the judgments found in ethical theories, principles, and rules.[15] Public policy is often formulated in contexts that are marked by profound social disagreements, uncertainties, and differing interpretations of history. No body of abstract moral principles and rules can fix policy in such circumstances, because abstract norms do not contain enough specific information to provide direct and discerning guidance. The implementation of moral principles and rules, through specification and balancing, must take into account factors such as feasibility, efficiency, cultural pluralism, political procedures, pertinent legal requirements, uncertainty about risk, and noncompliance by patients. Moral principles and rules provide a normative structure for policy formation and evaluation, but policies are also shaped by empirical data and by information available in fields such as medicine, nursing, public health, veterinary science, economics, law, biotechnology, and psychology.

When using moral norms to formulate or criticize public policies, we cannot move with assurance from a judgment that an *act* is morally right (or wrong) to a judgment that a corresponding *law* or *policy* is morally right (or wrong). The judgment that an act is morally wrong does not necessarily lead to the judgment that the government should prohibit it or refuse to allocate funds to support it. For example, one can argue without inconsistency that sterilization and abortion are morally wrong but that the law should not prohibit them, because they are fundamentally matters of personal choice beyond the legitimate reach of government (or, alternatively, because many persons would seek dangerous and unsanitary procedures from unlicensed practitioners). Similarly, the judgment that an act is morally acceptable does not imply that the law should permit it. For example, the belief that euthanasia is morally justified for terminally ill infants who face uncontrollable pain and suffering is consistent with the belief that the government should legally prohibit such euthanasia on grounds that it would not be possible to control abuses if it were legalized.

We are not defending any of these moral judgments. We are maintaining that the connections between moral norms and judgments about policy or law are complicated and that a judgment about the morality of acts does not entail an identical judgment about law or policy. Factors such as the symbolic value of law and the costs of a program and its enforcement often must be considered.

MORAL DILEMMAS

Common to all forms of practical ethics is reasoning through difficult cases, some of which constitute dilemmas. This is a familiar feature of decision making in morality, law, and public policy. Consider a classic case.[16] Some years ago, judges on the California Supreme Court had to reach a decision about the legal force and limits of medical confidentiality. A man had killed a woman after confiding to a therapist his intention to do so. The therapist had attempted unsuccessfully to have the man committed but, in accordance with his duty of medical confidentiality to the patient, did not communicate the threat to the woman when the commitment attempt failed.

The majority opinion of the Court held that "When a therapist determines, or pursuant to the standards of his profession should determine, that his patient presents a serious danger of violence to another, he incurs an obligation to use reasonable care to protect the intended victim against such danger." This obligation extends to notifying the police and warning the intended victim. The justices in the majority opinion argued that therapists generally ought to observe the rule of medical confidentiality, but that the rule must yield in this case to the "public interest in safety from violent assault." These justices recognized that rules of professional ethics have substantial public value, but they held that matters of greater importance, such as protecting persons against violent assault, can override these rules.

In a minority opinion, a judge disagreed and argued that doctors violate patients' rights if they fail to observe standard rules of confidentiality. If it were common practice to break these rules, he reasoned, the fiduciary nature of the relationship between physicians and patients would erode. The mentally ill would refrain from seeking aid or divulging critical information because of the loss of trust that is essential for effective treatment. Violent assaults would therefore increase.

This case presents straightforward moral and legal dilemmas in which both judges cite relevant reasons to support their conflicting judgments. Moral dilemmas are circumstances in which moral obligations demand or appear to demand that a person adopt each of two (or more) alternative but incompatible actions, such that the person cannot perform all the required actions. These dilemmas occur in at least two forms.[17] (1) Some evidence or argument indicates that an act is morally permissible and some evidence or argument indicates that it is morally wrong, but the evidence or strength of argument on both sides is inconclusive. Abortion, for example, is sometimes said to be a terrible dilemma for women who see the evidence in this way. (2) An agent believes that, on moral grounds, he or she is obligated to perform two or more mutually exclusive actions. In a moral dilemma of this form, one or more moral norms obligate an agent to do x and one or more moral norms obligate the agent to do y, but the agent cannot do both in the circumstance. The reasons behind alternatives x and y are weighty and neither set of reasons is overriding. If one acts on either set of reasons, one's actions will be morally acceptable in some respects and morally unacceptable in others. Some have viewed the withdrawal of life-prolonging therapies from patients in a persistent vegetative state as an instance of the second form of dilemma.

Popular literature, novels, and films often illustrate how conflicting moral principles and rules create difficult dilemmas. For example, an impoverished person who steals from a grocery store to save a family from starvation confronts such a dilemma. The only way to comply with one obligation is to contravene another obligation. Some obligation must be overridden or compromised no matter which course is chosen. From the perspective we defend in this volume, it is misleading to say that we are obligated to perform both actions in these dilemmatic circumstances. Instead, we should discharge the obligation that we judge to override what we would have been firmly obligated to perform were it not for the conflict.

Conflicts between moral requirements and self-interest sometimes create a *practical* dilemma, but not, strictly speaking, a *moral* dilemma. If moral reasons compete with nonmoral reasons, such as self-interest, questions about priority can still arise even though no moral dilemma is present. Examples appear in the work of anthropologist William R. Bascom, who collected hundreds of "African dilemma tales" transmitted for decades and sometimes centuries in African tribal societies. One traditional dilemma posed by the Hausa tribe of Nigeria is called *cure for impotence:*

> A friend gave a man a magical armlet that cured his impotence. Later he
> [the man with the armlet] saw his mother, who had been lost in a slave raid,
> in a gang of prisoners. He begged his friend to use his magic to release her.
> The friend agreed on one condition—that the armlet be returned. What
> shall his choice be?[18]

Difficult choice? Perhaps, but presumably not a difficult *moral* choice. The obligation to the mother is moral in character, whereas retaining the armlet is a matter of self-interest. (In this assessment, we are assuming that no moral obligation exists to a sexual partner; but in some circumstances, such an obligation would generate a moral dilemma.) A moral reason in conflict with a personal reason need not entail that the moral reason is overriding. If, for example, a physician must choose between saving his or her own life or that of a patient, in a situation of extreme scarcity of available drugs, the moral obligation to take care of the patient may not be overriding.

Some moral philosophers and theologians have argued that although many practical dilemmas involving moral reasons exist, no irresolvable moral dilemmas exist. They do not deny that agents experience moral perplexity or conflict in difficult cases. However, they claim that the purpose of a moral theory is to provide a principled procedure for resolving all deep conflicts. Some philosophers have defended this conclusion because they accept one supreme moral value as overriding all other conflicting values (moral and nonmoral) and because they regard it as incoherent to allow contradictory obligations in a properly structured moral theory. The only *ought,* they maintain, is the one generated by the supreme value.[19] We examine such theories, including both utilitarian and Kantian theories, in Chapter 9.

In contrast to the account of moral obligation offered by these theories, we maintain throughout this book that various moral principles, rules, and rights can and do conflict in the moral life. These conflicts sometimes produce irresolvable moral dilemmas. When forced to a choice, we may "resolve" the situation by choosing one option over another, but we still may believe that neither option is morally preferable. A physician with a limited supply of medicine may have to choose to save the life of one patient rather than another and still find his or her moral dilemma irresolvable. Explicit acknowledgment of such dilemmas helps deflate unwarranted expectations about what moral principles and theories can do. Although we often find ways of reasoning about what we should do, we may not be able to reach a reasoned resolution in many instances. In some cases the dilemma only becomes more difficult and remains unresolved even after the most careful reflection.

A Framework of Moral Norms

The moral norms that are central for biomedical ethics derive from the common morality, though they certainly do not exhaust the common morality. These norms are treated individually in Chapters 4 through 7 in Part II of this book. Most classical ethical theories accept these norms in some form, and traditional medical codes presuppose at least some of them.

Principles

The set of pivotal moral principles defended in this book functions as an analytical framework of general norms derived from the common morality that form a suitable starting point for biomedical ethics.[20] These principles are general guidelines for the formulation of more specific rules. In Chapters 4 through 7 we defend four clusters of moral principles: (1) *respect for autonomy* (a norm of respecting and supporting autonomous decisions), (2) *nonmaleficence* (a norm of avoiding the causation of harm), (3) *beneficence* (a group of norms pertaining to relieving, lessening, or preventing harm and providing benefits and balancing benefits against risks and costs), and (4) *justice* (a group of norms for fairly distributing benefits, risks, and costs).

Nonmaleficence and beneficence have played a central role in the history of medical ethics. By contrast, respect for autonomy and justice were neglected in traditional medical ethics and have risen to prominence only recently. In 1803, British physician Thomas Percival published *Medical Ethics,* the first comprehensive account of medical ethics in the long history of the subject. This book served as the prototype for the American Medical Association's first code of ethics in 1847. Percival argued, using somewhat different language, that nonmaleficence and beneficence fix the physician's primary obligations and triumph over the patient's preferences and decision-making rights in circumstances of conflict.[21] Percival greatly understated the importance of principles of respect for autonomy and distributive justice for physician conduct. However, in fairness to him, these considerations are now prominent in discussions of ethics in medicine in a way they were not when he wrote at the turn of the nineteenth century.

That these four clusters of moral principles are central to biomedical ethics is a conclusion the authors of this work have reached by examining *considered moral judgments* and *the way moral beliefs cohere,* two notions discussed in Chapter 10. The selection of these four principles, rather than some other clusters of principles, does not receive an argued defense in Chapters 1 through 3. However, in Chapters 4 through 7, we defend the vital role of each principle in biomedical ethics.

Rules

Our larger framework in this book encompasses several types of norms: principles, rules, rights, and virtues. Principles are more general and comprehensive norms than rules, but we draw only a loose distinction between rules and principles. Both are norms of obligation, but rules are more specific in content and more restricted in scope. Principles do not function as precise guides in each circumstance in the way that more detailed rules and judgments do. Finally, principles and rules of obligation have correlative rights, and virtues often have corresponding principles and rules (see Chapter 9).

We defend several types of rules, of which the most important categories are substantive rules, authority rules, and procedural rules.

Substantive rules. Rules of truth telling, confidentiality, privacy, forgoing treatment, informed consent, and rationing health care provide more specific guides to action than do abstract principles. An example of a rule that sharpens the requirements of the principle of respect for autonomy in certain contexts is "Follow an incompetent patient's advance directive whenever it is clear and relevant." To indicate how this rule *specifies* the principle of respect for autonomy, we may state it more fully as "Respect the autonomy of incompetent patients by following all clear and relevant formulations in their advance directives." This formulation shows how the initial norm of respect for autonomy endures even while becoming specified. (See the section "Specification" later in this chapter.)

Authority rules. We also defend rules of decisional authority—that is, rules regarding who may and should make decisions and perform actions. For example, *rules of surrogate authority* determine who should serve as surrogate agents when making decisions for incompetent persons; *rules of professional authority* determine who in professional ranks should make decisions to override or to accept a patient's decisions; and *rules of distributional authority* determine who should make decisions about allocating scarce medical resources.

Authority rules do not delineate substantive standards or criteria for making decisions. However, authority rules and substantive rules can interact. For instance, authority rules are justified, in part, by how well particular authorities can be expected to respect and comply with substantive rules and principles.

Procedural rules. We also defend rules that establish procedures to be followed. Procedures for determining eligibility for organ transplantation and procedures for reporting grievances to higher authorities are typical examples. We often

resort to procedural rules when we run out of substantive rules and when authority rules are incomplete or inconclusive. For example, if substantive or authority
rules are inadequate to determine which patients should receive scarce medical
resources, we resort to procedural rules such as queuing and lottery.[22]

Conflicting Moral Norms

Prima Facie Obligations and Rights

Principles, rules, obligations, and rights are not rigid or absolute standards that
allow no compromise. Although "a person of principle" is sometimes regarded
as strict and unyielding, principles must be balanced and specified so they can
function in particular circumstances. It is no objection to moral norms that, in
some circumstances, they can be justifiably overridden by other norms with
which they conflict. All general moral norms are justifiably overridden in some
circumstances. For example, we might justifiably not tell the truth to prevent
someone from killing another person; and we might justifiably disclose confidential information about a person to protect the rights of another person.

Actions that harm individuals, cause basic needs to go unmet, or limit liberties are often said to be wrong *prima facie* (i.e., wrongness is upheld unless the
act is justifiable because of norms that are more stringent in the circumstances) or
wrong *pro tanto* (i.e., wrong to a certain extent or wrong unless there is a compelling justification)—which is to say that the action is wrong in the absence of other
moral considerations that supply a compelling justification.[23] Compelling justifications are sometimes available. For example, in circumstances of a severe swine
flu pandemic, the forced confinement of persons through isolation and quarantine
orders might be justified. Here a justifiable infringement of liberty rights occurs.

W. D. Ross defended a distinction that we accept in principle between *prima
facie* and *actual* obligations. A *prima facie* obligation must be fulfilled unless it
conflicts with an equal or stronger obligation. Likewise, a *prima facie* right, we
maintain (here extending Ross), must prevail unless it conflicts with an equal
or stronger right (or conflicts with some other morally compelling alternative).
Obligations and rights always constrain us unless a competing moral obligation
or right can be shown to be overriding in a particular circumstance. As Ross
puts it, "the greatest balance" of right over wrong must be found. Agents can
determine their *actual* obligations in such situations by examining the respective
weights of competing prima facie obligations. What agents ought to do is, in the
end, determined by what they ought to do all things considered.[24]

As an example, imagine that a psychiatrist has confidential medical information about a patient who also happens to be an employee in the hospital where
the psychiatrist practices. The employee is seeking advancement in a stress-filled
position, but the psychiatrist has good reason to believe that this advancement

would be devastating for both the employee and the hospital. The psychiatrist has several prima facie duties in these circumstances, including those of confidentiality, nonmaleficence, beneficence, and respect for autonomy. Should the psychiatrist break confidence in this circumstance to meet these other duties? Could the psychiatrist make "confidential" disclosures to a hospital administrator and not to the personnel office? Addressing such questions through a process of moral deliberation and justification is required to establish an agent's actual duty in the face of these conflicting prima facie duties.

These matters are more complicated than Ross suggests, particularly when rights come into conflict. We often need to develop a structured moral system or set of guidelines in which (1) some rights in a certain class of rights have a fixed priority over others in another class and (2) it is extremely difficult for morally compelling social objectives to outweigh basic rights.

No moral theory or professional code of ethics has successfully presented a system of moral rules free of conflicts and exceptions, but this fact should not generate either skepticism or alarm. Ross's distinction between prima facie and actual obligations conforms closely to our experience as moral agents and provides indispensable categories for biomedical ethics. Almost daily we confront situations that force us to choose among conflicting values in our personal lives. For example, a person's financial situation might require that he or she choose between buying books and buying a train ticket to see friends. Not having the books will be an inconvenience and a loss, whereas not visiting home will disappoint the friends. Such a choice does not come effortlessly, but we are usually able to think through the alternatives, deliberate, and reach a conclusion. The moral life presents similar problems of choice.

Moral Regret and Residual Obligation

An agent who determines that an act is the best act to perform under circumstances of a conflict of obligations may still not be able to discharge all aspects of moral obligation by performing that act. Even the morally best action in the circumstances may still be regrettable and may leave a moral residue, also referred to as a moral trace.[25] Regret and residue over what is not done can arise even if the right action is clear and uncontested.

This point is about continuing obligation, not merely about feelings of regret and residue. Moral residue results because an overridden prima facie obligation does not simply go away when overridden. Often we have residual obligations because the obligations we were unable to discharge create new obligations. We may feel deep regret and a sting of conscience, but we also realize that we have a duty to bring closure to the situation.[26] We can sometimes make up for our inability to fulfill an obligation in one or more of several ways. For example, we may be able to notify persons in advance that we will not be able to keep a promise; we may be able to apologize in a way that heals a relationship; we may be able to change circumstances so that the conflict does not occur again; or we may be able to provide adequate compensation.

Specifying Principles and Rules

The four clusters of principles we present in this book do not constitute a general ethical theory. They provide only a framework of norms with which to get started in biomedical ethics. These principles must be specified in order to achieve more concrete guidance. Specification is a process of reducing the indeterminacy of abstract norms and generating rules with action-guiding content.[27] For example, without further specification, "do no harm" is too bare a starting point for thinking through problems such as whether it is permissible to hasten the death of a terminally ill patient.

Specification is not a process of producing or defending general norms such as those in the common morality; it assumes that the relevant norms are available. Specifying the norms with which one starts—whether those in the common morality or norms previously specified to some extent—is accomplished by narrowing the scope of the norms, not by explaining what the general norms mean. We narrow the scope, as Henry Richardson puts it, by "spelling out where, when, why, how, by what means, to whom, or by whom the action is to be done or avoided."[28] For example, the norm that we are obligated to "respect the autonomy of persons" cannot, unless specified, handle complicated problems in clinical medicine and research involving human subjects. A definition of "respect for autonomy" (e.g., as "allowing competent persons to exercise their liberty rights") clarifies one's meaning in using the norm, but it does not narrow the scope of the general norm or render it more specific in guiding actions.

Specification adds content. For example, as noted previously, one possible specification of "respect the autonomy of persons" is "respect the autonomy of competent patients by following their advance directives when they become incompetent." This specification will work well in some medical contexts, but it will confront limits in others, where additional specification will be needed. Progressive specification can continue indefinitely, but to qualify all along the way as a specification some transparent connection must be maintained to the initial general norm that gives moral authority to the resulting string of specifications. This process is a prime way in which general principles become practical instruments for moral reasoning; and the process also helps explain why the four-principles approach to biomedical ethics is not merely an abstract theory.[29]

An example of specification arises when psychiatrists conduct forensic evaluations of patients in a legal context. Psychiatrists cannot always obtain an informed consent and, in those circumstances, they risk violating their obligations to respect autonomy. However, obtaining informed consent is a central imperative of medical ethics. A specification aimed at handling this problem is "Respect the autonomy of persons who are the subjects of forensic evaluations, where consent is not legally required, by disclosing to the evaluee the nature and purpose of the evaluation." We do not claim that this formulation is the best specification, but it approximates the provision recommended in the "Ethical Guidelines for the Practice of Forensic Psychiatry" of the American Academy of Psychiatry and the Law.[30] This specification attempts to guide forensic psychiatrists in discharging their diverse moral obligations.

Another example of specification involves the oft-cited rule "Doctors should put their patients' interests first." In some countries patients can receive the best treatment available only if their physicians falsify information on insurance forms. The rule of patient priority does not imply that a physician should act illegally by lying or distorting the description of a patient's problem on an insurance form. Rules against deception, on the one hand, and for patient priority, on the other, are not categorical imperatives. When they conflict, we need some form of specification in order to know what we can and cannot do.

A survey of practicing physicians' attitudes toward deception illustrates how some physicians reconcile their dual commitment to patients and to non-deception. Dennis H. Novack and several colleagues used a questionnaire to obtain physicians' responses to difficult ethical problems that potentially could be resolved by deception. In one scenario, a physician recommends an annual screening mammography for a fifty-two-year-old woman who protests that her insurance company will not cover the test. The insurance company would cover the costs if the physician stated the reason as "rule out cancer" rather than "screening mammography," but the insurance company understands "rule out cancer" to apply only if there is a breast mass or other objective clinical evidence of the possibility of cancer, neither of which was present in this case. Almost 70% of the physicians responding to this survey indicated that they would state that they were seeking to "rule out cancer," and 85% of this group (85% of the 70%) insisted that their act would not involve "deception."[31]

These physicians' decisions are crude attempts to specify the rule that "Doctors should put their patients' interests first." Some doctors seem to think that it is properly specified as follows: "Doctors should put their patients' interests first by withholding information from or misleading someone who has no *right* to that information, including an insurance company that, through unjust policies of coverage, forfeits its right to accurate information." In addition, most physicians in the study apparently did not operate with the definition of deception favored by the researchers, which is "to deceive is to make another believe what is not true, to mislead." Some physicians apparently believed that "deception" occurs when one person unjustifiably misleads another, and that it was justifiable to mislead the insurance company in these circumstances. It appears that these physicians would not agree on how to specify rules against deception or rules assigning priority to patients' interests.

All moral rules are, in principle, subject to specification. They all will need some additional content, because, as Richardson puts it, "the complexity of the moral phenomena always outruns our ability to capture them in general norms."[32] Many already specified rules will need further specification to handle new circumstances of conflict. These conclusions are connected to our earlier discussion of particular moralities. Different persons and groups will offer conflicting specifications, potentially creating multiple particular moralities. In any problematic case, competing specifications are likely to be offered by reasonable and fair-minded parties, all of whom are committed to the common morality. Nothing in the model of specification suggests that we can avoid all circumstances of conflicting judgments.

To say that a problem or conflict is resolved or dissolved by specification is to say that norms have been made sufficiently determinate in content that, when cases fall under them, we know what ought to be done. Obviously some proposed specifications will not provide the most adequate or justified resolution. When competing specifications emerge, we should seek to discover which is superior. Proposed specifications should be based on deliberative processes of reasoning, as we discuss them in Chapter 10. In this way, we can connect specification as a method with a model of justification that will support some specifications and not others.

Finally, some specified norms are virtually absolute and need no further specification. Examples include prohibitions of cruelty that involves the unnecessary infliction of pain and suffering.[33] More interesting are norms that are intentionally formulated with the goal of including all legitimate exceptions. An example is, "Always obtain oral or written informed consent for medical interventions with competent patients, *except* in emergencies, in forensic examinations, in low-risk situations, or when patients have waived their right to adequate information." This norm needs further interpretation, including an analysis of what constitutes an informed consent, an emergency, a waiver, a forensic examination, and a low risk. However, this rule would be absolute if it were correct that all legitimate exceptions had successfully been incorporated in its formulation. If such rules exist, they are rare. In light of the range of possibilities for contingent conflicts among rules, even the firmest and most detailed rules are likely to encounter exceptive cases.

Weighing and Balancing

Principles, rules, obligations, and rights often must be balanced. Is balancing different from specification, and, if so, how?

The process of weighing and balancing. Balancing is the process of finding reasons to support beliefs about which moral norms should prevail. Balancing is concerned with the relative weights and strengths of different moral norms, whereas specification is concerned primarily with their scope (i.e., range). Accordingly, balancing consists of deliberation and judgment about these weights and strengths. Balancing seems particularly well suited for reaching judgments in *particular* cases, whereas specification seems especially useful for developing more specific *policies* from already accepted general norms.

The metaphor of larger and smaller weights moving a scale up and down has often been invoked to depict the balancing process, but this metaphor obscures what happens in balancing. Justified acts of balancing are supported by good reasons. They need not rest merely on intuition or feeling, although intuitive balancing is one form of balancing. Suppose a physician encounters an emergency case that would require her to extend an already long day, making her unable to keep a promise to take her son to the local library. She then engages in a process of deliberation that leads her to consider how urgently her son needs to get to the library, whether they could go to the library later, whether another physician could handle the emergency case, and so on. If she determines to stay deep into the night with the patient, she has judged this obligation to be overriding because she has found a good and sufficient reason for her action. The reason might be that a life hangs in the balance and she alone may have the knowledge to deal adequately with the circumstances. Canceling her evening with her son, distressing as it may be, could be justified by the significance of her reasons for doing what she does.

One way of analyzing the process of balancing merges it with specification. In our example, the physician's reasons can be generalized to similar cases: "If a patient's life hangs in the balance and the attending physician alone has the knowledge to deal adequately with the full array of the circumstances, then the physician's conflicting domestic obligations must yield." Even if we do not always state the way we balance considerations in the form of a specification, might not all deliberative judgments be made to conform to this model? If so, then deliberative balancing *is* nothing but deliberative specification.

The goal of merging specification and balancing is appealing, but it is not well-suited to handle all situations in which balancing occurs. Specification requires that a moral agent extend norms by both narrowing their scope and generalizing to relevantly similar circumstances. Thus, "respect the autonomy of competent patients when they become incompetent by following their advance directives" is a rule suited for all incompetent patients with advance directives. However, the responses of caring moral agents, such as physicians and nurses, are often highly specific to the needs of *this* patient or *this* family in *this* circumstance. Numerous considerations must be weighed and balanced, and any generalizations that could be formed might not hold even in closely related cases.

Generalizations conceived as policies might even be dangerous. For example, cases in which risk of harm and burden are involved for a patient are often circumstances unlikely to be decided by expressing, by rule, how much risk is allowable or how heavy the burden can be to secure a certain stated benefit. After levels of risk and burden are determined, these considerations must be balanced with the likelihood of the success of a procedure, the uncertainties involved, whether an adequately informed consent can be obtained, whether the family has a role to play, and the like. In this way, balancing allows for a due consideration of all the factors, including norms, bearing on a complex circumstance.

Consider the following discussion with a young woman who has just been told that she is HIV-infected, as recorded by physician Timothy Quill and nurse Penelope Townsend:[34]

> PATIENT: Please don't tell me that. Oh my God. Oh my children. Oh Lord have mercy. Oh God, why did He do this to me?...
> DR. QUILL: First thing we have to do is learn as much as we can about it, because right now you are okay.
> PATIENT: I don't even have a future. Everything I know is that you gonna die anytime. What is there to do? What if I'm a walking time bomb? People will be scared to even touch me or say anything to me.
> DR. QUILL: No, that's not so.
> PATIENT: Yes they will, 'cause I feel that way...
> DR. QUILL: There is a future for you...
> PATIENT: Okay, alright. I'm so scared. I don't want to die. I don't want to die, Dr. Quill, not yet. I know I got to die, but I don't want to die.
> DR. QUILL: We've got to think about a couple of things.

Quill and Townsend work to calm down and reassure this patient, while engaging sympathetically with her feelings and conveying the presence of knowledgeable medical authorities. Their emotional investment in the patient's feelings is joined with a detached evaluation of the patient. Too much compassion and emotional investment may doom the task at hand; too much detachment will be cold and may destroy the patient's trust and hope. A balance in the sense of a right mixture between engagement and detachment must be found.

Quill and Townsend could try to specify norms of respect and beneficence to indicate how caring physicians and nurses should respond to patients who are desperately upset. However, such a specification will ring hollow and will not be sufficiently subtle to provide practical guidance for this patient, let alone for all desperately upset patients. Each encounter calls for a response not adequately captured by general rules and their specifications. Behavior that is a caring response to one desperate patient will intrude on privacy or irritate the next desperate patient. A physician may, for example, find it appropriate to touch or caress a patient X, while appreciating that such behavior would be entirely inappropriate for another patient Y in a similar circumstance. How physicians and nurses balance different moral considerations often involves sympathetic insight, humane responsiveness, and the practical wisdom of discerning a particular patient's circumstance and needs.[35] Balancing often is a more complex set of activities than those involved in a straightforward case of balancing two conflicting principles or rules. Considerations of trust, compassion, objective assessment, caring responsiveness, reassurance, and the like are all being balanced. To act compassionately may be to undercut objective assessment. Not all of the norms at work can reasonably be said to be specifications, nor need there be a final specification.

In many clinical contexts it may be hopelessly complicated to engage in specification. For example, in cases of balancing harms of treatment against the benefits of treatment for incompetent patients, the cases are often so exceptional that it is perilous to generalize a conclusion that would reach out to other cases. These problems may be further complicated by disagreements among family members about what constitutes a benefit, poor decisions and indecision by a marginally competent patient, limitations of time and resources, and the like.[36]

We do not suggest that balancing is a matter of spontaneous, unreflective intuition without reasons. We are proposing a model of moral judgment that focuses on how balancing and judgment occur through practical astuteness, discriminating intelligence, and sympathetic responsiveness that are not reducible to the specification of norms. The capacity to balance many moral considerations is connected to what we discuss in Chapter 2 as capacities of moral character. Capacities in the form of virtues of compassion, attentiveness, discernment, caring, and kindness are integral to the way wise moral agents balance diverse, sometimes competing, moral considerations.

Practicability supplies another reason why the model of specification needs supplementation by the model of balancing. Progressive specification covering all areas of the moral life would eventually mushroom into a body of norms so bulky that the normative system would become unwieldy. A scheme of comprehensive specification would constitute a package of potentially hundreds, thousands, or millions of rules, each suited to a narrow range of conduct. In the ideal of specification, every type of action in a circumstance of the contingent conflict of norms would be covered by a rule, but the formulation of rules for every circumstance of contingent conflict would be a body of rules too cumbersome to be effective. The greater the number of rules and the more complex each rule, the less likely it is that the moral system will be functional and useful for guiding decisions.

Conditions that constrain balancing. To allay concerns that the model of balancing is too intuitive or too open-ended and lacks a commitment to firm principles and rigorous reasoning, we propose six conditions that should help reduce intuition, partiality, and arbitrariness. These conditions must be met to justify infringing one prima facie norm in order to adhere to another.

1. Good reasons can be offered to act on the overriding norm rather than on the infringed norm.
2. The moral objective justifying the infringement has a realistic prospect of achievement.
3. No morally preferable alternative actions are available.[37]
4. The lowest level of infringement, commensurate with achieving the primary goal of the action, has been selected.
5. All negative effects of the infringement have been minimized.
6. All affected parties have been treated impartially.

Although some of these conditions are obvious and noncontroversial, some are often overlooked in moral deliberation and would lead to different conclusions were they observed. For example, some proposals to use life-extending technologies, despite the objections of patients or their surrogates, violate condition 2 by endorsing actions in which no realistic prospect exists of achieving the goals of a proposed intervention. Typically, these proposals are made when health professionals regard the intervention as legally required, but in some cases the standard invoked is merely a traditional or deeply entrenched perspective.

Condition 3 is more commonly violated. Actions are regularly performed in some settings without serious consideration of alternative actions that might be performed. As a result, agents fail to identify a morally preferable alternative. For example, in animal care and use committees a common conflict involves the obligation to approve a good scientific protocol and the obligation to protect animals against unnecessary suffering. A protocol is often approved if it proposes a standard form of anesthesia. However, standard forms of anesthesia are not always the best way to protect the animal, and further inquiry is needed to determine the best anesthetic for the particular interventions proposed. In our schema of conditions, it is unjustifiable to approve the protocol or to conduct the experiment without this additional inquiry, which affects conditions 4 and 5 as well as 3.

Finally, consider this example: The principle of respect for autonomy and principles of beneficence (which require acts intended to prevent harm to others) sometimes come into contingent conflict in responding to situations that arise in the treatment of HIV/AIDS patients. Respect for autonomy sets a prima facie barrier to invasions of privacy and the mandatory testing of people at risk of HIV infection, yet their actions may put others at risk under conditions in which society has a prima facie obligation to act to prevent harm to those at risk. To justify overriding respect for autonomy, one must show that mandatory testing that invades the privacy of certain individuals is necessary to prevent harm to others and has a reasonable prospect of preventing such harm. If it meets these conditions, mandatory testing still must pass the least-infringement test (condition 4), and health workers must seek to reduce negative effects, such as the consequences that individuals fear from testing (condition 5).[38]

In our judgment, these six constraining conditions are morally demanding, at least in some circumstances. When conjoined with requirements of coherence that we propose in Chapter 10, these conditions provide a strong measure of protection against purely intuitive, subjective, or partial balancing judgments. We could try to introduce further criteria or safeguards, such as "rights override nonrights" and "liberty principles override nonliberty principles," but these rules are certain to fail in circumstances in which rights claims and liberty interests are relatively minor.

Moral Diversity and Moral Disagreement

Conscientious and reasonable moral agents understandably disagree over moral priorities in circumstances of a contingent conflict of norms. Morally conscientious persons may disagree, for example, about whether disclosure of a life-threatening condition to a fragile patient is appropriate, whether religious values about brain death have a place in secular biomedical ethics, whether teenagers should be permitted to refuse life-sustaining treatments, and hundreds of other issues. Such disagreement does not indicate moral ignorance or moral defect. We simply lack a single, entirely reliable way to resolve many disagreements, despite methods of specifying and balancing.

Moral disagreement can emerge because of (1) factual disagreements (e.g., about the level of suffering that an action will cause), (2) disagreements resulting from insufficient information or evidence, (3) disagreements about which norms are applicable or relevant in the circumstances, (4) disagreements about the relative weights or rankings of the relevant norms, (5) disagreements about appropriate forms of specification or balancing, (6) the presence of a genuine moral dilemma, (7) scope disagreements about who should be protected by a moral norm (e.g., whether embryos, fetuses, and sentient animals are protected; see Chapter 3), and (8) conceptual disagreements about a crucial moral notion (such as whether removal of nutrition and hydration at a family's request constitutes *killing*).

Different parties may emphasize different principles or assign different weights to principles even when they agree on which principles are relevant. Such disagreement may persist among morally committed persons who recognize all the demands that morality makes on them. If evidence is incomplete and different items of evidence are available to different parties, one individual or group may be justified in reaching a conclusion that another individual or group is justified in rejecting. Even when both parties have incorrect beliefs, each party may be justified in holding its beliefs. We cannot hold persons to a higher practical standard than to make judgments conscientiously in light of the relevant norms and relevant evidence.

When moral disagreements arise, a moral agent can—and usually should—defend his or her decision without disparaging or reproaching others who reach different decisions. Recognition of legitimate diversity, by contrast to moral violations that warrant criticism and perhaps even punishment, is vital when we evaluate the actions of others. One person's conscientious assessment of his or her obligations may differ from another's when they confront the same moral problem. Both evaluations may be appropriately grounded in the common morality. Similarly, what one institution or government determines it should do may differ from what another institution or government determines it should do. In such cases, we can assess one position as morally preferable to another only if we can show that the position rests on a more coherent set of specifications and interpretations of the common morality.[39]

CONCLUSION

In this chapter we have outlined what is sometimes called the *four-principles approach* to biomedical ethics,[40] now commonly designated *principlism*.[41] The four clusters of principles that we propose as a moral framework derive from the common morality, but when specifying and balancing these principles in later chapters we will also call upon historical experience in formulating professional obligations and virtues in health care, public health, biomedical research, and health policy. We will criticize many assumptions in traditional medical ethics, current medical codes, and other parts of contemporary bioethics, but we are also deeply indebted to the insights and commitments found in these moral viewpoints. Our goal in later chapters is to develop, specify, and balance the normative content of the four clusters of principles, and there we often seek to render our views consistent with professional traditions, practices, and codes.

Principlism, then, is not a mere list and analysis of four abstract principles. It is a theory about how principles link to and guide practice. We will be showing how these principles are connected to an array of transactions, practices, understandings, and forms of respect in health care settings, research institutions, and public health policies.

NOTES

1. See Albert R. Jonsen, *The Birth of Bioethics* (New York: Oxford University Press, 1998), pp. 3ff; Jonsen, *A Short History of Medical Ethics* (New York: Oxford University Press, 2000); and Edmund D. Pellegrino and David C. Thomasma, *The Virtues in Medical Practice* (New York: Oxford University Press, 1993), pp. 184–89.

2. These distinctions should be used with caution. Metaethics frequently takes a turn toward the normative. Likewise, normative ethics relies on metaethics. Just as no sharp distinction should be drawn between practical ethics and general normative ethics, so no clear line should be drawn to distinguish normative ethics and metaethics.

3. Although there is only one universal common morality, there is more than one theory of the common morality. For a diverse group of recent theories, see Alan Donagan, *The Theory of Morality* (Chicago: University of Chicago Press, 1977); Bernard Gert, *Common Morality: Deciding What to Do*

(New York: Oxford University Press, 2007); Bernard Gert, Charles M. Culver, and K. Danner Clouser, *Bioethics: A Return to Fundamentals,* 2nd ed. (New York: Oxford University Press, 2006); W. D. Ross, *The Foundations of Ethics* (Oxford: Oxford University Press, 1939); and the special issue of the *Kennedy Institute of Ethics Journal* 13 (2003), especially the introductory article by Robert Veatch, pp. 189–92.

4.   Compare the thesis of Martha Nussbaum that, in an Aristotelian philosophy, certain "non-relative virtues" are objective and universal. "Non-Relative Virtues: An Aristotelian Approach," in *Ethical Theory, Character, and Virtue,* ed. Peter French et al. (Notre Dame, IN: University of Notre Dame Press, 1988), pp. 32–53, especially pp. 33–4, 46–50.

5.   For an exceedingly broad account of common morality, see Rebecca Kukla, "Living with Pirates: Common Morality and Embodied Practice," forthcoming in *Cambridge Quarterly of Healthcare Ethics.* See also Bernard Gert's insistence on the role of the *whole moral system* and the perils of neglecting it. *Morality: Its Nature and Justification* (New York: Oxford University Press, 2005), pp. 3, 159–61, 246–47; and his "The Definition of Morality," in *The Stanford Encyclopedia of Philosophy,* 2002; revision of February 11, 2008, http://plato.stanford.edu/entries/morality-definition/ (accessed March 15, 2009).

6.   This charge is mistakenly directed at us by Leigh Turner, "Zones of Consensus and Zones of Conflict: Questioning the 'Common Morality' Presumption in Bioethics," *Kennedy Institute of Ethics Journal* 13 (2003): 193–218; and Turner, "An Anthropological Exploration of Contemporary Bioethics: The Varieties of Common Sense," *Journal of Medical Ethics* 24 (1998): 127–33.

7.   At least it does in all cultures in which there is the requisite core of morally committed persons.

8.   See Turner, "Zones of Consensus and Zones of Conflict"; Donald C. Ainslee, "Bioethics and the Problem of Pluralism," *Social Philosophy and Policy* 19 (2002): 1–28; and David DeGrazia, "Common Morality, Coherence, and the Principles of Biomedical Ethics," *Kennedy Institute of Ethics Journal* 13 (2003): 219–30.

9.   See Richard B. Brandt, "Morality and Its Critics," in his *Morality, Utilitarianism, and Rights* (Cambridge: Cambridge University Press, 1992), chap. 5.

10.   Talcott Parsons, *Essays in Sociological Theory,* rev. ed. (Glencoe, IL: Free Press, 1954), p. 372.

11.   The American Medical Association Code of Ethics of 1847 was largely adapted from Thomas Percival's *Medical Ethics; or a Code of Institutes and Precepts, Adapted to the Professional Conduct of Physicians and Surgeons* (Manchester, England: S. Russell, 1803). See Donald E. Konold, *A History of American Medical Ethics 1847–1912* (Madison, WI: State Historical Society of Wisconsin, 1962), chaps. 1–3; and Chester Burns, "Reciprocity in the Development of Anglo-American Medical Ethics," in *Legacies in Medical Ethics,* ed. Burns (New York: Science History Publications, 1977).

12.   Cf. the conclusions reached about medicine in N. D. Berkman, M. K. Wynia, and L. R. Churchill, "Gaps, Conflicts, and Consensus in the Ethics Statements of Professional Associations, Medical Groups, and Health Plans," *Journal of Medical Ethics* 30 (2004): 395–401; Robert D. Orr et al., "Use of the Hippocratic Oath: A Review of Twentieth Century Practice and a Content Analysis of Oaths Administered in Medical Schools in the U.S. and Canada in 1993," *Journal of Clinical Ethics* 8 (1997): 377–88; and A. C. Kao and K. P. Parsi, "Content Analyses of Oaths Administered at U.S. Medical Schools in 2000," *Academic Medicine* 79 (2004): 882–87.

13.   Jay Katz, ed., *Experimentation with Human Beings* (New York: Russell Sage Foundation, 1972), pp. ix–x.

14.   Omnibus Budget Reconciliation Act of 1990. Public Law 101–508 (Nov. 5, 1990), 4206, 4751. See 42 USC, scattered sections.

15.   See Will Kymlicka, "Moral Philosophy and Public Policy: The Case of New Reproductive Technologies," in *Philosophical Perspectives on Bioethics,* ed. L. W. Sumner and Joseph Boyle

(Toronto: University of Toronto Press, 1996); Dennis Thompson, "Philosophy and Policy," *Philosophy and Public Affairs* 14 (Spring 1985): 205–18; and a symposium on "The Role of Philosophers in the Public Policy Process: A View from the President's Commission," with essays by Alan Weisbard and Dan Brock, in *Ethics* 97 (July 1987): 775–95.

16.   *Tarasoff v. Regents of the University of California,* 17 Cal. 3d 425, 551 P.2d 334, 131 Cal. Rptr. 14 (Cal. 1976).

17.   John Lemmon, "Moral Dilemmas," *Philosophical Review* 71 (1962): 139–58; Daniel Statman, "Hard Cases and Moral Dilemmas," *Law and Philosophy* 15 (1996): 117–48; H. E. Mason, "Responsibilities and Principles: Reflections on the Sources of Moral Dilemmas," in *Moral Dilemmas and Moral Theory,* ed. H. E. Mason (New York: Oxford University Press, 1996).

18.   William R. Bascom, *African Dilemma Tales* (The Hague, Netherlands: Mouton, 1975), p. 145 (relying on anthropological research by Roland Fletcher).

19.   Christopher W. Gowans, ed., *Moral Dilemmas* (New York: Oxford University Press, 1987); Walter Sinnott-Armstrong, *Moral Dilemmas* (Oxford: Basil Blackwell, 1988); Edmund N. Santurri, *Perplexity in the Moral Life: Philosophical and Theological Considerations* (Charlottesville, VA: University Press of Virginia, 1987). For an approach to dilemmas offered as an addition to our accounts in this chapter, see J. P. DeMarco, "Principlism and Moral Dilemmas: A New Principle," *Journal of Medical Ethics* 31 (2005): 101–5.

20.   Some writers in biomedical ethics express reservations about the place of the particular principles we propose in this book. See numerous essays in *Principles of Health Care Ethics,* ed. Raanan Gillon and Ann Lloyd (London: Wiley, 1994); and *Principles of Health Care Ethics,* 2nd ed., ed. Richard E. Ashcroft et al. (Chichester, England: Wiley, 2007); K. Danner Clouser and Bernard Gert, "A Critique of Principlism," *Journal of Medicine and Philosophy* 15 (April 1990): 219–36; and Peter Herissone-Kelly, "The Principlist Approach to Bioethics, and Its Stormy Journey Overseas," in *Scratching the Surface of Bioethics,* ed. Matti Häyry and Tuija Takala (Amsterdam: Rodopi, 2003), pp. 65–77.

21.   Thomas Percival, *Medical Ethics.*

22.   Procedural rules might also be interpreted as grounded in substantive rules of equality. If so interpreted, the procedural rules could be said to have a justification in substantive rules.

23.   For a discussion of *pro tanto* and *prima facie,* see Shelly Kagan, *The Limits of Morality* (Oxford: Clarendon Press, 1989), p. 17. Kagan prefers *pro tanto,* rather than *prima facie,* but concedes that Ross used *prima facie* to mean the same.

24.   W. D. Ross, *The Right and the Good* (Oxford: Clarendon Press, 1930), esp. pp. 19–36, 88. On important cautions about both the meaning and use of the related notion of "prima facie rights," see Joel Feinberg, *Rights, Justice, and the Bounds of Liberty* (Princeton, NJ: Princeton University Press, 1980), pp. 226–29, 232; and Judith Jarvis Thomson, *The Realm of Rights* (Cambridge, MA: Harvard University Press, 1990), pp. 118–29.

25.   Robert Nozick, "Moral Complications and Moral Structures," *Natural Law Forum* 13 (1968): 1–50; James J. Brummer, "Ross and the Ambiguity of Prima Facie Duty," *History of Philosophy Quarterly* 19 (2002): 401–22. See also Thomas E. Hill, Jr., "Moral Dilemmas, Gaps, and Residues: A Kantian Perspective"; Walter Sinnott-Armstrong, "Moral Dilemmas and Rights"; and Terrance C. McConnell, "Moral Residue and Dilemmas"—all in *Moral Dilemmas and Moral Theory,* ed. Mason.

26.   For a similar view, see Ross, *The Right and the Good,* p. 28.

27.   Henry S. Richardson, "Specifying Norms as a Way to Resolve Concrete Ethical Problems," *Philosophy and Public Affairs* 19 (Fall 1990): 279–310; and "Specifying, Balancing, and Interpreting Bioethical Principles," *Journal of Medicine and Philosophy* 25 (2000): 285–307, also in *Belmont*

Revisited: Ethical Principles for Research with Human Subjects, ed. James F. Childress, Eric M. Meslin, and Harold T. Shapiro (Washington, DC: Georgetown University Press, 2005), pp. 205–27. See also David DeGrazia, "Moving Forward in Bioethical Theory: Theories, Cases, and Specified Principlism," *Journal of Medicine and Philosophy* 17 (1992): 511–39; and DeGrazia and Tom L. Beauchamp, "Philosophical Methods," in *Methods of Bioethics,* ed. Daniel Sulmasy and Jeremy Sugarman, 2nd ed. (Washington, DC: Georgetown University Press, 2010).

28.   Richardson, "Specifying, Balancing, and Interpreting Bioethical Principles," p. 289.

29.   For an outstanding critical examination and case study of how the four-principles approach can and should be used as a practical instrument, see John-Stewart Gordon, Oliver Rauprich, and Jochen Vollmann, "Applying the Four-Principle Approach," *Bioethics* 25 (2011): 293–300, with a reply by Tom Beauchamp, "Making Principlism Practical: A Commentary on Gordon, Rauprich, and Vollmann," *Bioethics* 25 (2011): 301–03.

30.   As revised and adopted May 2005, section III: "The informed consent of the person undergoing the forensic evaluation should be obtained when necessary and feasible. If the evaluee is not competent to give consent, the evaluator should follow the appropriate laws of the jurisdiction.... Psychiatrists should inform the evaluee that if the evaluee refuses to participate in the evaluation, this fact may be included in any report or testimony. If the evaluee does not appear capable of understanding the information provided regarding the evaluation, this impression should also be included in any report and, when feasible, in testimony." http://www.aapl.org/pdf/ETHICSGDLNS.pdf (accessed February 6, 2011).

31.   Dennis H. Novack et al., "Physicians' Attitudes Toward Using Deception to Resolve Difficult Ethical Problems," *Journal of the American Medical Association* 261 (May 26, 1989): 2980–85. We return to these problems in Chapter 8.

32.   Richardson, "Specifying Norms," p. 294. "Always" in this formulation should be understood to mean "in principle always." Specification may, in some cases, reach a final form.

33.   Other prohibitions, such as rules against murder, are absolute only because of the meaning of their terms. For example, to say "murder is categorically wrong" may be only to say "unjustified killing is unjustified."

34.   Timothy Quill and Penelope Townsend, "Bad News: Delivery, Dialogue, and Dilemmas," *Archives of Internal Medicine* 151 (March 1991): 463–64.

35.   See Alisa Carse, "Impartial Principle and Moral Context: Securing a Place for the Particular in Ethical Theory," *Journal of Medicine and Philosophy* 23 (1998): 153–69. For a defense of balancing as the best method in such situations, see Joseph P. DeMarco and Paul J. Ford, "Balancing in Ethical Deliberations: Superior to Specification and Casuistry," *Journal of Medicine and Philosophy* 31 (2006): 483–97, esp. 491–93.

36.   See similar reflections in Lawrence Blum, *Moral Perception and Particularity* (New York: Cambridge, 1994), p. 204.

37.   To the extent these six conditions incorporate norms, the norms are prima facie, not absolute. Condition 3 is redundant if it cannot be violated when all of the other conditions are satisfied; but we think it is best to be clear on this point, even if redundant.

38.   See James F. Childress, "Mandatory HIV Screening and Testing," in *Practical Reasoning in Bioethics* (Bloomington and Indianapolis, IN: Indiana University Press, 1997), chap. 6.

39.   For a criticism of our conclusion in this paragraph, see Marvin J. H. Lee, "The Problem of 'Thick in Status, Thin in Content' in Beauchamp and Childress' Principlism," *Journal of Medical Ethics* 36 (2010): 525–28. See further Angus Dawson and E. Garrard, "In Defence of Moral Imperialism: Four

Equal and Universal Prima Facie Principles," *Journal of Medical Ethics* 32 (2006): 200–4; Sinnott-Armstrong, *Moral Dilemmas,* pp. 216–27; and D. D. Raphael, *Moral Philosophy* (Oxford: Oxford University Press, 1981), pp. 64–65.

40.   See the articles in Gillon and Lloyd, eds., *Principles of Health Care Ethics* (the first edition of this work).

41.   See B. Gert, C. M. Culver, and K. D. Clouser, *Bioethics: A Return to Fundamentals,* 2nd ed. (New York: Oxford University Press, 2006), chap. 4; Clouser and Gert, "A Critique of Principlism," pp. 219–36; John H. Evans, "A Sociological Account of the Growth of Principlism," *Hastings Center Report* 30 (September–October 2000): 31–38; Evans, *The History and Future of Bioethics: A Sociological View* (New York: Oxford University Press, 2011); and Carson Strong, "Specified Principlism," *Journal of Medicine and Philosophy* 25 (2000): 285–307.

2
Moral Character

In Chapter 1 we concentrated on moral norms in the form of principles, rules, obligations, and rights. In this chapter, we concentrate on moral virtues, moral character, moral ideals, and moral excellence. These categories complement those in the previous chapter without undermining them. Whereas the moral norms discussed in Chapter 1 chiefly govern right action, character ethics or virtue ethics concentrates on the agent who performs actions and claims that an agent's virtues make him or her a morally worthy person.[1]

What often matters most in the moral life is not adherence to moral rules, but having a reliable character, a good moral sense, and an appropriate emotional responsiveness. Even specified principles and rules do not convey what occurs when parents lovingly play with and nurture their children or when physicians and nurses exhibit compassion, patience, and responsiveness in their encounters with patients and families. Our feelings and concerns for others lead us to actions that cannot be reduced to merely following rules, and morality would be a cold and uninspiring practice without appropriate sympathy, emotional responsiveness, excellence of character, and heartfelt ideals that reach beyond principles and rules.

Some philosophers have questioned the place of virtues in moral theory. They see virtues as less central than action-guiding norms and as difficult to unify in a systematic theory, in part because there are many largely independent virtues to be considered. Utilitarian Jeremy Bentham famously complained that there is "no marshaling" the virtues and vices and that "they are susceptible of no arrangement; they are a disorderly body, whose members are frequently in hostility with one another.... Most of them are characterized by that vagueness which is a convenient instrument for the poetical, but dangerous or useless to the practical moralist."[2]

Although principles and virtues are different and taught differently, virtues are no less important in the moral life. Indeed, the Aristotelian virtues are "valuable in large part because they are immunities from common forms of distortion in practical reasoning, arising from characteristically human desires, emotions, or feelings."[3] Moreover, the goals and structure of medicine, health care, public health, and research call for a deep appreciation of moral virtues.[4] In Chapter 9, we examine virtue ethics as a type of moral theory and address challenges and criticisms such as Bentham's. In the first few sections of the present chapter, we briefly analyze the concept of virtue; examine virtues in professional roles; treat the moral notions of care, caregiving, and caring as virtues in health care; and explicate five other focal virtues in both health care and research.

THE CONCEPT OF MORAL VIRTUE

A *virtue* is a dispositional trait of character that is socially valuable and reliably present in a person, and a *moral virtue* is a dispositional trait of character that is morally valuable and reliably present. If cultures or social groups approve a trait and regard it as moral, their approval is not sufficient to qualify the trait as a moral virtue. Some communities disvalue persons who are virtuous, and some communities admire persons for their vices, such as meanness and churlishness. Moral virtue, then, is more than a personal, dispositional trait that is socially approved in a particular group or culture.[5] This explanation accords with our conclusion in Chapter 1 that the common morality excludes provisions found in so-called cultural moralities and individual moralities.

Some define the term *moral virtue* as a disposition to act or a habit of acting in accordance with, and with the aim of following, moral principles, obligations, or ideals.[6] For example, they understand the moral virtue of nonmalevolence as the trait a person has of abstaining from causing harm to others when it would be wrong to cause harm. However, this definition unjustifiably views virtues as derivative from and dependent on principles, and it also fails to capture the importance of moral motives. We care morally about people's motives, and we care especially about their characteristic motives and dispositions. That is, we care about the motivational structures embedded in their character. Persons who are motivated through impartial sympathy and personal affection, for example, meet our moral approval, whereas others who act similarly, but are motivated merely by personal ambition, do not.

Imagine a person who discharges a moral obligation only because it is an obligation, but who intensely dislikes being placed in a position in which the interests of others override his or her own interests. This person does not feel friendly toward or cherish others and respects their wishes only because obligation requires it. This person nonetheless performs morally right actions and has a disposition to perform right actions. But if the motive is improper, a critical moral ingredient is missing; and if a person characteristically lacks this motivational structure, a necessary condition of virtuous character is absent. The act may be right and the actor blameless, but neither is *virtuous*. People may be disposed to do what is right, intend to do it, and do it, while simultaneously yearning to avoid doing it. Persons who characteristically perform morally right actions from such a motivational structure are not morally virtuous even if they invariably perform the morally right action.

Not only is such a person's character morally incomplete, but also it is morally incoherent in that he or she performs morally right actions for reasons or feelings disconnected from moral motivation. A philanthropist's gift of a new wing of a hospital will be recognized by hospital officials and by the general public as a generous gift, but if the philanthropist only feels the need for public praise and only makes the gift to gain such praise, there is a discordance between those feelings and the performance of the praised action. Feelings and a certain type of motivation are morally important in a virtue theory in a way that can be lost or obscured in an obligation-based theory.[7] Furthermore, there is an important distinction between the *virtuous person* as one whose character reliably leads to action motivated by morally admirable motives and a *virtuous action* as one performed in character by such a person.

VIRTUES IN PROFESSIONAL ROLES

Persons differ in the particular sets of character traits they possess. Most individuals have some virtues and some vices while lacking other virtues and vices. However, all persons with normal moral capacities can cultivate the character traits of chief importance to morality. In professional life the traits that warrant encouragement and admiration often derive from role responsibilities. Certain virtues are essential to the discharge of these professional roles, and certain vices are intolerable in professional life. Accordingly, we begin with virtues that are critically important in professional and institutional roles and practices in biomedical fields.

Virtues in Roles and Practices

Professional roles are usually tied to institutional expectations and standards of professional practice. Roles internalize conventions, customs, and procedures of teaching, nursing, doctoring, and the like. Professional practice has a tradition that requires professionals to cultivate certain virtues. Standards of virtue incorporate criteria of professional merit, and possession of these virtues disposes a person to act in accordance with the objectives of the practices.

Consider, for example, professional roles in the practice of medicine. Several goods are internal to the profession and are naturally associated with the idea of being a good physician. These include specific moral and nonmoral skills in the care of patients, the application of specific forms of knowledge, and the teaching of health behaviors. These goods are achievable if, and only if, one abides by the standards of the good physician, standards that have a history and that in part define the practice. A practice is not merely a set of technical skills. Practices should be understood in terms of the regard practitioners have for the goods internal to the practices. Although these practices are not immune to revision, historical development of a body of standards is definitive of the idea of medicine and nursing as practices.[8]

Roles and practices in medicine and nursing reflect social expectations as well as standards and ideals internal to these professions. Their traditional virtues derive primarily from experience with health care relationships.[9] The virtues we highlight are care—a fundamental virtue for traditional health care relationships—along with five focal virtues: compassion, discernment, trustworthiness, integrity, and conscientiousness, all of which support and promote caring and caregiving. Elsewhere in this chapter and in later chapters, we discuss other virtues, including respectfulness, nonmalevolence, benevolence, justice, truthfulness, and faithfulness.

To illustrate the difference between standards of moral character in a profession (and corresponding moral skills) and standards of technical performance in a profession (and corresponding technical skills), we begin with an instructive study of surgical error. Charles L. Bosk's influential *Forgive and Remember: Managing Medical Failure* presents an ethnographic study of the way two surgical services in "Pacific Hospital" handle medical failure, especially failures by surgical residents.[10] Bosk found that both surgical services distinguish, at least implicitly, between several different forms of error or mistake. The first is *technical:* The professional discharges role responsibilities conscientiously, but his or her technical training or information falls short of what the task requires. Every surgeon will occasionally make this sort of mistake. The second sort of error is *judgmental:* A conscientious professional develops and follows an incorrect strategy. These errors are also to be expected. Attending surgeons forgive momentary technical and judgmental errors but remember them in case a pattern develops indicating that a surgical resident lacks the technical and judgmental skills to be a competent surgeon. The third sort of error is *normative:* A physician violates a norm of conduct or fails to possess a moral skill, particularly by failing to discharge moral obligations conscientiously or by failing to acquire and exercise critical moral virtues such as conscientiousness. Bosk concludes that surgeons view technical and judgmental errors as less important than moral errors, because every conscientious person can be expected to make "honest errors" or "good faith errors." However, moral errors such as failures of conscientiousness are considered profoundly serious when a pattern indicates a defect of character.

As Bosk's study suggests, persons of high moral character acquire a reservoir of goodwill in assessments of either the praiseworthiness or the blameworthiness of their actions. If a conscientious surgeon and another surgeon who is not conscientious make the same technical or judgmental errors, the conscientious surgeon will not be subjected to moral blame to the same degree as the other surgeon.

Virtues in Alternative Professional Models

Professional virtues were historically integrated with professional obligations and ideals in codes of health care ethics. Insisting that the medical profession's "prime objective" is to render service to humanity, an American Medical Association (AMA) code in effect from 1957 to 1980 urged the physician to be "upright" and "pure in character and...diligent and conscientious in caring for the sick." It endorsed the virtues that Hippocrates commended: modesty, sobriety, patience, promptness, and piety. However, in sharp contrast to its first code in 1847, the AMA over the years has increasingly de-emphasized virtues in codes. The 1980 version for the first time eliminated all trace of the virtues except for the admonition to expose "those physicians deficient in character or competence." This pattern of de-emphasis regrettably continues today.

Thomas Percival's classic 1803 book, *Medical Ethics,* is an example of an attempt to establish the proper set of virtues in medicine. Starting from the assumption that the patient's best medical interest is the proper goal of medicine, Percival reached conclusions about the good physician's traits of character, which were invariably tied to responsibility for the patient's medical welfare.[11] Not surprisingly, this model supported medical paternalism with effectively no attention paid to respect for patients' autonomous choices.

Likewise, in traditional nursing, where the nurse was often viewed as the "handmaiden" of the physician, the nurse was counseled to cultivate the passive virtues of obedience and submission. In contemporary models in nursing, however, active virtues have become more prominent. For example, when the nurse's role is viewed as one of advocacy for patients, prominent virtues include respectfulness, considerateness, justice, persistence, and courage.[12] Attention to patients' rights and preservation of the nurse's integrity have become increasingly prominent in some contemporary models.

The conditions under which virtues are present in morally unworthy and condemnable actions present thorny ethical issues. Virtues such as loyalty, courage, generosity, kindness, respectfulness, and benevolence at times lead persons to act inappropriately and unacceptably. For instance, the physician who acts kindly and loyally by not reporting the incompetence of a fellow physician acts unethically. Such a failure to report professional misconduct does not suggest that loyalty and kindness are not virtues, only that the virtues need to be accompanied by an understanding of what is right and good, and of what deserves loyalty, kindness, generosity, and the like.

THE VIRTUE OF CARING

As the language of *health care, medical care,* and *nursing care* suggests, the virtue of care, or caring, is prominent in professional ethics in these contexts. We treat this virtue as fundamental in relationships, practices, and actions in health care. In explicating this virtue, or perhaps family of virtues, we draw on what has been called the *ethics of care,* which we interpret as a form of virtue ethics.[13] The ethics of care emphasizes traits valued in intimate personal relationships such as sympathy, compassion, fidelity, and love. *Caring,* in particular, refers to care for, emotional commitment to, and willingness to act on behalf of persons with whom one has a significant relationship. *Caring for* is expressed in actions of "caregiving," "taking care of," and "due care." The nurse's or physician's trust-worthiness and quality of care and sensitivity in the face of patients' problems, needs, and vulnerabilities are integral to their professional moral lives.

The ethics of care emphasizes not only what physicians and nurses do—for example, whether they break or maintain confidentiality—but also how they perform those actions, which motives and feelings underlie them, and whether their actions promote or thwart positive relationships. To take an example discussed in a later chapter, a caring clinician considers both whether to disclose the prognosis of a patient's death (in a few months) and how, when, and where to divulge that prognosis.

The Origins of the Ethics of Care

The ethics of care, interpreted as a form of philosophical ethics, originated primarily in feminist writings. The earliest works emphasized how women display an ethic of care, by contrast to men, who predominantly exhibit an ethic of rights and obligations. Psychologist Carol Gilligan advanced the influential hypothesis that "women speak in a different voice"—a voice that traditional ethical theory drowned out. She discovered "the voice of care" through empirical research involving interviews with girls and women. This voice, she said, stresses empathic association with others, not based on "the primacy and universality of individual rights, but rather on ... a very strong sense of being responsible."[14]

Gilligan identified two modes of moral thinking: an ethic of care and an ethic of rights and justice. She did not claim that these two modes of thinking strictly correlate with gender or that all women or all men speak in the same moral voice.[15] She maintained only that men tend to embrace an ethic of rights and justice that uses quasi-legal terminology and impartial principles, accompanied by dispassionate balancing and conflict resolution, whereas women tend to affirm an ethic of care that centers on responsiveness in an interconnected network of needs, care, and prevention of harm. The core notion in an ethics of care, then, is caring for and taking care of others.[16]

Criticisms of Traditional Theories by Proponents of an Ethics of Care

Proponents of the care perspective often criticize traditional ethical theories that seem to de-emphasize virtues of caring. Two criticisms merit consideration here.[17]

Challenging impartiality. According to some representations of the care perspective, theories of norms of obligation unduly telescope morality by overemphasizing detached fairness. This orientation is suitable for some moral relationships, especially those in which persons interact as equals in a public context of impersonal justice and institutional constraints, but moral detachment may also evince a lack of caring responsiveness. In the extreme case, detachment becomes uncaring indifference. Lost in the *detachment* of impartiality is an *attachment* to what we care about most and is closest to us—for example, our loyalty to family, friends, and groups. In the absence of public and institutional constraints, partiality toward others is morally permissible and is the expected form of interaction. It is also a feature of the human condition that cannot be eliminated. Without exhibiting partiality, we would impair or sever our most important relationships.[18]

Proponents of care ethics do not recommend a general abandonment of principles as long as principles allow room for discretionary and contextual judgment. At the same time, like many other proponents of virtue ethics, defenders of the ethics of care often find principles irrelevant, unproductive, ineffectual, or unduly constrictive in the moral life. A defender of principles could say that principles of care, compassion, and kindness tutor our responses in caring, compassionate, and kind ways. But this effort to rescue principles seems empty. Moral experience suggests that we often do rely on our emotions, our capacity for sympathy, our sense of friendship, and our sensitivity to determine appropriate moral responses. We can produce rough generalizations about how caring clinicians should respond to patients, but these generalizations cannot provide adequate guidance for all interactions with patients. Each situation calls for a set of responses beyond generalizations, and actions that are caring in one context may be offensive or even harmful in another.

Relationship and emotion. The ethics of care places special emphasis on mutual interdependence and emotional responsiveness. Many human relationships in health care and research involve persons who are vulnerable, dependent, ill, and frail. Feeling for and being immersed in the other person are vital aspects of a moral relationship with them.[19] A rights-based or obligation-based account may neglect appropriate forms of empathy because of its focus on protecting persons from wrongdoing by others. Having a certain emotional attitude and expressing the appropriate emotion in action are morally relevant factors, just as having appropriate motives is morally relevant. A person seems morally deficient who acts according to norms of obligation without appropriately aligned feelings, such as concern and sympathy for a suffering person. Good health care often involves insight into the needs of patients and considerate attentiveness to their circumstances, which may derive more from emotional or sympathetic responsiveness than from reason.[20]

In the history of human experimentation, those who first recognized that some subjects of research were brutalized, subjected to misery, or placed at unjustifiable risk were persons who were able to feel sympathy, compassion, disgust, and outrage about the situation of these research subjects. They exhibited perception of and sensitivity to the feelings of these subjects where others lacked comparable perceptions, sensitivities, and responses. This emphasis on the emotional dimension of the moral life does not entirely reduce moral response to emotional response. Caring itself has a cognitive dimension and requires a range of moral skills, because it involves insight into and understanding of another's circumstances, needs, and feelings.

One proponent of the ethics of care argues that, in a defensible ethical theory, action is sometimes principle-guided, but not necessarily always governed by or derived from principles.[21] This statement moves in the right direction for a comprehensive framework. We need not reject principles of obligation in favor of the virtues of caring, and we can conceive moral judgment as involving moral skills beyond those of specifying and balancing general principles. An ethic that emphasizes the virtues of caring can serve health care well because it is close to the relationships and processes of decision making found in clinical contexts, gives insight into basic commitments of caring and caretaking, and liberates health professionals from narrow conceptions of role responsibilities often found in professional codes of ethics.

FIVE FOCAL VIRTUES

We now examine five focal virtues for health professionals: compassion, discernment, trustworthiness, integrity, and conscientiousness. These virtues are important in part for the development and expression of caring, which we have presented as the fundamental orienting virtue in health care. These virtues provide a moral compass of character for health professionals, and some have played a prominent role for centuries in the ethics of physicians.[22] Other virtues are no less important, and we treat several of them later and in Chapter 9.

Compassion

Compassion is a "prelude to caring."[23] The virtue of compassion combines an attitude of active regard for another's welfare with an imaginative awareness and emotional response of sympathy, tenderness, and discomfort at another's misfortune or suffering.[24] Compassion presupposes sympathy, has affinities with mercy, and is expressed in acts of beneficence that attempt to alleviate the misfortune or suffering of another person. Unlike the virtue of integrity, which is focused on the self, compassion is directed at others.

Nurses and physicians must understand the feelings and experiences of patients to respond appropriately to them and their illnesses and injuries—hence the importance of empathy, which involves the reconstructing of another person's mental experience, whether that experience is negative or positive.[25] As important as empathy is for compassion and other virtues, the two are different and empathy does not always lead to compassion. Literature on professionalism in medicine and health care now often focuses on empathy rather than compassion. This literature may be making the mistake of viewing empathy alone as sufficient for humanizing medicine and health care.[26]

Compassion generally focuses on others' pain, suffering, disability, and misery—the typical occasions for compassionate responses in health care. Using the language of *sympathy,* eighteenth-century philosopher David Hume pointed to a typical circumstance of compassion in surgery and explained how it arises:

> Were I present at any of the more terrible operations of surgery, 'tis certain, that even before it begun, the preparation of the instruments, the laying of the bandages in order, the heating of the irons, with all the signs of anxiety and concern in the patient and assistants, wou'd have a great effect upon my mind, and excite the strongest sentiments of pity and terror. No passion of another discovers itself immediately to the mind. We are only sensible of its causes or effects. From *these* we infer the passion: And consequently *these* give rise to our sympathy.[27]

Those physicians and nurses who express no compassion in their behavior fail to provide what patients need most. The physician or nurse lacking altogether in the appropriate display of compassion has a moral weakness. However, compassion also may cloud judgment and preclude rational and effective responses. In one reported case, a long-alienated son wanted to continue a futile and painful treatment for his near-comatose father in an intensive care unit (ICU) to have time to "make his peace" with his father. Although the son understood that his alienated father had no cognitive capacity, the son wanted to work through his sense of regret. Some hospital staff argued that the patient's grim prognosis and pain, combined with the needs of others waiting to receive care in the ICU, justified stopping the treatment, as had been requested by the patient's close cousin and informal guardian. Another group in the unit regarded continued treatment as an appropriate act of compassion toward the son, who they thought should have time to express his farewells and regrets to make himself feel better about his father's death. The first group, by contrast, viewed compassion as misplaced because of the patient's prolonged agony and dying. In effect, those in the first group believed that the second group's compassion prevented clear thinking about primary obligations to this patient.[28]

Many writers in the history of ethical theory have proposed a cautious approach to compassion. They maintain that a passionate, or even a compassionate, engagement with others can blind reason and prevent impartial reflection.

Health care professionals understand and appreciate this phenomenon. Constant contact with suffering can overwhelm and even paralyze a compassionate physician or nurse. Impartial judgment can give way to impassioned decisions, and emotional burnout can occur. To counteract this problem, medical education and nursing education are designed to inculcate detachment alongside compassion. The language of *detached concern* and *compassionate detachment* appropriately appears in health care ethics expressly to identify a complex characteristic of the good physician or good nurse.

Discernment

The virtue of discernment brings sensitive insight, astute judgment, and understanding to bear on action. Discernment involves the ability to make fitting judgments and reach decisions without being unduly influenced by extraneous considerations, fears, personal attachments, and the like. Some writers closely associate discernment with practical wisdom, or *phronesis,* to use Aristotle's term. A person of practical wisdom knows which ends to choose, knows how to realize them in particular circumstances, and carefully selects from among the range of possible actions, while keeping emotions within proper bounds. In Aristotle's model, the practically wise person understands how to act with the right intensity of feeling, in just the right way, at just the right time, with a proper balance of reason and desire.[29]

The person of discernment is disposed to understand and perceive what circumstances demand in the way of human responsiveness. For example, a discerning physician will see when a despairing patient needs comfort rather than privacy, and vice versa. If comfort is the right choice, the discerning physician will find the right type and level of consolation to be helpful rather than intrusive. If a rule guides action in a particular case, seeing *how* to follow the rule involves a form of discernment that is independent of seeing *that* the rule applies.

The virtue of discernment involves understanding both that and how principles and rules apply in a variety of circumstances. For instance, acts of respect for autonomy and beneficence will vary in health care contexts, and the ways in which clinicians discerningly implement these principles in the care of patients will be as different as the ways in which devoted parents care for their children.

Trustworthiness

Virtues, Annette Baier maintains, "are personal traits that contribute to a good climate of trust between people, when trust is taken to be acceptance of being, to some degree and in some respects, in another's power."[30] This climate of trust is essential in medical and health care, where patients are vulnerable and must put themselves in the hands of health care professionals. Trust is a confident belief in and reliance on the moral character and competence of another person, often a person with whom one has an intimate or established relationship. Trust entails a confidence that another will reliably act with the right motives and feelings and in accordance with appropriate moral norms.[31] To be *trustworthy* is to merit confidence in one's character and conduct. Trustworthiness has the practical outcome of making health care effective. Nothing is more important in health care organizations than the maintenance of a culture of trust.

Traditional ethical theories rarely mention either trust or trustworthiness. However, Aristotle took note of one aspect of trust and trustworthiness. He maintained that when relationships are voluntary and among intimates, in contrast to legal relationships among strangers, it is appropriate for the law to forbid lawsuits for harms that occur. Aristotle reasoned that in intimate relationships "dealings with one another as good and trustworthy," rather than "bonds of justice," hold persons together.[32]

A true climate of trust is endangered in contemporary health care institutions, as is evidenced by the number of medical malpractice suits and adversarial relations between health care professionals and the public. Overt distrust has been engendered by mechanisms of managed care, because of the incentives some health care organizations create for physicians to limit the amount and kinds of care they provide to patients. Appeals have increased for ombudsmen, patient advocates, legally binding "directives" to physicians, and the like. Among the contributing causes of the erosion of a climate of trust are the loss of intimate contact between physicians and patients, the increased use of specialists, and the growth of large, impersonal, and bureaucratic medical institutions.[33]

Integrity

Some writers in bioethics claim that the primary virtue in health care is integrity.[34] People often justify their actions or refusals to act on grounds that they would otherwise compromise or sacrifice their integrity. Later in this chapter we discuss these appeals to integrity as invocations of *conscience,* but we confine attention here to the virtue of integrity.

The value of moral integrity is beyond serious dispute, but what we mean by the term is less clear. In its most general sense, "moral integrity" means soundness, reliability, wholeness, and integration of moral character. In a more restricted sense, the term refers to objectivity, impartiality, and fidelity in adherence to moral norms. Accordingly, the virtue of integrity represents two aspects of a person's character. The first is a coherent integration of aspects of the self— emotions, aspirations, knowledge, and the like—so that each complements and does not frustrate the others. The second is the character trait of being faithful to moral values and standing up in their defense when necessary. A person can lack moral integrity in several respects—for example, through hypocrisy, insincerity, bad faith, and self-deception. These vices represent breaks in the connections among a person's moral convictions, emotions, and actions. The most common deficiency is probably the simple lack of sincerely and firmly held moral convictions; but no less important is the failure to act on the correct moral beliefs that one does hold.

Problems in maintaining integrity arise not only from a lack of moral conviction or a conflict of moral norms, but also from moral demands that require persons to sacrifice in a way that causes them to abandon their personal goals and projects. Persons can feel violated by having to abandon their personal commitments to pursue moral objectives. For example, if a nurse is the only person in her family who can properly manage her mother's health, health care, prescription medications, nursing home arrangements, explanations to relatives, and negotiations with physicians, little time may be left for her personal projects and commitments. Such situations can deprive us of the liberty to structure and integrate our lives as we choose. If a person has structured his or her life around personal goals that are ripped away by the needs and agendas of others, a loss of personal integrity occurs.

Professional integrity presents issues about wrongful conduct in professions. Because breaches of professional integrity involve violations of professional standards of conduct, they are often viewed as violations of the rules of professional associations. This vision is too narrow.[35] Breaches of professional integrity also occur when a physician prescribes a drug that is not effective, enters into a sexual relationship with a patient, or follows a living will that asks for a medically outrageous "treatment"—whether or not professional associations disallow such conduct and whether or not the physician feels bound by the standards of conduct.

Sometimes conflicts arise between a person's sense of moral integrity and professional integrity. Consider, for example, medical practitioners who, because of their religious commitments to the sanctity of life, find it difficult to participate in decisions not to do everything possible to prolong life. To them, participating in removing ventilators and intravenous fluids from patients, even from patients with a clear advance directive, violates their integrity. Their evaluative commitments may create morally troublesome situations in which they must either compromise their fundamental commitments or withdraw from the care of the patient. Yet compromise seems what a person, or an organization, of integrity cannot do, because it involves the sacrifice of deep moral commitments.[36]

Health care facilities cannot entirely eliminate these and other problems of staff disagreement, but persons with the virtues of patience, humility, and tolerance can help to ameliorate these problems. Situations that compromise integrity can be ameliorated if participants anticipate the problem before it arises and recognize the limits and fallibility of their moral views. Participants in a dispute may also have recourse to consultative institutional processes, such as hospital ethics committees. However, it would be ill-advised to recommend that a person of integrity can and should always negotiate and compromise his or her values in an intrainstitutional confrontation. There is something ennobling and admirable about the person or organization that refuses to compromise beyond a certain carefully considered moral threshold. To compromise below the threshold of integrity is simply to lose it.

Conscientiousness

The topic of integrity and compromise leads directly to discussion of the virtue of conscientiousness and to accounts of conscience. An individual acts conscientiously if he or she is motivated to do what is right because it is right, has tried with due diligence to determine what is right, intends to do what is right, and exerts appropriate effort to do so. Conscientiousness is the character trait of acting in this way.

Conscience and conscientiousness. *Conscience* has often been viewed as a mental faculty of, and authority for, moral decision making.[37] Slogans such as, "Let your conscience be your guide" suggest that conscience is the final authority in moral justification. However, this account fails to capture the nature of either conscience or conscientiousness. We can see why by examining the following case put forward by Bernard Williams: Having recently completed his Ph.D. in chemistry, George has not been able to find a job. His family has suffered from his failure: They are short of money, his wife has had to take additional work, and their small children have been subjected to considerable strain, uncertainty, and instability. An established chemist can get George a position in a laboratory that pursues research in chemical and biological warfare. Despite his perilous financial and familial circumstances, George concludes that he cannot accept this position because of his conscientious opposition to chemical and biological warfare. The senior chemist notes that the research will continue no matter what George decides. Furthermore, if George does not take this position, it will be offered to another young man who would pursue the research vigorously. Indeed, the senior chemist confides, his concern about this other candidate's nationalistic fervor and uncritical zeal for research in chemical and biological warfare motivated him to recommend George for the job. George's wife is puzzled and hurt by George's reaction. She sees nothing wrong with the research. She is profoundly concerned about their children's problems and the instability of their family. Nonetheless, George forgoes this opportunity both to help his family and to prevent a destructive fanatic from obtaining the position because his conscience stands in the way.[38]

Conscience, as this example suggests, is not a special moral faculty or a self-justifying moral authority. It is a form of self-reflection about whether one's acts are obligatory or prohibited, right or wrong, good or bad, virtuous or vicious. It also involves an internal sanction that comes into play through critical reflection. When individuals recognize their acts as violations of an appropriate standard, this sanction often appears as a bad conscience in the form of feelings of remorse, guilt, shame, disunity, or disharmony. A conscience that sanctions conduct in this way does not signify bad moral character. To the contrary, this experience of conscience is most likely to occur in persons of strong moral character and may even be a necessary condition of morally good character.[39] For example, kidney donors have been known to say, "I had to do it. I couldn't have backed out, not that I had the feeling of being trapped, because the doctors offered to get me out. I just had to do it."[40] Such poignant statements indicate that some ethical standards are sufficiently powerful that violating them would diminish integrity and result in guilt or shame.[41]

When people claim that their actions are conscientious, they sometimes feel compelled by conscience to resist others' authoritative demands. Instructive examples are found in military physicians who believe they must answer first to their consciences and cannot plead "superior orders" when commanded by a superior officer to commit what they believe to be a moral wrong. In some cases agents even act out of character in order to perform what they judge to be the morally appropriate action. For example, a normally cooperative and agreeable physician may angrily, and justifiably, protest an insurance company's decision not to cover the costs of a patient's treatment. Such moral indignation and outrage are sometimes appropriate and admirable.

Conscientious refusals. Conscientious objections by physicians, nurses, pharmacists, and other health care professionals raise difficult issues for public policy, professional organizations, and health care institutions. Examples are found in a physician's refusal to honor a patient's valid advance directive to withdraw artificial nutrition and hydration, a nurse's refusal to participate in an abortion or sterilization procedure, and a pharmacist's refusal to fill a prescription for an emergency contraception. There are good reasons to promote conscientiousness and to respect acts of conscience, but some conscientious refusals adversely affect patients' and others' legitimate interests. Public policy, the professions, and institutions should seek to recognize and accommodate conscientious refusals as long as they can do so without seriously compromising patients' rights and interests.

The metaphor of balance, or balancing, is commonly used to guide efforts to protect both interest sets. Accordingly, no single model of appropriate response covers all cases.[42] Frequently, institutions such as hospitals and pharmacies can ensure the timely performance of needed or requested services while allowing particular conscientious objectors not to perform those services.[43] However, ethical complexities arise when, for example, a pharmacist refuses, on grounds of complicity in moral wrongdoing, to refer or transfer a consumer's prescription or to inform the consumer of pharmacies that would fill the prescription. According to one study, 14% of U.S. physicians surveyed do not feel obligated to disclose information about morally controversial medical procedures, and 29% of U.S. physicians do not recognize an obligation to refer patients for such procedures.[44]

At a minimum, health care professionals have an ethical duty to inform prospective employers and prospective patients, clients, and consumers in advance of their conscientious objections to performing vital services. Likewise, they have an ethical duty to disclose options for obtaining legal, albeit morally controversial, services and, in many cases, a duty to provide a referral for those services. They also have a duty to perform those services in emergency circumstances when the patient is at risk of adverse health effects and a timely referral is not possible.

Determining the appropriate scope of protectable conscientious refusals is a vexing problem that arises, for example, because of conscientious objections to expanded notions of participation in or assistance in the performance of an objectionable action. These expanded notions include actions that are only indirectly related to the objectionable procedure. For example, some nurses have claimed conscientious exemption from all forms of participation in the care of patients having an abortion or sterilization, even to the extent of declining to fill out admission forms or provide postprocedure care. It is difficult in institutions, and less clearly required from an ethical standpoint, to exempt objectors to such broadly delineated forms of participation in a procedure.

MORAL IDEALS

We argued in Chapter 1 that norms of obligation in the common morality constitute a moral minimum that pertains to everyone. These standards are notably different from extraordinary moral standards, which are neither required nor obligatory. However, general ideals such as extraordinary generosity are rightly admired and endorsed by all morally committed persons, and in this respect they form part of the common morality. Extraordinary moral standards come from a morality of aspiration in which individuals and communities adopt high ideals not demanded of others. We can praise and admire those who fulfill these ideals, but we cannot blame or criticize persons who do not pursue them.

A straightforward example of a moral ideal in biomedical ethics is found in "expanded access" or "compassionate use" programs that authorize access, prior to regulatory approval, to an investigational drug or device for patients with a serious or immediately life-threatening disease or condition. These patients have exhausted available therapeutic options and are situated so that they cannot participate in a clinical trial of a comparable investigational product. Although it is clearly compassionate and justified to provide some investigational products for therapeutic use, it is rarely obligatory to do so. These programs are compassionate, nonobligatory, and motivated by a goal of providing a good to these patients. The self-imposed moral commitment by the sponsors of the investigational product usually springs from a moral ideal of communal service. (We discuss expanded access programs further in Chapter 6.)

With the addition of moral ideals, we now have four categories of moral action: (1) actions that are right and obligatory (e.g., truth-telling); (2) actions that are wrong and prohibited (e.g., murder); (3) actions that are optional and morally neutral (neither wrong nor obligatory; e.g., playing chess with a friend); and (4) actions that are optional but morally meritorious and praiseworthy (e.g., sending flowers to a sick friend). We concentrated on the first two in Chapter 1, occasionally mentioning the third. We now focus exclusively on the fourth.

Supererogatory Acts

Supererogation is a category of moral ideals pertaining principally to ideals of action, but it has important links both to virtues and to Aristotelian ideas of moral excellence.[45] The etymological root of *supererogation* means paying or performing beyond what is owed or, more generally, doing more than is required. Supererogation has four defining conditions (which collectively state the meaning of category 4 listed in the previous paragraph). First, supererogatory acts are optional and neither required nor forbidden by common-morality standards of obligation. Second, supererogatory acts exceed what the common morality of obligation demands, but at least some moral ideals are endorsed by all who are committed to the common morality. Third, supererogatory acts are intentionally undertaken to promote the welfare interests of others. Fourth, supererogatory acts are morally good and praiseworthy in themselves; they are not merely acts that are undertaken from good intentions.

Despite the first condition, individuals who act on moral ideals do not always *consider* their actions to be morally optional. Many heroes and saints describe their actions in the language of *ought, duty,* and *necessity:* "I had to do it." "I had no choice." "It was my duty." The point of this language is to express a personal sense of obligation, not to state a general obligation. The agent accepts, as a pledge or assignment of personal responsibility, a norm that lays down what ought to be done. At the end of Albert Camus's *The Plague,* Dr. Rieux decides to make a record of those who fought the pestilence. It is to be a record, he says, of "what *had to be done* ... despite their personal afflictions, by all who, while unable to be saints but refusing to bow down to pestilences, strive their utmost to be healers."[46] Such healers accept exceptional risks and thereby exceed the obligations of the common morality and of their professional tradition.

Many supererogatory acts would be morally obligatory were it not for some abnormal adversity or risk in the face of which the individual elects not to invoke an exemption allowed because of the adversity or risk.[47] If persons have the strength of character that enables them to resist extreme adversity or assume additional risk to fulfill their own conception of their obligations, then it makes sense to accept their view that they are under a self-imposed obligation. The hero who says, "I was only doing my duty," is, from his or her perspective, speaking as one who accepts a standard of moral excellence. This hero does not make a mistake in regarding the action as personally required and can view failure as grounds for guilt, although no one else is free to so evaluate the act as a moral failure.

Despite our language of "exceptional" and "extreme adversity," not all supererogatory acts are extraordinarily arduous, costly, or risky. Examples of less demanding forms of supererogation include generous gift-giving, volunteering for public service, forgiving another's costly error, and special kindness. Many everyday actions exceed obligation without reaching the highest levels of super-erogation. For example, a nurse may put in extra hours of work during the day and return to the hospital at night to visit patients without becoming a saint or hero.

Often we are uncertain whether an action exceeds obligation because the boundaries of obligation and supererogation are ill defined. There may be no clear norm of action, only a virtue of character at work. For example, what is a nurse's role obligation to desperate, terminally ill patients who cling to the nurse for comfort in their few remaining days? If the obligation is that of spending forty hours a week in conscientiously fulfilling a job description, then the nurse exceeds that obligation by a few off-duty visits to patients. If the obligation is simply to help patients overcome burdens and meet a series of challenges, then a nurse who does so while displaying extraordinary patience, fortitude, and friendliness exceeds the demands of obligation. There are also cases of health care professionals living up to what would ordinarily be a role obligation (e.g., complying with standards of care), while making a significant sacrifice or taking an exceptional risk.

The Continuum from Obligation to Supererogation

Our analysis may suggest that any given action can be readily classified as either obligatory or beyond the obligatory. However, some actions do not fit neatly into these categories because they fall between the two. Common morality distinctions and ethical theory are not precise enough to determine whether these actions are morally required or morally elective. This problem is compounded in professional ethics, because professional roles engender obligations that do not bind persons who do not occupy the relevant professional roles. Hence, the two "levels" of the obligatory and the supererogatory lack sharp boundaries both in the common morality and in professional ethics.

There is a critical distinction between actions that are strictly obligatory, actions that are borderline, and actions that are beyond the obligatory. A continuum runs from strict obligation (the core principles and rules in the common morality) through weaker obligations (the periphery of ordinary expectations in the common morality) and on to the domain of the morally nonrequired and the exceptionally virtuous. The nonrequired starts with lower level supererogation, such as walking a visitor lost in a hospital's corridors to a doctor's office. Here an absence of generosity or kindness in helping someone constitutes a defect in the moral life, although not a failure of obligation. The continuum ends with higher level supererogation, such as heroic acts of self-sacrifice, as in highly risky medical self-experimentation. A continuum exists on each level and across their boundaries. The following diagram represents the continuum.

Obligation		*Beyond Obligation (Supererogation)*	
Strict obligation [1]	Weak obligation [2]	Ideals beyond the obligatory [3]	Saintly and heroic ideals [4]

This continuum moves from the strictest obligation to the most arduous and elective moral ideal. The horizontal line represents a continuum with rough, not sharply defined, breaks. The middle vertical line divides the two general categories, but does not indicate a sharp break. Accordingly, the horizontal line expresses a continuum across the four lower categories and expresses the scope of the common morality in the domain of obligations and nonobligatory ideals.

Joel Feinberg argued that supererogatory acts are "located on an altogether different scale than obligations."[48] The preceding diagram suggests that this comment is correct in one respect, but potentially misleading in another. The right half of the diagram is not scaled by obligation, whereas the left half is. In this respect, Feinberg's comment is correct. However, the full horizontal line is connected by a single scale of moral value in which the right is continuous with the left. For example, obligatory acts of beneficence and supererogatory acts of beneficence are on the same scale because they are morally of the same kind. The domain of supererogatory ideals is continuous with the domain of norms of obligation by *exceeding* those obligations in accordance with the several defining conditions of supererogation listed previously.

The Place of Ideals in Biomedical Ethics

Many beneficent actions by health care professionals straddle the territory marked in the preceding diagram between Obligation and Beyond Obligation (in particular, between [2] and [3]). Matters become more complicated when we introduce the distinction discussed in Chapter 1 between professional obligations and obligations incumbent on everyone. Many moral duties established by roles in health care are not moral obligations from the perspective of persons not in these roles. These duties in medicine and nursing are profession-relative, and some are role obligations even when not formally stated in professional codes. For example, the expectation that physicians and nurses will encourage and cheer patients is a profession-imposed obligation, though not one usually incorporated in a professional code of ethics.

Some customs in the medical community are not well established as obligations, such as the belief that physicians and nurses should efface self-interest and take risks in attending to patients. The nature of "obligations" when caring for patients with severe acute respiratory syndrome (SARS) and other diseases with a significant risk of transmission has been controversial, and professional codes and medical association pronouncements have varied.[49] One of the strongest statements of physician duty appeared in the original 1847 Code of Medical Ethics of the American Medical Association (AMA): "when pestilence prevails, it is their [physicians'] duty to face the danger, and to continue their labours for the alleviation of the suffering, even at the jeopardy of their own lives."[50] This statement was retained in subsequent versions of the AMA code until the 1950s, when, perhaps in part because of a false sense of the permanent conquest of dangerous contagious diseases, it was eliminated.

We cannot resolve controversies about duty in face of risk without determining the level of risk—in terms of both the probability and the seriousness of harm—that professionals are expected to assume and setting a threshold beyond which the level of risk is so high that it renders an act optional rather than obligatory. The difficulty of drawing this line should help us appreciate why some medical associations have urged their members to be courageous and treat patients with potentially lethal infectious diseases, while other associations have advised their members that treatment is optional in those circumstances.[51] Still others have taken the view that both virtue and obligation converge to the conclusion that particular health care professionals should set aside self-interest, within limits, and that the health care professions should take actions to ensure appropriate care.[52]

It is doubtful that health care professionals fail to discharge moral *obligations* when they fall short of the highest possible standards in the profession. Confusion arises because of the indeterminate boundaries of what is required in the common morality, what is required in professional communities, and what is a matter of moral character beyond the requirements of moral obligations.

MORAL EXCELLENCE

Aristotelian ethical theory closely connects moral excellence to moral character as well as virtues and moral ideals. Aristotle succinctly presents this idea: "A truly good and intelligent person...from his resources at any time will do the finest actions he can, just as a good general will make the best use of his forces in war, and a good shoemaker will produce the finest shoe he can from the hides given him, and similarly for all other craftsmen."[53] This passage indicates the demanding nature of Aristotle's account in contrast to ethical theories that focus entirely on the moral minimum of obligations.

The value of this vision of excellence is highlighted by John Rawls, in conjunction with what he calls the "Aristotelian principle":

> The excellences are a condition of human flourishing; they are goods from everyone's point of view. These facts relate them to the conditions of self-respect, and account for their connection with our confidence in our own value.... [T]he virtues are [moral] excellences.... The lack of them will tend to undermine both our self-esteem and the esteem that our associates have for us.[54]

We now draw on this general background in Aristotelian theory and on our prior analysis of moral ideals and supererogation for an account of moral excellence.

The Place of Moral Excellence

We begin with four reasons that motivate us to treat this subject. First, we hope to overcome an undue imbalance in contemporary ethical theory and bioethics, which focus narrowly on the moral minimum of obligations while ignoring supererogation and moral ideals.[55] This concentration dilutes the moral life, including our expectations for ourselves, our close associates, and health professionals. If we expect only the moral minimum of obligation, we may lose an ennobling sense of moral excellence. A second and related reason is that we hope to overcome skepticism in contemporary ethical theory concerning high ideals in the moral life. Some influential writers note that high moral ideals must compete with other goals and responsibilities in life, and consequently that these ideals can lead persons to neglect other matters worthy of attention, including personal projects, family relationships, friendships, and experiences that broaden outlooks.[56] A third reason concerns what we call in Chapter 9 the *criterion of comprehensiveness* in an ethical theory. Recognizing the value of moral excellence will allow us to incorporate a broad range of moral virtues and forms of supererogation beyond the obligations, rights, and virtues that comprise ordinary morality. Fourth, and finally, a model of moral excellence merits pursuit because it indicates what is worthy of aspiration. Morally exemplary persons and acts provide ideals that help guide and inspire us to higher goals and morally better lives.

Aristotelian Ideals of Moral Character

Aristotle maintained that we acquire virtues much as we do skills such as carpentry, playing a musical instrument, and cooking.[57] Both moral and nonmoral skills require training and practice. Obligations play a less central role in his account. Consider, for example, a person who undertakes to expose scientific fraud in an academic institution. It is easy to frame this objective as a matter of obligation, especially if the institution has a policy on fraud. However, suppose this person's reports of fraud to superiors are ignored, and eventually her job is in jeopardy and her family receives threats. At some point, she has fulfilled her obligations and is not morally required to pursue the matter further. However, when she does persist her continued pursuit would be praiseworthy. Her efforts to bring about institutional reform could even take on heroic dimensions. Aristotelian theory frames this situation in terms of the person's level of commitment, the perseverance and endurance shown, the resourcefulness and discernment in marshalling evidence, and the courage, as well as the decency and diplomacy, displayed in confronting superiors.

An analogy to education illustrates why setting goals beyond the moral minimum is important, especially when discussing moral character. Most of us are trained to aspire to an ideal of education. We are taught to prepare ourselves as best we can. No educational aspirations are too high unless they exceed our abilities and cannot be attained. If we stop at a level below our educational potential, we will consider our achievement a matter of disappointment and regret even if we obtain a degree. As we fulfill our aspirations, we sometimes expand our goals beyond what we had originally planned. We think of getting another degree, learning another language, or reading widely beyond our specialized training. We do not say at this point, however, that we have an *obligation* to achieve as high a level of education as we can achieve.

The Aristotelian model suggests that moral character and moral achievement similarly are functions of self-cultivation and aspiration. Goals of moral excellence can and should enlarge as moral development progresses. Each individual should seek to reach a level as elevated as his or her ability permits, not as a matter of obligation but of aspiration. Just as persons vary in the quality of their performances in athletics and medical practice, so too in the moral life some persons are more capable than others and deserve more acknowledgment, praise, and admiration. Some persons are sufficiently advanced morally that what they can achieve far exceeds what those who are less morally developed can expect to achieve.

Wherever a person is on the continuum of moral development, there will be a goal of excellence that exceeds what he or she has already achieved. This potential to revise our aspirations explains why ideals are of such central importance in our account. Consider, for example, the clinical investigator who uses human subjects in research but who asks only (as is typical in protocol review), "What am I obligated to do to protect human subjects?" The presumption is that once this question has been addressed by reference to a checklist of obligations, the researcher can ethically proceed with the research. By contrast, in the model we are proposing, this approach is only the starting point. The most important question is, "How could I conduct this research to maximally protect and minimally inconvenience subjects, commensurate with achieving the objectives of the research?" Evading this question indicates that one is morally less committed than one could be.

The Aristotelian model we have sketched does not expect perfection, only that persons strive toward perfection. The model might seem impractical, but, in fact, moral ideals are practical instruments. As *our* ideals, they motivate us and set out a path that we can climb in stages, with a renewable sense of progress and achievement.

Exceptional Moral Excellence: Saints, Heroes, and Others

Extraordinary persons function as models of excellence whose examples we aspire to follow. Among the many models, the moral hero and the moral saint are the most celebrated, and deservedly so.

The term *saint* has a long history in religious, especially Christian, traditions (where a person is recognized for exceptional holiness), and, like *hero*, it also has a secular moral use (where a person is recognized for exceptional virtue). Exceptional other-directedness, altruism, and benevolence are prominent features of the moral saint.[58] Saints do their duty and realize moral ideals where most people would fail to do so. Saintliness requires regular fulfillment of duty and realization of ideals over time; it demands consistency and constancy. We likely cannot make an adequate or final judgment about a person's moral saintliness until the record is complete. By contrast, a person may become a moral hero through a single exceptional action, such as accepting extraordinary risk while discharging duty or realizing ideals. The hero resists fear and the desire for self-preservation in undertaking risky actions that most people would avoid, but the hero also may lack the constancy over a lifetime that distinguishes the saint.

Many persons who serve as moral models or as persons from whom we draw moral inspiration are not so advanced morally that they qualify as saints or heroes. We learn about good moral character from persons with a limited repertoire of exceptional virtues, such as conscientious health professionals. Consider, for example, John Berger's biography of the English physician John Sassall, who chose to practice medicine in a poverty-ridden, culturally deprived country village in a remote region of northern England. Under the influence of works by Joseph Conrad, Sassall chose this village from an "ideal of service" that reached beyond "the average petty life of self-seeking advancement." Sassall was aware that he would have almost no social life and that the villagers had few resources with which to pay him, to develop their community, and to attract better medicine, but he focused on their needs rather than his own. Progressively, Sassall grew morally as he interacted with members of the community. He developed a deep understanding of, and profound respect for, the villagers. He became a person of exceptional caring, devotion, discernment, conscientiousness, and patience when taking care of the villagers. His moral character grew and deepened year after year in caring for them. They, in turn, trusted him under the most adverse and personally difficult circumstances.[59]

From exemplary lives such as that of John Sassall and from our previous analysis, we can extract four criteria of moral excellence.[60] First, Sassall is faithful to a *worthy moral ideal* that he keeps constantly before him in making judgments and performing actions. The ideal is deeply devoted service to a poor and needy community. Second, he has a *motivational structure* that conforms closely to our earlier description of the motivational patterns of virtuous persons, who are prepared to forgo certain advantages for themselves in the service of a moral ideal. Third, he has an *exceptional moral character;* that is, he possesses moral virtues that dispose him to perform supererogatory actions of a high order and quality.[61] Fourth, he is a *person of integrity*—both of moral integrity and of a deep personal integrity—and thus is not overwhelmed by distracting conflicts, self-interest, or personal projects in making judgments and performing actions.

These four conditions are sufficient conditions of moral *excellence.* They are also relevant, but not sufficient, conditions of moral *saintliness* and moral *heroism.* John Sassall, exceptional as he is, is neither a saint nor a hero. To achieve this elevated status, he would have to satisfy additional conditions. Sassall is not a person who faces deep adversity (although he faces modest adversity), extremely difficult tasks, or a high level of risk, and these are typically the sorts of conditions that contribute to making a person a saint or a hero.

Examples of prominent moral saints, under the analysis we have now offered, are St. Francis, Mother Teresa, and Albert Schweitzer. Examples of prominent moral heroes include soldiers, political prisoners, and ambassadors who take substantial risks to save endangered persons by such acts as falling on hand grenades or resisting political tyrants. Scientists and physicians who experiment on themselves to generate knowledge that may benefit others may be heroes. There are many examples: Daniel Carrion injected blood into his arm from a patient with verruga peruana (an unusual disease marked by many vascular eruptions of the skin and mucous membranes as well as fever and severe rheumatic pains), only to discover that it had given him a fatal disease (Oroya fever). Werner Forssman performed the first heart catheterization on himself, walking to the radiological room with the catheter sticking into his heart.[62] A French researcher, Dr. Daniel Zagury, injected himself with an experimental AIDS vaccine, maintaining that his act was "the only ethical line of conduct."[63]

A person can qualify as a moral hero or a moral saint only if he or she meets some combination of the previously listed four conditions of moral excellence. It is too demanding to say that a person must satisfy all four conditions to qualify as a moral hero, but a person must satisfy all four to qualify as a moral saint. This appraisal does not imply that moral saints are more valued or more admirable than moral heroes. We are simply proposing conditions of moral excellence that are more stringent for moral saints than for moral heroes.[64]

To test the analysis we have put forward, consider physician David Hilfiker's *Not All of Us Are Saints,* which offers an instructive model of very exceptional but not quite saintly or heroic conduct in medicine—in his case resulting from his efforts to practice "poverty medicine" in Washington, DC.[65] His decision to leave a rural medical practice in the Midwest to provide medical care to the very poor, including the homeless, reflected both an ambition and a felt obligation. Many health problems he encountered stemmed from an unjust social system, in which his patients had limited access to health care and to other basic social goods that contribute to health. He experienced severe frustration as he encountered major social and institutional barriers to providing poverty medicine, and his patients were often difficult and uncooperative. His frustrations generated stress, depression, and hopelessness, along with vacillating feelings and attitudes including anger, pain, impatience, and guilt. His wellspring of compassion exhausted by his sense of endless needs and personal limitations, he one day failed to respond as he felt he should have: "Like those whom on another day I would criticize harshly, I harden myself to the plight of a homeless man and leave him to the inconsistent mercies of the city police and ambulance system. Numbness and cynicism, I suspect, are more often the products of frustrated compassion than of evil intentions."

Hilfiker declared that he is "anything but a saint." He considered the label "saint" to be inappropriate for people, like himself, who have a safety net to protect them. Blaming himself for "selfishness," he redoubled his efforts, but recognized a "gap between who I am and who I would like to be," and he considered that gap "too great to overcome." He abandoned "in frustration the attempt to be Mother Teresa," observing that "there are few Mother Teresas, few Dorothy Days who can give everything to the poor with a radiant joy." Hilfiker did think that many of the people with whom he worked counted as heroes, in the sense that they "struggle against all odds and survive; people who have been given less than nothing, yet find ways to give."

In *What Really Matters: Living a Moral Life Amidst Uncertainty and Danger,* psychiatrist and anthropologist Arthur Kleinman presents half-a-dozen real-life stories about people who, as the book's subtitle suggests, attempt to live morally in the context of unpredictability and hazard.[66] One powerful story, which provided the impetus for his book, portrays a woman he names Idi Bosquet-Remarque, a French-American who for more than fifteen years was a field representative for several different international aid agencies and foundations, mainly in sub-Saharan Africa. Her humanitarian assistance, carried out almost anonymously, involved working with vulnerable refugees and displaced women and children as well as with the various professionals, public officials, and others who interacted with them. Kleinman presents her as a "moral exemplar," who expressed "our finest impulse to acknowledge the suffering of others and to devote our lives and careers to making a difference (practically and ethically) in their lives, even if that difference must be limited and transient."

At times Bosquet-Remarque was dismayed by various failures, including her own mistakes; she despaired about the value of her work given the overwhelming odds against the people she sought to help; and she recognized some truth in several criticisms of humanitarian assistance. Faced with daunting obstacles, she persisted because of her deep commitment but eventually experienced physical and emotional burnout, numbness, and demoralization. Nevertheless, she returned to the field because her work mattered so much to her. Bosquet-Remarque recognized that her motives might be mixed. In addition to her altruism and compassion, she could also be working out family guilt or seeking to liberate her soul. Despite the ever-present risk of serious injury and even death from violence, she was not comfortable with the image of humanitarian worker as "hero."

After Bosquet-Remarque's death in an automobile accident, Kleinman informed her family that he wanted to tell her story. Her mother requested that her daughter not be identified by name: "That way, you will honor what she believed in. Not saints or heroes, but ordinary nameless people doing what they feel they must do, even in extraordinary situations. As a family, we believe in this too."

These observations about ordinary persons who act in extraordinary ways also pertain to what has been called moral heroism in living organ and tissue donation—a topic to which we now turn.

Living Organ Donation and Tissue Donation

In light of our account in this chapter, how should we assess the offer or the act of donating a kidney by a friend or a stranger?

Health care professionals frequently function as moral gatekeepers to determine who may undertake living donation of organs and tissues for transplantation. Blood donation raises few questions, but in cases of bone marrow donation and the donation of kidneys or portions of livers or lungs, health care professionals have to consider whether, when, and from whom to invite, accept, and effectuate acts of donation. Living organ donation raises complex ethical issues because the transplant team subjects a healthy person to a variably risky surgical procedure, with no medical benefit to him or her. It is therefore appropriate for transplant teams to probe the prospective donor's understanding, voluntariness, and motives.

Transplant teams have traditionally been suspicious of living, genetically unrelated donors—particularly of strangers and mere acquaintances but even of emotionally related donors such as spouses and friends. This suspicion has several sources, including concerns about donors' motives and worries about their competence to decide, their understanding of the risks, and the voluntariness of their decisions. This suspicion increases in cases of nondirected donation, that is, donation not to a particular known individual, but to anyone in need. However, in contrast to professionals' attitudes,[67] a majority of the public in the United States believes that the gift of a kidney to a stranger is reasonable and proper and that the transplant team should accept it.[68] The offer to donate a kidney by a friend, acquaintance, or stranger typically does not involve such high risks that questions automatically arise about the donor's competence, understanding, voluntariness, and motivation.[69]

Transplant teams can and should decline some heroic offers of organs for moral reasons—even when the donors are competent, their decisions informed and voluntary, and their moral excellence beyond question. For instance, transplant teams have good grounds to decline a mother's offer to donate her heart to save her dying child, because the donation would involve others in directly causing her death. A troublesome case arose when an imprisoned, 38-year-old father who had already lost one of his kidneys wanted to donate his remaining kidney to his 16-year-old daughter whose body had already rejected one kidney transplant.[70] The family insisted that medical professionals and ethics committees had no right to evaluate, let alone reject, the father's act of donation. However, questions arose about the voluntariness of the father's offer (in part because he was in prison), about the risks to him (many patients without kidneys do not thrive on dialysis), about the probable success of the transplant (because of his daughter's problems with her first transplant), and about the costs to the prison system (approximately $40,000 to $50,000 a year for dialysis for the father if he donated the remaining kidney).

We propose that society and health care professionals start with the presumption that living organ donation is praiseworthy but optional. Transplant teams need to subject their criteria for selecting and accepting living donors to public scrutiny to ensure that the teams do not inappropriately use their own values about sacrifice, risk, and the like, as the basis for their judgments.[71] Policies and practices of encouraging prospective living donors are ethically acceptable as long as they do not turn into undue influence or coercion. In the final analysis, live organ donors may not rise to the level of heroes, depending on the risks involved, but many embody moral excellence and merit society's praise.

CONCLUSION

In this chapter we have moved to a moral territory distinct from the principles, rules, obligations, and rights treated in Chapter 1. We have tried to render the two domains entirely consistent, without assigning priority to one over the other. We have discussed how standards of virtue and character are closely connected to other moral norms. Virtues, ideals, and aspirations of moral excellence support and enrich the rights, principles, and rules discussed in Chapter 1. There is no reason to consider one domain inferior to or derivative from the other, and there is reason to believe that these categories all have a significant place in the common morality.

There are still other domains of the moral life, and in Chapter 3 we turn to the chief domain not yet addressed: criteria of moral status.

NOTES

1. For relevant literature on the subjects discussed here in Chapter 2 and also in the last section of Chapter 9, see Stephen Darwall, ed., *Virtue Ethics* (Oxford: Blackwell Publishing, 2003); Roger Crisp and Michael Slote, eds., *Virtue Ethics* (Oxford: Oxford University Press, 1997); Roger Crisp, ed., *How Should One Live? Essays on the Virtues* (Oxford: Oxford University Press, Clarendon, 1996); and Daniel Statman, ed., *Virtue Ethics: A Critical Reader* (Washington, DC: Georgetown University Press, 1997). Many constructive discussions of virtue theory are indebted to Aristotle. For a range of treatments, see Julia Annas, *Intelligent Virtue* (New York: Oxford University Press, 2011); Christine Swanton, *Virtue Ethics: A Pluralistic View* (New York: Oxford University Press, 2003); Nancy Sherman, *The Fabric of Character: Aristotle's Theory of Virtue* (Oxford: Clarendon, 1989); Alasdair MacIntyre, *After Virtue: A Study in Moral Theory,* 3rd ed. (Notre Dame, IN: University of Notre Dame Press, 2007) and *Dependent Rational Animals: Why Human Beings Need the Virtues* (Chicago: Open Court, 1999); and Timothy Chappell, ed., *Values and Virtues: Aristotelianism in Contemporary Ethics* (Oxford: Clarendon, 2006). See also Robert Merrihew Adams, *A Theory of Virtue: Excellence in Being for the Good* (Oxford: Clarendon, 2006).

2. Bentham, *Deontology or the Science of Morality* (Chestnut Hill, MA: Adamant Media Corporation, 2005; reprinted in the Elibron Classics Series of the 1834 edition, originally published in London by Longman et al., 1834), p. 196.

3. Talbot Brewer, *The Retrieval of Ethics* (New York: Oxford University Press, 2009), p. 209.

4. Compare, favorably, the analysis of the virtues in Annas, *Intelligent Virtue,* esp. chaps. 2, 5; and Edmund D. Pellegrino and David C. Thomasma, *The Virtues in Medical Practice* (New York: Oxford University Press, 1993).

5. This is an intentionally broad sense of "virtue." We do not require, as did Aristotle, that virtue involve habituation rather than a natural character trait. *Nicomachean Ethics,* trans. Terence Irwin (Indianapolis, IN: Hackett Publishing, 1985), 1103ª18–19. Nor do we follow St. Thomas Aquinas (relying on a formulation by Peter Lombard), who additionally held that virtue is a good quality of mind by which we live rightly and therefore cannot be put to bad use. See *Treatise on the Virtues* (from *Summa Theologiae,* I–II), Question 55, Arts. 3–4. We treat problems of the definition of "virtue" in more detail in Chapter 9.

6. This definition is the primary use reported in the *Oxford English Dictionary* (*OED*). It is defended by Alan Gewirth, "Rights and Virtues," *Review of Metaphysics* 38 (1985): 751; and R. B. Brandt, "The Structure of Virtue," *Midwest Studies in Philosophy* 13 (1988): 76. See also the consequentialist account in Julia Driver, *Uneasy Virtue* (Cambridge: Cambridge University Press, 2001), esp. chap. 4. Edmund Pincoffs presents a definition of virtue in terms of desirable dispositional qualities of persons, in *Quandaries and Virtues: Against Reductivism in Ethics* (Lawrence, KS: University Press of Kansas, 1986), pp. 9, 73–100; see also MacIntyre, *After Virtue,* chaps. 10–18, on various definitions; and Raanan Gillon, "Ethics Needs Principles," *Journal of Medical Ethics* 29 (2003): 307–12, esp. 309.

7. See the pursuit of this Aristotelian theme in Annas, *Intelligent Virtue,* chap. 5.

8. This analysis is influenced by Alasdair MacIntyre, *After Virtue,* esp. chap. 14; and Dorothy Emmet, *Rules, Roles, and Relations* (New York: St. Martin's, 1966). See also Justin Oakley and Dean Cocking, *Virtue Ethics and Professional Roles* (Cambridge: Cambridge University Press, 2001).

9. A similar thesis is defended, in dissimilar ways, in Edmund D. Pellegrino, "Toward a Virtue-Based Normative Ethics for the Health Professions," *Kennedy Institute of Ethics Journal* 5 (1995): 253–77. See also John Cottingham, "Medicine, Virtues and Consequences," in *Human Lives: Critical Essays on Consequentialist Bioethics,* ed. David S. Oderberg (New York: Macmillan, 1997); and Alan E. Armstrong, "Towards a Strong Virtue Ethics for Nursing Practice," *Nursing Philosophy* 7 (2006): 110–24.

10. Charles L. Bosk, *Forgive and Remember: Managing Medical Failure* (Chicago: University of Chicago Press, 1979). Bosk also recognizes a fourth type of error: "quasi-normative errors," based on the attending's special protocols.

11. Thomas Percival, *Medical Ethics; or a Code of Institutes and Precepts, Adapted to the Professional Conduct of Physicians and Surgeons* (Manchester, England: S. Russell, 1803), pp. 165–66. This book formed the substantive basis of the first AMA code.

12. See the virtue-based approach to nursing ethics in Alan F. Armstrong, *Nursing Ethics: A Virtue-Based Approach* (Houndmills, England: Palgrave Macmillan, 2007).

13. Contrast Virginia Held's argument for a sharp distinction between the ethics of care and virtue ethics on the grounds that the former focuses on relationships and the latter on individuals' dispositions: *The Ethics of Care: Personal, Political, and Global* (New York: Oxford University Press, 2006). We reject this treatment.

14. Carol Gilligan, *In a Different Voice* (Cambridge, MA: Harvard University Press, 1982), esp. p. 21. See also her "Mapping the Moral Domain: New Images of Self in Relationship," *Cross Currents* 39 (Spring 1989): 50–63.

15. Indeed, Gilligan and many others deny that the two distinct voices correlate strictly with gender. See Gilligan and Susan Pollak, "The Vulnerable and Invulnerable Physician," in *Mapping the Moral Domain,* ed. C. Gilligan, J. Ward, and J. Taylor (Cambridge, MA: Harvard University Press, 1988), pp. 245–62.

16. See Gilligan and G. Wiggins, "The Origins of Morality in Early Childhood Relationships," in *The Emergence of Morality in Young Children,* ed. J. Kagan and S. Lamm (Chicago: University of Chicago Press, 1988). See also Margaret Olivia Little, "Care: From Theory to Orientation and Back," *Journal of Medicine and Philosophy* 23 (1998): 190–209.

17. Our formulation of these criticisms is influenced by Alisa L. Carse, "The 'Voice of Care': Implications for Bioethical Education," *Journal of Medicine and Philosophy* 16 (1991): 5–28, esp. 8–17. For analysis and assessment of such criticisms, see Abraham Rudnick, "A Meta-Ethical Critique of Care Ethics," *Theoretical Medicine* 22 (2001): 505–17.

18. Alisa L. Carse, "Impartial Principle and Moral Context: Securing a Place for the Particular in Ethical Theory," *Journal of Medicine and Philosophy* 23 (1998): 153–69.

19. See Nel Noddings, *Caring: A Feminine Approach to Ethics and Moral Education,* 2nd ed. (Berkeley, CA: University of California Press, 2003), and the evaluation of her work in Raja Halwani, "Care Ethics and Virtue Ethics," *Hypatia* 18 (2003), esp. pp. 162ff.

20. See Nancy Sherman, *The Fabric of Character* (Oxford: Oxford University Press, 1989), pp. 13–55; and Martha Nussbaum, *Love's Knowledge* (Oxford: Oxford University Press, 1990). On "attention" in medical care, see Margaret E. Mohrmann, *Attending Children: A Doctor's Education* (Washington, DC: Georgetown University Press, 2005).

21. Carse, "The 'Voice of Care,'" p. 17.

22. On the historical role of a somewhat different collection of central virtues in medical ethics and their connection to vices, especially since the eighteenth century, see Frank A. Chervenak and Laurence B. McCullough, "The Moral Foundation of Medical Leadership: The Professional Virtues of the Physician as Fiduciary of the Patient," *American Journal of Obstetrics and Gynecology* 184 (2001): 875–80.

23. Pellegrino, "Toward a Virtue-Based Normative Ethics," p. 269.

24. See Lawrence Blum, "Compassion," in *Explaining Emotions,* ed. Amélie Oksenberg Rorty (Berkeley, CA: University of California Press, 1980); and David Hume, *A Dissertation on the Passions,* Sect. 3, §§ 4–5 (London, 1772 ed.), pp. 208–9.

25. Martha Nussbaum, *Upheavals of Thought: The Intelligence of Emotions* (Cambridge: Cambridge University Press, 2001), p. 302. Part II of this book is devoted to compassion.

26. See Jodi Halpern, *From Detached Concern to Empathy: Humanizing Medical Practice* (New York: Oxford University Press, 2001).

27. David Hume, *A Treatise of Human Nature,* ed. David Fate Norton and Mary Norton (Oxford: Clarendon, 2007), 3.3.1.7.

28. Baruch Brody, "Case No. 25. 'Who Is the Patient, Anyway': The Difficulties of Compassion," in *Life and Death Decision Making* (New York: Oxford University Press, 1988), pp. 185–88.

29. Aristotle, *Nicomachean Ethics,* trans. Irwin, 1106^{b}15–29, 1141^{a}15–1144^{b}17.

30. Annette Baier, "Trust, Suffering, and the Aesculapian Virtues," in *Working Virtue: Virtue Ethics and Contemporary Moral Problems,* ed. Rebecca L. Walker and Philip J. Ivanhoe (Oxford: Clarendon, 2007), p. 137.

31. See Annette Baier's "Trust and Antitrust" and two later essays on trust in her *Moral Prejudices* (Cambridge, MA: Harvard University Press, 1994); Nancy N. Potter, *How Can I Be Trusted: A Virtue Theory of Trustworthiness* (Lanham, MD: Rowman & Littlefield, 2002); Philip Pettit, "The Cunning of Trust," *Philosophy and Public Affairs* 24 (1995): 202–25; and Pellegrino and Thomasma in *The Virtues in Medical Practice,* chap. 5.

32. Aristotle, *Eudemian Ethics,* 1242^{b}23–1243^{a}13, in *The Complete Works of Aristotle,* ed. Jonathan Barnes (Princeton, NJ: Princeton University Press, 1984).

33. For a discussion of the erosion of trust in medicine, see David Mechanic, "Public Trust and Initiatives for New Health Care Partnerships," *Milbank Quarterly* 76 (1998): 281–302; Pellegrino and Thomasma in *The Virtues in Medical Practice,* pp. 71–77; and Mark A. Hall, "The Ethics and Empirics of Trust," in *The Ethics of Managed Care: Professional Integrity and Patient Rights,* ed. W. B. Bondeson and J. W. Jones (Dordrecht, Netherlands: Kluwer, 2002), pp. 109–26. Broader explorations of trustworthiness, trust, and distrust appear in Russell Hardin's *Trust and Trustworthiness,* The Russell Sage Foundation Series on Trust, vol. 4 (New York: Russell Sage Foundation Publications, 2004). Onora O'Neill offers proposals to restore trust in medical and other contexts where mistrust results largely from such factors as bureaucratic structures of accountability, excessive transparency, and public culture. See her *A Question of Trust* (Cambridge: Cambridge University Press, 2002) and *Autonomy and Trust in Bioethics* (Cambridge: Cambridge University Press, 2003).

34. Brody, *Life and Death Decision Making*, p. 35.

35. See Edmund Pellegrino, "Codes, Virtue, and Professionalism," in *Methods of Medical Ethics,* ed. Jeremy Sugarman and Daniel P. Sulmasy (Washington, DC: Georgetown University Press, 2010),

pp. 91–107, esp. 94; and Michael Wreen, "Medical Futility and Physician Discretion," *Journal of Medical Ethics* 30 (2004): 275–78.

36. For useful discussions of this question in nursing, see Martin Benjamin and Joy Curtis, *Ethics in Nursing: Cases, Principles, and Reasoning,* 4th ed. (New York: Oxford University Press, 2010), pp. 122–26; and Betty J. Winslow and Gerald Winslow, "Integrity and Compromise in Nursing Ethics," *Journal of Medicine and Philosophy* 16 (1991): 307–23. For a broader discussion, see also Benjamin, *Splitting the Difference: Compromise and Integrity in Ethics and Politics* (Lawrence, KS: University Press of Kansas, 1990).

37. For a historically grounded critique of such conceptions and a defense of conscience as a virtue, see Douglas C. Langston, *Conscience and Other Virtues: From Bonaventure to MacIntyre* (University Park, PA: Pennsylvania State University Press, 2001).

38. Williams, "A Critique of Utilitarianism," in *Utilitarianism: For and Against,* ed. J. J. C. Smart and Williams (Cambridge: Cambridge University Press, 1973), pp. 97–98.

39. We here draw from two sources: Hannah Arendt, *Crises of the Republic* (New York: Harcourt, Brace, Jovanovich, 1972), p. 62; and John Stuart Mill, *Utilitarianism,* chap. 3, pp. 228–29, and *On Liberty,* chap. 3, p. 263, in *Collected Works of John Stuart Mill,* vols. 10, 18 (Toronto, Canada: University of Toronto Press, 1969, 1977).

40. Carl H. Fellner, "Organ Donation: For Whose Sake?" *Annals of Internal Medicine* 79 (October 1973): 591.

41. See Larry May, "On Conscience," *American Philosophical Quarterly* 20 (1983): 57–67; C. D. Broad, "Conscience and Conscientious Action," in *Moral Concepts,* ed. Joel Feinberg (Oxford: Oxford University Press, 1970), pp. 74–79; and James F. Childress, "Appeals to Conscience," *Ethics* 89 (1979): 315–35.

42. For several models, see Rebecca Dresser, "Professionals, Conformity, and Conscience," *Hastings Center Report* 35 (November–December 2005): 9–10. See also Mark R. Wicclair, *Conscientious Objection in Health Care: An Ethical Analysis* (Cambridge: Cambridge University Press, 2011); Alta R. Charo, "The Celestial Fire of Conscience—Refusing to Deliver Medical Care," *New England Journal of Medicine* 352 (2005): 2471–73; and Elizabeth Fenton and Loren Lomasky, "Dispensing with Liberty: Conscientious Refusal and the 'Morning-After Pill,'" *Journal of Medicine and Philosophy* 30 (2005): 579–92.

43. See Holly Fernandez Lynch, *Conflicts of Conscience: An Institutional Compromise* (Cambridge, MA: MIT Press, 2008).

44. Farr A. Curlin et al., "Religion, Conscience, and Controversial Clinical Practices," *New England Journal of Medicine* 356 (February 8, 2007): 593–600.

45. Our analysis is indebted to David Heyd, *Supererogation: Its Status in Ethical Theory* (Cambridge: Cambridge University Press, 1982); Heyd, "Tact: Sense, Sensitivity, and Virtue," *Inquiry* 38 (1995): 217–31; Heyd, "Obligation and Supererogation," *Encyclopedia of Bioethics,* 3rd ed. (New York: Thomson Gale, 2004), vol. 4, pp. 1915–20; and Heyd, "Supererogation," *Stanford Encyclopedia of Philosophy,* first published November 4, 2002; substantive revision, September 27, 2011, http://plato. stanford.edu/entries/supererogation/ (accessed December 27, 2011). We are also indebted to J. O. Urmson, "Saints and Heroes," *Essays in Moral Philosophy,* ed. A. I. Melden (Seattle, WA: University of Washington Press, 1958), pp. 198–216; John Rawls, *A Theory of Justice* (Cambridge, MA: Harvard University Press, 1971; rev. ed. 1999), pp. 116–17, 438–39, 479–85 (1999: 100–01, 385–86, 420–25); Joel Feinberg, "Supererogation and Rules," *Ethics* 71 (1961): 276–88; Roderick M. Chisholm, "Supererogation and Offense: A Conceptual Scheme for Ethics," *Ratio* 5 (June 1963): 1–14; and Gregory Mellema, *Beyond the Call of Duty: Supererogation, Obligation, and Offence* (Albany, NY: State University of New York Press, 1991).

46. Albert Camus, *The Plague,* trans. Stuart Gilbert (New York: Knopf, 1988), p. 278.

47. The formulation in this sentence relies in part on Rawls, *A Theory of Justice,* p. 117 (1999: 100).

48. Feinberg, "Supererogation and Rules," 397.

49. See Dena Hsin-Chen and Darryl Macer, "Heroes of SARS: Professional Roles and Ethics of Health Care Workers," *Journal of Infection* 49 (2004): 210–15; Bernard Lo, "Obligations to Care for Persons with Human Immunodeficiency Virus," *Issues in Law & Medicine* 4 (1988): 367–81; Doran Smolkin, "HIV Infection, Risk Taking, and the Duty to Treat," *Journal of Medicine and Philosophy* 22 (1997): 55–74; and John Arras, "The Fragile Web of Responsibility: AIDS and the Duty to Treat," *Hastings Center Report* 18 (April–May 1988): S10–20.

50. American Medical Association (AMA), *Code of Medical Ethics* (Chicago: American Medical Association, 1847), p. 105. Available at http://www.ama-assn.org/resources/doc/ethics/1847code.pdf (accessed January 10, 2012).

51. See American Medical Association, Council on Ethical and Judicial Affairs, "Ethical Issues Involved in the Growing AIDS Crisis," *Journal of the American Medical Association* 259 (March 4, 1988): 1360–61.

52. Health and Public Policy Committee, American College of Physicians and Infectious Diseases Society of America, "The Acquired Immunodeficiency Syndrome (AIDS) and Infection with the Human Immunodeficiency Virus (HIV)," *Annals of Internal Medicine* 108 (1988): 460–61; Edmund Pellegrino, "Character, Virtue, and Self-Interest in the Ethics of the Professions," *Journal of Contemporary Health Law and Policy* 5 (1989): 53–73, esp. 70–71.

53. Aristotle, *Nicomachean Ethics,* trans. Irwin, 1101^{a}1–7.

54. Rawls, *A Theory of Justice,* pp. 443–45 (1999: 389–91). On the Aristotelian principle, see pp. 424–33 (1999: 372–80).

55. Urmson recognized this problem in "Saints and Heroes," pp. 206, 214. Imbalance is found in forms of utilitarianism that make strong demands of obligation. However, see the attempt to revise consequentialism to bring it in line with common moral intuitions in Douglas W. Portman, "Position-Relative Consequentialism, Agent-Centered Options, and Supererogation," *Ethics* 113 (2003): 303–32.

56. This skepticism is evident in some influential philosophical works, including those of Susan Wolf, Philippa Foot, Bernard Williams, and Thomas Nagel.

57. Aristotle, *Nicomachean Ethics,* trans. Irwin, 1103^{a}32–1103^{b}1.

58. Edith Wyschogrod defines a "saintly life" as "one in which compassion for the other, irrespective of cost to the saint, is the primary trait." Wyschogrod, *Saints and Postmodernism: Revisioning Moral Philosophy* (Chicago: University of Chicago Press, 1990), pp. xiii, xxii, et passim.

59. John Berger (and Jean Mohr, photographer), *A Fortunate Man: The Story of a Country Doctor* (London: Allen Lane, the Penguin Press, 1967), esp. pp. 48, 74, 82ff, 93ff, 123–25, 135. Lawrence Blum pointed us to this book and influenced our perspective on it.

60. Our conditions of moral excellence are indebted to Lawrence Blum, "Moral Exemplars," *Midwest Studies in Philosophy* 13 (1988): 204. See also Blum's "Community and Virtue," in *How Should One Live?: Essays on the Virtues,* ed. Crisp.

61. Our second and third conditions are influenced by the characterization of a saint in Susan Wolf's "Moral Saints," *Journal of Philosophy* 79 (1983): 419–39. For a pertinent critique of Wolf's interpretation, see Robert Merrihew Adams, "Saints," *Journal of Philosophy* 81 (1984), reprinted in Adams,

The Virtue of Faith and Other Essays in Philosophical Theology (New York: Oxford University Press, 1987), pp. 164–73.

62.   Jay Katz, ed., *Experimentation with Human Beings* (New York: Russell Sage Foundation, 1972), pp. 136–40.

63.   Philip J. Hilts, "French Doctor Testing AIDS Vaccine on Self," *Washington Post,* March 10, 1987, p. A7; and see Lawrence K. Altman, *Who Goes First?: The Story of Self-Experimentation in Medicine,* 2nd ed. (Berkeley, CA: University of California Press, 1998).

64.   We will not consider whether these conditions point to another and still higher form of moral excellence: the combination of saint and hero in one person. There have been such extraordinary persons, and we could make a case that some of these extraordinary figures are more excellent than others. But at this level of moral exemplariness, such fine distinctions serve no purpose.

65.   David Hilfiker, *Not All of Us Are Saints: A Doctor's Journey with the Poor* (New York: Hill & Wang, 1994). The summaries and quotations that follow come from this book.

66.   Arthur Kleinman, *What Really Matters: Living a Moral Life Amidst Uncertainty and Danger* (New York: Oxford University Press, 2006), chap. 3. The quotations are from this work.

67.   For the attitudes of nephrologists, transplant nephrologists, and transplant surgeons, see Carol L. Beasley, Alan R. Hull, and J. Thomas Rosenthal, "Living Kidney Donation: A Survey of Professional Attitudes and Practices," *American Journal of Kidney Diseases* 30 (October 1997): 549–57. Even though there is now strong support for living kidney donation, there are discrepancies with actual practice.

68.   See Aaron Spital and Max Spital, "Living Kidney Donation: Attitudes Outside the Transplant Center," *Archives of Internal Medicine* 148 (May 1988): 1077–80.

69.   From 1996 to 2005, as living kidney donation overall doubled in the United States, the annual percentage of genetically unrelated kidney donors (excluding spouses) rose from 5.9% to 22%. *2006 Annual Report of the U.S. Organ Procurement and Transplantation Network and the Scientific Registry of Transplant Recipients: Transplant Data 1996–2005* (Rockville, MD: Health Resources and Services Administration, Healthcare Systems Bureau, Division of Transplantation, 2006). For a few years, 2001–03, the acts of living organ donation outnumbered the acts of deceased organ donation, but living organ donation, which had increased for the preceding five years, declined steadily after 2004 for both kidneys and livers. See A. S. Klein, E. E. Messersmith, L. E. Ratner, et al., "Organ Donation and Utilization in the United States, 1999–2008," *American Journal of Transplantation* 10 (Part 2) (2010): 973–86.

70.   Evelyn Nieves, "Girl Awaits Father's 2nd Kidney, and Decision by Medical Ethicists," *New York Times,* December 5, 1999, pp. A1, A11.

71.   For guidelines, see Linda Wright, Karen Faith, Robert Richardson, and David Grant, "Ethical Guidelines for the Evaluation of Living Organ Donors," *Canadian Journal of Surgery* 47 (December 2004): 408–12. For an examination of the ethical issues in living organ donation, see James F. Childress and Cathryn T. Liverman, eds., *Organ Donation: Opportunities for Action* (Washington, DC: National Academies Press, 2006), chap. 9.

3
Moral Status

The previous two chapters concentrated on moral agents and their obligations, rights, virtues, and relationships. We gave little consideration to whom the obligations are owed, why we have obligations to some individuals and not others, and which beings have rights and which do not. In this chapter we inquire into these questions of moral status, also referred to as moral standing and moral considerability.[1]

The terms *status* and *standing* have been transported into ethics from law and its notion of legal standing. In a weak sense, "moral status" refers to a status, grade, or rank of moral importance. In a strong sense, "status" means to have rights or the functional equivalent of rights. The concept of moral status basically entails that any being X has moral status if moral agents have moral obligations to X, X has basic welfare interests, and the moral obligations owed to X are based on X's interests.[2]

THE PROBLEM OF MORAL STATUS

The problem of moral status begins with questions about which individuals and groups are, or should be, protected by moral norms. For example, what are we to say about human eggs? Embryos? Human embryonic stem cells? Fetuses? Newborn infants? Anencephalic babies? The mentally disabled? Persons who are unable to distinguish right from wrong? The seriously demented? Those incurring a permanent loss of consciousness? The brain-dead? Cadavers? Nonhuman animals used in medical research? A biologically modified animal designed to carry a human fetus to term? Chimeric animals, transgenic animals, and other new life forms created in research? Do the members of each of these groups deserve moral protections or have moral rights? If so, do they deserve the same complement of protections and rights afforded to humans? If not, what elevates normally functioning humans above members of the groups just listed?

Throughout much of human history, certain groups of human beings (e.g., racial groupings, tribes, or enemies in war) and effectively all nonhuman animals have been treated as less than persons. They have been treated as incapable of morality and as having either no moral status or a low-level moral status. Individuals without moral status have been regarded as having no moral rights (historically, slaves in many societies). Those with a lower moral status have fewer or weaker rights (historically, women in many societies).[3] In these morally blemished societies, having either a full or a partial moral status determines whether an individual or group has a full or a partial set of moral rights. A still common, though controversial, presumption in medicine and biomedical ethics is that some groups have no moral rights (e.g., animals used in biomedical research) and that some groups have fewer or weaker rights (e.g., human embryos used in research).

Surrogate decision making (see Chapter 6) also raises questions about moral status. When a person is deemed incompetent and needs a surrogate decision maker, the person does not lose all moral protections and forms of moral respect. Many obligations to these individuals continue, and some obligations may increase. Nonetheless, the recognition of a surrogate as the rightful decision maker entails that the incompetent individual has lost some rights of decision making, and in this respect the individual's moral status has been lowered. Any "decision" that such an individual might reach (e.g., to leave a nursing home or mental institution) does not have the same moral authority that it had prior to the determination of incompetency. At least some of our obligations to the person have shifted and some have ceased. For example, we are no longer required to obtain first-party informed consent from this individual; instead, consent must be obtained from the surrogate decision maker. The criterion of mental incompetence is one among many we use in assessing moral status and in determining rights and obligations.

Similar questions arise about what we owe to small children when we involve them in pediatric research that holds out no promise of direct benefit for the child subjects, because the goal of the research is to develop new treatments to help children in the future. Often we assert that we owe vulnerable parties more, not fewer, protections. Yet children involved in research that is not intended to benefit them have sometimes been treated as if they have a diminished moral status and even as utilitarian means to the advancement of research goals.

Another example of problems of moral status comes from cases of pregnant women who are brain-dead but whose biological capacities are artificially maintained for several weeks to enable the fetus they are carrying to be born.[4] Ordinarily, we would not think of dead people as having a moral status affording them a right to be kept biologically functioning. Indeed, some might argue that maintaining a brain-dead pregnant woman's body against her formerly stated wishes implies that she has been categorized as having a *lower* moral status than other corpses because her body is subjected to extreme measures—sometimes for months—to benefit the fetus, the woman's partner, or the next of kin in the family.[5] The central ethical question is whether anyone, principally a fetus, has rights stronger than those of a brain-dead pregnant woman who filed an advance directive expressing a wish to have her body cease cardiorespiratory functions at the point of death. Beliefs about the moral status of the fetus are powerful motivating considerations in some cases, but the fetus is not the only individual with moral status and rights at the point of the pregnant woman's brain death. Discussion continues about whether a brain-dead woman in this situation has any rights, as asserted in her advance directive, and whether maintaining her body to sustain the pregnancy violates those rights.[6]

Finally, views of and practices toward the many nonhuman animals that we use in biomedical research merit consideration. At times we appear to treat them primarily as utilitarian means to the ends of science, facilitated by the decisions of some person or group said to be their "stewards." The implication is that laboratory animals are not morally protected against invasive, painful, and harmful forms of experimentation, and perhaps that they lack moral status altogether. However, an outright denial of moral status is implausible in light of the fact that virtually every nation and major scientific association has guidelines to alleviate, diminish, or otherwise limit what can be done to animals in biomedical research. It is today generally accepted that experimental animals have some form of moral status, though it remains unclear precisely what warrants this judgment and whether our obligations to these animals also imply that they have rights.

At the root of these and related questions is a rich body of theoretical issues and practical problems about moral status.

THEORIES OF MORAL STATUS

To have moral status is to deserve at least some of the protections afforded by moral norms, including the principles, rules, obligations, and rights discussed in Chapter 1. These protections are afforded only to entities that can be morally wronged by actions. Here is a simple example: We wrong a person by intentionally infecting his or her computer with a virus, but we do not wrong the computer itself even if we damage it irreparably and render it nonfunctional. It is possible to have duties *with regard to* some entities, such as someone's computer, without having duties *to* those entities.[7] By contrast, if we deliberately infect a person's dog with a harmful virus, then it seems that we have wronged not only the dog's owner, but also the dog. Why are persons and dogs direct moral objects and thereby distinguished from computers and houses, which are only indirect moral objects? Presumably the answer is that direct moral objects count in their own right,[8] whereas indirect moral objects do not. But how is the line to be drawn between what counts in its own right and what does not?

The mainstream approach has been to ask whether a being is *the kind of entity* to which moral principles or other moral categories can and should be applied and, if so, based on which *properties* of the being. In some theories, one and only one property confers moral status. For example, some say that this property is human dignity—a very unclear notion that moral theory has done little to clarify. Others say that another property, or perhaps several properties, is needed to acquire moral status—for example, sentience, rationality, or moral agency.

We argue in this chapter that the properties identified in five prominent theories of moral status will not, by themselves, resolve the main issues about moral status, but that *collectively* these theories provide us with a general, although untidy, framework for handling such problems. We begin by looking at each of the five theories and assessing why each one is attractive, yet deeply problematic if taken as the only acceptable theory. Each theory presents a plausible perspective on moral status that merits attention, but no theory by itself is adequate. We conclude that each theory fails to account adequately for some of the ways we do, and should, approach issues of moral status, but that all five theories contribute to our understanding of moral status.

We doubt that it is possible to resolve definitively all controversies about moral status, and we make no pretense to do so. However, we will explain why disagreement persists regarding the moral status of some individuals, and we will offer suggestions for reducing problems of conflict.

A Theory Based on Human Properties

The first theory might be called the traditional account of moral status. It holds that distinctively human properties, those of *Homo sapiens,* confer moral status. All humans have full moral status and only humans have that status. Distinctively human properties demarcate that which has *moral value* and delineate which beings constitute the *moral community.* An individual has moral status if and only if that individual is conceived by human parents—or, alternatively, if and only if it is an organism with a human genetic code. To be a living member of the species *Homo sapiens* is a necessary and sufficient condition of moral respect. The following is a concise statement of such a position by two members of the President's Council on Bioethics (2001–2009):

> Fertilization produces a new and complete, though immature, human organism. The same is true of successful cloning. Cloned embryos therefore ought to be treated as having the same moral status as other human embryos. A human embryo is, then, a whole living member of the species Homo sapiens in the earliest stage....Human embryos possess the epigenetic primordia for self-directed growth into adulthood....We were then, as we are now distinct and complete....To deny that embryonic human beings deserve

full respect, one must suppose that not every whole living human being is deserving of full respect. To do that, one must hold that those human beings who deserve full respect deserve it not in virtue of the kind of entity they are, but, rather, in virtue of some acquired characteristic that some human beings…have and others do not, and which some human beings have in greater degree than others….[Even embryos] are quite unlike cats and dogs….As humans they are members of a natural kind—the human species….Since human beings are intrinsically valuable and deserving of full moral respect in virtue of what they are, it follows that they are intrinsically valuable from the point at which they come into being.[9]

Many find such a theory attractive because it unequivocally covers all human beings and demands that no human be excluded on the basis of a property such as being a fetus, having brain damage, or having a congenital anomaly. We expect a moral theory to cover everyone, without making arbitrary or rigged exceptions. This theory meets that standard. The moral status of human infants, mentally disabled humans, and those with a permanent loss of consciousness (in a persistent vegetative state) is not in doubt or subject to challenge in this theory. This theory also fits well, intuitively, with the moral belief that all humans have "human rights" precisely because they are human, whether or not the rights are legally recognized in a political state.[10]

Despite its attractive features, this theory is problematic when taken as a general theory that one and only one "natural kind" deserves moral status. If we were to train nonhuman apes to converse with us and engage in moral relationships with us, as some believe has already occurred, it would be baseless and prejudicial to say that they have a lesser status merely because of a *biological* difference in species. If we were to encounter a being with properties such as intelligence, memory, and moral capacity, we would frame our moral obligations toward that being not only or even primarily by asking whether it is or is not biologically human. We would look to see if such a being has capacities of reasoning and planning, has a conception of itself as a subject of action, is able to act autonomously, is able to engage in speech, and can make moral judgments. If the individual does have one or more of these properties, its moral status (at some level) is assured, whereas if it had no such properties, its moral status would be in question, depending on the precise properties it had. Accordingly, human biological properties are not necessary conditions of moral status.

The criterion of "human properties" using species criteria is also not as clear as adherents of this first theory often seem to think. Consider the example of a monkey–human chimera created for the purposes of stem-cell research. This research, which has the objective of alleviating or curing neurological diseases and injuries, is conducted by inserting a substantial human cell contribution into a developing monkey's brain. Investigators implant human neural stem cells into a fetal bonnet monkey's brain to see what the cells do and where they are located.[11] Thus far, no such chimeric being has been allowed to progress past early fetal stages, but such a chimera might be born. There are cells in this chimera that are distinctly human and cells that are distinctly monkey. The monkey's brain is developing under the influence of the human cells. Should it be born, it could possibly think and behave in humanlike ways. In theory, the larger the proportion of engrafted human cells relative to host cells, the higher the likelihood of humanlike features or responses. Such a chimera would possess a substantial human biological contribution and could possibly have capacities for speech and moral behavior, especially if the great apes were the selected species. There also are transgenic animals, that is, animals that possess and express genes from a different species. An example is the much discussed Harvard oncomouse, which has only mouse cells but also has bits of human DNA and develops human skin cancers.[12]

There has been little opposition, other than a few concerns about human safety, to most mixtures of human and animal tissues and cells in the context of medical care (e.g., transplantation of animal parts or insertion of animal-derived genes or cells) and biomedical research (e.g., several kinds of insertion of human stem cells into animals). Matters become more complicated, from an ethical standpoint, when animal–human *hybrids* are created. In 2004 the President's Council on Bioethics found "especially acute" the ethical concerns raised by the possibility of mixing human and nonhuman gametes or blastomeres to create a hybrid. It opposed creating animal–human hybrid embryos by ex vivo fertilization of a human using animal sperm or of an animal egg using human sperm. One reason is the difficulty society would face in judging the humanity and the moral status of such an "ambiguous hybrid entity."[13] These and other possible developments in scientific research challenge the belief that there are fixed species boundaries determinative of moral status.[14]

The first theory of moral status confronts a related problem as well: It is correct to say that the commonsense concept of *person* is, in ordinary language, functionally identical to the concept of *human being,* but there is no warrant for the stronger assertion that *only* properties distinctive of the human species count toward personhood or that species membership determines moral status. Even if certain properties strongly correlated with membership in the human species qualify humans for moral status more readily than the members of other species, these properties are only contingently connected to being human. Such properties could be possessed by members of nonhuman species or by entities outside the sphere of natural species, such as God, chimeras, robots, and genetically manipulated species (and biological humans could, in principle, lack these properties).[15]

"Person" is itself too vague a category to resolve these problems of moral status.[16] Some people maintain that what it means to be a person is simply to have some human biological properties; others maintain that personhood is delineated not biologically, but in terms of certain cognitive capacities, moral capacities, or both. What counts as a person seems to expand or contract as theorists construct their theories so that precisely the entities for which they advocate will be judged to be persons and other entities will not. In one theory, human embryos are declared persons and the great apes are not, whereas in another theory the great apes are persons and human embryos are not. The concept of "personhood" is so inherently contestable that we avoid it in this book insofar as possible. This is one reason, among others, that we shy away from the language of "respect for persons" in this book. This language is too unclear regarding what is to be respected and how it is to be respected. Our goal is to be as precise as possible about what is and must be respected. Use of the vague language of "person" tends to undercut this goal.

This first theory of moral status might seem salvageable if we include both human biological properties and distinctively human psychological properties, that is, properties exhibiting distinctively human mental functions of awareness, emotion, cognition, motivation, intention, volition, and action. This broader scope, however, will not rescue the theory. If nonhuman animals are not morally protected—in a context of biomedical research, say—because they lack certain psychological characteristics such as self-determination, moral motivation, language use, and moral emotions, then consistency requires us to say that humans who lack these characteristics do not qualify for moral protections for the same reason. For any human psychological property we select, some human beings will lack this characteristic (or lack it to the relevant degree); and frequently some nonhuman animal will possess this characteristic. Primates, for example, often possess humanlike properties that some humans lack, such as intellectual quickness, the capacity to feel pain, and the ability to enter into meaningful social relationships. This first theory, then, is not an adequate account of moral status.

Nonetheless, it would be morally perilous to give up the idea that properties of humanity form a basis of moral status. This position is entrenched in morality and provides the foundation of the claim that all humans have human rights. Accordingly, the proposition that *some* set of human properties is a sufficient, but not necessary, condition of moral status is an acceptable position.[17] We leave it an open question precisely which set of properties counts, and we acknowledge that argument is needed to show that some properties count whereas others do not. It could turn out that this first theory will ultimately be absorbed by a more precise theory that is not developed in terms of *species* properties. It also could turn out that the properties we regard as the critical, distinctively human properties are not distinctively human at all.

The acceptance of a criterion of human properties as supplying a sufficient condition of moral status does not rule out the possibility that properties other than distinctively human ones also constitute sufficient conditions. To test this hypothesis, we need to consider the other four theories.

A Theory Based on Cognitive Properties

A second theory of moral status moves beyond biological criteria and species membership to a specific set of cognitive properties. "Cognition" refers to processes of awareness such as perception, memory, understanding, and thinking. This theory does not assume that only humans have such properties, although the starting model for these properties is again the competent human adult. The theory is that individuals have moral status because they are able to reflect on their lives through their cognitive capacities and are self-determined by their beliefs in ways that incompetent humans and nonhuman animals are not.

Properties found in theories of this second type include (1) self-consciousness (consciousness of oneself as existing over time, with a past and future); (2) freedom to act and the capacity to engage in purposeful actions; (3) ability to give and to appreciate reasons for acting; (4) capacity for beliefs, desires, and thoughts; (5) capacity to communicate with other persons using a language; and (6) rationality and higher order volition.[18] The goal of these theories is often to identify a set of cognitive properties possessed by all and only persons, under the assumption that persons and only persons have moral status. One is a person if and only if one possesses the cognitive properties that distinguish higher level beings from lower level beings. Any being with the higher level properties has moral status. We set aside disputes internal to these theories about precisely which cognitive properties are jointly necessary and/or sufficient for personhood, and therefore for moral status. To investigate the problems with this general type of theory, it does not matter whether only one or more than one of these criteria must be satisfied to qualify for moral status, and it also does not matter whether the category of "persons" is used in the theory.

The model of an autonomous human being, or person, is conceived in these theories in terms of such cognitive properties as self-awareness, processing information, choosing, and authorizing. The theory that these properties form the foundation of moral status acknowledges that if a nonhuman animal, a hybrid human, or a brain-damaged human is in all relevant respects like a cognitively capable human being, then it has a similar (and presumably identical) moral status. A corollary is that if one is *not* in the relevant respects like a cognitively competent human being, one's moral status is correspondingly reduced or vacated.

This second general type of theory allows for different interpretations with different mixtures of the six aforementioned criteria forming a particular theory. As the number or level of the required cognitive abilities is increased, there will be a reduction in the number of individuals who satisfy the theory's conditions, and therefore fewer individuals will qualify for moral status or at least for elevated moral status. For example, if all six of the previously mentioned criteria must be satisfied, many humans would be excluded from moral status. Likewise, reducing the quality or level of required cognitive skill would increase the number of individuals who qualify for protection under the theory. If only understanding and intentional action were required, even some nonhuman animals would qualify.

A worrisome feature of this theory is that infants, the senile elderly, persons with a severe mental disability, and others who we generally view as having a secure moral status lack the cognitive capacities required to attain moral status. Most nonhuman animals also lack such cognitive capacities. The level of cognitive abilities demanded also varies from theory to theory. In explicating a Kantian position, Christine Korsgaard writes that "Human beings are distinguished from animals by the fact that practical reason rather than instinct is the determinant of our actions."[19] If this were the sole criterion, then biological humans are animals (by contrast to "human beings") whenever they lack practical rationality.

An objection to this theory, often directed against theories predicated primarily on human dignity and autonomy, is generally referred to as "the argument from marginal cases": This argument maintains that every major cognitive criterion of moral status (intelligence, agency, self-consciousness, etc.) excludes some humans, including young children and humans with serious brain damage. These "marginal" cases of cognitive human capacities can be at the same level of cognitive and other capacities as some animals, and hence to exclude these animals is also to exclude comparably situated humans. If animals can be treated as mere means to human ends, then comparable "marginal" cases of human capacity can also be treated as mere means to human ends.[20] This claim is especially dangerous for weak, vulnerable, and incapacitated humans.

This theory therefore does not function, as does the first theory, to ensure that vulnerable human beings will be morally protected. The more vulnerable the individual, by virtue of cognitive deficiency, the weaker the moral protection afforded. The fact that individuals who are members of the human species will typically exhibit higher levels of cognitive capacities than members of other species does not alleviate this problem. In this theory, a nonhuman animal in principle can overtake a human in moral status once the human loses a measure of mental abilities after a cataclysmic event or a decline of capacity. For example, once the primate training in a language laboratory exceeds a deteriorating Alzheimer's patient on the relevant scale of cognitive capacities, the primate attains a higher moral status.[21]

Writers in both science and biomedical ethics often assume that nonhuman animals lack the relevant cognitive abilities, including self-consciousness (even basic consciousness), autonomy, or rationality, and are therefore not elevated in status by this theory. However, this premise is more assumed than demonstrated, and it is a philosophically dubious assumption.[22] Much has been demonstrated about cognition in animal minds by ethologists who investigate animal cognition and mental properties using evolutionary and comparative studies as well as naturalistic and laboratory techniques of observation and experimentation.[23] Comparative studies of the brain show many relevant similarities between the human species and various other species. In behavioral studies, some great apes appear to make self-references or at least to show self-awareness or self-recognition, and many animals learn from the past and then use their knowledge to forge intentional plans of action for hunting, stocking reserve foods, and constructing dwellings.[24] These animals are aware of their bodies and their interests, and they distinguish them from the bodies and interests of others. In play and social life, they understand assigned functions and either follow designated roles or decide for themselves what roles to play.[25] Moreover, many animals seem to understand and intend in ways that some incapacitated humans cannot. These are all *cognitively* significant properties, and therefore, in this second theory, they are *morally* significant properties that award a more elevated moral status to nonhuman animals with the properties than to humans who lack them. This conclusion should not be taken as a problem for a consistent defender of the second theory. It is a problem only for those who assume a priori that only *humans* have the requisite cognitive capacities.

However, defenders of this second theory need to address how to establish the importance and relevance of the connection asserted between cognitive properties and moral protections. Why do *cognitive* properties of individuals determine anything at all about their *moral* status? We are not asserting that a theory of moral status cannot be based on nonmoral properties. It can, but a theory of moral status must make a connection between its preferred nonmoral properties and moral status that will supply the basis of the claim that the lack of a certain property entails a lack of moral status. Defenders need to explain why the absence of this property (e.g., self-consciousness) makes a critical moral difference and precisely what that difference is. If a fetus or an individual with advanced dementia lacks cognitive properties, it does not follow, without supporting argument, that moral status and moral protections are absent.

To conclude this section, this second theory, like the first, fails to establish that cognitive capacity is a *necessary condition* of moral status. However, the theory does arguably succeed in showing that cognitive capacity is a *sufficient condition* of moral status; and we accept this conclusion. Cognitive capacities such as reasoned choice occupy a central place in what we respect in an individual when we invoke moral principles such as "respect for autonomy." The main problem with this second theory is not that it invokes these properties, but that it considers *only* cognitive properties and neglects other potentially relevant properties, most notably properties on the basis of which individuals can suffer and enjoy well-being. We will see in Chapters 5 and 6—and in examining the fourth theory of moral status later in this chapter—that these noncognitive properties ground the principles of nonmaleficence and beneficence in important ways. This problem takes us to the remaining three theories.

A Theory Based on Moral Agency

In the third theory, moral status derives from the capacity to act as a moral agent. The category of a *moral agent* is subject to different interpretations, but at a minimum an individual is a moral agent if two conditions are satisfied: (1) the individual is capable of making moral judgments about the rightness and wrongness of actions, and (2) the individual has motives that can be judged morally. These are moral-capacity criteria, not conditions of morally correct action or character. An individual could make immoral judgments or have immoral motives and still be a moral agent.[26]

Several theories fall under this general type, some with more stringent conditions of moral agency than the two just listed. Historically, Immanuel Kant advanced what is today the most influential theory of moral agency. He concentrated on moral worth, autonomy, and dignity, but some of his formulations suggest that he is proposing conditions of moral status. Moral autonomy of the will is central to his theory. It occurs if and only if one knowingly governs oneself in accordance with universally valid moral principles. This governance gives an individual "an intrinsic worth, i.e., dignity," and "hence autonomy is the ground of the dignity of human nature and of every rational creature." One has dignity "only insofar as" one is an autonomous agent.[27]

Kant and many after him have suggested that capacity for moral agency gives an individual a moral respect and dignity not possessed by individuals incapable of moral agency—human or nonhuman. This account, which we interpret as one of moral status, has one clearly attractive feature: Being a moral agent is indisputably a *sufficient* condition of moral status. Moral agents are the paradigmatic bearers of moral status. They know that we can condemn their motives and actions, blame them for irresponsible actions, and punish them for immoral behavior.[28]

Like the first two theories, this third theory again supplies a *sufficient* condition of moral status, but, like the first two, it fails to identify a *necessary* condition of moral status. If being a moral agent (or being morally autonomous) were a necessary condition of moral status, then many humans to whom we extend moral protections would be stripped of their moral status, as would all nonhuman animals. Many psychopaths, patients with severe brain damage, patients with advanced dementia, and animal subjects in research would lack moral status in this theory. Yet individuals in these classes deserve to have their interests attended to by many parties, including institutions of medical care. However, the reason for such protections cannot be a capacity of moral agency, because these individuals have none.

The theory of moral agency as a necessary condition of moral status is, in the final analysis, strongly counterintuitive. A morally appropriate response to vulnerable parties such as young children, the severely retarded, patients with senile dementia, and vulnerable research animals is that they deserve *special* protection, not that they merit no protection. Whether these individuals are moral agents is not the primary consideration in assessing their moral status.

In short, the third theory yields a sufficient condition of moral status but not a necessary one. We have already seen that there are other ways to acquire moral status. We will now see that a fourth theory lends additional support to this conclusion.

A Theory Based on Sentience

Humans as well as nonhuman animals have properties that are neither *cognitive* nor *moral* properties, and yet count toward moral status. These properties include a range of emotional and affective responses, the single most important being *sentience*—that is, consciousness in the form of feeling, especially the capacity to feel pain and pleasure and to suffer, as distinguished from consciousness as perception or thought. Proponents of the fourth theory claim that having the capacity of sentience is a sufficient condition of moral status. Some defenders also claim that this capacity is both *necessary and sufficient* for moral status—a more difficult claim to support.[29]

In its most basic form, the central line of argument in the fourth theory is the following: Pain is an evil, pleasure a good. To cause pain to any entity is to harm it. Many beings can experience pain and suffering.[30] To harm these individuals is to *wrong* them. These harm-causing actions are morally prohibited unless one has moral reasons sufficient to justify them.

This simple argument, which is further pursued in Chapter 5, is directly pertinent to the issue of moral status. The properties of experiencing pain and suffering are almost certainly sufficient to confer some measure of moral status. One of the main objectives of morality is to minimize pain and suffering and to prevent or limit indifference and antagonism toward those who are experiencing pain and suffering. It is fundamental to morality that actions that cause pain and suffering to others are prohibited unless one has a morally good and sufficient reason for performing those actions. We need look no further than ourselves to find this point convincing: Pain is an evil to each of us, and the intentional infliction of pain is a moral-bearing action, from the perspective of anyone so afflicted. Pain and suffering are very real even to individuals who are not cognitively capable, morally capable, or biologically human. What matters, with respect to pain, is not species membership or the complexity of intellectual or moral capacities, but the actual pain. From this perspective, all entities that can experience pain and suffering have moral status and can be morally wronged when others cause them pain and suffering.

This theory has broad scope. It reaches to vulnerable humans as well as to animals used in research. Most vertebrate animals are sentient (mammals, birds, reptiles, amphibians, and fish), and some invertebrate animals may be sentient or at least capable of subjective experience. We study animals in biomedical research because of their similarities with humans, and in so studying them a moral problem arises: The reason to use animals in research is that they are so similar to humans, and the reason not to use animals in research is that they are so similar to us in their experience of pain and suffering. Most notably in the case of primates, their lives are damaged and their suffering often resembles human suffering because they are remarkably similar to us physically, cognitively, and emotionally.

This view underlies Jeremy Bentham's famous statement: "The question is not, Can they *reason?* nor, Can they *talk?* but, Can they *suffer?*"[31] Moral claims on behalf of any individual, human or nonhuman, need have nothing to do with intelligence, capacity for moral judgment, self-consciousness, rationality, personality, or any other such fact about the individual. Sentience is a *sufficient* condition of moral status independent of these properties of individuals.

Exactly *who* or *what* is covered by this conclusion, and *when,* is disputed in literature on human fetal research and abortion. If sentience confers moral status, then a human fetus acquires moral status no earlier and no later than the point of sentience. Growth to sentience in the sense of a biological process is gradual over time, but the acquisition of sentience, or the first glimmer of sentience, is not itself a gradual process. That point is, in the theory presently under consideration, the point at which moral status is obtained. Some writers argue that development of a functioning central nervous system and brain is the proper point of moral status for the human fetus, because it is the biological condition of sentience.[32] This approach does not protect human blastocysts or embryos and has proved to be an uncertain basis on which to build arguments allowing or disallowing abortion, because there is disagreement about when the brain has developed sufficiently for sentience. However, in this theory a fetus does have moral status at some point after several weeks of development, and thus abortions at that point and later would be (prima facie) impermissible. This point is prior to the stage of development at which some legal abortions now occur.[33] We are not, in making these observations, presenting objections to sentience theory or to any version of it. We are simply noting that these problems must be handled by a viable comprehensive theory.

The theory that sentience is a sufficient condition of moral status makes more modest claims than the theory that sentience is a necessary and sufficient condition and thus the only criterion of moral status. The latter theory is embraced by several philosophers who hold that properties and capacities other than sentience, such as human biological life and cognitive and moral capacities, are not defensible bases of moral status.[34] Nonsentient beings, such as computers, robots, and plants (and also nonsentient animals), lack the stuff of moral status precisely because they have no capacity for pain; all other beings deserve moral consideration because and only because they are sentient.

Several problems arise for this strong version of the fourth theory. First, problems confront the claim that any individual lacking the capacity for sentience lacks moral status. On the human side, this theory disallows moral status for early-stage fetuses as well as for all who have irreversibly lost the capacity for sentience, such as patients with severe brain damage. It also has the potential to exclude all nonsentient, nonhuman beings, most notably the lower animals, from any degree of moral status. To see this outcome as a problem, we need not hold that these classes of beings actually do have moral status. It is arguable that they do not. For example, it can be argued that presentient fetuses are morally equivalent to human tissue, that absence of significant brain activity denies moral status to patients in a persistent vegetative state, and the like. A defense of the fourth theory requires that argument along these lines be successful. It is not satisfactory merely to assert that absence of sentience is sufficient for absence of moral status. Proponents of the sentience theory might seek to defend it in several ways, and some defenses will add another criterion of moral status to that of sentience. This maneuver would give up the claim that sentience is a necessary and sufficient condition of moral status, thereby abandoning the theory itself.

A second problem with some strong versions of the fourth theory is their *impracticability*. We could not hope to implement these strong versions in our conduct with regard to all species whose members are capable of sentience, and certainly we could not do so without grave danger to human beings. Virtually no one believes, or defends the view, that we cannot have public health policies that vigorously control for pests and pestilence by extermination. The most plausible argument by a sentience theorist who holds the view that sentience is necessary for moral status is that the theory only grants *some level* of moral status. However, this is a dangerous retreat if the actual level of moral status is then fixed by features other than sentience itself. For example, if features such as higher cognitive capacities or moral agency are required to attain a higher level of moral status, this supplementation abandons a pure sentience theory.

We might try to rescue the theory that sentience is both necessary and sufficient for moral status by recognizing (1) that not all sentient creatures have the same level of sentience, and (2) that, even among creatures with the same level of sentience, sentience may not have the same significance because of its interaction with other properties they possess. Some writers believe that there is a gradation of richness or quality of life, depending on complexity of consciousness, social relationships, ability to derive pleasure, creativity, and the like. A continuum of moral status scaled from the autonomous adult human down through the lowest levels of sentience can in this way be layered into the sentience theory. Through this or some similar maneuver, it can be argued that merely because many sentient animals have moral status, it does not follow that humans should be treated no differently than other animals. There may be many good reasons for differential treatment.

In one version of this theory, recognition of a continuum of moral status need not assign different value to different species. We might, as Martha Nussbaum argues, hold that species with more "complex forms of life" are vulnerable to greater and different types of harm and suffering: "The type and degree of harm a creature can suffer varies with its form of life."[35] However, we would also have to allow for the possibility that species with less complex forms of life may also, in some cases, be more vulnerable, not less vulnerable.[36]

In a second, quite different, version of a theory that complexity creates a relevant difference, the argument is that a human life with the capacity for richness of consciousness has a higher moral status and value than even a very richly flourishing animal life such as that of a dog or a bonobo. This judgment has nothing to do with species membership, but with "the fact that [rich, conscious] human life is more valuable than animal life" by virtue of experiences such as real autonomy.[37]

However, these theories have deep problems. They hold that, even among sentient beings, the degree of moral status and the level of moral protection can vary according to conditions such as the quality, richness, or complexity of life. The moral status of a life and its protection therefore can decline by degrees as conditions of welfare and richness diminish. As loss of capacity occurs, for example, humans and nonhumans alike will have a decreased moral status. In this way, highly vulnerable beings can justifiably become vulnerable to abuse or exploitation because of their reduced moral status. No theory that yields this conclusion is morally acceptable.

In light of the several problems surrounding the theory that sentience is both a necessary and sufficient condition of moral status, we conclude that this fourth theory—like the first three theories—is best interpreted as providing a sufficient, but not a necessary, condition of some level of moral status. This theory needs supplementation by the other theories previously discussed. Sentience theory could be used to determine which beings have moral status, whereas the other theories could be called on to determine the degree of moral status. Nothing in this theory indicates the precise level of status or the proper scope of moral protections, and the other theories can potentially be called upon to help resolve this problem.

A Theory Based on Relationships

A fifth and final theory is based on relational properties. This theory holds that relationships between parties account for moral status, primarily relationships that establish roles and obligations. An example is the patient–physician relationship, which is a relationship of medical need and provision of care. Once this relationship is initiated, the patient gains a right to care that other persons who are not the physician's patient lack. The patient does not have this status independent of the established relationship, and the physician does not have the same obligations to those outside such a relationship. This relationship may deepen and gain new dimensions of status as the parties come to know and trust one another. Trusting and caring relationships in which both parties understand and agree are paradigm cases of rights and obligations established and maintained through relationships. Other examples are found in relationships that do *not* involve a formal understanding between the parties, such as our bonds with persons with whom we work closely, and in relationships that involve no mutual understanding between the parties, such as human initiatives that establish relations with laboratory animals and thereby change what is owed to these animals. These relationships bring value to our lives and moral obligations arise from them.

This fifth theory tries to capture the conditions under which certain relationships, especially those involving social interaction and reciprocity, are stronger and more influential than relationships with strangers and outsiders. It also tries to account for our degrees of sensitivity to and sympathy for the interests and capacities of other individuals. In the case of both humans and nonhumans, some individuals are in closer contact with us than others; some engage our affections more easily than others; and some become close to us because the relationship occurs over a long period of time.

One version of this theory of moral status depicts the relevant relationships as developing in diverse ways and often firmly established only after some period of time. Moral status does not necessarily come through a decisive event that can, independently of communal relationships, be determined at a particular time. Moral status is arguably accorded to classes of beings such as human fetuses, Alzheimer's patients, and experimental animals by virtue of a history in which the human moral community has assessed the importance of its relationship to these classes as well as the burdens of offering moral protections to entities in these classes. We usually owe protection and care to those with whom we have established these relationships, and when they are vulnerable to harm because of the relationship, obligations of protection and care will increase.[38]

Some proponents of relationship theory argue that the human fetus and the newborn are examples of those who gradually come to have a significant moral status through special social relationships. Conversely, the less the fetus is part of a nexus of social relationships, the weaker is the fetus's claim to moral status:

> The social role in question develops over time, beginning prior to birth.…A matrix of social interactions between fetus and others is usually present well before parturition. Factors contributing to this social role include the psychological attachment of parents to the fetus, as well

as advances in obstetric technology that permit monitoring of the health status of the fetus....The less the degree to which the fetus can be said to be part of a social matrix, the weaker the argument for regarding her/him as having the same moral status as persons. Near the borderline of viability,...the fetus might be regarded as part of a social network to a lesser degree than at term. If so, the degree of weight that should be given to the fetus's interests varies, being stronger at term but relatively weaker when viability is questionable.[39]

It is not clear how determinative this theory can be made. Once fetuses, for example, are detected in utero by stethoscope or sonogram, they become in significant respects part of a social matrix. They therefore seem to gain some measure of moral status at that point, according to this theory. If fetuses late in pregnancy have a significant moral status, it would be difficult to explain why fetuses earlier in pregnancy do not have the same form and level of moral status.

Despite its attractions, this fifth theory cannot do more than account for how moral status and associated protections are sometimes established. If taken as the sole basis of moral status, then only social bonds and special relationships determine moral status. Critical rights such as the right to life or the right not to be confined have no force in such a theory independent of either a community's conferral or rejection of those rights or acts such as the creation of a relationship of dependence. The theory is unsustainable as an account of moral status if it rejects, neglects, or omits insights in the previous four theories. Those theories recognize moral status on the basis of qualities (cognition, sentience, etc.) that can be acknowledged independently of an established relationship. For example, in the fourth theory, the property of sentience is status conferring. When we wrongfully harm a human research subject or a human population through environmental pollution, it is not correct to say that the harming is wrong because we have an established laboratory, clinical, or social relationship with either that individual or that population. We behave wrongly because we cause gratuitous and unnecessary risk, pain, or suffering, and this would be so whether or not an established relationship exists.

The problem of moral status is fundamentally about which beings have moral status, and this fifth theory does not directly address this problem. Instead, it addresses problems having to do with the basis on which beings sometimes gain or lose specific moral rights or create or decline specific moral obligations. Accordingly, this fifth theory clearly does not supply a necessary condition of moral status, and, in contrast to the other theories we have examined, it does not provide a sufficient condition of moral status.[40] Many loving and caring relationships, with many kinds of beings, do not confer moral status on those beings. No matter how much we love our children's closest friends or a neighbor's pet, they do not gain some form of moral status by virtue of our relationship to them—a relationship that may, however, engender specific moral rights and obligations. Nor does the lack of such a relationship indicate a lack of moral status; an individual still may gain status under criteria drawn from one of the four previous theories (humanity, cognition, moral agency, and sentience). This seems the best way to maximally preserve claims of moral status for those individuals who no longer have significant interpersonal relationships. They will not be stripped of moral status merely because certain relationships have been lost.

This fifth theory's contribution is to show that certain relationships account for how one gains or loses a specific moral right or obligation, and therefore the theory helps account for different degrees of moral status, as discussed in the section below on Degrees of Moral Status.

FROM THEORIES TO PRACTICAL GUIDELINES

Each of the five theories that we have examined has elements that merit acceptance. However, each theory risks making the mistake of isolating a singular property or type of property—biological species, cognitive capacity, moral agency, sentience, or special relationships—as the sole criterion of moral status. Each theory proposes using its preferred property for both including certain individuals (those who have this property) and excluding others (those who lack this property); and each theory becomes unduly narrow as a general theory of moral status unless it accepts some of the criteria in the other four theories.

From ancient Hellenic times to the present, we have witnessed different motives and theories at work when groups of people (e.g., slaves and women) have been refused a certain social standing because they lack some highly valued property that would secure them full moral status. Over time, views about the moral acceptability of these presumed criteria changed, thereby altering beliefs about the moral status of members of these groups. For example, women and many minority groups who had been denied equal moral status later received from society the equal status that ought never to have been denied in the first place. The worry today is that some groups, especially vulnerable groups, may still be in a discriminatory social situation: They fail to satisfy criteria of moral status precisely because the dominant criteria have been tailored specifically to deny them partial or full moral status. Discussion in biomedical ethics has focused principally, though not exclusively, on whether the following are vulnerable groups of this description: human embryos, human fetuses, anencephalic children, research animals, and individuals in a persistent vegetative state.[41]

The evident first step toward addressing these problems, and the one we recommend, is to accept the criteria advanced in each of the first four theories as an acceptable general criterion of moral status—as sufficient but not necessary for moral status—and the fifth theory as adding another relevant dimension to these theories. Unfortunately, more work than we can undertake is needed to develop the nature and limits of these criteria and to determine whether they are hierarchically ranked. The primary norms in each theory—which we hereafter refer to as *criteria* of moral status (rather than as *theories* or *conditions* of moral status)—work well for some problems and circumstances in which decisions must be made, but not as well for other problems and circumstances.

Appropriation of the Five Theories

Ideally, we will be able to appropriate the best from each of the five theories and meld these elements together into a multicriterial, coherent account of moral status.[42] This strategy will help accommodate the diversity of views about moral status, will allow a balancing of the interests of different parties to public controversies such as the interests of scientists in new knowledge and the interests of research subjects, and will help avoid intractable clashes of rights, such as conflicts between the rights of scientists to engage in research and the rights of human embryos. We hereafter assume that, in principle, the ideal of a coherent, multicriterial account of moral status can be satisfied. However, a unified and comprehensive account of moral status is a massive project and we make no claim to have achieved it. In this section we principally treat three problems that confront a multicriterial account.

First, interpretation and analysis are required of some of the central concepts that are inherently contestable. For instance, the concept of "human life" has long been problematic in the literature of biomedical ethics, as we hinted in treating the five theories of moral status. "Human life" carries at least two substantially different meanings. On one hand, it can mean *biological human life,* the biological characteristics that set the human species apart from nonhuman species, as in the first theory we examined. On the other hand, "human life" can mean *life that is distinctively human,* that is, a life characterized more by cognitive than biological properties or abilities. This meaning is closer to the considerations brought forward in the second and third theories. For example, the ability to use symbols, to imagine, to love, and to perform higher intellectual skills may be distinctive human properties, but not all biologically human individuals possess these capacities.

A simple example illustrates the gap and the tension between these two senses of "human life": Some infants with extreme disabilities die shortly after birth. They are born of human parents and they are biologically human, but they never exhibit the distinctively human cognitive traits mentioned in the second and third theories and in many cases lack the potential to do so. For these individuals it is not possible to make their human lives, in the biological sense, human lives in the psychological sense. In discussions of moral status that use the language of "human life," the properties that are excluded and included in the use of the term should be specified. The choice of properties is almost certain to be contested.

Second, the problem of potentiality is prominent and deeply contested in theories of moral status. Human embryos and fetuses are often the centerpiece of discussion because they are developing individuals with the potential for, without yet having acquired, cognitive properties and moral agency. This potentiality is present in the form of existing natural capacities that will develop into other capacities. If unimpaired and uninterrupted in development, embryos have the potential to satisfy every condition of full moral status set out in all five theories. Some writers argue that because of this potential, embryos and fetuses have a right to life, and therefore it is as wrong to harm or kill them as it is to harm or kill beings that actually possess the advanced capacities. The thesis is that it is morally wrong to intentionally cause a being with the potential to develop status-conferring properties to lose or to fail to realize that potential.

Less clear in literature on the potentiality of embryos is how to interpret the nature of the protections afforded by "the right to life." A plausible reason for saying that embryos have this right is that their destruction would deprive them of valuable futures. If embryos have a right to life of this description, they could not ethically be disabled or destroyed, which would have the effect of disallowing practices such as the use of extracorporeal human embryos in stem-cell research. However, it does not follow from this right to life (grounded in the principle of nonmaleficence) that an embryo has a right to be provided with an appropriate environment in which its potential can be realized (a right that would have to be grounded in beneficence and/or justice). The two proclaimed rights are distinct, and independent arguments are required in their defense.[43] They also have quite different implications for the debate about abortion. For instance, if the debate focuses on duties of beneficence rather than nonmaleficence, the question becomes whether the pregnant woman has an obligation—and how far that obligation extends—to provide bodily life support to the fetus, rather than whether she has an obligation not to kill the fetus.[44]

Moral responsibilities to the fetus in utero have long been discussed in biomedical ethics, and over the last few decades discussion has also focused on moral responsibilities to the embryo created by in vitro fertilization and located in the Petri dish or freezer. Three general positions have emerged regarding the moral status of both the developing fetus in utero and of the embryo in the Petri dish or freezer: (1) mere tissue, (2) potential human life (with some, perhaps intermediate, moral status), and (3) full human life (with full moral status). The first position has many defenders, especially, it appears, among scientists, whereas the third position prominently appears in certain religious traditions. For instance, the official Roman Catholic position holds that human life begins at conception, and it treats this potentiality as morally equivalent to actuality or fulfillment. The second position (potential human life) seems to be the dominant view in most Protestant and Jewish traditions, as well as in secular thought. It often includes a moral presumption against abortion and embryo destruction, while holding that both can be justified under some conditions. In one such view, early-stage embryos have an "intermediate moral status" and thus deserve "special respect," but this special respect is compatible with using the embryos for biomedical research if a reasonable prospect exists that such research will save human lives. Although this research may be undertaken and supported with a "heavy heart,"[45] it is widely accepted, however controversially, that the research is justified if necessary to achieve promising and consequential biomedical goals. Problems of potentiality are nuanced and compelling, and they need more analysis than we can provide. However, we again note that whatever degree of moral status is possessed by a being with the potential for status-conferring properties, the individual's rights still may be justifiably overridden by the rights of others in certain circumstances.

Third, and finally, the criteria advanced in the five theories themselves come into moral conflict in some circumstances. How can we ease or resolve these conflicts? We treat this problem in the next two sections. Related questions concern whether these five criteria can be shown to be coherent. We treat some problems of coherence in Chapter 10.

Degrees of Moral Status

In many accounts of moral status, not all individuals who have moral status have it categorically, without qualification, or fully. In some theories, competent, adult humans—or persons—have a broader array of rights than other beings, especially rights of self-determination and liberty, because of their capacities of autonomy and moral agency. Despite the now pervasive view that nonhuman animals have some level of moral status, it is rare to find a theory of moral status that asserts that these animals have the same degree of moral status as human persons. If we had to choose between the welfare interest of a person and the identical welfare interest of the person's cat (e.g., when a house is ablaze), only the exceptional person would argue that we morally should not prefer the person's welfare to that of the cat. Almost everyone will at some point apply a principle of unequal consideration of interests because they believe that the person has a higher moral status than does the cat.[46] Even animal rights theorists generally acknowledge that it is worse to exterminate a person than to exterminate a rat because rats have a lower moral status. Similarly, a common view is that early human embryos and the human fetus (at least in some stages of development) do not have the same moral status as human persons. But are these views about degrees of moral status defensible?

We can start toward an answer by examining a representative example in public policy of the idea of degrees of moral status, one taken from the history of debate and legislation of embryo research in the United Kingdom. The morally contentious issues surrounding embryo research were first considered by the Committee of Inquiry into Human Fertilisation and Embryology (the Warnock Committee, 1984[47]) and later were debated in Parliament during passage of the Human Fertilisation and Embryology Act of 1990. Regulations in 2001 set regulatory policy governing the use of embryos in research. These regulations were indebted to a 2000 report by the Chief Medical Officer's Expert Group.[48] This report indicates that British policy reaffirms the following moral principles deriving from the Warnock Committee Report and views these principles as the moral basis of British law and regulation on the subject of the use of embryos in stem-cell research:

> The 1990 Act reflects the majority conclusion of the Warnock Committee. The use of embryos in research in the UK is currently based on the [following] principles expressed in their Report:
>
> • The embryo of the human species has a special status but not the same status as a living child or adult.
>
> • The human embryo is entitled to a measure of respect beyond that accorded to an embryo of other species.
>
> • Such respect is not absolute and may be weighed against the benefits arising from proposed research.
>
> • The embryo of the human species should be afforded some protection in law....
>
> The Expert Group accepted the 'balancing' approach which commended itself to the majority of the Warnock Committee. On this basis, extending the permitted research uses of embryos appears not to raise new issues of principle.[49]

This is a vague, but common—and, in this case, influential—expression of an account of degrees of moral status. Depending on the theory at work (these four principles are only a sketch of a theory), a being has moral status only to the extent or degree that it has cognitive properties, is a moral agent, stands in a relationship of created dependence, and the like. The five theories we have addressed can each be interpreted so that moral status is expressible in terms of degrees. For example, in the fourth theory, based on sentience, moral status is arguably proportional to degree of sentience and perhaps to the quality and richness of sentient life. Similarly, in the fifth theory, based on relationships, moral status is expressible in terms of degrees of relationship: Relationships come in different degrees of closeness, and relations of dependence can be far more significant in some cases than in others. Arguably, all morally relevant properties in all of these theories are degreed. Capacity for language use, sentience, moral agency, rationality, autonomous decision making, and self-consciousness all come in degrees and are not merely properties of human beings.[50] From this perspective, there are higher and lower levels of moral status, and we can conceive a continuum running from full moral status to no moral status.

However, is an account of degrees of moral status superior to an all-or-nothing account of moral status?[51] The notion of a lesser moral status (including the notion of being subhuman) has been troublesome throughout history, and its remnants linger in many cultural practices. Is it, then, best to deny or to affirm that there are degrees of moral status? We could reformulate the problem of degrees of moral status entirely in terms of different sets of obligations and rights, which increase or decrease in various contexts. In this way we could altogether dispatch the concept of degrees of moral status.

While this view has the virtue of simplicity,[52] it is too simple for an adequate understanding of moral status. Even if all sentient beings (and even some not-yet sentient beings) are direct moral objects that count in their own right, a being's moral status is still contingent on its properties. For example, persons have more at stake in being denied a future than do nonpersons, which is an important reason for giving them a higher degree of moral status. Presumably (though we will not pursue the point) there is a continuum of degrees of moral status, not merely a two-tiered species difference between humans and nonhumans (as theory 1 seems to suggest).

These problems of degrees of moral status should not obscure the fact that all beings with moral status, even though they may have less than full status, still have *some* moral status. It is morally unacceptable to treat any being lacking in full status as if it therefore has no significant status (or does not even reach a crucial threshold of status), as two-tiered theories tend to do. Such treatment would be a deep misunderstanding and misappropriation of the account of degrees of status under discussion in this section.

Nevertheless, disagreement is inevitable regarding whether the concept of degrees is suitable for the analysis of all properties that confer moral status. Examples of disagreement appear in strong commitments to the first theory, based on properties of humanity. One problematic and controversial case, as we have seen, involves the potential of a human fetus to become a sentient, cognitively aware, moral agent. In some theories this potential is not expressible by degrees because full potential is there from the start of an individual's existence; a fetus therefore has full moral status at its origins and throughout its existence. In other theories, by contrast, human fetuses, and possibly infants, have a lower degree of moral status precisely because they are only potential persons, not yet actual persons.

In one version of continuum theory, the moral status of human zygotes, embryos, and fetuses increases gradually during gestation.[53] This theory can also be developed to make potentiality itself a matter of degree (degree of potential). For example, brain defects in a fetus or infant can affect the potential for cognitive and moral awareness and also for the relationships that can be formed with others. This theory can also be expressed in terms of different sets of rights—for instance, pregnant women may have more rights, as well as a higher level of moral status, than their fetuses, at least at some stages of fetal development.

A practically oriented theory of moral status will need to determine with precision what an individual's or a group's status is, not merely that the individual or group has some form of status. Because "status" refers to a grade or rank of moral importance, the precise grade or rank and its implications must be specified. A comprehensive theory will explain whether and, if so, how the rank will change as properties that contribute to status are progressively gained or lost. We ought not to be optimistic that such a theory can be developed to cover all problems of moral status, but we can hope to achieve a more comprehensive and coherent theory than has thus far been made available, even if it is unlikely to be the only coherent theory.

The Connection between Moral Norms and Moral Status

At the beginning of this chapter we distinguished questions of moral status from the questions of moral norms addressed in Chapter 1. Moral norms are principles and rules that state obligations and, correlatively, rights. We reaffirm the distinction between problems of criteria of moral status and problems of moral norms, but we also now qualify it: *Criteria of moral status are moral norms in the generic sense of "moral norm."* A norm in the most general sense is a (prima facie) standard that has the authority to judge or direct human belief, reasoning, or behavior. A norm guides, commands, requires, or commends. Failure to follow a norm warrants censure, criticism, disapproval, or some other negative appraisal. Criteria of moral status satisfy this description. Although not the same type of norm as principles and rules, they are normative standards.

Criteria of moral status also should be understood in light of the discussions in Chapter 1 of moral conflict, moral dilemmas, prima facie norms, and the specification and balancing of norms. Criteria of moral status can and often do come into conflict. For example, the criterion of sentience (drawn from theory 4) and the criterion of human species membership (drawn from theory 1) can come into conflict in the attempt to determine the moral status of the early-stage human fetus. The sentience criterion suggests that the fetus gains status only at the point of sentience; the criterion of human properties (as expressed in theory 1) suggests that moral status accrues at human biological inception. Also, to complicate the picture, on one interpretation of the criterion of relational properties in theory 5, moral status is gained only when certain relationships are formed after birth, but on another interpretation relationships also could be formed in utero—for instance, after ultrasound visualization.

Guidelines Governing Moral Status: Putting Specification to Work

Such conflicts of theory and interpretation can and should be addressed using the account of specification delineated in Chapter 1. Deliberating about and reaching conclusions about cases will require becoming more specific about the content of criteria of moral status than the five theories discussed thus far. As we become increasingly specific, we will continue to encounter additional conflicts, some of which may be resolvable through further specification and some of which produce unresolvable moral dilemmas of the sort discussed in Chapter 1.

We have seen that having moral status does not entail having an absolute claim or right. Criteria of moral status afford moral protection, but the rights established will in some cases be overridden by competing moral considerations. Consider the case of a human fetus that, at some designated stage of development, has a level of moral status that bestows a right not to be harmed by a research intervention or an abortifacient. There still may be cases of justified intervention and abortion. A pregnant woman may legitimately abort the fetus if she will die unless she terminates the pregnancy. Moral conflict here is a conflict of rights: The unborn possess some rights, including a right to life, and pregnant women also possess some rights, including a right to life. Those who possess rights have a (prima facie) moral claim to be treated in accordance with their rights, but it is not possible to avoid all conflicts among rights and therefore there will be a need to specify rights in situations of conflict.

Norms are specified by narrowing their scope, which allows us to create what we will call *guidelines* governing moral status. Others might call them rules rather than guidelines, but in our framework rules specify principles whereas guidelines specify criteria of moral status. The goal is to extract content from the criteria in each of the five theories to show how that content can be shaped into progressively more practical guidelines. We will state these guidelines using the language of a "level of moral status." This idea of a level should be interpreted in light of our previous discussion of degrees of moral status. This theory provides for a continuum of moral status, running from a limited range of moral protections to a broad range of moral protections. For example, infants, the mentally handicapped, and many persons who are cognitively incompetent have some level of moral status, but they do not have the same level of moral status as autonomous persons. For instance, those who lack substantial cognitive and autonomy capacities do not have the same decision-making rights as those who are substantially autonomous.

To show how norms can be made progressively practical, we treat some illustrative specifications that qualify as guidelines. We are not recommending the guidelines we mention. Our goal is merely to clarify the nature and basis of these guidelines and to show how they are formed using the method of specification.

Consider first a circumstance in which the criterion "All living human beings have some level of moral status" comes into conflict with the criterion "All sentient beings have some level of moral status." Here are two possible specifications (guidelines 1 and 2) that engage the criteria put forward in theories 1 (the criterion of human life) and 4 (the criterion of sentience):

> **Guideline 1.** All human beings who are sentient or have the biological potential for sentience have some level of moral status; all human beings

who are not sentient and have no biological potential for sentience have moral status.

This specification allows for a further specification to particular such as anencephalic individuals (those without a cerebrum and cerebellum) and individuals who have sufficient brain damage that they are not sentient and have no potential for sentience. Guideline 1 says that individuals in such groups have no moral status. By contrast, the guideline assigns (some level of) moral status to all healthy human embryos and fetuses because they are either sentient or have the potential to be sentient. This guideline cannot be used to support human embryonic stem-cell research or abortions, and so would not support the transplantation of human fetal stem cells into a Parkinson's patient. Guideline 1 stands opposed to these practices (though it can be further specified).

A different, and obviously *competitive,* guideline achieved through specification is this:

> **Guideline 2.** All human beings who are sentient have some level of moral status; all human beings who are not sentient, including those with a mere potential for sentience, have no moral status.

This second guideline has implications for whether embryos and early-stage fetuses have moral status, and therefore implications for moral debates about human embryonic stem-cell research and early-stage abortions. This guideline states that although life prior to sentience is morally unprotected, the fetus is protected against abortion and research interventions once it becomes sentient.[54] Unlike guideline 1, this guideline does support the transplantation (after proper research) of human fetal stem cells into a Parkinson's patient.

Clarifying the exact implications of this second guideline would require further specification(s). In the case of abortion in particular, even when a fetus is sentient its continued existence could threaten the life or health of the pregnant woman. On one line of further specification, sentient fetuses possess the *same* rights possessed by all sentient human beings, and an abortion is a maleficent act as objectionable as the killing of an innocent person. On a different line of specification, sentient fetuses have a diminished set of rights if their presence threatens the life of a pregnant woman. In its abstract form, as here presented, guideline 2 is only a first step in grappling with problems governing several classes of individuals, and therefore a first step in what might be a long line of specification.

Here is a third guideline reached by specification that makes an appeal both to theory 4 (sentience) and to theory 2 (cognitive capacity):

> **Guideline 3.** All sentient beings have some level of moral status; the level is elevated in accordance with the level of sentience and the level of cognitive complexity.

According to this guideline, the more sentient the individual and the richer the cognitive or mental life of the individual, the higher the individual's level of moral status. The capacities of creatures for an array of valuable experiences vary widely, which prompts the judgment that not all lives are lived at the same high level of perception, cognition, appreciation, esthetic experience, and the like. The issue here is not one of whether a life has value, but rather of different levels of value because of differences in sentience and the quality of mental life. This guideline is a first step toward working out the common intuition that great apes deserve stronger protections than pigs, which deserve more protection than rats, and so forth. However, there is no guarantee that this guideline will support an intuition of species preference; for example, pigs could turn out to have a richer mental life and therefore a higher moral status than dogs.

Depending on how this guideline is further specified, it might or might not support use of a ready-to-transplant pig heart valve into a human heart. According to this guideline, the level of the pig's capacities of sentience and cognition makes a critical moral difference in whether the valve can be harvested in the first place. Questions of the comparative value of the human life saved and the pig's life sacrificed can only be decided by inquiry into the levels of their sentience and cognition.

Consider now a fourth guideline, this one a specification of the criterion of moral agency (theory 3) in conflict with the criterion of human-species properties (theory 1):

> **Guideline 4.** All human beings capable of moral agency have equal basic rights; all sentient human beings not capable of moral agency have a diminished set of rights.

This guideline elevates the status of moral agents and gives a lesser status to all other sentient creatures, including all members of the human species not capable of moral agency. Defense of this guideline requires an account of equal basic rights and of which rights are held and not held by those incapable of moral agency (a subject treated in Chapter 4).

This guideline is, from one perspective, obviously correct and noncontroversial: Competent individuals capable of moral agency have a set of rights—for example, decision-making rights—not held by individuals who are not capable of moral agency, whether the latter are human or nonhuman. Far more controversial, however, is the underlying premise that human individuals who lack capacity for moral agency have a reduced moral status. Proponents of theory 1 would resist this premise in their specifications. The categorization of reduced moral status could affect many decisions in bioethics. For example, in specifications of how to rank order who qualifies first in the competition for organ transplants, the value of individuals with no capacity for moral agency, and thereby a reduced moral status, might well be discounted.

Consider, as a final example, a possible guideline that engages the demands of the fifth theory (of status through relationships) and the fourth theory (of sentience). This specification brings the two criteria to bear on the circumstance of laboratory animals. The following formulation assumes the moral proposition that the "communal" relationship between persons in charge of a laboratory and the animals in it is morally significant:

> **Guideline 5.** All sentient laboratory animals have a level of moral status that affords them some protections against being caused pain or suffering; as the likelihood or the magnitude of potential pain or suffering increases, the level of moral status increases and protections must be increased accordingly.

This guideline is the first step in making precise the idea that laboratory animals who benefit human communities gain a higher moral status than would be acquired by sentience alone. Human initiatives that establish relations with animals change what is owed to them, and they thereby hold a higher status than do wild animals of the same species. The main conditions of interest are the vulnerability and dependence engendered in animals when humans establish relations with them in laboratories. The more vulnerable we make the animals to pain and suffering, the more our duties of animal care and protection increase. This guideline has sometimes been expressed, though poorly, in terms of our stewardship over the animals—that is, the careful and responsible oversight and protection of the conditions of an animal entrusted to one's care. However, a far better model is grounded in obligations of reciprocity and nonmaleficence: Animal research subjects gain a higher moral status because of the use made of their bodies and the harm or risk of harm imposed on them.

These five guidelines are so abstract and indeterminate that they may seem doubtfully practicable. If their abstractness cannot be further reduced, this outcome would be unfortunate because practicability is an important criterion of an ethical theory. We recognize, of course, that these guidelines need further development and defense and that they will be difficult to bring to bear on the world of biomedical research and all areas of medical practice that present difficult cases. Nonetheless, these and other guidelines can be progressively specified to the point of practicability, just as moral principles can (as we argued in Chapter 1). In addition, constrained balancing (also analyzed in Chapter 1) will often have a central role in determining justifiable courses of action. For instance, the use of sentient animals in research designed to benefit humans cannot be justified if there are other ethically acceptable ways to gain the relevant knowledge, if the harms such as pain and discomfort to the animals cannot be adequately minimized, if those harms are disproportionate to the end sought, and the like.

THE MORAL SIGNIFICANCE OF MORAL STATUS

Some writers challenge the need for the category of moral status. They argue that moral theory can and should go directly to discussion of how individuals ought to be treated and to the roles of moral virtues and moral character as suitable guides. Mary Midgley and Rosalind Hursthouse, two representative theorists, argue that moral status accounts of the sort examined thus far offer a superficially attractive but overly simplistic picture of how we "expand the circle of our concern" beyond autonomous adult humans to human fetuses, brain-damaged humans, laboratory animals, and the like. They argue that such theories blind us to the range of features that are morally relevant in decision making. If a creature has a property such as sentience, this fact does not inform us how we should treat or otherwise respond to members of the class of sentient beings; nor does it give us an account of moral priorities. Thus, we do not need the concept and theory of moral status, and we would be better off without it.[55]

This thesis about moral judgment requires that we attend to various morally relevant features of situations that give us moral reasons for acting or abstaining from acting in regard to others that no theory of moral status is well suited to address. For example, we often make distinctions that lead us to justifiably give preferential treatment to either individuals or classes of individuals, such as preferences to our own children, to companion animals that live with us, and the like. We have to sort through which preferences are justifiable and which not, but no theory of moral status can direct us in this task.

These cautions rightly warn us about the limits of the theory of moral status. Nonetheless, moral status is a matter of paramount moral importance and should be carefully analyzed, not discarded. We take a similar view about basic rights in Chapter 9. It would be a catastrophic moral loss if we did not have available either basic norms of moral status or basic rights. Practices of slavery as well as abuses of human research subjects have thrived historically in part because of defective criteria of moral status and inattention to basic rights. In our lifetimes, some children who were institutionalized as mentally infirm, some elderly patients in chronic disease hospitals, and some racial groups were treated in the United States as if they had little or no moral status by some of the finest centers of biomedical research in the world and by the sponsors of the research.[56] It is easy to forget how recognition of moral status can generate interest in and support vital moral protections.[57]

VULNERABLE POPULATIONS AND VULNERABLE INDIVIDUALS

Concern about moral status in biomedical ethics has often grown out of concern about ostensibly vulnerable populations. Rules requiring additional protections for populations judged to be vulnerable are a foundation stone of both clinical ethics and research ethics. These protections arose from concerns about exploitation and the inability of the members of some groups to consent.[58] Reduced capacity to consent is regarded as justifying additional protections such as surrogate consent and lowered limits of acceptable risk. Vulnerable persons in biomedical contexts are incapable of protecting their own interests because of sickness, debilitation, mental illness, immaturity, cognitive impairment, and the like. They often are socioeconomically impoverished, which adds to the potential for harmful outcomes. Accordingly, populations such as homeless families, political refugees, and illegal aliens—whose members have sometimes been human research subjects and who often go without medical care—can also be considered *vulnerable*. However, this term should be used with caution, because it can function to stereotype and to unduly protect.[59]

Guidelines for Vulnerable Populations

In controversies over uses of vulnerable populations in biomedical research, one of three positions might be taken on the justification of any particular research practice:

1. Do not allow the practice (a policy of full prohibition).
2. Allow the practice without regard to conditions (a policy of full permissibility).
3. Allow the practice only under certain conditions (a policy of partial permissibility).

Public opinion is deeply divided over which of the three is the most appropriate policy to govern various uses of fetuses in research—in utero and after deliberate abortions. Many prefer the first, many the second, and many the third. Such split opinions are slightly, but only slightly, less typical of debates about experimentation with animals, experimentation with children, and experimentation with incompetent individuals. Few today defend either full prohibition or full permissibility of research involving these groups, but many would support a prohibition on the use of some classes of these individuals, such as the great apes and seriously ill children. To reject the first two guidelines—as is common—is to accept the third, which in turn requires that we establish the precise set of moral protections to be provided and determine the conditions that allow us to proceed or not to proceed.

Problems of moral coherence bedevil these issues. Near-universal agreement exists that humans who lack certain capacities should not be used in biomedical research that is risky and does not offer them a prospect of direct benefit. Protections for these vulnerable populations should be at a high level because of their vulnerability. Nonhuman animals are usually not treated equivalently, though the reasons for this differential treatment are often unclear. Their limited cognitive and moral capacities have traditionally provided the substantive justification for, rather than against, their use in biomedical research when human subjects cannot ethically be used. How we can justify causing harm and premature death to these animals, but not to humans with similarly limited capacities, is an unresolved issue in biomedical ethics, and one that threatens coherence in moral theory. History now seems unlikely to side with the traditional view that the level of some animal subjects' moral status is either zero or vastly below that of human subjects.[60]

Practices of abortion, particularly where fetuses are capable of sentience, raise directly related issues of moral coherence. The long and continuing strug- gle over abortion primarily concerns two questions: (1) What is the moral status of the fetus (at various developmental points)? (2) What should we do when the rights generated by this status conflict with the rights of women to control their futures? Near-universal agreement exists that a very late-term fetus is not relevantly different from a newborn. Another month earlier in development will also show little difference in morally relevant differences, and coherence threat- ens any point on the continuum at which a decision is made about moral status. As with animal subjects, the status of human fetuses tends to be downgraded because of their lack of sentient, cognitive, and moral capacities, which usually plays a role in attempts to justify abortion. Questions about whether we can jus- tify such downgrading and whether we can justify causing premature death to the fetus remain among the most difficult questions in biomedical ethics.

There are benefits to humans from a system in which the lives of embryos, fetuses, and research animals can be terminated with relative ease. The range of benefits produced by animal research, for example, raises questions about whether such research should be restricted, and, if so, in which ways. All research involves some level of risk or harm, and the most promising justifica- tion for introducing these risks is its potential benefits. The moral challenge is to make our answers to these questions coherent in a way that allows different levels of risk of harm for different classes of individuals only when a criterion of moral status permits unequal treatment.

Sympathy and Impartiality

Problems of moral status and vulnerable populations can be profitably discussed in terms of our capacity to sympathize with the predicament of others. In previ- ous sections of this chapter we have connected our reflections on moral status to the discussion of *moral norms* in Chapter 1. Now we connect these reflections to our account of *moral character* in Chapter 2. In particular, we focus on moral sympathy as a trait similar to compassion and usually involving empathy, both of which we discussed in Chapter 2.

The capacity for sympathy enables us to enter into, however imperfectly, the thoughts and feelings of another being. Through sympathy, we form a con- cern for the other's welfare. Such sympathizing does not necessarily imply gen- erosity or favorable responsiveness. A convicted criminal who is put to death may engage our sympathy without engaging our generosity, mercy, leniency, or assistance. Research investigators, veterinarians, and animal trainers may have a rich and sympathetic understanding of the humans or the nonhuman animals they encounter, without exhibiting generosity or mercy toward them.

David Hume discerningly argued that most human beings have only a *limited* sympathy with the plight of others, but also have some level of capacity to overcome these limits through calm, reflective judgments:

> [T]he generosity of men is very limited, and…seldom extends beyond their friends and family, or, at most, beyond their native country.…[T]ho' [our] sympathy [for others] be much fainter than our concern for ourselves, and a sympathy with persons remote from us much fainter than that with persons near and contiguous; yet we neglect all these differences in our calm judgments concerning the characters of men.[61]

Hume notes that bias and partiality enter into many relationships and judgments. Our sympathy for others, he judges, is almost always fainter than our concern for ourselves. After we attend to ourselves, our sympathy reaches out most naturally to our intimates, such as the members of our family. From there sympathy typically moves to a wider, but still relatively small, group of acquaintances, such as those with whom we have the most frequent contact or in whose lives we have most heavily invested. Our sympathy with those truly remote from us, such as strangers or persons in other nations, is usually diminished by comparison to sympathy with those close to us. The "distance or contiguity," as Hume puts it, between others and us makes a critical motivational difference in how we regard and think about our obligations to them.

Both *dissimilarity to* and *distance from* other persons function to limit our sympathy. People in nursing homes are often both dissimilar to and distant from other persons, as are people with diseases such as Lesch-Nyhan, human embryos, and animals used in research, among others. Hence, it is harder for us to view these individuals as having a significant moral status that places demands on us and holds us accountable. Even though we know that individuals in vulnerable populations suffer, our sympathy and moral responsiveness do not come easily, especially when the individuals are hidden from our view or are of another species.

Not surprisingly, many persons among the "moral saints" we discussed in Chapter 2 exhibit an expanded sympathy with the plight of those who suffer— a form of sympathy beyond the level most of us achieve or even hold as a moral ideal. Severely limited sympathy, together with severely limited generosity, helps explain such social phenomena as child abuse, animal abuse, and the neglect of enfeebled elderly persons in nursing homes. It is regrettable, of course, that enlarged affections are not commonplace in human interactions, but this fact is predictable given what we know about human nature.

One way that Hume proposes to address limited sympathy for those different from us is the deliberate exercise of impartiality through "calm judgments":

"It is necessary for us, in our calm judgments and discourse...to neglect all these differences, and render our sentiments more public and social."[62] He asks us to reach out for a more extensive sympathy. His proposal accords with our discussion in Chapter 2 of "moral excellence." A morally excellent person will work both to enlarge his or her sympathy for those who suffer and to reach calm and unbiased judgments. Hume characterizes his ideal as a "common" or "general" point of view in moral judgment—an impartial viewpoint. This perspective, which some philosophers call "the moral point of view," controls for the distortions and biases created by our closeness to some individuals, and also opens us up to a more extensive sympathy.[63]

This perspective could help us address several problems encountered in this chapter, but it would be unreasonable to insist on a moral point of view that incorporates such a deep sympathy and extensive impartiality that it applies equally across cultures, geography, and species. Extensive sympathy is a regulative, but arduous, ideal of conduct. When consistently achieved across a lifetime, it is a morally beautiful adornment of character.

CONCLUSION

In this chapter we have used the language of "theories," "criteria," "guidelines," and "degrees" of moral status, rather than the language of "principles," "virtues," and "character" that dominated Chapters 1 and 2. These forms of discourse and the territories they cover should be carefully distinguished. We have not argued that the common morality—as discussed in Chapters 1 and 2—gives us an adequate and workable framework of criteria of moral status, and we have left many issues about moral status undecided. There is justified uncertainty in arguments about the moral status of embryos, fetuses, brain-damaged humans, and animals used in research—and about whether there are degrees of moral status. Reasoned disagreement is to be expected, but those who engage these issues need to be clear about the models they use and their defense, a matter that has yet to be made abundantly clear in the literature of bioethics. If the model accepts degrees of moral status, that model needs to be stated with precision. If the model rejects degrees of moral status, that account, too, needs more penetrating analysis than is presently available.

We return to some of these problems near the end of Chapter 10, where we discuss both the common morality and the possibility of "moral change" in conceptions of moral status.

NOTES

1. Cf. Mark H. Bernstein, *On Moral Considerability: An Essay on Who Morally Matters* (New York: Oxford University Press, 1998).

2. This conceptual thesis is indebted to David DeGrazia, "Moral Status as a Matter of Degree," *Southern Journal of Philosophy* 46 (2008): 181–98, esp. 183.

3. This history and its relevance for biomedical ethics—with special attention to slavery—are presented in Ronald A. Lindsay, "Slaves, Embryos, and Nonhuman Animals: Moral Status and the Limitations of Common Morality Theory," *Kennedy Institute of Ethics Journal* 15 (December 2005): 323–46. On the history of problems about moral status for nonhuman animals, see the four chapters by Stephen R. L. Clark, Aaron Garrett, Michael Tooley, and Sarah Chan and John Harris, in *The Oxford Handbook of Animal Ethics,* ed. Tom L. Beauchamp and R. G. Frey (New York: Oxford University Press, 2011), chaps. 1–2, 11–12.

4. D. J. Powner and I. M. Bernstein, "Extended Somatic Support for Pregnant Women after Brain Death," *Critical Care Medicine* 31 (2003): 1241–49; David R. Field et al., "Maternal Brain Death During Pregnancy," *JAMA: Journal of the American Medical Association* 260 (August 12, 1988): 816–22; Xavier Bosch, "Pregnancy of Brain-Dead Mother to Continue," *Lancet* 354 (December 18–25, 1999): 2145.

5. See Hilde Lindemann Nelson, "The Architect and the Bee: Some Reflections on Postmortem Pregnancy," *Bioethics* 8 (1994): 247–67; D. Sperling, "From the Dead to the Unborn: Is There an Ethical Duty to Save Life?" *Medicine and Law Journal* 23 (2004): 567–86; and Christoph Anstotz, "Should a Brain-Dead Pregnant Woman Carry Her Child to Full Term?: The Case of the 'Erlanger Baby,'" *Bioethics* 7 (1993): 340–50.

6. Daniel Sperling, *Management of Post-Mortem Pregnancy: Legal and Philosophical Aspects* (Aldershot, England: Ashgate Publishing, 2006) (addressing questions of both the moral and the legal status of the fetus); Sarah Elliston, "Life after Death? Legal and Ethical Considerations of Maintaining Pregnancy in Brain-Dead Women," in *Intersections: Women on Law, Medicine and Technology,* ed. Kerry Petersen (Aldershot, England: Ashgate Publishing, 1997), pp. 145–65. Our discussion here does not suppose that dead persons have legally protected interests and rights; we are focusing on a case where the dead pregnant woman had an advance directive requesting that treatment be withheld or withdrawn under conditions that included her death.

7. On this distinction, see Mary Midgley, "Duties Concerning Islands," in *Environmental Ethics,* ed. Robert Elliott (Oxford: Oxford University Press, 1995); Christopher W. Morris, "The Idea of Moral Standing," in *Oxford Handbook of Animal Ethics* (2011), pp. 261–62; and David Copp, "Animals, Fundamental Moral Standing, and Speciesism," in *Oxford Handbook of Animal Ethics* (2011), pp. 276–77.

8. On why something counts "in its own right," see Allen Buchanan, "Moral Status and Human Enhancement," *Philosophy & Public Affairs* 37 (2009): 346–81, esp. 346; Frances M. Kamm, "Moral Status," in *Intricate Ethics: Rights, Responsibilities, and Permissible Harm* (New York: Oxford University Press, 2006), pp. 227–30; and L. Wayne Sumner, "A Third Way," in *The Problem of Abortion,* 3rd edition, ed. Susan Dwyer and Joel Feinberg (Belmont, CA: Wadsworth, 1997), p. 99. We thank Chris Morris for these references.

9. Robert P. George and Alfonso Gómez-Lobo, "The Moral Status of the Human Embryo," *Perspectives in Biology and Medicine* 48 (2005): 201–10, quotation spanning pp. 201–05.

10. Cf. the Preamble and Articles in the *United Nations Universal Declaration of Human Rights,* http://www.un.org/Overview/rights.html (accessed May 19, 2007).

11. On September 7, 2001, V. Ourednik et al. published an article entitled "Segregation of Human Neural Stem Cells in the Developing Primate Forebrain," *Science* 293 (2001): 1820–24. This article is the first report of the implanting of human neural stem cells into the brains of a primate, creating a monkey–human chimera.

12. "Chimeric" usually refers to the cellular level, whereas "transgenic" concerns the genetic level. See the argument in Mark K. Greene et al., "Moral Issues of Human—Non-Human Primate Neural Grafting," *Science* 309 (July 15, 2005): 385–86. See also the conclusions of Julian Savulescu, "Genetically Modified Animals: Should There Be Limits to Engineering the Animal Kingdom?"

in *Oxford Handbook of Animal Ethics* (2011), esp. pp. 644–64; Jason Robert and Françoise Baylis, "Crossing Species Boundaries," *American Journal of Bioethics* 3 (2003): 1–13 (and commentaries following); Henry T. Greely, "Defining Chimeras...and Chimeric Concerns," *American Journal of Bioethics* 3 (2003): 17–20; and Robert Streiffer, "At the Edge of Humanity: Human Stem Cells, Chimeras, and Moral Status," *Kennedy Institute of Ethics Journal* 15 (2005): 347–70.

13.   A common view is that permitting the creation of animal–human hybrids for research purposes is defensible, as long as they are destroyed within a specified period of time. See Henry T. Greely, "Human/ Nonhuman Chimeras: Assessing the Issues," in *Oxford Handbook of Animal Ethics* (2011), pp. 671–72, 676, 684–86. However, a federal ban on their creation was recommended by the President's Council on Bioethics, *Reproduction & Responsibility: The Regulation of New Biotechnologies* (Washington, DC: President's Council on Bioethics, 2004), available at http://bioethics.georgetown.edu/pcbe/ (accessed January 28, 2012). See also Scottish Council on Human Bioethics, *Embryonic, Fetal and Post-Natal Animal–Human Mixtures: An Ethical Discussion* (Edinburgh, U.K.: Scottish Council on Human Bioethics, 2006), available at http://www.schb.org.uk/ (accessed January 28, 2012).

14.   National Research Council, National Academy of Science, Committee on Guidelines for Human Embryonic Stem Cell Research, *Guidelines for Human Embryonic Stem Cell Research* (Washington, DC: National Academies Press, 2005); Amendments 2007 available online; Mark Greene, "On the Origin of Species Notions and Their Ethical Limitations," in *Oxford Handbook of Animal Ethics* (2011), pp. 577–602.

15.   The language of "person" has a long history in theology, especially in Christian theological efforts to explicate the three individualities of the Trinity. On the potential of chimeras, see Greene et al., "Moral Issues of Human–Nonhuman Primate Neural Grafting."

16.   See further Tom L. Beauchamp, "The Failure of Theories of Personhood," *Kennedy Institute of Ethics Journal* 9 (1999): 309–24; and Lisa Bartolotti, "Disputes over Moral Status: Philosophy and Science in the Future of Bioethics," *Health Care Analysis* 15 (2007): 153–58, esp. 155–57.

17.   At least one adherent of the first theory reaches precisely this conclusion. See Patrick Lee, "Personhood, the Moral Standing of the Unborn, and Abortion," *Linacre Quarterly* (May 1990): 80–89, esp. 87; and Lee, "Soul, Body and Personhood," *American Journal of Jurisprudence* 49 (2004): 87–125.

18.   See the variety of accounts in Michael Tooley, "Are Nonhuman Animals Persons?" in *Oxford Handbook of Animal Ethics* (2011), pp. 332–73; Harry G. Frankfurt, *Necessity, Volition, and Love* (Cambridge: Cambridge University Press, 1999), chaps. 9, 11; Mary Anne Warren, *Moral Status* (Oxford: Oxford University Press, 1997), chap. 1; H. Tristram Engelhardt, Jr., *The Foundations of Bioethics,* 2nd ed. (New York: Oxford University Press, 1996), chaps. 4, 6; and Lynne Rudder Baker, *Persons and Bodies* (Cambridge: Cambridge University Press, 2000), chaps. 4, 6.

19.   Korsgaard, "Kant's Formula of Humanity," in *Creating the Kingdom of Ends* (Cambridge: Cambridge University Press, 1996), pp. 110–11. See further on this point her general Kantian views in "Interacting with Animals: A Kantian Account," in *Oxford Handbook of Animal Ethics* (2011), pp. 91–118, esp. p. 103.

20.   See Tom Regan, *The Case for Animal Rights* (Berkeley, CA: University of California Press, 1983; updated ed. 2004), pp. 178, 182–84.

21.   Exactly how this conclusion should be developed is morally disputable. It would clearly be wrong to treat a late-stage Alzheimer patient in the way in which biomedical researchers often treat experimental animals, but it can be argued for the same reasons that we should treat primate research subjects as well as we treat late-stage Alzheimer patients. Similarly, if it is outlandish to assert that "marginal" cases of human capacity can be treated as mere means to human ends, then it is arguably the case that the way researchers often use animals as mere means is morally outlandish.

22. See Korsgaard's similar assessment of its lack of merit in "Interacting with Animals: A Kantian Account," p. 101.

23. Colin Allen and Marc Bekoff, *Species of Mind: The Philosophy and Biology of Cognitive Ethology* (Cambridge, MA: MIT Press, 1997); Colin Allen, "Assessing Animal Cognition: Ethological and Philosophical Perspectives," *Journal of Animal Science* 76 (1998): 42–47.

24. See Donald R. Griffin, *Animal Minds: Beyond Cognition to Consciousness,* 2nd ed. (Chicago: University of Chicago Press, 2001); and Rosemary Rodd, *Ethics, Biology, and Animals* (Oxford: Clarendon, 1990), esp. chaps. 3–4, 10.

25. Cf. Gordon G. Gallup, "Self-Recognition in Primates," *American Psychologist* 32 (1977): 329–38; and David DeGrazia, *Taking Animals Seriously: Mental Life and Moral Status* (New York: Cambridge University Press, 1996), esp. p. 302.

26. These criteria also would require, in a deeper analysis than we can provide, explication in terms of some of the cognitive conditions discussed previously. For example, the capacity to make moral judgments requires a certain level of the capacity for understanding.

27. Kant, *Grounding for the Metaphysics of Morals,* trans. James W. Ellington, in Kant, *Ethical Philosophy* (Indianapolis, IN: Hackett, 1983), pp. 38–41, 43–44 (Preussische Akademie, pp. 432, 435, 436, 439–40).

28. Examples of such theories, focused on the claim that there is sufficient evidence to count some nonhuman animals as moral agents and therefore as members of the moral community, are Marc Bekoff and Jessica Pierce, *Wild Justice: The Moral Lives of Animals* (Chicago: University of Chicago Press, 2009); Michael Bradie, "The Moral Life of Animals," in *Oxford Handbook of Animal Ethics* (2011), pp. 547–73, esp. pp. 555–70; and Tom Regan, *The Case for Animal Rights,* esp. pp. 151–56.

29. See two opposed theories on the latter issue in L. Wayne Sumner, *Abortion and Moral Theory* (Princeton, NJ: Princeton University Press, 1981); and Bonnie Steinbock, *Life Before Birth: The Moral and Legal Status of Embryos and Fetuses,* 2nd ed. (New York: Oxford University Press, 2011).

30. Although we use both terms, *pain* and *suffering*, which are sometimes used interchangeably, a distinction is often drawn between them on grounds that suffering may require more cognitive ability than the mere experience of pain. Suffering may occur from aversive or harmful states such as misery that are not attended by pain.

31. Bentham, *An Introduction to the Principles of Morals and Legislation,* ed. J. H. Burns and H. L. A. Hart; with a new introduction by F. Rosen; and an interpretive essay by Hart (Oxford: Clarendon, 1996), p. 283.

32. Baruch Brody, *Abortion and the Sanctity of Life* (Cambridge, MA: MIT Press, 1975). Brain birth is said to be analogous to brain death at critical transition points.

33. This point is made in Stephen Griffith, "Fetal Death, Fetal Pain, and the Moral Standing of a Fetus," *Public Affairs Quarterly* 9 (1995): 117.

34. See, for example, Peter Singer, *Animal Liberation,* 2nd ed. (London: Pimlico, 1995), p. 8; and Sumner, *Abortion and Moral Theory.*

35. Nussbaum, *Frontiers of Justice: Disability, Nationality, Species Membership* (Cambridge, MA: Harvard University Press, 2006), p. 361. Nussbaum argues that species membership is not "morally and politically irrelevant" because it can give us "the appropriate benchmark for judging whether a given creature has decent opportunities for flourishing." Hence, efforts should be undertaken to bring a child with serious mental handicaps up to a certain level of function, for instance, in the use of language,

whereas such efforts are not required for a chimpanzee who has a comparable level of mental function, but for whom language use is a "frill." *Frontiers of Justice,* pp. 357–66.

36.   This thesis is defended in Sahar Akhtar, "The Relationship between Cognitive Sophistication and Pain in Animals," in *Oxford Handbook of Animal Ethics* (2011), pp. 495–518, esp. pp. 499–511; see also David DeGrazia and Andrew Rowan, "Pain, Suffering, and Anxiety in Animals and Humans," *Theoretical Medicine and Bioethics* 12 (1991): 193–211.

37.   In this theory, life is valuable and has moral status only under certain conditions of quality of life. Life, therefore, can lose its value and moral status by degrees as conditions of welfare and richness of experience decrease. Frey, "Moral Standing, the Value of Lives, and Speciesism," *Between the Species* 4 (Summer 1988): 191–201; "Animals," in *The Oxford Handbook of Practical Ethics* (New York: Oxford University Press, 2003), esp. pp. 163, 178; and "Autonomy and the Value of Animal Life," *Monist* 70 (January 1987): 50–63.

38.   Ronald Green, "Stem Cell Research:…Determining Moral Status," *American Journal of Bioethics* 2 (Winter 2002): 20–30; Diane Jeske, "Special Obligations," *Stanford Encyclopedia of Philosophy,* http://plato.stanford.edu/entries/special-obligations/#6 (accessed November 13, 2011); Clare Palmer, "The Moral Relevance of the Distinction between Domesticated and Wild Animals," *Oxford Handbook of Animal Ethics* (2011), pp. 701–25.

39.   Carson Strong and Garland Anderson, "The Moral Status of the Near-Term Fetus," *Journal of Medical Ethics* 15 (1989): 25–26.

40.   See the related conclusion in Nancy Jecker, "The Moral Status of Patients Who Are Not Strict Persons," *Journal of Clinical Ethics* 1 (1990): 35–38.

41.   For a broader set of patients than the latter category suggests—especially various terminally ill patients—see Felicia Cohn and Joanne Lynn, "Vulnerable People: Practical Rejoinders to Claims in Favor of Assisted Suicide," in *The Case against Assisted Suicide: For the Right to End-of-Life Care,* ed. Kathleen Foley and Herbert Hendin (Baltimore: Johns Hopkins University Press, 2002), pp. 238–60.

42.   An influential general strategy of melding diverse theories is proposed in Warren, *Moral Status,* though her set of melded theories differs from ours. A similar strategy, again with a different set of melded theories, appears in Lawrence J. Nelson and Michael J. Meyer, "Confronting Deep Moral Disagreements: The President's Council on Bioethics, Moral Status, and Human Embryos," *American Journal of Bioethics* 5 (2005): 33–42 (with a response to critics, pp. W14–16).

43.   See Don Marquis, "How Not to Argue that Embryos Lack Full Moral Status," *American Journal of Bioethics* 5 (2005): 54–56; and a criticism of Marquis's general position by David DeGrazia, "Moral Status, Human Identity, and Early Embryos: A Critique of the President's Approach," *Journal of Law, Medicine, and Ethics* 34 (2006): 49–57.

44.   See Judith Jarvis Thomson's classic discussion in "A Defense of Abortion," *Philosophy and Public Affairs* 1 (1971): 47–66; and Patricia Beattie Jung, "Abortion and Organ Donation: Christian Reflections on Bodily Life Support," *Journal of Religious Ethics* 16 (1988): 273–305.

45.   This quotation is in the voice of some members of the President's Council on Bioethics who support human cloning for biomedical research. See The President's Council on Bioethics, *Human Cloning and Human Dignity* (New York: Public Affairs, 2002), pp. 153–58. See also the National Bioethics Advisory Commission (NBAC), *Ethical Issues in Human Stem Cell Research, Vol. I, Report and Recommendations* (Rockville, MD: NBAC, September 1999), which accepts "an intermediate position…that the embryo merits respect as a form of human life, but not the same level of respect accorded persons" (p. 50). This rules out the sale of embryos but does not rule out their use in destructive research that is deemed necessary for a justifiable goal. A thesis about "respectful destruction" is developed by Susanne Gibson, "Uses of Respect and Uses of the Human Embryo," *Bioethics* 21 (2007): 370–78. "Respect" that accepts destruction obviously provides only minimal protections.

46.   The problem of equal and unequal consideration of interests, and different degrees of consideration, is discussed in DeGrazia, "Moral Status as a Matter of Degree," esp. pp. 188, 191.

47.   [Mary Warnock], *Report of the Committee of Inquiry into Human Fertilisation and Embryology: Presented to Parliament* (London: H.M.S.O., July 1984). [The Warnock Committee Report.]

48.   Chief Medical Officer's Expert Group, *Stem Cell Research: Medical Progress with Responsibility* (London: Department of Health, 2000).

49.   Chief Medical Officer's Expert Group, *Stem Cell Research,* sects. 4.6, 4.12, pp. 38–39.

50.   See David DeGrazia, "Great Apes, Dolphins, and the Concept of Personhood," *Southern Journal of Philosophy* 35 (1997): 301–20.

51.   For an all-or-nothing account that rejects degrees of moral status, see Elizabeth Harman, "The Potentiality Problem," *Philosophical Studies* 114 (2003): 173–98.

52.   Morris reaches this conclusion in "The Idea of Moral Standing," p. 264.

53.   Carson Strong, "The Moral Status of Preembryos, Embryos, Fetuses, and Infants," *Journal of Medicine and Philosophy* 22 (1997): 457–78.

54.   Cf. the similar conclusion, with an argued defense, in Mary Anne Warren, "Moral Status," in *A Companion to Applied Ethics,* ed. R. G. Frey and Christopher Wellman (Oxford: Blackwell, 2003), p. 163.

55.   Mary Midgley, *Animals and Why They Matter* (Athens, GA: University of Georgia Press, 1983), pp. 28–30, 100; Rosalind Hursthouse, "Virtue Ethics and the Treatment of Animals," in *Oxford Handbook of Animal Ethics* (2011), chap. 4; and Hursthouse, *Ethics, Humans and Other Animals* (London: Routledge, 2000), pp. 127–32.

56.   Classic cases in the United States are the Tuskegee syphilis experiment, the use of mentally retarded children at the Willowbrook State School, and the injection of cancer cells into debilitated patients at the Jewish Chronic Disease Hospital in Brooklyn. For the first, see James H. Jones, *Bad Blood: The Tuskegee Syphilis Experiment,* rev. ed. (New York: Free Press, 1993), and Susan Reverby, ed., *Tuskegee's Truths: Rethinking the Tuskegee Syphilis Study* (Chapel Hill, NC: University of North Carolina Press, 2000); for the others, see Jay Katz et al., eds., *Experimentation with Human Beings: The Authority of the Investigator, Subject, Professions, and State in the Human Experimentation Process* (New York: Russell Sage Foundation, 1972).

57.   Parallel debates in environmental ethics focus on the moral status of dimensions of nature beyond human and nonhuman animals; for example, whether individual trees, plants, species, and ecosystems have moral status. See Kenneth Goodpaster, "On Being Morally Considerable," *Journal of Philosophy* 75 (1978): 308–25; Paul Taylor, *Respect for Nature: A Theory of Environmental Ethics,* 25th Anniversary Edition (Princeton, NJ: Princeton University Press, 2011); Gary Varner, "Environmental Ethics, Hunting, and the Place of Animals," *Oxford Handbook of Animal Ethics* (2011), pp. 855–76; and Lawrence E. Johnson, *A Morally Deep World: An Essay on Moral Significance and Environmental Ethics* (Cambridge: Cambridge University Press, 1993).

58.   National Commission for the Protection of Human Subjects of Biomedical and Behavioral Research, *The Belmont Report: Ethical Principles and Guidelines for the Protection of Human Subjects of Research* (Washington, DC: DHEW Publication OS 78–0012, 1978); Code of Federal Regulations, Title 45 (Public Welfare), Part 46 (Protection of Human Subjects), http://www.hhs.gov/ohrp/humansubjects/guidance/45cfr46.html (accessed July 15, 2011).

59.   On analysis of vulnerability, see Kenneth Kipnis, "Vulnerability in Research Subjects: A Bioethical Taxonomy," in National Bioethics Advisory Commission (NBAC), *Ethical and Policy Issues in Research Involving Human Participants,* vol. 2 (Bethesda, MD: NBAC, 2001), pp. G-1–13.

60.   A major document to illustrate this trend is an Institute of Medicine committee report: Committee on the Use of Chimpanzees in Biomedical and Behavioral Research, *Chimpanzees in Biomedical and Behavioral Research: Assessing the Necessity* (Washington, DC: National Academies Press, 2011).

61.   Hume, *A Treatise of Human Nature,* ed. David Fate Norton and Mary J. Norton (Oxford: Oxford University Press, 2006), 3.3.3.2 [SBN 602–3].

62.   Hume, *An Enquiry Concerning the Principles of Morals,* ed. Tom L. Beauchamp (Oxford: Oxford University Press, 1998), 5.42 [SBN 229].

63.   We are concentrating on the role impartiality can play in expanding sympathy, but impartiality also can help to correct misdirected and exaggerated sympathy that borders on sentimentality. For a critique of a kind of sentimentality that stands opposed to potentially effective measures to obtain transplantable organs from brain-dead individuals, see Joel Feinberg, "The Mistreatment of Dead Bodies," *Hastings Center Report* 15 (February 1985): 31–37.

PART II

MORAL PRINCIPLES

4
Respect for Autonomy

The principle of respect for the autonomous choices of persons runs as deep in the common morality as any principle, but determining its nature, scope, or strength requires careful analysis. We employ the concept of autonomy and the principle of respect for autonomy in this chapter largely to examine individuals' decision making in health care and research, both as patients and as subjects (or "participants"[1]).

Although we begin our analysis of a framework of principles of biomedical ethics with the principle of respect for autonomy, the order of our chapters does not imply that this principle has moral priority over other principles. We do not hold, as some of our critics have suggested, that the principle of respect for autonomy always has priority over all other moral considerations. We also argue, in contrast to some of our commentators, that respect for autonomy is not excessively individualistic (to the neglect of the social nature of individuals and the impact of individual choices and actions on others), is not excessively focused on reason (to the neglect of the emotions), and is not unduly legalistic (highlighting legal rights while downplaying social practices and responsibilities).

THE CONCEPT OF AUTONOMY AND THE PRINCIPLE OF RESPECT FOR AUTONOMY

The word *autonomy,* derived from the Greek *autos* ("self") and *nomos* ("rule," "governance," or "law"), originally referred to the self-rule or self-governance of independent city-states. Autonomy has since been extended to individuals, but the precise meaning of the term is disputed. At a minimum, personal autonomy encompasses self-rule that is free from both controlling interference by others and limitations that prevent meaningful choice, such as inadequate understanding. The autonomous individual acts freely in accordance with a self-chosen plan, analogous to the way an independent government manages its territories and sets its policies. In contrast, a person of diminished autonomy is in some material respect controlled by others or incapable of deliberating or acting on the basis of his or her desires and plans. For example, cognitively challenged individuals and prisoners often have diminished autonomy. Mental incapacitation limits the autonomy of a person with a severe mental handicap, whereas coercive institutionalization constrains a prisoner's autonomy.

Virtually all theories of autonomy view two conditions as essential for autonomy: *liberty* (independence from controlling influences) and *agency* (capacity for intentional action). However, disagreement exists over the meaning of these two conditions and over whether additional conditions are required.[2] How a theory can be constructed from these basic conditions is the first subject we will consider.

Theories of Autonomy

Some theories of autonomy feature the abilities, skills, or traits of the *autonomous person,* which include capacities of self-governance such as understanding, reasoning, deliberating, managing, and independent choosing.[3] However, our focus in this chapter on decision making leads us to concentrate on *autonomous choice* rather than on general capacities for governance and self-management. Even autonomous persons who have self-governing capacities and are, on the whole, good managers of their health sometimes fail to govern themselves in particular choices because of temporary constraints caused by illness, depression, ignorance, coercion, or other conditions that limit their judgment or their options.

An autonomous person who signs a consent form for a procedure without reading or understanding the form has the capacity to act autonomously, but fails to so act in this circumstance. Depending on the context, we might be able to correctly describe the act as one of placing trust in one's physician and therefore as an act that autonomously authorizes the physician to proceed. However, even if this claim were accurate, the act is not an autonomous authorization *of the procedure* because this person lacks material information about it. Similarly, some persons who are generally incapable of autonomous decision making can at times make autonomous choices. For example, some patients in mental institutions who cannot care for themselves and have been declared legally incompetent may still make some autonomous choices, such as stating preferences for meals, refusing medications, and making phone calls to acquaintances.

Split-level theories of autonomy. An influential group of philosophers has presented a theory of autonomy that requires having the capacity to reflectively control and identify with or oppose one's basic (first-order) desires or preferences through higher level (second-order) desires or preferences.[4] Gerald Dworkin offers a "content-free" definition of autonomy as a "second-order capacity of persons to reflect critically upon their first-order preferences, desires, wishes, and so forth and the capacity to accept or attempt to change these in the light of higher-order preferences and values."[5] An example is an alcoholic who has a desire to drink, but also a higher order desire to stop drinking. In a second example, a dedicated physician may have a first-order desire to work exceptionally long hours in the hospital, while also having a higher order commitment to spend all of her evening hours with her family. Whenever she wants to work late in the evening and does so, she wants what she does not autonomously want, and therefore acts nonautonomously. Action from a first-order desire that is not endorsed by a second-order volition is not autonomous and represents animal behavior. Accordingly, in this theory an autonomous person has the capacity to reflectively accept, identify with, or repudiate a lower order desire independent of others' manipulations of that desire. This higher order capacity to accept or repudiate first-order preferences *constitutes* autonomy, and no person is autonomous without this capacity.

This theory is problematic, however, because nothing prevents a reflective acceptance, preference, or volition at the second level from being caused by and assured by a strong first-order desire. The individual's second-level acceptance of, or identification with, the first-order desire would then be the causal result of an already formed structure of preferences. Potent first-order desires from a condition such as alcohol addiction are antithetical to autonomy and can cause second-order desires. If second-order desires (decisions, volitions, etc.) are generated by prior desires or commitments, then the process of identifying with one desire rather than another does not distinguish autonomy from nonautonomy.

This theory needs more than a convincing account of second-order preferences and acceptable influences. It needs a way for ordinary persons to qualify as deserving respect for their autonomy even when they have not reflected on their preferences at a higher level. This theory also risks running afoul of the criterion of coherence with the principle of respect for autonomy discussed throughout this chapter. If reflective identification with one's desires or second-order volitions is a necessary condition of autonomous action, then many ordinary actions that are almost universally considered autonomous, such as cheating on one's spouse (when one truly wishes not to be such a person) or selecting tasty snack foods when grocery shopping (when one has never reflected on one's desires for snack foods), would be rendered *non*autonomous in this theory. Requiring reflective identification and stable volitional patterns deeply narrows the scope of actions protected by a principle of respect for autonomy.

Agnieszka Jaworska insightfully argues that choosing contrary to one's stable or accepted values need not constitute an abandonment of autonomy even if a choice contradicts the person's own professed, fixed set of values. For example, a patient might request a highly invasive treatment at the end of life against his previous judgment about his best interests because he has come to a conclusion that surprises him: He cares more about living a few extra days than he had thought he would. Despite his long-standing and firm view that he would reject such invasive treatments, he now accepts them. Jaworska's case is not uncommon in medical contexts.[6]

Few decision makers and few choices would be autonomous if held to the standards of higher order reflection in this split-level theory, which seems to present an aspirational ideal of autonomy rather than a suitable theory of autonomy for decision making of the sort under study in this chapter. A theory should not be inconsistent with pretheoretical assumptions implicit in the principle of respect for autonomy, and no theory of autonomy is acceptable if it presents an ideal beyond the reach of ordinary, competent agents and choosers.

Our three-condition theory. Instead of depicting such an ideal theory of autonomy, our analysis focuses on nonideal conditions. We analyze autonomous action in terms of normal choosers who act (1) intentionally, (2) with understanding, and (3) without controlling influences that determine their action. This account of autonomy is specifically designed to be coherent with the premise that the everyday choices of generally competent persons are autonomous.

1. *Intentionality.* Intentional actions require plans in the form of representations of the series of events proposed for the execution of an action. For an act to be intentional, as opposed to accidental, it must correspond to the actor's conception of the act in question, although a planned outcome might not materialize as projected.[7] Nothing about intentional acts rules out actions that one wishes one did not have to perform. Our motivation often reflects *conflicting* wants and desires, but this fact does not render an action less than intentional or autonomous. Foreseen but undesired outcomes are often part of a plan of intentional action.

2. *Understanding.* Understanding is the second condition of autonomous action. An action is not autonomous if the actor does not adequately understand it. Conditions that limit understanding include illness, irrationality, and immaturity. Deficiencies in the communication process also can hamper understanding. In our account, an autonomous action needs only a substantial degree of understanding and freedom from constraint, not a full understanding or a complete absence of influence. To restrict adequate decision making by patients and research subjects to the ideal of fully or completely autonomous decision making strips their acts of any meaningful place in the practical world, where people's actions are rarely, if ever, fully autonomous.

3. *Noncontrol.* The third of the three conditions of autonomous action is that a person be free of controls exerted either by external sources or by internal states that rob the person of self-directedness. Influence and resistance to influence are basic concepts for this analysis. Not all influences exerted on another person are controlling. Our analysis of noncontrol and voluntariness later in this chapter focuses on coercion and manipulation as key categories of influence. We there concentrate on *external* controlling influences—usually influences of one person on another—but no less important to autonomy are *internal* influences on the person, such as those caused by mental illness. All of these conditions can limit voluntariness.

The first of the three conditions of autonomy—intentionality—is not a matter of degree: Acts are either intentional or nonintentional. However, acts can satisfy both the conditions of understanding and absence of controlling influence to a greater or lesser extent. For example, threats can be more or less severe; understanding can be more or less complete; and mental illness can be more or less controlling. Children provide a good example of the continuum running from being in control to not being in control. In the early months of life children are heavily controlled and display only limited ability to be in control: They exhibit different degrees of resistance to influence as they mature, and their capacity to take control and perform intentional actions, as well as to understand, gradually increases as they develop.

Acts therefore can be autonomous by degrees, as a function of satisfying these two conditions of understanding and voluntariness to different degrees. A continuum of both understanding and noncontrol runs from full understanding and being entirely noncontrolled to absence of relevant understanding and being fully controlled. Cutoff points on these continua are required for the classification of an action as either autonomous or nonautonomous. The lines between adequate and inadequate degrees of understanding and degrees of control must be determined in light of specific objectives of decision making such as deciding about surgery, choosing a university to attend, and hiring a new employee.

The line between what is substantial and what is insubstantial may appear arbitrary. However, thresholds marking substantially autonomous decisions can be carefully fixed in light of specific objectives such as meaningful decision making. Patients and research subjects can achieve substantial autonomy in their decisions, just as substantially autonomous choice occurs in other areas of life such as choice of diet. The appropriate criteria for substantial autonomy are best addressed in a particular context.

Autonomy, Authority, Community, and Relationships

Some theorists argue that autonomous action is incompatible with the authority of governments, religious organizations, and other communities that prescribe behavior. They maintain that autonomous persons must act on their own reasons and can never submit to an authority or choose to be ruled by others without losing their autonomy.[8] However, no fundamental inconsistency exists between autonomy and authority if individuals exercise their autonomy in choosing to accept an institution, tradition, or community that they view as a legitimate source of direction.

Choosing to follow medical authority is a prime example. Other examples are a Jehovah's Witness who accepts the authority of that tradition and who therefore refuses a recommended blood transfusion and a Roman Catholic who accepts the authority of the church and chooses against an abortion. That persons share moral norms with authoritative institutions does not prevent these norms from being autonomously accepted, even if these principles derive from traditions or from institutional authority. If a Jehovah's Witness who insists on adhering to the doctrines of his faith in refusing a blood transfusion is deemed nonautonomous on the basis of his religious upbringing and convictions, many of our choices based on our confidence in institutional authority will be likewise deemed unworthy of respect. In our account, a theory of autonomy that takes this course is morally unacceptable.

We encounter many limitations of autonomous choice in medical contexts because of the patient's dependent condition and the medical professional's authoritative position. On some occasions authority and autonomy are incompatible, but not because the two *concepts* are incompatible. Conflict arises because authority has not been properly presented or accepted. For example, an undue influence may have been exerted. Some critics of autonomy's prominent role in biomedical ethics question what they deem to be a model of an independent, rational will that is inattentive to emotions, communal life, social context, interdependence, reciprocity, and the development of persons over time. They charge that such an account of autonomy focuses too narrowly on the self as independent and rationally controlling. For instance, some writers have sought to affirm autonomy while interpreting it through relationships.[9] This conception of "relational autonomy" is motivated by the conviction that persons' identities are shaped through social interactions and complex intersecting social determinants, such as race, class, gender, ethnicity, and authority structures. Persons are both interdependent and in danger of oppressive socialization and oppressive social relationships that impair their autonomy by conditions that unduly form their desires, beliefs, emotions, and attitudes and improperly thwart the development of the capacities and competencies essential for autonomy.[10]

We will largely address the challenges of relational autonomy through the ethical principles analyzed in Chapters 5 through 7. For instance, principles of justice provide a basis for condemning oppressive relationships and for determining which constraints on autonomous choice are and which are not ethically justified. In our view, relational conceptions of autonomy are defensible as long as they do not neglect or obscure the principal features of autonomy, as we analyze the concept in this chapter.

The Principle of Respect for Autonomy

To respect autonomous agents is to acknowledge their right to hold views, to make choices, and to take actions based on their values and beliefs. Such respect involves respectful *action,* not merely a respectful *attitude.* It also requires more than noninterference in others' personal affairs. It includes, in some contexts, building up or maintaining others' capacities for autonomous choice while helping to allay fears and other conditions that destroy or disrupt autonomous action. Respect, so understood, involves acknowledging the value and decision-making rights of autonomous persons and enabling them to act autonomously, whereas disrespect for autonomy involves attitudes and actions that ignore, insult, demean, or are inattentive to others' rights of autonomous action.

The principle of respect for autonomy can be stated as both a negative obligation and a positive obligation. As a *negative* obligation, the principle requires that autonomous actions not be subjected to controlling constraints by others. It asserts a broad obligation that is free of exceptive clauses such as "We must respect individuals' views and rights so long as their thoughts and actions do not seriously harm other persons." Of course, the principle of respect for autonomy needs specification in particular contexts to function as a practical guide to conduct, and appropriate specification will incorporate valid exceptions. This process of specification will affect rights and obligations of liberty, privacy, confidentiality, truthfulness, and informed consent—all of which receive attention in this and subsequent chapters.

As a *positive* obligation, the principle requires both respectful treatment in disclosing information and actions that foster autonomous decision making. Many autonomous actions could not occur without others' material cooperation in making options available. Respect for autonomy obligates professionals in health care and research involving human subjects to disclose information, to probe for and ensure understanding and voluntariness, and to foster adequate decision making. As some contemporary Kantians have argued, the demand that we treat others as ends requires that we assist them in achieving their ends and foster their capacities as agents, not merely that we avoid treating them solely as means to our ends.[11]

These negative and positive sides of respect for autonomy are capable of supporting many more specific moral rules, some of which may also be justified, in whole or in part, by other moral principles discussed in this book. Examples of such rules include the following:

1. Tell the truth.
2. Respect the privacy of others.
3. Protect confidential information.
4. Obtain consent for interventions with patients.
5. When asked, help others make important decisions.

Respect for autonomy has only prima facie standing, and competing moral considerations sometimes override this principle. Examples include the following: If our autonomous choices endanger the public health, potentially harm innocent others, or require a scarce resource for which no funds are available, others can justifiably restrict our exercises of autonomy. The principle of respect for autonomy often does not determine what, on balance, a person ought to be free to know or do or what counts as a valid justification for constraining autonomy. For example, a patient with an inoperable, incurable carcinoma once asked specifically, "I don't have cancer, do I?" The physician lied, saying, "You're as good as you were ten years ago." This lie infringed the principle of respect for autonomy by denying the patient information he may have needed to determine his future courses of action. Although the matter is controversial, such a lie might be justified by a principle of beneficence if certain major benefits will flow to the patient. (For the justification, see our discussions of paternalism in Chapter 6 and veracity in Chapter 8.)

Obligations to respect autonomy do not extend to persons who cannot act in a sufficiently autonomous manner—and who cannot be rendered autonomous—because, for instance, they are immature, incapacitated, ignorant, coerced, or exploited. Infants, irrationally suicidal individuals, and drug-dependent patients are examples. This standpoint does not presume that these individuals are not owed moral respect.[12] In our framework, they have a significant moral status (see Chapter 3) that obligates us to protect them from harm-causing conditions and to supply medical benefits (see Chapters 5–7).

The Triumph or Failure of Respect for Autonomy?

Some writers lament the "triumph of autonomy" in American bioethics. They charge that autonomy's proponents sometimes disrespect patients by forcing them to make choices, even though many patients do not want to receive information about their condition or to make decisions. Carl Schneider, for example, claims that stout proponents of autonomy, whom he labels "autonomists," concern themselves less with what patients *do want* than with what they *should want*. He concludes that "while patients largely wish to be informed about their medical circumstances, a substantial number of them [especially the elderly and the very sick] do not want to make their own medical decisions, or perhaps even to participate in those decisions in any very significant way."[13]

The duty of respect for autonomy has a correlative *right* to choose, but there is no correlative *duty* to choose. Several empirical studies of the sort cited by Schneider seem to misunderstand, as he does, how autonomous choice functions in a theory such as ours and how it should function in clinical medicine. In one study, UCLA researchers examined the differences in the attitudes of elderly subjects (sixty-five years or older) from different ethnic backgrounds toward (a) disclosure of the diagnosis and prognosis of a terminal illness, and (b) decision making at the end of life. The researchers summarize their main findings, based on 800 subjects (200 from each ethnic group): "Korean Americans (47%)

and Mexican Americans (65%) were significantly less likely than European Americans (87%) and African Americans (88%) to believe that a patient should be told the diagnosis of metastatic cancer. Korean Americans (35%) and Mexican Americans (48%) were less likely than African Americans (63%) and European Americans (69%) to believe that a patient should be told of a terminal prognosis and less likely to believe that the patient should make decisions about the use of life-supporting technology (28% and 41% vs. 60% and 65%). Korean Americans and Mexican Americans tended to believe that the family should make decisions about the use of life support." Investigators in this study stress that "belief in the *ideal* of patient autonomy is far from universal" (italics added), and they contrast this ideal with a "family-centered model" focused on an individual's web of relationships and "the harmonious functioning of the family."[14]

Nevertheless, the investigators themselves conclude that "physicians should ask their patients if they wish to receive information and make decisions or if they prefer that their families handle such matters." Far from abandoning or supplanting the moral demand that we respect individual autonomy, their recommendation accepts the normative position that the choice is rightly the patient's. Even if the patient delegates that right to someone else, the choice to delegate can itself be autonomous.

In a second study, this time of Navajo values and the disclosure of risk and medical prognoses, two researchers sought to determine how health care providers "should approach the discussion of negative information with Navajo patients" to provide "more culturally appropriate medical care." Frequent conflicts emerge, these researchers report, between autonomy and the traditional Navajo conception that "thought and language have the power to shape reality and to control events." According to the traditional conception, telling a Navajo patient recently diagnosed with a disease the potential complications of that disease may actually produce those complications, because "language does not merely describe reality, language shapes reality." Traditional Navajo patients may process various forms of negative information as dangerous to them. They expect instead a "positive ritual language" that promotes or restores health.

One middle-aged Navajo nurse reported that a surgeon explained the risks of bypass surgery to her father in such a way that he refused to undergo the procedure: "The surgeon told him that he may not wake up, that this is the risk of every surgery. For the surgeon it was very routine, but the way that my Dad received it, it was almost like a death sentence, and he never consented to the surgery." The researchers therefore found ethically troublesome those policies that, in compliance with the Patient Self-Determination Act, attempt to "expose all hospitalized Navajo patients to the idea, if not the practice, of advance care planning."[15]

These two studies enrich our understanding of diverse cultural beliefs and values. However, several studies misrepresent what the principle of respect for autonomy and many related laws and policies require. They view their results as opposing rather than enriching the principle of respect for autonomy. A fundamental obligation exists to ensure that patients have the right to choose, as well as the right to accept or to decline information. Forced information and forced choice are usually inconsistent with this obligation. From this perspective, a tension exists between the two studies just discussed. One study recommends inquiring in advance to ascertain patients' preferences about information and decision making, whereas the other suggests, tenuously, that even informing certain patients of a right to decide may cause harm. The practical question is whether it is possible to inform patients of their rights to know and to decide without compromising their systems of belief and values or otherwise disrespecting them.

Health professionals should almost always inquire about their patients' wishes to receive information and to make decisions, and they should not assume that because a patient belongs to a particular community or culture, he or she affirms that community's worldview and values. The fundamental requirement is to respect a particular person's autonomous choices, whatever they may be. Respect for autonomy is not a mere ideal in health care; it is a professional obligation.

Complexities in Respecting Autonomy

Varieties of autonomous consent. Consent sometimes grants permission for others to act in ways that normally would be unjustifiable—for instance, engaging in sexual relations or performing surgery. However, when examining autonomy and consent in this chapter, we do not presume that consent is either necessary or sufficient for certain interventions to be justified. It is not always necessary in emergencies, in public health interventions, in research involving anonymized data, and so forth; and it is not always sufficient because other ethical principles too must be satisfied—for example, research involving human subjects must pass a benefit–risk test and a fairness test in the recruitment of participants.[16]

The basic paradigm of the exercise of autonomy in health care and in research is *express* or *explicit* consent (or refusal), usually informed consent (or refusal).[17] However, the informed consent paradigm captures only one form of consent. Consent may also be implied, tacit, or presumed; and it may be general or specific.

Implicit (or *implied*) consent is inferable from actions. Consent to a medical procedure may be implicit in a specific consent to another procedure, and providing general consent to treatment in a teaching hospital may imply consent to various roles for physicians, nurses, and others in training. Another form is *tacit* consent, which occurs silently or passively through omissions. For example, if the staff of a long-term care facility asks residents whether they object to having the time of dinner changed by one hour, a uniform lack of objection constitutes consent.

Presumed consent is subject to a variety of interpretations. It is a form of implied consent if consent is presumed on the basis of what is known about a particular person's choices; in certain contexts, presumed consent is tacit consent that gives good grounds for accepting the consent as valid. By contrast, presuming consent on the basis of human goods that are desirable or what a rational will would accept is morally perilous. Consent should refer to an individual's actual choices or known preferences, not to presumptions about the choices the individual would or should make.

Different conceptions of consent have appeared in debates about teaching medical students how to perform intimate examinations, especially pelvic and rectal examinations.[18] Often medical students have learned and practiced on anesthetized patients, some of whom have not given an explicit informed consent. For instance, many teaching hospitals have allowed one or two medical students to participate in the examination of women who are under anesthesia in preparation for surgery. Anesthetized patients have been considered ideal for teaching medical students how to perform a pelvic examination because the patients are relaxed and would not feel any mistakes. When questioned about this practice, some directors of obstetrics and gynecology programs have appealed to the patient's general consent upon entering a teaching hospital. Such consent typically authorizes medical students and residents to participate in patients' care for teaching and learning purposes. However, it is not specific as to which procedures might involve participation by medical students.

It is debatable whether general consent is sufficient or whether specific informed consent is necessary in these circumstances. We often seek specific informed consent when a procedure is invasive, as in the case of surgery, or when it is risky. Although pelvic examinations are not invasive or particularly risky by comparison to surgery, patients may object to the intrusion into their bodies, especially for education and training. Some women readily consent to the participation of medical students in such examinations, but others view the practice as a violation of their dignity and privacy. One commentator appropriately states that "the patient must be treated as the student's teacher, not as a training tool."[19]

Using anesthetized women who have given only a general consent may be highly efficient in clinical training, but in view of the importance of respect for autonomy, there are ethically preferable alternatives such as using anesthetized patients who have given specific informed consent or using healthy volunteers who are willing to serve as trainers or models. Either of these alternatives respects personal autonomy and avoids negative medical education. A study of medical students in the Philadelphia area found that the practice of conducting pelvic exams on anesthetized patients without specific informed consent desensitized physicians to the need for patients to give their consent before such procedures. For students who had finished an obstetrics/gynecology clerkship, consent was significantly less important (51%) than for students who had not completed a clerkship (70%). The authors conclude that "to avoid this decline in attitudes toward seeking consent, clerkship directors should ensure that students perform examinations only after patients have given consent explicitly."[20]

Nonexpress forms of consent have been considered and sometimes adopted. In late 2006, the U.S. Centers for Disease Control and Prevention (CDC) changed its recommendations about HIV screening for patients in health care settings where various other diagnostic and screening tests are regularly performed. The recommendations moved away from specific, explicit informed consent, usually in written form, to general, implicit consent as part of the acceptance of medical care. Previous policies required specific disclosure of information and a decision to accept or refuse testing.[21] For many commentators, this shift indicated that conventional public health measures were now being applied to HIV infection and AIDS, rather than being excluded on grounds of respect for the autonomy of patients and associated principles such as privacy and confidentiality.[22]

The CDC justified its new recommendations on two main grounds. First, because HIV and AIDS are chronic conditions that can be effectively treated, although not cured, the new screening approach would enable more people who are infected to take advantage of available therapies that could extend their lives at a higher quality. Second, the information gained from screening could enable persons who are infected with HIV to take steps to protect their sex partners or drug-use partners from infection. The CDC estimated that in 2008, over 1,175,000 people in the United States were HIV-infected, but that over 236,000 infected individuals were not aware of their infection. More recently it has become evident that treating individuals to reduce their viral load is very effective in reducing the spread of HIV infection to their sexual partners.[23]

The CDC's new approach did not eliminate patient autonomy in health care settings—patients could still refuse testing—but, by shifting the default from "opt in" to "opt out," the CDC expected that more people previously unaware of their HIV infection would be tested and would gain knowledge that could benefit themselves and others. Despite its potential benefits, some critics of the "opt-out" policy warned that in the absence of a requirement for explicit, written informed consent, compromises of autonomy are inevitable and "compulsory" screening would occur in some contexts. According to one AIDS activist, "This is not informed consent, and it is not even consent, [but rather an attempt] to ram HIV testing down people's throats without their permission."[24] Although an "opt-out" approach can be justified in such circumstances, this strategy can be ethically improved by the use of *notification* while retaining the possibility of "opting out."

Another context in which an opt-out approach, in the form of presumed or tacit consent, could, in principle, be justified is organ donation from deceased individuals. In the opt-in system in the United States, deceased organ donation requires express, explicit consent, whether by an individual while alive or by the next of kin after his or her death. Even though the information disclosed for the individual's consent is usually quite limited—for instance, in a cursory exchange when obtaining a license to operate an automobile—it is arguably adequate for purposes of postmortem organ donation. In view of the tremendous gap between the number of organs donated each year and the number of patients awaiting a transplant, many propose that the United States adopt an opt-out model for organ removal from deceased persons, as several European countries have done. This model shifts the default so that an individual's silence, or nonregistration of dissent, counts as consent. Two questions arise: Is such a policy of presumed consent ethically acceptable? Could it be adopted and would it be effective in the United States?

To be ethically justifiable, such a policy would require vigorous efforts to ensure the public's understanding of the options they face as individuals, as well as a reliable, easy, and nonburdensome mechanism to use to opt out. Such a policy will not likely be adopted in the United States because of historical and legal commitments to individual choice. Even if it were adopted, it probably would not increase the number of organs for transplantation overall because, according to survey data, too many citizens would opt out; and opting out would prevent postmortem familial donations, which now provide a large number of transplantable organs.[25]

The varieties of consent we have now examined point to a fundamental question in this chapter: Who should seek what kind of consent from whom and for what?

Consents and refusals over time. Beliefs and choices shift over time. Ethical and interpretive problems arise when a person's present choices contradict his or her previous choices, which, in some cases, he or she explicitly designed to prevent possible future changes of mind from affecting an outcome. In one case, a twenty-eight-year-old man decided to terminate chronic renal dialysis because of his restricted lifestyle and the burdens his medical conditions imposed on his family. He had diabetes, was legally blind, and could not walk because of progressive neuropathy. His wife and physician agreed to provide medication to relieve his pain and further agreed not to put him back on dialysis even if he requested this action under the influence of pain or other bodily changes. (Increased amounts of urea in the blood, which result from kidney failure, can sometimes lead to altered mental states, for example.) While dying in the hospital, the patient awoke complaining of pain and asked to be put back on dialysis. The patient's wife and physician decided to act on the patient's earlier request not to intervene, and he died four hours later.[26] Although their decision was understandable, respect for autonomy suggests that the spouse and physician should have put the patient back on dialysis to flush the urea out of his blood-stream and then to determine if he had autonomously revoked his prior choice. If the patient later indicated that he had not revoked his prior choice, he could have refused again, thereby providing the caregivers with increased assurance about his settled preferences.

In shifts over time the key question is whether people are autonomously revoking their prior decisions. Discerning whether current decisions are autonomous may depend, in part, on whether they are in character or out of character. Out-of-character actions can raise caution flags that warn others to seek explanations and to probe more deeply into whether the actions are autonomous, but they may turn out to be autonomous. Actions are more likely to be substantially autonomous if they are in character (e.g., when a committed Jehovah's Witness refuses a blood transfusion), but acting in character does not necessarily indicate an autonomous choice. How, then, are we to determine whether actions are autonomous?

THE CAPACITY FOR AUTONOMOUS CHOICE

Many patients and potential research subjects are not competent to give a valid consent or refusal. Inquiries about competence focus on whether such persons are capable, cognitively, psychologically, and legally, of adequate decision making. Competence in decision making is closely connected to autonomous decision making, as well as to the validity of consent. Several commentators distinguish judgments of capacity from judgments of competence on the grounds that health professionals assess capacity and incapacity, whereas courts determine competence and incompetence. However, this distinction breaks down in practice, and we will not use it. When clinicians judge that patients lack decision-making capacity, the practical effects of these judgments may not differ from those of a legal determination of incompetence.[27]

The Gatekeeping Function of Competence Judgments

Competence or capacity judgments in health care serve a gatekeeping role by distinguishing persons whose decisions should be solicited or accepted from persons whose decisions need not or should not be solicited or accepted. Health professionals' judgments of a person's incompetence may lead them to override that person's decisions, to turn to informal surrogates for decision making, to ask the court to appoint a guardian to protect his or her interests, or to seek that person's involuntary institutionalization. When a court establishes legal incompetence, it appoints a surrogate decision maker with either partial or plenary (full) authority over the incompetent individual. Physicians and other health professionals do not have the authority to declare patients incompetent as a matter of law, but, within limits, they often have the de facto power to override or constrain patients' decisions about care based on assessments of limited capacity or incapacity.

Competence judgments have the distinctive *normative* function of qualifying or disqualifying persons for certain decisions or actions, but those in control sometimes incorrectly present these judgments as *empirical*. For example, a person who appears irrational or unreasonable to others might fail a psychiatric test, and therefore be declared incompetent. The test is an empirical measuring device, but normative judgments establish how the test is to be used to sort persons into the two classes of competent and incompetent, which determines how persons ought to be, or may permissibly be, treated.

The Concept of Competence[28]

Some commentators hold that we lack both a single acceptable *definition* of competence and a single acceptable *standard* of competence. They also contend that no nonarbitrary *test* exists to distinguish between competent and incompetent persons. We will engage these issues by distinguishing between definitions, standards, and tests—focusing first on problems of definition.

A single core meaning of the word *competence* applies in all contexts. That meaning is "the ability to perform a task."[29] By contrast to this core meaning, the *criteria* of particular competencies vary from context to context because the criteria are relative to specific tasks. The criteria for someone's competence to stand trial, to raise dachshunds, to answer a physician's questions, and to lecture to medical students are radically different. The competence to decide is therefore relative to the particular decision to be made. Rarely should we judge a person incompetent with respect to every sphere of life. We usually need to consider only some type of competence, such as the competence to decide about treatment or about participation in research. These judgments of competence and incompetence affect only a limited range of decision making. For example, a person who is incompetent to decide about financial affairs may be competent to decide to participate in medical research, or able to handle simple tasks easily while faltering before complex ones.

Competence may vary over time and may be intermittent. Many persons are incompetent to do something at one point in time but competent to perform the same task at another point in time. Judgments of competence about such persons can be complicated by the need to distinguish categories of illness that result in *chronic* changes of intellect, language, or memory from those characterized by *rapid reversibility* of these functions, as in the case of transient ischemic attack or transient global amnesia. In some of the latter cases competence varies from hour to hour. Here a determination of specific incompetence may prevent vague generalizations that exclude these persons from all forms of decision making.

These conceptual distinctions have practical significance. The law has traditionally presumed that a person who is incompetent to manage his or her estate is also incompetent to vote, make medical decisions, get married, and the like. The global sweep of these laws, based on a total judgment of the person, at times has extended too far. In one classic case, a physician argued that a patient was incompetent to make decisions because of epilepsy,[30] although many persons who suffer from epilepsy are competent to decide in most contexts. Such judgments defy much that we now know about the etiology of various forms of incompetence, even in hard cases involving persons with mental retardation, with psychosis, or with uncontrollably painful afflictions. In addition, persons who are incompetent by virtue of dementia, alcoholism, immaturity, and mental retardation present radically different types and problems of incompetence.

Sometimes a competent person who can usually select appropriate means to reach his or her goals will act incompetently in some circumstances. Consider the following actual case of a hospitalized patient who has an acute disc problem and whose goal is to control back pain. The patient decided to manage the problem by wearing a brace, a method she had used successfully in the past. She believes strongly that she should return to this treatment modality. This approach conflicts, however, with her physician's unwavering and near-insistent advocacy of surgery. When the physician, an eminent surgeon who alone in her city is suited to treat the patient, asks her to sign the surgical permit, she is psychologically unable to refuse. Her illness increases both her hopes and her fears, and, in addition, she has a deferential personality. In these circumstances, it is psychologically too risky for her to act as she desires. Even though she is competent to choose in general, she is not competent to choose on this occasion.

This case indicates how close the concept of competence in decision making is to the concept of autonomy. Patients or prospective subjects are competent to make a decision if they have the capacity to understand the material information, to make a judgment about this information in light of their values, to intend a certain outcome, and to communicate freely their wishes to caregivers or investigators. Law, medicine, and, to some extent, philosophy presume a context in which the characteristics of the competent person are also the properties possessed by the autonomous person. Although *autonomy* and *competence* differ in meaning (*autonomy* meaning self-governance; *competence* meaning the ability to perform a task or range of tasks), the criteria of the autonomous person and of the competent person are strikingly similar.

Persons are more and less able to perform a specific task to the extent that they possess a certain level or range of abilities, just as persons are more and less intelligent and athletic. For example, in the emergency room an experienced and knowledgeable patient is likely to be more qualified to consent to or refuse a procedure than a frightened, inexperienced patient. It would be confusing to view this continuum of abilities in terms of degrees of *competency.* For practical and policy reasons, we need *threshold levels* below which a person with a certain level of abilities for a particular task is incompetent. Not all competent persons are equally able, and not all incompetent persons are equally unable, but competence determinations sort persons into these two basic classes, and thus treat persons as either competent or incompetent for specific purposes. Above the threshold, we treat persons as equally competent; below the threshold we treat them as equally incompetent. Gatekeepers test to determine who is above and who is below the threshold. Where we draw the line depends on the particular tasks involved.[31]

Standards of Competence

Questions about competence often center on the standards for its determination, that is, the conditions a competence judgment must satisfy. Standards of competence feature mental skills or capacities closely connected to the attributes of autonomous persons, such as cognitive skills and independent judgment. In criminal law, civil law, and clinical medicine, standards for competence cluster around various abilities to comprehend and process information and to reason about the consequences of one's actions. In medical contexts, physicians usually consider a person competent if he or she can understand a procedure, deliberate with regard to its major risks and benefits, and make a decision in light of this deliberation.

The following case illustrates some difficulties encountered in attempts to judge competence. A man who generally exhibits normal behavior patterns is involuntarily committed to a mental institution as the result of bizarre self-destructive behavior (pulling out an eye and cutting off a hand). This behavior results from his unusual religious beliefs. The institution judges him incompetent, despite his generally competent behavior and despite the fact that his peculiar actions coherently follow from his religious beliefs.[32] This troublesome case is not one of intermittent competence. Analysis in terms of limited competence at first appears plausible, but this analysis perilously suggests that persons with unorthodox or bizarre religious beliefs are less than competent, even if they reason coherently in light of their beliefs. This policy would not be ethically acceptable unless specific and careful statements spelled out the reasons under which a finding of incompetence is justified.

Rival standards of incompetence. We focus on standards of *incompetence,* rather than *competence,* because of the legal, medical, and practical presumption that an adult is competent and should be treated as such in the absence of a determination of incompetence or incapacity. In the clinical context, an inquiry into a patient's competence to make decisions usually occurs only when the medical decision at stake is complex and involves significant risks or when the patient does not accept the physician's recommendation.[33] The following schema expresses the range of inabilities currently required under competing standards of incompetence presented in literature on the subject.[34]

1. Inability to express or communicate a preference or choice
2. Inability to understand one's situation and its consequences
3. Inability to understand relevant information
4. Inability to give a reason
5. Inability to give a rational reason (although some supporting reasons may be given)
6. Inability to give risk/benefit-related reasons (although some rational supporting reasons may be given)
7. Inability to reach a reasonable decision (as judged, for example, by a reasonable person standard)

These standards cluster around three kinds of abilities or skills. Standard 1 looks for the simple ability to formulate a preference, an elementary standard. Standards 2 and 3 probe for abilities to understand information and to appreciate one's situation. Standards 4 through 7 concentrate on the ability to reason through a consequential life decision. These standards have been and still are used, either alone or in combination, to determine incompetence.

Testing for incompetence. A clinical need exists to turn one or more of these general standards into an operational test of incompetence that establishes passing and failing evaluations. Dementia rating scales, mental status exams, and similar devices test for factors such as time-and-place orientation, memory, understanding, and coherence. Although these clinical assessments are empirical tests, normative judgments underlie each test. The following ingredients incorporate normative judgments:[35]

1. Choosing the relevant abilities for competence
2. Choosing a threshold level of the abilities in item 1
3. Choosing an empirical test for item 2

For any test already accepted under item 3, it is an empirical question whether someone possesses the requisite level of abilities, but this empirical question can only be addressed if normative criteria have already been fixed under items 1 and 2. Institutional rules or traditions usually establish these criteria, but the standards should be open to periodic review and modification.

It is beyond the scope of our discussion to analyze and evaluate the numerous tests and instruments that have been developed to assess decisional capacity for clinical treatment or research. Several reviews[36] of these instruments—one review examined twenty-three such instruments—have found that, even though these instruments can aid clinicians' and researchers' assessment of decision-making competence, they produce variable results. Accordingly, it is premature to conclude that any one of them provides a satisfactory and reliable way to assess decision-making capacity. In the final analysis, the assessment of decisional capacity remains heavily a matter of clinical judgment, although some studies indicate that these clinical judgments too are often not reliable.[37]

The sliding-scale strategy. Properties of autonomy and of mental and psychological capacity are not the only criteria used in delineating competence standards. Many policies use pragmatic criteria such as efficiency, feasibility, and social acceptability to determine whether a person is competent to make decisions about medical care. For example, age has conventionally been used as an operational criterion of valid authorization or refusal of medical procedures. Established thresholds of age vary in accordance with a community's standards, with the degree of risk involved, and with the importance of the prospective benefits. From this perspective, standards of competence are connected to levels of experience, maturity, responsibility, and welfare.

Some writers offer a sliding-scale strategy for how to realize this goal. They argue that, as the risks of a medical intervention increase for patients, so should the level of ability required for a judgment of competence to elect or refuse the intervention. As the consequences for well-being become less substantial, we should lower the level of capacity required for competence. For example, Grisso and Appelbaum present a "competence balance scale." An autonomy cup is suspended from the end of one arm of a measuring scale, and a protection cup is suspended from the other; the fulcrum is set initially to give more weight to the autonomy cup. The balancing judgment depends "on the balance of (1) the patient's mental abilities in the face of the decisional demands, weighed against (2) the probable gain-risk status of the patient's treatment choice."[38] If a serious risk such as death is present, then a correspondingly stringent standard of competence should be used; if a low or insignificant risk is present, then a relaxed or lower standard of competence is permissible. Thus, the same person—a child, for example—might be competent to decide whether to take a tranquilizer but incompetent to decide whether to authorize surgery.[39]

This sliding-scale strategy is attractive. A decision about which standard to use to determine competence depends on several factors that are risk-related. The sliding-scale strategy rightly recognizes that our interests in ensuring good outcomes legitimately contribute to the way we create standards. If the consequences for welfare are grave, the need to certify that the patient possesses the requisite capacities increases; but if little in the way of welfare is at stake, we can lower the level of capacity required for decision making. For example, if a patient with reversible dementia needs enteral nutrition to recover, a powerful reason exists for protecting that patient against rash or imprudent decision making and, accordingly, for adopting a more stringent standard of decision-making capacity.

Although the sliding-scale strategy may function as a valuable protective device, it creates confusion regarding the nature of both competence judgments and competence itself because of certain conceptual and moral difficulties. This strategy suggests that a person's *competence* to decide is contingent on the decision's importance or on some harm that might follow from the decision. This thesis is dubious: A person's competence to decide whether, for example, to participate in cancer research does not depend on the decision's consequences. As risks increase or decrease, we can legitimately increase or reduce the rules, procedures, or measures we use to *ascertain* whether someone is competent; but in formulating what we are doing, we need to distinguish between a person's *competence* and the *modes of ascertaining* that person's competence. Leading proponents of the sliding-scale strategy hold the reverse view that *competence itself* varies with risk. For example, according to Allen Buchanan and Dan Brock, "Because the appropriate level of competence properly required for a particular decision must be adjusted to the consequences of acting on that decision, no single standard of decision-making competence is adequate. Instead, the level of competence appropriately required for decision making varies along a full range from low/minimum to high/maximal."[40]

This account is conceptually and morally perilous. It is correct to say that the level of a person's capacity to decide will rise as the *complexity* or *difficulty* of a task increases (deciding about spinal fusion, say, as contrasted with deciding whether to take a minor tranquilizer), but the level of competence to decide does not rise as the *risk* of an outcome increases. It is confusing to blend a decision's complexity or difficulty with the risk at stake. No basis exists for believing that risky decisions require more ability at decision making than less risky decisions.

We can sidestep these problems by recognizing that the level of *evidence* for determining competence should vary according to risk. As examples, some statutes have required a higher standard of evidence for competence in making than in revoking advance directives, and the National Bioethics Advisory Commission recommended a higher standard of evidence of competence to consent to participate in most research than to object to participation.[41] These are counsels of prudence that protect patient-subjects. Whereas Brock and Buchanan propose that the level of decision-making *competence itself* belongs on a sliding scale from low to high in accordance with risk, we recommend placing only the required *standards of evidence* for determining decision-making competence on a sliding scale.

The Meaning and Justification of Informed Consent

At least since the Nuremberg trials, which exposed the Nazis' horrific medical experiments, biomedical ethics has placed consent at the forefront of its concerns. The term *informed consent* did not appear until a decade after these trials (held in the late 1940s). It did not receive detailed examination until the early 1970s. In recent years the focus has shifted from the physician's or researcher's obligation to disclose information to the quality of a patient's or subject's understanding and consent. The forces behind this shift of emphasis were autonomy driven. In this section, we treat standards of informed consent as they have evolved through the regulation of research, case law, changes in the patient–physician relationship, and ethical analysis.

The Justification of Informed Consent Requirements

Virtually all prominent medical and research codes and institutional rules of ethics now hold that physicians and investigators must obtain the informed consent of patients and subjects prior to a substantial intervention. Throughout the early history of concern about research subjects, consent requirements were proposed primarily as a way to minimize the potential for harm. However, since the mid-1970s the primary justification advanced for requirements of informed consent has been to protect autonomous choice, a goal that institutions often bury in broad statements about protecting the rights of patients and research subjects.

In a series of books and articles on informed consent and autonomy, British philosopher Onora O'Neill has argued against the view that informed consent is justified in terms of respect for personal autonomy.[42] O'Neill is suspicious of contemporary conceptions of autonomy and respect for autonomy, which she finds variable, vague, and difficult to tailor to acceptable requirements of informed consent. We agree that clarifications are needed, but we think that respect for autonomy does provide the primary justification of rules, policies, and practices of informed consent. O'Neill argues that practices and rituals of informed consent are best understood as ways to prevent deception and coercion; the process of informed consent provides reasonable assurance that a patient, subject, or tissue donor "has not been deceived or coerced."[43] However, respect for autonomy in health care relationships requires much more than avoiding deception and coercion. It requires an attempt to instill relevant understanding, to avoid forms of manipulation, and to respect persons' rights.

The Meaning and Elements of Informed Consent

Some commentators have attempted to analyze the idea of informed consent in terms of shared decision making between doctor and patient, thus rendering *informed consent* and *mutual decision making* synonymous.[44] However, informed consent should not be equated with shared decision making. Professionals obtain and will continue to obtain informed consent in many contexts of research and medicine in which shared decision making is a misleading model. We should distinguish (1) informational exchanges and communication through which patients elect interventions, often based on medical advice, from (2) acts of approving and authorizing those interventions. Shared decision making may be a worthy ideal in medicine, but the proposed process of decisions being shared is vague—with different conceptions of what exactly is shared. However interpreted, shared decision making as effective communication neither defines nor displaces informed consent.[45] If shared decision making is presented as a plea merely for patients to be allowed to participate in decision making about diagnostic and treatment procedures, it continues the legacy of medical paternalism by ignoring patients' rights to consent or to refuse those procedures.

Two meanings of "informed consent."[46] Two different senses of "informed consent" appear in current literature, policies, and practices. In the first sense, informed consent is analyzable through the account of autonomous choice presented earlier in this chapter: An informed consent is an individual's *autonomous authorization* of a medical intervention or of participation in research. In this first sense, a person must do more than express agreement or comply with a proposal. He or she must *authorize* something through an act of informed and voluntary consent. In an early and classic case, *Mohr v. Williams* (1905), a physician obtained Anna Mohr's consent to an operation on her right ear. While operating, the surgeon determined that the left ear actually needed surgery. A court found that the physician should have obtained the patient's consent to the surgery on the left ear: "If a physician advises a patient to submit to a particular operation, and the patient weighs the dangers and risks incident to its performance, and finally consents, the patient thereby, in effect, enters into a contract authorizing the physician to operate to the extent of the consent given, but no further."[47] An informed consent in this first sense occurs if and only if a patient or subject, with substantial understanding and in absence of substantial control by others, intentionally authorizes a professional to do something quite specific.

In the second sense, informed consent refers to *conformity to the social rules of consent* that require professionals to obtain legally or institutionally valid consent from patients or subjects before proceeding with diagnostic, therapeutic, or research procedures. Informed consents are not necessarily autonomous acts under these rules and sometimes are not even meaningful authorizations. *Informed consent* refers here only to an institutionally or legally effective authorization, as determined by prevailing social rules. For example, a mature minor may autonomously authorize an intervention, but the minor's authorization may not be an effective consent under existing legal or institutional rules. Thus, a patient or subject can *autonomously* authorize an intervention, and so give an informed consent in the first sense, without *effectively* authorizing the intervention (because of some set of rules), and thus without giving an informed consent in the second sense.

Institutional rules of informed consent have typically not been assessed by the demanding standard of autonomous authorization. As a result, institutions, as well as laws and courts, sometimes impose on physicians and hospitals nothing more than an obligation to warn of risks of proposed interventions. "Consent" under these circumstances is not bona fide informed consent. The problem arises from the gap between the two senses of informed consent: Physicians who obtain consent under institutional criteria can and often do fail to meet the rigorous standards of the autonomy-based model.

It is easy to criticize institutional rules as superficial, but health care professionals cannot reasonably be expected to obtain a consent that satisfies the demands of rigorous autonomy-protecting rules in all circumstances. Autonomy-protecting rules may turn out to be excessively difficult or even impossible to implement. Hence, we should evaluate institutional rules not only in terms of respect for autonomy and autonomous authorization, but also in terms of the probable consequences of imposing unfairly burdensome requirements on institutions and professionals. Policies may legitimately take account of what is fair and reasonable to require of health care professionals and researchers. Nevertheless, we take as axiomatic that the model of autonomous choice (following the first sense of "informed consent") ought to serve as the benchmark for the moral adequacy of institutional rules of consent.

Franklin Miller and Alan Wertheimer challenge our view that the first sense of "informed consent" is the benchmark for judging the moral adequacy of institutional understandings and rules of informed consent. They propose a "fair transaction model" of the doctrine of informed consent in which, for example, investigators and their subjects are all treated fairly by giving due consideration to the reasonable limits of an investigator's responsibilities to ensure adequate understanding on the part of subjects who consent to research, the modest levels of comprehension expectable of some subjects, and the overall interests of subjects in participating in research. We welcome this approach as a way of interpreting our second sense of institutional informed consent, but the Miller-Wertheimer theory moves into unacceptably dangerous territory by altogether, and by design, abandoning the first sense of autonomous authorization and substituting the "fair transaction" model. Their model would be more suitable if it were presented as an explication of our second sense of "informed consent" and as a fairness-based analysis of requirements for various practical contexts in which informed consent is obtained. However, as their theory stands, these authors give a priority to fairness to all parties that loses sight of the central role of respect for the subject's or patient's autonomy. We see no justification for their claims that their model merits adoption "in place of the autonomous authorization model" and that "consent is a bilateral transaction," rather than the "one-sided focus on the quality of the subject's consent" to which the autonomous authorization model is committed. We earlier argued, in treating the "shared decision-making" conception, that informed consent is misconceived as bilateral. Bilateral transactions of informational exchange often appropriately occur in consent contexts, but genuine informed *consent* is not reducible to a bilateral transaction.[48]

The elements of informed consent. Some commentators have attempted to define *informed consent* by specifying the elements of the concept, in particular by dividing the elements into an information component and a consent component. The information component refers to the disclosure (and often the comprehension) of information. The consent component refers to both a voluntary decision and an authorization to proceed. Legal, regulatory, philosophical, medical, and psychological literatures tend to favor the following elements as the components of informed consent:[49] (1) competence, (2) disclosure, (3) understanding, (4) voluntariness, and (5) consent. Some writers present these elements as the building blocks of a definition of *informed consent:* A person gives an informed consent to an intervention if (and perhaps only if) he or she is competent to act, receives a thorough disclosure, comprehends the disclosure, acts voluntarily, and consents to the intervention.

This five-element definition is superior to the one-element definition in terms of *disclosure* that courts and medical literature have often relied on.[50] However, in this chapter we accept and treat each of the following seven elements:

I. Threshold elements (preconditions)
    1. Competence (to understand and decide)
    2. Voluntariness (in deciding)

II. Information elements
    3. Disclosure (of material information)
    4. Recommendation (of a plan)
    5. Understanding (of 3 and 4)

III. Consent elements
    6. Decision (in favor of a plan)
    7. Authorization (of the chosen plan)

This list requires a brief explanation. First, *an informed refusal* entails a modification of items under III, thereby turning the categories into refusal elements, for example, "6. Decision (against a plan)." Whenever we use the expression "informed consent," we allow for the possibility of an informed refusal. Second, providing information for potential participants in research does not, and should not, necessarily involve making a recommendation (number 4). Third, competence should perhaps be classified as a *presupposition* of obtaining informed consent, rather than as an *element.*

Having examined competence previously, we now concentrate on the critical elements of disclosure, understanding, and voluntariness.

DISCLOSURE

Disclosure is the third of our seven elements of informed consent. Some institutions and legal authorities have presented the obligation to disclose information to patients as the only major condition of informed consent. The legal doctrine of informed consent in the United States primarily has focused on disclosure because of a physician's obligation to exercise reasonable care in providing information. Civil litigation has emerged over informed consent because of injuries (measured in terms of monetary damages) that physicians intentionally or negligently have caused by their failures to disclose. The term *informed consent* was born in this legal context. However, from the moral viewpoint, informed consent has little to do with the liability of professionals as agents of disclosure and everything to do with the autonomous choices of patients and subjects.

Even so, disclosure usually does play a pivotal role in the consent process. Absent professionals' provision of information, many patients and subjects will have an insufficient basis for decision making. Professionals are usually obligated to disclose a core set of information, including (1) those facts or descriptions that patients or subjects consider material when deciding whether to refuse or consent to a proposed intervention or involvement in research, (2) information the professional believes to be material, (3) the professional's recommendation (if any), (4) the purpose of seeking consent, and (5) the nature and limits of consent as an act of authorization. If research is involved, disclosures should generally cover the aims and methods of the research, anticipated benefits and risks, any anticipated inconvenience or discomfort, and the subjects' right to withdraw, without penalty, from the research.

We could easily expand the list of basic information. For example, in one controversial decision, the California Supreme Court held that, when seeking an informed consent, "a physician must disclose personal interests unrelated to the patient's health, whether research or economic, that may affect the physician's professional judgment."[51] Such a disclosure requirement has acquired greater moral significance as conflicts of interest have become more pronounced and problematic. We will examine this subject in Chapter 8.

Standards of Disclosure

Courts in the United States have struggled to determine which norms should govern the disclosure of information. Two competing standards of disclosure have become most prominent: the professional practice standard and the reasonable person standard. A third, the subjective standard, has also received some support, although courts have usually avoided it. These standards are morally, not merely legally, important.

The professional practice standard. The first standard holds that a professional community's customary practices determine adequate disclosure. That is, professional custom establishes the amount and type of information to be disclosed. Disclosure, like treatment, is a responsibility of physicians because of their professional expertise and commitment to the patient's welfare. As a result, only expert testimony from members of this profession can count as evidence that a physician violated a patient's right to information.

Several difficulties plague this standard, which some call a reasonable doctor standard. First, it is uncertain in many situations whether a customary standard actually exists for the communication of information in medicine. Second, if custom alone were conclusive, pervasive negligence could be perpetuated with impunity. The majority of professionals could offer the same inadequate level of information. Third, based on empirical studies, it is questionable whether many physicians have developed the skills to determine the information that serves their patients' best interests.[52] The weighing of risks in the context of a person's subjective beliefs, fears, and hopes is not an expert skill, and information provided to patients and subjects sometimes needs to be freed from the entrenched values and goals of medical professionals. Finally, the professional practice standard ignores and may subvert patients' rights of autonomous choice. Professional standards in medicine are fashioned for medical judgments, but decisions for or against medical care, which are nonmedical decisions, belong to the patient.

The reasonable person standard. Although many legal jurisdictions rely on the traditional professional practice standard, a reasonable person standard has gained acceptance in many states in the United States. According to this standard, the information to be disclosed should be determined by reference to a hypothetical reasonable person. Whether information is pertinent or material is to be measured by the significance a reasonable person would attach to it in deciding whether to undergo a procedure. Hence, the authoritative determination of informational needs shifts from the physician to the patient, and physicians may be found guilty of negligent disclosures even if their behavior conforms to recognized professional practice.

Whatever its merits, the reasonable person standard presents conceptual, moral, and practical difficulties. No one has carefully defined the concepts of "material information" and "reasonable person," and questions arise about whether and how physicians and other health care professionals can employ the reasonable person standard in practice. Its abstract and hypothetical character makes it difficult for them to use because they have to project what a reasonable patient would need to know.

The subjective standard. The "subjective model" judges the adequacy of information by reference to the specific informational needs of the individual person, rather than by the hypothetical "reasonable person." Individual needs can differ: Persons may have unconventional beliefs, unusual health problems, or unique family histories that require a different informational base than the reasonable person needs. For example, a person with a family history of reproductive problems might desire information that other persons would not need or want before becoming involved in research on sexual and familial relations. If a physician knows or has reason to believe that a person wants such information, then withholding it may undermine autonomous choice. The key issue is whether a standard should be tailored to the individual patient and thus made subjective. The subjective standard requires the physician to disclose the information a particular patient needs to know to the extent it is reasonable to expect the physician to be able to determine that patient's informational needs.[53]

The subjective standard is the preferable moral standard of disclosure, because it alone meets persons' specific informational needs. Nevertheless, an exclusive reliance on the subjective standard would not suffice for either law or ethics because patients often do not know what information is relevant for their deliberations, and we cannot reasonably expect a doctor to do an exhaustive background and character analysis of each patient to determine the relevant information. Hence, we should use the reasonable person standard as the initial standard of disclosure and then supplement it by investigating the informational needs of particular patients or potential research subjects.

Intentional Nondisclosure

Some types of research are incompatible with complete disclosure, and in some clinical situations physicians claim that nondisclosures benefit the patient. Are these intentional nondisclosures justifiable?

The therapeutic privilege. Legal exceptions to the rule of informed consent allow the health professional to proceed without consent in cases of emergency, incompetence, and waiver. These three exceptive conditions are not controversial. However, one controversial exception is the therapeutic privilege, which states that a physician may legitimately withhold information based on a sound medical judgment that divulging the information would potentially harm a depressed, emotionally drained, or unstable patient. Possible and harmful outcomes include endangering life, causing irrational decisions, and producing anxiety or stress.[54] Despite the protected status this doctrine traditionally has enjoyed, U.S. Supreme Court Justice Byron White once vigorously attacked the idea that possibly increasing a person's anxiety about a procedure provides grounds for an exception to rules of informed consent.[55] White suggested that the legally protected status of the doctrine of therapeutic privilege lacks the security it once had.

All attempts to justify the therapeutic privilege are beneficence- and nonmaleficence-based because nondisclosure is aimed at the patient's good and at preventing harm from occurring. However, the precise content and formulation of the therapeutic privilege varies significantly across legal jurisdictions and institutional practices. Some formulations permit physicians to withhold information if disclosure would cause *any* deterioration in the patient's condition. Other formulations permit the physician to withhold information if and only if the patient's knowledge of the information would have serious health-related consequences, for example, by jeopardizing the treatment's success or by critically impairing relevant decision-making processes.

The narrowest formulation of the therapeutic privilege appeals to a circumstance of incompetence: A physician may invoke the therapeutic privilege only if he or she has sufficient reason to believe that disclosure would render the patient incompetent to consent to or refuse the treatment. This criterion does not conflict with respect for autonomy, because the patient would not be capable of an autonomous decision at the point a decision is needed. However, in our judgment it is ethically indefensible, even if legally permissible, to invoke the therapeutic privilege merely on grounds that the disclosure of relevant information might lead a competent patient to refuse a proposed treatment. (Related issues appear in our discussion of paternalism in Chapter 6 and of veracity in Chapter 8.)

Therapeutic use of placebos.   The therapeutic use of placebos typically involves lack of transparency, incomplete disclosure, or even intentional deception. A placebo is a substance or intervention that the clinician believes to be pharmacologically or biomedically inert or inactive for the condition being treated. While "pure" placebos, such as a sugar pill, are pharmacologically inactive, active medications are sometimes used as "impure" placebos for conditions for which they are not medically indicated—for example, the prescription of an antibiotic for a common cold. Systematic evidence is lacking for the clinically significant benefits of most placebos, but patient and clinician reports indicate that placebos relieve some symptoms in as many as one-third of patients who suffer from conditions such as angina pectoris, cough, anxiety, depression, hypertension, headache, and the common cold.[56] Placebos have also been reported to help some patients with irritable bowel syndrome, pain, and nausea.[57]

The provision or prescription of placebos is common in clinical practice, despite a weak body of evidence about their clinical benefits. In a national study of U.S. internists and rheumatologists, approximately half of the respondents reported that over the previous year they had prescribed placebo treatments on a regular basis, most often over-the-counter analgesics and vitamins. Slightly more than 10% had prescribed antibiotics or sedatives as placebo treatments; only a few had used saline or sugar pills as placebo treatments. Over 60% of those surveyed expressed a belief that the practice of prescribing placebos is ethically permissible.[58]

Beyond arguments against deception and failure to respect autonomy,[59] objections to the therapeutic provision or prescription of placebos without adequate disclosure focus on their possible negative consequences, such as damage to a specific clinical relationship or to clinical relationships in general because of reduced trust. Some defenses of the use of placebos without specific disclosure require only that a patient consent to a generic treatment, using language such as "an effective pill" or "a powerful medicine." A related defense of placebos appeals to the patient's prior consent to the goals of treatment. Although such consent is not informed consent, these proposals might be acceptable if, prior to the initiation of the patient's care, the patient were informed that a placebo might be used at some point in the treatment and he or she consented to this arrangement.[60]

The American Medical Association (AMA) has taken a similar approach by adopting a policy that bans the provision or prescription of a substance that the physician believes will have "no specific pharmacological effect upon the condition being treated" unless the patient has given an informed consent to the use of such a substance. The rationale is that this policy enables the physician to respect the patient's autonomy and to foster a trusting relationship, "while the patient still may benefit from the placebo effect."[61] The AMA's position is strongly justified because it removes the major ethical objection to deceptive placebo use, namely, that it violates the principle of respect for autonomy and the requirements of informed consent.

Evidence indicates that the placebo response or placebo effect can sometimes be produced without nondisclosure or deception. For example, the placebo response sometimes occurs even if patients have been informed that a particular substance is pharmacologically inert and still consent to its use.[62] The mechanisms of placebo responses are poorly understood, but several hypotheses have been proposed, frequently centering on the healing context, with its symbolic significance and its rituals, including the ritual of taking medications, and on the professional's care, compassion, and skill in fostering trust and hope.[63] However, in prescribing placebos, clinicians sometimes bypass opportunities for effective communication with patients. Communication and understanding can be fostered by admitting uncertainty; exploring patients' concerns, outlooks, and values; and inviting patients to be partners in the search for therapeutic options.[64]

Withholding information from research subjects. Problems of intentional nondisclosure in clinical practice have parallels in research in which investigators sometimes need to withhold some information from subjects. Occasionally, good reasons support nondisclosure. Scientists could not conduct vital research in fields such as epidemiology if they always had to obtain consent from subjects for access to medical records. Officials often justify using such records without consent to establish the prevalence of a particular disease. This research is commonly only the first phase of an investigation intended to determine whether to trace and contact particular individuals who are at risk of disease, and the researchers often must obtain their permission for further participation in research. Sometimes, however, researchers need not contact individuals at all, for example, when hospitals strip personal identifiers from their records so that epidemiologists cannot identify individual patients. In other circumstances, researchers only need to notify persons in advance about how they will use data and to offer these persons the opportunity to refuse to participate. In short, disclosures, warnings, and opportunities to decline involvement are sometimes legitimately substituted for informed consent.

Many other forms of intentional nondisclosure in research are more difficult to justify. For instance, debate arose about a study, designed and conducted by two physicians at the Emory University School of Medicine, to determine the prevalence of cocaine use and the reliability of self-reports of drug use among male patients in an Atlanta walk-in, inner-city hospital clinic serving low-income, predominantly black residents. In this study, approved by the institutional human investigations committee, researchers asked weekday outpatients at Grady Memorial Hospital to participate in a study about asymptomatic carriage of sexually transmitted diseases (STDs). The participants provided informed consent for the STD study, but not for an *unmentioned* piggy-back study on recent cocaine use and the reliability of self-reports of such use. Researchers informed patients that their urine would be tested for STDs, but neglected to inform them that their urine would also be tested for cocaine metabolites. Of the 415 eligible men who agreed to participate, 39% tested positive for a major cocaine metabolite, although 72% of those with positive urinary assays denied any illicit drug use in the three days prior to sampling. Researchers concluded: "Our findings underscore the magnitude of the cocaine abuse problem for young men seeking care in inner-city, walk-in clinics. Health care providers need to be aware of the unreliability of patient self-reports of illicit drug use."[65]

These researchers deceived their subjects about some aims and purposes of the research and did not disclose the means they would use. Investigators thought they faced a dilemma: On the one hand, they needed accurate information about illicit drug use for health care and public policy. On the other hand, obtaining adequate informed consent would be difficult, because many potential subjects would either refuse to participate or would offer false information to researchers. The critical matter is that rules requiring informed consent have been designed to protect subjects from manipulation and abuse during the research process. Reports of the strategy used in this cocaine study could increase suspicion of medical institutions and professionals and could make patients' self-reports of illegal activities even less reliable.[66] Investigators should have resolved their dilemma by developing alternative research designs, including sophisticated methods of using questions that can either reduce or eliminate response errors without violating rules of informed consent.

In general, research cannot be justified if significant risk is involved and subjects are not informed that they are being placed at risk. This conclusion does not imply that researchers can never justifiably undertake studies involving deception. Relatively risk-free research involving deception or incomplete disclosure is common in fields such as behavioral and physiological psychology. However, researchers should use deception only if it is essential to obtain vital information, it involves no substantial risk, they inform subjects that deception or incomplete disclosure is part of the study, and subjects consent to participate under these conditions. (In Chapter 8, we examine nondisclosure in blinded randomized clinical trials.)

UNDERSTANDING

Understanding is the fifth element of informed consent in our earlier list. Clinical experience and empirical data indicate that patients and research subjects exhibit wide variation in their understanding of information about diagnoses, procedures, risks, probable benefits, and prognoses.[67] For instance, in a study of participants in cancer clinical trials, 90% indicated they were satisfied with the informed consent process and most of them thought they were well informed. However, approximately three-fourths of them did not understand that the trials included nonstandard and unproven treatment, and approximately one-fourth did not appreciate that the primary purpose of the trials was to benefit future patients and that the benefits to them personally were uncertain.[68]

Many factors account for limited understanding in the informed consent process. Some patients and subjects are calm, attentive, and eager for dialogue, whereas others are nervous or distracted in ways that impair or block understanding. Other conditions that limit understanding include illness, irrationality, and immaturity. Important institutional and situational factors include pressures of time, limited or no remuneration to professionals for time spent in communication, and professional conflicts of interest.

The Nature of Understanding

No consensus exists about the nature and level of understanding needed for an informed consent, but an analysis sufficient for our purposes is that persons understand if they have acquired pertinent information and have relevant beliefs about the nature and consequences of their actions. Their understanding need not be *complete,* because a grasp of central facts is generally sufficient. Some facts are irrelevant or trivial; others are vital, perhaps decisive. In some cases, a person's lack of awareness of even a single risk or missing fact can deprive him or her of adequate understanding. Consider, for example, the classic case of *Bang v. Miller Hospital* (1958), in which patient Bang did not intend to consent to a sterilization entailed in prostate surgery.[69] Bang did, in fact, consent to prostate surgery, but without being told that sterilization was an inevitable outcome. (Although sterilization is not necessarily an outcome of prostate surgery, it is inevitable in the specific procedure recommended in this case.) Bang's failure to understand this one surgical consequence compromised what was otherwise an adequate understanding and invalidated what otherwise would have been a valid consent.

Patients and subjects usually should understand, at a minimum, what an attentive health care professional or researcher believes a reasonable patient or subject needs to understand to authorize an intervention. Diagnoses, prognoses, the nature and purpose of the intervention, alternatives, risks and benefits, and recommendations typically are essential. Patients or subjects also need to share an understanding with professionals about the terms of the authorization before proceeding. Unless agreement exists about the essential features of what is authorized, there can be no assurance that a patient or subject has made an autonomous decision and provided a valid consent. Even if physician and patient both use a word such as *stroke* or *hernia,* their interpretations will diverge if standard medical conceptions have no meaning for the patient.

Some argue that many patients and subjects cannot comprehend enough information or sufficiently appreciate its relevance to make autonomous decisions about medical care or participation in research. Such statements overgeneralize, perhaps because of an improper ideal of full disclosure and full understanding. If we replace this unrealistic standard with a more defensible account of the understanding of material information, we can avoid this skepticism. From the fact that actions are never fully informed, voluntary, or autonomous, it does not follow that they are never adequately informed, voluntary, or autonomous.[70]

However, some patients have such limited knowledge bases that communication about alien or novel situations is exceedingly difficult, especially if physicians introduce new concepts and cognitive constructs. Studies indicate that these patients likely will have an impoverished and distorted understanding of scientific goals and procedures.[71] Even in these difficult situations enhanced understanding and adequate decision making can often be achieved. Professionals may be able to communicate novel or specialized information to laypersons by drawing analogies between this information and more ordinary events familiar to the patient or subject. Similarly, professionals can express risks in both numeric and nonnumeric probabilities, while helping the patient or subject to assign meanings to the probabilities through comparison with more familiar risks and prior experiences, such as risks involved in driving automobiles or using power tools.[72]

Even with the assistance of these and other strategies, enabling a patient to both comprehend and appreciate risks and probable benefits is a formidable task. For example, patients confronted with various forms of surgery understand that they will suffer postoperative pain. Nevertheless, their projected expectations of pain are often inadequate. Many patients cannot in advance adequately appreciate the nature and severity of the pain, and many ill patients reach a point when they can no longer balance with clear judgment the threat of pain against the benefits of surgery. At this point, they may find the benefits of surgery overwhelmingly attractive, while discounting the risks. These patients correctly understand basic facts about procedures that involve pain, but their understanding is nonetheless inadequate.

Many studies focus on patients' and research participants' failures to comprehend the risks involved, but problems also arise in the understanding of expected benefits—their nature, probability, and magnitude. These problems were evident in a study of the understanding of patients with stable coronary artery disease who chose to undergo percutaneous coronary intervention (PCI). In contrast to the best available evidence and the views of their cardiologists, the overwhelming majority of these patients thought that PCI would reduce their risk of a heart attack (88%) and their risk of death from a heart attack (82%), even though PCI's major expected benefit for such patients is only symptomatic, namely, relief from chest pain or discomfort. PCI may be lifesaving for patients who have an acute or unstable angina, and the patients who had only stable angina may have confused the two conditions because both involve chest pain and discomfort. According to the investigators and a commentator, direct communication about these and other matters, accompanied by decision aids, could have been helpful, especially when accompanied by improvements in the level of reading difficulty and the information provided in the consent form.[73]

Although studies suggest that modest efforts may significantly improve informed consent in clinical care,[74] special concerns about adequate understanding for valid consent arise in the context of research, which is designed to generate generalizable knowledge rather than to benefit the participant. The "therapeutic misconception" is a widely discussed problem of informed consent that must be addressed in research, where subjects may fail to distinguish between clinical care and research and may fail to understand the purpose and aim of research, thereby misconceiving their participation as therapeutic in nature.[75] In a stringent interpretation of the standard of adequate understanding, the therapeutic misconception invalidates a subject's consent because he or she is not truly consenting to participation *in research*. A partial solution is twofold: first, to recognize that the label "therapeutic misconception" is too broad, and second, to find specific interventions to address the different misunderstandings under that rubric.[76]

Sam Horng and Christine Grady appropriately distinguish therapeutic misconception in the strict sense from therapeutic misestimation and therapeutic optimism.[77] The therapeutic misconception, if uncorrected, invalidates subjects' consent because they do not have the facts straight enough to truly consent to participate in research. However, some participants who understand that they are involved in research, rather than clinical care, still overestimate the therapeutic possibilities and probabilities, that is, the odds that participants will benefit. Such a therapeutic misestimation, Horng and Grady argue, should be tolerated if "modest misestimates do not compromise a reasonable awareness of possible outcomes." By contrast, in therapeutic optimism participants accurately understand the odds that participants will benefit but are overly optimistic about their own chances of beating those odds. This therapeutic optimism usually does not compromise or invalidate the individual's informed consent because it is more like a legitimate hope than an informational bias.

Problems of Information Processing

With the exception of a few studies of comprehension, studies of patients' decision making pay insufficient attention to information processing. Information overload may prevent adequate understanding, and physicians exacerbate these problems when they use unfamiliar medical terms.

Some studies have uncovered difficulties in processing information about risks, indicating that risk disclosures commonly lead subjects to distort information, promote inferential errors, and create disproportionate fears of some risks. Some ways of framing information are so misleading that both health professionals and patients regularly misconstrue the content. For example, choices between risky alternatives can be influenced by whether the same risk information is presented as providing a gain or an opportunity for a patient or as constituting a loss or a reduction of opportunity.[78] One study asked radiologists, outpatients with chronic medical problems, and graduate business students to make a hypothetical choice between two alternative therapies for lung cancer: surgery and radiation therapy.[79] Researchers framed the information about outcomes in terms of (1) survival and (2) death. This difference of framing affected the preferences of all three groups. When faced with outcomes framed in terms of probability of *survival,* 25% chose radiation over surgery. However, when the identical outcomes were presented in terms of probability of *death,* 42% preferred radiation. The mode of presenting the risk of immediate death from surgical complications, which has no counterpart in radiation therapy, appears to have made the decisive difference.

These framing effects reduce understanding, with direct implications for autonomous choice. If a misperception prevents a person from adequately understanding the risk of death and this risk is material to the person's decision, then the person's choice of a procedure does not reflect a substantial understanding and his or her consent does not qualify as an autonomous authorization. The lesson is the need for better understanding of techniques that enable professionals to communicate both the positive and the negative sides of information—for example, both the survival and the mortality probabilities.

Decision aids are increasingly used to prepare individuals to participate in medical decisions that involve balancing probable benefits and risks in contexts of scientific uncertainty where decisions about screening or therapeutic interventions are difficult to evaluate. Studies show that the use of decision aids can provide important information and enable patients to reflect on their own values and preferences in relation to their circumstances and options. The use of these decision aids correlates with patients' increased knowledge and more active participation in decision making. Other benefits include a reduction in patients' decisional conflict based on inadequate information or unclarity about their personal values and preferences and fewer decisions for elective procedures, such as PCI for stable coronary artery disease.[80]

However, caution is in order. As a result of some studies of decision aids, questions have emerged about their health effects. In a randomized controlled trial, investigators studied the impact of a decision aid to enhance informed choices and involvement in decision making about screening for bowel cancer among adults with low levels of education. The decision aid—an interactive booklet and a DVD—presented quantitative information about the relative risks of (1) testing occult fecal blood versus (2) no testing. The control group received standard information about the relative risks. The decision aid effectively enhanced informed choices, as indicated by the participants' knowledge and participation in decisions about screening. However, only 59% in the decision aid group chose to be tested in comparison with 75% in the control group.[81] Some critics charge that informed choice initiatives may be harmful in some cases, especially when solid evidence exists about a procedure's value. One critic even proposes that in efforts to reduce mortality from bowel cancer, the purpose of information interventions should be to "support uptake" rather than to "prepare or enable decision making."[82] For this critic, the presentation of information to describe the risks and benefits of screening should occur "within a framework that encourages adherence to recommendations." Defenders of improving informed choice challenge this proposal as a paternalistic manipulation of information to ensure the use of screening.[83] Moreover, in many cases physicians do not agree among themselves about what, if anything, is to be recommended.

Problems of Nonacceptance and False Belief

A breakdown in a person's ability to accept information as true or untainted, even if he or she adequately comprehends the information, also can compromise decision making. A single false belief can invalidate a patient's or subject's consent, even when there has been a suitable disclosure and comprehension. For example, a seriously ill patient who has been adequately informed about the nature of the illness and has been asked to make a treatment decision might refuse under the false belief that he or she is not ill. Even if the physician recognizes the patient's false belief and adduces conclusive evidence to prove to the patient that the belief is mistaken, and the patient comprehends the information provided, the patient may go on believing that what has been reported is false.

If ignorance prevents an informed choice, it may be permissible or possibly even obligatory to promote autonomy by attempting to impose unwelcome information. Consider the following case in which a false belief played a major role in a patient's refusal of treatment:[84]

> A 57-year-old woman was admitted to the hospital because of a fractured hip....During the course of the hospitalization, a Papanicolaou test and biopsy revealed stage 1A carcinoma of the cervix....Surgery was strongly recommended, since the cancer was almost certainly curable by a hysterectomy....The patient refused the procedure. The patient's treating physicians at this point felt that she was mentally incompetent. Psychiatric and neurological consultations were requested to determine the possibility of dementia and/or mental incompetency. The psychiatric consultant felt that the patient was demented and not mentally competent to make decisions regarding her own care. This determination was based in large measure on the patient's steadfast "unreasonable" refusal to undergo surgery. The neurologist disagreed, finding no evidence of dementia. On questioning, the patient stated that she was refusing the hysterectomy because she *did not believe* she had cancer. "Anyone knows," she said, "that people with cancer are sick, feel bad and lose weight," while she felt quite well. The patient continued to hold this view despite the results of the biopsy and her physicians' persistent arguments to the contrary.

The physician seriously considered overriding the patient's refusal, because solid medical evidence indicated that she was unjustified in believing that she did not have cancer. As long as this patient continues to hold a false belief that is material to her decision, her refusal is not an *informed* refusal. The case illustrates some complexities involved in effective communication: The patient was a poor white woman from Appalachia with a third-grade education. The fact that her treating physician was black was the major reason for her false belief that she did not have cancer. She would not believe what a black physician told her. However, intense and sometimes difficult discussions with a white physician and with her daughter eventually corrected her belief and led her to consent to

a successful hysterectomy. This example illustrates why it is sometimes necessary for clinicians to vigorously challenge patients' choices in order to further
enhance the quality of their autonomous choices rather than merely accept their
choices at face value.

Problems of Waivers

Further problems about understanding arise in waivers of informed consent.
In the exercise of a waiver, a patient voluntarily relinquishes the right to an
informed consent and relieves the physician of the obligation to obtain informed
consent.[85] The patient delegates decision-making authority to the physician or
to a third party, or simply asks not to be informed. The patient makes a decision
not to make an informed decision.

Some courts have held that physicians need not make disclosures of risk if a
patient requests not to be informed,[86] and some writers in biomedical ethics hold
that rights are always waivable.[87] It is usually appropriate to recognize waivers
of rights because we enjoy discretion over whether to exercise such rights. For
example, if a committed Jehovah's Witness informed a doctor that he wished to
have everything possible done for him, but did not want to know if the hospital
utilized transfusions or similar procedures, it is difficult to imagine a moral argument sufficient to support the conclusion that he must give a specific informed
consent to the transfusions. Nevertheless, a general practice of allowing waivers
is dangerous. Many patients have an inordinate trust in physicians, and a widespread acceptance of waivers of consent in research and therapeutic settings
could make subjects and patients more vulnerable to those who omit consent
procedures for convenience, which is already a serious problem in health care.

No solution to these problems about waivers is likely to emerge that fits all
cases. Although each case or situation of waiver needs to be considered sepa-
rately, there may be appropriate procedural responses. For example, institutions
can develop rules that disallow waivers except when they have been approved
by deliberative bodies, such as institutional review committees and hospital
ethics committees. If a committee determines that recognizing a waiver would
best protect a person's interest in a particular case, then the waiver could be
sustained.

VOLUNTARINESS

Voluntariness is the second element of informed consent in our list and also
the third of our three conditions of autonomous action. Because it was so often
neglected in the history of research, this element has come to have a prominent
role in biomedical ethics. The Nuremberg Code, for example, insists on voluntariness: A research subject "should be so situated as to be able to exercise free

power of choice, without the intervention of any element of force, fraud, deceit, duress, over-reaching, or other ulterior form of constraint or coercion."[88]

We use the term *voluntariness* more narrowly than some writers do. Some have analyzed voluntariness in terms of the presence of adequate knowledge, the absence of psychological compulsion, and the absence of external constraints.[89] If we were to adopt such a broad meaning, we would be equating voluntariness with autonomy. We hold only that a person acts voluntarily if he or she wills the action without being under the control of another person or condition. We will consider here only the condition of control by other individuals, but we note that conditions such as debilitating disease, psychiatric disorders, and drug addiction can also diminish or destroy voluntariness, thereby precluding autonomous choice and action.

Forms of Influence

Not all influences exerted on another person are controlling. If a physician orders a reluctant patient to undergo cardiac catheterization and coerces the patient into compliance through a threat of abandonment, then the physician's influence controls the patient. If, by contrast, a physician persuades the patient to undergo the procedure when the patient is at first reluctant to do so, then the physician's actions influence, but do not control, the patient. Many influences are resistible, and some are welcomed rather than resisted.

The broad category of influence includes acts of love, threats, education, lies, manipulative suggestions, and emotional appeals, all of which can vary dramatically both in their impact on persons and in their ethical justification. Our analysis focuses on three categories of influence: coercion, persuasion, and manipulation. Coercion occurs if and only if one person intentionally uses a credible and severe threat of harm or force to control another.[90] The threat of force used by some police, courts, and hospitals in acts of involuntary commitment for psychiatric treatment is coercive. Some threats will coerce virtually all persons (e.g., a credible threat to kill the person), whereas others will coerce only a few persons (e.g., an employee's threat to an employer to quit a job unless a raise is offered). Whether coercion occurs depends on the subjective responses of the coercion's intended target. However, a subjective response in which persons comply because they *feel* threatened even though no threat has actually been issued does not qualify as coercion. Coercion occurs only if an intended and credible threat displaces a person's self-directed course of action, thereby rendering even intentional and well-informed behavior nonautonomous. We reject a common tendency in biomedical ethics to use "coercion" as a broad term of ethical criticism that obscures relevant and distinctive ethical concerns. For instance, coercion is not identical to taking advantage of a person in dire circumstances. Both are wrong in many contexts, often for different reasons.[91]

In *persuasion* a person must come to believe in something through the merit of reasons another person advances. Appeal to reason—that is, attempted persuasion—is distinguishable from influence by appeal to emotion. In health care, the problem is how to distinguish emotional responses from cognitive responses and to determine which are likely to be evoked. Disclosures or approaches that might rationally persuade one patient might overwhelm another whose fear or panic undercuts reason.

Manipulation is a generic term for several forms of influence that are neither persuasive nor coercive. The essence of manipulation is swaying people to do what the manipulator wants by means other than coercion or persuasion. In health care, the most likely form of manipulation is informational manipulation, a deliberate act of managing information that alters a person's understanding of a situation and motivates him or her to do what the agent of influence intends. Many forms of informational manipulation are incompatible with autonomous decision making. For example, lying, withholding information, and misleading by exaggeration with the intent to lead persons to believe what is false all compromise autonomous choice. The manner in which a health care professional presents information—by tone of voice, by forceful gesture, and by framing information positively ("we succeed most of the time with this therapy") rather than negatively ("we fail with this therapy in 35% of the cases")—can also manipulate a patient's perception and response.

Nevertheless, it is easy to inflate control by manipulation beyond its actual significance in health care. We typically make decisions in a context of competing influences, such as personal desires, familial constraints, legal obligations, and institutional pressures. These influences usually do not control decisions to a morally worrisome degree. In biomedical ethics we need only establish general criteria for the point at which influence threatens autonomous choice.

The Obligation to Abstain from Controlling Influence

Coercion and controlling manipulation are occasionally justified—infrequently in medicine, more often in public health, and even more often in law enforcement. If a physician taking care of a disruptive and noncompliant patient threatens to discontinue treatment unless the patient alters certain behaviors, the physician's mandate may be justified even if it is coercive. The most difficult problems about manipulation do not involve threat and punishment, which are almost always unjustified in health care and research. Rather, they involve the effect of rewards, offers, and encouragement.

A classic example of an unjustified offer occurred during the Tuskegee syphilis study. Researchers used various offers to stimulate and sustain the subjects' interest in continued participation; these offers included free burial assistance and insurance, free transportation to and from the examinations, and a free stop in town on the return trip. Subjects also received free medicines and free hot meals on the days of the examination. The subjects' socioeconomic deprivation made them vulnerable to these overt and unjustified forms of manipulation.[92]

The conditions under which an influence both controls persons and lacks moral justification may be clear in theory, but they are often unclear in concrete situations. For example, many patients report feeling severe pressure to enroll in clinical trials, even though their enrollment is voluntary.[93] Some difficult cases in health care involve manipulation-like situations in which patients or subjects are in desperate need of a given medication or a source of income. Attractive offers such as free medication or extra money can leave a person without a meaningful choice. A threatening situation can constrain a person even in the absence of another's intentional manipulation. Influences that persons ordinarily find resistible can control abnormally weak, dependent, and surrender-prone patients.[94] In short, people's vulnerabilities differ, thereby producing variations in what constitutes an "undue" influence.[95]

The threat of exploitation for research and other purposes is substantial in institutions where populations are confined involuntarily, but even if persons voluntarily admit themselves to institutions, rules, policies, and practices can work to compromise autonomous choice. This compromise is often evident in long-term care. The elderly in nursing homes can experience constricted choices in everyday matters. Many suffer a decline in their ability to carry out personal choices because of physical impairments, but this decline in *executional* autonomy need not be accompanied by a decline in *decisional* autonomy.[96] On the one hand, the problem is that caregivers in nursing homes may neglect, misunderstand, or override residents' autonomous decisions in everyday decisions that range over food, roommates, possessions, exercise, sleep, and clothes, along with baths, medications, and restraints. On the other hand, institutional needs for structure, order, safety, and efficiency are sometimes legitimately invoked to override residents' autonomous choices.

CONCLUSION

The intimate connection between autonomy and decision making in health care and research, especially in circumstances of consent and refusal, unifies this chapter's several sections. Although we have justified the obligation to solicit decisions from patients and potential research subjects by the principle of respect for autonomy, we have also acknowledged that the principle's precise demands remain unsettled and open to legitimate interpretation and specification.

We have criticized various approaches that have been taken to obtaining consents, but we should be mindful that the history of informed consent and the place of autonomy in biomedical ethics are still under development. Current deficiencies may be no less apparent to future generations than the past failures we have occasionally pointed to in this chapter.

Finally, we again stress that construing respect for autonomy as a principle with priority over all other moral principles, rather than as one principle in a framework of prima facie principles, is indefensible. The human moral community—indeed, morality itself—is rooted no less deeply in the three clusters of principles to be discussed in the next three chapters.

NOTES

1.   Generally we refer to those who enroll in research as *subjects,* but occasionally as *participants.* See the discussion of this distinction in National Bioethics Advisory Commission (NBAC), *Ethical and Policy Issues in Research Involving Human Participants, Vol. I: Report and Recommendations* (Bethesda, MD: NBAC, August 2001), pp. 32–33.

2.   The core idea of autonomy is treated by Joel Feinberg, *Harm to Self,* vol. III in *The Moral Limits of Criminal Law* (New York: Oxford University Press, 1986), chaps. 18–19; various essays in Franklin G. Miller and Alan Wertheimer, eds., *The Ethics of Consent: Theory and Practice* (New York: Oxford University Press, 2010); and several essays in James Stacey Taylor, ed., *Personal Autonomy: New Essays on Personal Autonomy and Its Role in Contemporary Moral Philosophy* (Cambridge: Cambridge University Press, 2005).

3.   For a theory that points to the importance of a broader theory of the autonomous person than we provide, see Rebecca Kukla, "Conscientious Autonomy: Displacing Decisions in Health Care," *Hastings Center Report* 35 (March–April 2005): 34–44.

4.   Gerald Dworkin, *The Theory and Practice of Autonomy* (New York: Cambridge University Press, 1988), chaps. 1–4; Harry G. Frankfurt, "Freedom of the Will and the Concept of a Person," *Journal of Philosophy* 68 (1971): 5–20, as reprinted in *The Importance of What We Care About* (Cambridge: Cambridge University Press, 1988), pp. 11–25. Frankfurt may be primarily focused on a theory of freedom rather a theory of autonomy; but see his uses of the language of "autonomy" in his *Necessity, Volition, and Love* (Cambridge: Cambridge University Press, 1999), chaps. 9, 11, especially pp. 95–110, 137.

5.   Dworkin, *The Theory and Practice of Autonomy,* p. 20.

6.   Agnieszka Jaworska, "Caring, Minimal Autonomy, and the Limits of Liberalism," in *Naturalized Bioethics: Toward Responsible Knowing and Practice,* ed. Hilde Lindemann, Marian Verkerk, and Margaret Urban Walker (New York: Cambridge University Press, 2009), pp. 80–105, esp. 82.

7.   For a "planning theory" and its relation to theories of autonomy, see Michael Bratman, "Planning Agency, Autonomous Agency," in *Personal Autonomy,* ed. Taylor, pp. 33–57.

8.   See Arthur Kuflik, "The Inalienability of Autonomy," *Philosophy and Public Affairs* 13 (1984): 271–98; Joseph Raz, "Authority and Justification," *Philosophy and Public Affairs* 14 (1985): 3–29; and Christopher McMahon, "Autonomy and Authority," *Philosophy and Public Affairs* 16 (1987): 303–28.

9.   See several essays in *Relational Autonomy: Feminist Perspectives on Autonomy, Agency, and the Social Self,* ed. Catriona Mackenzie and Natalie Stoljar (New York: Oxford University Press, 2000); Marilyn Friedman, *Autonomy, Gender, and Politics* (New York: Oxford University Press, 2003); John Christman, "Feminism and Autonomy," in *Nagging Questions: Feminist Ethics in Everyday Life,* ed. Dana Bushnell (Lanham, MD: Rowman & Littlefield, 1995); and Alasdair Maclean on "relational consent" in his *Autonomy, Informed Consent and Medical Law: A Relational Challenge* (Cambridge: Cambridge University Press, 2009).

10. See, further, Carolyn Ells, "Shifting the Autonomy Debate to Theory as Ideology," *Journal of Medicine and Philosophy* 26 (2001): 417–30; Stoljar, "Informed Consent and Relational Conceptions of Autonomy," *Journal of Medicine and Philosophy* 36 (2011): 375–84; Susan Sherwin, "A Relational Approach to Autonomy in Health-Care," in *The Politics of Women's Health: Exploring Agency and Autonomy,* The Feminist Health Care Ethics Research Network (Philadelphia: Temple University Press, 1998); and Anne Donchin, "Understanding Autonomy Relationally," *Journal of Medicine and Philosophy* 23, no. 4 (1998).

11. See Barbara Herman, "Mutual Aid and Respect for Persons," *Ethics* 94 (July 1984): 577–602, esp. 600–2; and Onora O'Neill, "Universal Laws and Ends-in-Themselves," *Monist* 72 (1989): 341–61.

12. This misunderstanding of our claim is seen in M. Therese Lysaught, "Respect: or, How Respect for Persons Became Respect for Autonomy," *Journal of Medicine and Philosophy* 29 (2004): 665–80, esp. 676.

13. Carl E. Schneider, *The Practice of Autonomy: Patients, Doctors, and Medical Decisions* (New York: Oxford University Press, 1998), esp. p. xi. See also Paul Root Wolpe, "The Triumph of Autonomy in American Bioethics: A Sociological View," in *Bioethics and Society: Constructing the Ethical Enterprise,* ed. Raymond DeVries and Janardan Subedi (Upper Saddle River, NJ: Prentice Hall, 1998), pp. 38–59; Daniel Callahan, "Autonomy: A Moral Good, Not a Moral Obsession," *Hastings Center Report* 14 (October 1984): 40–42; Robert M. Veatch, "Autonomy's Temporary Triumph," *Hastings Center Report* 14 (October 1984): 38–40; James F. Childress, "The Place of Autonomy in Bioethics," *Hastings Center Report* 20 (January–February 1990): 12–16; and Thomas May, "The Concept of Autonomy in Bioethics: An Unwarranted Fall from Grace," in *Personal Autonomy,* ed. Taylor, pp. 299–309.

14. Leslie J. Blackhall, Sheila T. Murphy, Gelya Frank, et al., "Ethnicity and Attitudes toward Patient Autonomy," *JAMA: Journal of the American Medical Association* 274 (September 13, 1995): 820–25.

15. Joseph A. Carrese and Lorna A. Rhodes, "Western Bioethics on the Navajo Reservation: Benefit or Harm?" *JAMA: Journal of the American Medical Association* 274 (September 13, 1995): 826–29.

16. We make these points to forestall misunderstanding. Some critics of theories that connect respect for autonomy to informed consent mistakenly presume that defenders of these views, including us, view them as necessary and sufficient. See Neil C. Manson and Onora O'Neill, *Rethinking Informed Consent in Bioethics* (Cambridge: Cambridge University Press, 2007), pp. 19, 185ff.

17. For a fuller discussion of the relation between autonomy and consent, see Tom L. Beauchamp, "Autonomy and Consent," in *The Ethics of Consent,* ed. Miller and Wertheimer, chap. 3.

18. See Avram Goldstein, "Practice vs. Privacy on Pelvic Exams: Med Students' Training Intrusive and Needs Patient Consent, Activists Say," *Washington Post,* May 10, 2003, p. A1.

19. Britt-Ingjerd Nesheim, "Commentary: Respecting the Patient's Integrity Is the Key," *BMJ: British Medical Journal* 326 (January 11, 2003): 100.

20. Peter A. Ubel, Christopher Jepson, and Ari Silver-Isenstadt, "Don't Ask, Don't Tell: A Change in Medical Student Attitudes after Obstetrics/Gynecology Clerkships toward Seeking Consent for Pelvic Examinations on an Anesthetized Patient," *American Journal of Obstetrics and Gynecology* 188 (February 2003): 575–79.

21. Bernard M. Branson, H. Hunter Handsfield, Margaret A. Lampe, et al., "Revised Recommendations for HIV Testing of Adults, Adolescents, and Pregnant Women in Health-Care Settings," *Morbidity and Mortality Weekly Report, Recommendations and Report* 55 (RR-14) (September 22, 2006): 1–17. Under these recommendations, specific, explicit informed consent is still expected in nonclinical settings.

22. See Ronald Bayer and Amy L. Fairchild, "Changing the Paradigm for HIV Testing—The End of Exceptionalism," *New England Journal of Medicine* 355 (August 17, 2006): 647–49; Lawrence

O. Gostin, "HIV Screening in Health Care Setting: Public Health and Civil Liberties in Conflict?" *JAMA: Journal of the American Medical Association* 296 (October 25, 2006): 2023–25; and Thomas R. Frieden et al., "Applying Public Health Principles to the HIV Epidemic," *New England Journal of Medicine* 353 (December 1, 2005): 2397–402. For a cost-effectiveness analysis, see Gillian D. Sanders et al., "Cost-Effectiveness of Screening for HIV in the Era of Highly Active Antiretroviral Therapy," *New England Journal of Medicine* 352 (February 10, 2005): 570–85.

23. See Carl W. Dieffenbach and Anthony S. Fauci, "Thirty Years of HIV and AIDS: Future Challenges and Opportunities," *Annals of Internal Medicine* 154, no. 11 (June 2011): 766–72.

24. Quoted in Bayer and Fairchild, "Changing the Paradigm for HIV Testing," p. 649.

25. For a fuller discussion of the issues raised by "opt-out" policies to increase the supply of transplantable organs, see Institute of Medicine, Committee on Increasing Rates of Organ Donation, *Organ Donation: Opportunities for Action,* ed. James F. Childress and Catharyn Liverman (Washington, DC: National Academies Press, 2006), chap. 7. See also Richard H. Thaler and Cass R. Sunstein, *Nudge: Improving Decisions about Health, Wealth, and Happiness* (New Haven, CT: Yale University Press, 2008), chap. 11, "How to Increase Organ Donations."

26. This case was developed by Gail Povar, M.D.

27. See Thomas Grisso and Paul S. Appelbaum, *Assessing Competence to Consent to Treatment: A Guide for Physicians and Other Health Professionals* (New York: Oxford University Press, 1998), p. 11.

28. The analysis in this section has profited from discussions with Ruth R. Faden, Nancy M. P. King, and Dan Brock.

29. See the analysis of the core meaning in Charles M. Culver and Bernard Gert, *Philosophy in Medicine* (New York: Oxford University Press, 1982), pp. 123–26.

30. *Pratt v. Davis,* 118 Ill. App. 161 (1905), aff'd, 224 Ill. 300, 79 N.E. 562 (1906).

31. See Daniel Wikler, "Paternalism and the Mildly Retarded," *Philosophy and Public Affairs* 8 (1979): 377–92; and Kenneth F. Schaffner, "Competency: A Triaxial Concept," in *Competency,* ed. M. A. G. Cutter and E. E. Shelp (Dordrecht, Netherlands: Kluwer Academic, 1991), pp. 253–81.

32. This case was prepared by P. Browning Hoffman, M.D., for presentation in the series of "Medicine and Society" conferences at the University of Virginia.

33. Laura L. Sessums, Hanna Zembrzuska, and Jeffrey I. Jackson, "Does This Patient Have Medical Decision-Making Capacity?" *JAMA: Journal of the American Medical Association* 306 (July 27, 2011): 420. See also J. B. Jourdan and L. Glickman, "Reasons for Requests for Evaluation of Competency in a Municipal General Hospital," *Psychomatics* 32 (1991): 413–16.

34. This schema is indebted to Paul S. Appelbaum and Thomas Grisso, "Assessing Patients' Capacities to Consent to Treatment," *New England Journal of Medicine* 319 (December 22, 1988): 1635–38; and Jessica W. Berg, Paul S. Appelbaum, Charles W. Lidz, and Lisa S. Parker, *Informed Consent: Legal Theory and Clinical Practice,* 2nd ed. (New York: Oxford University Press, 2001).

35. For additional ways in which values are incorporated, see Loretta M. Kopelman, "On the Evaluative Nature of Competency and Capacity Judgments," *International Journal of Law and Psychiatry* 13 (1990): 309–29. For conceptual and epistemic problems in available tests, see E. Haavi Morreim, "Competence: At the Intersection of Law, Medicine, and Philosophy," in *Competency,* ed. Cutter and Shelp, pp. 93–125, esp. pp. 105–8.

36. See Sander P. K. Welie, "Criteria for Patient Decision Making (In)competence: A Review of and Commentary on Some Empirical Approaches," *Medicine, Health Care and Philosophy* 4 (2001):

139–51; Jennifer Moye, Ronald J. Guerrera, Michele J. Karel, et al., "Empirical Advances in the Assessment of the Capacity to Consent to Medical Treatment: Clinical Implications and Medical Needs," *Clinical Psychology Review* 26 (2006): 1054–77; Laura B. Dunn, Milap A. Nowrangi, Barton W. Palmer, et al., "Assessing Decisional Capacity for Clinical Research or Treatment: A Review of Instruments," *American Journal of Psychiatry* 163 (2006): 1323–34; and Sessums, Zembrzuska, and Jackson, "Does This Patient Have Medical Decision-Making Capacity?" Various factors enter into the assessment of these instruments; for example, the last article listed stresses their suitability for use in an office visit, robust likelihood ratios, moderate to strong levels of evidence, and consistency with U.S. or Canadian law.

37. See Sessums, Zembzuska, and Jackson, "Does This Patient Have Medical Decision-Making Capacity?" which shows that physicians count as competent many persons who lack capacity but usually count as incompetent only those who lack capacity.

38. Grisso and Appelbaum, *Assessing Competence to Consent to Treatment,* p. 139.

39. See Willard Gaylin, "The Competence of Children: No Longer All or None," *Hastings Center Report* 12 (April 1982): 33–38, esp. 35; Allen Buchanan and Dan Brock, *Deciding for Others* (Cambridge: Cambridge University Press, 1989), pp. 51–70; and Eric Kodish, "Children's Competence for Assent and Consent: A Review of Empirical Findings," *Ethics & Behavior* 14 (2004): 255–95.

40. Buchanan and Brock, *Deciding for Others,* pp. 52–55. For elaboration and defense, see Brock, "Decisionmaking Competence and Risk," *Bioethics* 5 (1991): 105–12.

41. *Report and Recommendations of the National Bioethics Advisory Commission, Research Involving Persons with Mental Disorders That May Affect Decision Making Capacity,* vol. I (Rockville, MD: National Bioethics Advisory Commission, December 1998), p. 58.

42. Onora O'Neill, *Autonomy and Trust in Bioethics* (Cambridge: Cambridge University Press, 2002); O'Neill, "Autonomy: The Emperor's New Clothes," *Proceedings of the Aristotelian Society,* supp. vol. 77 (2003): 1–21; O'Neill, "Some Limits of Informed Consent," *Journal of Medical Ethics* 29 (2003): 4–7; and Manson and O'Neill, *Rethinking Informed Consent in Bioethics.*

43. O'Neill, "Some Limits of Informed Consent," p. 5.

44. See Jay Katz, *The Silent World of Doctor and Patient* (New York: Free Press, 1984), pp. 86–87 [Reprint ed. (Baltimore, MD: The Johns Hopkins University Press, 2002)]; and President's Commission for the Study of Ethical Problems in Medicine and Biomedical and Behavioral Research, *Making Health Care Decisions,* vol. I (Washington, DC: U.S. Government Printing Office, 1982), p. 15.

45. For extensions of this thesis, see Simon Whitney, Amy McGuire, and Laurence McCullough, "A Typology of Shared Decision Making, Informed Consent, and Simple Consent," *Annals of Internal Medicine* 140 (2003): 54–59.

46. The analysis in this subsection is based in part on Faden and Beauchamp, *A History and Theory of Informed Consent,* chap. 8.

47. *Mohr v. Williams,* 95 Minn. 261, 265; 104 N.W. 12, 15 (1905).

48. Franklin G. Miller and Alan Wertheimer, "The Fair Transaction Model of Informed Consent: An Alternative to Autonomous Authorization," *Kennedy Institute of Ethics Journal* 21 (2011): 201–18. At pp. 210–12 these authors recognize the importance of our second sense of "informed consent" and the qualifications it allows, but they seem not to appreciate the critical importance of maintaining the first sense as the primary model of an informed consent. See also their "Preface to a Theory of Consent Transactions: Beyond Valid Consent," in *The Ethics of Consent,* ed. Miller and Wertheimer, pp. 79–105.

49. See, for example, Alan Meisel and Loren Roth, "What We Do and Do Not Know about Informed Consent," *JAMA: Journal of the American Medical Association* 246 (1981): 2473–77; President's

Commission, *Making Health Care Decisions,* vol. II, pp. 317–410, esp. p. 318, and vol. I, chap. 1, esp. pp. 38–39; National Commission for the Protection of Human Subjects of Biomedical and Behavioral Research, *The Belmont Report* (Washington, DC: DHEW Publication OS 78-0012, 1978), p. 10.

50. A classic case is *Planned Parenthood of Central Missouri v. Danforth,* 428 U.S. 52 at 67 n.8 (1976) (U.S. Supreme Court).

51. *Moore v. Regents of the University of California,* 793 P.2d 479 (Cal. 1990) at 483.

52. See, for example, Clarence H. Braddock et al., "How Doctors and Patients Discuss Routine Clinical Decisions: Informed Decision Making in the Outpatient Setting," *Journal of General Internal Medicine* 12 (1997): 339–45; and John Briguglio et al., "Development of a Model Angiography Informed Consent Form Based on a Multiinstitutional Survey of Current Forms," *Journal of Vascular and Interventional Radiology* 6 (1995): 971–78.

53. The Oklahoma Supreme Court supported this standard in *Scott v. Bradford,* 606 P.2d 554 (Okla. 1979) at 559 and *Masquat v. Maguire,* 638 P.2d 1105, Okla. 1981.

54. *Canterbury v. Spence,* 464 F.2d 772 (1977), at 785–89; and see Nathan A. Bostick, Robert Sade, John W. McMahon, and Regina Benjamin, "Report of the American Medical Association Council on Ethical and Judicial Affairs: Withholding Information from Patients: Rethinking the Propriety of 'Therapeutic Privilege,'" *Journal of Clinical Ethics* 17 (Winter 2006): 302–6. For studies of levels of anxiety and stress produced by informed consent disclosures, see Jeffrey Goldberger et al., "Effect of Informed Consent on Anxiety in Patients Undergoing Diagnostic Electrophysiology Studies," *American Heart Journal* 134 (1997): 119–26; and Kenneth D. Hopper et al., "The Effect of Informed Consent on the Level of Anxiety in Patients Given IV Contrast Material," *American Journal of Roentgenology* 162 (1994): 531–35.

55. *Thornburgh v. American College of Obstetricians,* 476 U.S. 747 (1986) (White, J., dissenting).

56. Howard Brody, *Placebos and the Philosophy of Medicine: Clinical, Conceptual, and Ethical Issues* (Chicago: University of Chicago Press, 1980), pp. 10–11.

57. Ted J. Kaptchuk, Elizabeth Friedlander, John M. Kelley, et al, "Placebos without Deception: A Randomized Controlled Trial in Irritable Bowel Syndrome," *PloS One* 5 (2010), available at http://www.plosone.org/article/info:doi/10.1371/journal.pone.0015591 (accessed October 19, 2011).

58. Jon C. Tilburt, Ezekiel J. Emanuel, Ted J. Kaptchuk, et al., "Prescribing 'Placebo Treatments': Results of National Survey of US Internists and Rheumatologists," *BMJ: British Medical Journal* 337 (2008): a1938. Similar results have been reported in studies in other countries.

59. On the merit of these arguments, see Anne Barnhill, "What It Takes to Defend Deceptive Placebo Use," *Kennedy Institute of Ethics Journal* 21 (2011): 219–50.

60. For a similar proposal, see Armand Lione, "Ethics of Placebo Use in Clinical Care" (Correspondence), *Lancet* 362 (September 20, 2003): 999. For cases involving the different appeals to "consent," along with analysis and assessment, see P. Lichtenberg, U. Heresco-Levy, and U. Nitzan, "The Ethics of the Placebo in Clinical Practice," *Journal of Medical Ethics* 30 (2004): 551–54; "Case Vignette: Placebos and Informed Consent," *Ethics and Behavior* 8 (1998): 89–90, with commentaries by Jeffrey Blustein, Walter Robinson, and Gregory S. Loeben and Benjamin S. Wilfond; and Philip Levendusky and Loren Pankratz, "Self-Control Techniques as an Alternative to Pain Medication," *Journal of Abnormal Psychology* 84 (1975): 165–68.

61. Nathan A. Bostick, Robert Sade, Mark A. Levine, and Dudley M. Steward, Jr., "Placebo Use in Clinical Practice: Report of the American Medical Association Council on Ethical and Judicial Affairs," *Journal of Clinical Ethics* 19, no. 1 (Spring 2008): 58–61. For a criticism of this policy, see both Bennett Foddy, "A Duty to Deceive: Placebos in Clinical Practice," *American Journal of Bioethics* 9, no. 12 (2009): 4–12 (and his response to commentaries in the same issue, W1–2); and Adam Kolber,

"A Limited Defense of Clinical Placebo Deception," *Yale Law & Policy Review* 26 (2007–08): 75–134. For a defense of the American Medical Association policy, see Kavita R. Shah and Susan Door Goold, "The Primacy of Autonomy, Honest, and Disclosure—Council on Ethical and Judicial Affairs' Placebo Opinions," *American Journal of Bioethics* 9, no. 12 (2009): 15–17; and for an analysis of the science and ethics of placebo treatment, see Franklin G. Miller and Luana Colloca, "The Legitimacy of Placebo Treatments in Clinical Practice: Evidence and Ethics," *American Journal of Bioethics* 9, no. 12 (2009): 39–47.

62.   Kaptchuk, Friedlander, Kelley, et al., "Placebos without Deception"; Brody, *Placebos and the Philosophy of Medicine,* pp. 110, 113, et passim; Brody, "The Placebo Response: Recent Research and Implications for Family Medicine," *Journal of Family Practice* 49 (July 2000): 649–54. For a broader defense of placebos, see Howard Spiro, *Doctors, Patients, and Placebos* (New Haven, CT: Yale University Press, 1986).

63.   See Fabrizio Benedetti, "Mechanisms of Placebo and Placebo-Related Effects across Diseases and Treatments," *Annual Review of Pharmacology and Toxicology* 48 (2008): 33–60, more fully developed in his *Placebo Effects: Understanding the Mechanisms in Health and Disease* (New York: Oxford University Press, 2009). Benedetti focuses on the "psychosocial-induced biochemical changes in a person's brain and body."

64.   See Yael Schenker, Alicia Fernandez, and Bernard Lo, "Placebo Prescriptions Are Missed Opportunities for Doctor-Patient Communication," and Howard Brody, "Medicine's Continuing Quest for an Excuse to Avoid Relationships with Patients," both in *American Journal of Bioethics* 9, no. 12 (2009): 48–54 and 13–15, respectively.

65.   Sally E. McNagy and Ruth M. Parker, "High Prevalence of Recent Cocaine Use and the Unreliability of Patient Self-Report in an Inner-City Walk-in Clinic," *JAMA: Journal of the American Medical Association* 267 (February 26, 1992): 1106–8.

66.   Sissela Bok, "Informed Consent in Tests of Patient Reliability," *JAMA: Journal of the American Medical Association* 267 (February 26, 1992): 1118–19.

67.   Barbara A. Bernhardt et al., "Educating Patients about Cystic Fibrosis Carrier Screening in a Primary Care Setting," *Archives of Family Medicine* 5 (1996): 336–40.

68.   Steven Joffe et al., "Quality of Informed Consent in Cancer Clinical Trials: A Cross-Sectional Survey," *Lancet* 358 (November 24, 2001): 1772–77.

69.   *Bang v. Charles T. Miller Hospital,* 251 Minn. 427, 88 N.W. 2d 186 (1958).

70.   See also Gopal Sreenivasan, "Does Informed Consent to Research Require Comprehension?" *Lancet* 362 (December 13, 2003): 2016–18.

71.   C. K. Dougherty et al., "Perceptions of Cancer Patients and Their Physicians Involved in Phase I Clinical Trials," *Journal of Clinical Oncology* 13 (1995): 1062–72; Paul R. Benson et al., "Information Disclosure, Subject Understanding, and Informed Consent in Psychiatric Research," *Law and Human Behavior* 12 (1988): 455–75.

72.   See further Edmund G. Howe, "Approaches (and Possible Contraindications) to Enhancing Patients' Autonomy," *Journal of Clinical Ethics* 5 (1994): 179–88.

73.   See Michael B. Rothberg, Senthil K. Sivalingam, Javed Ashraf, et al., "Patients' and Cardiologists Perceptions of the Benefits of Percutaneous Coronary Intervention for Stable Coronary Disease," *Annals of Internal Medicine* 153 (2010): 307–13. See also the commentary by Alicia Fernandez, "Improving the Quality of Informed Consent: It Is Not All about the Risks," *Annals of Internal Medicine* 153 (2010): 342–43.

74.   Yael Schenker, Alica Fernandez, Rebecca Sudore, and Dean Schillinger, "Intervention to Improve Patient Comprehension in Informed Consent for Medical and Surgical Procedures: A Systematic Review," *Medical Decision Making* 31 (2011): 151–73.

75.   This label was apparently coined by Paul S. Appelbaum, Loren Roth, and Charles W. Lidz in "The Therapeutic Misconception: Informed Consent in Psychiatric Research," *International Journal of Law and Psychiatry* 5 (1982): 319–29. See also Appelbaum, Lidz, and Thomas Grisso, "Therapeutic Misconception in Clinical Research: Frequency and Risk Factors," *IRB: Ethics and Human Research* 26 (2004): 1–8; Walter Glannon, "Phase I Oncology Trials: Why the Therapeutic Misconception Will Not Go Away," *Journal of Medical Ethics* 32 (2006): 252–55; Appelbaum and Lidz, "The Therapeutic Misconception," in *The Oxford Textbook of Clinical Research Ethics,* ed. Ezekiel Emanuel, Christine Grady, Robert Crouch, et al. (New York: Oxford University Press, 2008); and Franklin G. Miller, "Consent to Clinical Research," in *The Ethics of Consent: Theory and Practice,* ed. Miller and Wertheimer, chap. 15.

76.   A broader problem and one more difficult to address is that the frame of discourse in interactions between researchers and potential subjects may incorporate the therapeutic misconception. See Philip J. Candilis and Charles W. Lidz, "Advances in Informed Consent Research," in *The Ethics of Consent,* ed. Miller and Wertheimer, p. 334; David E. Ness, Scott Kiesling, and Charles W. Lidz, "Why Does Informed Consent Fail? A Discourse Analytic Approach," *Journal of the American Academy of Psychiatry and the Law* 37, no. 3 (2009): 349–62.

77.   Sam Horng and Christine Grady, "Misunderstanding in Clinical Research: Distinguishing Therapeutic Misconception, Therapeutic Misestimation, & Therapeutic Optimism," *IRB: Ethics and Human Research* 25 (January–February 2003): 11–16.

78.   The pioneering work was done by Amos Tversky and Daniel Kahneman. See "Choices, Values and Frames," *American Psychologist* 39 (1984): 341–50; and "The Framing of Decisions and the Psychology of Choice," *Science* 211 (1981): 453–58. See also Daniel Kahneman and Amos Tversky, eds., *Choices, Values, and Frames* (Cambridge: Cambridge University Press, 2000). On informed consent specifically, see Dennis J. Mazur and Jon F. Merz, "How Age, Outcome Severity, and Scale Influence General Medicine Clinic Patients' Interpretations of Verbal Probability Terms," *Journal of General Internal Medicine* 9 (1994): 268–71.

79.   S. E. Eraker and H. C. Sox, "Assessment of Patients' Preferences for Therapeutic Outcome," *Medical Decision Making* 1 (1981): 29–39; Barbara McNeil et al., "On the Elicitation of Preferences for Alternative Therapies," *New England Journal of Medicine* 306 (May 27, 1982): 1259–62.

80.   See A. M. O'Connor, C. L. Bennett, D. Stacey, et al., "Decision Aids for People Facing Health Treatment or Screening Decisions," *Cochrane Database of Systematic Reviews,* no. 3 (2009), Art. No. CD001431.

81.   Sian K. Smith, Lyndal Trevena, Judy M. Simpson, et al., "A Decision Aid to Support Informed Choices about Bowel Cancer Screening among Adults with Low Education: Randomised Controlled Trial," *BMJ: British Medical Journal* 341 (2010): c5370. By contrast with this Australian study, a study in Germany found that evidence-based risk information on colorectal cancer screening (along with two optional Internet modules on risk and diagnostic tests) did not affect planned and actual uptake of screening even though it, too, increased informed choices and improved knowledge. See Anke Steckelberg, Christian Hülfenhaus, Burkhard Haastert, and Ingrid Mühlhauser, "Effect of Evidence Based Risk Information on 'Informed Choice' in Colorectal Cancer Screening: Randomised Controlled Trial," *BMJ: British Medical Journal* 342 (2011): d3193. The authors conclude that those "designing and implementing screening programmes should respect the ethical right of consumers for evidence based information and informed choices."

82.   Hilary L. Bekker, "Decision Aids and Uptake of Screening," *BMJ: British Medical Journal* 341 (2010), c5407.

83.   For criticisms of the editorial by Bekker, see C. B. Dalton, "Decision Aids and Screening. Editorial Was Amoral," *BMJ: British Medical Journal* 341 (2010): c6648; and Ben Hudson, "Decision Aids and Screening. Information v Promotion," *BMJ: British Medical Journal* 341 (2010): c6650.

84.   Ruth Faden and Alan Faden, "False Belief and the Refusal of Medical Treatment," *Journal of Medical Ethics* 3 (1977): 133–36.

85.   Neil Manson and Onora O'Neill interpret all consent as a waiver of rights. Although this interpretation is not incorrect, it is often more illuminating to describe informed consent as an exercise of rights rather than a waiver of rights. See Manson and O'Neill, *Rethinking Informed Consent in Bioethics,* esp. pp. 72–77, 187–89.

86.   *Cobbs v. Grant,* 502 P.2d 1, 12 (1972).

87.   Baruch Brody, *Life and Death Decision Making* (New York: Oxford University Press, 1988), p. 22.

88.   The Nuremberg Code, in *Trials of War Criminals Before the Nuernberg Military Tribunals under Control Council Law no. 10* (Washington, DC: U.S. Government Printing Office, 1949).

89.   See Joel Feinberg, *Social Philosophy* (Englewood Cliffs, NJ: Prentice Hall, 1973), p. 48; *Harm to Self,* pp. 112–18. For a notably different view of the concept of voluntariness and its connection to consent—one heavily influenced by law—see Paul S. Appelbaum, Charles W. Lidz, and Robert Klitzman, "Voluntariness of Consent to Research: A Conceptual Model," *Hastings Center Report* 39 (January–February 2009): 30–39, esp. 30–31, 33; and a criticism of Appelbaum, Lidz, and Klitzman in Robert M. Nelson, Tom Beauchamp, Victoria A. Miller, et al. "The Concept of Voluntary Consent," *American Journal of Bioethics* 11 (2011): 6–16, esp. 12–13.

90.   Our formulation is indebted to Robert Nozick, "Coercion," in *Philosophy, Science and Method: Essays in Honor of Ernest Nagel,* ed. Sidney Morgenbesser, Patrick Suppes, and Morton White (New York: St. Martin's, 1969), pp. 440–72; and Bernard Gert, "Coercion and Freedom," in *Coercion: Nomos XIV,* ed. J. Roland Pennock and John W. Chapman (Chicago: Aldine, Atherton, 1972), pp. 36–37. See also Alan Wertheimer, *Coercion* (Princeton, NJ: Princeton University Press, 1987).

91.   Cf. Jennifer S. Hawkins and Ezekiel J. Emanuel, "Clarifying Confusions about Coercion," *Hastings Center Report* 35 (September–October 2005): 16–19.

92.   See James H. Jones, *Bad Blood,* rev. ed. (New York: Free Press, 1993); David J. Rothman, "Were Tuskegee & Willowbrook 'Studies in Nature'?" *Hastings Center Report* 12 (April 1982): 5–7; Susan M. Reverby, ed., *Tuskegee's Truths: Rethinking the Tuskegee Syphilis Study* (Chapel Hill, NC: University of North Carolina Press, 2000); Reverby, *Examining Tuskegee: The Infamous Syphilis Study and Its Legacy* (Chapel Hill, NC: University of North Carolina Press, 2009); and Ralph V. Katz and Rueben Warren, eds., *The Search for the Legacy of the USPHS Syphilis Study at Tuskegee: Reflective Essays Based upon Findings from the Tuskegee Legacy Project* (Lanham, MD: Lexington Books, 2011).

93.   See Sarah E. Hewlett, "Is Consent to Participate in Research Voluntary," *Arthritis Care and Research* 9 (1996): 400–4; Virginia Miller et al., "Challenges in Measuring a New Construct: Perception of Voluntariness for Research and Treatment Decision Making," *Journal of Empirical Research on Human Research Ethics* 4 (2009): 21–31; and Nancy E. Kass et al., "Trust: The Fragile Foundation of Contemporary Biomedical Research," *Hastings Center Report* 25 (September–October 1996): 25–29.

94.   See Charles W. Lidz et al., *Informed Consent: A Study of Decision Making in Psychiatry* (New York: Guilford, 1984), chap. 7, esp. pp. 110–11, 117–23.

95.   Although the U.S. federal regulations for research involving human subjects require additional "safeguards" to protect groups—prisoners, children, pregnant women, mentally disabled persons, and

persons who are economically or educationally disadvantaged—all of whom are deemed "likely to be vulnerable to coercion or undue influence," the key concepts are inadequately analyzed and the list of groups is controversial. For examinations of possible types of vulnerability in research involving human subjects, see Kenneth Kipnis, "Vulnerability in Research Subjects: A Bioethical Taxonomy," in National Bioethics Advisory Commission, *Ethical and Policy Issues in Research Involving Human Participants,* vol. 2 (Bethesda, MD: National Bioethics Advisory Commission, 2001): G1–13; and James DuBois, "Vulnerability in Research," in *Institutional Review Board: Management and Function,* 2nd ed., ed. Robert Amdur and Elizabeth Bankert (Boston: Jones & Bartlett, 2005), pp. 337–40.

96.   For the distinction between decisional autonomy and executional autonomy, see Bart J. Collopy, "Autonomy in Long Term Care," *Gerontologist* 28, Supplementary Issue (June 1988): 10–17. On failures to appreciate both capacity and incapacity, see C. Dennis Barton et al., "Clinicians' Judgement of Capacity of Nursing Home Patients to Give Informed Consent," *Psychiatric Services* 47 (1996): 956–60; and Meghan B. Gerety et al., "Medical Treatment Preferences of Nursing Home Residents," *Journal of the American Geriatrics Society* 41 (1993): 953–60.

5

Nonmaleficence

The principle of nonmaleficence obligates us to abstain from causing harm to others. In medical ethics this principle has been treated as effectively identical to the celebrated maxim *Primum non nocere:* "Above all [or first] do no harm." Often proclaimed as the fundamental principle in the Hippocratic tradition, this principle does not appear in the Hippocratic corpus, and a venerable statement sometimes confused with it—"at least, do no harm"—is a strained translation of a single Hippocratic passage.[1] Nonetheless, the Hippocratic oath incorporates both an obligation of nonmaleficence and an obligation of beneficence: "I will use treatment to help the sick according to my ability and judgment, but I will never use it to injure or wrong them."

This chapter explores the principle of nonmaleficence and its implications for several areas of biomedical ethics where harms may occur. We examine distinctions between killing and allowing to die, intending and foreseeing harmful outcomes, withholding and withdrawing life-sustaining treatments, and extraordinary and ordinary treatments. The terminally ill and the seriously ill and injured are featured in many of these discussions. The framework for decision making about life-sustaining procedures and assistance in dying that we defend would alter current medical practice for both competent and incompetent patients. Central to this framework is a commitment to, rather than suppression of, quality-of-life judgments. In this chapter we also show several implications of the principle of nonmaleficence by addressing moral problems of risk of harm to children; the underprotection and the overprotection of subjects of research through public and institutional policies; harms that result from unduly broad forms of consent; and the protection of incompetent patients through advance directives and surrogate decision makers.

The Concept of Nonmaleficence and the Principle of Nonmaleficence

The Distinction between Nonmaleficence and Beneficence

Many types of ethical theory recognize a principle of nonmaleficence.[2] Some philosophers combine nonmaleficence with beneficence to form a single principle. William Frankena, for example, divides the principle of beneficence into four general obligations, the first of which we identify as the principle and obligation of nonmaleficence and the other three of which we refer to as principles and obligations of beneficence:

1. One ought not to inflict evil or harm.
2. One ought to prevent evil or harm.
3. One ought to remove evil or harm.
4. One ought to do or promote good.[3]

If we were to bring these ideas of benefiting others and not injuring them under a single principle, we would be forced to note, as did Frankena, the several distinct obligations embedded in this general principle. In our view, conflating nonmaleficence and beneficence into a single principle obscures critical moral distinctions as well as different types of moral theory. Obligations to not harm others, such as those prohibiting theft, disablement, and killing, are distinct from obligations to help others, such as those prescribing the provision of benefits, protection of interests, and promotion of welfare.

Obligations not to harm others are sometimes more stringent than obligations to help them, but the reverse is also true. If in a particular case a health care provider inflicts a very minor injury—swelling from a needlestick, say—but simultaneously provides a major benefit such as a lifesaving intervention, then we consider the obligation of beneficence to take priority over the obligation of nonmaleficence.[4] The point is that causing some risks of surgical harm, introducing social costs to protect the public health, and placing burdens on some research subjects can all be justified by the benefits in some cases.

One might try to reformulate the idea of nonmaleficence's increased stringency as follows: Obligations of nonmaleficence are usually more stringent than obligations of beneficence, and nonmaleficence may override beneficence, even if the best utilitarian outcome would be obtained by acting beneficently. If a surgeon, for example, could save two innocent lives by killing a prisoner on death row to retrieve his heart and liver for transplantation, this outcome would have the highest net utility under the circumstances, but the surgeon's action would be morally indefensible. This formulation of stringency with respect to nonmaleficence may have an initial ring of plausibility, but we should be cautious about constructing axioms regarding priority. Nonmaleficence typically does override other principles, but the weights of these moral principles vary in different circumstances. In our view, no rule in ethics favors avoiding harm over providing benefit in every circumstance. The claim that an order of priority exists among elements 1 through 4 in Frankena's scheme is unsustainable.

Rather than attempting to structure a hierarchical ordering, we group the principles of nonmaleficence and beneficence into four norms that do not have an a priori rank order:

Nonmaleficence
   1. One ought not to inflict evil or harm.

Beneficence
   2. One ought to prevent evil or harm.
   3. One ought to remove evil or harm.
   4. One ought to do or promote good.

Each of the three principles of beneficence requires taking action by *helping*—preventing harm, removing harm, and promoting good—whereas nonmaleficence requires only *intentional avoidance* of actions that cause harm. Rules of nonmaleficence therefore take the form "Do not do X." Some philosophers accept only principles or rules that take this proscriptive form. They even limit rules of respect for autonomy to rules of the form "Do not interfere with a person's autonomous choices." These philosophers reject all principles or rules that require helping, assisting, or rescuing other persons, although they recognize these norms as legitimate *moral ideals.* Mainstream moral philosophy, however, does not accept this *sharp* distinction between obligations of refraining from harming and obligations of helping. Instead, it recognizes and preserves the relevant distinctions in other ways. We take this same path, and in Chapter 6 we explain further the nature of the distinction.

Legitimate disagreements arise about how to classify actions under categories 1 through 4, as well as about the nature and stringency of the obligations that arise from them. Consider the following case: Robert McFall was dying of aplastic anemia, and his physicians recommended a bone marrow transplant from a genetically compatible donor to increase his chances of living one additional year from 25% to a range of 40% to 60%. The patient's cousin, David Shimp, agreed to undergo tests to determine his suitability as a donor. After completing the test for tissue compatibility, he refused to undergo the test for genetic compatibility. He had changed his mind about donation. Robert McFall's lawyer asked a court to compel Shimp to undergo the second test and donate his bone marrow if the test indicated a good match.[5]

Public discussion focused on whether Shimp had an obligation of beneficence toward McFall in the form of an obligation to prevent harm, to remove harm, or to promote McFall's welfare. Though ultimately unsuccessful, McFall's lawyer contended that even if Shimp did not have a legal obligation of benef-icence to rescue his cousin, he did have a legal obligation of nonmaleficence, which required that he not make McFall's situation worse. The lawyer argued that when Shimp agreed to undergo the first test and then backed out, he caused a "delay of critical proportions" that constituted a violation of the obligation of nonmaleficence. The judge ruled that Shimp did not violate any legal obligation but also held that his actions were "morally indefensible."[6]

This case illustrates difficulties of identifying specific obligations under the principles of beneficence and nonmaleficence. Again we see the importance of *specifying* these principles to handle circumstances such as those of donating organs or tissues, withholding life-sustaining treatments, hastening the death of a dying patient, and biomedical research involving both human and animal subjects.

The Concept of Harm

The concept of nonmaleficence has been explicated by the concepts of *harm* and *injury,* but we will confine our analysis to harm. This term has both a normative and a nonnormative use. "X harmed Y" sometimes means that X wronged Y or treated Y unjustly, but it sometimes only means that X's action had an adverse effect on Y's interests. As we use these notions, *wronging* involves violating someone's rights, but *harming* need not signify such a violation. People are harmed without being wronged through attacks by disease, natural disasters, bad luck, and acts of others to which the harmed person has consented.[7] People can also be wronged without being harmed. For example, if an insurance company improperly refuses to pay a patient's hospital bill and the hospital shoulders the full bill, the insurance company wronged the patient without harming him or her.

We construe harm in the second sense: A harm is a thwarting, defeating, or setting back of some party's interests, but a harmful action is not always a wrong or unjustified. Harmful actions that involve justifiable setbacks to anoth-er's interests are not wrong—for example, justified amputation of a patient's leg, justified punishment of physicians for incompetence or negligence, justified demotion of an employee for poor performance in a job, and some forms of research involving animals. Nevertheless, the principle of nonmaleficence is a prima facie principle that requires the justification of harmful actions. This justi-fication may come from showing that the harmful actions do not infringe specific obligations of nonmaleficence or that the infringements are outweighed by other ethical principles and rules.

Some definitions of harm are so broad that they include setbacks to inter-ests in reputation, property, privacy, and liberty or, in some writings, discom-fort, humiliation, offense, and annoyance. Such broad conceptions can still distinguish trivial harms from serious harms by the magnitude of the interests affected. Other accounts with a narrower focus view harms exclusively as setbacks to physical and psychological interests, such as those in health and survival.

Whether a broad or a narrow construal is preferable is not a matter we need to decide here. Although harm is a contested concept, significant bodily harms and setbacks to other significant interests are paradigm instances of harm. We concentrate on physical harms, especially pain, disability, suffering, and death, while still affirming the importance of mental harms and other setbacks to interests. In particular, we concentrate on intending, causing, and permitting death or the risk of death.

Rules Specifying the Principle of Nonmaleficence

The principle of nonmaleficence supports several more specific moral rules (although principles other than nonmaleficence help justify some of these rules).[8] Examples of more specific rules include the following:[9]

1. Do not kill.
2. Do not cause pain or suffering.
3. Do not incapacitate.
4. Do not cause offense.
5. Do not deprive others of the goods of life.

Both the principle of nonmaleficence and its specifications in these moral rules are prima facie, not absolute.

Negligence and the Standard of Due Care

Obligations of nonmaleficence include not only obligations not to inflict harms, but also obligations not to impose *risks* of harm. A person can harm or place another person at risk without malicious or harmful intent, and the agent of harm may or may not be morally or legally responsible for the harms. In some cases agents are causally responsible for a harm that they did not intend or know about. For example, if cancer rates are elevated at a chemical plant as the result of exposure to a chemical not previously suspected as a carcinogen, the employer has placed its workers at risk by its actions or decisions, even though the employer did not intentionally or knowingly cause the harm.

In cases of risk imposition, both law and morality recognize a standard of due care that determines whether the agent who is causally responsible for the risk is legally or morally responsible as well. This standard is a specification of the principle of nonmaleficence. Due care is taking appropriate care to avoid causing harm, as the circumstances demand of a reasonable and prudent person. This standard requires that the goals pursued justify the risks that must be imposed to achieve those goals. Grave risks require commensurately momentous goals for their justification. Serious emergencies justify risks that many nonemergency situations do not justify. For example, attempting to save lives after a major accident justifies, within limits, the dangers created by rapidly moving emergency vehicles. A person who takes due care in this context does not violate moral or legal rules, even in imposing significant risk on other parties.

Negligence is the absence of due care. In the professions negligence involves a departure from the professional standards that determine due care in given circumstances. The term *negligence* covers two types of situations: (1) intentionally imposing unreasonable risks of harm (advertent negligence or recklessness) and (2) unintentionally but carelessly imposing risks of harm (inadvertent negligence). In the first type, an agent knowingly imposes an unwarranted risk: For example, a nurse knowingly fails to change a bandage as scheduled, creating an increased risk of infection. In the second type, an agent unknowingly performs a harmful act that he or she should have known to avoid: For example, a physician acts negligently if he or she forgets that a patient does not want to receive certain types of information and discloses that information, causing fear and shame in the patient. Both types of negligence are morally blameworthy, although some conditions may mitigate the blameworthiness.[10]

In treating negligence, we will concentrate on conduct that falls below a standard of due care that law or morality establishes to protect others from the careless imposition of risks. Courts must determine responsibility and liability for harm, because a patient, client, or consumer seeks compensation for setbacks to interests or punishment of a responsible party, or both. We will not concentrate on legal liability, but the legal model of responsibility for harmful action presents a framework that we will adapt to express moral responsibility for harm caused by health care professionals. The following are essential elements in a professional model of the failure of due care:

1. The professional must have a duty to the affected party.
2. The professional must breach that duty.
3. The affected party must experience a harm.
4. The harm must be caused by the breach of duty.

Professional malpractice is an instance of negligence that involves failure to follow professional standards of care.[11] By entering into the profession of medicine, physicians accept a responsibility to observe the standards specific to their profession. If their conduct falls below these standards, they act negligently. However, even if the therapeutic relationship proves harmful or unhelpful, malpractice occurs if and only if physicians do not meet professional standards of care. For example, in *Adkins v. Ropp* the Supreme Court of Indiana considered a patient's claim that a physician acted negligently in removing foreign matter from the patient's eye:

When a physician and surgeon assumes to treat and care for a patient, in the absence of a special agreement, he is held in law to have impliedly contracted that he possesses the reasonable and ordinary qualifications of his profession and that he will exercise at least reasonable skill, care and diligence in his treatment of him. This implied contract on the part of the physician does not include a promise to effect a cure and negligence cannot be imputed because a cure is not effected, but he does impliedly promise that he will use due diligence and ordinary skill in his treatment of the patient so that a cure may follow such care and skill. This degree of care and skill is required of him, not only in performing an operation or administering first treatments, but he is held to the same degree of care and skill in the necessary subsequent treatments unless he is excused from further service by the patient himself, or the physician or surgeon upon due notice refuses to further treat the case.[12]

The line between due care and inadequate care is often difficult to draw. Increased safety measures in epidemiological and toxicological studies, educational and health promotional programs, and other training programs can sometimes reduce health risks. A substantial question, however, remains about the lengths to which physicians, employers, and others must go to avoid or to lower risks—a problem in determining the scope of obligations of nonmaleficence.

Whose Risk and Whose Benefit?: Problems of the Underprotection and Overprotection of Research Subjects

We have thus far concentrated on harm in clinical care, but we now turn to ethical issues of harm in research.

Historical problems of underprotection. Historically, the risks of harm to human subjects in medical research have often been placed heavily on the economically disadvantaged, the very sick, and the vulnerable, owing to their ready availability. The unjustified overutilization of members of these populations has long been a matter of deep moral concern. Even though there is general agreement that we need a system of research ethics with enough internal controls to protect subjects from utilitarian exploitation, disagreement surrounds questions about the conditions under which protections are needed and how best to ensure those protections. For over four decades the predominant concern has been that we underprotect human subjects, especially vulnerable groups such as children, the mentally handicapped, and the institutionalized. Although much has been made of the harms caused by the underprotection of research subjects (see our discussions in Chapters 3 and 7), relatively little has been said about harms caused by the overprotection of subjects. Such overprotection can create serious delays in the progress of research, thereby causing harm to those who do not receive the medical benefits of the research in a timely fashion. We emphasize the latter in the following section.

Recent problems of overprotection. An eye-opening case of such problems involves allegedly inappropriate human-subjects research on catheter-related bloodstream infections, which cause thousands of deaths each year in intensive care units (ICUs).[13] Dr. Peter Pronovost of the Johns Hopkins University was working with 103 ICUs in 67 Michigan hospitals to implement and evaluate what had been established at Johns Hopkins and other ICUs to be a successful infection-control measure. The work was halted by federal regulators in the Office for Human Research Protections (OHRP) on grounds that Pronovost and the hospitals were using patients in human-subjects research without informed consent. Pronovost's activities were part of a study to improve medical care sponsored by the Michigan Hospital Association. The aim was to control infections in ICUs by strictly implementing preventive procedures that had already been recommended by the Centers for Disease Control and Prevention, such as washing hands, using certain infection control precautions, and the like. The team studied the effect on infection rates of a careful implementation in practice of all the recommended procedures, following a checklist. They found that infection rates fall substantially if the checklist is scrupulously followed.

A published report of the study led to a complaint to the OHRP that the research violated U.S. regulations. After investigating, the OHRP demanded that Johns Hopkins and Michigan hospitals correct this mistake and undertake a full ethics review of the study. The Johns Hopkins institutional review board (IRB) had already examined the project and found that full IRB review and informed consent were *not* required for such a study. This IRB had a different understanding of federal regulations and research ethics than did the OHRP—a result most likely explained by regulatory statements that are vague and unspecific. One problem is the lack of clarity surrounding the concept of "research involving human subjects." If an IRB has one interpretation and a regulatory office another, both research and advances in practice can be held up and might even lead to disastrous federal penalties if the wrong judgment is made.

In the Pronovost case the activities involved no new interventions and posed no risk for patients. Research was fully integrated with practice, and physicians were following the safest practices known to exist—without introducing new research activities. OHRP officials made the judgment that because infection rates were being studied in *patients,* the work called for full committee review and for the informed consent of *subjects.* But this research was by its design an attempt to improve medical care. The invocation of regulations intended to protect research subjects caused a delay in the use of effective preventive measures in hospitals, which could have caused multiple patient deaths and could have eventuated in unjustified penalties to the medical research institutions and hospitals involved.

Eventually the OHRP issued a statement that in effect admitted that it had been wrong. It acknowledged that the work was "being used...solely for clinical purposes, not medical research or experimentation." The OHRP further acknowledged that the activity, from the start, "would likely have been eligible for both expedited IRB review and a waiver of the informed consent requirement."[14] While laudable, this acknowledgment of error is puzzling. Pronovost's work was an empirical study and therefore research. Perhaps the OHRP means that the study is research, though not "research involving human subjects." This estimate is probably correct, but it also indicates that the notion of research involving human subjects is systematically unclear and can lead to overprotection, as in this case, and cause harm.

Government regulations always need some form of interpretation, but we should not tolerate a system in which lives might be lost because of an obsolete conception of human-subjects research that presents obstructions to riskless studies aimed at improving medical practice. When such work is unduly retarded through requirements of regulation and review, the requirements should be adjusted. In the case of Pronovost's research, the system of oversight worked more to present risks to current and future patients than to protect them.

Distinctions and Rules Governing Nontreatment

Religious traditions, philosophical discourse, professional codes, public policy, and law have developed many guidelines to specify the requirements of nonmaleficence in health care, particularly with regard to treatment and nontreatment decisions. Some of these guidelines are helpful, but others need revision or replacement. Many draw heavily on at least one of the following distinctions:

1. *Withholding* and *withdrawing* life-sustaining treatment
2. *Extraordinary* (or heroic) and *ordinary* treatment
3. *Sustenance technologies* and *medical treatments*
4. *Intended* effects and *merely foreseen* effects

Although at times influential in medicine and law, these distinctions, we will argue, are outmoded and need to be replaced. The venerable position that these traditional distinctions have occupied in professional codes, institutional policies, and writings in biomedical ethics by itself provides no warrant for retaining them, and some of these distinctions are now morally dangerous.

Withholding and Withdrawing Treatments

Debate about the principle of nonmaleficence and forgoing life-sustaining treatments has centered on the omission–commission distinction, especially the distinction between withholding (not starting) and withdrawing (stopping) treatments. Many professionals and family members feel justified in withholding treatments they never started, but not in withdrawing treatments already initiated. They sense that decisions to stop treatments are more momentous and consequential than decisions not to start them. Stopping a respirator, for example, seems to many to cause a person's death, whereas not starting the respirator does not seem to have this same causal role.[15]

In one case, an elderly man suffered from several major medical problems with no reasonable chance of recovery. He was comatose and unable to communicate. Antibiotics to fight infection and an intravenous (IV) line to provide nutrition and hydration kept him alive. No evidence indicated that he had expressed his wishes about life-sustaining treatments while competent, and he had no family member to serve as a surrogate decision maker. The staff quickly agreed on a "no code" or "do not resuscitate" (DNR) order, a signed order not to attempt cardiopulmonary resuscitation if a cardiac or respiratory arrest occurred. In the event of such an arrest, the physicians would allow the patient to die. The staff felt comfortable with this decision because of the patient's overall condition and prognosis, and because they could view not resuscitating the patient as withholding rather than withdrawing treatment.

Questions arose about whether to continue the interventions in place. Some members of the health care team thought that they should stop all medical treatments, including antibiotics and artificial nutrition and hydration, because they were "extraordinary" or "heroic" measures. Others thought it wrong to stop these treatments once they had been started. A disagreement erupted about whether it would be permissible not to insert the IV line again if it became infiltrated—that is, if it broke through the blood vessel and began leaking fluid into surrounding tissue. Some who had opposed stopping treatments were comfortable with not inserting the IV line again, because they viewed the action as withholding rather than withdrawing. They emphatically opposed reinsertion if it required a cutdown (an incision to gain access to the deep large blood vessels) or a central line. Others viewed the provision of artificial nutrition and hydration as a single process and felt that inserting the IV line again was simply continuing what had been interrupted. For them, not restarting was equivalent to withdrawing and thus, unlike withholding, morally wrong.[16]

In many similar cases caregivers' discomfort about withdrawing life-sustaining treatments appears to reflect the view that such actions render them causally responsible and culpable for a patient's death, whereas they are not responsible if they never initiate a life-sustaining treatment. The conviction that starting a treatment often creates valid claims or expectations for its continuation frequently serves as another source of caregiver discomfort. Only if patients waive the claim for continued treatment does it seem legitimate to many caregivers to stop procedures. Otherwise, stopping procedures appears to breach expectations, promises, or contractual obligations to the patient, family, or surrogate decision maker. Patients for whom physicians have not initiated treatment seem to hold no parallel claim.[17]

Feelings of reluctance about withdrawing treatments are understandable, but the distinction between withdrawing and withholding treatments is morally irrelevant and potentially dangerous. The distinction is unclear, inasmuch as withdrawing can happen through an omission (withholding) such as not recharging batteries that power respirators or not putting the infusion into a feeding tube. In multistaged treatments, decisions not to start the next stage of a treatment plan can be tantamount to stopping treatment, even if the early phases of the treatment continue.

Both not starting and stopping can be justified, depending on the circumstances. Both can be instances of allowing to die, and both can be instances of killing. Courts recognize that individuals can commit a crime by omission if they have an obligation to act, just as physicians can commit a wrong by omission in medical practice. Such a judgment depends on whether a physician has an obligation either not to withhold or not to withdraw treatment. In these cases if a physician has a duty to treat, omission of treatment breaches this duty, whether or not withholding or withdrawing is involved. However, if a physician does not have a duty to treat or has a duty not to treat, omission of either type involves no moral violation. Indeed, if the physician has a duty not to treat, it would be a moral violation not to withdraw the treatment if it has already begun.

In the classic case of Earle Spring, a court raised a legal problem about continuing kidney dialysis as follows: "The question presented by...modern technology is, once undertaken, at what point does it cease to perform its intended function?" The court held that "a physician has no duty to continue treatment, once it has proven to be ineffective." The court emphasized the need to balance benefits and burdens to determine overall effectiveness.[18] Although legal responsibility cannot be equated with moral responsibility in such cases, the court's conclusion is consistent with the moral conclusions about justified withdrawal for which we are presently arguing. Approximately one in four deaths of patients with end-stage renal disease occurs after decisions to withdraw dialysis.[19] The practice is common, and the decisions are often justified.

Giving priority to withholding over withdrawing treatment can lead to *overtreatment* in some cases, that is, the continuation of no longer beneficial or desirable treatment for the patient. Less obviously, the distinction can lead to *undertreatment*. Patients and families worry about being trapped by biomedical technology that, once begun, cannot be stopped. To circumvent this problem, they become reluctant to authorize the technology, even when it could possibly benefit the patient. Health care professionals often exhibit the same reluctance. In one case, a seriously ill newborn died after several months of treatment, much of it against the parents' wishes, because a physician was unwilling to stop the respirator once it had been connected. Later this physician reportedly felt "less eager to attach babies to respirators now."[20]

The moral burden of proof often is heavier when the decision is to withhold rather than to withdraw treatments. Only after starting treatments will it be possible, in many cases, to make a proper diagnosis and prognosis as well as to balance prospective benefits and burdens. This trial period can reduce uncertainty about outcomes. Patients and surrogates often feel less stress and more in control if they can reverse or otherwise change a decision to treat after the treatment has started. Accordingly, responsible health care may propose a trial with periodic reevaluation. Caregivers then have time to judge the effectiveness of the treatment, and the patient or surrogate has time to evaluate its benefits and burdens. Not to propose or allow the trial is morally worse than not trying. Hence, withholding may be worse than withdrawing in such cases.

The withholding–withdrawing distinction has shaped an intense debate about cardiovascular implantable electronic devices (CIEDs), which include pacemakers and implantable cardioverter-defibrillators (ICDs). These devices are increasingly common and often helpful and necessary. While clinicians have generally been comfortable in not implanting these devices when patients or their surrogates do not want them, they have often been uncomfortable discontinuing them, particularly pacemakers, even though each one can be stopped noninvasively, without surgery. Horror stories abound. In one case, a woman described the struggle to have her elderly, severely demented, significantly incapacitated father's battery-powered pacemaker turned off. The pacemaker had been inserted because, without it, a cardiologist would not clear her father for surgery to correct a painful intestinal hernia; the family later realized that a temporary version would have sufficed. When her father's health problems worsened, and her mother requested deactivation of the pacemaker, the physician refused because "it would have been like putting a pillow over [his] head."[21]

Many physicians, over 60% in one study,[22] see an ethical distinction between deactivating a pacemaker and deactivating an ICD. For many, deactivation of pacemakers is similar to active euthanasia. The problem seems to be that pacemakers provide continuous rather than intermittent treatment and their removal may lead to immediate death, thereby increasing the professional's sense of causal and moral responsibility.[23] A major consensus statement in 2010, involving several professional groups, rightly dismissed any ethical and legal distinctions among CIEDs, viewing all of them as life-sustaining treatments that patients and their surrogates may legitimately request to be withdrawn in order to allow the underlying disease to take its course.[24] The consensus statement recognized clinicians' rights not to participate in the withdrawal while, at the same time, emphasizing their responsibility to refer patients to clinicians or others who would deactivate the devices. As it happens, industry representatives deactivate the pacemaker about half the time and the ICD about 60% of the time.[25]

We conclude that the distinction between withholding and withdrawing is morally untenable and can be morally dangerous. If a caregiver makes decisions about treatment using this irrelevant distinction, or allows a surrogate (without efforts at dissuasion) to make such a decision, the caregiver is morally blameworthy for negative outcomes. The felt importance of the distinction between not starting and stopping procedures undoubtedly accounts for, but does not justify, the speed and ease with which hospitals and health care professionals accepted no code or DNR orders and formed hospital policies regarding cardiopulmonary resuscitation (CPR). Policies regarding CPR often stand independent of other policies regarding life-sustaining technologies, such as respirators, in part because many health care professionals view not providing CPR as withholding rather than withdrawing treatment. Their decisions are especially problematic when made without advance consultation with patients or their families.[26]

Ordinary and Extraordinary Treatments

The distinction between ordinary and extraordinary treatments was once widely invoked both to justify and to condemn decisions to use or to forgo life-sustaining treatments. The rule was that extraordinary treatments can legitimately be forgone, whereas ordinary treatments cannot legitimately be forgone. The distinction has a prominent history in medical practice, judicial decisions, and Roman Catholic casuistry. It has also been used to determine whether an act that results in death counts as killing. As developed by Roman Catholic theologians to deal with problems of surgery (prior to the development of antisepsis and anesthesia), this distinction was used to determine whether a patient's refusal of treatment should be classified as suicide.[27] Refusal of ordinary means of life-sustaining treatment was long considered suicide, but refusal of extraordinary means was not. Likewise, families and physicians did not commit homicide if they withheld or withdrew extraordinary means of treatment from patients.

Unfortunately, neither a long history nor precedent guarantees clarity or adequacy. The distinction between ordinary and extraordinary means of treatment is unacceptably vague and morally misleading. Throughout its history, the distinction has acquired a confusing array of meanings and functions. Interpreters have often taken *ordinary* to mean "usual" or "customary" and *extraordinary* to mean "unusual" or "uncustomary"—under either the professional practice standard discussed in Chapter 4 or the due care standard discussed earlier in this chapter. According to this interpretation, treatments are extraordinary if they are unusual or uncustomary for physicians to use in the relevant contexts. Over time, the terms thus became attached to particular technologies and alterable standards of practice.

Criteria other than usual and unusual medical practice have also been proposed for classifying procedures as extraordinary. These criteria include whether the treatment is simple or complex, natural or artificial, noninvasive or highly invasive, inexpensive or expensive, and routine or heroic. These substitutions, classifications, or distinctions have rarely been analyzed with care and offer no improvement over *usual* and *unusual*. A treatment that is simple, natural, noninvasive, inexpensive, or routine is more likely to be viewed as ordinary (and thus obligatory) than a treatment that is complex, artificial, invasive, expensive, or heroic (and thus optional). However, these various criteria are relevant only if some deeper moral considerations make them relevant.

More consequential than these conceptual problems is whether such distinctions give sound moral guidance for treatment and nontreatment decisions. The principal consideration should always be whether a treatment is beneficial or burdensome.[28] All of these distinctions are irrelevant except insofar as they point to a quality-of-life criterion that requires balancing benefits against burdens. We conclude that the distinction between ordinary and extraordinary treatment is morally irrelevant. The distinction between optional and obligatory treatment, as determined by the balance of benefits and burdens to the patient, is the pertinent distinction.

Sustenance Technologies and Medical Treatments

Widespread debate has occurred about whether health care institutions can legitimately use the distinction between *medical* technologies and *sustenance* technologies to distinguish between justified and unjustified forgoing of life-sustaining treatments. Some argue that technologies for dispensing sustenance—namely, those that supply nutrition and hydration using needles, tubes, catheters, and the like—are *nonmedical* means of maintaining life that are unlike optional forms of medical life-sustaining technologies, such as respirators and dialysis machines.

To help determine whether this distinction is more acceptable than the previous distinctions, we examine some cases, beginning with the case of a seventy-nine-year-old widow who had resided in a nursing home for several years, frequently visited by her daughter and grandchildren, who loved her deeply. In the past she experienced repeated transient ischemic attacks caused by reductions or stoppages of blood flow to the brain. Because of progressive organic brain syndrome, she had lost most of her mental abilities and had become disoriented. She also had thrombophlebitis (inflammation of a vein associated with clotting) and congestive heart failure. One day she suffered a massive stroke. She made no recovery, remained nonverbal, manifested a withdrawal reaction to painful stimuli, and exhibited a limited range of purposeful behaviors. She strongly resisted a nasogastric tube being placed into her stomach to introduce nutritional formulas and water. At each attempt she thrashed about violently and pushed the tube away. When the tube was finally placed, she managed to remove it. After several days the staff could not find new sites for inserting IV lines, and debated whether to take further "extraordinary" measures to maintain fluid and nutritional intake for this elderly patient, who did not improve and was largely unaware and unresponsive. After lengthy discussions with nurses on the floor and with the patient's family, the physicians in charge concluded that they should not provide further IVs, cutdowns, or a feeding tube. The patient had minimal oral intake and died quietly the following week.[29]

Second, in a groundbreaking case in 1976, the New Jersey Supreme Court ruled it permissible for a guardian to disconnect Karen Ann Quinlan's respirator and allow her to die.[30] After the respirator was removed, Quinlan lived for almost ten years, protected by antibiotics and sustained by nutrition and hydration provided through a nasogastric tube. Unable to communicate, she lay comatose in a fetal position, with increasing respiratory problems, bedsores, and weight loss from 115 to 70 pounds. A moral issue developed over those ten years. If it is permissible to remove the respirator, is it permissible to remove the feeding tube? Several Roman Catholic moral theologians advised the parents that they were not morally required to continue medically administered nutrition and hydration (MN&H) or antibiotics to fight infections. Nevertheless, the Quinlans continued MN&H because they believed that the feeding tube did not cause pain, whereas the respirator did.

U.S. courts have since generally placed MN&H under the same substantive and procedural standards as other medical treatments such as the respirator.[31] In the famous Terri Schiavo case, the husband and parents of a woman who was in a persistent vegetative state (PVS) were in conflict over whether it was justifiable to withdraw her feeding tube. Despite legal challenges and ferocious political conflicts, the court applying Florida's laws allowed the husband, expressing what he represented as Terri Schiavo's wishes, to withdraw MN&H to allow her to die, approximately fifteen years after she entered the PVS.[32]

In our judgment, caregivers may justifiably forego MN&H for patients in some circumstances, as holds true for other life-sustaining technologies. No morally relevant difference exists between the various life-sustaining technologies, and the right to refuse medical treatment for oneself or others is not contingent on the type of treatment. There is no reason to believe that MN&H is always an essential part of palliative care or that it necessarily constitutes a beneficial medical treatment.

Intended Effects and Merely Foreseen Effects

Another venerable attempt to specify the principle of nonmaleficence appears in the rule of double effect (RDE), often called the principle or doctrine of double effect. This rule incorporates an influential distinction between intended effects and merely foreseen effects.

Functions and conditions of the RDE. The RDE is invoked to justify claims that a single act, which has one good effect and one harmful effect (such as death), is not always morally prohibited.[33] As an example of the use of the RDE, consider a patient experiencing terrible pain and suffering who asks a physician for help in ending his life. If the physician injects the patient with a chemical to end the patient's pain and suffering, he or she intentionally causes the patient's death as a means to end pain and suffering. The physician's action is wrong because it involves the intention to cause the patient's death. In contrast, suppose the physician could provide medication to relieve the patient's pain and suffering at a substantial risk that the patient would die as a result of the medication. If the physician refuses to administer the medication, the patient will endure continuing pain and suffering; if the physician provides the medication, it may hasten the patient's death. If the physician intended, through the provision of medication, to relieve grave pain and suffering and did not intend to cause death, then the act of indirectly hastening death is not wrong, according to the RDE.

Classical formulations of the RDE identify four conditions or elements that must be satisfied for an act with a double effect to be justified. Each is a necessary condition, and together they form sufficient conditions of morally permissible action:[34]

1. *The nature of the act.* The act must be good, or at least morally neutral, independent of its consequences.
2. *The agent's intention.* The agent intends only the good effect, not the bad effect. The bad effect can be foreseen, tolerated, and permitted, but it must not be intended.
3. *The distinction between means and effects.* The bad effect must not be a means to the good effect. If the good effect were the causal result of the bad effect, the agent would intend the bad effect in pursuit of the good effect.
4. *Proportionality between the good effect and the bad effect.* The good effect must outweigh the bad effect. That is, the bad effect is permissible only if a proportionate reason compensates for permitting the foreseen bad effect.

All four conditions are controversial. We begin to investigate the cogency of the RDE by considering four cases of what many call therapeutic abortion (limited to protecting maternal life in these examples): (1) A pregnant woman has cervical cancer; she needs a hysterectomy to save her life, but this procedure will result in the death of the fetus. (2) A pregnant woman has an ectopic pregnancy—the nonviable fetus is in the fallopian tube—and physicians must remove the tube to prevent hemorrhage, which will result in the death of the fetus. (3) A pregnant woman has a serious heart disease that probably will result in her death if she attempts to carry the pregnancy to term. (4) A pregnant woman in difficult labor will die unless the physician performs a craniotomy (crushing the head of the unborn fetus). Some interpretations of Roman Catholic teachings hold that the actions that produce fetal death in the first two cases sometimes satisfy the four conditions of the RDE and therefore can be morally acceptable, whereas the actions that produce fetal death in the latter two cases never meet the conditions of the RDE and therefore are always morally unacceptable.[35]

In the first two cases, according to proponents of the RDE, a physician undertakes a legitimate medical procedure aimed at saving the pregnant woman's life with the foreseen but unintentional result of fetal death. When viewed as unintended side effects (rather than as ends or means), these fetal deaths are said to be justified by the proportionately grave reason of saving the pregnant woman's life. In both of the latter two cases, the action of terminating fetal life is a *means* to save the pregnant woman's life. As such, it requires intending the fetus's death even if the death is not desired. Therefore, in those cases, criteria 2 and 3 are violated and the act cannot be justified by proportionality (criterion 4).

However, it is not likely that a morally relevant difference can be established between cases such as a hysterectomy or a craniotomy in terms of the abstract conditions that comprise the RDE. In neither case does the agent want or desire the death of the fetus, and the descriptions of the acts in these cases do not indicate morally relevant differences between intending, on the one hand, and foreseeing but not intending, on the other. More specifically, it remains unclear why advocates of RDE conceptualize craniotomy as killing the fetus rather than as the act of crushing the skull of the fetus with the unintended result that the fetus dies. Similarly, it remains unclear why in the hysterectomy case the death of the fetus is foreseen but not intended. Proponents of the RDE must have a practicable way to distinguish the intended from the merely foreseen, but they face major difficulties in providing a theory of intention precise enough to draw defensible moral lines between the hysterectomy and craniotomy cases.

A problematic conception of intention. Adherents of the RDE need an account of intentional actions and intended effects of action to distinguish them from nonintentional actions and unintended effects. The literature on intentional action is itself controversial and focuses on diverse conditions such as volition, deliberation, willing, reasoning, and planning. One of the few widely shared views in this literature is that intentional actions require that an agent have a plan—a blueprint, map, or representation of the means and ends proposed for the execution of an action.[36] For an action to be intentional, it must correspond to the agent's plan for its performance.

Alvin Goldman uses the following example in an attempt to prove that agents do not intend merely foreseen effects.[37] Imagine that Mr. G takes a driver's test to prove competence. He comes to an intersection that requires a right turn and extends his arm to signal for a turn, although he knows it is raining and that he will get his hand wet. According to Goldman, Mr. G's signaling for a turn is an intentional act. By contrast, his getting a wet hand is an unintended effect or "incidental by-product" of his hand-signaling. A defender of the RDE must elect a similarly narrow conception of what is intended to avoid the conclusion that an agent intentionally brings about all the consequences of an action that the agent foresees. The defender distinguishes between acts and effects, and then between effects that are desired or wanted and effects that are foreseen but not desired or wanted. The RDE views the latter effects as foreseen, but not intended.

It is more suitable in these contexts to discard the language of "wanting" and to say that foreseen, undesired effects are "tolerated."[38] These effects are not so undesirable that the actor would avoid performing the act that results in them; the actor includes them as a part of his or her plan of intentional action. To account for this point, we use a model of intentionality based on what is *willed* rather than what is *wanted*. On this model intentional actions and intentional effects include any action and any effect specifically willed in accordance with a plan, including tolerated as well as wanted effects.[39] In this conception a physician can desire not to do what he intends to do, in the same way that one can be willing to do something but, at the same time, reluctant to do it or even detest doing it.

Under this conception of intentional acts and intended effects, the distinction between what agents intend and what they merely foresee in a planned action is not viable.[40] For example, if a man enters a room and flips a switch that he knows turns on both a light and a fan, but desires only to activate the light, he cannot say that he activates the fan unintentionally. Even if the fan made an obnoxious whirring sound that he is aware of and wants to avoid, it would be mistaken to say that he unintentionally brought about the obnoxious noise by flipping the switch. More generally, a person who knowingly and voluntarily acts to bring about an effect brings about that effect intentionally. The person intends the effect, but does not desire it, does not will it for its own sake, and does not intend it as the goal of the action.

Now we can reconsider the moral relevance of the RDE and its distinctions. Is it plausible to distinguish morally between intentionally causing the death of a fetus by craniotomy and intentionally removing a cancerous uterus that causes the death of a fetus? In both actions the intention is to save the woman's life with knowledge that the fetus will die. No agent in either scenario desires the negative result (the fetus's death) for its own sake, and none would have tolerated the negative result if its avoidance were morally preferable to the alternative outcome. All parties accept the bad effect only because they cannot eliminate it without sacrificing the good effect.

In the standard interpretation of the RDE, the fetus's death is a *means* to saving a woman's life in the unacceptable case, but merely a *side effect* in the acceptable case. That is, an agent intends a means, but does not intend a side effect. This approach seems to allow persons to foresee almost anything as a side effect rather than as an intended means. It does not follow, however, that people can create or direct intentions as they please. For example, in the craniotomy case, the surgeon might not intend the death of the fetus but only intend to remove it from the birth canal. The fetus will die, but is this outcome more than an unwanted and, in double effect theory, unintended consequence?[41]

The RDE might appear to fare better in care of dying patients, where there is no conflict between different parties. It is often invoked to justify a physician's administration of medication to relieve pain and suffering (the primary intention and effect) even though it will probably hasten the patient's death (the unintended, secondary effect). A related practice, terminal sedation, challenges the boundaries and use of the RDE. In terminal sedation, physicians induce a deep sleep or unconsciousness to relieve pain and suffering in the expectation that this state will continue until the patient dies. Some commentators contend that some cases of terminal sedation can be justified under the RDE, whereas others argue that terminal sedation directly, although slowly, kills the patient and thus is a form of euthanasia.[42] Much depends on the description of terminal sedation in a particular set of circumstances, including the patient's overall condition, the proximity of death, and the availability of alternative means to relieve pain and suffering, as well as the intention of the physician and other parties. Interpretations of the RDE to cover some cases of terminal sedation allow compassionate acts of relieving pain, suffering, and discomfort that will foreseeably hasten death.

Often in dispute is whether death is good or bad for a particular person, and nothing in the RDE settles this dispute. The RDE applies only in cases with both a bad and a good effect, but determining the goodness and badness of different effects is a separate judgment. Accordingly, the goodness or badness of death for a particular person, whether it occurs directly or indirectly, must be determined and defended on independent grounds.[43]

Defenders of the RDE eventually may solve the puzzles and problems that critics have identified, but they have not succeeded thus far. One constructive effort to retain an emphasis on intention without entirely abandoning the larger point of the RDE focuses on the way actions display a person's motives and character. In the case of performing a craniotomy to save a pregnant woman's life, a physician may not *want* or *desire* the death of the fetus and may regret performing a craniotomy just as much as he or she would in the case of removing a cancerous uterus. Such facts about the physician's motivation and character can make a decisive difference to a moral assessment of the action and the agent. But this moral conclusion also can be reached independently of the RDE.

OPTIONAL TREATMENTS AND OBLIGATORY TREATMENTS

We have now rejected several leading distinctions and rules about forgoing life-sustaining treatment and causing death that are accepted in some traditions of medical ethics. In their place we propose a basic distinction between obligatory and optional treatments. We will rely heavily on quality-of-life considerations that are generally incompatible with the distinctions and rules that we have already rejected. The following categories are central to our arguments:

  I. Obligatory to Treat (Wrong Not to Treat)
  II. Obligatory Not to Treat (Wrong to Treat)
  III. Optional Whether to Treat (Neither Required nor Prohibited)

Under III, the question is whether it is morally neutral and therefore optional to provide or not to provide a treatment.

The principles of nonmaleficence and beneficence have often been specified to establish a presumption in favor of providing life-sustaining treatments for sick and injured patients. This presumption does not entail that it is always obligatory to provide the treatments. The use of life-sustaining treatments occasionally violates patients' interests. For example, pain can be so severe and physical restraints so burdensome that these factors outweigh anticipated benefits, such as brief prolongation of life. Providing the treatment may then be inhumane or cruel. Even for an incompetent patient, the burdens can so outweigh the benefits that the treatment is wrong, not merely optional.

Conditions for Overriding the Prima Facie Obligation to Treat

Several conditions justify decisions by patients, surrogates, or health care professionals to withhold or withdraw treatment. We introduce these conditions (in addition to valid refusal of treatment) in this section.

Futile or pointless treatment. Physicians have no obligation to provide pointless, futile, or contraindicated treatment. In an extreme example, if a patient has died but remains on a respirator, cessation of treatment cannot harm him or her, and a physician has no obligation to continue to treat. However, some religious and personal belief systems do not consider a patient dead according to the same criteria health care institutions recognize. For example, if there is heart and lung function, some religious traditions hold that the person is not dead, and the treatment is, from this perspective, not futile even if health care professionals deem it useless and wasteful. This example is the tip of an iceberg of controversies about futility.

Typically the term *futile* refers to a situation in which irreversibly dying patients have reached a point at which further treatment provides no physiological benefit or is hopeless and becomes optional. Palliative interventions may still be continued. This model of futility covers only a narrow range of treatments. Less typically, in the literature on futility, all of the following have been labeled futile: (1) whatever physicians cannot perform, (2) whatever will not produce a physiological effect, (3) whatever is highly unlikely to be efficacious, (4) whatever probably will produce only a low-grade, insignificant outcome (i.e., qualitatively, the results are expected to be exceedingly poor), (5) whatever is highly likely to be more burdensome than beneficial, (6) whatever is completely speculative because it is an untried "treatment," and (7) whatever—in balancing effectiveness, potential benefit, and potential burden—warrants withdrawing or withholding treatment.[44] Thus, the term *futility* is used to cover many situations of predicted improbable outcomes, improbable success, and unacceptable benefit–burden ratios. This situation of competing conceptions and ambiguity suggests that we should generally avoid the term *futility* in favor of more precise language. Judgments of futility presuppose an accepted goal in relation to which an intervention is deemed to be useless or, in alternative language, medically inappropriate.[45]

Ideally, health care providers will focus on objective medical factors in their decisions involving the dead and the irreversibly dying. Realistically, however, this ideal is difficult to satisfy. Disagreement often exists among health professionals, and conflicts may arise from a family's belief in a possible miracle, a religious tradition's insistence on doing everything possible in such circumstances, and the like. It is sometimes difficult to know whether a judgment of futility is based on a probabilistic prediction of failure or on something closer to medical certainty. If an elderly patient has a 1% chance of surviving an arduous and painful regimen, one physician may call the procedure futile while another may view survival as unlikely, but a possibility meriting consideration. At stake is a value judgment about what is worth the effort, as well as scientific knowledge and evidence. Decision makers typically use "futility" to express a combined value judgment and scientific judgment.

A physician is not morally required to provide a genuinely futile or contraindicated treatment and in some cases may be required *not* to provide the treatment. The physician may not even be required to discuss the treatment.[46] These circumstances often involve incompetent persons, especially patients in a PVS, where physicians or hospital policies sometimes impose decisions to forgo life support on patients or surrogates. Hospitals are increasingly adopting policies aimed at denying therapies that physicians knowledgeably judge to be futile, especially after trying them for a reasonable period of time. Although the possibility of judgmental error by physicians should lead to caution in formulating these policies, unreasonable demands by patients and families should not be given priority over reasonable policies in health care institutions. Respect for the autonomy of patients or authorized surrogates is not a trump that allows them alone to determine whether a treatment is futile.

Our conclusion is that a genuinely futile medical intervention—one that has no chance of being efficacious in relation to accepted goals—is morally optional and in many cases ought not be introduced or continued. However, undertaking a futile intervention, such as CPR, may be an act of compassion and care toward the grief-stricken family of a seriously ill child, and could be justified, within limits.[47] Legitimate disagreements about whether a medical intervention is futile in particular circumstances may necessitate institutional procedures, such as mediation, ethics consultations, or ethics committee review, or, on occasion, judicial review.[48]

Burdens of treatment outweigh benefits. Medical codes and institutional policies often mistakenly assume that physicians may terminate life-sustaining treatments for persons not able to consent to or refuse the treatments only if the patient is terminally ill. Even if the patient is not terminally ill, life-sustaining medical treatment is not obligatory if its burdens outweigh its benefits to the patient. Medical treatment for those not terminally ill is sometimes optional even if it could prolong life indefinitely and the patient is incompetent and lacks an advance directive. Moral considerations of nonmaleficence do not demand the maintenance of biological life and do not require the initiation or continuation of treatment without regard to the patient's pain, suffering, and discomfort.

As an example, seventy-eight-year-old Earle Spring developed numerous medical problems, including chronic organic brain syndrome and kidney failure. Hemodialysis controlled the latter problem. Although several aspects of this case were never resolved—such as whether Spring was aware of his surroundings and able to express his wishes—a plausible argument existed that the family and health care professionals were not morally obligated to continue hemodialysis because of the balance of benefits and burdens to a patient whose compromised mental condition and kidney function would gradually worsen regardless of what was done. However, in this case, as in many others, a family conflict of interest complicated the situation: The family had to pay mounting health care costs while attempting to make judgments in the patient's best interests. (We return later in this chapter to procedures designed to protect incompetent patients.)

Quality-of-Life Judgments

Controversies about quality-of-life judgments. Our arguments thus far give considerable weight to quality-of-life judgments in determining whether treatments are optional or obligatory. We have relied on the premise that when quality of life is sufficiently low and an intervention produces more harm than benefit for the patient, caregivers may justifiably withhold or withdraw treatment. These judgments require defensible criteria of benefits and burdens that avoid reducing quality-of-life judgments to arbitrary personal preferences or to the patient's social worth.

In a landmark case involving quality-of-life judgments, sixty-eight-year-old Joseph Saikewicz, who had an IQ of 10 and a mental age of approximately two years and eight months, suffered from acute myeloblastic monocytic leukemia. Chemotherapy would have produced extensive suffering and possibly serious side effects. Remission under chemotherapy occurs in only 30% to 50% of such cases and typically only for between two and thirteen months. Without chemotherapy, doctors expected Saikewicz to live for several weeks or perhaps several months, during which he would not experience severe pain or suffering. In not ordering treatment, the lower court considered "the quality of life available to him [Saikewicz] even if the treatment does bring about remission."

The Supreme Judicial Court of Massachusetts rejected the lower court's judgment that the value of life could be equated with one measure of the quality of life—in particular, Saikewicz's lower quality of life due to mental retardation. Instead, the court interpreted "the vague, and perhaps ill-chosen, term 'quality of life'...as a reference to the continuing state of pain and disorientation precipitated by the chemotherapy treatment."[49] It balanced prospective benefit against pain and suffering, finally determining that the patient's interests supported a decision to not provide chemotherapy. From a moral standpoint, we agree with the court's conclusion in this legal opinion.

"Quality of life," however, needs further qualification. Some writers have argued that we should reject *moral* or otherwise *evaluative* judgments about quality of life and rely exclusively on *medical* indications for treatment decisions. Paul Ramsey argues that, for incompetent patients, we need only determine which treatment is medically indicated to know which treatment is obligatory and which is optional. For imminently dying patients, responsibilities are not fixed by obligations to provide treatments that serve only to extend the dying process; they are fixed by obligations to provide appropriate care in dying. Ramsey predicts that, unless we use these guidelines, we will gradually move toward a policy of active, involuntary euthanasia for unconscious or incompetent, nondying patients, based on arbitrary and inappropriate quality-of-life judgments.[50]

However, putatively objective medical factors, such as criteria used to determine medical indications for treatment, cannot provide the objectivity that Ramsey seeks. These criteria undermine his fundamental distinction between the medical and the moral (or evaluative). It is impossible to determine what will benefit a patient without presupposing some quality-of-life standard and some conception of the life the patient will live after a medical intervention. Accurate medical diagnosis and prognosis are indispensable. But a judgment about whether to use life-prolonging measures rests unavoidably on the anticipated quality of life of the patient, and cannot be reduced to a standard of what is medically indicated.[51]

Ramsey maintains that a quality-of-life approach improperly shifts the focus from whether treatments benefit patients to whether patients' lives are beneficial to them—a shift that opens the door to active, involuntary euthanasia.[52] The underlying issue is whether we can state criteria of quality of life with sufficient precision and cogency to avoid such dangers. We think we can, although the vagueness surrounding terms such as *dignity* and *meaningful life* is a cause for concern, and cases in which seriously ill or disabled newborn infants have been "allowed to die" under questionable justifications do provide a reason for caution.

We should exclude several conditions of patients from consideration. For example, mental retardation is irrelevant in determining whether treatment is in the patient's best interest. Proxies should not confuse quality of life for the patient with the value of the patient's life for others. Instead, criteria focused on the incompetent patient's best interests should be decisive for a proxy, even if the patient's interests conflict with familial or societal interests in avoiding burdens or costs.

This position contrasts with that of the U.S. President's Commission for the Study of Ethical Problems in Medicine and Biomedical and Behavioral Research, which recognized a broader conception of "best interests" that includes the welfare of the family: "The impact of a decision on an incapacitated patient's loved ones may be taken into account in determining someone's best interests, for most people do have an important interest in the well-being of their families or close associates."[53] Patients often do have an interest in their family's welfare, but it is a long step from this premise to a conclusion about whose interests should be overriding (unless the patient explicitly so states). When the incompetent patient has never been competent or has never expressed his or her wishes while competent, it is improper to impute altruism or any other motive to that patient against his or her medical best interest.

Children with serious illnesses or disabilities. Endangered near-term fetuses, seriously ill newborns, and young children also present difficult questions about quality of life and treatment omission. Prenatal obstetric management and neonatal intensive care can now salvage the lives of many anomalous fetuses and disabled newborns with physical conditions that would have been fatal a few decades ago. However, the resultant quality of life is sometimes so low that it becomes questionable whether aggressive obstetric management or intensive care has produced more harm than benefit for the patient. Some commentators argue that avoidance of harm (including iatrogenic harm) is the best guide to decisions on behalf of near-term fetuses and infants in neonatal nurseries,[54] and others argue that aggressive intervention violates the obligation of nonmaleficence if any one of three conditions is present: (1) inability to survive infancy, (2) inability to live without severe pain, and (3) inability to minimally participate in human experience.[55]

Managing high-risk pregnancies nonaggressively and allowing seriously disabled newborns to die are, under some conditions, morally permissible actions that do not violate obligations of nonmaleficence. When a patient has such a low quality of life that aggressive intervention or intensive care produces more harm than benefit, physicians justifiably may withhold or withdraw treatment from near-term fetuses, newborns, or infants, just as they do with older persons. The conditions that lead to a sufficiently poor quality of life include a number of antenatal conditions that eventuate in stillbirth; severe brain damage caused by birth asphyxia; Tay–Sachs disease, which involves increasing spasticity and dementia and usually results in death by age three or four; and Lesch–Nyhan disease, which involves uncontrollable spasms, mental retardation, compulsive self-mutilation, and early death. Severe cases of neural tube defects in which newborns lack all or most of the brain and will inevitably die also occasion a justifiable decision not to treat.

Consistent with our arguments at the end of Chapter 4, the most appropriate standard in cases of never-competent patients, including seriously ill newborns, is that of best interests, as judged by the best estimate of what reasonable persons would consider the highest net benefit among the available options. Competent patients and authorized surrogates can legitimately use quality-of-life considerations to determine whether treatments are optional or obligatory (or in extreme cases, wrong). We conclude that these categories of optional and obligatory should replace the traditional distinctions and rules examined earlier in this chapter.

KILLING AND LETTING DIE

The distinction between killing and letting die (or allowing to die) is the most difficult and the most important of all of the distinctions that have been used to determine acceptable decisions about treatment and acceptable forms of professional conduct with seriously ill or injured patients. This distinction has long been critical in law, medicine, and moral philosophy to distinguish appropriate from inappropriate ways for death to occur. A large body of distinctions and rules about life-sustaining treatments derives from the killing–letting die distinction, which in turn draws on the act–omission and active–passive distinctions.[56] The killing–letting die distinction has also affected distinctions between suicide and forgoing treatment and between homicide and natural death.[57] It has been widely used to separate permissible practices from condemnable ones.

In considering whether this distinction is coherent, defensible, and useful for moral guidance, this section addresses three sets of questions. (1) *Conceptual questions:* What conceptually is the difference between killing and letting die? (2) *Moral questions:* Is killing in itself morally wrong, whereas allowing to die is not in itself morally wrong? (3) *Combined conceptual and causal questions:* Is forgoing life-sustaining treatment sometimes a form of killing? If so, is it sometimes suicide and sometimes homicide?

Conceptual Questions about the Nature of Killing and Letting Die

Can we define *killing* and *letting die* so that they are conceptually distinct and do not overlap? The following two cases suggest that we cannot: (1) A newborn with Down syndrome needed an operation to correct a tracheoesophageal fistula (a congenital deformity in which a connection exists between the trachea and the esophagus, thereby allowing food or milk to get into the lungs). The parents and physicians judged that survival was not in this infant's best interests and decided to let the infant die rather than perform the operation. However, a public outcry erupted over the case, and critics charged that the parents and physicians had killed the child by negligently allowing the child to die. (2) Dr. Gregory Messenger, a dermatologist, was charged with manslaughter after he unilaterally disconnected his premature (twenty-five weeks gestation, 750 g.) son's life-support system in a Lansing, Michigan, neonatal intensive care unit. He thought he had merely acted compassionately in letting his son die after a neonatologist had failed to fulfill a promise not to resuscitate the infant.[58]

Can we legitimately describe actions that involve intentionally not treating a patient as "allowing to die" or "letting die," rather than "killing"? Do at least some of these actions involve both killing and allowing to die? Is "allowing to die" a euphemism in some cases for "acceptable killing" or "acceptable taking of life"? These conceptual questions have moral implications. Unfortunately, both ordinary discourse and legal concepts are vague and equivocal. In ordinary language, *killing* is a causal action that brings about death, whereas *letting die* is an intentional avoidance of causal intervention so that disease, system failure, or injury causes death. Killing extends to animal and plant life. Neither in ordinary language nor in law does the word *killing* entail a wrongful act or a crime, or even an intentional action. For example, we can say properly that, in automobile accidents, one driver killed another even when no awareness, intent, or negligence was present.

Conventional definitions are unsatisfactory for drawing a sharp distinction between killing and letting die. They allow many acts of letting die to count as killing, thereby defeating the very point of the distinction. For example, under these definitions, health professionals kill patients when they intentionally let them die in circumstances in which they have a duty to keep the patients alive. It is unclear in literature on the subject how to distinguish killing from letting die so as to avoid even simple cases that satisfy the conditions of both killing and letting die. The meanings of "killing" and "letting die" are vague and inherently contestable. Attempts to refine their meanings likely will produce controversy without closure. We use these terms because they are prominent in mainstream literature, but we avoid them insofar as possible.

Connecting Right and Wrong to Killing and Letting Die

"Letting die" is prima facie acceptable in medicine under one of two conditions: (1) a medical technology is *useless* in the strict sense of medical futility, as discussed earlier in this chapter, or (2) patients or their authorized surrogates have *validly refused* a medical technology. That is, letting a patient die is acceptable if and only if it satisfies the condition of futility or the condition of a valid refusal of treatment. If neither of these two conditions is satisfied, then letting a patient die constitutes killing (perhaps by negligence).

In medicine and health care, "killing" has traditionally been conceptually and morally connected to unacceptable acts. The conditions of medical practice make this connection understandable, but killing's absolute unacceptability is not assumed outside of medical circles. The term *killing* does not necessarily entail a wrongful act or a crime, and the rule "Do not kill" is not an absolute rule. Standard justifications of killing, such as killing in self-defense, killing to rescue a person endangered by other persons' wrongful acts, and killing by misadventure (accidental, nonnegligent killing while engaged in a lawful act) prevent us from prejudging an action as wrong merely because it is a killing. Correctly applying the label "killing" or the label "letting die" to a set of events (outside of traditional assumptions in medicine) will therefore fail to determine whether an action is acceptable or unacceptable.[59]

It may be the case that killing is usually wrong and letting die only rarely wrong, but, if so, this conclusion is contingent on the features of particular cases. The general wrongness of killing and the general rightness of letting die are not surprising features of the moral world inasmuch as killings are rarely authorized by appropriate parties (excepting contexts of warfare and capital punishment) and cases of letting die generally are validly authorized. Be that as it may, the *frequency* with which one kind of act is justified, in contrast to the other kind of act, cannot determine whether either kind of act is legally or morally justified. Forgoing treatment to allow patients to die can be both as intentional and as immoral as actions that in some more direct manner take their lives, and both can be forms of killing.

In short, the labels "killing" and "letting die," even when correctly applied, do not determine that one form of action is better or worse, or more or less justified, than the other. Some particular instance of killing, such as a brutal murder, may be worse than some particular instance of allowing to die, such as forgoing treatment for a PVS patient; but some particular instance of letting die, such as not resuscitating a patient whom physicians could potentially save, also may be worse than some particular instance of killing, such as mercy killing at the patient's request. Nothing about either killing or allowing to die entails judgments about actual wrongness or rightness. Rightness and wrongness depend on the merit of the justification underlying the action, not on whether it is an instance of killing or of letting die. Neither killing nor letting die is per se wrong. In this regard, we can distinguish them from murder, which is per se wrongful.

Accordingly, judging whether an act of either killing or letting die is justified or unjustified requires that we know something else about the act besides these characteristics. We need to know about the circumstances, the actor's motive (e.g., whether it is benevolent or malicious), the patient's preferences, and the act's consequences. These additional factors will allow us to place the act on a moral map and make an informed normative judgment.

Forgoing Life-Sustaining Treatment: Killing or Allowing to Die?

Many writers in medicine, law, and ethics have construed a physician's intentionally forgoing a medical technology as letting die if and only if an underlying disease or injury causes death. When physicians withhold or withdraw medical technology, according to this interpretation, a natural death occurs, because natural conditions do what they would have done if the physicians had never initiated the technology. By contrast, killings occur when acts of persons rather than natural conditions cause death. From this perspective, one acts nonmaleficently in allowing to die and maleficently in killing.

Although this view is influential in law and medicine, it is flawed. To attain a satisfactory account, we must add that the forgoing of the medical technology is validly authorized and for this reason justified. If the physician's forgoing of technology were unjustified and a person died from "natural" causes of injury or disease, the result would be unjustified killing, not justified allowing to die. The validity of the authorization—not some independent assessment of causation—determines the morality of the action. For example, withdrawing treatment from a competent patient is not morally justifiable unless the patient has made an informed decision authorizing this withdrawal. If a physician removes a respirator from a patient who needs it and wants to continue its use, the action is wrong, even though the physician has only removed artificial life support and let nature take its course. The lack of authorization by the patient is the relevant consideration in assessing the act as unacceptable, not the distinction between letting die and killing.

Even from a legal perspective, we can provide a better causal account than "the preexisting disease caused the death." The better account is that legal liability should not be imposed on physicians and surrogates unless they have an obligation to provide or continue the treatment. If no obligation to treat exists, then questions of causation and liability do not arise. If the categories of obligatory and optional are primary, we have a reason for avoiding discussions about killing and letting die altogether and for focusing instead on health care professionals' obligations and problems of moral and legal responsibility.

In conclusion, the distinction between killing and letting die suffers from vagueness and moral confusion. Specifically, the language of killing is so confusing—causally, legally, and morally—that it provides little, if any, help in discussions of assistance in dying. In the next section we further support this conclusion.

THE JUSTIFICATION OF INTENTIONALLY ARRANGED DEATHS

We now address a set of moral questions about the causation of death that are largely free of the language of "killing." The general question is, "Under which conditions, if any, is it permissible for a patient and a health professional to arrange for assistance in intentionally ending the patient's life?"

Withholding or withdrawing treatment will hasten death only for those individuals who could be or are being sustained by a technology. Many other individuals, including some patients with cancer, face a protracted period of dying when respirators and other life-preserving technology are not being utilized. Great improvements in and extensions of palliative care adequately address the needs of many, perhaps most, of these patients.[60] However, for some, palliative care and the refusal of particular treatments do not adequately address all their concerns. During their prolonged period of dying, they may endure a loss of functional capacity, unremitting pain and suffering, an inability to experience the simplest of pleasures, and long hours aware of the hopelessness of their condition. Some patients find this prospect unbearable and desire a painless means to hasten their deaths.

In addition to withholding or withdrawing treatments or technologies, and prescribing medications that may relieve pain and suffering while indirectly hastening death (see our discussion earlier of the rule of double effect), physicians sometimes use what is viewed as a more active means to bring about a patient's death. Some argue that the use of an active means in medicine to bring about death constitutes an inappropriate killing, but there are several problems inherent in the idea that we can determine appropriate and inappropriate conduct by considering whether an active means was involved. An example is the Oregon Death with Dignity Act (ODWDA),[61] where the distinction between "letting die" and "killing" is not used and is not helpful in addressing particular cases. Physicians who act under the ODWDA do not "kill"; as permitted under the law, they write prescriptions for a lethal medication at a patient's request. The patient must make a conscious decision to use the drug. About one-third of the patients who fill a prescription never ingest the lethal drug. For those who take the drug, the physician's writing of the prescription is a necessary step in the process that leads to the patient's death, but it is not the determinative or even the final step. Under any reasonable interpretation of the term, the Oregon physician does not "kill" the patient, nor does a physician "let the patient die." Here the terms *letting die* and *killing* do not illuminate or help evaluate what happens when a physician helps a person escape the ravages of a fatal illness.

Literature often treats issues about active physician assistance under the umbrella of the legal protection of a "right to die,"[62] but underlying the legal issues is a powerful struggle in law, medicine, and ethics over the nature, scope, and foundations of the right to choose the manner of one's death. We here offer a few judgments about legalization, public policy, and institutional policy, but we are primarily interested in whether acts of assistance by health professionals are morally justified. We begin with the important distinction between acts and policies. From there we work back to some foundational moral issues.

Acts, Practices, and Slippery-Slope Problems

Justifying an act is distinct from justifying a practice or a policy that permits or even legitimates the act's performance. A rule of practice or a public policy or a law that prohibits various forms of assistance in dying in medicine may be justified even if it excludes some acts of causing a person's death that in themselves are *morally* justifiable. For example, sufficient reasons may justify a law that prohibits physicians from prescribing a lethal drug. However, in a particular case, it could be ethically justifiable to provide the drug to a patient who suffers from terrible pain, who will probably die within a few weeks, and who requests a merciful assisted death. Accordingly, a valid and ethically justifiable law might forbid an action that is morally justified in such an individual case.

A much-discussed problem is that a practice or policy that allows physicians to intervene to cause deaths or to prescribe lethal drugs runs risks of abuse and might cause more harm than benefit. The argument is not that serious abuses will occur immediately, but that they will grow incrementally over time. Society could start by severely restricting the number of patients who qualify for assistance in dying, but later loosen these restrictions so that cases of unjustified killing begin to occur. Unscrupulous persons would learn how to abuse the system, just as they do now with methods of tax evasion on the margins of the system of legitimate tax avoidance. In short, the slope of the trail toward the unjustified taking of life could be so slippery and precipitous that we ought never to embark on it.

Many dismiss such slippery-slope, or wedge, arguments because of a lack of empirical evidence to support the claims involved, as well as because of their heavily metaphorical character ("the thin edge of the wedge," "the first step on the slippery slope," "the foot in the door," and "the camel's nose under the tent"). However, some slippery-slope arguments should be taken with utmost seriousness.[63] They force us to think about whether unacceptable harm may result from attractive, and apparently innocent, first steps. If society removes certain restraints against interventions that cause death, various psychological and social forces would likely make it more difficult to maintain the relevant distinctions in practice.

Opponents of legalization of physician-assisted dying have maintained that the practice inevitably would be expanded to include euthanasia, that the quality of palliative care for all patients would deteriorate, that patients would be manipulated or coerced into requesting assistance in hastening death, that patients with impaired judgment would be allowed to request such assistance, and that members of possibly vulnerable groups (the economically disadvantaged, the elderly, immigrants, members of racial and ethnic minorities, etc.) would be adversely affected in disproportionate numbers. Such slippery-slope claims seem credible in light of the effects of social discrimination based on disability, cost-cutting measures in the funding of health care, and the growing number of elderly persons with medical problems that require larger and larger proportions of a family's or the public's financial resources. If rules allowing physician-assisted dying became public policy, the risk would increase that persons in these populations will be neglected or otherwise abused. For example, the risk would increase that families and health professionals may abandon treatments for disabled newborns and adults with severe brain damage to avoid social and familial burdens. If decision makers reach judgments that some newborns and adults have overly burdensome conditions or lives with no value, the same logic can be extended to other populations of feeble, debilitated, and seriously ill patients who are financial and emotional burdens on families and society.

These fears are understandable. Rules in a moral code against passively or actively causing the death of another person are not isolated fragments. They are threads in a fabric of rules that uphold respect for human life. The more threads we remove, the weaker the fabric may become. If we focus on the modification of attitudes and beliefs, not merely on rules, shifts in public policy may also erode the general attitude of respect for life. Prohibitions are often both instrumentally and symbolically important, and their removal could weaken critical attitudes, practices, and restraints.

Rules against bringing about another's death also provide a basis of trust between patients and health care professionals. We expect health care professionals to promote our welfare under all circumstances. We may risk a loss of public trust if physicians become agents of intentionally causing death in addition to being healers and caregivers. On the other side, however, we may also risk a loss of trust if patients and families believe that physicians abandon them in their suffering because the physicians lack the courage to offer the assistance needed in the darkest hours of their lives.[64]

The success or failure of slippery-slope arguments ultimately depends on speculative predictions of a progressive erosion of moral restraints. If dire consequences will flow from the legalization of physician-assisted dying in a jurisdiction, then these arguments are cogent and such practices are justifiably prohibited in that jurisdiction. But how good is the evidence that dire consequences will occur? Does the evidence indicate that we cannot maintain firm distinctions in public policies between, for example, patient-requested death and involuntary euthanasia?[65]

Scant evidence supports any of the answers traditionally given to these questions. Those of us, including the authors of this book, who take seriously some versions of the slippery-slope argument should admit that it requires a premise on the order of a precautionary principle, such as "better safe than sorry." The likelihood of the projected moral erosion is not something we presently can assess by appeal to good evidence. Arguments on every side are speculative and analogical, and different assessors of the same evidence reach different conclusions. Intractable controversy likely will persist over what counts as good and sufficient evidence. How Oregon's procedural safeguards work, or fail to work, will continue to be carefully watched. That state's experience is likely to shape the next steps taken in other states and countries. Failure of the ODWDA would be a major setback for proponents of the right to die by use of prescribed drugs.

However, to date, none of the abuses some predicted have materialized in Oregon.[66] The Oregon statute's restrictions have been neither loosened nor broadened. There is no evidence that any patient has died other than in accordance with his or her own wishes. The number of patients seeking prescriptions under the statute has been both low and stable (at around sixty per year), and hastened death has not been used primarily by individuals who might be thought vulnerable to intimidation or abuse. Those choosing assisted death have had, on average, a higher level of education and better medical coverage than terminally ill Oregonians who did not seek assistance in dying. Women, people with disabilities, and members of disadvantaged racial minorities have not sought assistance in dying in disproportionate numbers. The overwhelming number of persons requesting assistance in dying are caucasian, and the gender of the requesters reflects the general population. Meanwhile, reports indicate that the quality of palliative care has improved in Oregon. About one-third of the patients requesting assistance in dying ultimately decide not to use the prescribed drug.[67]

Oregon's experiment in physician-assisted suicide is instructive and reassuring in many respects, but questions inevitably arise about its generalizability as a model for the whole United States and for other countries, just as they arise about other national experiments—for example, in the Netherlands, with euthanasia.[68]

Valid Requests for Aid-in-Dying

We can now go to the central question—whether some acts of assisting another in dying are morally justified. The frontier of expanded rights to control one's death has shifted from *refusal* of treatment to *requests* for aid-in-dying.[69] Assuming that the principles of respect for autonomy and nonmaleficence justify forgoing treatment, the same justification might be extended to physicians prescribing barbiturates or providing other forms of help requested by seriously ill patients. This strategy rests on the premise that professional ethics and legal rules should avoid the apparent inconsistency between (1) the strong rights of autonomous choice that allow persons in grim circumstances to refuse treatment so as to bring about their deaths and (2) the denial of a similar autonomy right to arrange for death by mutual agreement between patient and physician under equally grim circumstances. The argument for reform is particularly compelling when a condition overwhelmingly burdens a patient, pain management fails to adequately comfort the patient, and only a physician can and is willing to bring relief. At present, medicine and law in most jurisdictions in the United States are in the awkward position of having to say to such patients, "If you were on life-sustaining treatment, you would have a right to withdraw the treatment and then we could let you die. But since you are not, we can only allow you to refuse nutrition and hydration or give you palliative care until you die a natural death, however painful, undignified, and costly."

Clearly the two types of authorization—refusal of treatment and request for aid-in-dying—are not perfectly analogous. A health professional is obligated to honor an autonomous refusal of a life-prolonging technology, but he or she is not obligated under ordinary circumstances to honor an autonomous request for aid-in-dying. However, the key issue is not whether physicians are *obligated* to lend assistance in dying, but whether valid requests render it *permissible* for a physician (or some other person) to lend aid-in-dying. Refusals in medical settings have a moral force not found in requests, but requests do not lack all power to confer on another a moral right to act in response.

A physician's precise responsibilities to a patient may depend on the nature of the request made as well as on the nature of the preestablished patient–physician relationship. In some cases of physician compliance with requests, the patient and the physician pursue the patient's best interest under an agreement that the physician will not abandon the patient and will undertake to serve what they jointly determine are the patient's best interests. In some cases, patients in a close relationship with a physician both refuse a medical technology and request a hastened death to lessen pain or suffering. Refusal and request may be parts of a single plan. If the physician accepts the plan, some form of assistance grows out of the preestablished relationship. From this perspective, a valid request for aid-in-dying frees a responder of moral culpability for the death, just as a valid refusal precludes culpability.

These arguments suggest that causing a person's death is morally wrong, when it is wrong, because an unauthorized intervention thwarts or sets back a person's interests. It is an unjustified act when it deprives the person who dies of opportunities and goods.[70] However, if a person freely authorizes death, making an autonomous judgment that cessation of pain and suffering through death constitutes a personal benefit rather than a setback to interests, then active aid-in-dying at the person's request involves neither harming nor wronging. Aiding an autonomous person at his or her request for assistance in dying is, from this perspective, a way of showing respect for the person's autonomous choices. Similarly, denying the person access to other individuals who are willing and qualified to comply with the request shows a fundamental disrespect for the person's autonomy.

Unjustified Physician Assistance in Dying

The fact that the autonomous requests of patients for aid-in-dying should be respected in some circumstances does not entail that *all* cases of physician-assisted death by the patient's request are justifiable. Jack Kevorkian's practices provide an important historical example of the kind of *unjustified* physician assistance that society should discourage and even prohibit. In his first case of assisting in suicide, Janet Adkins, an Oregon grandmother with Alzheimer's disease, had reached a decision that she wanted to take her life rather than lose her cognitive capacities, which she was convinced were slowly deteriorating. After Adkins read in news reports that Kevorkian had invented a "death machine," she communicated with him by phone and then flew from Oregon to Michigan to meet with him. Following brief discussions, she and Kevorkian drove to a park in northern Oakland County. He inserted a tube in her arm and started saline flow. His machine was constructed so that Adkins could then press a button to inject other drugs, culminating in potassium chloride, which would physically cause her death. She then pressed the button.[71]

This case raises several concerns. Janet Adkins was in the fairly early stages of Alzheimer's and was not yet debilitated. At fifty-four years of age, she was still capable of enjoying a full schedule of activities with her husband and playing tennis with her son, and she might have been able to live a meaningful life for several more years. A slight possibility existed that the Alzheimer's diagnosis was incorrect, and she might have been more psychologically depressed than Kevorkian appreciated. She had limited contact with him before they collaborated in her death, and he did not administer examinations to confirm either her diagnosis or her level of competence to commit suicide. Indeed, he lacked the professional expertise to evaluate her medically or psychologically. The glare of media attention also raises the question whether Kevorkian acted imprudently to generate publicity for his social goals and for his forthcoming book.

Lawyers, physicians, and writers in bioethics have almost universally condemned Kevorkian's actions. The case raises all the fears present in the arguments mentioned previously about physician-assisted dying: lack of social control, inadequate medical knowledge, absence of accountability, and unverifiable circumstances of a patient's death. Although Kevorkian's approach to assisted suicide was regrettable, some of his "patients" raise distressing questions about the lack of a support system in health care for handling their problems. Having thought for over a year about her future, Janet Adkins decided that the suffering of continued existence exceeded its benefits. Her family supported her decision. She faced a bleak future from the perspective of a person who had lived an unusually vigorous life, both physically and mentally. She believed that her brain would slowly deteriorate, with progressive and devastating cognitive loss and confusion, fading memory, immense frustration, and loss of all capacity to take care of herself. She also believed that the full burden of responsibility for her care would fall on her family. From her perspective, Kevorkian's offer was preferable to what other physicians had offered, which was a flat refusal to help her die as she wished.

Justified Physician Assistance in Dying

Balancing the errors of Kevorkian's strategy are cases of *justified* assisted suicide. Consider the actions of physician Timothy Quill in prescribing the barbiturates desired by a forty-five-year-old patient who had refused a risky, painful, and often unsuccessful treatment for leukemia. She had been his patient for many years and she and members of her family had, as a group, come to this decision with his counsel. She was competent and had already discussed and rejected all available alternatives for the relief of suffering. This case satisfied the conditions that are sufficient for justified physician assistance in ending life. These conditions include:

1. A voluntary request by a competent patient
2. An ongoing patient–physician relationship
3. Mutual and informed decision making by patient and physician
4. A supportive yet critical and probing environment of decision making
5. A considered rejection of alternatives
6. Structured consultation with other parties in medicine
7. A patient's expression of a durable preference for death
8. Unacceptable suffering by the patient
9. Use of a means that is as painless and comfortable as possible

Although Quill's actions satisfied all of these conditions, some people found his involvement as a physician unsettling and unjustified. Several critics invoked the slippery-slope argument, because acts like Quill's, if legalized, could potentially affect many patients, especially the elderly. Others were troubled by the fact that Quill apparently violated a New York State law against assisted suicide. Furthermore, to reduce the risks of criminal liability, Quill lied to the medical examiner by informing him that a hospice patient had died of acute leukemia.[72]

Despite these problems, we do not criticize Quill's basic intentions in responding to the patient, the patient's decision, or their relationship. Suffering and loss of cognitive capacity can ravage and dehumanize patients so severely that death is in their best interests. In these tragic situations—or in anticipation of them, as in this case—physicians such as Quill do not act wrongly in assisting competent patients, at their request, to bring about their deaths. Public policy issues regarding how to avoid abuses and discourage unjustified acts should be a central part of our discussion about forms of appropriate physician assistance, but these issues should not affect the moral justifiability of the physician's act of assisting in the patient's death in the context of caring for the patient.

Physician assistance in hastening death should be viewed as part of a continuum of medical care. A physician who encounters a sick patient should initially seek, if possible, to rid the patient's body of its ills. Restoration of health is a morally mandatory goal if a reasonable prospect of success exists and the patient supports the means necessary to this end. However, to confine the practice of medicine to measures designed to cure diseases or heal injuries is an unduly narrow way of thinking about what the physician has to offer the patient. When, in the patient's assessment, the burdens of continued attempts to cure outweigh their probable benefits, the caring physician should redirect the course of treatment so that its primary focus is the relief of pain and suffering. For many patients, palliative care with aggressive use of analgesics will prove sufficient to accomplish this goal. For other patients, relief of intolerable suffering will come only with death, which some will seek to hasten.

A favorable response by a physician to a request for assistance in facilitating death by *hastening* it through prescribing lethal medication is not relevantly different from a favorable response to requests for assistance in facilitating death by *easing* it through removal of life-prolonging technology or use of coma-inducing medications. The two acts of physician assistance are morally equivalent as long as no other differences are present in the cases. That is, if the disease is relevantly similar, the request by the patient is relevantly similar, and the desperateness of the patient's circumstance is relevantly similar, responding to a request to provide the means to hasten death is morally equivalent to responding to a request to ease death by withdrawing treatment, sedating to coma, and the like.

With due caution, we should be able to devise social policies and laws that maintain a bright line between justified and unjustified physician assistance in dying. Principles of respect for autonomy and beneficence and virtues of care and compassion all offer strong reasons for recognizing the legitimacy of physician-assisted death. Major opposition stems from interpretations of the principle of nonmaleficence and its specifications in various distinctions and rules. We have argued that those distinctions and rules break down on closer examination. In arguing for changes in laws and policies to allow physician-assisted dying in certain contexts, we do not maintain that these changes will handle all important issues. They mainly address last-resort situations, which can often be avoided by better social policies and practices, including improved palliative care, which of course we strongly recommend.

In presenting a case involving the disconnection of a ventilator maintaining the life of a patient with amyotrophic lateral sclerosis (ALS, or Lou Gehrig's disease) at an international conference on "Ethical Issues in Disability and Rehabilitation," some clinicians framed it as an "end-of-life case," in which the "patient" decided to discontinue the ventilator. They were surprised when the audience, many of whom had disabilities and had themselves experienced long-term ventilator use, disputed this classification and argued instead that this was a "disability" case in which the clinicians should have provided better care, fuller information, and more options to the "consumer," particularly to help him overcome his felt isolation after the recent death of his spouse: "What to the clinicians was a textbook case of 'end-of-life' decision making was, for their audience, a story in which a life was ended as a result of failures of information and assistance by the presenters themselves."[73]

Few doubt that we need further improvements in supporting people who suffer from serious medical problems. Control of pain and suffering is a moral imperative. However, significant progress in control of pain and suffering will not obviate all last-resort situations, in which individuals reasonably seek control over their dying in ways that have often been denied them.

PROBLEMS OF GROUP HARM

In Chapter 4, we presented a theory of valid informed consent. We there paid little attention to the practice of "broad consent," also called "global consent" and "blanket consent." Under this form of consent, harms may occur for individuals and groups as a result of inadequate information and understanding. The problems can be acute when biological samples are banked and then used in unanticipated ways.

The Banking of Samples

Advances in science have introduced confusion about how we can efficiently promote research while protecting the rights of donors of samples. Samples collected for future research may not be adequately described in a protocol or consent form when the collection occurs. The wording in the form may be dictated by shadowy anticipated future uses of samples, with little expectation of harmful outcomes. The challenge is both not to cause harm to personal and group interests and not to violate privacy and confidentiality. The question is whether it is possible to meet this challenge.[74]

Samples and data frequently derive from sources external to a research setting, including industry, government, and university sources, and it may be difficult to determine whether adequately informed consent was obtained and whose interests might be at risk. Using samples or data to achieve goals other than those initially disclosed to subjects negates even an originally valid consent process and threatens the trust between subjects and investigators. Even anonymized samples can harm some personal and group interests and may violate the investigator–subject trust relationship. We will not try to resolve all of these complicated issues. We will simply present a case that compellingly exemplifies the pitfalls and risks of harm in research that permits broad consents.

Diabetes Research on Havasupai Indians

This case involves research conducted at Arizona State University using as research subjects the Havasupai Indians of the Grand Canyon. Investigators used a broad consent, which was not as carefully scrutinized by university committee review as it should have been. The history starts in 1990 when members of the fast-disappearing Havasupai tribe gave DNA samples to university researchers with the goal of providing genetic information about the tribe's distressing, indeed, alarming, rate of diabetes. Dating from the 1960s, the Havasupai had experienced a high incidence of type 2 diabetes that led to amputations and had forced many tribal members to leave their village in the Grand Canyon for dialysis.

From 1990 to 1994, approximately 100 members of the tribe signed a broad consent that indicated the research was to "study the causes of behavioral/medical disorders." The consent form was intentionally confined to clear, simply written, basic information, because English is a second language for many Havasupai, and few of the tribe's remaining 650 members had graduated from high school. From the researchers' perspective, tribe members had consented to collecting the blood and to its use in genetic research well beyond the research on their particular disease. The Havasupai, by contrast, denied that they gave permission for any nondiabetes research or that they received adequate information about and had an adequate understanding of the risks of the research before they agreed to participate.

In the course of the research, diabetes was investigated, but the roughly 200 blood samples were also put to several additional uses in genetics research having nothing to do with diabetes. One use was to study mental illness, especially schizophrenia, and another was to examine inbreeding in the tribe. Approximately two dozen scholarly articles were published on the basis of research on the samples. The Havasupai viewed some of this research as offensive, insulting, stigmatizing, harmful, and provocative. They filed a lawsuit charging research investigators with fraud, breach of fiduciary duty, negligence, and trespass.[75]

Both the researchers and the review committee at the university apparently did not notice the serious risks of harm, disrespect, and abuse inherent in the research they conducted subsequent to the broad consent. One article eventually published by investigators theorized that the tribe's ancestors had crossed the frozen Bering Sea to arrive in North America. This thesis contradicted the tribe's traditional stories and cosmology, which have quasi-religious significance. According to their tradition, the tribe originated in the Grand Canyon and was assigned to be the canyon's guardian. To be told that the tribe was instead of Asian origin and that this hypothesis was developed from studies on their blood, which also has a special significance to the Havasupai, was disorienting and abhorrent. The thesis also set off legal alarms in the community, because the Havasupai had argued that their origin in the Grand Canyon was the legal basis of their entitlement to the land.[76]

This case presents paradigmatic problems of risk of harm, adequacy of consent, and human rights. In particular, it underlines the need to attend to group, as well as individual, harms, and to a richer conception of harms in research than often occurs. Research on samples, especially genetics research, can create psychosocial risks in the absence of physical risks to individual sources of the samples. In this case the tribe was harmed by the damage to its traditional self-understanding. This case also raises questions about whether scientists took advantage of a vulnerable population by exploiting its members' lack of understanding. In the end, the university made a monetary payment to forty-one of the tribe's members and acknowledged that the payment was to "remedy the wrong that was done."[77] The university had worked for years to establish good relationships with Native American tribes in Arizona, but this reservoir of trust was profoundly set back by this case.

PROTECTING INCOMPETENT PATIENTS

In Chapter 6 we will develop standards of surrogate decision making for incompetent patients. Here we consider *who* should make decisions for patients who are incompetent. Determining the best system for protecting patients from negligence and harm is the central problem.[78] We think first of families as the proper decision makers because they usually have the deepest interest in protecting their incompetent members. However, we need a system that will shield incompetent individuals from family members who care little or are caught in conflicts of interest, while protecting residents of nursing homes, psychiatric hospitals, and facilities for the disabled and mentally handicapped who rarely, if ever, see a family member. The appropriate roles of families, courts, guardians, conservators, hospital committees, and health professionals all merit consideration.

Advance Directives

In an increasingly popular procedure rooted as much in respect for autonomy as in obligations of nonmaleficence, a person, while competent, either writes a directive for health care professionals or selects a surrogate to make decisions about life-sustaining treatments during periods of incompetence.[79] Two types of *advance directive* aim at governing future decisions: (1) *living wills,* substantive or instructional directives regarding medical procedures in specific circumstances, and (2) *durable power of attorney* (DPA) for health care, or proxy directives. A DPA is a legal document in which one person assigns another person authority to perform specified actions on behalf of the signer. The power is "durable" because, unlike the usual power of attorney, it continues in effect when the signer becomes incompetent.

However, these documents generate practical and moral problems.[80] First, relatively few persons compose them, and when they do, they often fail to leave sufficiently explicit instructions. Second, a designated decision maker might be unavailable when needed, might be incompetent to make good decisions for the patient, or might have a conflict of interest, for example, because of a prospective inheritance or an improved position in a family-owned business. Third, some patients who change their preferences about treatment fail to change their directives, and a few, when legally incompetent, protest a surrogate's decision. Fourth, laws often severely restrict the use of advance directives. For example, advance directives have legal effect in some locations if and only if the patient is terminally ill and death is imminent. Decisions must be made, however, in some cases in which death is not imminent or the patient does not have a medical condition appropriately described as a terminal illness. Fifth, living wills provide no basis for health professionals to overturn a patient's instructions; yet prior decisions by the patient could turn out not to be in the patient's best medical interest. Patients while competent often could not have reasonably anticipated the precise circumstances they actually encountered. Surrogate decision makers also sometimes make decisions with which physicians sharply disagree, in some cases asking the physician to act against his or her conscience. Even when the patient has a living will and has designated a surrogate, he or she may have failed to indicate which has priority in case of a conflict.

Nonetheless, the advance directive is a valid way for competent persons to exercise their autonomy, and implementing the procedures for informed consent discussed in Chapter 4 can overcome many of the practical problems. As in informed consent situations, we should distinguish the *process* from the *product* (here, the advance directive). Efforts are under way to enhance the entire process of advance care planning, for instance, through in-depth dialogue, improved communication, values histories, and the use of a variety of scenarios and decision aids.[81] In contrast to earlier studies that found little if any impact of advance directives on subsequent decisions and care,[82] recent research indicates that elderly patients who lose their capacity to make decisions but who have advance directives tend to receive care that is strongly associated with their previously stated preferences.[83]

Surrogate Decision Making without Advance Directives

When an incompetent patient has not left an advance directive, who should make the decision, and with whom should the decision maker consult?

Qualifications of surrogate decision makers. We propose the following list of qualifications for decision makers for incompetent patients (including newborns):

1. Ability to make reasoned judgments (competence)
2. Adequate knowledge and information
3. Emotional stability
4. A commitment to the incompetent patient's interests, free of conflicts of interest and free of controlling influence by those who might not act in the patient's best interests

The first three conditions follow from the discussions of informed consent and competence in Chapter 4. The only potentially controversial condition is the fourth. Here we endorse a criterion of *partiality*—acting as an advocate in the incompetent patient's best interests—rather than *impartiality,* which requires neutrality in consideration of the interests of the various affected parties.

Four classes of decision makers have been proposed and used in cases of withholding and terminating treatment for incompetent patients: families, physicians and other health care professionals, institutional committees, and courts. If a court-appointed guardian exists, that person will act as the primary responsible party. The following analysis is meant to provide a defensible structure of decision-making authority that places the caring family as the presumptive authority when the patient cannot make the decision and has not previously designated a decision maker.

The role of the family. Wide agreement exists that the patient's closest family member is the first choice as a surrogate. Many patients strongly prefer family members to interact with physicians as the decision-making authorities about their medical fate.[84] The family's role should be primary because of its presumed identification with the patient's interests, depth of concern about the patient, and intimate knowledge of his or her wishes, as well as its traditional position in society. Unfortunately, the term *family* is imprecise, especially if it includes the extended family. The reasons that support assigning presumptive priority to the patient's closest family member(s) also support assigning relative priority to other family members. However, even the patient's closest family members sometimes make unacceptable decisions, and the authority of the family is not final or ultimate.[85] The closest family member can have a conflict of interest, can be poorly informed, or can be too distant personally and even estranged from the patient.[86]

Consider an illustrative case: Mr. Lazarus was a fifty-seven-year-old male patient who was brought into the hospital after suffering a heart attack while playing touch football. He lapsed into a coma and became ventilator-dependent. After twenty-four hours his wife asked that the ventilator be withdrawn and dialysis stopped so that he could be allowed to die. The attending physician was uncomfortable with this request because he thought that Mr. Lazarus had a good chance of full recovery. Mrs. Lazarus insisted that treatment be withdrawn, and she produced a DPA for health care that designated her as the surrogate. She became angry when the health care team expressed its reluctance to withdraw care, and she threatened to sue the hospital if her decision was not honored. An ethics consult was called because the attending and staff remained unwilling to carry out her wishes. The ethics consultant carefully read the DPA, only to discover that Mr. Lazarus had designated his wife as surrogate only if he was deemed to be in a PVS. Furthermore, Mr. Lazarus had stipulated on the DPA that if he was not in a PVS, he wanted "everything done." He awoke after three days and immediately revoked his DPA when told of his wife's demand.[87]

Health care professionals should seek to disqualify any decision makers who are significantly incompetent or ignorant, are acting in bad faith, or have a conflict of interest. Serious conflicts of interest in the family may be more common than either physicians or the courts have generally appreciated.

Health care professionals can and should recognize and help address the burdens of decision making on familial and other surrogates. According to one review of the relevant research, at least one-third of the surrogates involved in decision making about treatment for incapacitated adults experienced emotional burdens, such as stress, guilt, and doubt about whether they had made the best decisions in the circumstances. However, when surrogates were confident that the treatment decision accorded with the patient's own preferences, their emotional burden was reduced.[88]

The role of health care professionals. Physicians and other health care professionals can help the family become more adequate decision makers and can safeguard the patient's interests and preferences, where known, by monitoring the quality of surrogate decision making. Often the physician will best serve both the family and the patient by helping surrogates see that rapid functional decline has set in and the time has come to shift from life-prolonging measures to palliative care centered on increasing comfort and reducing the burdens of treatments.[89] Such guidance can be wrenchingly difficult and emotionally challenging for the physician.

In the comparatively rare situation in which physicians contest a surrogate's decision and disagreements persist, an independent source of review, such as a hospital ethics committee or the judicial system, is advisable. In the event that a surrogate, a member of the health care team, or an independent

reviewer asks a caregiver to perform an act that the caregiver regards as contraindicated, futile, or unconscionable, the caregiver is not obligated to perform
the act but may still be obligated to help the surrogate or patient make other
arrangements for care.

Institutional ethics committees. Surrogate decision makers sometimes refuse
treatments that would serve the interests of those they should protect, and physicians sometimes too readily acquiesce in their preferences. In other cases, surrogates need help in reaching difficult decisions. The involved parties then may
need a mechanism or procedure to help make a decision or to break a private
circle of refusal and acquiescence. A similar need exists for assistance in decisions regarding residents of nursing homes and hospices, psychiatric hospitals,
and residential facilities in which families often play only a small role, if any.

Institutional ethics committees differ widely in their composition and function. Many create or recommend explicit policies to govern actions such as
withholding and withdrawing treatment, and many serve educational functions
in the hospital. Controversy centers on additional functions, such as whether
committees should make, facilitate, or monitor decisions about patients in particular cases. The decisions of committees on occasion need to be reviewed or
criticized, perhaps by an auditor or impartial party. Nonetheless, the benefits of
good committee review generally outweigh its risks, and these committees have
a robust role to play in circumstances in which physicians acquiesce too readily
to parental, familial, or guardian choices that prove contrary to a patient's best
interests.

The judicial system. Courts are sometimes unduly intrusive as final decision
makers, but in many cases they represent the last and the fairest recourse. When
good reasons exist to appoint guardians or to disqualify familial decision makers or health care professionals to protect an incompetent patient's interests, the
courts may legitimately be involved. The courts also sometimes need to intervene in nontreatment decisions for incompetent patients in mental institutions,
nursing homes, and the like. If no family members are available or willing to
be involved, and if the patient is confined to a state mental institution or is in a
nursing home, it may be appropriate to establish safeguards beyond the health
care team and the institutional ethics committee.[90]

Conclusion

We have concentrated in this chapter on the principle of nonmaleficence and its
implications for refusals of treatment and requests for assistance in dying when
death is a high probability or certainty. From the principle that we should avoid
causing harm to persons, there is no direct step to the conclusion that a positive
obligation exists to provide benefits such as health care and various forms of

assistance. We have not entered this territory in this chapter on nonmaleficence because obligations to provide positive benefits are the territory of beneficence and justice. We treat these principles in Chapters 6 and 7.

NOTES

1.   W. H. S. Jones, *Hippocrates,* vol. I (Cambridge, MA: Harvard University Press, 1923), p. 165. See also Albert R. Jonsen, "Do No Harm: Axiom of Medical Ethics," in *Philosophical and Medical Ethics: Its Nature and Significance,* ed. Stuart F. Spicker and H. Tristram Engelhardt, Jr. (Dordrecht, Netherlands: D. Reidel, 1977), pp. 27–41; and Steven H. Miles, *The Hippocratic Oath and the Ethics of Medicine* (New York: Oxford University Press, 2004).

2.   W. D. Ross, *The Right and the Good* (Oxford: Clarendon, 1930), pp. 21–26; John Rawls, *A Theory of Justice* (Cambridge, MA: Harvard University Press, 1971; rev. ed., 1999), p. 114 (1999: p. 98).

3.   William Frankena, *Ethics,* 2nd ed. (Englewood Cliffs, NJ: Prentice Hall, 1973), p. 47.

4.   On the priority of avoiding harm, see criticisms by N. Ann Davis, "The Priority of Avoiding Harm," in *Killing and Letting Die,* 2nd ed., ed. Bonnie Steinbock and Alastair Norcross (New York: Fordham University Press, 1999), pp. 298–354.

5.   *McFall v. Shimp,* no. 78-1771 in Equity (C. P. Allegheny County, PA, July 26, 1978); Barbara J. Culliton, "Court Upholds Refusal to Be Medical Good Samaritan," *Science* 201 (August 18, 1978): 596–97; Mark F. Anderson, "Encouraging Bone Marrow Transplants from Unrelated Donors," *University of Pittsburgh Law Review* 54 (1993): 477ff.

6.   Alan Meisel and Loren H. Roth, "Must a Man Be His Cousin's Keeper?" *Hastings Center Report* 8 (October 1978): 5–6.

7.   Joel Feinberg, *Harm to Others,* vol. I of *The Moral Limits of the Criminal Law* (New York: Oxford University Press, 1984), esp. pp. 32–36.

8.   On some of the roles of harm and nonmaleficence in bioethics, see Bettina Schöne-Seifert, "Harm," in *Encyclopedia of Bioethics,* rev. ed., ed. Warren Reich (New York: Simon & Schuster Macmillan, 1995), pp. 1021–26.

9.   For an account of the central rules of nonmaleficence and their role in bioethics, see Bernard Gert, *Morality: Its Nature and Justification* (New York: Oxford University Press, 2005); and Bernard Gert, Charles M. Culver, and K. Danner Clouser, *Bioethics: A Systematic Approach* (New York: Oxford University Press, 2006).

10.   H. L. A. Hart, *Punishment and Responsibility* (Oxford: Clarendon, 1968), esp. pp. 136–57; Joel Feinberg, *Doing and Deserving* (Princeton, NJ: Princeton University Press, 1970), esp. pp. 187–221; Eric D'Arcy, *Human Acts: An Essay in Their Moral Evaluation* (Oxford: Clarendon, 1963), esp. p. 121.

11.   On medical negligence, physician-caused harm, and their connection to medical ethics, see Virginia A. Sharpe and Alan I. Faden, *Medical Harm: Historical, Conceptual, and Ethical Dimensions of Iatrogenic Illness* (New York: Cambridge University Press, 1998).

12.   As quoted in Angela Roddy Holder, *Medical Malpractice Law* (New York: Wiley, 1975), p. 42.

13.   The facts of the case and observations about it are found in Peter Pronovost et al. "An Intervention to Decrease Catheter-Related Bloodstream Infections in the ICU," *New England Journal of Medicine* 355 (2006): 2725–32; Mary Ann Baily, "Harming through Protection?" *New England Journal of Medicine* 358 (2008): 768–69; and U.S. Department of Health and Human Services, Office for Human

Research Protections, *OHRP Statement Regarding The New York Times Op-Ed Entitled "A Lifesaving Checklist,"* News, January 15, 2008, http://www.hhs.gov/ohrp/news/recentnews.html#20080215 (accessed January 22, 2010).

14.   *OHRP Statement Regarding The New York Times Op-Ed Entitled "A Lifesaving Checklist,"* http://www.hhs.gov/ohrp/news/recentnews.html#20080215 (accessed December 5, 2011).

15.   Cf. the conclusions about physicians' reservations in Arthur R. Derse, "Limitation of Treatment at the End-of-Life: Withholding and Withdrawal," *Clinics in Geriatric Medicine* 21 (2005): 223–38; Neil J. Farber et al., "Physicians' Decisions to Withhold and Withdraw Life-Sustaining Treatments," *Archives of Internal Medicine* 166 (2006): 560–65; and Sharon Reynolds, Andrew B. Cooper, and Martin McKneally, "Withdrawing Life-Sustaining Treatment: Ethical Considerations," *Surgical Clinics of North America* 87 (2007): 919–36, esp. 920–23.

16.   This case was presented to one of the authors during a consultation. On some of the intuitions at work in this and similar cases, see Anna Maria Cugliari and Tracy E. Miller, "Moral and Religious Objections by Hospitals to Withholding and Withdrawing Life-Sustaining Treatment," *Journal of Community Health* 19 (1994): 87–100.

17.   For defenses of the distinction along these or similar lines, see Daniel P. Sulmasy and Jeremy Sugarman, "Are Withholding and Withdrawing Therapy Always Morally Equivalent?" *Journal of Medical Ethics* 20 (1994): 218–22 (commented on by John Harris, pp. 223–24); and Kenneth V. Iserson, "Withholding and Withdrawing Medical Treatment: An Emergency Medicine Perspective," *Annals of Emergency Medicine* 28 (1996): 51–54.

18.   *In the matter of Spring,* Mass. 405 N.E. 2d 115 (1980), at 488–89.

19.   Lewis Cohen, Michael Germain, and David Poppel, "Practical Considerations in Dialysis Withdrawal," *JAMA: Journal of the American Medical Association* 289 (2003): 2113–19.

20.   Robert Stinson and Peggy Stinson, *The Long Dying of Baby Andrew* (Boston: Little, Brown, 1983), p. 355.

21.   Katy Butler, "What Broke My Father's Heart," *New York Times Magazine,* June 18, 2010, available at http://www.nytimes.com/2010/06/20/magazine/20pacemaker-t.html?pagewanted=all (accessed February 10, 2012). For clinicians' views and ethical analyses, see Michael B. Bevins, "The Ethics of Pacemaker Deactivation in Terminally Ill Patients," *Journal of Pain and Symptom Management* 41 (June 2011): 1106–10; T. C. Braun et al., "Cardiac Pacemakers and Implantable Defibrillators in Terminal Care," *Journal of Pain and Symptom Management* 18 (1999): 126–31; and A. S. Kelley et al., "Implantable Cardioverter-Defibrillator at End-of-Life: A Physician Survey," *American Heart Journal* 157 (2009): 702–8.

22.   Paul Mueller et al., "Deactivating Implanted Cardiac Devices in Terminally Ill Patients: Practices and Attitudes," *Pacing and Clinical Electrophysiology* 31, no. 5 (2008): 560–68.

23.   Rachel Lampert et al., "HRS Expert Consensus Statement on the Management of Cardiovascular Implantable Electronic Devices (CIEDs) in Patients Nearing End of Life or Requesting Withdrawal of Therapy," *Heart Rhythm* 7, no. 7 (July 2010): 1008–25, available at http://www.hrsonline.org/ClinicalGuidance/upload/ceids_mgmt_eol.pdf (accessed January 28, 2012).

24.   Lampert, "HRS Expert Consensus Statement on the Management of Cardiovascular Implantable Electronic Devices (CIEDs)."

25.   Mueller et al., "Deactivating Implanted Cardiac Devices in Terminally Ill Patients: Practices and Attitudes," p. 560.

26.   Susanna E. Bedell and Thomas L. Delbanco, "Choices about Cardiopulmonary Resuscitation in the Hospital: When Do Physicians Talk with Patients?" *New England Journal of Medicine* 310 (April

26, 1984): 1089–93; Marcia Angell, "Respecting the Autonomy of Competent Patients," *New England Journal of Medicine* 310 (April 26, 1984): 1115–16; J. P. Burns et al., "Do-Not-Resuscitate Order after 25 Years," *Critical Care Medicine* 31, no. 5 (2003): 1534–50.

27.   On the nature and evolution of the doctrine, see Scott M. Sullivan, "The Development and Nature of the Ordinary/Extraordinary Means Distinction in the Roman Catholic Tradition," *Bioethics* 21 (2007): 386–97; and Donald E. Henke, "A History of Ordinary and Extraordinary Means," *National Catholic Bioethics Quarterly* 5 (2005): 555–75.

28.   The clearer language of "proportionate" and "disproportionate" now commonly explains or replaces the language of "ordinary" and "extraordinary" in Roman Catholic thought. See, for example, U.S. Conference of Catholic Bishops (USCB), *Ethical and Religious Directives for Catholic Health Care Services,* 5th ed. (Washington, DC: USCB, November 17, 2009), part five, available at http://www.ncbcenter.org/document.doc?id=147 (accessed January 28, 2012); and Jos V. M. Welie, "When Medical Treatment Is No Longer in Order: Toward a New Interpretation of the Ordinary-Extraordinary Distinction," *National Catholic Bioethics Quarterly* 5 (2005): 517–36.

29.   This case has been adapted with permission from a case presented by Dr. Martin P. Albert of Charlottesville, Virginia. On problems in nursing homes, see Alan Meisel, "Barriers to Forgoing Nutrition and Hydration in Nursing Homes," *American Journal of Law and Medicine* 21 (1995): 335–82; and Sylvia Kuo et al., "Natural History of Feeding-Tube Use in Nursing Home Residents With Advanced Dementia," *Journal of the American Medical Directors Association* 10 (2009): 264–70, which concludes that most feeding tubes are inserted during an acute care hospitalization and are associated with poor survival and subsequent heavy use of health care. O'Brien and colleagues determined that close to 70% of nursing home residents prefer not to have a feeding tube placed in cases of permanent brain damage, and many others shared that preference when they learned that physical restraints might be required: Linda A. O'Brien et al., "Tube Feeding Preferences Among Nursing Home Residents," *Journal of General Internal Medicine* 12 (1997): 364–71.

30.   *In the matter of Quinlan,* 70 N.J. 10, 355 A.2d 647, cert. denied, 429 U.S. 922 (1976). The New Jersey Supreme Court ruled that the Quinlans could disconnect the mechanical ventilator so that the patient could "die with dignity."

31.   In *Cruzan v. Director, Missouri Dep't of Health,* 497 U.S. 261 (1990), the U.S. Supreme Court concluded that a competent person has a constitutionally protected right to refuse lifesaving hydration and nutrition. Its dicta reflected no distinction between medical and sustenance treatments.

32.   See Lois Shepherd, *If That Ever Happens to Me: Making Life and Death Decisions after Terri Schiavo* (Chapel Hill, NC: University of North Carolina Press, 2009); Timothy E. Quill, "Terri Schiavo—A Tragedy Compounded," *New England Journal of Medicine* 352, no. 16 (2005): 1630–33; and George J. Annas, "'Culture of Life' Politics at the Bedside—The Case of Terri Schiavo," *New England Journal of Medicine* 352, no. 16 (2005): 1710–15. See further Thomas S. Shannon, "Nutrition and Hydration: An Analysis of the Recent Papal Statement in the Light of the Roman Catholic Bioethical Tradition," *Christian Bioethics* 12 (2006): 29–41.

33.   The RDE has rough precedents that predate the writings of St. Thomas Aquinas (e.g., in St. Augustine and Abelard). However, the history primarily flows from St. Thomas. See Anthony Kenny, "The History of Intention in Ethics," in *Anatomy of the Soul* (Oxford: Basil Blackwell, 1973), Appendix; Joseph T. Mangan, S.J., "An Historical Analysis of the Principle of Double Effect," *Theological Studies* 10 (1949): 41–61; and T. A. Cavanaugh, *Double-Effect Reasoning: Doing Good and Avoiding Evil* (New York: Oxford University Press, 2006), chap. 1.

34.   Joseph Boyle reduces the RDE to two conditions: intention and proportionality. "Who Is Entitled to Double Effect?" *Journal of Medicine and Philosophy* 16 (1991): 475–94; and "Toward Understanding the Principle of Double Effect," *Ethics* 90 (1980): 527–38. For criticisms of intention-weighted views, see Sophie Botros, "An Error about the Doctrine of Double Effect," *Philosophy* 74 (1999): 71–83; Timothy E. Quill, Rebecca Dresser, and Dan Brock, "The Rule of Double Effect—A Critique of Its

Role in End-of-Life Decision Making," *New England Journal of Medicine* 337 (1997): 1768–71; and Alison MacIntyre, "Doing Away with Double Effect," *Ethics* 111, no. 2 (2001): 219–55. T. M. Scanlon rejects the RDE on the grounds that it is not clear how an agent's intentions determine the permissibility of an agent's actions as the doctrine claims; however, it may still be appropriate in assessing the reasons an agent saw as bearing on his actions. Scanlon, *Moral Dimensions: Permissibility, Meaning, Blame* (Cambridge, MA: Harvard University Press, 2008), esp. Introduction and chaps. 1, 2. Intention may be relevant in judging an agent's character rather than in judging the rightness or wrongness of his or her actions. For an overview of the doctrine of double effect, see Suzanne Uniacke, "The Doctrine of Double Effect," in *Principles of Health Care Ethics,* 2nd ed., ed. Richard E. Ashcroft et al. (Chichester, England: John Wiley & Sons, 2007), pp. 263–68. For representative philosophical positions, see P. A. Woodward, ed., *The Doctrine of Double Effect: Philosophers Debate a Controversial Moral Principle* (Notre Dame, IN: Notre Dame University Press, 2001).

35. For assessments, see Daniel Sulmasy, "Reinventing the Rule of Double Effect," in *The Oxford Handbook of Bioethics,* ed. Bonnie Steinbock (New York: Oxford University Press, 2010), pp. 114–49; David Granfield, *The Abortion Decision* (Garden City, NY: Image Books, 1971); and Susan Nicholson, *Abortion and the Roman Catholic Church* (Knoxville, TN: Religious Ethics, 1978). See the criticisms of the RDE in Donald Marquis, "Four Versions of Double Effect," *Journal of Medicine and Philosophy* 16 (1991): 515–44, reprinted in *The Doctrine of Double Effect,* ed. Woodward, pp. 156–85.

36. See Michael Bratman, *Intention, Plans, and Practical Reason* (Cambridge, MA: Harvard University Press, 1987).

37. Alvin I. Goldman, *A Theory of Human Action* (Englewood Cliffs, NJ: Prentice Hall, 1970), pp. 49–85.

38. Hector-Neri Castañeda, "Intensionality and Identity in Human Action and Philosophical Method," *Nous* 13 (1979): 235–60, esp. 255.

39. Our analysis draws from Ruth R. Faden and Tom L. Beauchamp, *A History and Theory of Informed Consent* (New York: Oxford University Press, 1986), chap. 7.

40. We follow John Searle in thinking that we cannot reliably distinguish, in many situations, among acts, effects, consequences, and events. Searle, "The Intentionality of Intention and Action," *Cognitive Science* 4 (1980): 65.

41. This interpretation of double effect is defended by Boyle, "Who Is Entitled to Double Effect?"

42. See Joseph Boyle, "Medical Ethics and Double Effect: The Case of Terminal Sedation," *Theoretical Medicine* 25 (2004): 51–60; Alison McIntyre, "The Double Life of Double Effect," *Theoretical Medicine* 25 (2004): 61–74; Sulmasy and Pellegrino, "The Rule of Double Effect"; Lynn A. Jansen and Daniel Sulmasy, "Sedation, Alimentation, Hydration, and Equivocation: Careful Conversation about Care at the End of Life," *Annals of Internal Medicine* 136 (June 4, 2002): 845–49; and Johannes J. M. van Delden, "Terminal Sedation: Source of a Restless Debate," *Journal of Medical Ethics* 33 (2007): 187–88.

43. See Quill, Dresser, and Brock, "The Rule of Double Effect"; and McIntyre, "The Double Life of Double Effect."

44. Debates about the concept of medical futility have been vigorous over the last twenty-five years. See D. J. C. Wilkinson and J. Savulescu, "Knowing When to Stop: Futility in the Intensive Care Unit," *Current Opinion in Anesthesiology* 24 (April 2011): 160–65; D. K. Sokol, "The Slipperiness of Futility," *BMJ: British Medical Journal* 338 (June 5, 2009); E. Chwang, "Futility Clarified," *Journal of Law, Medicine, and Ethics* 37 (2009): 487–95; Baruch A. Brody and Amir Halevy, "Is Futility a Futile Concept?" *Journal of Medicine and Philosophy* 20 (1995): 123–44; R. Lofmark and T. Nilstun, "Conditions and Consequences of Medical Futility," *Journal of Medical Ethics* 28 (2002): 115–19; and

Loretta M. Kopelman, "Conceptual and Moral Disputes about Futile and Useful Treatments," *Journal of Medicine and Philosophy* 20 (1995): 109–21.

45. Wilkinson and Savulescu, in "Knowing When to Stop," propose the language of "medically inappropriate" to highlight that medical professionals are making value judgments and that a treatment is appropriate or inappropriate for realizing some goal of treatment. For a discussion of the limits of providing requested "nonbeneficial interventions," see Allan S. Brett and Laurence B. McCullough, "Addressing Requests by Patients for Nonbeneficial Interventions," *JAMA: Journal of the American Medical Association* 307 (January 11, 2012): 149–50.

46. Susan B. Rubin, *When Doctors Say No: The Battleground of Medical Futility* (Bloomington, IN: Indiana University Press, 1998); Lawrence J. Schneiderman and Nancy S. Jecker, *Wrong Medicine: Doctors, Patients, and Futile Treatment,* 2nd ed. (Baltimore: Johns Hopkins University Press, 2011).

47. For a defense of an occasional compassionate futile intervention, see Robert D. Truog, "Is It Always Wrong to Perform Futile CPR?" *New England Journal of Medicine* 362 (2010): 477–79. A counterargument, based on the individual's right to die with dignity, appears in J. J. Paris, P. Angelos, and M. D. Schreiber, "Does Compassion for a Family Justify Providing Futile CPR?" *Journal of Perinatology* 30 (December 2010): 770–72.

48. For an overview, see John Luce, "A History of Resolving Conflicts over End-of-Life Care in Intensive Care Units in the United States," *Critical Care Medicine* 38 (August 2010): 1623–29. For constructive proposals that take account of legitimate disagreement, see Amir Halevy and Baruch A. Brody, "A Multi-Institution Collaborative Policy on Medical Futility," *JAMA: Journal of the American Medical Association* 276 (1996): 571–75; Robert L. Fine, "Point: The Texas Advance Directives Act Effectively and Ethically Resolves Disputes about Medical Futility," *Chest* 136 (2009): 963–67; Robert D. Truog, "Counterpoint: The Texas Advance Directives Act Is Ethically Flawed: Medical Futility Disputes Must Be Resolved by a Fair Process," *Chest* 136 (2009): 968–71, followed by discussion 971–73; Wilkinson and Savulescu, "Knowing When To Stop"; and Carolyn Standley and Bryan A. Liang, "Addressing Inappropriate Care Provision at the End-of-Life: A Policy Proposal for Hospitals," *Michigan State University Journal of Medicine and Law* 15 (Winter 2011): 137–76. For a proposal for retaining the possibility of appeal to the courts, see Douglass B. White and Thaddeus M. Pope, "The Courts, Futility, and the Ends of Medicine," *JAMA: Journal of the American Medical Association* 307, no. 2 (2012): 151–52.

49. *Superintendent of Belchertown State School v. Saikewicz,* Mass., 370 N.E. 2d 417 (1977), at 428.

50. Ramsey, *Ethics at the Edges of Life* (New Haven, CT: Yale University Press, 1978), p. 155.

51. See President's Commission for the Study of Ethical Problems in Medicine and Behavioral Research, *Deciding to Forego Life-Sustaining Treatment: Ethical, Medical, and Legal Issues in Treatment Decisions* (Washington, D.C.: U.S. Government Printing Office, March 1983), chap. 5, and the articles on "The Persistent Problem of PVS," *Hastings Center Report* 18 (February–March 1988): 26–47.

52. Ramsey, *Ethics at the Edges of Life,* p. 172.

53. President's Commission, *Deciding to Forego Life-Sustaining Treatment.*

54. See Frank A. Chervenak and Laurence B. McCullough, "Nonaggressive Obstetric Management," *JAMA: Journal of the American Medical Association* 261 (June 16, 1989): 3439–40; and their "The Fetus as Patient: Implications for Directive versus Nondirective Counseling for Fetal Benefit," *Fetal Diagnosis and Therapy* 6 (1991): 93–100.

55. Albert R. Jonsen and Michael J. Garland, "A Moral Policy for Life/Death Decisions in the Intensive Care Nursery," in *Ethics of Newborn Intensive Care,* ed. Jonsen and Garland (Berkeley, CA: University of California, Institute of Governmental Studies, 1976), p. 148. A report from the Nuffield

Council on Bioethics uses the concept of "intolerability" to describe situations where life-sustaining treatment would not be in the baby's "best interests" because of the burdens imposed by "irremediable suffering." *Critical Care Decisions in Fetal and Neonatal Medicine: Ethical Issues* (London: Nuffield Council on Bioethics, 2006). An overview of the development of "neonatal bioethics" indicates that physicians' judgments about neonatal intensive care now include both the baby's chances for survival and his or her anticipated quality of life. See John Lantos and William L. Meadow, *Neonatal Bioethics: The Moral Challenges of Medical Innovation* (Baltimore: Johns Hopkins University Press, 2006), p. 10 et passim.

56.   See Steinbock and Norcross, *Killing and Letting Die,* 2nd ed.; Tom L. Beauchamp, ed., *Intending Death* (Upper Saddle River, NJ: Prentice Hall, 1996); Jeff McMahan, "Killing, Letting Die, and Withdrawing Aid," *Ethics* 103 (1993): 250–79; David Orentlicher, "The Alleged Distinction between Euthanasia and the Withdrawal of Life-Sustaining Treatment: Conceptually Incoherent and Impossible to Maintain," *University of Illinois Law Review* (1998): 837–59; and James Rachels, "Killing, Letting Die, and the Value of Life," in his *Can Ethics Provide Answers? And Other Essays in Moral Philosophy* (Lanham, MD: Rowman & Littlefield, 1997), pp. 69–79.

57.   *Assisted suicide* is the term often used to describe this practice. Although we sometimes use this term, we also use broader language, such as "physician-assisted dying" or "physician-arranged dying," not because of a desire to find euphemisms but because the broader language provides a more accurate description. Although the term *suicide* has the small advantage of indicating that the one whose death is brought authorizes or performs the final act, other conditions such as prescribing and transporting fatal substances may be as causally relevant as the "final act" itself. For related conceptual problems, see Franklin G. Miller, Robert D. Truog, and Dan W. Brock, "Moral Fictions and Medical Ethics," *Bioethics* 24 (2010): 453–60.

58.   Howard Brody, "Messenger Case: Lessons and Reflections," *Ethics-In-Formation* 5 (1995): 8–9; John Roberts, "Doctor Charged for Switching off His Baby's Ventilator," *British Medical Journal* 309 (August 13, 1994): 430.

59.   Cf. James Rachels, "Active and Passive Euthanasia," *New England Journal of Medicine* 292 (January 9, 1975): 78–80; Franklin G. Miller, Robert D. Truog, and Dan W. Brock, "Moral Fictions and Medical Ethics," *Bioethics* 24 (2010): 453–60; Roy W. Perrett, "Killing, Letting Die and the Bare Difference Argument," *Bioethics* 10 (1996): 131–39; and Dan W. Brock, "Voluntary Active Euthanasia," *Hastings Center Report* 22 (March–April 1992): 10–22.

60.   See Joseph J. Fins, *A Palliative Ethic of Care: Clinical Wisdom at Life's End* (Sudbury, MA: Jones & Bartlett, 2006); and Joanne Lynn et al., *Improving Care for the End of Life: A Sourcebook for Health Care Managers and Clinicians* (New York: Oxford University Press, 2007).

61.   Oregon Death with Dignity Act, Ore. Rev. Stat. § 127.800 *et seq.* This act explicitly rejects the language of "physician-assisted suicide." It prefers the language of a right patients have to make a "request for medication to end one's life in a humane and dignified manner."

62.   See Lawrence O. Gostin, "Deciding Life and Death in the Courtroom: From Quinlan to Cruzan, Glucksberg, and Vacco—A Brief History and Analysis of Constitutional Protection of the 'Right to Die,'" *JAMA: Journal of the American Medical Association* 278 (November 12, 1997): 1523–28; and Yale Kamisar, "When Is There a Constitutional Right to Die? When Is There *No* Constitutional Right to Live?" *Georgia Law Review* 25 (1991): 1203–42.

63.   For discussions, see Douglas Walton, *Slippery Slope Arguments* (Oxford: Clarendon, 1992); Govert den Hartogh, "The Slippery Slope Argument," in *A Companion to Bioethics,* 2nd ed., ed. Helga Kuhse and Peter Singer (Malden, MA: Wiley-Blackwell, 2009): 321–31; Christopher James Ryan, "Pulling up the Runaway: The Effect of New Evidence on Euthanasia's Slippery Slope," *Journal of Medical Ethics* 24 (1998): 341–44; Bernard Williams, "Which Slopes Are Slippery?" in *Moral Dilemmas in Modern Medicine,* ed. Michael Lockwood (Oxford: Oxford University Press, 1985), pp. 126–37; and James Rachels, *The End of Life: Euthanasia and Morality* (Oxford: Oxford University Press, 1986), chap. 10.

64.   See Timothy E. Quill and Christine K. Cassel, "Nonabandonment: A Central Obligation for Physicians," in *Physician-Assisted Dying: The Case for Palliative Care and Patient Choice,* ed. Quill and Margaret P. Battin (Baltimore: Johns Hopkins University Press, 2004), chap. 2.

65.   See Franklin G. Miller, Howard Brody, and Timothy E. Quill, "Can Physician-Assisted Suicide Be Regulated Effectively?" *Journal of Law, Medicine and Ethics* 24 (1996): 225–32. Defenders of slippery-slope arguments in this context include John Keown, *Euthanasia, Ethics and Public Policy: An Argument Against Legislation* (Cambridge: Cambridge University Press, 2002); J. Pereira, "Legalizing Euthanasia or Assisted Suicide: The Illusion of Safeguards and Controls," *Current Oncology* 18 (April 2011): e38–45; and David Albert Jones, "Is There a Logical Slippery Slope from Voluntary to Nonvoluntary Euthanasia?" *Kennedy Institute of Ethics Journal* 21 (2011): 379–404. Opponents include L. W. Sumner, *Assisted Death: A Study in Ethics and Law* (New York: Oxford University Press, 2011); and Report of the Royal Society of Canada Expert Panel, *End-of-Life Decision Making* (Ottawa, ON: The Royal Society of Canada, December 2011), available at http://www.rsc.ca/ documents/RSC_EOL_1_3_25_Twenty-five_EN_FINAL.pdf (accessed February 3, 2012). After examining the laws and practical experience of jurisdictions around the world that authorize assisted dying in some cases, the latter concludes: "Despite the fears of opponents, it is…clear that the much-feared slippery slope has not emerged following decriminalization, at least not in those jurisdictions for which evidence is available" (p. 90).

66.   See, for example, Timothy E. Quill, "Legal Regulation of Physician-Assisted Death—The Latest Report Cards," *New England Journal of Medicine* 356 (May 10, 2007): 1911–13; Susan Okie, "Physician-Assisted Suicide—Oregon and Beyond," *New England Journal of Medicine* 352 (April 21, 2005): 1627–30; and Courtney Campbell, "Ten Years of 'Death with Dignity,'" *New Atlantis* (Fall 2008): 33–46.

67.   The information in this paragraph appears in the annual reports by the Oregon Department of Human Services. See *Oregon's Death with Dignity Act—2010,* and previous annual reports, available at http://public.health.oregon.gov/ProviderPartnerResources/EvaluationResearch/DeathwithDignityAct/ Pages/index.aspx (accessed February 3, 2012). See also *The Oregon Death with Dignity Act: A Guidebook for Health Care Professionals Developed by The Task Force to Improve the Care of Terminally-Ill Oregonians,* convened by The Center for Ethics in Health Care, Oregon Health & Science University. First Edition (print): March 1998; Current Edition (2008 online; updated as information becomes available): http://www.ohsu.edu/xd/education/continuing-education/center-for-ethics/ ethics-outreach/upload/Oregon-Death-with-Dignity-Act-Guidebook.pdf (accessed December 6, 2011).

68.   See Report of the Royal Society of Canada Expert Panel, *End-of-Life Decision Making,* which examines the international experience with laws authorizing assisted dying; and Guenter Lewy, *Assisted Death in Europe and America: Four Regimes and Their Lessons* (New York: Oxford University Press, 2011).

69.   See Bernard Gert, James L. Bernat, and R. Peter Mogielnicki, "Distinguishing between Patients' Refusals and Requests," *Hastings Center Report* 24 (July–August 1994): 13–15; Leigh C. Bishop et al., "Refusals Involving Requests" (Letters and Responses), *Hastings Center Report* 25 (July–August 1995): 4; and Diane E. Meier et al., "On the Frequency of Requests for Physician Assisted Suicide in American Medicine," *New England Journal of Medicine* 338 (April 23, 1998): 1193–1201.

70.   Cf. Allen Buchanan, "Intending Death: The Structure of the Problem and Proposed Solutions," in *Intending Death,* ed. Beauchamp, esp. pp. 34–38; Frances M. Kamm, "Physician-Assisted Suicide, the Doctrine of Double Effect, and the Ground of Value," *Ethics* 109 (1999): 586–605; and Matthew Hanser, "Why Are Killing and Letting Die Wrong?" *Philosophy and Public Affairs* 24 (1995): 175–201.

71.   *New York Times,* June 6, 1990, pp. A1, B6; June 7, 1990, pp. A1, D22; June 9, 1990, p. A6; June 12, 1990, p. C3; *Newsweek,* June 18, 1990, p. 46. Kevorkian's own description is in his *Prescription: Medicide* (Buffalo, NY: Prometheus Books, 1991), pp. 221–31.

72.   Timothy E. Quill, "Death and Dignity: A Case of Individualized Decision Making," *New England Journal of Medicine* 324 (March 7, 1991): 691–94, reprinted with additional analysis in Quill, *Death and Dignity* (New York: Norton, 1993).

73. J. K. Kaufert and T. Koch, "Disability or End-of-Life: Competing Narratives in Bioethics," *Theoretical Medicine* 24 (2003): 459–69. See also Kristi L. Kirschner, Carol J. Gill, and Christine K. Cassel, "Physician-Assisted Death in the Context of Disability," in *Physician-Assisted Suicide,* ed. Robert F. Weir (Bloomington and Indianapolis, IN: Indiana University Press, 1997), pp. 155–66.

74. Allen Buchanan, "An Ethical Framework for Biological Samples Policy," in National Bioethics Advisory Commission, *Research Involving Human Biological Materials: Ethical Issues and Policy Guidance,* vol. 2 (Rockville, MD: National Bioethics Advisory Commission, January 2000); Karen J. Maschke, "Wanted: Human Biospecimens," *Hastings Center Report* 40, no. 5 (2010): 21–23; Rebecca D. Pentz, Laurent Billot, and David Wendler, "Research on Stored Biological Samples: Views of African American and White American Cancer Patients," *American Journal of Medical Genetics,* published online March 7, 2006, http://onlinelibrary.wiley.com/doi/10.1002/ajmg.a.31154/full.

75. *Havasupai Tribe of Havasupai Reservation v. Arizona Bd. of Regents,* 204 P.3d 1063 (Ariz. Ct. App. 2008); Dan Vorhaus, "The Havasupai Indians and the Challenge of Informed Consent for Genomic Research," *Genomics Law Report,* published online April 21, 2010, http://www .genomicslawreport.com/index.php/2010/04/21/the-havasupai-indians-and-the-challenge-of-informed-consent-for-genomic-research/; Amy Harmon, "Indian Tribe Wins Fight to Limit Research of Its DNA," *New York Times,* April 21, 2010, p. A1, available at http://www.nytimes.com/2010/04/22/us/22dna.html; and Amy Harmon, "Havasupai Case Highlights Risks in DNA Research," *New York Times,* April 22, 2010, available at http://www.nytimes.com/2010/04/22/us/22dnaside.html

76. See Michelle M. Mello and Leslie E. Wolf, "The Havasupai Indian Tribe Case—Lessons for Research Involving Stored Biological Samples," *New England Journal of Medicine* 363 (July 15, 2010): 204–7.

77. Amy Harmon, "Where'd You Go with My DNA?" *New York Times,* April 25, 2010, available at http://www.nytimes.com/2010/04/25/weekinreview/25harmon.html?ref=us

78. For an examination of current U.S. law, see Norman L. Cantor, *Making Medical Decisions for the Profoundly Mentally Disabled* (Cambridge, MA: MIT Press, 2005).

79. See Hans-Martin Sass, Robert M. Veatch, and Rihito Kimura, eds., *Advance Directives and Surrogate Decision Making in Health Care: United States, Germany, and Japan* (Baltimore: Johns Hopkins University Press, 1998); and Nancy M. P. King, *Making Sense of Advance Directives* (Dordrecht, Netherlands: Kluwer Academic, 1991; rev. ed. 1996).

80. See, for example, The President's Council on Bioethics, *Taking Care: Ethical Caregiving in Our Aging Society* (Washington, DC: President's Council on Bioethics, 2005), chap. 2; Alasdair R. MacLean, "Advance Directives, Future Selves and Decision-Making," *Medical Law Review* 14 (2006): 291–320; A. Fagerlin and C. E. Schneider, "Enough: The Failure of the Living Will," *Hastings Center Report* 34, no. 2 (2004): 30–42; M. R. Tonelli, "Pulling the Plug on Living Wills: A Critical Analysis of Advance Directives," *Chest* 110 (1996): 816–22; D. I. Shalowitz, E. Garrett-Mayer, and D. Wendler, "The Accuracy of Surrogate Decision Makers: A Systematic Review," *Archives of Internal Medicine* 165 (2006): 493–97.

81. See, for instance, Benjamin H. Levi and Michael J. Green, "Too Soon to Give Up: Re-Examining the Value of Advance Directives," *American Journal of Bioethics* 10 (April 2010): 3–22 (and responses thereafter); Bernard Lo and Robert Steinbrook, "Resuscitating Advance Directives," *Archives of Internal Medicine* 164 (2004): 1501–6; and Joanne Lynn and N. E. Goldstein, "Advance Care Planning for Fatal Chronic Illness: Avoiding Commonplace Errors and Unwarranted Suffering," *Annals of Internal Medicine* 138 (2003): 812–18.

82. See, for example, J. M. Teno, J. Lynn, R. S. Phillips, et al., "Do Formal Advance Directives Affect Resuscitation Decisions and the Use of Resources for Seriously Ill Patients?" SUPPORT Investigators: Study to Understand Prognoses and Preferences for Outcomes and Risks of Treatments, *Journal of Clinical Ethics* 5 (1994): 23–30.

83.   Maria J. Silveira, Scott Y. H. Kim, and Kenneth M. Langa, "Advance Directives and Outcomes of Surrogate Decision Making Before Death," *New England Journal of Medicine* 362 (April 1, 2010): 1211–18; K. M. Detering et al., "The Impact of Advance Care Planning on End of Life Care in Elderly Patients: Randomised Controlled Trial," *BMJ: British Medical Journal* 340 (2010): c1345. Debate continues about whether advance directives have—or for that matter, should have—an impact on health care costs. See Douglas B. White and Robert M. Arnold, "The Evolution of Advance Directives," *JAMA: Journal of the American Medical Association* 306 (October 5, 2011): 1485–86.

84.   Su Hyun Kim and Diane Kjervik, "Deferred Decision Making: Patient's Reliance on Family and Physicians for CPR Decisions in Critical Care," *Nursing Ethics* 12 (2005): 493–506.

85.   See Judith Areen, "The Legal Status of Consent Obtained from Families of Adult Patients to Withhold or Withdraw Treatment," *JAMA: Journal of the American Medical Association* 258 (July 10, 1987): 229–35; Charles B. Sabatino, "The Evolution of Health Care Advance Planning Law and Policy," *Milbank Quarterly* 88 (2010): 211–38; and Commission on Law and Aging, *Default Surrogate Consent Statutes as of November 2009* (Washington, DC: American Bar Association, 2009), available at http://www.americanbar.org/content/dam/aba/migrated/aging/PublicDocuments/famcon_2009 .authcheckdam.pdf (accessed February 4, 2012).

86.   Patricia King, "The Authority of Families to Make Medical Decisions for Incompetent Patients after the Cruzan Decision," *Law, Medicine & Health Care* 19 (1991): 76–79.

87.   Mark P. Aulisio, "Standards for Ethical Decision Making at the End of Life," in *Advance Directives and Surrogate Decision Making in Illinois,* ed. Thomas May and Paul Tudico (Springfield, IL: Human Services Press, 1999), pp. 25–26.

88.   David Wendler, "The Effect on Surrogates of Making Treatment Decisions for Others," *Annals of Internal Medicine* 154 (March 1, 2011): 336–46.

89.   David E. Weissman, "Decision Making at a Time of Crisis Near the End of Life," *JAMA: Journal of the American Medical Association* 292 (2004): 1738–43.

90.   For an analysis of the role of courts and the connection to valid consent, see M. Stratling, V. E. Scharf, and P. Schmucker, "Mental Competence and Surrogate Decision-Making Towards the End of Life," *Medicine, Health Care and Philosophy* 7 (2004): 209–15.

6
Beneficence

Morality requires not only that we treat persons autonomously and refrain from harming them, but also that we contribute to their welfare. These beneficial actions fall under the heading of "beneficence." Principles of beneficence potentially demand more than the principle of nonmaleficence, because agents must take positive steps to help others, not merely refrain from harmful acts. There is an implicit assumption of beneficence in all medical and health care professions and their institutional settings: Attending to the welfare of patients—not merely avoiding harm—embodies medicine's goal, rationale, and justification. Likewise, preventive medicine, public health, and biomedical research embrace values of public beneficence.

We distinguish and examine two principles of beneficence in this chapter: positive beneficence and utility. *Positive beneficence* requires agents to provide benefits to others. *Utility* requires that agents balance benefits, risks, and costs to produce the best overall results. We explore the virtue of benevolence, obligatory beneficence, and nonobligatory ideals of beneficence. We then show how to handle conflicts between beneficence and respect for autonomy that occur in paternalistic refusals to accept a patient's wishes and in public policies designed to protect or improve individuals' health. Thereafter, the chapter focuses on two discrete areas. First, we discuss the ways in which systems of surrogate decision making should function to protect and promote the welfare interests of patients. Second, we treat ideas of balancing benefits, risks, and costs through analytical methods designed to implement the principle of utility in both health policy and clinical care. We conclude that these analytical methods have a useful, albeit limited, role as aids in decision making.

THE CONCEPT OF BENEFICENCE AND PRINCIPLES OF BENEFICENCE

In ordinary English, the term *beneficence* connotes acts of mercy, kindness, friendship, charity, and the like. We use the term in this chapter to cover beneficent action in a broad sense, so that it includes all forms of action intended to benefit other persons. *Benevolence* refers to the character trait or virtue of being disposed to act for the benefit of others. *Principle of beneficence* refers to a statement of moral obligation to act for the benefit of others. Many acts of beneficence are not obligatory, but some forms of beneficence are obligatory.

Beneficence and benevolence have played central roles in certain ethical theories. Utilitarianism, for example, is systematically arranged on a principle of beneficence (the principle of utility in this theory). During the Scottish Enlightenment, major figures such as Francis Hutcheson and David Hume made benevolence the centerpiece of their common-morality theories. These theories closely associate beneficence with the goal of morality itself. We concur that obligations to confer benefits, to prevent and remove harms, and to weigh an action's possible goods against its costs and possible harms are central to the moral life. However, principles of beneficence are not sufficiently broad or foundational, in our account, that they determine or justify all other principles.

The principle of utility in our account is thus not identical to the classic utilitarian principle of utility. Whereas utilitarians view utility as the sole or fundamental principle of ethics, we treat it as only one among a number of prima facie principles, and it does not determine the overall balance of moral obligations. Although utilitarians allow society's interests to override individual interests, the principle of utility that we defend can be legitimately overridden by other moral principles in a variety of circumstances.

OBLIGATORY BENEFICENCE AND IDEAL BENEFICENCE

Some deny that morality includes any positive obligations. They hold that beneficence is purely a virtuous ideal or an act of charity, and thus that persons do not violate obligations of beneficence if they fail to act beneficently. These views rightly point to a need to clarify and specify beneficence, stating the points at which beneficence is optional rather than obligatory.

An instructive and classic example of this problem appears in the New Testament parable of the Good Samaritan, which illustrates several problems in interpreting beneficence. In this parable, robbers beat and abandon a "half-dead" man traveling from Jerusalem to Jericho. After two travelers pass by the injured man without rendering help, a Samaritan sees him, has compassion, binds up his wounds, and brings him to an inn to take care of him. In having compassion and showing mercy, the Good Samaritan expressed an attitude of caring about the injured man and he also took care of him. Both the Samaritan's motives and his actions were beneficent. Common interpretations of the parable suggest that positive beneficence is here an ideal rather than an obligation, because the Samaritan's act seems to exceed ordinary morality. But even if the case of the Samaritan does present an ideal of conduct, there are obligations of beneficence.

Virtually everyone agrees that the common morality does not contain a principle of beneficence that requires severe sacrifice and extreme altruism—for example, putting one's life in grave danger to provide medical care or giving both of one's kidneys for transplantation. Only ideals of beneficence incorporate such extreme generosity. Likewise, we are not morally required to benefit persons on all occasions, even if we are in a position to do so. For example, we are not morally required to perform all possible acts of generosity or charity that would benefit others. Much beneficent conduct therefore does constitute ideal, rather than obligatory, conduct, and the line between an obligation of beneficence and a moral ideal of beneficence is often unclear. Nonetheless, the principle of positive beneficence supports an array of prima facie rules of obligation, including the following:

1. Protect and defend the rights of others.
2. Prevent harm from occurring to others.
3. Remove conditions that will cause harm to others.
4. Help persons with disabilities.
5. Rescue persons in danger.

Distinguishing Rules of Beneficence from Rules of Nonmaleficence

Rules of beneficence differ in several ways from those of nonmaleficence. In the previous chapter we argued that rules of nonmaleficence (1) are negative prohibitions of action, (2) must be followed impartially, and (3) provide moral reasons for legal prohibitions of certain forms of conduct. By contrast, rules of beneficence (1) present positive requirements of action, (2) need not always be followed impartially, and (3) generally do not provide reasons for legal punishment when agents fail to abide by them.

The second condition of impartial adherence asserts that we are morally prohibited by rules of nonmaleficence from causing harm to anyone. We are obligated to act nonmaleficently toward all persons at all times. By contrast, beneficence permits us to help or benefit those with whom we have special relationships, and we often are not required to help or benefit those with whom we have no such relationship. With family, friends, and others of our choice morality ordinarily allows us to practice beneficence with partiality. Nonetheless, we will show that we are obligated to follow impartially *some* rules of beneficence, such as those requiring efforts to rescue strangers when the rescue efforts pose little risk.

General and Specific Beneficence

A distinction between specific and general beneficence eliminates some of the confusion that surrounds the distinction between obligatory beneficence and

nonobligatory moral ideals. Specific beneficence usually rests on moral relations, contracts, or special commitments and is directed at particular parties,
such as children, friends, contractors, or patients. For instance, many specific
obligations of beneficence in health care—often referred to as duties—rest on
a health professional's assumption of obligations through entering a profession
and taking on professional roles. By contrast, general beneficence is directed
beyond special relationships to all persons.

Virtually everyone agrees that all persons are obligated to act in the interests
of their children, friends, and other parties in special relationships, but the idea
of a general obligation of beneficence is controversial. W. D. Ross suggests that
obligations of general beneficence "rest on the mere fact that there are other
beings in the world whose condition we can make better."[1] From this perspective, general beneficence obligates us to benefit persons whom we do not know
or with whose views we are not sympathetic. The notion that we have the same
impartial obligations of beneficence to persons we do not know as we have to
our own families is overly romantic and impractical. It is also perilous because
this standard may divert attention from our obligations to those with whom we
have special moral relationships, and to whom our responsibilities are clear
rather than clouded. The more widely we generalize obligations of beneficence,
the less likely we will be to meet our primary responsibilities. For this reason,
among others, the common morality recognizes significant limits to the demands
of beneficence.

Some writers try to set limits to our obligations by distinguishing between
the removal of harm, the prevention of harm, and the promotion of benefit. In
developing a principle of "the obligation to assist," Peter Singer distinguishes
preventing evil from promoting good, and contends that "if it is in our power to
prevent something bad from happening, without thereby sacrificing anything of
comparable moral importance, we ought, morally, to do it."[2] Singer's criterion
of comparable importance sets a limit on sacrifice: We ought to donate time
and resources until we reach a level at which, by giving more, we would sacrifice something of comparable moral importance. For example, at this point we
might cause as much suffering to ourselves as we would relieve through our gift.
While Singer leaves open the question of what counts as morally important, his
argument implies that morality sometimes requires us to make large personal
sacrifices to rescue needy persons around the world. As judged by common-
morality standards, this account is overdemanding. The requirement that persons
seriously disrupt reasonable life plans in order to benefit the sick, undereducated,
or starving exceeds the limits of basic obligations. Singer identifies a commendable moral ideal, not an obligation.

Singer resists this assessment. He regards ordinary morality as endorsing a
highly demanding harm prevention principle. He assesses the almost universal
lack of concern for poverty relief as a failure to draw the correct implications from

the moral principle(s) of beneficence that all moral persons accept. We respond, constructively, to this line of argument in the next section, where we treat obligations of rescue. The claim that Singer-type beneficence makes excessively strong demands is best tested by these rescue cases. We there offer a five-condition analysis of beneficence that we judge more satisfactory than Singer's principle.

Singer has contested objections that his principle sets too high a standard. Although he still adheres to his challenging principle of beneficence, he acknowledges that it may be maximally productive to *publicly advocate* a less demanding principle. He once suggested "a round percentage of one's income like, say, 10 per cent—more than a token donation, yet not so high as to be beyond all but saints."[3] This revised thesis more appropriately sets limits on the scope of the obligation of beneficence—limits that reduce required costs and impacts on the agent's life plans and that make meeting one's obligations a realistic possibility.

Recently, Singer has been less concerned to precisely fix obligations of beneficence and more concerned to identify the social conditions that will motivate people to give.[4] He responds to critics[5] by conceding that the limit of what we should publicly advocate as a level of giving is a person's "fair share" of what is needed to relieve poverty and other problems. A fair share is a lower threshold of obligations than his earlier formulations suggested and a more realistic goal. His attention to motivation to contribute to others illuminates one dimension of the nature and limits of beneficence. Of course, obligation and motivation are distinguishable, and, as Singer appreciates, it will prove difficult in many circumstances to motivate people to live up to obligations (as Singer conceives them) to rescue individuals in need.

The Duty of Rescue as Obligatory Beneficence

Some circumstances eliminate discretionary choice regarding beneficiaries of our beneficence. Consider the stock example of a passerby who observes someone drowning, but stands in no special moral relationship to the drowning person. The obligation of beneficence is not sufficiently robust to require a passerby who is a poor swimmer to risk his or her life by trying to swim a hundred yards to rescue someone drowning in deep water. Nonetheless, the passerby who is well-placed to help the victim in some manner has a moral obligation to do so. If the passerby does nothing (e.g., fails to alert a nearby lifeguard or fails to call out for help), the failure is morally culpable.

Apart from close moral relationships, such as contracts or the ties of family or friendship, we propose that a person X has a prima facie obligation of beneficence, in the form of a duty of rescue, toward a person Y if and only if each of the following conditions is satisfied (assuming that X is aware of the relevant facts):[6]

1. Y is at risk of significant loss of or damage to life, health, or some other basic interest.
2. X's action is necessary (singly or in concert with others) to prevent this loss or damage.
3. X's action (singly or in concert with others) will probably prevent this loss or damage.[7]
4. X's action would not present significant risks, costs, or burdens to X.
5. The benefit that Y can be expected to gain outweighs any harms, costs, or burdens that X is likely to incur.

Although it is difficult to state the precise meaning of "significant risks, costs, or burdens" in the fourth condition, reasonable threshold lines can be drawn and this condition, like the other four, seems essential to render the action *obligatory* on grounds of beneficence.

We can now test these five conditions expressing the demands of beneficence with two previously mentioned cases. The first is a borderline case of specific obligatory beneficence, involving rescue, whereas the second presents a clear-cut case of specific obligatory beneficence. After these two cases we examine the notion of a duty to rescue in the context of research.

In the first case, which was originally introduced in Chapter 5, Robert McFall was diagnosed as having aplastic anemia, which is often fatal, but his physician believed that a bone marrow transplant from a genetically compatible donor could increase his chances of surviving. David Shimp, McFall's cousin, was the only relative willing to undergo the first test, which established tissue compatibility. Shimp then unexpectedly refused to undergo the second test for genetic compatibility. When McFall sued to force his cousin to undergo the second test and to donate bone marrow if he turned out to be compatible, the judge ruled that the *law* did not allow him to force Shimp to engage in such acts of positive beneficence. However, the judge also stated his view that Shimp's refusal was "*morally* indefensible."

The judge's moral assessment is questionable because it is unclear that Shimp shirked an obligation. Conditions 1 and 2 listed previously were met for an obligation of specific beneficence in this case, but condition 3 was not satisfied. McFall's chance of surviving one year (at the time) would have only increased from 25% to between 40% and 60%. These contingencies make it difficult to determine whether a principle of beneficence can be validly specified so that it demands a particular course of action in this case. Although most medical commentators agreed that the risks to the donor were minimal, Shimp was concerned about condition 4. Bone marrow transplants, he was told, require 100 to 150 punctures of the pelvic bone. These punctures can be painlessly performed under anesthesia, and the major risk at the time was a 1 in 10,000 chance of death from anesthesia. Shimp, however, believed that the risks were greater ("What if I become a cripple?" he asked) and that they outweighed the probability and magnitude of benefit to McFall. This case, then, is a borderline case of obligatory beneficence.

In the *Tarasoff* case, the opening case in Chapter 1, a therapist, on learning of his patient's intention to kill an identified woman, notified the police but not the intended victim, because of constraints of confidentiality. Suppose we modify the actual circumstances in this case to create the following hypothetical situation: A psychiatrist informs all patients that he may not keep information confidential if serious threats to other persons are disclosed. The patient agrees to treatment under these conditions and subsequently reveals an unmistakable intention to kill an identified woman. The psychiatrist may now either remain aloof or take measures to protect the woman by notifying her or the police, or both. What does morality—and specifically beneficence—demand of the psychiatrist in this case?

Only a remarkably narrow account of moral obligation would assert that the psychiatrist is under no obligation to protect the woman by contacting her or the police or both. The psychiatrist is not at significant risk and will suffer virtually no inconvenience or interference with his life plans. If morality does not demand this much beneficence, it is difficult to see how morality imposes any positive obligations at all. Even if a competing obligation exists, such as protection of confidentiality, requirements of beneficence will in some cases override it. For example, health care professionals may have an overriding moral obligation to warn spouses or lovers of HIV-infected patients who refuse to disclose their status and who refuse to engage in safer sex practices.

What, now, is the morally relevant difference between these rescue cases involving individuals and those discussed in the previous section? We suggested that rescuing a drowning person involves a special obligation not present with global poverty, because the rescuer is "well-placed at that moment to help the victim." However, we are all placed well enough to help people in poverty by giving modest sums of money; we can do so at little risk to ourselves and with a significant probability of some degree of success. One response is that in the drowning case there is a specific individual toward whom we have an obligation, whereas in the poverty cases we have vast obligations toward entire populations of people, only a few of whom we can hope to help through a gift. Perhaps we are obligated only when there are specific individuals whom we can help, not when there is a whole group and we can only help some of the members.

This line of argument has implausible implications, particularly when the size of groups is smaller in scale. Consider a situation in which an epidemic breaks out in a reasonably small community, calling for immediate quarantine, and hundreds of persons who are not infected cannot return to their homes if infected persons are in the home. They are also not allowed to leave the city limits, and all hotel rooms are filled. Authorities project that you could prevent the deaths of approximately twenty noninfected persons by offering them your house. Conditions would become unsanitary if more than twenty persons were housed in one home, but there are enough homes to house every stranded person if each house in the community takes twenty persons. It seems implausible to say that no person is morally obligated to open their houses to these people for the weeks needed to control the epidemic, even though no one person has a specific obligation to any one of the stranded people. The hypothesis might be offered that this obligation arises only because they are all members of the community, but this principle is implausible because it would arbitrarily exclude visitors who were stranded. Accordingly, we sometimes have obligations beyond those to specific individuals.

It is doubtful that ethical theory and practical deliberation can establish precise, determinate limits on the scope of obligations of beneficence. Attempts to do so will involve setting a revisionary line in the sense that they will draw a sharper boundary for our obligations than the common morality recognizes. Although the limits of beneficence are not precise, we can still appropriately fix or specify some obligations of beneficence.

We will now take these conclusions about the duty to rescue and connect them to a difficult problem of policies and programs in research ethics.

Expanded Access and Continued Access in Research

An excellent test for our analysis of obligations of beneficence and the duty of rescue is found in programs and policies of expanded access and continued access to investigational (experimental) products such as drugs and medical devices.

Expanded access to investigational products. Is it either morally acceptable or morally obligatory to provide an investigational product to seriously ill patients, often persons with life-threatening disorders, who cannot enroll in a clinical trial? Policies that do so are commonly called either "expanded access" or "compassionate use" programs. The two terms are not synonymous, but they both identify the same type of program, namely, one that authorizes access to an investigational product even though as yet it does not have regulatory approval.[8]

The primary goal of clinical research is scientific understanding that can lead to sound clinical interventions. Research is not aimed at immediately providing treatments, but rather at ensuring that potential treatments are safe and efficacious. Research on new products therefore does not carry clinical obligations of health care, and clinical investigators and research sponsors are not morally obligated to provide access to an investigational product outside of a clinical trial. However, there are circumstances in which a program of expanded access is reasonably safe, based on available data, and has a possibility of providing a benefit to some patients; no alternative therapies are available; and therapeutic use of the product does not threaten the scheduled completion or the results of a clinical trial. In these cases, it is morally permissible to adopt a program of expanded access, and in some cases investigational treatments have worked for patients enrolled in these programs. The use of the drug AZT in the treatment of AIDS is a classic case in which compassionate use would have been justified had there been an adequate supply of the drug available at the time. (See our discussion of this case in Chapter 8, pp. 337–39.)

Part of the reason for the virtue-derived language of "compassionate use" is that, though it is clearly compassionate and justified to provide some investigational products for therapeutic use, it is generally not obligatory to do so. In some cases it is obligatory to not provide access either because the risks are too high for patients or because access might endanger clinical trial goals. Most investigational products do not survive clinical trials to achieve regulatory approval, and many turn out to have harmful side effects. If it is justified to proceed with a "compassionate use" program, the justification will likely appeal to a moral ideal, as analyzed in Chapter 2, rather than a moral obligation. It would be obligatory to undertake an expanded access program only if the situation conformed to all five conditions in the analysis of a duty of rescue that we discussed in the previous section.

In the normal course of investigational products, the prospect that all five conditions will be satisfied in any given new case is unlikely. In most possible compassionate use programs, condition 3 (will probably prevent a loss), condition 4 (will not present significant risks, costs, or burdens), or condition 5 (potential benefit can be expected to outweigh harms, costs, or burdens likely to be incurred) will not be satisfied. Often predictions and hopes about innovative treatments are not met. An apt illustration comes from the experimental treatment of breast cancer with high-dose chemotherapy followed by bone marrow transplantation. Perceptible initial improvement using aggressive applications in early-phase trials led to requests for expanded access from many patients. Approximately 40,000 women were given expanded access to this investigational approach—despite weak evidence of efficacy—and only 1,000 women participated in the clinical trial. The completed clinical trial established that this investigational strategy provided no benefits over standard therapies and, indeed, elevated the risk of mortality. In short, this expanded access program increased risks for thousands of patients without additional benefits.[9]

Conditions 4 and 5 in our analysis will be met in a number of circumstances, but condition 3 can involve very complicated decision making. However, we can easily imagine an extraordinary circumstance, such as a public health emergency, in which all of these conditions are satisfied and create an ethical obligation, not merely a moral ideal, of rescue through expanded access. The unusual case of the antiviral drug ganciclovir represents an interesting clinical situation of compassionate use because it satisfies all five conditions of the duty of rescue independently of a clinical trial and yet only questionably created an obligation on the part of the pharmaceutical company to provide the product. Ganciclovir had been shown to work in the laboratory against a previously untreatable viral infection, but a clinical trial was still years away. Authorization was given to first use the drug in a few emergency compassionate use cases. The drug was demonstrated to be efficacious by evidence of a different nature than the information collected in a clinical trial. For example, retinal photographs showed changes in eye infections after treatment.[10] Although the provision of ganciclovir in this compassionate use program was controversial from the beginning, the program in retrospect clearly was justified, even though it cannot be said to have been morally obligatory when initiated. Syntex, the pharmaceutical company that developed the drug, created what would become a five-year expanded access program. The company was trapped into continuing the program, which it had planned to be only short-term, because the U.S. Food and Drug Administration (FDA) would not accept ganciclovir in the absence of a scientific trial.

In most circumstances a more likely candidate than expanded access for being an obligation of specific beneficence is continued access, a related but notably different situation.

Continued access to investigational products. The moral problem of continued access is how to identify the conditions under which it is morally obligatory, after a clinical trial has ended, to continue to provide an investigational product to research subjects who have favorably responded to the product during the trial. Continued access may occur in a number of ways. The former subjects might continue as subjects in an extension of the trial on the same product or they might simply be given the product by the research sponsor. When subjects have responded favorably to an investigational product during the course of a trial and their welfare interests will be set back if the effective intervention is no longer available to them, two moral considerations distinguish this situation from that of expanded access. First, our analysis of the principle of nonmaleficence in Chapter 5 suggests that sponsors and investigators would be causing harm to research subjects by denying them further access to a product that is helping them escape serious health problems or death. Second, obligations of reciprocity (a moral notion treated in the next section in this chapter) suggest that research subjects are owed access to an apparently successful treatment at the end of their service in a clinical trial because they undertook risks to help produce knowledge about that product, which is also knowledge that advances science and benefits sponsors and investigators involved in the research.

These two moral considerations differentiate the continued access situation from the expanded access situation. They warrant the conclusion that there can be—and we think frequently are—moral obligations to provide continued access to investigational products for former research subjects. These obligations are independent of those created by our five-condition analysis of the duty of rescue. Although most of these five conditions are satisfied in many cases of continued access, condition 3 (will probably prevent loss or damage) often is not satisfied. Our view is that even if condition 3 is not satisfied, there still can be sufficient moral grounds to create an obligation to provide a continued access program because of demands of reciprocity and nonmaleficence. These moral grounds apply when there is good evidence that the research subject is currently benefiting even if there is inconclusive evidence that he or she will benefit in the long run.

Unlike the ordinary expanded access situation, it is unethical to withdraw an effective investigational product when a research subject with a serious disorder or facing a significant risk of death has been shown to respond favorably to the investigational product. Sponsors and investigators should make conscientious efforts before a trial begins to ensure that a program of continued access is in place for all subjects for whom an investigational product proves effective. They also have an obligation to state the conditions of continued access in the research protocol and to inform all potential subjects as part of the consent process what will happen if they respond favorably. Disclosures should be made regarding both the nature and duration of the continued access program, as well as the source of financing. If a protocol and consent form lack such information, the review committee should require investigators to justify the omission.[11]

However, these demanding conclusions need a proviso. In some cases, a product under study may be in such an early stage of development that information about efficacy and safety is inadequate to assess risk and potential benefits. In other cases it may be unclear whether subjects have genuinely responded favorably to interventions. Under these conditions, continued access programs may not be obligatory for some early-stage studies. In some difficult cases the provision of an investigational drug that has been shown to be seriously unsafe for most patients—that is, to carry an unreasonably high level of risk—can justifiably be discontinued altogether, even if some patients have responded favorably. However, because risk and safety indexes vary significantly in subjects, what is unsafe for one group of patients may not be unduly risky for another group. A high level of risk in general therefore may not be a sufficient reason to discontinue availability to individual subjects who have responded favorably.

A Reciprocity-Based Justification of Obligations of Beneficence

Obligations of general and specific beneficence can be justified in several ways. In addition to our observations about obligations of specific beneficence based on special moral relations and roles and about the duty of rescue in particular circumstances, another type of justification is based on reciprocity. This approach is well-suited to some areas of biomedical ethics, as we saw in the earlier discussion of expanded access. David Hume argued that the obligation to benefit others in society arises from social interactions: "All our obligations to do good to society seem to imply something reciprocal. I receive the benefits of society, and therefore ought to promote its interests."[12] Reciprocity is the act or practice of making an appropriate and often proportional return—for example, returning benefit with proportional benefit, countering harm-causing activities with proportional criminal sentencing, and reciprocating friendly and generous actions with gratitude. Hume's reciprocity account appropriately maintains that we incur obligations to help or benefit others at least in part because we have received, will receive, or stand to receive beneficial assistance from them.

Reciprocity pervades social life. It is implausible to maintain that we are largely free of, or can free ourselves from, indebtedness to our parents, researchers in medicine and public health, and teachers. The claim that we make our way independent of our benefactors is as unrealistic as the idea that we can always act autonomously without affecting others.[13] Codes of medical ethics have sometimes inappropriately viewed physicians as independent, self-sufficient philanthropists whose beneficence is analogous to generous acts of giving. The Hippocratic oath states that physicians' obligations to patients represent philanthropic service, whereas obligations to their teachers represent debts incurred in the course of becoming physicians. Today many physicians and health care professionals owe a large debt to society (e.g., for formal education and training in hospitals) and to their patients, past and present (e.g., for learning gained from both research and practice). Because of this indebtedness, the medical profession's role of beneficent care of patients is misconstrued if modeled on philanthropy, altruism, and personal commitment. This care is rooted in a moral reciprocity of the interface of receiving and giving in return.[14]

A compelling instance of reciprocity, and one with a promising future in medicine, occurs in what an Institute of Medicine report calls "a learning healthcare system." The report defines this type of system as "one in which knowledge generation is so embedded into the core of the practice of medicine that it is a natural outgrowth and product of the healthcare delivery process and leads to continual improvement in care."[15] A true learning health system will be structured so that professionals have obligations of care to patients and patients have specific obligations of reciprocity to facilitate learning in the health system so that care for all patients can be improved. In this institutional structure—which will in the near future increasingly become an integral part of the design of health care institutions all over the world—patients are on the receiving end of informational benefits in which the quality of their health care depends on a rapid and regular flow of information received from other patients and from other health care systems. Obligations of reciprocity call for all patients to supply information by participating in the same sort of learning activities and burdens that others have shouldered in the past to benefit them. In these circumstances, research and practice are merged in a constantly updated environment of learning designed to benefit everyone involved in the institution.

A reciprocity-based approach to beneficence has also emerged as a possible way to overcome the chronic shortage of deceased donor organs for transplantation. Appeals to obligatory or ideal beneficence to strangers have fallen far short of generating the number of organs needed to save the lives and enhance the quality of lives of patients with end-stage organ failure, many of whom die while awaiting a transplant. A reciprocity-based system would give preferential access to patients in need who previously agreed, some years earlier, to donate their own organs after their deaths. (Declared donors' immediate family members would also be included in some proposals.) Some private organizations, including LifeSharers, have taken this approach, and in 2012 Israel became the first country to implement a reciprocity-based system.

Two models have been proposed for such a program: (1) a model of pure reciprocity restricts the pool of potential organ recipients to declared donors; (2) a model of preferential access or preferred status gives declared donors additional points toward access in an allocation point system. Both models encounter difficult questions of fairness to persons in need who were not eligible because of age or disqualifying medical conditions to declare their status as donors; but the second, nonexclusionary, preferred-status model, which Israel adopted, can handle it more easily. However, other justice-based moral concerns focus on how a policy might disadvantage those who are uninformed about organ donation and on how much weight should be given to declared donor status and how much to medical need.[16]

PATERNALISM: CONFLICTS BETWEEN BENEFICENCE AND RESPECT FOR AUTONOMY

The thesis that beneficence expresses the primary obligation in health care is ancient. A venerable expression appears in the Hippocratic work *Epidemics:* "As to disease, make a habit of two things—to help, or at least to do no harm."[17] Traditionally, physicians relied almost exclusively on their own judgments about their patients' needs for information and treatment. However, medicine in the modern world has increasingly confronted assertions of patients' rights to receive information and to make independent judgments. As assertions of autonomy rights increased, problems of paternalism became more evident.

Whether respect for the autonomy of patients should have priority over professional beneficence directed at those patients is a central problem in clinical ethics. We begin to address paternalism by considering some key conceptual issues.

The Nature of Paternalism

The *Oxford English Dictionary* (*OED*) dates the term *paternalism* to the 1880s, giving its root meaning as "the principle and practice of paternal administration; government as by a father; the claim or attempt to supply the needs or to regulate the life of a nation or community in the same way a father does those of his children." The analogy with the father presupposes two features of the paternal role: that the father acts beneficently (i.e., in accordance with his conception of his children's welfare interests) and that he makes all or at least some of the decisions relating to his children's welfare, rather than letting them make those decisions. In health care relationships, the analogy is that a professional has superior training, knowledge, and insight and is thus in an authoritative position to determine the patient's best interests.

Examples of paternalism in medicine include the provision of blood transfusions when patients have refused them, involuntary commitment to institutions for treatment, intervention to stop suicides, resuscitation of patients who have asked not to be resuscitated, withholding of medical information that patients have requested, denial of an innovative therapy to someone who wishes to try it, and some governmental efforts to promote health.

Paternalistic acts sometimes use forms of influence such as deception, lying, manipulation of information, nondisclosure of information, or coercion, but they may also simply involve a refusal to carry out another's wishes. According to some definitions in the literature, paternalistic actions restrict only *autonomous* choices, whereas restricting nonautonomous conduct is not paternalistic. Although one author of this text prefers this conception,[18] we here accept and build on the broader definition suggested by the *OED:* intentional nonacquiescence or intervention in another person's preferences, desires, or actions with the intention of either preventing or reducing harm to or benefiting that person. Even if a person's desires, intentional actions, and the like are not substantially autonomous, overriding them can be paternalistic under this definition.[19] For example, if a man ignorant of his fragile, life-threatening condition and sick with a raging fever attempts to leave a hospital, it is paternalistic to detain him, even if his attempt to leave does not derive from a substantially autonomous choice.

Accordingly, we define "paternalism" as *the intentional overriding of one person's preferences or actions by another person, where the person who overrides justifies this action by appeal to the goal of benefiting or of preventing or mitigating harm to the person whose preferences or actions are overridden.* This definition is normatively neutral—it does not presume that paternalism is either justified or unjustified. Although the definition assumes an act of beneficence analogous to parental beneficence, it does not prejudge whether the beneficent act is justified, obligatory, misplaced, or wrong.

Problems of Medical Paternalism

Throughout the history of medical ethics the principles of nonmaleficence and beneficence have both been invoked as a basis for paternalistic actions. For example, physicians have traditionally held that disclosing certain kinds of information can cause harm to patients under their care and that medical ethics obligates them not to cause such harm. Here is a typical case: A man brings his father, who is in his late sixties, to his physician because he suspects that his father's problems in interpreting and responding to daily events may indicate Alzheimer's disease. The man also makes an "impassioned plea" that the physician not tell his father if the tests suggest Alzheimer's. Tests subsequently indicate that the father probably does have this disease. The physician now faces a dilemma, because of the conflict between demands of respect for autonomy, assuming that the father still has substantial autonomy and is competent at least some of the time, and demands of beneficence. The physician first considers the now recognized obligation to inform patients of a diagnosis of cancer. This obligation typically presupposes accuracy in the diagnosis, a relatively clear course of the disease, and a competent patient—none of which is clearly present in this case. The physician also notes that disclosure of Alzheimer's disease sometimes adversely affects patients' coping mechanisms, and thus could harm the patient, particularly by causing further decline, depression, agitation, and paranoia.[20] (See also our discussion of veracity in Chapter 8.)

Some patients—for example, those who are depressed or addicted to potentially harmful drugs—are unlikely to reach adequately reasoned decisions. Other patients who are competent and deliberative may make poor choices, as judged by their physicians' recommendations. When patients of either type choose harmful courses of action, some health care professionals respect autonomy by not interfering beyond attempts at persuasion, whereas others act beneficently by attempting to protect patients against the potentially harmful consequences of their own stated preferences. Discussions of medical paternalism focus on how to specify or balance these principles, which principle to follow under which conditions, and how to intervene in the decisions and affairs of such patients when intervention is warranted.

Soft and Hard Paternalism

A crucial distinction exists between soft and hard paternalism.[21] In soft paternalism, an agent intervenes in the life of another person on grounds of beneficence or nonmaleficence with the goal of preventing substantially nonvoluntary conduct.

Substantially nonvoluntary actions include cases such as poorly informed consent or refusal, severe depression that precludes rational deliberation, and addiction that prevents free choice and action. Hard paternalism, by contrast, involves interventions intended to prevent or mitigate harm to or to benefit a person, despite the fact that the person's risky choices and actions are informed, voluntary, and autonomous.

A hard paternalist will restrict forms of information available to the person or will otherwise override the person's informed and voluntary choices. For example, it is an act of hard paternalism to refuse to release a competent hospital patient who will probably die outside the hospital but who requests the release in full awareness of the probable consequences. Hard paternalism usurps autonomy by either restricting the information available to a person or overriding the person's informed and voluntary choices. For example, a hard paternalist might prevent a patient capable of making reasoned judgments from receiving diagnostic information if the information would lead the patient to a state of depression. For the interventions to qualify as hard paternalism, the intended beneficiary's choices need not be fully informed or voluntary, but they must be substantially autonomous.

Soft paternalistic actions are morally complicated largely because of the difficulty of determining whether a person's actions are substantially nonautonomous and of determining appropriate means of action. That we should protect persons from harm caused to them by conditions beyond their control is not controversial. Soft paternalism therefore does not involve a deep conflict between the principles of respect for autonomy and beneficence. Soft paternalism only tries to prevent the harmful consequences of a patient's actions that the patient did not choose with substantial autonomy.

This conclusion is not inconsistent with our earlier definition of paternalism as involving an intentional overriding of one person's known preferences or actions by another person. Some behaviors that express preferences are not autonomous. For example, some patients on medication or recovering from surgery insist that they do not want a certain physician to touch or examine them. They may be experiencing temporary hallucinations around the time of the statement. A day later they may have no idea why they stated this preference. A person's preferences can be motivated by many states and desires.

Paternalistic policies. Debates about paternalism have emerged in health policy as well as in clinical ethics. Often health policies—for example, requiring a doctor's prescription for a type of medical device—have the goal of avoiding a harm or providing a benefit in a population in which most affected parties are not consulted. Policymakers understand that some percentage of the population does not support the policy on grounds that it is autonomy depriving, whereas others strongly approve of the policy. In effect, the policy is intended to benefit all members of a population without consulting the autonomous preferences of individuals, and with the knowledge that many individuals would reject the control that the policy exerts over their lives.

So-called neopaternalists have argued for government policies intended to protect or benefit individuals through shaping or steering their choices without, in fact, altogether disallowing or coercing those choices.[22] In clinical care, similar arguments have supported the physician's manipulation of some patients to select proper goals of care.[23] Some soft paternalists recommend policies and actions that pursue values that an intended beneficiary already, at least implicitly, holds but cannot realize because of limited capacities or limited self-control.[24] The individual's own *stated* preferences, choices, and actions are deemed unreasonable in light of *other* standards the person embraces. By contrast, in hard paternalism the intended beneficiary does not accept the values used to define his or her own best interests. Hard paternalism requires that the benefactor's conception of best interests prevail, and it may ban, prescribe, or regulate conduct in ways that manipulate individuals' actions to secure the benefactor's intended result. Soft paternalism, by contrast, reflects the intended beneficiary's conception of his or her best interests, even if the intended beneficiary fails to adequately understand or recognize those interests or to fully pursue them because of inadequate voluntariness, commitment, or self-control.

This conception of soft paternalism faces difficulties. Our knowledge of what an informed and competent person chooses to do is generally the *best evidence* we have of what his or her values are. For example, if a deeply religious man fails to follow the dietary restrictions of his religion, although he is in the abstract strongly committed to all aspects of the religion, his departures from dietary laws may be the best evidence we have of his true values on the particular matter of dietary restrictions. Because it seems correct—short of counterevidence in particular cases—that competent informed choice is the best evidence of a person's values, a justified paternalism must have adequate evidence that this assumption is misguided in a particular case.

Some proponents of soft paternalism reach the conclusion that the position is compatible with, rather than contrary to, autonomous choice. Cass Sunstein and Richard Thaler maintain that "The idea of libertarian paternalism might seem to be an oxymoron, but it is both possible and desirable for private and public institutions to influence behavior while also respecting freedom of choice."[25] "Libertarian paternalism" is indeed counterintuitive, but sense can be made of it. Suppose that available evidence were to establish that smokers psychologically discount the risks of smoking because of an "optimism bias" (among other factors). It does not follow that a government would violate their autonomy through programs intended to correct their biases—for example, through television advertisements that graphically present the suffering that often results from smoking.[26]

Libertarian paternalism is premised on the view that people have limited rationality or limited self-control that reduces their capacity to choose and act autonomously. A critical assumption is that all autonomous persons would value health over the ill health caused by smoking, and in this sense a person's deepest autonomous commitment is to be a nonsmoker. The thesis is that we are justified on autonomy grounds in arranging their choice situation in a way that likely will correct their cognitive biases and bounded rationality. However, if this position holds that we should use our knowledge of cognitive biases not only to correct for failures of rationality, but also to manipulate substantially autonomous people into doing what is good for them, then this position is *hard* paternalism. Depending on the nature of the manipulation and the nature of the affected choices, the account could turn out to be either a hard or a soft paternalism.

There is a good reason for caution about libertarian paternalism.[27] The theory's supposed advantage may actually be an ethical disadvantage. This paternalism reflects many values that individuals would recognize or realize themselves if they did not encounter internal limits of rationality and control. The means employed, whether by health care professionals or the government, shape and steer persons without thwarting their free choice. These prima facie appealing paternalistic policies and practices may face little opposition and be implemented without the transparency and publicity needed for public assessment. Paternalistic governmental policies or health care practices are susceptible to abuse if they lack high-level public scrutiny.

Social norms and stigmatization. Soft paternalistic policies sometimes stigmatize conduct such as smoking. While stigmatization can change behavior in some contexts, it often has psychosocial costs. Proponents insist that they target *acts,* not *persons.* However, in practice, stigmatizing conduct may slide into stigmatizing people who engage in that conduct. For example, antismoking measures such as prohibitive "sin taxes" levied on cigarettes often have paternalistic goals of forcing changes in unhealthy behavior. Nevertheless, they sometimes slide from stigmatization of acts (smoking) to stigmatization of people (smokers), leading to hostility and antipathy directed at population subgroups.[28] Because smoking is now more common among lower socioeconomic groups in some countries, stigmatization is directed at socially vulnerable members of society and may involve discriminatory actions—a matter of moral concern from the standpoint of both beneficence and justice.[29]

So-called soft paternalistic interventions may promote social values that eventually pave the way for hard paternalistic interventions. The campaign against cigarette smoking is again instructive. It moved from disclosure of information, to sharp warnings, to soft paternalistic measures to reduce addiction-controlled unhealthy behavior, to harder paternalistic measures such as significantly increasing the taxes on cigarettes.[30] In this example, paternalistic interventions remain beneficent, but increasingly lose touch with, and may even violate, respect for autonomy.

The Justification of Paternalism and Antipaternalism

Three general positions appear in literature on the justification of paternalism: (1) antipaternalism, (2) paternalism that appeals to the principle of respect for autonomy as expressed through some form of consent, and (3) paternalism that appeals to principles of beneficence. All three positions agree that some acts of soft paternalism are justified, such as preventing a man under the influence of a hallucinogenic drug from killing himself. Even antipaternalists do not object to such interventions, because substantially autonomous actions are not at stake.

Antipaternalism. Antipaternalists oppose hard paternalistic interventions for several reasons. One motivating concern focuses on the potential adverse consequences of giving paternalistic authority to the state or to a group such as physicians. Another influential reason is that rightful authority resides in the individual. The argument for this conclusion rests on the analysis of autonomy rights discussed in Chapter 4: Hard paternalistic interventions display disrespect toward autonomous agents and fail to treat them as moral equals, treating them instead as less-than-independent determiners of their own good. If others impose their conception of the good on us, they deny us the respect they owe us, even if they have a better conception of our needs than we do.[31]

Antipaternalists also hold that paternalistic standards are too broad and authorize and institutionalize too much intervention when made the basis of policy. Hence, paternalism allows an unacceptable latitude of judgment. For example, suppose a sixty-five-year-old man who has donated a kidney to one of his sons now volunteers to donate his second kidney when another son needs a transplant, an act most would think not in his best interests even though he contends that he could survive on dialysis. Are we to commend him, ignore him, or deny his request? Hard paternalism suggests that it would be permissible and perhaps obligatory to restrain him as well as to refuse to carry out his request. If so, antipaternalists argue, the state is permitted, in principle, to restrain its morally heroic citizens if they act in a manner "harmful" to themselves.

A medical example with an extensive antipaternalistic literature is the involuntary hospitalization of persons who have neither been harmed by others nor actually harmed themselves, but who are thought to be at risk of such harm because of their mental disorders. In this case, a double paternalism is common—a paternalistic justification for both commitment and therapy. Antipaternalists would regard the intervention as justified by the intent to benefit, emphasizing that, in such a case, beneficence does not conflict with respect for autonomy because the intended beneficiary lacks substantial autonomy.

Paternalism justified by consent. Some appeal to *consent* to justify paternalistic interventions—be it rational consent, subsequent consent, hypothetical consent, or some other type of consent. As Gerald Dworkin puts it, "The basic notion of consent is important and seems to me the only acceptable way to try to delimit an area of justified paternalism." Paternalism, he says, is a "social insurance policy" to which fully rational persons would subscribe in order to protect themselves.[32] Such persons would know, for example, that they might be tempted at times to make decisions that are far-reaching, potentially dangerous, and irreversible. At other times, they might suffer irresistible psychological or social pressures to take actions that are unreasonably risky. In still other cases, persons might not sufficiently understand the dangers of their actions, such as medical facts about the effects of smoking, although they might believe that they have a sufficient understanding. Those who use consent as a justification conclude that, as fully rational persons, we would consent to a limited authorization for others to control our actions if our autonomy becomes defective or we are unable to make the prudent decision that we otherwise would make.[33]

A theory that appeals to rational consent to justify paternalistic interventions has attractive features, particularly its attempt to harmonize principles of beneficence and respect for autonomy. However, this approach does not incorporate an individual's actual consent, and is therefore not truly consent-based. It is best to keep autonomy-based justifications at arm's length from both paternalism and hypothetical, rational-persons arguments. Beneficence alone justifies truly paternalistic actions, exactly as it justifies parental actions that override children's preferences.[34] Children are controlled not because we believe that they will subsequently consent to or rationally approve our interventions. We control them because we believe they will have better, or at least less dangerous, lives.

Paternalism justified by prospective benefit. Accordingly, the justification of paternalistic actions that we recommend places benefit on a scale with autonomy interests and balances both: As a person's interests in autonomy increase and the benefits for that person decrease, the justification of paternalistic action becomes less plausible; conversely, as the benefits for a person increase and that person's autonomy interests decrease, the justification of paternalistic action becomes more plausible. Preventing minor harms or providing minor benefits while deeply disrespecting autonomy lacks plausible justification, but actions that prevent major harms or provide major benefits while only trivially disrespecting autonomy have a plausible paternalistic rationale. As we will now argue, even hard paternalistic actions can sometimes be justified.[35]

Justified hard paternalism. An illustrative case provides a good starting point for reflection on the conditions of justified hard paternalism: A physician obtains the results of a myelogram (a graph of the spinal region) following examination of a patient. Although the test yields inconclusive results and needs to be repeated, it also suggests a serious pathology. When the patient asks about the test results, the physician decides on grounds of beneficence to withhold potentially negative information, knowing that, on disclosure, the patient will be distressed and anxious. Based on her experience with other patients and her ten-year knowledge of this particular patient, the physician is confident that the information would not affect the patient's decision to consent to another myelo-gram. Her sole motivation in withholding the information is to spare the patient the emotional distress of processing negative information, which seems prema-ture and unnecessary. However, the physician intends to be completely truthful with the patient about the results of the second test and intends to disclose the information well before the patient would need to decide about surgery. This physician's act of temporary nondisclosure is morally justified, although benef-icence has, temporarily, received priority over respect for autonomy.[36] Such minor hard paternalistic actions are common in medical practice, and in our view are sometimes warranted.

To consolidate the discussion thus far, hard paternalism is justified in health care only if the following conditions are satisfied (see further our conditions for constrained balancing in Chapter 1):

1. A patient is at risk of a significant, preventable harm.
2. The paternalistic action will probably prevent the harm.
3. The prevention of harm to the patient outweighs risks to the patient of the action taken.
4. There is no morally better alternative to the limitation of autonomy that occurs.
5. The least autonomy-restrictive alternative that will secure the benefit is adopted.

We could add a sixth condition requiring that a paternalistic action not damage *substantial* autonomy interests, as would occur if one were to override the decision of a Jehovah's Witness patient who, from deep conviction, refuses a blood transfusion. To intervene forcefully by providing the transfusion would substantially infringe the patient's autonomy and could not be justified under this additional condition. However, some cases of justified hard paternalism do cross the line of minimal infringement. In general, as the risk to a patient's welfare increases or the likelihood of an irreversible harm increases, the likelihood of a justified paternalistic intervention correspondingly increases.

The following case plausibly supports hard paternalistic intervention, though it involves more than minimal infringement of respect for autonomy: A psychi-atrist is treating a patient who is sane, but who acts in what appear to be bizarre ways. He is acting conscientiously on his unique religious views. He asks a psy-chiatrist a question about his condition, a question that has a definite answer but which, if answered, would lead the patient to engage in seriously self-maiming behavior such as plucking out his right eye to fulfill what he believes to be his religion's demands. Here the doctor acts paternalistically, and justifiably, by con-cealing information from this patient, who is rational and otherwise informed. Because the infringement of the principle of respect for autonomy is more than minimal in this case (the religious views being central to the patient's life plan), a sixth condition requiring no substantial infringement of autonomy cannot be a necessary condition for all cases of justified hard paternalism.

Problems of Suicide Intervention

The state, religious institutions, and health care professionals have traditionally assumed jurisdiction to intervene in suicide attempts. Those who intervene do not always justify their actions on paternalistic grounds, but paternalism has been the primary justification.

Several conceptual questions about the term *suicide* make it difficult to categorize acts as suicides.[37] A classic example of these difficulties involves Barney Clark, who became the first human to receive an artificial heart. He was given a key that he could use to turn off the compressor if he decided he wanted to die. As Dr. Willem Kolff noted, if the patient "suffers and feels it isn't worth it any more, he has a key that he can apply....I think it is entirely legitimate that this man whose life has been extended should have the right to cut it off if he doesn't want it, if [his] life ceases to be enjoyable."[38] Would Clark's use of the key to turn off the artificial heart have been an act of suicide? If he had refused to accept the artificial heart in the first place, few would have labeled his act a suicide. His overall condition was extremely poor, the artificial heart was experimental, and no suicidal intention was evident. If, on the other hand, Clark had intentionally shot himself with a pistol while on the artificial heart, his act would have been classified as suicide.

Our main concern here is paternalistic intervention in acts of attempted suicide. The primary moral issue is the following: If suicide is a protected moral right, then the state, health professionals, and others have no legitimate grounds for intervention in autonomous suicide attempts. No one doubts that we should intervene to prevent suicide by substantially nonautonomous persons, and few wish to return to the days when suicide was a criminal act. However, if there is an autonomy right to commit suicide, then we could not legitimately attempt to prevent an autonomous but imprudent individual from committing suicide.

A clear and relevant example of attempted suicide appears in the following case, involving John K., a thirty-two-year-old lawyer. Two neurologists independently confirmed that his facial twitching, which had been evident for three months, was an early sign of Huntington's disease, a neurological disorder that progressively worsens, leads to irreversible dementia, and is uniformly fatal in approximately ten years. His mother suffered a horrible death from the same disease, and John K. had often said that he would prefer to die than to suffer the way his mother had suffered. Over several years he was anxious, drank heavily, and sought psychiatric help for intermittent depression. After he received this diagnosis, he told his psychiatrist about his situation and asked for help in committing suicide. After the psychiatrist refused to help, John K. attempted to take his own life by ingesting his antidepressant medication, leaving a note of explanation to his wife and child.[39]

Several interventions occurred or could have occurred in this case. First, the psychiatrist refused to assist John K.'s suicide and would have sought involuntary commitment had John K. not insisted that he did not plan to kill himself anytime soon. The psychiatrist appears to have thought that he could provide appropriate psychotherapy over time. Second, John K.'s wife found him unconscious and rushed him to the emergency room. Third, the emergency room staff decided to treat him despite the suicide note. The question is which, if any, of these possible or actual interventions is justifiable?

A widely accepted account of our obligations relies on a strategy of *temporary* intervention devised by John Stuart Mill. On this account, provisional intervention is justified to ascertain whether a person is acting autonomously; further intervention is unjustified once it is clear that the person's actions are substantially autonomous. Glanville Williams used this strategy in a classic statement of the position:

> If one suddenly comes upon another person attempting suicide, the natural and humane thing to do is to try to stop him, for the purpose of ascertaining the cause of his distress and attempting to remedy it, or else of attempting moral dissuasion if it seems that the act of suicide shows lack of consideration for others, or else again from the purpose of trying to persuade him to accept psychiatric help if this seems to be called for.... But nothing longer than a temporary restraint could be defended. I would gravely doubt whether a suicide attempt should be a factor leading to a diagnosis of psychosis or to compulsory admissions to a hospital. Psychiatrists are too ready to assume that an attempt to commit suicide is the act of mentally sick persons.[40]

This strong antipaternalist stance might be questioned on two grounds. First, failure to intervene in a more forceful manner than Williams allows symbolically communicates to potentially suicidal persons a lack of communal concern and seems to diminish communal responsibility. Second, many persons who commit or attempt to commit suicide are mentally ill, clinically depressed, or destabilized by a crisis and are, therefore, not acting autonomously. Many mental health professionals believe that suicides almost always result from maladaptive attitudes or illnesses needing therapeutic attention and social support. In a typical circumstance the suicidal person plans how to end life while simultaneously holding fantasies about how rescue will occur, rescue from death and also from the negative circumstances prompting the suicide. If the suicide springs from clinical depression or constitutes a call for help, a failure to intervene shows disrespect for the person's deepest autonomous wishes, including his or her hopes for the future.

Nonetheless, caution is needed in calls for communal beneficence, which may be expressed paternalistically through unjustifiably forceful interventions. Although suicide has been decriminalized, a suicide attempt, irrespective of motive, almost universally provides a legal basis for public officers to intervene, as well as grounds for at least temporary involuntary hospitalization.[41] Here the burden of proof is rightly placed on those who claim that the patient's judgment is insufficiently autonomous. Consider the following instructive example involving Ida Rollin, seventy-four years old and suffering from ovarian cancer. Her physicians truthfully told her that she had only a few months to live and that her dying would be painful and upsetting. Rollin indicated to her daughter that she wanted to end her life and requested assistance. The daughter secured some pills and conveyed a doctor's instructions about how they should be taken. When the daughter expressed reservations about these plans, her husband reminded her that they "weren't driving, she [Ida Rollin] was," and that they were only "navigators."[42]

This metaphor-laden reference to rightful authority is a reminder that those who propose suicide intervention to prevent such persons from control over their lives require a moral justification that fits the context. Occasions arise in health care and beyond when it is appropriate to step aside and allow a person to bring life to an end, and perhaps even to assist in facilitating the death, just as occasions exist when it is appropriate to intervene. (See further Chapter 5 on physician-assisted forms of ending life.)

Denying Requests for Nonbeneficial Procedures

Patients and surrogates sometimes request medical procedures that the clinician is convinced will not be beneficial. Sometimes denials of such requests are paternalistic.

Passive paternalism. A passive paternalism occurs when professionals refuse, for reasons of beneficence, to execute a patient's positive preferences for an intervention.[43] The following is a case in point: Elizabeth Stanley, a sexually active twenty-six-year-old intern, requests a tubal ligation, insisting that she has thought about this request for months, dislikes available contraceptives, does not want children, and understands that tubal ligation is irreversible. When the gynecologist suggests that she might someday want to get married and have children, she responds that she would either find a husband who did not want children or adopt children. She thinks that she will not change her mind and wants the tubal ligation to make it impossible for her to reconsider. She has scheduled vacation time from work in two weeks and wants the surgery then.[44]

If a physician refuses to perform the tubal ligation on grounds of the patient's benefit, the decision is paternalistic. However, if the physician refuses purely on grounds of conscience ("I won't do such procedures as a matter of personal moral policy"), it may not be a paternalistic decision. Passive paternalism is usually easier to justify than active paternalism, because physicians do not have a moral obligation to carry out their patients' wishes when they are incompatible with acceptable standards of medical practice or are against the physicians' conscience.

Medical futility. Passive paternalism is present in some forms of medical futility, a topic we introduced in Chapter 5. Consider the classic case of eighty-five-year-old Helga Wanglie, who was maintained on a respirator in a persistent vegetative state. The hospital sought to stop the respirator on grounds that it was nonbeneficial in that it could not heal her lungs, palliate her suffering, or enable her to experience the benefits of life. Surrogate decision makers—her husband, a son, and a daughter—wanted life support continued on grounds that Mrs. Wanglie would not be better off dead, that a miracle could occur, that physicians should not play God, and that efforts to remove her life support epitomize "moral decay in our civilization."[45]

If life support for such patients truly is futile, denying patients' or surrogates' requests for treatment is warranted. In these circumstances "clinically nonbeneficial interventions" is preferable to the term *futility.*[46] Typically a claim of futility is not that an intervention will harm the patient in violation of the principle of nonmaleficence, but that it will not produce the benefit the patient or the surrogate seeks. A justified belief in futility cancels a professional's obligation to provide a medical procedure. However, it is not clear that the language of futility illuminates the range of relevant ethical issues in passive paternalism, in part because of its variable and vague uses, which we discussed in Chapter 5.

SURROGATE DECISION MAKING FOR INCOMPETENT PATIENTS

We turn now from paternalistic protections to the related domain of surrogate decision makers who are duly authorized to make decisions for doubtfully autonomous and nonautonomous patients. Surrogates daily make decisions to terminate or continue treatment for incompetent patients, for example, those suffering from stroke, Alzheimer's disease, Parkinson's disease, chronic depression affecting cognitive function, senility, and psychosis. If a patient is not competent to accept or refuse treatment, a hospital, a physician, or a family member may justifiably exercise a decision-making role, depending on legal and institutional rules, or go before a court or other authority to resolve uncertainties about decision-making authority.

Three general standards have been proposed for use by surrogate decision makers: *substituted judgment,* which is sometimes presented as an autonomy-based standard; *pure autonomy;* and *the patient's best interests.* Our objective is to restructure and to integrate this set of standards for surrogate decision making into a coherent framework. Although we evaluate these standards for law and policy, our underlying moral argument is concerned with how to protect both patients' former autonomous preferences and current best interests. (In Chapter 5 we consider *who* should be the surrogate decision maker.)

The Substituted Judgment Standard

The standard of substituted judgment is constructed on the premise that decisions about treatment properly belong to the incompetent or nonautonomous patient, by virtue of his or her rights of autonomy and privacy. Patients thus have the right to decide and to have their values and preferences taken seriously even though they lack the capacity to exercise those rights. It would be unfair to deprive an incompetent patient of decision-making rights merely because he or she is no longer (or has never been) autonomous.

This is a weak standard of autonomy. It requires the surrogate decision maker to "don the mental mantle of the incompetent," as a judge in a classic court case put it—that is, to make the decision the incompetent person would have made if competent. In this case, the court invoked the standard of substituted judgment to decide that Joseph Saikewicz, an adult who had never been competent, would have refused treatment had he been competent. Acknowledging that what the majority of reasonable people would choose might differ from the choice of a particular incompetent person, the court said that "[T]he decision in many cases such as this should be that which would be made by the incompetent person, if that person were competent, but taking into account the present and future incompetency of the individual as one of the factors which would necessarily enter into the decision-making process of the competent person."[47]

The standard of substituted judgment could and should be used for once-competent patients, but only if reason exists to believe that the surrogate decision maker can make a judgment that the patient would have made. In such cases, the surrogate should have such a deep familiarity with the patient that the particular judgment made reflects the patient's views and values. Merely knowing something in general about the patient's personal values is not sufficient. Accordingly, if the surrogate can reliably answer the question, "What would *the patient* want in this circumstance?" substituted judgment is an appropriate standard that approximates first-person consent. However, if the surrogate can only answer the question, "What do *you* want for the patient?" then a choice should be made on the basis of the patient's best interests, rather than an autonomy standard. We obviously cannot follow a substituted judgment standard for never-competent patients, because no basis exists for a judgment of their autonomous choice.

The Pure Autonomy Standard

A second standard eliminates the dubious autonomy reflected in substituted judgment and replaces it with real autonomy. The pure autonomy standard applies exclusively to formerly autonomous, now-incompetent patients who expressed a relevant, autonomous treatment preference. The principle of respect for autonomy compels us to respect such preferences, even if the person can no longer express the preference for himself or herself. This standard asserts that, whether or not a formal advance directive exists, caretakers should act on the patient's prior autonomous judgments, sometimes called "precedent autonomy."

Disputes arise, however, about the criteria of satisfactory evidence for action under this standard. In the absence of explicit instructions, a surrogate decision maker might, for example, select from the patient's life history values that accord with the surrogate's own values, and then use only those values in reaching decisions. The surrogate might also base his or her findings on the patient's values that are only distantly relevant to the immediate decision (e.g., the patient's expressed dislike of hospitals). It is reasonable to ask what a surrogate decision maker can legitimately infer from a patient's prior conduct, especially from conditions such as fear and avoidance of doctors and earlier refusals to consent to physician recommendations. Even when the patient has provided an oral or written advance directive, surrogates need to determine carefully whether it displays an autonomous preference that is directly pertinent to the decision at hand.[48]

The Best Interests Standard

Often a patient's relevant autonomous preferences cannot be known. Under the best interests standard, a surrogate decision maker must then determine the highest probable net benefit among the available options, assigning different weights to interests the patient has in each option balanced against their inherent risks, burdens, or costs. The term *best* applies because of the surrogate's obligation to act beneficently by maximizing benefit through a comparative assessment that locates the highest probable net benefit. The best interests standard protects an incompetent person's welfare interests by requiring surrogates to assess the risks and probable benefits of various treatments and alternatives to treatment. It is therefore inescapably a quality-of-life criterion.

The best interests standard can in some circumstances validly override advance directives executed by formerly autonomous patients, as well as consents or refusals by minors and by other incompetent patients. This overriding can occur, for example, in a case in which a person by durable power of attorney has designated a surrogate to make medical decisions on his or her behalf. If the designated surrogate makes a decision that threatens the patient's best interests, the decision morally can and should be overridden unless the patient while competent executed a clearly worded document that specifically supports the surrogate's decision.

Challenges to reliance on advance directives often stress the formerly autonomous person's failure to anticipate the state or condition that actually emerged.

Examples are cases of apparently contented, nonsuffering, incompetent patients who can be expected to survive if treated against their advance directive, but who otherwise would die. Several discussions have focused on "Margo," a patient with Alzheimer's who, according to the medical student who visited her regularly, is "one of the happiest people I have ever known."[49] Some discussants ask us to imagine what should be done if Margo had a living will, executed just at the onset of her Alzheimer's, stating that she did not want life-sustaining treatment if she developed another life-threatening illness. In that circumstance caregivers would have to determine whether to honor her advance directive, and thereby to respect her precedent autonomy by not using antibiotics to treat her pneumonia, or to act in accord with what may appear to be her current best interests given her overall happiness.

As persons slip into incompetence, their condition can be very different from, and sometimes better than, they had anticipated. If so, it seems unfair to the now happily situated incompetent person to be bound by a prior decision that may have been underinformed and shortsighted. In Margo's case, not using antibiotics would arguably harm what Ronald Dworkin calls, in discussing this case, her "experiential interests"—her contentment with her current life. However, providing antibiotics would violate her living will, which expresses her considered values, her life story and commitments, and the like. Dworkin argues that Margo should not be treated in these circumstances.[50] By contrast, the President's Council on Bioethics concludes that "Margo's apparent happiness would seem to make the argument for overriding the living will morally compelling in this particular case."[51]

Except in unusual cases, such as Margo's, we are obligated to respect the previously expressed autonomous wishes of the now-nonautonomous person because of the continuing force of the principle of respect for the autonomy of the person who made the decision. However, advance directives raise complex issues and occasionally should be overridden.

In this section we have argued that previously competent patients who autonomously expressed clear preferences in an oral or written advance directive should generally be treated under the pure autonomy standard, and we have suggested an economy of standards by viewing the first standard (substituted judgment) and second standard (pure autonomy) as essentially identical. However, if the previously competent person left no reliable traces of his or her preferences—or if the individual was never competent—surrogate decision makers should adhere to the best interests standard.

Balancing Benefits, Costs, and Risks

Thus far, we have concentrated on the role of the principle of beneficence in clinical medicine, health care, and public policy. We now examine and evaluate beneficent health policies through tools that analyze and assess appropriate benefits relative to costs and risks. These tools often are morally unobjectionable and may even be morally required, but problems do attend their use.

Physicians routinely base judgments about the most suitable medical treatments on the balance of probable benefits and harms for patients. This criterion is also used in judgments about the ethical acceptability of research involving human subjects. These judgments consider whether the probable overall benefits—usually for society—outweigh the risks to subjects. In submitting a research protocol involving human subjects to an institutional review board (IRB) for approval, an investigator is expected to array the risks to subjects and probable benefits to both subjects and society, and then to explain why the probable benefits outweigh the risks. When IRBs array risks and benefits, determine their respective weights, and reach decisions, they typically use informal techniques such as expert judgments based on reliable data and analogical reasoning based on precedents. We focus in this section on techniques that employ formal, quantitative analysis of costs, risks, and benefits.

The Nature of Costs, Risks, and Benefits

Costs include the resources required to bring about a benefit, as well as the negative effects of pursuing and realizing that benefit. We concentrate on costs expressed in monetary terms—the primary interpretation of costs in cost–benefit and cost-effectiveness analysis. The term *risk,* by contrast, refers to a possible future harm, where harm is defined as a setback to interests, particularly in life, health, or welfare. Expressions such as *minimal risk, reasonable risk,* and *high risk* usually refer to the chance of a harm's occurrence—its probability—but often also to the severity of the harm if it occurs—its magnitude.

Statements of risk are descriptive inasmuch as they state the probability that harmful events will occur. They are *evaluative* inasmuch as they attach a value to the occurrence or prevention of these events. Statements of risk presume a prior negative evaluation of some condition. At its core, a circumstance of risk involves a possible occurrence of something that has been evaluated as harmful along with an uncertainty about its actual occurrence that can be expressed in terms of its probability. Several types of risks exist, including physical, psychological, financial, and legal risks. The term *benefit* sometimes refers to cost avoidance and risk reduction, but more commonly in biomedicine it refers to something of positive value, such as life or improvement in health. Unlike *risk, benefit* is not a probabilistic term. Probable benefit is the proper contrast to risk, and benefits are comparable to harms rather than to risks of harm. Thus, we can best conceive risk–benefit relations in terms of a ratio between the probability and magnitude of an anticipated benefit and the probability and magnitude of an anticipated harm.

Cost-Effectiveness and Cost–Benefit Analyses

Cost-effectiveness analysis (CEA) and cost–benefit analysis (CBA) are widely used, but controversial, tools of formal analysis underlying public policies regarding health, safety, and medical technologies.[52] Some policies are directed at burgeoning demands for expensive medical care and the need to contain costs. In assessing such policies, CEA and CBA appear precise and helpful because they present trade-offs in quantified terms.[53]

Defenders of these techniques praise them as ways to reduce the intuitive weighing of options and to avoid subjective and political decisions. Critics claim that these methods of analysis are not sufficiently comprehensive, that they fail to include all relevant values and options, that they frequently conflict with principles of justice, and that they are often themselves subjective and biased. Critics also charge that these techniques concentrate decision-making authority in the hands of narrow, technical professionals (e.g., health economists) who often fail to understand moral, social, legal, and political constraints that legitimately limit use of these methods.

CEA and CBA use different terms to state the value of outcomes. CBA measures both the benefits and the costs in monetary terms, whereas CEA measures the benefits in nonmonetary terms, such as years of life, quality-adjusted life-years, or cases of disease. CEA offers a bottom line such as "cost per year of life saved," whereas CBA offers a bottom line of a benefit–cost ratio stated in monetary figures that express the common measurement. Although CBA often begins by measuring different quantitative units (such as number of accidents, statistical deaths, and number of persons treated), it attempts to convert and express these seemingly incommensurable units of measurement into a common figure.

Because it uses the common metric of money, CBA in theory permits a comparison of programs that save lives with, for example, programs that reduce disability or accomplish other goals, such as public education. By contrast, CEA does not permit an evaluation of the inherent worth of programs or a comparative evaluation of programs with different aims. Instead, CEA functions best to compare and evaluate different programs sharing an identical aim, such as saving years of life.

Many CEAs involve comparing alternative courses of action that have similar health benefits to determine which is the most cost-effective. A simple and now classic example is the use of the guaiac test, an inexpensive test for detecting minute amounts of blood in the stool. Such blood may result from several problems, including hemorrhoids, benign intestinal polyps, or colonic cancer. A guaiac test cannot identify the cause of the bleeding, but if there is a positive stool guaiac and no other obvious cause for the bleeding, physicians undertake other tests. In the mid-1970s, the American Cancer Society proposed using six sequential stool guaiac tests to screen for colorectal cancers. Two analysts prepared a careful CEA of the six stool guaiac tests. They assumed that the initial test costs four dollars, that each additional test costs one dollar, and that each successive test detects many fewer cases of cancer. They then determined that the marginal cost per case of *detected* cancer increased dramatically: $1,175 for one test; $5,492 for two tests; $49,150 for three tests; $469,534 for four tests; $4.7 million for five tests; and $47 million for the full six-test screen.[54] Such findings do not dictate a conclusion, but the analysis provides relevant data for a society needing to allocate resources, for insurance companies and hospitals setting policies, for physicians making recommendations to patients, and for patients considering diagnostic procedures.

Conceptual confusion often mars uses of CEA. In some cases, when two programs are compared, the cost savings of one may be sufficient to view it as more cost-effective than the other. Yet some analysts contend that we should not confuse CEA with either reduced costs or increased effectiveness, because it often depends on both together. A program may be more cost-effective than another even if it (1) costs more, because it may increase medical effectiveness, or (2) leads to an overall decrease in medical effectiveness, because it may greatly reduce the costs. No form of analysis has the moral power to dictate the use of a particular medical procedure simply because that procedure has the lowest cost-effectiveness ratio. To assign priority to the alternative with the lowest cost-effectiveness ratio is to view medical diagnosis and therapy in unjustifiably narrow terms.

Risk Assessment and Values in Conflict

Risk assessment, another analytic technique, involves the analysis and evaluation of probabilities of negative outcomes, especially harms. Risk *identification* involves locating some hazard. Risk *estimation* determines the probability and magnitude of harms from that hazard. Risk *evaluation* determines the acceptability of the identified and estimated risks, often in relation to other objectives. Evaluation of risk in relation to probable benefits is often labeled *risk–benefit analysis* (RBA), which may be formulated in terms of a ratio of expected benefits to risks and may lead to a judgment about the acceptability of the risk under assessment. Risk identification, estimation, and evaluation are all stages in risk assessment. The next stage in the process is risk control or management—the set of individual, institutional, or policy responses to the analysis and assessment of risk, including decisions to reduce or control risks.[55] For example, risk management in hospitals includes setting policies to reduce the risk of medical malpractice suits.

Risk assessment informs technology assessment, environmental impact statements, and public policies protecting health and safety. The following schema of magnitude and probability of harm helps in understanding risk assessment:

	Magnitude of Harm	
	Major	*Minor*
High	1	2
Low	3	4

Probability of Harm

As category 4 suggests, questions arise about whether some risks are so insignificant, in terms of either probability or magnitude of harm or both, as not to merit attention. So-called *de minimis* risks are acceptable risks because they can be interpreted as effectively zero. According to the FDA, a risk of less than one cancer per million persons exposed is *de minimis*. However, the quantitative threshold or cutoff point used in a *de minimis* approach is problematic. For instance, an annual risk of one cancer per million persons for the U.S. population would produce the same number of fatalities (i.e., 300) as a risk of one per one hundred in a town with a population of 30,000. In focusing on the annual risk of cancer or death to one individual per million, the *de minimis* approach may neglect the cumulative, overall level of risk created for individuals over their lifetimes by the addition of several one-per-million risks.[56]

Risk assessment also focuses on the acceptability of risks relative to the benefits sought. With the possible exception of *de minimis* risks, most risks will be considered acceptable or unacceptable in relation to the probable benefits of the actions that carry those risks—for example, the benefits of radiation or a surgical procedure in health care or the benefits of nuclear power or toxic chemicals in the workplace.[57]

Risk–benefit analyses in the regulation of drugs and medical devices. Some of the conceptual, normative, and empirical issues in risk assessment and in RBA are evident in the FDA's regulation of drugs and medical devices.

The FDA requires three phases of human trials of drugs prior to regulatory approval. Each stage involves RBA to determine whether to proceed to the next stage and whether to approve a drug for wider use. Patients, physicians, and other health care professionals have often criticized the process of drug approval because of the length of time required. Some critics contend that the standard of evidence for a favorable risk–benefit ratio is too high and thus severely limits patients' access to promising new drugs, often in times of dire need created by serious, even fatal, medical conditions. Other critics charge that the process is not rigorous enough in view of the problems that sometimes appear after drug approval.[58] A related criticism is that approved drugs that nonetheless turn out to be inefficacious or unsafe sometimes are not removed quickly enough from the market.

In the absence of satisfactory alternatives, many patients and their families have been keenly interested in gaining access to promising drugs that are in clinical trials but not yet approved. Societal perceptions of clinical research have shifted significantly. In the 1970s and early 1980s, the major concern was to protect individuals from burdens and risks associated with research. Beginning in the 1980s, the emphasis shifted to increasing access to clinical trials. Particularly in response to requests from AIDS activists, the FDA developed mechanisms to provide expanded access to experimental drugs, as discussed earlier in this chapter.[59] Other FDA initiatives included a "fast track" of expedited approval and a "parallel track." The fast track allows patients with "seriously debilitating" or "life-threatening" conditions to accept greater risks in taking new drugs in the absence of acceptable alternatives.

An example from medical devices presents another classic case of difficult RBAs and assessments undertaken by the FDA in its regulatory decisions. For more than thirty years, thousands of women used silicone-gel breast implants to augment their breast sizes, to reshape their breasts, or to reconstruct their breasts following mastectomies for cancer or other surgery. These implants were already on the market when legislation in 1976 required that manufacturers provide data about safety and efficacy for certain medical devices. As a result, implant manufacturers were not required to provide these data unless questions arose. The health and safety concerns that subsequently emerged centered on the implants' longevity, rate of rupture, and link with various diseases.

Defenders of complete prohibition contended that no woman should be allowed to take a risk of unknown but potentially serious magnitude because her consent might not be adequately informed. FDA Commissioner David Kessler and others defended a restrictive policy, which was implemented in 1992. Kessler argued that for "patients with cancer and others with a need for breast reconstruction," a favorable risk–benefit ratio could exist in carefully controlled circumstances.[60] He sharply distinguished candidates for reconstruction following surgery from candidates for augmentation and held that a favorable risk–benefit ratio existed only for candidates for reconstruction.

Because candidates for augmentation still had breast tissue, they were considered to be at "higher risk" from these implants. In the presence of an implant, the argument went, mammography might not detect breast cancer, and the use of mammography could create a risk of radiation exposure in healthy young women with breast tissue who have silent ruptures of the silicone-gel implant without symptoms. Kessler wrote: "In our opinion the risk–benefit ratio does not at this time favor the unrestricted use of silicone breast implants in healthy women."

Although Kessler denied that this decision involved "any judgment about values," critics rightly charged that, in fact, it was based on contested values and was inappropriately paternalistic. There is evidence that the FDA gave an unduly heavy weight to unknown risks largely because the agency discounted the self-perceived benefits of breast implants for women except in cases of reconstruction. The agency then held these implants to a high standard of safety, instead of allowing women to decide for themselves whether to accept the risks for their own subjective benefits.[61]

If the evidence had indicated high risk relative to benefit, as well as unreasonable risk-taking by women, a different conclusion might have been sustained, but evidence available at the time and since points in the other direction. The FDA policy was unjustifiably paternalistic, noticeably so when compared to the less restrictive public decisions reached in European countries.[62] A more defensible, nonpaternalistic policy would have permitted the continued use of silicone-gel breast implants, regardless of the users' biological conditions and aims, while requiring adequate disclosure of information about risks. Raising the level of disclosure standards, as the FDA has done in some cases, would have been more appropriate than restraining choice.

In 2006, as a result of new data from manufacturers and assessments by its advisory committees, the FDA approved the marketing of two companies' silicone-gel breast implants to women of all ages for breast reconstruction and to women twenty-two years and older for breast augmentation.[63] Even though these breast implants have "frequent local complications and adverse outcomes," the FDA determined that their benefits and risks are "sufficiently well understood for women to make informed decisions about their use."[64] The FDA continues to monitor data about implants and communicate new safety information. It has also called for manufacturers and physicians to provide current and balanced information to help inform women's decisions.

We reach two general conclusions from this discussion. First, it is morally legitimate and often obligatory for society to act beneficently through the government and its agencies to protect citizens from medical drugs and devices that are harmful or that have not been established to be safe and efficacious. Hence, the FDA and comparable agencies play a justifiable regulatory role. Our conclusion that the FDA should not have severely restricted or prohibited the use of silicone-gel breast implants should not be interpreted as an argument against the agency's indispensable social role. Second, RBAs are not value-free. Values are evident in various RBA-based decisions, including those made in the breast implant case.

Risk perception. An individual's perception of risks may differ from an expert's assessment. Variations may reflect not only different goals and "risk budgets," but also different qualitative assessments of particular risks, including whether the risks in question are voluntary, controllable, highly salient, novel, or dreaded.[65]

Differences in risk perception suggest some limits of attempts to use quantitative statements of probability and magnitude in reaching conclusions about the acceptability of risk. The public's informed but subjective perception of a harm should be considered and given substantial weight when formulating public policy, but the appropriate weighting will vary with each case. The public sometimes holds factually mistaken views about risks that experts can identify. Accordingly, mistaken public views can and should be corrected through a fair public policy process.[66]

Precaution: Principle or Process?

Occasionally a new technology such as nanotechnology or a novel activity such as injecting bovine growth hormone into dairy cows appears to pose a health threat or create a hazard, thereby evoking public concern. Scientists may lack evidence to determine the magnitude of the possible negative outcome or the probabilities of its occurrence, perhaps because of uncertain cause–effect relations. The risks cannot be quantified and an appropriate benefit–risk–cost analysis is not constructible. At most, beneficence can be implemented only through *precautionary* measures. Which actions, if any, are justifiable in the face of uncertain risks?

Several common maxims come to mind: Better safe than sorry; look before you leap; and an ounce of prevention is worth a pound of cure. As rough guides for decision making, these maxims are unobjectionable. A so-called "precautionary principle" has been implemented in some international treaties as well as in laws and regulations in several countries to protect the environment and public health.[67] However, it is difficult to talk about *the* precautionary principle because there are so many different versions, with different strengths and weaknesses. One assessment reports that there are as many as nineteen different formulations.[68] Moreover, views expressed about particular precautionary measures are rarely expressed in the form of a *principle.*

A general and universal precautionary principle is incoherent. There are different threats, hazards, and uncertain risks; and efforts to avoid any single one must attend to the others. The failure to develop some technologies may create risks just as much as the failure to stop development of those technologies. A precautionary principle, in its most demanding versions, could be a recipe for paralysis; it may be too abstract to give substantive, practical guidance, and appeals to it may lead parties to carefully examine only one narrow set of risks, while ignoring other risks and potential benefits.[69] For example, appealing to this principle to prevent scientific research using human cells and animal chimeras, because of a perceived but vague risk of adverse consequences, may neglect significant potential health benefits that could result from the research. Perils created by some versions and uses of a precautionary principle include distortion of public policy as a result of speculative and theoretical threats that divert attention from real, albeit less dramatic, threats.

However, if properly formulated, some precautionary approaches, processes, and measures are justified. Depending on what is valued and what is at risk, it may be ethically justifiable and even obligatory to take steps, in the absence of conclusive scientific evidence, to avoid a hazard where the harm would be both serious and irreversible—in short, a catastrophe.[70] Triggering conditions for these measures include plausible evidence of possible major harm where it is not possible to adequately characterize and quantify risk because of scientific uncertainty and ignorance. The precautionary process should not be viewed as an alternative to risk analysis and scientific research. It should instead be viewed as a way to supplement risk appraisals when the available scientific evidence does not permit firm characterizations of the probability or magnitude of plausible risks.

Prudent use of precaution is more a process than a genuine principle, and it needs to be justified by a rigorous interpretation of the principles of beneficence and nonmaleficence. Measures commonly associated with a precautionary process include transparency, involvement of the public, and consultation with experts about possible responses to threats marked by uncertainty or ignorance about probabilities and magnitudes. Although transparency sometimes heightens fears, the public good is best served by risk-avoidance or risk-reduction policies that are generally consistent with the society's basic values and the public's reflective preferences. The acceptance or rejection of any precautionary approach will depend on a careful weighing of social, cultural, and psychological perspectives.[71]

It is easy to oversimplify and unduly magnify cultural differences by suggesting, for instance, that Europe is more precaution-oriented than the United States. Even if precautionary approaches appear to have more traction in laws, regulations, and discourse in Europe than in the United States, both adopt a variety of precautionary measures in response to the same and to different perceived threats or hazards.[72]

THE VALUE AND QUALITY OF LIFE

We turn, finally, to controversies regarding how to place a value on life, which have centered on CBAs. We also examine controversies over the value of quality-adjusted life-years (QALYs), which have centered on CEAs.

Valuing Lives

One approach assigns an economic value to human life. A society may spend amount x to save a life in one setting (e.g., by reducing the risk of death from cancer), but only spend amount y to save a life in another setting (e.g., by reducing the risk of death from mining accidents). One objective in determining the value of a life is to develop consistency across practices and policies.

Analysts have developed several methods to determine the value of human life. These include discounted future earnings (DFE) and willingness to pay (WTP). According to DFE, we can determine the monetary value of lives by considering what people at risk of some disease or accident could be expected to earn if they survived. Although this approach can help measure the costs of diseases, accidents, and death, it risks reducing people's value to their potential economic value and gives an unfair priority to those who would be expected to have greater future earnings.

WTP considers how much individuals would be willing to pay to reduce the risks of death, either through their revealed preferences (i.e., decisions people actually make in their lives) or through their expressed preferences (i.e., what people say in response to hypothetical questions). For revealed preferences to be meaningful, individuals would have to understand the risks in their lives and voluntarily assume those risks—assumptions that often are not met. Individuals' answers to hypothetical questions also may not accurately indicate how much they would be willing to spend on actual programs to reduce their (and others') risk of death. Additionally, individuals' financial situations (including their household income, real estate, and financial solvency) can have an impact on their expressed willingness to pay.[73]

Although we rarely put an explicit monetary value on human life, proponents of CBA urge precisely this strategy. Qualitative factors, such as how deaths occur, are often more important to many people than these purely economic considerations. Moreover, beneficence is often expressed in policies, such as rescuing trapped coal miners, that symbolize societal benevolence and affirm the value of victims, even though these policies would often not be supported by a CBA focused on the economic value of life, determined by either DFE or WTP.

In our judgment, data gained from CBA and other analytic techniques are relevant to the formulation and assessment of public policies and can provide very valuable insights, but they provide only one set of indicators of appropriate social beneficence. It is often not necessary to put a specific economic value on human life to evaluate possible risk-reduction policies and to compare their costs. Evaluation may reasonably focus on the life-years saved, without attempting to convert them into monetary terms. In health care, CBA has, quite appropriately, diminished in importance by comparison to CEA, which often promotes the goal of maximizing QALYs, a topic to which we now turn.[74]

Valuing Quality-Adjusted Life-Years

Quality of life and QALYs. Quality of life is as important as saving lives and years of life in many areas of health policy and health care. Many individuals, when contemplating different treatments for a particular condition, are willing to trade some life-years for improved quality of life during their remaining years. Hence, researchers and policymakers have sought measures, called health-adjusted life-years (HALYs), that combine longevity with health status. QALYs are the most widely used type of HALY.[75] The National Institute for Health and Clinical Excellence (NICE) in the United Kingdom, which uses QALYs in evaluations that are designed for the British system of resource allocation, defines a QALY as "a measure of health outcome which looks at both length of life and quality of life. QALYS are calculated by estimating the years of life remaining for a patient following a particular care pathway and weighting each year with a quality of life score."[76] In short, a QALY is a calculation that takes into account both the quantity and the quality of life produced by medical interventions.

An influential premise underlying use of QALYs is that, "if an extra year of healthy (i.e., good quality) life-expectancy is worth one, then an extra year of unhealthy (i.e., poor quality) life-expectancy must be worth less than one (for why otherwise do people seek to be healthy?)."[77] On this scale, the value of the condition of death is zero. Various states of illness or disability better than death but short of full health receive a value between zero and one. Health conditions assessed as worse than death receive a negative value. The value of particular health outcomes depends on the increase in the utility of the health state and the number of years it lasts.[78]

The goal of QALY analysis is to bring length of life and quality of life into a single framework of evaluation.[79] QALYs can be used to monitor the effects of treatments on patients in clinical practice or in clinical trials, to determine what to recommend to patients, to provide information to patients about the effects of different treatments, and to assist in resource allocation in health care. The goal is to make the basis for choices between options as clear and rational as possible.

British health economist Alan Williams used QALYs to examine the cost-effectiveness of coronary artery bypass grafting. In his analysis, bypass grafting compares favorably with pacemakers for heart block. It is superior to heart transplantation and the treatment of end-stage renal failure. He also found that bypass grafting for severe angina and extensive coronary artery disease is more cost-effective than for less severe cases. The rate of survival can be misleading for coronary artery bypass grafting and many other therapeutic procedures that have a major impact on quality of life. Ultimately, Williams recommended that resources "be redeployed at the margin to procedures for which the benefits to patients are high in relation to the costs."[80]

How to determine quality of life poses related difficulties. Analysts often start with rough measures, such as physical mobility, freedom from pain and distress, and the capacity to perform the activities of daily life and to engage in social interactions. Quality-of-life discussions are theoretically attractive as a way to provide information about the ingredients of a good life, but practically difficult to implement. However, some instruments can and should be developed and refined to present meaningful and accurate measures of health-related quality of life. Without such instruments, we are likely to operate with implicit and unexamined views about trade-offs between quantity and quality of life in relation to cost.

Ethical assumptions of QALYs. Many ethical assumptions are involved in QALY-based CEA. Utilitarianism is CEA's philosophical parent, and some of its problems carry over to its offspring, even though there are differences.[81] Implicit in QALY-based CEA is the idea that health maximization is the only relevant objective of health services. But some nonhealth benefits or utilities of health services also contribute to quality of life. As our discussion of silicone-gel breast implants noted, conditions such as asymmetrical breasts may affect a person's subjective estimate of quality of life and may constitute a source of distress. The problem is that QALY-based CEA may be used so that it attaches utility only to selected outcomes while neglecting values such as how care is provided (e.g., whether it is personal care) and how it is distributed (e.g., whether universal access is provided).[82]

Related issues arise about whether the use of QALYs in CEA is adequately egalitarian. Proponents of QALY-based CEA hold that each healthy life-year is equally valuable for everyone. A QALY is a QALY, regardless of who possesses it.[83] However, QALY-based CEA may discriminate against older people, because, conditions being equal, saving the life of a younger person is likely to produce more QALYs than saving the life of an older person.[84]

QALY-based CEA also does not attend adequately to some aspects of justice. It does not consider how life-years are distributed among patients, and it may not include efforts to reduce the number of individual victims in its attempts to increase the number of life-years. From this standpoint, no difference exists between saving one person who can be expected to have forty QALYs and saving two people who can be expected to have twenty QALYs each. In principle, CEA will give priority to saving one person with forty expected QALYs over saving two persons with only nineteen expected QALYs each. Hence, QALY-based CEA favors life-years over individual lives, and the number of life-years over the number of individual lives, while failing to recognize that societal and professional obligations of beneficence sometimes require rescuing endangered individual lives.[85]

A tension can emerge between QALY-based CEA and the duty to rescue, even though both are ultimately grounded on beneficence. This tension appeared in an effort by the Oregon Health Services Commission to develop a prioritized list of health services so that the state of Oregon could expand its Medicaid coverage to all of its poor citizens. In commenting on a draft priority list that ranked some life-saving procedures below some routine procedures, David Hadorn noted that, "The cost-effectiveness analysis approach used to create the initial list conflicted directly with the powerful 'Rule of Rescue'—people's perceived duty to save endangered life whenever possible."[86] If unqualified by further ethical considerations, QALY-based CEA's methodological assignment of priority to life-years over individual lives implies that beneficence-based rescue (especially life-saving) is less significant than cost utility, that the distribution of life-years is unimportant, that saving more lives is less important than maximizing the number of life-years, and that quality of life is more important than quantity of life. Each of these priorities needs careful scrutiny in each context in which QALYs are used.

CONCLUSION

In this chapter we have distinguished two principles of beneficence and have defended the theoretical and practical importance of the distinction between obligatory beneficence and ideal beneficence. We have developed a type of paternalism that makes it possible to justify a restricted range of both soft and hard paternalistic actions. We have nonetheless acknowledged that, in addition to its disrespect for personal autonomy, a policy or rule permitting a hard paternalism in professional practice is usually not worth the risk of abuse that it invites. The fact that physicians are situated to make sound and caring decisions from a position of professional expertise should be one factor, but only one factor, in the on-balance consideration of whether paternalistic interventions in medicine are warranted.

In examining standards of decision making for surrogate decision makers, we have proposed an integrated set of standards of (1) respect for the patient's prior autonomous choices where reliably known and (2) the patient's best interest in the absence of reliable knowledge of the patient's prior autonomous choices (and occasionally (2) justifiably overrides (1) in circumstances of conflict).

Finally, we examined formal techniques of analysis—CEA, CBA, and RBA—and concluded that they can function as morally unobjectionable ways to implement the principle of utility—as one principle of beneficence—but that principles of respect for autonomy and justice often justifiably set limits on the uses of these techniques. The next chapter develops an account of some of the relevant principles of justice that began to surface in the final parts of this chapter.

NOTES

1. W. D. Ross, *The Right and the Good* (Oxford: Clarendon, 1930), p. 21.

2. Peter Singer, "Famine, Affluence, and Morality," *Philosophy and Public Affairs* 1 (1972): 229–43.

3.   Peter Singer, *Practical Ethics,* 2nd ed. (Cambridge: Cambridge University Press, 1993), p. 246.

4.   Peter Singer, *The Life You Can Save: Acting Now to End World Poverty* (New York: Random House, 2009).

5.   In particular to Liam B. Murphy, "The Demands of Beneficence," *Philosophy and Public Affairs* 22 (1993): 267–92.

6.   Our formulations are indebted to Eric D'Arcy, *Human Acts: An Essay in Their Moral Evaluation* (Oxford: Clarendon, 1963), pp. 56–57. We added the fourth condition and altered others in his formulation. Our reconstruction also profited from Joel Feinberg, *Harm to Others,* vol. I of *The Moral Limits of the Criminal Law* (New York: Oxford University Press, 1984), chap. 4.

7.   This third condition will need a finer grained analysis to avoid some problems of what is required if there is a small (but not insignificant) probability of saving millions of lives at minimal cost to a person. It is not plausible to hold that a person has *no obligation* to so act. Condition 3 here could be refined to show that there must be some appropriate proportionality between probability of success, the value of outcome to be achieved, and the sacrifice that the agent would incur. Perhaps the formulation should be "a high ratio of probable benefit relative to the sacrifice made."

8.   Our discussion of these issues is intended to cover a variety of actual and possible expanded access programs or studies. It is not limited to programs that fall under the policies of the Food and Drug Administration. For the latter and for a link to some ongoing expanded access studies, see "Access to Investigational Drugs Outside of a Clinical Trial (Expanded Access)," updated June 30, 2010, http://www.fda.gov/ForConsumers/ByAudience/ForPatientAdvocates/AccesstoInvestigationalDrugs/ucm176098.htm (accessed March 24, 2012).

9.   Michelle M. Mello and Troyen A. Brennan, "The Controversy Over High-Dose Chemotherapy with Autologous Bone Marrow Transplant for Breast Cancer," *Health Affairs* 20 (2001): 101–17; Edward A. Stadtmauer et al., "Conventional-Dose Chemotherapy Compared with High-Dose Chemotherapy Plus Autologous Hematopoietic Stem-Cell Transplantation for Metastatic Breast Cancer," *New England Journal of Medicine* 342 (2000): 1069–76; Rabiya A. Tuma, "Expanded-Access Programs: Little Heard Views from Industry," *Oncology Times* 30 (August 10, 2008): 19, 22–23.

10.   William C. Buhles, "Compassionate Use: A Story of Ethics and Science in the Development of a New Drug," *Perspectives in Biology and Medicine* 54 (2011): 304–15. The case is far more complicated than we can report here.

11.   Cf. conclusions about posttrial access in National Bioethics Advisory Commission (NBAC), *Ethical and Policy Issues in International Research: Clinical Trials in Developing Countries* (Bethesda, MD: National Bioethics Advisory Commission, April 2001), vol. 1, pp. 64–65, 74, especially Recommendation 4.1; and Nuffield Council on Bioethics, *The Ethics of Research Related to Healthcare in Developing Countries* (London: Nuffield Council on Bioethics, 2002), chap. 9, "What Happens Once Research is Over?" Sects. 9.21–31, available at http://nuffieldbioethics.org/go/ourwork/developingcountries/publication_309.html.

12.   David Hume, "Of Suicide," in *Essays Moral, Political, and Literary,* ed. Eugene Miller (Indianapolis, IN: Liberty Classics, 1985), pp. 577–89.

13.   See David A. J. Richards, *A Theory of Reasons for Action* (Oxford: Clarendon, 1971), p. 186; Lawrence Becker, *Reciprocity* (Chicago: University of Chicago Press, 1990); Aristotle, *Nicomachean Ethics,* bks. 8–9.

14.   See William F. May, "Code and Covenant or Philanthropy and Contract?" in *Ethics in Medicine,* ed. Stanley Reiser, Arthur Dyck, and William Curran (Cambridge, MA: MIT Press, 1977), pp. 65–76; and May, *The Healer's Covenant: Images of the Healer in Medical Ethics,* 2nd ed. (Louisville, KY: Westminster-John Knox Press, 2000).

15.   Institute of Medicine of the National Academies, Roundtable on Evidence-Based Medicine, *The Learning Healthcare System: Workshop Summary,* ed. LeighAnne Olsen, Dara Aisner, and J. Michael McGinnis (Washington, DC: National Academies Press, 2007), esp. chap. 3, available at http://www .nap.edu/catalog/11903.html (accessed October 31, 2011).

16.   For an analysis and assessment of the two models, see James F. Childress and Catharyn T. Liverman, eds., *Organ Donation: Opportunities for Action* (Washington, DC: National Academies Press, 2006), pp. 253–59, which argues against both models "because of insuperable practical problems in implementing them fairly" (p. 253). See further LifeSharers at http://www.lifesharers.org/ (accessed March 10, 2012); Gil Siegal and Richard Bonnie, "Closing the Organ Donation Gap: A Reciprocity-Based Social Contract Approach," *Journal of Law, Medicine & Ethics* 34 (2006): 415–23; and Danielle Ofri, "In Israel, a New Approach to Organ Donation," *New York Times,* February 17, 2012.

17.   *Epidemics,* 1:11, in *Hippocrates,* vol. I, ed. W. H. S. Jones (Cambridge, MA: Harvard University Press, 1923), p. 165.

18.   See Tom L. Beauchamp and Laurence B. McCullough, *Medical Ethics: The Moral Responsibilities of Physicians* (Englewood Cliffs, NJ: Prentice Hall, 1984), p. 84.

19.   See Donald VanDeVeer, *Paternalistic Intervention: The Moral Bounds on Benevolence* (Princeton, NJ: Princeton University Press, 1986), pp. 16–40; and John Kleinig, *Paternalism* (Totowa, NJ: Rowman & Allanheld, 1983), pp. 6–14.

20.   This case has been formulated on the basis of and incorporates language from Margaret A. Drickamer and Mark S. Lachs, "Should Patients with Alzheimer's Be Told Their Diagnosis?" *New England Journal of Medicine* 326 (April 2, 1992): 947–51. For diagnostic procedures for Alzheimer's disease (updated in January 2011), see the information provided by the National Institute of Aging, Alzheimer's Disease Education and Referral Center, at http://www.nia.nih.gov/Alzheimers/ AlzheimersInformation/Diagnosis/ (accessed May 20, 2011). The available diagnostic methods and tools enable physicians to determine with a fair degree of accuracy whether a patient with memory problems has "possible Alzheimer's disease," "probable Alzheimer's disease," or some other non-Alzheimer's disease problem. Only an autopsy after the patient's death can provide a definitive diagnosis of Alzheimer's disease.

21.   First introduced as the distinction between strong and weak paternalism by Joel Feinberg, "Legal Paternalism," *Canadian Journal of Philosophy* 1 (1971): 105–24, esp. 113, 116. See, further, Feinberg, *Harm to Self,* vol. III of *The Moral Limits of the Criminal Law* (New York: Oxford University Press, 1986), esp. pp. 12ff.

22.   See Cass R. Sunstein and Richard H. Thaler, "Libertarian Paternalism Is Not an Oxymoron," *University of Chicago Law Review* 70 (Fall 2003): 1159–202.

23.   Erich H. Loewy, "In Defense of Paternalism," *Theoretical Medicine and Bioethics* 26 (2005): 445–68.

24.   James F. Childress, *Who Should Decide? Paternalism in Health Care* (New York: Oxford University Press, 1982), p. 18.

25.   Sunstein and Thaler, "Libertarian Paternalism Is Not an Oxymoron," p. 1159. See also Richard H. Thaler and Cass R. Sunstein, "Libertarian Paternalism," *American Economics Review* 93 (2003): 175–79.

26.   Jolls and Sunstein, "Debiasing through Law," *Journal of Legal Studies* 33 (January 2006): 232.

27.   See Edward L. Glaeser, "Symposium: Homo Economicus, Homo Myopicus, and the Law and Economics of Consumer Choice: Paternalism and Autonomy," *University of Chicago Law Review* 73 (Winter 2006): 133–57.

28.   Ronald Bayer and Jennifer Stuber, "Tobacco Control, Stigma, and Public Health: Rethinking the Relations," *American Journal of Public Health* 96 (January 2006): 47–50; Glaeser, "Symposium: Homo Economicus, Homo Myopicus, and the Law and Economics of Consumer Choice," pp. 152–53.

29.   Bayer and Stuber, "Tobacco Control, Stigma, and Public Health: Rethinking the Relations," p. 49.

30.   W. Kip Vicusi, "The New Cigarette Paternalism," *Regulation* (Winter 2002–03): 58–64.

31.   For interpretations of (hard) paternalism as insult, disrespect, and treatment of individuals as unequals, see Ronald Dworkin, *Taking Rights Seriously* (Cambridge, MA: Harvard University Press, 1978), pp. 262–63; and Childress, *Who Should Decide?* chap. 3.

32.   Gerald Dworkin, "Paternalism," *Monist* 56 (January 1972): 65.

33.   See Dworkin, "Paternalism"; and John Rawls, *A Theory of Justice* (Cambridge, MA: Harvard University Press, 1971; rev. ed., 1999), pp. 209, 248–49 (1999: pp. 183–84, 218–20).

34.   Dworkin says, "The reasons which support paternalism are those which support any altruistic action—the welfare of another person." "Paternalism," in *Encyclopedia of Ethics,* ed. Lawrence Becker (New York: Garland, 1992), p. 940. For a variety of consent and nonconsent defenses of paternalism, see Kleinig, *Paternalism,* pp. 38–73; and see Kultgen, *Autonomy and Intervention,* esp. chaps. 9, 11, 15.

35.   We here take a constrained-balancing approach to the conflict between respect for autonomy and beneficence to a particular person. Another approach would develop a specification of beneficence— including both positive beneficence and utility—and respect for autonomy that would rule out all hard paternalistic interventions. The specification could take the following form: "when a person's actions are substantially autonomous and create the risk of harm to himself or herself, without imposing significant harms or burdens on others or the society, we should not act paternalistically beyond the use of modest means such as persuasion." Determining whether such a specification could be rendered coherent with our overall approach would require more attention than we can devote here.

36.   See also our discussion of staged disclosure of information in Chapter 8.

37.   We do not here address philosophical problems surrounding the definition of suicide. See Tom L. Beauchamp, "Suicide," in *Matters of Life and Death,* 3rd ed., ed. Tom Regan (New York: Random House, 1993), esp. part I; John Donnelly, ed., *Suicide: Right or Wrong?* (Buffalo, NY: Prometheus Books, 1991), part I; and Michael Cholbi, *Suicide: The Philosophical Dimensions* (Toronto: Broadview Press, 2011), chap. 1.

38.   See James Rachels, "Barney Clark's Key," *Hastings Center Report* 13 (April 1983): 17–19, esp. 17.

39.   This case is presented in Marc Basson, ed., *Rights and Responsibilities in Modern Medicine* (New York: Alan R. Liss, 1981), pp. 183–84.

40.   Glanville Williams, "Euthanasia," *Medico-Legal Journal* 41 (1973): 27.

41.   See President's Commission for the Study of Ethical Problems in Medicine and Biomedical and Behavioral Research, *Deciding to Forego Life-Sustaining Treatment: Ethical, Medical, and Legal Issues in Treatment Decisions* (Washington, D.C.: U.S. Government Printing Office, March 1983), p. 37.

42.   Betty Rollin, *Last Wish* (New York: Linden Press/Simon & Schuster, 1985).

43.   Childress, *Who Should Decide?* chap. 1. See also Timothy E. Quill and Howard Brody, "Physician Recommendations and Patient Autonomy: Finding a Balance between Physician Power and Patient Choice," *Annals of Internal Medicine* 125 (1996): 763–69; Allan S. Brett and Laurence B. McCullough,

"When Patients Request Specific Interventions: Defining the Limits of the Physician's Obligation," *New England Journal of Medicine* 315 (November 20, 1986): 1347–51; and Brett and McCullough, "Addressing Requests by Patients for Nonbeneficial Interventions," *JAMA: Journal of the American Medical Association* 307 (January 11, 2012): 149–50.

44. We have adapted this case from "The Refusal to Sterilize: A Paternalistic Decision," in *Rights and Responsibilities in Modern Medicine,* ed. Basson, pp. 135–36.

45. See Steven H. Miles, "Informed Demand for Non-Beneficial Medical Treatment," *New England Journal of Medicine* 325 (August 15, 1991): 512–15; and Ronald E. Cranford, "Helga Wanglie's Ventilator," *Hastings Center Report* 21 (July–August 1991): 23–24.

46. Catherine A. Marco and Gregory L. Larkin, "Case Studies in 'Futility'—Challenges for Academic Emergency Medicine," *Academic Emergency Medicine* 7 (2000): 1147–51.

47. *Superintendent of Belchertown State School v. Saikewicz,* Mass. 370 N.E. 2d 417 (1977).

48. See, for example, *In the Matter of the Application of John Evans against Bellevue Hospital,* Supreme Court of the State of New York, Index No. 16536/87 (1987).

49. A. D. Firlik, "Margo's Logo" (Letter), *JAMA: Journal of the American Medical Association* 265 (1991): 201.

50. Ronald Dworkin, *Life's Dominion: An Argument about Abortion, Euthanasia, and Individual Freedom* (New York: Knopf, 1993), pp. 221–29.

51. President's Council on Bioethics, *Taking Care: Ethical Caregiving in Our Aging Society* (Washington, DC: President's Council on Bioethics, September 2005), p. 84. The President's Council draws in part on the work of one of its members, Rebecca Dresser, "Dworkin on Dementia: Elegant Theory, Questionable Policy," *Hastings Center Report* 25 (1995): 32–38.

52. Some examinations of analytic methods include cost-utility analysis (CUA), as distinguished from CEA, while other discussions, particularly in the United States, treat CUA as a subset of CEA, as we do. For a sharp distinction between CUA and CEA, see Michael F. Drummond, Mark J. Sculpher, George W. Torrance, et al., *Methods for the Economic Evaluation of Health Care Programmes,* 3rd ed. (New York: Oxford University Press, 2005), esp. chaps. 5 and 6; contrast Marthe R. Gold, Joanna E. Siegel, Louise B. Russell, and Milton C. Weinstein, eds., *Cost-Effectiveness in Health and Medicine* (New York: Oxford University Press, 1996).

53. Our description of these analytic techniques draws on Gold, Siegel, Russell, and Weinstein, eds., *Cost-Effectiveness in Health and Medicine;* and Wilhelmine Miller, Lisa A. Robinson, and Robert S. Lawrence, eds., *Valuing Health for Regulatory Effectiveness Analysis* (Washington, DC: National Academies Press, 2006). See also Peter J. Neumann, *Using Cost-Effectiveness Analysis to Improve Health Care: Opportunities and Barriers* (New York: Oxford University Press, 2005). The recent attention to comparative effectiveness analysis in the United States appears, in part, to be an attempt to avoid facing the trade-offs between costs, on the one hand, and effectiveness and benefits, on the other. See Uwe E. Reinhardt, "'Cost-Effectiveness Analysis' and U.S. Health Care," *New York Times,* March 13, 2009.

54. On this now classic example, see Duncan Neuhauser and Ann M. Lewicki, "What Do We Gain from the Sixth Stool Guaiac?" *New England Journal of Medicine* 293 (July 31, 1975): 226–28. See also "American Cancer Society Report on the Cancer-Related Checkup," *CA—A Cancer Journal for Clinicians* 30 (1980): 193–240, which recommended the full set of six guaiac tests.

55. See, for example, Charles Yoe, *Primer on Risk Analysis: Decision Making under Uncertainty* (Boca Raton, FL: CRC Press, 2012).

56. See Sheila Jasanoff, "Acceptable Evidence in a Pluralistic Society," in *Acceptable Evidence: Science and Values in Risk Management,* ed. Deborah G. Mayo and Rachelle D. Hollander (New York: Oxford University Press, 1991).

57.   See Richard Wilson and E. A. C. Crouch, "Risk Assessment and Comparisons: An Introduction," *Science* 236 (April 17, 1987): 267–70; and Wilson and Crouch, *Risk-Benefit Analysis* (Cambridge, MA: Harvard University Center for Risk Analysis, 2001).

58.   Curt D. Burberg, Arthur A. Levin, Peter A. Gross, et al., "The FDA and Drug Safety," *Archives of Internal Medicine* 166 (October 9, 2006): 1938–42; Alina Baciu, Kathleen Stratton, and Sheila P. Burke, eds., *The Future of Drug Safety: Promoting and Protecting the Health of the Public* (Washington, DC: National Academies Press, 2006).

59.   On the significant role of AIDS activists, see Steven Epstein, *Impure Science: AIDS, Activism, and the Politics of Knowledge* (Berkeley, CA: University of California Press, 1996); Loretta M. Kopelman, "How AIDS Activists Are Changing Research," in *Health Care Ethics: Critical Issues,* ed. John Monagle and David C. Thomasma (Gaithersburg, MD: Aspen, 1994), pp. 199–209; and Robert J. Levine, "The Impact of HIV Infection on Society's Perception of Clinical Trials," *Kennedy Institute of Ethics Journal* 4 (1994): 93–98.

60.   David A. Kessler, "Special Report: The Basis of the FDA's Decision on Breast Implants," *New England Journal of Medicine* 326 (June 18, 1992): 1713–15. All references to Kessler's views are to this article.

61.   See Marcia Angell, "Breast Implants—Protection or Paternalism?" *New England Journal of Medicine* 326 (June 18, 1992): 1695–96. Angell's criticisms also appear in her *Science on Trial: The Clash of Medical Evidence and the Law in the Breast Implant Case* (New York: Norton, 1996).

62.   For reviews and evaluations of the scientific data, see E. C. Janowsky, L. L. Kupper, and B. S. Hulka, "Meta-Analyses of the Relation between Silicone Breast Implants and the Risk of Connective Tissue Diseases," *New England Journal of Medicine* 342 (2000): 781–90; *Silicone Gel Breast Implants: Report of the Independent Review Group* (Cambridge, MA: Jill Rogers Associates, 1998); and S. Bondurant, V. Ernster, and R. Herdman, eds., *Safety of Silicone Breast Implants* (Washington, DC: National Academies Press, 2000).

63.   "FDA Approves Silicone Gel-Filled Breast Implants after In-Depth Evaluation," *FDA News* (November 17, 2006), http://www.fda.gov/bbs/topics/NEWS/2006/NEW01512.html. On March 9, 2012, the FDA approved a third company's silicone-gel-filled breast implants. See http://www.fda.gov/NewsEvents/Newsroom/PressAnnouncements/ucm295437.htm (accessed March 10, 2012).

64.   Center for Devices and Radiological Health, U.S. Food and Drug Administration, *FDA Update on the Safety of Silicone Gel-Filled Breast Implants* (June 2011), http://www.fda.gov/downloads/MedicalDevices/ProductsandMedicalProcedures/ImplantsandProsthetics/BreastImplants/UCM260090.pdf (accessed March 10, 2012).

65.   See Paul Slovic, "Perception of Risk," *Science* 236 (April 17, 1987): 280–85; and Slovic, *The Perception of Risk* (London and Sterling, VA: Earthscan, 2000).

66.   See Cass Sunstein, *Laws of Fear: Beyond the Precautionary Principle* (Cambridge: Cambridge University Press, 2005) and *Risk and Reason* (Cambridge: Cambridge University Press, 2002).

67.   For cautious defenses of the precautionary principle, see United Nations Educational, Scientific and Cultural Organization (UNESCO), *The Precautionary Principle* (2005), http://unesdoc.unesco.org/images/001395/139578ee.pdf; Poul Harremoes, David Gee, Malcolm MacGarvin, et al., *The Precautionary Principle in the 20th Century: Lessons from Early Warnings* (London: Earthscan, 2002); Tim O'Riordan, James Cameron, and Andrew Jordan, eds., *Reinterpreting the Precautionary Principle* (London: Earthscan, 2001); Carl Cranor, "Toward Understanding Aspects of the Precautionary Principle," *Journal of Medicine and Philosophy* 29 (June 2004): 259–79; and Elizabeth Fisher, Judith Jones, and René von Schomberg, eds., *Implementing the Precautionary Principle: Perspectives and Prospects* (Northampton, MA: Edward Elgar Publishing, 2006). For critical perspectives on the

precautionary principle, see Sunstein, *Laws of Fear: Beyond the Precautionary Principle;* H. Tristram Engelhardt, Jr. and Fabrice Jotterand, "The Precautionary Principle: A Dialectical Reconsideration," *Journal of Medicine and Philosophy* 29 (June 2004): 301–12; and Russell Powell, "What's the Harm? An Evolutionary Theoretical Critique of the Precautionary Principle," *Kennedy Institute of Ethics Journal* 20 (2010): 181–206.

68.   See P. Sandin, "Dimensions of the Precautionary Principle," *Human and Ecological Risk Assessment* 5 (1999): 889–907.

69.   Sunstein, *Laws of Fear: Beyond the Precautionary Principle.* See also Engelhardt and Jotterand, "The Precautionary Principle: A Dialectical Reconsideration"; and Søren Holm and John Harris, "Precautionary Principle Stifles Discovery" (correspondence), *Nature* 400 (July 1999): 398.

70.   Cf. Cass Sunstein, *Laws of Fear: Beyond the Precautionary Principle;* and Richard A. Posner, *Catastrophe: Risk and Response* (New York: Oxford University Press, 2004).

71.   See several chapters in O'Riordan, Cameron, and Jordan, eds., *Reinterpreting the Precautionary Principle.*

72.   See Jonathan Zander, *The Application of the Precautionary Principle in Practice: Comparative Dimensions* (New York: Cambridge University Press, 2010), which notes variations in the application of the precautionary principle in Europe, as well as in the United States.

73.   See Emma McIntosh et al., "Applied Cost-Benefit Analysis in Health Care: An Empirical Application in Spinal Surgery," in *Applied Methods of Cost-Benefit Analysis in Health Care,* ed. Emma McIntosh et al. (New York: Oxford University Press, 2010), pp. 139–57, esp. 153–54, which focuses on one type of willingness to pay in the context of spinal surgery.

74.   For a philosophical critique of CBA, see Elizabeth Anderson, *Values in Ethics and Economics* (Cambridge, MA: Harvard University Press, 1993), esp. chap. 9; Matthew D. Adler, *Well-Being and Fair Distribution: Beyond Cost-Benefit Analysis* (New York: Oxford University Press, 2012), esp. pp. 88–114; and Peter A. Ubel, *Pricing Life: Why It's Time for Health Care Rationing* (Cambridge, MA: MIT Press, 2000), esp. p. 68.

75.   See Miller, Robinson, and Lawrence, eds., *Valuing Health for Regulatory Cost-Effectiveness Analysis.* For an examination and a call for further clarification of different types of measures, see Marthe R. Gold, David Stevenson, and Dennis G. Fryback, "HALYs and QALYs and DALYs, Oh My: Similarities and Differences in Summary Measures of Population Health," *Annual Review of Public Health* 23 (2002): 115–34. For a critical examination of DALYs, see Sudhir Anand and Kara Hanson, "Disability-Adjusted Life Years: A Critical Review," in *Public Health, Ethics, and Equity,* ed. Sudhir Anand, Fabienne Peter, and Amartya Sen (Oxford: Oxford University Press, 2004), chap. 9.

76.   National Institute for Health and Clinical Excellence (NICE), *Social Value Judgements: Principles for the Development of NICE Guidance,* 2nd ed., p. 35, http://www.nice.org.uk/media/ C18/30/SVJ2PUBLICATION2008.pdf (accessed November 6, 2011).

77.   Alan Williams, "The Importance of Quality of Life in Policy Decisions," in *Quality of Life: Assessment and Application,* ed. Stuart R. Walker and Rachel M. Rosser (Boston: MTP Press, 1988), p. 285.

78.   See Erik Nord, *Cost-Value Analysis in Health Care: Making Sense out of QALYs* (Cambridge: Cambridge University Press, 1999), passim; and Gold et al., *Cost-Effectiveness in Health and Medicine,* passim.

79.   See David Eddy, "Cost-Effectiveness Analysis: Is It up to the Task?" *Journal of the American Medical Association* 267 (June 24, 1992): 3344.

80. Alan Williams, "Economics of Coronary Artery Bypass Grafting," *British Medical Journal* 291 (August 3, 1985): 326–29. See also M. C. Weinstein and W. B. Stason, "Cost-Effectiveness of Coronary Artery Bypass Surgery," *Circulation* 66, Suppl. 5, pt. 2 (1982): III, 56–66.

81. See Paul Menzel, Marthe R. Gold, Erik Nord, et al., "Toward a Broader View of Values in Cost-Effectiveness Analysis of Health," *Hastings Center Report* 29 (May–June 1999): 7–15. For a defense of the utilitarian perspective of CEA and QALYs, see John McKie, Jeff Richardson, and Helga Kuhse, *The Allocation of Health Care Resources: An Ethical Evaluation of the 'QALY' Approach* (Aldershot, England: Ashgate, 1998). See also Joshua Cohen, "Preferences, Needs and QALYs," *Journal of Medical Ethics* 22 (1996): 267–72; Dan W. Brock, "Ethical Issues in the Use of Cost Effectiveness Analysis for the Prioritisation of Health Care Resources," in *Public Health, Ethics, and Equity,* ed. Anand, Peter, and Sen, chap. 10; and Madison Powers and Ruth Faden, *Social Justice: The Moral Foundations of Public Health and Health Policy* (Oxford: Oxford University Press, 2006), chap. 6.

82. Gavin Mooney, "QALYs: Are They Enough? A Health Economist's Perspective," *Journal of Medical Ethics* 15 (1989): 148–52.

83. Alan Williams, "The Importance of Quality of Life in Policy Decisions," in *Quality of Life,* ed. Walker and Rosser, p. 286; Williams, "Economics, QALYs and Medical Ethics—A Health Economist's Perspective," *Health Care Analysis* 3 (1995): 221–26.

84. Some proposals to modify or limit QALY-based CEA by societal values would require even lower weight for the elderly, in line with dominant societal values. See, for example, Nord, *Cost-Value Analysis in Health Care;* Menzel et al., "Toward a Broader View of Values in Cost-Effectiveness Analysis of Health"; and Ubel, *Pricing Life.*

85. But see the careful and qualified framework surrounding the use of QALYs by NICE, *Social Value Judgements,* sections 3–4, 7–8, esp. 4.2. John Harris argues that QALYs are a "life-threatening device," because they suggest that life-years rather than individual lives are valuable. "QALYfying the Value of Life," *Journal of Medical Ethics* 13 (1987): 117. See also Peter Singer, John McKie, Helga Kuhse, and Jeff Richardson, "Double Jeopardy and the Use of QALYs in Health Care Allocation," *Journal of Medical Ethics* 21 (1995): 144–50; John Harris, "Double Jeopardy and the Veil of Ignorance—A Reply," *Journal of Medical Ethics* 21 (1995): 151–57; McKie, Kuhse, Richardson, and Singer, "Double Jeopardy, the Equal Value of Lives and the Veil of Ignorance: A Rejoinder to Harris," *Journal of Medical Ethics* 22 (1996): 204–8.

86. David C. Hadorn, "Setting Health Care Priorities in Oregon: Cost-Effectiveness Meets the Rule of Rescue," *Journal of the American Medical Association* 265 (May 1, 1991): 2218. See, further, Peter Ubel, D. Scanlon, and M. Kamlet, "Individual Utilities Are Inconsistent with Rationing Choices: A Partial Explanation of Why Oregon's Cost-Effectiveness List Failed," *Medical Decision Making* 16 (1996): 108–16; and John McKie and Jeff Richardson, "The Rule of Rescue," *Social Science & Medicine* 56 (2003): 2407–19. We will return to the Oregon experiment in the next chapter.

7
Justice

Inequalities in access to health care and in health status, combined with dramatic increases in the costs of health care, have fueled debates about what, if anything, justice requires of particular societies and the global community. But are problems of inequality and cost truly problems of *justice* in health policy and health care institutions? If so, is the problem that inequality and cost threaten access to, and proper distribution of, health care? If the answer is again affirmative, by which principles of justice should health care be distributed?

In "The Lottery in Babylon," Jorge Luis Borges depicts a society that distributes all social benefits and burdens solely on the basis of a periodic lottery. Each person is assigned a social role such as slave, factory owner, priest, or executioner, purely by the lottery. This random selection system disregards criteria of distribution such as achievement, education, merit, experience, contribution, need, deprivation, and effort. The ethical and political oddity of the system described in Borges's story is jolting because assigning positions in this way does not cohere with conventional principles of justice. Borges's system appears capricious and unfair, because we expect valid principles to determine how social burdens, benefits, opportunities, and positions ought to be distributed.[1]

However, attempts to specify principles of justice for the many contexts in which they might be employed have proved as inconclusive as the lottery method seems capricious. Both the construction of a unified theory of justice that captures our diverse conceptions and use of principles of justice in biomedical ethics continue to be controversial and hard to pin down. We begin work on these problems in this chapter by analyzing the terms *justice* and *distributive justice*. Then we examine several general theories of distributive justice. Later we examine problems of national and international health policy and consider some enduring problems of social justice, including the nature of fair opportunity and unfair discrimination in health care, issues of vulnerability and exploitation in research, the defensibility of a right to health care and a right to health, the plausibility of a theory of global justice, the place of allocation and priority setting in health policy, and proper criteria of rationing health care in circumstances of scarcity.

THE CONCEPT OF JUSTICE AND PRINCIPLES OF JUSTICE

The terms *fairness, desert* (what is deserved), and *entitlement* have all been used by philosophers as a basis on which to explicate the term *justice.* These accounts interpret justice as fair, equitable, and appropriate treatment in light of what is due or owed to persons. The term *distributive justice* refers to fair, equitable, and appropriate distribution of benefits and burdens determined by norms that structure the terms of social cooperation.[2] Its scope includes policies that allot diverse benefits and burdens such as property, resources, taxation, privileges, and opportunities.

A compelling example of difficulties in determining the scope of distributive justice appears in the recent history of research involving human subjects. Until the 1990s, the paradigm problem in ethical assessment of research was the risks and burdens of research and the need to protect subjects from harm, abuse, and exploitation, especially when research offers no prospect of direct therapeutic benefit to the subjects and unfairly burdens a specific class of subjects. However, a paradigm shift occurred in the 1990s, in part because of the interest of patients with HIV/AIDS in gaining expanded access to new, experimental drugs both within and outside of clinical trials. The focus shifted to the possible benefits of clinical trials, while de-emphasizing their risks. As a result, justice as fair access to research—both participation in research and access to the results of research—became as important as protection from harm and exploitation.[3]

No single moral principle is capable of addressing all problems of justice. In this chapter we discuss several principles and consider how they can be balanced and specified in contexts of health care and public health. We argue that conditions of scarcity sometimes force a society to make tragic choices and in the process even valid principles of justice may be infringed, compromised, or sacrificed.[4] We start in this section with one basic *formal* principle and then turn to principles that have been proposed as *material,* that is, substantive principles of justice.

The Formal Principle of Justice

Common to all theories of justice is a minimal requirement traditionally attributed to Aristotle: Equals must be treated equally, and unequals must be treated unequally. This principle of formal justice—sometimes called the principle of formal equality—is "formal" because it identifies no particular respects in which equals ought to be treated equally and provides no criteria for determining whether two or more individuals are in fact equals. It merely asserts that persons equal in whichever respects are deemed relevant should be treated equally.

This formal principle lacks all substance. That equals ought to be treated equally provokes no debate, but significant problems surround decisions about what constitutes an equal and which differences are relevant in comparing individuals or groups. As a matter of human rights (see our account in Chapter 9), all citizens in a political state should have equal political rights, equal access to public services, and equal treatment under the law, but how far do principles of equality extend? Consider the following situation: Virtually all accounts of justice in health care hold that delivery programs and services designed to assist persons of a certain class, such as the poor, the elderly, pregnant women, and the disabled, should be made available to all members of that class. To deny benefits to some when others in the same class receive benefits is unjust, but is it also unjust to deny access to equally needy persons outside the delineated class, such as workers with no health insurance? How do we determine which classes, if any, should be designated? Answers require material principles of justice.

Material Principles of Justice and Morally Relevant Properties of Persons

Principles that specify the relevant characteristics for equal treatment are *material* because they identify the substantive properties for distribution. A relatively simple example is what we will call the principle of need, which declares that essential social resources, including health care, should be distributed according to need. To say that a person needs something is to say that, without it, that person will suffer a harm, or at least be detrimentally affected. However, we are not required to distribute all goods and services to satisfy all needs, such as needs for athletic equipment and cell phones. Presumably our obligations are limited to fundamental needs for essential resources. To say that someone has a fundamental need is to say that the person will be harmed or detrimentally affected in a fundamental way if the need is not met. For example, the person might be harmed through malnutrition, bodily injury, or nondisclosure of critical information. (See our discussion of harm in Chapter 5.)

If we were to continue to analyze this notion of fundamental needs, we could progressively specify and shape the material principle of need into a public policy for purposes of distribution—for example, a public policy regarding access to hospitals. For the moment, however, we are emphasizing only the significance of accepting a principle of need as a valid material principle of justice. This principle is only one among several plausible material principles of justice. If, by contrast, one were to accept only a principle of free-market distribution, then one would oppose a principle of need as a basis for public policy. All public and institutional policies based on distributive justice ultimately derive from the acceptance or rejection of some material principles and some procedures for specifying, refining, or balancing them.

Material principles identify morally relevant properties that persons must possess to qualify for particular distributions, but theoretical and practical difficulties confront the justification of allegedly relevant properties. Tradition, convention, and moral and legal principles sometimes point to relevant properties in some cases, but in many contexts it is appropriate either to institute a new policy that establishes relevant properties where none previously existed or that revises entrenched criteria. For example, nation-states need to establish a policy about whether nonresident aliens will be allowed on waiting lists for cadaveric organ transplantation. The government must decide whether citizenship is a relevant property and, if so, on which basis, in which ways, and with which exceptions.

Courts have sometimes mandated policies that revise entrenched notions about morally relevant properties. For example, the U.S. Supreme Court decided in the case of *Auto Workers v. Johnson Controls, Inc.*[5] that employers cannot legally adopt "fetal protection policies" that specifically exclude women of childbearing age from a hazardous workplace, because these policies unfairly discriminate based on the morally irrelevant property of gender. Under the policy that was challenged, fertile men could choose whether they wished to assume reproductive risks, whereas fertile women could not. The majority of justices held that this policy used the irrelevant property of gender despite the fact that mutagenic substances affect sperm as well as eggs.

Material Principles in Theories of Justice

Material principles have often been presented through general theories of justice. We too will introduce problems of distributive justice using this approach, turning first to what we call four *traditional theories*. We then consider two *recent theories*. Little beyond history depends on the terms *traditional* and *recent*. Our main interest in examining these six theories is to call attention to various general principles that help us think through problems of justice in different contexts of biomedical ethics, health care, public health, and health policy.

The four *traditional* theories are as follows: *Utilitarian* theories emphasize a mixture of criteria for the purpose of maximizing public utility; *libertarian* theories lay emphasis on individual rights to social and economic liberty, while invoking fair procedures as the basis of justice, rather than substantive outcomes such as increases of welfare; *communitarian* theories underscore principles of justice as derived from conceptions of the good developed in moral communities; and *egalitarian* theories emphasize equal access to the goods in life that every rational person values, often invoking material criteria of need and equality. The two *recent* theories are these: *Capabilities* theories identify capabilities and forms of freedom that are essential for a flourishing life and identify ways social institutions can protect them, whereas *well-being* theories emphasize essential core dimensions of well-being, such as health, and what is required to realize these states of well-being.

Each theory articulates a general, notably abstract, material principle of distributive justice:

1. To each person according to rules and actions that maximize social utility
2. To each person a maximum of liberty and property resulting from the exercise of liberty rights and participation in fair free-market exchanges
3. To each person according to principles of fair distribution derived from conceptions of the good developed in moral communities
4. To each person an equal measure of liberty and equal access to the goods in life that every rational person values
5. To each person the means necessary for the exercise of capabilities essential for a flourishing life
6. To each person the means necessary for the realization of core dimensions of well-being.

No obvious barrier prevents acceptance of more than one of these principles as valid—perhaps all six—in a pluralistic theory of justice. However, these principles are usually considered competitive. To retain them all, one would have to argue that each of these material principles identifies a prima facie obligation whose weight cannot be assessed independently of particular goods and domains in which they are applicable, and one would have to show how these principles can be rendered coherent.

Arguably, most societies do invoke more than one of these material principles in framing public policies for different contexts. For example, the resources available for public health programs and for women's and children's health programs might be distributed on the basis of either social utility or individual need to have a basic capability restored; salaries and the higher incomes of some persons might be allowed and even encouraged on grounds of free-market wage exchanges and competition; the resources needed for a basic education, for overcoming poverty, and for a decent level of health care might be distributed either equally to all citizens or as needed for citizens to achieve a basic level of well-being; and jobs and promotions in many sectors might be awarded on the basis of demonstrated achievement and merit, as assessed by criteria in individual communities.

TRADITIONAL THEORIES OF JUSTICE

Theories of distributive justice link the morally relevant properties of persons to morally justifiable distributions of benefits and burdens. By the last quarter of the twentieth century it became clear that the four traditional theories we will now examine had emerged as the most widely discussed theories of justice. We do not suggest that these theories are of equal importance, and we make no attempt to rank one over the others. In referring to them as "traditional," we are not signaling that they have a lower status, as if they were merely a matter of tradition and not currently defensible. Indeed, egalitarianism—the third theory— has been the most widely discussed and the most influential type of theory over the last few decades. It is still the starting point for almost all writers on distributive justice. Egalitarianism is also the logical transition point from "traditional" theories to the "recent" theories that we treat in the following section, because the recent theories show significant egalitarian influence.

Utilitarian Theories

Utilitarian theories, which rose to prominence in the nineteenth century at the hands of John Stuart Mill and Jeremy Bentham, are treated as general moral theories in some detail in Chapter 9 (pp. 354–61). Principles of distributive justice, in particular, are presented in utilitarian theories as among several principles and rules that maximize utility, that is, welfare. Any standard or rule of justice must be grounded in the principle of utility, which requires that we seek to produce the maximal balance of positive value over disvalue—or the least possible disvalue, if only undesirable results can be achieved. As Mill maintained, justice is the name for the paramount and most stringent forms of obligation set by the principle of utility.[6] However, the idea of maximizing utility is imprecise and has led to issues regarding which welfare functions should be maximized. In effect, all benefits stand to improve welfare—for example, nutritious foods, hygiene, annual medical physical examinations, and public health measures. A utilitarian with a practical account of justice must explain how welfare is to be understood and how to weight conditions of welfare in the system.

Typically, utilitarian obligations of justice establish correlative rights for individuals that should be enforced by law. These rights are strictly contingent upon social arrangements that maximize net social utility. Human rights and principles of obligation have no other basis than utility maximization in utilitarian theory. Disputes have abounded among utilitarians as to whether rights have a meaningful place in utilitarian theory, but if a system of rights such as an international code of the rights of research subjects is justified entirely on the grounds that its existence will maximize social utility, utilitarians cannot consistently object to those rights.

However, as even many utilitarians point out, moral problems surround the use of utilitarian principles to justify rights such as the right to health care and the rights of human subjects. Rights grounded in justice could be viewed as having a tenuous foundation when they rest on overall utility maximization, because the balance of social utility could change at any time. One coherent utilitarian view is that just as conditions of social utility can change, so the range of protected rights can change. For example, legal rights to health care in the United States have been limited to a few populations, especially the poor and the elderly, but conditions of social utility could shift so that every citizen is granted a right to health care.

Although utilitarian theories face serious challenges as general theories of justice, they can help form just health policies in publicly supported institutions, especially when the policies are formulated using cost–benefit or risk–benefit analysis, as we note later in this chapter and in other chapters (especially Chapter 6).

Libertarian Theories

Libertarian theories date at least to early modern theories of natural rights, most notably in passages in John Locke's philosophy, which recognizes "just and natural rights" to liberty.[7] These theories are both general moral accounts and accounts of justice because they state general duties all members of society owe to one another, usually conceived as duties to respect liberty and to enforce individual liberty rights by coercive power when necessary. A libertarian interpretation of justice focuses not on public utility or on acting to meet the health and welfare needs of citizens, but on the unfettered operation of fair procedures and transactions under conditions of law and order.

Robert Nozick has for several decades been the most influential libertarian philosopher. He argues for a theory of justice in which government action is justified if and only if it protects citizens' liberty and property rights.[8] Here a theory of justice affirms individual liberty rights rather than creating patterns of distribution in which governments redistribute the wealth originally acquired by persons in the free market. Governments act coercively and unjustly when they tax the wealthy at a progressively higher rate than those who are less wealthy and then use the proceeds to underwrite state support of the indigent through welfare payments and unemployment compensation.

Nozick proposes three and only three principles of justice, all centered on private property rights: justice in acquisition, justice in transfer, and justice in rectification. No pattern of just distribution exists independent of free-market procedures of acquiring property, legitimately transferring that property, and providing rectification for those whose property was illegitimately taken or who otherwise were illegitimately obstructed in the free market. Accordingly, justice consists in the operation of just procedures, not in the production of just outcomes such as an equal distribution of health resources. There are no welfare rights, and therefore no rights or justified claims to health care can be based on justice.

Libertarians do not oppose utilitarian or egalitarian patterns of distribution if these patterns are freely chosen by all participants affected. Any distribution of goods, including public health measures and health care, is just and justified if and only if individuals in the relevant community freely choose it. The state must not coercively take anyone's personal property to benefit another, but it can justifiably restrict by coercive means those who violate the liberty rights of others.

In this system, investors in health care have property rights, physicians have liberty rights, and society is not morally obligated to provide health care. Indeed, society is morally obligated to refrain from collecting such public funding by coercive taxation and from assigning physicians to communities by conscription. The United States, with some exceptions, traditionally accepted what approximates a libertarian ideal according to which distributions of health insurance and health care were best left to a material principle of ability to pay for insurance and medical care, supplemented by voluntary charitable acts and institutions such as charitable hospitals. Under this conception, a just society protects rights of property and liberty, allowing all persons the freedom to improve their circumstances and protect their health on their own initiative. Health care is not a right, the ideal system of health insurance is privatized, and charitable care institutions are nonprofit and untaxed.

Egalitarian Theories

Egalitarian theories have a history as old as religious traditions that have held that all humans must be treated as equals because they are created as equals and have equal moral status. In moral and political philosophy, at least since Locke and other seventeenth-century writers, egalitarian thought has had a large presence. These theories explicate the idea of equality in terms of treating persons as equals *in certain respects*. No prominent egalitarian theory has contained a distributive principle that requires equal sharing of all social benefits to all persons. The dominant egalitarian theories are qualified ones that identify basic equalities while permitting some inequalities.

Rawls's celebrated egalitarian theory starts with the view that "what justifies a conception of justice is not its being true to an order antecedent and given to us, but its congruence with our deeper understanding of ourselves and our aspirations."[9] A theory of justice uses central judgments of equal respect for persons and fairness to help us establish principles of justice. Rawls argues that impartial persons would agree on two fundamental principles. The first principle requires that each person be permitted the maximum amount of basic liberty compatible with a similar measure of liberty for others. The second principle requires that social inequalities must satisfy two conditions: (1) the first condition stipulates that inequalities in social primary goods (including, for example, income, rights, and opportunities) may be allowed, but only if they benefit everyone (the difference principle); (2) the second condition requires that social offices and positions be open to all under circumstances of fair equality of opportunity (a fair opportunity rule, as we will treat it later in this chapter).[10] Rawls considers nations and social institutions just if and only if they conform to each of these basic principles. He neither states how large the inequalities in income, rights, and opportunities might be nor speculates about how much better off the least advantaged must be under the difference principle. This leaves uncertain how far the difference principle pushes in the direction of allowing inequalities.

Although Rawls never pursued the implications of his theory for health policy, others have. In an influential interpretation and extension, Norman Daniels argues for a just health care system based primarily on these principles, with a special emphasis on what Rawls called "fair equality of opportunity." Daniels argues that health care needs are special and that fair opportunity is central to any acceptable theory of justice. Social institutions affecting health care distribution thus should be arranged, as far as possible, to allow each person to achieve a fair share of the normal range of opportunities present in that society.

Daniels's theory, like Rawls's, recognizes a positive societal obligation to reduce or eliminate barriers that prevent fair equality of opportunity, an obligation that extends to programs to correct or compensate for disadvantages. It views disease and disability as undeserved restrictions on persons' opportunities to realize basic goals. Health care is needed to achieve, maintain, or restore adequate or "species-typical" levels of functioning so that individuals can realize basic goals. A health care system designed to meet these needs should attempt to prevent disease, illness, or injury from reducing the range of opportunity open to individuals. The allocation of health care resources, then, should be structured to ensure justice through fair equality of opportunity.[11]

This Rawls-inspired theory has far-reaching egalitarian implications for national health policies and perhaps for international policy as well. On this account, each member of society, irrespective of wealth or position, would have equal access to an adequate, although not maximal, level of health care—the exact level of access being contingent on available social resources and public processes of decision making.

Communitarian Theories

Communitarian theories of justice can and have laid claim to a tradition traceable to Aristotle, Hegel, and other figures in the history of philosophy. However, few philosophers have self-identified as "communitarian," a label that collects a variety of theories. In its recent forms, these theories have largely been devised as critical reactions to Rawls's theory, and secondarily to Nozick's theory. Communitarians have little sympathy with theories based on individual rights and contracts. They see societies constructed on these principles as lacking in a commitment to the general welfare, to common purposes, and to education in citizenship. Conventions, traditions, loyalties, and the social nature of life and institutions figure prominently in communitarian theories.[12]

Every major communitarian thinker has contested the thesis of the priority of individual rights over the common good. Charles Taylor's challenge is straightforward: He argues that claims of the priority of individual rights over communal decision making are premised on a conception of the human good (e.g., the good of autonomous moral agency), as if individuals are isolated atoms existing independently of communities. Even the type of autonomy suggested by individualism, Taylor argues, cannot be developed in the absence of the family and other community structures and interests.[13]

Communitarians regard principles of justice as pluralistic, deriving from as many different conceptions of the good as there are diverse moral communities. What is owed to individuals and groups depends on these community-derived standards.[14] As an example of communitarians' promotion of the common good in biomedical ethics, consider their difference from libertarians and others over policies for obtaining cadaveric organs for transplantation. Based on principles of individual rights, all states in the United States adopted the Uniform Anatomical Gift Act in the late 1960s and early 1970s. This act gives individuals the right to donate their organs after death. Some communitarians challenge whether the right to donate is the relevant consideration. A strongly stated communitarian policy supports the routine removal of organs in the absence of registered objections. Arguments for such a policy stress either the individual's obligation to donate to help others or the society's ownership of cadaveric organs. Some communitarians argue for such a policy on grounds that members of a community should be willing to provide others objects of lifesaving value when they can do so at no cost to themselves. Others recommend policies of routine removal that assume communal, rather than individual or familial, ownership of cadaveric body parts.[15]

An emphasis on the community and the common good also appears in recommended policies for the allocation of health care. According to Daniel Callahan's communitarian account, we should enact public policy from a shared consensus about the good of society rather than on the basis of individual rights. We should relax liberal assumptions about government neutrality, and society should be free to implement a substantive concept of the good. Callahan would have us ask, "What is most conducive to a good society?" rather than simply, "Is it harmful, or does it violate autonomy?"[16]

RECENT THEORIES OF JUSTICE

Since roughly the beginning of the twenty-first century, some innovative theories have reoriented discussions about justice in biomedical ethics. Responses to Rawls's egalitarianism have guided much of this literature, but the new work cannot be accurately described as fundamentally Rawlsian, though it is egalitarian. This literature has also been heavily influenced by Aristotelian moral theory, especially the role and importance of states of human flourishing (see our discussion of Aristotelian theories of moral virtue and moral excellence in Chapter 2 and the modest extension in Chapter 9). This section is dedicated to recent theories that are heavily influenced by both Aristotle and Rawls and that are important and relevant for concerns in biomedical ethics.

Capabilities Theories

An approach known as capabilities theory starts from the premise that the opportunity to reach states of proper functioning and well-being are of basic moral significance and that the freedom to reach these states is to be analyzed in the language of "capabilities." The quality of persons' lives is contingent on what they are able to achieve, and a life well lived is one in which individuals sustain and exercise a group of core capabilities. This theory was pioneered by Amartya Sen[17] and developed in numerous ways relevant to biomedical ethics by Martha Nussbaum,[18] who uses the theory to address "social justice" and the "frontiers of justice"—the latter including justice for the disabled, the globally poor, and nonhuman animals. The theory holds that a minimal level of social justice requires "the availability to all citizens of ten core 'capabilities,'"[19] which are the following:[20]

1. *Life.* Being able to live a normal life without dying prematurely or existing in a reduced state making life not worth living
2. *Bodily health.* Being able to have good health, nutrition, and shelter
3. *Bodily integrity.* Being able to move freely, to be secure against violence, and to have opportunities for sexual satisfaction and reproductive choice
4. *Senses, imagination, and thought.* Being able to use these capacities in an informed and human way aided by an adequate and diverse education and in a context of freedom of expression
5. *Emotions.* Being able to have emotional attachments to things and people so that one can love, grieve, and feel gratitude without having one's emotional development blunted by fear, anxiety, and the like
6. *Practical reason.* Being able to form a conception of the good and to critically reflect in planning one's life
7. *Affiliation.* Being able to live meaningfully in the company of others, with self-respect and without undue humiliation
8. *Other species.* Being able to live with concern for animals, plants, and nature generally
9. *Play.* Being able to play and enjoy recreational activities

10. *Control over one's environment.* Being able to participate as an active citizen in political choices pertaining to one's life and property

Each capability is essential for a human life to not be impoverished below the level of the dignity of a person, and each capability is the basis of a human right or entitlement. Our natural "basic capabilities" must be developed so that we have trained capacities: We innately have capacities for speech, learning, and free action, which can then be developed into more advanced capabilities such as literacy, job skills, and knowledge about how to avoid poverty and disease.

Nussbaum's account holds that these capabilities, which are essential to flourishing, must be socially sustained and protected: *"all ten of these plural and diverse ends are minimum requirements of justice,* at least up to [a] threshold level."[21] Justice requires that we, as a society, ensure that the world does not interfere with individuals' development of their core capabilities or block political participation in a way that stunts or harms them. Society sometimes must equip persons with capabilities, including provision of the resources necessary for living appropriately such as food, education, nondiscriminatory institutions, and health care. This approach focuses on putting persons in circumstances or conditions in which they are enabled to set their own goals and live as they choose. Nussbaum insists that "the political entitlements of all citizens are equal and the same."[22]

In addressing the "frontiers of justice" Nussbaum's theory is remarkably broad, covering not only human capabilities and functioning for disabled and socially oppressed persons, but also nonhuman animals. Treating an individual justly requires, negatively, *not obstructing* the individual's attempts at flourishing through acts of coercion, violence, or cruelty and also requires, positively, support of efforts to flourish.[23] This is an extremely demanding theory of justice, perhaps as demanding as any ever devised. It is also what we will later refer to as a global theory inasmuch as it extends "justice to all world citizens, showing theoretically how we might realize a world that is just as a whole" by providing the "necessary conditions for a decently just society."[24]

Well-Being Theories

Capabilities theories are centered on the *abilities* and *opportunities* requisite for well-being, but other recent theories focus on *well-being itself.* In these accounts the liberty to act, innate capabilities, training that enables, and resources that enable are not fundamental to justice, because these conditions are valuable only as means to well-being and its proper distribution. The distribution that needs to occur is a distribution of welfare. Utilitarianism is one such theory, but only one. In this section we concentrate on a different type of theory devised explicitly for bioethics, public health, and health policy by Madison Powers and Ruth Faden.

They start with a basic premise: "Social justice is concerned with human well-being." It is concerned not merely with capabilities for well-being or with a single form of well-being, such as health. They argue that a theory of social justice should be concerned with six core dimensions of well-being:

1. Health
2. Personal security
3. Reasoning
4. Respect
5. Attachment
6. Self-determination

This list may seem similar to Nussbaum's—for example, "attachment" resembles Nussbaum's "affiliation"—but Powers and Faden reject the language of capabilities as confusing and wide of the target of a theory of justice. Theirs is a list of essential core dimensions of well-being, rather than a list of core capabilities.[25] Being healthy, being secure, and being respected are desirable states of being, not merely capabilities or functionings. For example, we want not merely the *capability* to be well-nourished, but to *be* well-nourished. Justice is concerned with the achievement of well-being, not merely the capabilities to pursue it.

The "job of justice" in this theory is to secure a sufficient level of each dimension for each person. Each of the six dimensions is an independent concern of justice, but they also interact with each other. The justice of health policy in societies and in the global order can be judged by how well these dimensions are implemented. Powers and Faden see the major problem of justice as reducing inequality in international health, especially reducing the role that poverty plays in causing and perpetuating poor health. Here the major concern is the right to *health,* not the right to *health care.*

Powers and Faden see their basic principle and focus as egalitarian justice, not merely beneficence or social utility. The goal is to reduce inequality in the world as we encounter it—a world characterized by profound inequalities in well-being and resources. Although only the first of the six dimensions of well-being in this account is health, Powers and Faden argue that the moral justification for health policies depends as much on the other five dimensions of well-being as it does on health. An absence of any of the other conditions can be seriously destructive to health. A constellation of inequalities can systemically magnify and reinforce initial conditions of ill health, creating ripple effects that impact other dimensions of health. The interactive effects include poor education and lack of respect, which can affect core forms of reasoning and health status. Social structures can compound these adverse effects. The result is a mixture of interactive and cascading effects that require urgent attention from the point of view of justice.[26]

Conclusion

We can expect the six theories we have now displayed to succeed only partially in bringing coherence and comprehensiveness to our multilayered and sometimes fragmented conceptions of social justice. Policies for health care access and distribution in many nations provide excellent cases of the problems that confront these theories. These countries seek to make available high-quality health care for all citizens, while protecting public resources through cost-containment programs and policies that set fair limits. Many of their policies also promote the ideal of equal access to health care for everyone, including the indigent, while maintaining aspects of a competitive, free-market environment. These laudable goals of superior care, equal access, free choice, social efficiency, and well-being are all justifiable in some domain (or at least we will here so assume), but they are also difficult to render coherent in a social system and in a theory of justice; pursuing one goal may function to undercut another.

It seems likely that there has never been a political state or a world order fashioned *entirely* on one and only one of the several theories of justice that we have now discussed. Some commentators see these theories as having the weakness of Plato's ideal state in the *Republic:* They provide models, but not truly practical instruments. This skeptical caution is prudent, but it can lead to an underevaluation. Intelligent use of the principles of justice at work in these theories has enormous practical significance for biomedical ethics and for the citizens of political states, as we will try to show in the remainder of this chapter. We will not attempt to assess the relative merits of these theories. Rather, we will use them as resources, with special attention to egalitarian thinking and the distribution of health care and public health resources.

FAIR OPPORTUNITY AND UNFAIR DISCRIMINATION

Among the most influential features of egalitarian thinking, especially in Rawlsian theory, is the rule of fair opportunity. We begin with the question, "What kind of fair opportunity does justice require?"

To address this question, we consider first the properties that have often served, unjustly, as bases of distribution. These properties include gender, race, IQ, linguistic accent, ethnicity, national origin, and social status. In anomalous contexts (e.g., in casting for film or theater), these properties may be relevant and acceptable. However, general rules such as "To each according to gender" and "To each according to IQ" are unacceptable as prima facie material principles of justice. These properties are irrelevant and based on differences for which the affected individual is not responsible. Basing actions or policies on them is discriminatory.

The Fair-Opportunity Rule

The fair-opportunity rule descends from Rawls's conditions of fair equality of opportunity. The rule, as we present it, asserts that individuals should not receive social benefits on the basis of undeserved advantageous properties and should not be denied social benefits on the basis of undeserved disadvantageous properties, because they are not responsible for these properties. Properties distributed by the lotteries of social and biological life do not provide grounds for morally acceptable discrimination between persons in social allocations if people do not have a fair chance to acquire or overcome these properties.

The goal of supplying all citizens with a basic education raises moral problems analogous to problems of justice in health care. Imagine a community that offers a high-quality education to all students with basic abilities, regardless of gender or race, but does not offer a comparable educational opportunity to students with reading difficulties or mental deficiencies. This system is unjust. The students with disabilities lack basic skills and require special training to overcome their problems. They should receive an education suitable to their needs and opportunities, even if it costs more. The fair-opportunity rule requires that they receive benefits that will ameliorate the unfortunate effects of life's lottery. By analogy, persons with functional disabilities lack critical capacities and need health care to reach a suitable level of function and have a fair opportunity in life. When persons are not responsible for their disabilities, the fair-opportunity rule demands that they receive help to reduce or overcome the unfortunate effects of life's lottery of health.

Fair Opportunity as a Rule of Redress: Mitigating the Negative Effects of Life's Lotteries

Numerous properties might be disadvantageous and undeserved—for example, a squeaky voice, an ugly face, inarticulate speech, an inadequate early education, malnutrition, and disease. But which undeserved properties create a right *in justice* to some form of assistance?

A particularly strong claim is that virtually all abilities and disabilities are functions of what Rawls calls the natural lottery and the social lottery. "Natural lottery" refers to the distribution of advantageous and disadvantageous genetic properties, and "social lottery" refers to the distribution of assets or deficits through family property, school systems, tribal affiliation, government agencies, and the like. It is conceivable that all talents, disabilities, and disadvantaging properties result from sources such as heredity, natural environment, family upbringing, education, and inheritance. Even the ability to work long hours, the ability to compete, and a warm smile may be biologically, environmentally, and socially engendered. If so, talents, abilities, and successes are not to our credit, just as genetic disease is acquired through no fault of the afflicted person.

Rawls uses fair opportunity as a rule of redress. To overcome undeserved disadvantaging conditions, whether they derive from the natural lottery or the social lottery, the rule demands compensation for disadvantages. The implications of this theory have never been made clear, but Rawls's conclusions are demanding:

> [A free-market arrangement] permits the distribution of wealth and income to be determined by the natural distribution of abilities and talents. Within the limits allowed by the background arrangements, distributive shares are decided by the outcome of the natural lottery; and this outcome is arbitrary from a moral perspective. There is no more reason to permit the distribution of income and wealth to be settled by the distribution of natural assets than by historical and social fortune. Furthermore, the principle of fair opportunity can be only imperfectly carried out, at least as long as the institution of the family exists. The extent to which natural capacities develop and reach fruition is affected by all kinds of social conditions and class attitudes. Even the willingness to make an effort, to try, and so to be deserving in the ordinary sense is itself dependent upon happy family and social circumstances.[27]

Current social systems of distributing benefits and burdens might undergo massive revision if this approach were accepted. Instead of permitting broad inequalities in access to health care and quality of care—based on employer contributions, wealth, and the like—justice is achieved only if opportunity-reducing inequalities are first addressed. Of course, at some point the process of reducing inequalities created by life's lotteries must stop.[28] From this perspective, a strict fair-opportunity rule is overly demanding. Libertarians rightly stress that limited resources will constrain the implementation of this rule, but their criticisms go too far when they maintain that some disadvantages are merely *unfortunate,* whereas others are *unfair* and therefore obligatory in justice to correct. Tristram Engelhardt provides an example. He argues that society should call a halt to claims of fairness or justice precisely at the point of this distinction between the unfair and the unfortunate.[29]

We will eventually argue both that no bright lines distinguish the unfair from the unfortunate—or fair from unfair allocation schemes—and that emphasizing fair opportunity without reference to welfare makes for an inadequate account of justice.

Racial, Ethnic, Gender, and Social Status Disparities in Health Care

Many disparities in health care and research based on racial, ethnic, and gender properties as well as social status are problems of fair opportunity. Health care goods and research risks have often been covertly distributed on the basis of these properties, resulting in a differential impact in many countries on the health of racial and ethnic minorities, women, and the poor.[30] Many studies in the United States indicate that African Americans, women, and the economically disadvantaged have poorer access to various forms of health care and to valued research in comparison to white males. For example, gender and racial inequities in employment situations have an impact on job-based health insurance, and serving as research subjects falls disproportionately on socially and economically disadvantaged patients or groups of patients such as individuals who have low incomes or are homeless. Similarly, the advantages of some forms of health care and research disproportionately benefit patients who are already socially and economically advantaged.

In the face of such disparities, numerous efforts have emerged to overcome racial, ethnic, gender, and social-status disparities.[31] One controversy centers on disparities in rates of coronary artery bypass grafting (CABG) between white and black Medicare patients, as well as between male and female Medicare patients. Differences in use, which have been evident since the 1980s, cannot be entirely accounted for by differential need, and it remains unclear to what extent the rates can be explained by physician supply, poverty, awareness of health care opportunities, reluctance among blacks and women to undergo surgery, and racial prejudice. One study found that, after controlling for age, payer, and appropriateness and necessity for CABG, African American patients in New York State had significant access problems unrelated to patient refusals.[32]

Disparities have persisted in the management of acute myocardial infarction and acute coronary syndromes,[33] as well as in cholesterol control among patients with cardiovascular diseases, in cancer screening,[34] in the diagnosis and treatment of conditions such as colorectal cancer and glucose control for patients with diabetes,[35] and in pain care.[36] Disparities in use do not always amount to injustices, but they require close scrutiny to determine their causes and to be on guard against injustice. In some disparities, there is both overutilization by some groups and underutilization by others.[37]

A report from the U.S. Institute of Medicine on racial and ethnic disparities in health care identifies several "unacceptable" racial and ethnic disparities across a range of medical conditions and health care services, leading to worse health outcomes. Whereas insurance status, income, and level of education are critically important to health care access in the United States, the report argues that other, independent factors are likewise significant, including historic and continuing social and economic inequality; cultural preferences; biological differences; system-level factors, such as language barriers, time constraints in health care, and geographic availability; and care process–level variables, including bias, stereotyping, and uncertainty based in part on racial and ethnic differences and on clinicians' needs to make medical decisions under pressures of time and limited information.[38]

Renal transplantation provides another example. In U.S. policy, financial barriers play a less significant role in kidney transplantation than in most areas of health care. The federal End-Stage Renal Disease (ESRD) Program ensures coverage for kidney dialysis and transplantation for virtually every citizen who needs them if their private insurance does not provide the coverage. However, concerns about costs can still be a factor because immunosuppressant medications needed for life are not covered under the ESRD program after three years. Evidence suggests that discrimination against blacks, other minorities, women, and the poor occurs leading up to and at the point of referral to transplantation centers and admission to waiting lists, where criteria may vary considerably. For instance, black Americans are much less likely than white Americans to be referred for evaluation at transplant centers and to be placed on a waiting list or to receive a transplant.[39] Factors include minority distrust of the system, delayed or limited access to health care, and inadequate guidance through the system by health care professionals.

Once patients are admitted to the waiting list, the criteria for selecting recipients of deceased donor organs are public and are, to a significant extent, represented through point systems. Disputes continue regarding how much weight to give to different factors in the distribution of kidneys for transplantation, with particular attention to human lymphocyte antigen (HLA) matching. The degree of HLA match between a donor and a recipient affects the long-term survival of the transplanted kidney. Assigning priority to tissue matching—and giving less weight to time on the waiting list and other factors—has been shown to produce disparate effects for minorities. Most organ donors are white; certain HLA phenotypes are different in white, black, and Hispanic populations; and the identification of HLA phenotypes is less complete for blacks and Hispanics. Yet nonwhites have a higher rate of end-stage renal disease and are also disproportionately represented on dialysis rolls. Blacks on the waiting list also, on average, wait longer than whites to receive a first kidney transplant, if they receive one at all.

After extensive discussion and deliberation, including professional and public input, the United Network for Organ Sharing in 2003 changed its kidney allocation criteria to eliminate the priority given to HLA-B matching with the goal of reducing the disparity in deceased donor kidney transplants between African Americans and whites. The revised policy was defended on the grounds that it would resolve "the tension inherent in the current allocation policy by improving equity without sacrificing utility."[40] It succeeded in reducing the disparity: Before the policy change, African Americans had 37% lower rates of deceased donor kidney transplants, but after the change they had 23% lower rates.[41] Perhaps because of unaddressed or unknown factors, disparity was not eliminated. We do not know whether, or to what extent, the policy change decreased the number of years of transplant function. Normatively, the tension

between maximizing utility and providing fair opportunity persists, and critics
have challenged the use of disparate impact tests to shift from policies that seek
to maximize the number of quality-adjusted life-years per transplanted organ to
trying to increase the access of racial or ethnic groups to transplantation.[42]

VULNERABILITY, EXPLOITATION, AND DISCRIMINATION IN RESEARCH

We turn now to a different set of problems about fair opportunity, these deriving
from the vulnerability of human research subjects who are at risk of exploitation.
We concentrate on the recruitment and enrollment in clinical research (primarily
pharmaceutical trials) of the economically disadvantaged.

By "economically disadvantaged," we mean persons who are impoverished, may lack significant access to health care, may be homeless, or may be
malnourished, and yet possess the mental capacity to volunteer to participate
in, for example, safety and toxicity (phase I) drug studies. We will consider in
this section only persons who possess a basic competence to reason, deliberate,
decide, and consent. Somewhere between 50% and 100% of research subjects
who are healthy volunteers self-report that financial need or financial reward is
their primary motive for volunteering.[43] We know little about the full extent of
their involvement, just as we do not know the scope of the use of poor persons
as research subjects.[44]

Vulnerability and Vulnerable Groups

The relevant literature has sometimes viewed the class of the economically disadvantaged and vulnerable as narrow, at other times as broad. The persons so
classified may or may not include individuals living on the streets, low-income
persons who are the sole financial support of a large family, persons desperately
lacking access to health care, persons whose income falls below a certain threshold level, and so forth.

The notion of a "vulnerable group" was a major category in bioethics and
health policy between the 1970s and the 1990s. However, over the years it suffered from overexpansion because so many groups were declared vulnerable—
from the infirm elderly, to the undereducated, to those with inadequate resources,
to whole countries whose members lack rights or are subject to exploitation.[45]
The language of "vulnerable groups" suggests that all members of a vulnerable
group—for example, all prisoners, all poor people, and all pregnant women—are
by category vulnerable. However, for many groups a label covering all members
of the group serves to overprotect, stereotype, and even disqualify members capable of making their own decisions.[46] "Vulnerable" is an inappropriate label for any
class of persons when some members of the class are not vulnerable in the relevant

respects. For example, pregnant women as a class are not vulnerable, although some pregnant women are. Accordingly, we will not here speak of the economically disadvantaged as a vulnerable group. Instead, we speak of *vulnerabilities*.[47]

A tempting strategy to protect their interests is to exclude economically disadvantaged persons categorically, even if they are not categorically vulnerable. This remedy would eliminate the problem of unjust exploitation but also would deprive these individuals of the freedom to choose and would often be harmful to their financial interests. Nothing about economically disadvantaged persons justifies their exclusion, as a group, from participation in research, just as it does not follow from their status as disadvantaged that they should be excluded from any legal activity. To be sure, there is an increased risk of taking advantage of the economically distressed, but to exclude them categorically would be an unjust and paternalistic form of discrimination that may only serve to further marginalize, deprive, or stigmatize them.

Undue Inducement, Undue Profit, and Exploitation

We turn now to moral problems about enrolling the economically disadvantaged in research. These are problems of undue inducement, undue profit, and exploitation. Some persons report feeling heavily pressured to enroll in clinical trials, even though their enrollment is classified as voluntary.[48] These individuals are in desperate need of money. Attractive offers of money and other goods can leave a person with a sense of being constrained and having no meaningful choice but to accept research participation.

Constraining situations. These constraining situations are sometimes misleadingly termed *coercive situations*.[49] Here a person feels controlled by the constraints of a situation, such as severe illness or lack of food and shelter, rather than by the design or threat of another person. There is no coercion because no one has intentionally issued a threat to gain compliance or forced a person to consent. Still, persons feel "threatened," and sometimes feel compelled to prevent or ameliorate perceived harms of illness, powerlessness, and lack of resources. The prospect of another night on the streets or another day without food can constrain a person to accept an offer of research participation, just as such conditions could constrain a person to accept an unpleasant or risky job that the person would otherwise not accept.

Undue inducement. In constraining situations, monetary payments and related offers such as shelter or food give rise to problems of justice commonly referred to as *undue inducement,* on the one hand, and *undue profit,* on the other. The "Common Rule" in the United States requires investigators to "minimize the possibility of" coercion and undue inducement, but it does not define, analyze, or explain these notions.[50] The bioethics and public policy literatures also do not adequately handle the problems.

Monetary payments seem unproblematic if the payments are welcome offers that persons do not want to refuse and the risks are at the level of everyday activities.[51] But inducements become increasingly problematic as (1) risks are increased, (2) more attractive inducements are offered, and (3) the subjects' economic disadvantage is greater. The problem of exploitation centers on whether solicited persons are situationally disadvantaged and lack viable alternatives, feel forced or compelled to accept attractive offers that they otherwise would not accept, and assume increased risk in their lives. As these conditions are mitigated, problems of exploitation diminish and may vanish altogether. As these conditions are increased, the problem of exploitation looms larger.

The presence of an irresistibly attractive offer is a necessary condition of "undue inducement," but this condition is not by itself sufficient to make an inducement undue. A situation of undue inducement must also involve a person's assumption of a serious risk of harm that he or she would not ordinarily assume. We will not try to pinpoint a precise threshold level of risk, but it would have to be above the level of common job risks such as those of unskilled construction work. Inducements are not undue unless they are both above the level of standard risk (hence excessive in risk) and irresistibly attractive (hence excessive in payment) in light of a constraining situation.

Undue profit. Undue inducements should be distinguished from *undue profits*, which occur from a distributive injustice of too small a payment to subjects, rather than an irresistibly attractive, large payment. In the undue-profit situation, the subjects in research receive an unfairly low payment, while the sponsor of research garners more than is justified. Often, this seems to be what critics of pharmaceutical research are asserting: Researchers approach potential subjects who are in a weak to nonexistent bargaining situation, constrained by their poverty, and offered an unjustly small amount of money and an unjustly low share of the benefits, while companies reap unseemly profits. If this is the worry, the basic question is how to determine a nonexploitative, fair payment for service as a research subject, which might include benefits of successful research such as free medication.

How should we handle these two moral problems of exploitation—undue inducement (unduly large and irresistible payments) and undue profit (unduly small and unfair payments)? One approach is to prohibit research that involves excessive risk, even if a good oversight system is in place. This answer is appealing, but we would still need to determine in each case what constitutes excessive risk, irresistibly attractive payment, unjust underpayment, and constraining situations—all difficult and unresolved problems.

These problems resist a tidy solution: To avoid undue inducement, payment schedules must be kept reasonably low, approximating an unskilled labor wage, or possibly even lower. Even at this low level, payment might still be sufficiently large to constitute an undue inducement for some research subjects.

As payments are lowered to avoid undue inducement, research subjects in some circumstances will be recruited largely or entirely from the ranks of the economically disadvantaged. Somewhere on this continuum the amount of money paid will be so little that it is exploitative by virtue of undue profits yielded by taking advantage of a person's misfortune. If the payment scales were increased to avoid undue profit, they would at some point become high enough to attract persons from the middle class. At or around this point, the offers would be declared excessively attractive and judged undue inducements for impoverished persons interested in the payments.[52] This dilemma is a profound problem of social injustice if the pool of research subjects is composed more or less exclusively of the economically disadvantaged.

Finally, an important reason for caution about prohibiting research or about encouraging pharmaceutical companies to pull out of poor communities is that payments for studies may be a vital source of needed funds for the economically disadvantaged and a way to build an infrastructure and create jobs in these communities. Among the few readily available sources of money for some economically distressed persons are jobs such as day labor that expose them to more risk and generate less money than the payments generated by participation in phase I clinical trials.[53] To deny these persons the right to participate in clinical research on grounds of the potential exploitation we have discussed can be paternalistic and demeaning, as well as economically distressing. It would in many circumstances be unjust.

NATIONAL HEALTH POLICY AND THE RIGHT TO HEALTH CARE

Problems of justice in access to health care differ substantially in diverse parts of the world, but questions about who shall receive what share of a society's resources are at the center of the discussion almost everywhere. In this and later sections we examine several controversies about appropriate national health policies, inequalities of distribution, and rationing of health-related goods and services.

The primary economic barrier to health care access in many countries is the lack of adequate insurance or funding for care. Fifty million U.S. citizens, approximately 16.3% of the total population and 18% of the nonelderly population, lack health insurance of any kind.[54] Inadequate insurance affects persons who are uninsured, uninsurable, underinsured, or only occasionally insured. Some problems of unfairness arise in the United States because of the system's reliance on employers for financing health insurance. Persons with medium- to large-sized employers are not only better covered, but also subsidized by tax breaks. When employed persons who are not covered become ill, taxpayers (and not free-riding employers) usually pick up the cost. The financing of health care is also regressive. Low-income families pay premiums comparable to and often higher than the premiums paid by high-income families, and many individuals who do not qualify for group coverage pay dramatically more for the same coverage than those who qualify in a group.

A social consensus appears to exist in the United States that all citizens should be able to secure equitable access to health care, including insurance coverage. However, this consensus is content-thin regarding the role of government, methods of financing insurance and health care, and the meaning of "equitable access." It is unclear whether such a fragile consensus can generate a secondary consensus about how to implement a system of equitable access. Similar issues appear in many nations.

Arguments Supporting Rights to Health Care

Two principal arguments support a moral right to government-funded health care: (1) an argument from collective social protection and (2) an argument from fair opportunity.

The first argument focuses on the similarities between health needs and other needs that government has traditionally protected. Threats to health are relevantly similar to threats presented by crime, fire, and pollution. Collective actions and resources have conventionally been used to resist such threats, and many collective schemes to protect health exist in virtually all societies, including programs of public health and environmental protection. Consistency suggests that critical health care assistance in response to threats to health should likewise be a collective responsibility. This argument by analogy appeals to coherence: If the government has an obligation to provide one type of essential service, then it must have an obligation to provide another relevantly similar essential service.

This argument has been criticized on grounds that government responsibilities are neither obligatory nor essential. However, this perspective is favored by few beyond those committed to libertarianism. On each of the nonlibertarian theories of justice previously explicated, the argument from other comparable government services generates a public obligation to provide some level of goods and services to protect health. Relevant dissimilarities do exist, however, between the good of health care *for individuals* and other public programs, including social goods such as public health. The argument from collective social protection therefore might seem to fail or at least to be incomplete.

However, additional premises supporting the right to health care are found in society's right to expect a decent return on the investment it has made in physicians' education, funding for biomedical research, and funding for various parts of the medical system that pertain to health care. This argument appeals to reciprocity: Society should give a proportional return on benefits received from individuals, with all alike sharing the burdens of taxation necessary to produce these benefits. The return to be expected on individuals' taxed investments is protection of their health. The scope of protection extends beyond public health measures to access to physicians and the products of research. Nevertheless, we cannot reasonably expect a direct individual return on all collective investments. Some investments are only for the purpose of discovering treatments, not for the provision of treatments once discovered. Even if the government funds drug research and regulates the drug industry, this activity does not justify the expectation that the government will subsidize or reimburse individuals' drug purchases. Accordingly, this first argument in support of a moral right to health care secures only a right to a decent return on society's investment, not a full return.

A second argument buttresses this first argument by appeal to the previously discussed fair-opportunity rule, which asserts that the justice of social institutions should be judged by their tendency to counteract lack of opportunity caused by unpredictable misfortune over which the person has no meaningful control. The need for health care is greater among the seriously diseased and injured, because the costs of health care for them can be uncontrollable and overwhelming, particularly as their health status worsens. Insofar as injuries, diseases, or disabilities create profound disadvantages and reduce agents' capacity to function properly, justice requires that we use societal health care resources to counter these effects and to give persons a fair chance to use their capacities.[55]

The Right to a Decent Minimum of Health Care

One problem about the right to health-related goods and services is how to specify the entitlements. One approach proposes a right of *equal access* to health resources. At a minimum, this goal entails that all persons have a right not to be prevented from obtaining health care, but this thin expression of a right does not entail that others must provide anything in the way of goods, services, or resources. Some libertarians favor not providing anything from public funds, but their proposal is not supported by the other general theories of justice we have examined. A more meaningful right of access to health care includes the right to obtain specified goods and services to which every entitled person has an equal claim. A demanding interpretation of this right is that everyone everywhere has equal access to all goods and services available to anyone. Unless the world's economic systems are radically revised, this conception of a right is utopian. Rights to health-related resources will likely always have severe limits (see our later discussions of "Setting Limits" and "Rationing Scarce Treatments").

The right to a decent minimum of health care therefore presents a more attractive goal—and, realistically, probably the only goal that can be achieved.[56] This moderate egalitarian goal is one of universal accessibility (at least in a political community) to fundamental health care and health-related resources.

The standard conception is a two-tiered system of health care: enforced social coverage for basic and catastrophic health needs (tier 1), together with voluntary private coverage for other health needs and desires (tier 2). At the second tier, better services, such as luxury hospital rooms and optional, cosmetic dental work, are available for purchase at personal expense through private health insurance or direct payment. The first tier meets needs by universal access to basic services. This tier presumably covers at least public health protections and preventive care, primary care, acute care, and special social services for those with disabilities. This model of a safety net for everyone acknowledges that society's obligations are not limitless.

The decent minimum, so conceived, offers a possible compromise among various theories of justice, because it incorporates some moral premises that most theories stress. It guarantees basic health care for all on a premise of equal access while allowing unequal additional purchases by individual initiative, thereby mixing private and public forms of distribution. An egalitarian should be able to see an opportunity to use an equal access principle and to embed fair opportunity in the distributional system. Utilitarians should find the proposal attractive because it serves to minimize public dissatisfaction, to maximize social utility, and to permit allocation decisions based on cost-effectiveness analysis. Similarly, supporters of a capabilities theory or a well-being theory can see the likelihood of increases in the capability of many to afford better quality care and achieve better states of health. The libertarian may dislike these outcome-oriented approaches, but should see a substantial opportunity for free-market production and distribution since one tier is left entirely up to free choice and private insurance. A health care system that finds pockets of support from each of these accounts could also turn out to be the fairest approach to democratic reform of the system.[57] We do not now have—and are not likely ever to have—a single viable theory of justice.

Although attractive theoretically, the decent-minimum proposal will be difficult to specify in social policy and to implement practically. The plan raises questions about whether society can fairly, consistently, and unambiguously devise a public policy that recognizes a right to care for primary needs without creating a right to expansive and expensive forms of treatment, such as liver transplantation, that reduce the resources that could be put to good use elsewhere. Nonetheless, in light of the current flux in national health systems, constructing such systems is the major task confronting the ethics of health policy in many, and perhaps all, countries today. We include in this domain the problem of *setting priorities* in the distribution and use of health resources, a problem handled in a later section of this chapter.

Fair public participation is indispensable in any process of setting the threshold of a decent minimum and in fixing the precise content of the package of goods and services to be offered (and to be withheld). Issues of allocating, rationing, and setting priorities, as discussed later in this chapter, must be confronted as part of the process. When substantive standards are contested regarding a decent or sufficient level of health care, fair procedures for reaching agreement may be our only recourse. Ronald Dworkin has proposed a hypothetical test of what "ideal prudent insurers" would choose.[58] He rightly criticizes an undue use of the "rescue principle," which asserts that it is intolerable for a society to allow people to die who could have been saved by spending more money on health care. He argues that this principle grows out of an "insulation model" that treats health care as different from and superior to all other goods. Instead, Dworkin envisions a "prudent insurance" ideal involving "a free and unsubsidized market." This ideal market presupposes a fair distribution of wealth and income; full information about the benefits, costs, and risks of various medical procedures; and ignorance about the likelihood that any particular person will experience morbidity, either life-threatening or non-life-threatening, from diseases and accidents. Under these circumstances, whatever aggregate amount a well-informed community decides to spend on health care is just, as is the distribution pattern it chooses. Dworkin's strategy will be difficult to implement, but it provides a good model for determination of what justice requires in the way of a decent minimum.

Forfeiting the Right to Health Care

If we assume that all citizens enjoy a right to a decent minimum of health care, can individuals forfeit that right even though they wish to retain it? The question is whether a person forfeits the right to certain forms of care through avoidable risk-assuming actions that result in personal ill health and that generate health care needs. Examples include patients who acquire AIDS as a result of unsafe sexual activities or intravenous drug use, smokers with lung cancer, workers who fail to use protective equipment in the workplace, and alcoholics who develop liver disease. In the case of insurance schemes, some regard it as unfair to ask individuals to pay higher premiums or higher taxes to support people in the scheme who voluntarily engage in risky actions.[59] This conclusion does not conflict with the rule of fair opportunity, they argue, because risk-takers' voluntary actions reduce their opportunity.

However, the question remains whether society can fairly exclude risk-takers from coverage in even the most prominent cases, such as smoking. In answering this question, society would first have to identify and differentiate the various causal factors in morbidity, such as natural causes, the social environment, and personal actions. Once these factors have been identified, solid evidence must establish that a particular disease or illness resulted from personal activities, rather than some other causal condition. Second, the personal actions in question must have been autonomous. If risks are unknown at the time of action, individuals cannot be justly held responsible for their choices.

It is virtually impossible to isolate causal factors in many cases of ill health because of complex causal links and limited knowledge. Medical needs often result from the conjunction of genetic predispositions, personal actions, effects of prior disease, and environmental and social conditions. The respective roles of these different factors are often not established, as in attempts to determine whether a particular individual's lung cancer resulted from personal cigarette smoking, passive smoking, environmental pollution, occupational conditions, or heredity (or some combination of these causal conditions). If ill health is broadly rooted in socially induced causes such as environmental pollutants and infant feeding practices, then the class of diseases covered by the right to a decent minimum will presumably expand as evidence about the causal roles of these factors increases.

Despite these problems, it would be fair in some circumstances to require individuals to pay higher premiums or taxes if they accept well-documented risks that may result in costly medical attention. Risk-takers could be required to contribute more to particular pools, such as insurance plans, or to pay a tax on their risky conduct, such as an increased tax on cigarettes.[60]

Another more difficult question is whether it is justifiable to deny individual risk-takers equal access to scarce health care that they need when these needs derive from their own actions. One issue concerns patients with alcohol-related end-stage liver failure (ESLF) who need liver transplants. Donated livers are scarce, and many patients suffering from end-stage liver failure die before they can obtain transplants. A major cause of ESLF is excessive alcohol intake that causes cirrhosis of the liver. Hence, the question arises whether patients who have alcohol-related ESLF should be excluded from waiting lists for liver transplants or should be given lower priority scores. Arguments for their lower priority or total exclusion often appeal to the probability that they will resume a pattern of alcohol abuse and again experience ESLF, thereby wasting the transplanted liver. However, studies have demonstrated that patients with alcohol-related ESLF who receive a liver transplant and abstain from alcohol do as well as patients whose ESLF resulted from other causes (although conditions such as a smoking history complicate this generalization).[61] Accordingly, a good case can be made for not excluding alcohol-related ESLF patients altogether, and instead for requiring demonstrated and extended abstention from alcohol.

Alvin Moss and Mark Siegler have proposed that patients with alcohol-related ESLF (over 50% of the patients with ESLF) automatically receive a lower priority ranking in the allocation of donated livers than patients who develop ESLF through no fault of their own.[62] They appeal to fairness, fair opportunity, and utility. They maintain that it is fair to hold people responsible for their decisions, and then to allocate organs with a view to utilitarian outcomes. They believe that the public will be less willing to donate livers if many go to persons with alcohol-related ESLF. They judge that it is "fairer to give a child dying of biliary atresia an opportunity for a first normal liver than it is to give a patient with [alcohol-related ESLF] who was born with a normal liver a second one."[63] Even if it were established that alcoholism is a chronic disease for which individuals are not responsible, Moss and Siegler contend that individuals who have this disease have the responsibility to seek and use available and effective treatments to control their alcoholism and to prevent late-stage complications, including liver failure; and their failure to do so is a morally relevant consideration.

In our assessment, all patients should be evaluated on a case-by-case basis, considering medical need and probability of successful transplantation, rather than being excluded altogether (few argue for this) or automatically receiving a lower priority.[64] An individual can then receive a lower priority rating, as warranted. There are clear examples of conditions under which personal responsibility should affect priorities and lead to a lower rating: (1) The alcoholic who fails to seek effective treatment for alcoholism and develops alcohol-related ESLF should receive a lower priority, but a diagnosis of alcohol-related ESLF is not itself categorically sufficient for a lower priority score. (2) A transplant recipient who through personal negligence does not take regular and sufficient immuno-suppressant medication, causing the transplant to fail, should be given a lower priority or be rejected for a second transplant.

GLOBAL HEALTH POLICY AND THE RIGHT TO HEALTH

Some of the theories examined early in this chapter could be presented either as global theories (principles of justice operate globally, not merely locally) or as statist theories (their principles operate locally, not globally). A statist theory holds that normative requirements of justice apply within the political state, whereas a global theory applies moral norms irrespective of political boundaries.[65] The capabilities theory and the well-being theory examined earlier are explicitly global. Communitarianism and libertarianism are statist theories. Utilitarian and many egalitarian theories could be fashioned as either global or local.

The issues here concern (1) whether the territory in which theories, principles, and rules of justice operate should be restricted to the nation-state or should be understood as applying internationally and (2) whether traditional theories of justice have failed to provide the central concepts and principles that should govern global theories of justice. Reaction to Rawls's egalitarianism has guided much of this literature, but these global theories cannot be accurately described as primarily erected on Rawls's model.

Statist Theories and Global Theories

In Rawls's theory, and until very recently, approaches to justice in health care and health policy (and in areas beyond health) have been conceived in terms of the rules and policies of nation-states, where governments have historically engaged in changes of law and policy that affect the distribution of opportunities and use of economic resources. Taxation and the use of money garnered from taxation are largely local matters of distributive justice, but some policies of states, including the expenditure of funds, are global. For example, a policy of expending state funds to eliminate malaria from the world is a global policy.

In an eighteenth-century theory of justice that deeply affected Rawls's ideas about the circumstances of justice,[66] David Hume argued that all rules of justice are inherently local, even though the reasons why rules of justice are needed in states are universal.[67] Rawls, as we have seen, argued that there are universal principles of justice, even though specific rules of justice such as those found in national health policies are not universal. The dominant conception in both Hume and Rawls is statist, not globalist.

However, the idea of a right to goods and services such as a decent minimum of health through public health measures, sanitation, supply of clean drinking water, and the like can and, many today argue, should be modeled on the global order that reaches beyond national health systems. A globalized world has brought a realization that protecting health and maintaining healthy conditions are international in nature and will require a justice-based restructuring of the global order. One model of international justice is found in a statement of the United Nations:

> [T]he right of everyone to the enjoyment of the highest attainable standard of physical and mental health is a human right.... [F]or millions of people throughout the world, the full realization of th[is] right...still remains a distant goal and..., especially for those living in poverty, this goal is becoming increasingly remote....[P]hysical and mental health is a most important worldwide social goal, the realization of which requires action by many other social and economic sectors in addition to the health sector.[68]

Ethical and political theories that explicitly address questions of global justice are sometimes referred to as "cosmopolitan theories," though "global theories" is currently the preferred term. This approach, which has deeply influenced the authors of this volume, takes as its starting point large and usually catastrophic social conditions—in particular, famine, poverty, and epidemic disease. The theory then attempts to delineate which obligations extend across national borders to address these problems. The obligations advanced are similar to those traditionally found in moral and political theory, but now globalized.

An early influence on global theories came from Peter Singer's utilitarian theory, which we discussed in Chapter 6. One reason for Singer's influence in turning philosophers' attention in a global direction was his trenchant way of pointing to the gap between the demands of fundamental *principles* of morality, such as those we treat in this book, and the *practice* of those principles at the international level. Singer succeeded in convincing many philosophers that, despite the seemingly overdemanding nature of his moral conclusions, morality requires more of us—beyond the actions and obligations of individuals, communities, and nation-states—than many had thought, especially in addressing global poverty and ill health.

Singer's theory, grounded in utilitarian beneficence, is oriented toward the obligations of agents such as persons and governments. By contrast, the perspective of egalitarian social justice—a perspective we often embrace in this chapter—proposes that we orient theory around the moral evaluation of social institutions and their responsibilities, legitimacy, and weaknesses. The focus is not on the morality of individual choices, but on the morality of the basic structure of society within which moral choices are made. The most influential global theories attempt to use a theory of justice as a model for global institutional reform—for example, reform in the structure and commitments of the World Health Organization and reform in pharmaceutical pricing.

Thomas Pogge, a prominent defender of a global theory of this sort, argues that Rawls's thesis that the principles of justice are limited to specific nation-states unduly restricts the scope of the theory of justice. A consistent moral theory that embraces universal principles will apply those principles everywhere. If the worst-off are the focal point of concern, as they are in Rawls's theory, then the situation of the truly worst-off—the global poor—should be addressed. The basic structure of society lies in the scattered norms and institutions that affect almost everyone, including those found in commerce and public policy, and here there is no clear way to, or good reason to, separate citizens from foreigners. The criterion of national citizenship, from the point of view of justice, is as morally arbitrary as race, class, or gender. Applying rules of justice exclusively within given nations also will increase disparities in wealth and well-being rather than alleviate the fundamental problems.[69]

Global theory typically begins with problems of poor health and inequalities that are the result of many interactive effects. It would be absurd for a theory of justice to look only at the distribution of health care, while ignoring the many causes of poor health and poor delivery of care. Deprivations of education cause deprivations of health, just as ill health can make it difficult to obtain a good education. Any one dimension of well-being can affect the other dimensions of well-being, and all can make for poor health. In some societies, there is a constantly compounding body of deprivations. Inequalities in these circumstances are among the most urgent for a theory of justice to address, regardless of the nation in which they occur.

Inequalities are not merely a matter of bad luck or personal failings. They are often distributed by social institutions that can be structured explicitly to reduce the inequalities. If, for example, lower level public schools distribute woeful educational outcomes, which in turn contribute to poor diet and poor health, it is within our power to alter this situation. Rawls was right to point to the pervasive effects of these institutions and their place in the theory of justice. In three theories previously discussed, Pogge, Powers-Faden, and Nussbaum all sensibly argue that inequalities in health and well-being brought about by severe poverty have a moral urgency at the global level. In addition to radical inequalities in health care, somewhere around twenty million people in the developing world die each year, including several million young children, from malnutrition and diseases that can be inexpensively prevented or treated by cheap and available means. If the reach of social justice is global, this kind of inequality from disadvantaging conditions would be at the top of the list of conditions to be remedied.

While the best strategy for attacking these problems remains unclear, we can again hold out the model of a decent minimum, but here the goal is likely to be a decent minimum standard of *health,* by contrast to *health care.* It would be a significant gain in global justice if all persons could have a fair opportunity at reasonably good health and welfare over the course of a decent life span.

ALLOCATING, SETTING PRIORITIES, AND RATIONING

Rights to health and health care encounter theoretical and practical difficulties of allocating, rationing, and setting priorities. We begin to work on these problems of justice by treating basic conceptual and structural matters, with primary attention to intrastate decisions.

Allocation

Decisions about allocation of particular goods and services often have far-reaching effects on other allocations. For example, the funds allocated for medical and biological research may affect the availability of training programs for physicians. Allocation decisions usually involve selection among desirable programs. Four distinct, but interrelated, types of allocation can be distinguished. The third and fourth are of particular importance for the discussion of rationing later in this chapter.

> **1.** *Partitioning the comprehensive social budget.* Every large political unit operates with a budget, which includes allocations for health and for other social goods, such as housing, education, culture, defense, and recreation. Health is not our only value or goal, and expenditures for other goods inevitably compete for limited resources with health-targeted expenditures. However, apart from an emergency state of affairs, if a well-off society fails to allocate sufficient funds to provide adequate public health measures and access to a decent minimum of health care, its allocation system is likely to be unjust.

2. *Allocating within the health budget.* Health allocation decisions must be made from within the budget portion devoted to health-connected budgets. We protect and promote health in many ways besides the provision of medical care. Health policies and programs for public health, disaster relief, poverty aid, occupational safety, environmental protection, injury prevention, consumer protection, and food and drug control are all parts of society's effort to protect and promote the health of its citizens and often citizens of other nations as well.

3. *Allocating within targeted budgets.* Once society has determined its budget for sectors such as public health and health care, it still must allocate its resources within each sector by selecting projects and procedures for funding. For example, determining which categories of injury, illness, or disease should receive a priority ranking in the allocation of health care resources is a major aspect of allocation. Policymakers will examine various diseases in terms of their communicability, frequency, cost, associated pain and suffering, and impact on length of life and quality of life, among other factors. It might be justified, for instance, to concentrate less on fatal diseases, such as some forms of cancer, and more on widespread disabling diseases, such as arthritis.

4. *Allocating scarce treatments for patients.* Because health needs and desires are virtually limitless, every health care system faces some form of scarcity, and not everyone who needs a particular form of health care can gain access to it. At various times and in various places, medical resources and supplies such as penicillin, insulin, kidney dialysis, cardiac transplantation, and space in intensive care units have been allocated for specific patients or classes of patients. These decisions are more difficult when an illness is life-threatening and the scarce resource potentially life-saving. The question can become, "Who shall live when not everyone can live?"

Allocation decisions of type 3 and type 4 interact. Type 3 decisions partially determine the necessity and extent of patient selection by determining the availability and supply of a particular resource. Distress in making difficult choices through explicit decisions of type 4 sometimes leads a society to modify its allocation policies at the level of type 3 to increase the supply of a particular resource. For example, because of controversies about criteria of access to a limited supply of dialysis machines,[70] the U.S. Congress passed legislation in 1972 that provided funds to ensure near-universal access to kidney dialysis and kidney transplantation for its citizens without regard for ability to pay.

Setting Priorities

Setting priorities, both in health care and in public health, is a widely discussed and urgent topic about just health policy.[71] Structuring clear priorities in type 3 allocation decisions has been difficult in many countries, and costs continue to rise dramatically as a result of several factors—in particular, insurance costs, new technologies, deteriorating health conditions, and longer life expectancy. These problems of contemporary health policy are extraordinarily complicated. The difficulty in setting priorities is how to determine what ought to be done when resources are inadequate to provide all of the health benefits that it is technically possible to provide. A now classic example of the problem in health policy comes from the state of Oregon.

Lessons from the Oregon plan. Legislators and citizens in Oregon engaged in a pioneering effort to set priorities in allocating health care in order to extend health insurance coverage to uninsured state residents below the poverty line. Oregon's Basic Health Services Act became a focal point for debates about justice and setting limits in health policy, including issues such as access to care, cost-effectiveness, rationing, and a decent minimum. This act attempted to put into practice what has typically been discussed only at the level of theory. Many believed that the Oregon plan would mark the beginning of a new era in coming to grips with problems of rationing in the United States, and in important respects it lived up to these expectations.[72]

The Oregon Health Services Commission (OHSC) was charged with producing a ranked priority list of services that would define a decent minimum of coverage by Medicaid, which is the state and federal program that provides funds to cover medical needs for financially impoverished citizens. The goal was to expand coverage to those below the poverty level and to fund as many top priority–ranked services as possible. In 1990, the OHSC listed 1,600 ranked medical procedures ranging "from the most important to the least important" services, based in part on data about quality of well-being after treatment and cost-effectiveness analysis. The ranking was widely criticized as unjust and arbitrary. Critics pointed to the state's ranking of tooth-capping above appendectomies as a particularly egregious example. Later Oregon reduced the list to 709 ranked services, while abandoning cost-effectiveness analysis and broadening citizen participation. The goal became to rank items on the prioritized list by clinical effectiveness and social value. These spare categories need specificity, and much ingenuity went into these efforts in Oregon.

Within the state, there was initially a strong endorsement of the list of covered services, because it succeeded in expanding access. However, many procedures, such as incapacitating hernias, tonsillectomy, and adenoidectomy, fell below the cutoff line of the priority list.[73] Oregon has had to modify the plan in numerous ways over the years, with the consequence of high rates of coverage loss and disenrollment from the plan, difficulty in meeting the needs of the chronically ill, increased unmet health needs, reduced access to health care services, and financial strain.[74] Oregon's priority list has also had trouble managing recurring budget shortfalls.

Just strategies for setting priorities.[75] Even before the Oregon experiment, an influential literature on setting priorities had emerged from health economics, as briefly discussed in Chapter 6. This literature urged use of cost-effectiveness analysis (CEA), the most important version being cost–utility analysis (CUA). In this strategy health benefits are measured in terms of anticipated health gains, and costs are measured in terms of expenditures of resources. The goal is basically utilitarian: the greatest health benefits for the money expended. Health benefits are quantified, and an attempt is made to incorporate the outcome directly into public policy by measuring the impact of interventions on both the length and quality of life.

Representatives of almost all types of theory of justice other than utilitarians have raised objections to this strategy for setting limits. Charges of discrimination against infants, the elderly, and the disabled (especially those with permanent incapacitation and the terminally ill), as well as uncertainties about how to judge gains in quality of life, have led many to conclude that appeals to the forms of cost analysis used allow unjust and impermissible trade-offs in setting priorities. One problem is whether lifesaving interventions such as heart transplantation should lose out altogether in the competition for priority if other interventions such as arthritis medication provide a greater improvement in quality of life.

To address such questions, numerous decisions must be made, including whether priority should go to prevention or treatment and whether lifesaving procedures take priority over other interventions. Policymakers commonly labor to set priorities in the absence of any precise or powerful decision-making instrument and in the absence of significant systems of accountability.[76] Expenditures for treatment, rather than prevention, are far higher in the current health care systems of most industrialized nations, and government officials might justifiably choose, for example, to concentrate on preventing heart disease rather than on providing individuals with heart transplants or artificial hearts. In many cases preventive care is more effective and more efficient in saving lives, reducing suffering, raising levels of health, and lowering costs. Preventive care typically reduces morbidity and premature mortality for unknown "statistical lives," whereas critical interventions concentrate on known "identifiable lives." Many societies have favored identified persons and have allocated resources for critical care, but good evidence shows that public health expenditures targeted at poorer communities for preventive measures, such as prenatal care, save many times that amount in future care. Accordingly, our moral intuitions and institutional commitments may distort our thinking about the moral dilemma of whether to allocate more to rescue persons in medical need or to allocate more to prevent persons from falling into such need.

Although no consensus is found either in health policy or in biomedical ethics, many are now open to the use of various utility-driven strategies to generate data that the public and policymakers can weigh, together with other considerations. Public preferences, sound arguments for various policy options, and knowledge of the literature of ethics and health policy could help replace or constrain morally objectionable trade-offs indicated by economic analysis.[77] Perhaps the major problem, as we indicated in Chapter 6, is how to establish constraints that are strongly recommended by justice. For example, it seems unfair and unacceptable to allow forms of cost-effective rationing that adversely affect or ignore levels of health among the most disadvantaged populations, in effect worsening their condition. This generalization may seem obvious, but it has proved and will continue to prove extremely difficult to implement at both the national level and, especially, the global level.

Procedural strategies for setting priorities. One tempting strategy is to either abandon recourse to theories of justice altogether or unite them with use of democratic deliberation among fair-minded persons who seek to cooperatively reach decisions about priorities. So-called pure procedural justice and fair deliberative mechanisms capable of supporting democratic procedures anchor this approach, together with back-up processes of review and appeal. A central feature is the inclusion of a representative body of fair-minded persons capable of enhancing accountability for reasonableness in priority setting, thereby contributing to the "goal of having all relevant reasons considered" (an idea connected to the method of reflective equilibrium that we accept in Chapter 10).[78]

One option is to use direct appeals to the public's preferences when questions of trade-offs arise. The answers given by the public are often remarkably different from those found in economic analyses, because the public weighs factors such as severe incapacity and lifesaving technologies more heavily.[79] However, this approach confronts problems. It is unclear how to solicit and aggregate the preferences of members of the public—and also unclear when, if ever, preferences alone should count heavily in the public policy process. There are problems of how to frame a question fairly, so that the question does not itself determine the outcome, and problems of how to assess the validity of preferences. Attempts to eliminate unduly biased preferences will likely invoke some appeal to justice that itself merits careful scrutiny for adequacy.

Majority preferences, no matter how well-informed and fair, will sometimes eventuate in unjust outcomes. The literature remains relatively unclear about how to protect against such unfair outcomes, whether citizen deliberators could ever satisfy the demands of true deliberative democracy, and how much real agreement they could reach. The upshot is that at present we lack a reliable, practicable strategy for setting priorities and limits by this method. Although some in biomedical ethics are ready to forsake the major theories of justice previously discussed, these theories continue to have staying power. What seems unlikely is that one of these theories will oust the others in the bid to capture our sense of justice in the distribution of health care.

Several target goals, consistent with justice and national health policies, can be identified. The first objective is unobstructed access to a decent minimum of health care through some form of universal insurance coverage that operationalizes the right to health care. The second objective is to develop acceptable incentives for physicians and consumer-patients. Unless cost consciousness and cost controls are introduced and maintained, expenditures will spiral out of control, and the necessity for rationing at the first tier will then threaten the goal of providing a decent minimum. The third objective is to construct a fair system of rationing that does not violate the decent minimum standard. Although rationing is sometimes required at the first tier—for example, when a new vaccine or drug is in scarce supply or when a public health emergency strikes—heavy rationing at the first tier would sabotage the moral foundations of the enterprise. Finally, the fourth objective is to implement a system that can be put into effect incrementally, without drastic disruption of basic institutions that finance and deliver health care.

Several carefully reasoned proposals attempt to meet these objectives at least partially. Despite many differences, these proposals fall into two families: unified systems and pluralist systems. Unified plans look primarily to egalitarian justice, with utility a second-level consideration, whereas pluralist plans look primarily to utility (efficiency and broad coverage) and freedom of choice for consumers, patients, and providers, with egalitarian justice a second-level consideration. Although we cannot consider the details of any one plan or develop an ideal plan, we have argued in this chapter in favor of a unitary system at the first tier of health care and a pluralist system at the second tier, thus allowing, and strongly endorsing, a two-tier system.

Rationing

We now further address the types of allocation decision categorized on pp. 279–80 as types 3 and 4. Both are often discussed under the topic of *rationing* and related terms, such as *triage*.[80] The choice of terms makes a difference, because each term has a different history in which changes in meaning have occurred.[81] *Rationing* originally did not suggest harshness or an emergency. It meant a form of allowance, share, or portion, as when food is divided into rations in the military. Only recently has *rationing* been linked to limited resources and the setting of priorities in health care budgets.

Rationing has at least three relevant meanings or types. The first is related to "denial from lack of resources." In a market economy, all types of goods— including health care—are to some extent rationed by ability to pay. A second sense of *rationing* derives not from market limits but from social policy limits: The government determines an allowance or allotment, and individuals are denied access beyond the allotted amount. Rationing gasoline and types of food during a war is a well-known example, but national health systems that do not allow purchases of goods or insurance beyond an allotted amount provide equally good examples. Finally, in a third sense of *rationing,* an allowance or allotment is distributed equitably, but those who can afford additional goods are not denied access beyond the allotted amount. In this third form, rationing involves elements of each of the first two forms: Public policy fixes an allowance, and those who cannot afford or arrange for additional units are thereby effectively denied access beyond the allowance. We will occasionally use "rationing" in each of the three senses, while concentrating on the third.

The term *rationing* sometimes carries a negative connotation, especially in public political debates where it is often used to condemn putatively unwarranted activities of denying health care. However, public policies of health protection and health care delivery necessarily involve some form and level of rationing. Prioritizing health care resources is itself an exercise in rationing.

We turn next to two case studies in problems of rationing. The first focuses on rationing by age and the second on rationing highly expensive treatments, using the example of heart transplantation.

Rationing by age. Policies sometimes exclude or give a lower priority to persons in a particular age group and also sometimes provide advantages to a group such as the elderly, as in Medicare entitlements in the United States. In the United Kingdom implicit rationing policies have excluded elderly, end-stage kidney patients from kidney dialysis and transplantation because of their age or expected quality of life.[82] In another example, policies for allocating transplantable kidneys sometimes give priority to young patients by assigning them additional points in a point system.

Various arguments have been proposed to justify the use of age in allocation policies. Some rest on judgments about the probability of successful treatment; these arguments are usually a matter of medical utility. For instance, age may be an indicator of the probability of surviving a major operation and also a factor in the likely success of the procedure. Judgments of the probability of success also may include the length of time that the recipient of an organ is expected to survive, a period that is usually shorter for an older patient than for a younger patient. If one criterion is quality-adjusted life-years (QALYs, as discussed in Chapter 6), younger patients will typically fare better than older patients in the allocation. An example is found in a proposal by the United Network for Organ Sharing that focuses on predicted life years from transplantation as a criterion for allocating organs to patients. Critics charge that using this assessment would unfairly disadvantage older patients by reducing their opportunities for kidneys.[83]

Norman Daniels has offered an influential argument for viewing age as different from properties of race and gender for purposes of fair health care allocation.[84] He appeals to prudential individual decisions about health care from the perspective of an entire lifetime. Each age group can be conceived as representing a stage in a person's life span. The goal is to allocate resources prudently throughout all of the stages of life within a social system that provides a fair lifetime share of health care for each citizen. As prudent deliberators, he argues, impartial persons would choose under conditions of scarcity to distribute health care over a lifetime in a way that improves their chance of attaining at least a normal life span. We would reject a pattern that reduced our chances of reaching a normal life span but that increased our chances of living beyond a normal life span if we did become elderly. Daniels maintains that an impartial person would choose to shift resources that might otherwise be consumed in prolonging the lives of the elderly to the treatment of younger persons. This policy increases each person's chance of living at least a normal life span.

Another and related theory uses a "fair-innings" argument. It considers a person's whole lifetime experience and seeks equality. Alan Williams, a fair-innings proponent, stresses that this conception of intergenerational equity would *require,* not merely *permit,* "greater discrimination against the elderly than would be dictated simply by efficiency objectives."[85]

All calls for age-based rationing face challenges.[86] Such rationing runs the risk of perpetuating injustice by stereotyping the elderly, treating them as scapegoats because of increased health care costs, and creating unnecessary conflicts between generations. Elderly persons in each generation will complain that, when they were younger, they did not have access to new technologies that were later developed, using their taxes for funding; and they will claim that it would be unfair to deny them beneficial technologies now. Nonetheless, to protect the health of children and many vulnerable parties, we are certain to find that we have to set a threshold age beyond which funding for various conditions is not publicly available. This choice may be perceived as tragic, yet it may be an entirely just and justifiable policy. Indeed, it may be unjust to adopt any other policy.

Still, even if age-based allocations of health care do not violate the fair-opportunity rule, they have often been unjust in the way they have been implemented in many countries. These allocations are a prime example of a need for society to take a systematic, publicly announced, and closely scrutinized approach to decisions about equitable access.

Rationing heart transplantation. Controversies about rationing heart transplantation began shortly after cardiac transplantation became effective in the 1980s. The number of heart transplants performed is small, but the cost is large. The current U.S. average billed charge per transplant is $1,000,000, and $1,150,000 for heart-lung transplants.[87] Changing medical and political circumstances over the years have led to alterations of policy that close one gap in equity only to open other equity issues. The process that led to the Oregon

Health Act in part arose from concern about the soaring expense of organ transplants.

Despite the high cost of coverage for heart transplants, arguments have been offered for publicly funding them. As an example, the federal Task Force on Organ Transplantation, appointed by the U.S. Department of Health and Human Services, recommended that "a public program should be set up to cover the costs of people who are medically eligible for organ transplants but who are not covered by private insurance, Medicare, or Medicaid and who are unable to obtain an organ transplant due to the lack of funds."[88] The task force grounded its recommendation on two arguments from justice.

The first argument emphasizes the continuity between heart and liver transplants and other forms of medical care, including kidney transplants, that are already accepted as part of the decent minimum of health care that should be provided in a country as well off as the United States: Heart and liver transplants are comparable to other funded or fundable procedures in terms of their effectiveness in saving lives and enhancing the quality of life. In response to the claim that heart and liver transplants are too expensive, the task force argued that any burdens created by saving public funds for health should be distributed equitably rather than imposed on particular groups of patients, such as those suffering from end-stage heart or liver failure. It would be arbitrary to exclude one lifesaving procedure while funding others of comparable lifesaving potential and cost.

The second argument for equitable access focuses on practices of organ donation and procurement. Various public officials, including heads of state, participate in efforts to increase the supply of donated organs by appealing to all citizens to donate organs. It would be unfair and perhaps exploitative to solicit people, rich and poor alike, to donate organs if the organs are then distributed on the basis of ability to pay.[89] Furthermore, it is morally inconsistent to prohibit the sale of organs while distributing donated organs according to ability to pay. It is morally problematic to distinguish buying an organ for transplantation from buying an organ transplant procedure when a donated organ is used in the procedure.

These arguments are attractive appeals to coherence, but they do not establish that justice requires expensive health care irrespective of its cost or that it is arbitrary to use a reasonably structured system of rationing that involves tough choices in setting priorities. Once a society has achieved a fair threshold determination of funding at the decent-minimum level, it legitimately may select some procedures while excluding others when they are of equal lifesaving potential and of equal cost, as long as it identifies relevant differences through a fair procedure. Substantial public participation along the way helps legitimate these determinations.

Heart transplantation is certain to be rationed by one system or another. In this section we focused entirely on limited funds, without consideration of the severely limited supply of hearts available for transplantation. In the end, we should situate recommendations about funding heart transplants and all other expensive treatments in the larger context of a just social policy of procurement and allocation, which will require that we systematically and fairly set priorities and limits.

Rationing Scarce Treatments to Patients

Health care professionals and policymakers often must decide who will receive an available scarce medical resource that cannot be provided to all needy people. We concentrate here on priority schemes for selecting recipients in urgent circumstances. Two broad approaches vie for primacy: (1) a utilitarian strategy that emphasizes maximal benefit to patients and society, and (2) an egalitarian strategy that emphasizes the equal worth of persons and fair opportunity. We argue that these two broad approaches can justifiably and coherently be combined in policies and practices of distribution.

We defend a system that uses two stages of substantive standards and procedural rules for rationing scarce medical resources: (1) criteria and procedures to determine a qualifying pool of potential recipients, such as patients eligible for heart transplantation; and (2) criteria and procedures for final selection of recipients, such as the patient to receive a particular heart.

The constituency factor. Criteria for screening potential recipients of care fall into three basic categories: constituency, progress of science, and prospect of success.[90] The first criterion uses social rather than medical factors. It is determined by clientele boundaries, such as veterans served by medical centers established for veterans; geographic or jurisdictional boundaries, such as being citizens of a legal jurisdiction served by a publicly funded hospital; and ability to pay, such as the wealthy and the highly insured. These criteria are entirely nonmedical, and they involve moral judgments that often are not impartial, such as excluding noncitizens or including only veterans. These clientele boundaries are sometimes acceptable, but often have been dubious.

For example, the Task Force on Organ Transplantation in the United States proposed that donated organs be considered national, public resources to be distributed primarily according to both the needs of patients and the probability of successful transplantation.[91] However, the task force judged that foreign nationals do not have the same moral claim on organs donated in the United States as its own citizens and residents do. The judgment apparently is that citizenship and residency are morally relevant properties for distribution, but the task force also determined that compassion and fairness support the admission of some nonresident aliens. In a split vote, it recommended that nonresident aliens comprise no more than 10% of the waiting list for cadaver kidneys donated for transplantation and that all patients on the waiting list, including nonresident aliens, have access to organs according to the same criteria of need, probability of success, and time on the waiting list.[92]

Progress of science. The second criterion of scientific progress is research-oriented and is relevant during an experimental phase in the development of a treatment. For example, physician-investigators may justifiably exclude patients who suffer from other diseases that might obscure the research result. The objective is to determine whether an experimental treatment is effective and how it can be improved. This criterion rests on moral and prudential judgments about the efficient and proper use of resources. The factors used to include or to exclude patients for participation in such research can be controversial, especially if persons who potentially could benefit are excluded for reasons of scientific efficiency or persons who are unlikely to benefit are continued in a clinical trial to make trial results acceptable to the scientific community.

Prospect of success. Whether a treatment is experimental or routine, the likelihood of success in treating the patient is a relevant criterion because scarce medical resources should be distributed only to patients who have a reasonable chance of benefit. Ignoring this factor is unjust if it wastes resources, as in the case of organs that can be transplanted only once. Heart transplant surgeons sometimes list their patients as urgent priority candidates for an available heart because the patients will soon die if they do not receive a transplant, but some of these patients are virtually certain to die even if they do receive the heart. Good candidates may be passed over in the process. A classification and queuing system that permits the urgency of a situation alone to determine priority is as unjust as it is inefficient.

Medical utility. We turn now to standards proposed for *final selection* of patients. Controversy centers on standards of medical utility and social utility and on impersonal mechanisms such as lotteries and queuing.

We assume the generally accepted rule that judgments about medical utility should figure into decisions to ration scarce medical resources. Differences in patients' prospects for successful treatment are relevant considerations, as is maximizing the number of lives saved. However, both need and prospect of success are value-laden concepts, and uncertainty often exists about likely outcomes and about the factors that contribute to success. For example, kidney transplant surgeons dispute the importance of having a good tissue match, because minor tissue mismatches can be managed by immunosuppressant medications that reduce the body's tendency to reject transplanted organs. Insisting on the seemingly objective criterion of tissue match in distributing kidneys also can disadvantage persons with a rare tissue type and racial minorities, as we saw earlier in this chapter.

The criteria of medical need and prospect of success sometimes come into conflict. In intensive care units trying to save a patient whose need is medically urgent sometimes inappropriately consumes resources that could be used to save other people who will die without those resources.[93] A rule of giving priority to the sickest patients or those with the most urgent medical needs will produce unfairness, because it will lead in some cases to inefficient uses of resources. Rationing schemes that altogether exclude considerations of medical utility are indefensible, but judgments of medical utility are not always sufficient by themselves. This problem leads to the subject of chance and queuing.

Impersonal mechanisms of chance and queuing. We began this chapter by noting the oddity and unacceptability of using a lottery to distribute all social positions. However, a lottery or another system of chance is not always odd and unacceptable.[94] Although, as Peter Stone notes, lotteries "prevent decisions from being made on the basis of reasons,"[95] they or other methods of random selection are justifiable in some circumstances. Consider the following scenario: If medical resources are scarce and not divisible into portions, and if no major disparities exist in medical utility for patients (particularly when selection determines life or death), then considerations of fair opportunity and equal respect may justify a lottery, randomization, or queuing—depending on which procedure is the most appropriate and feasible in the circumstances.

Similar judgments have supported the use of lotteries to determine who would gain access to new drugs available only in limited supply, either because they had only recently been approved or because they remained experimental. For instance, Berlex Laboratories held a lottery to distribute Betaseron, a new genetically engineered drug that appeared to slow the deterioration caused by multiple sclerosis, and several drug companies held lotteries to distribute a new class of compounds to patients with AIDS. The symbolic value of the lotteries also can be morally significant: Lotteries send the message that all persons deserve an equal chance at social goods.[96] These methods also make the selection with little investment of time and financial resources and can create less stress for all involved, including patients.[97] Even bypassed candidates may feel less distress at being rejected by chance than by judgments of comparative merit.

However, some impersonal selection procedures present both theoretical and practical problems. For example, the rule "first come, first served" carries the potential for injustice. Under some conditions a patient already receiving a particular treatment has a severely limited chance of survival, virtually to the point of futility, whereas other patients who need the treatment have a far better chance of survival. Does "first come, first served" imply that those already receiving treatment have absolute priority over those who arrive later but have either more urgent needs or better prospects of success? Intensive care units (ICUs) again provide a good example. Although admission to the ICU establishes a presumption in favor of continued treatment, it does not give a person an absolute claim. In decisions in neonatal intensive care about the use of extracorporeal membrane oxygenation (ECMO), a form of cardiopulmonary bypass used to support newborns with life-threatening respiratory failure, a truly scarce resource is being provided, because it is not widely available and requires the full-time presence of well-trained personnel. Robert Truog argues, rightly in our judgment, that ECMO should be withdrawn from a newborn with a poor prognosis in favor of another with a good prognosis if the latter is far more likely to survive, requires the therapy, and cannot be safely transferred to another facility.[98] Such displacement of a child from the ICU requires justification, but it need not constitute abandonment or injustice if other forms of care are provided.

Whether queuing or chance is preferable will depend largely on practical considerations, but queuing appears to be feasible and acceptable in many health care settings, including emergency medicine, ICUs, and organ transplant lists. A complicating factor is that some people do not enter the queue or a lottery in time because of factors such as slowness in seeking help, inadequate or incompetent medical attention, delay in referral, or overt discrimination. A system is unfair if some people gain an advantage in access over others because they are better educated, are better connected, or have more money for frequent visits to physicians.

Social utility. Although criteria of social utility are controversial, the comparative social value of potential recipients is, under some conditions, a relevant and even decisive consideration. An often-used analogy comes from World War II, when, according to some reports, the scarce resource of penicillin was distributed to U.S. soldiers suffering from venereal disease rather than to those suffering from battle wounds. The rationale was military need: The soldiers suffering from venereal disease could be restored to battle more quickly.[99]

An argument in favor of social-utilitarian selection is that medical institutions and personnel are trustees of society and must consider the probable future contributions of patients. We argue later that, in rare and exceptional cases involving persons of critical social importance, criteria of social value—narrow and specific as opposed to broad and general social utility—are appropriately overriding. However, in general we need to protect the relationship of personal care and trust between patients and physicians, and it would be threatened if physicians were trained to look beyond their patients' needs to society's needs.

Triage: Medical utility and narrow social utility. Some have invoked the model of *triage*, a French term meaning "sorting," "picking," or "choosing." It has been applied to sorting items such as wool and coffee beans according to their quality. In the delivery of health care, triage is a process of developing and using criteria for prioritization. It has been used in war, in community disasters, and in emergency rooms where injured persons have been sorted for medical attention according to their needs and prospects. Decisions to admit and to discharge patients from ICUs often involve triage. The objective is to use available medical resources as effectively and as efficiently as possible, here a utilitarian rationale.[100]

Triage decisions usually appeal to *medical* utility rather than *social* utility. For example, disaster victims are generally sorted according to medical need. Those who have major injuries and will die without immediate help, but who can be salvaged, are ranked first; those whose treatment can be delayed without immediate danger are ranked second; those with minor injuries are ranked third; and those for whom no treatment will be efficacious are ranked fourth. This priority scheme is fair and does not involve judgments about individuals' comparative social worth.

However, narrow or specific judgments of comparative social worth are inescapable and acceptable in some situations.[101] For example, in an earthquake disaster in which some injured survivors are medical personnel who suffer only minor injuries, they can justifiably receive priority for treatments if they are needed to help others. Similarly, in an outbreak of pandemic influenza, it is justifiable to inoculate physicians and nurses first to enable them to care for others. Under such conditions, a person may receive priority for treatment on grounds of narrow social utility if and only if his or her contribution is indispensable to attaining a major social goal. As in analogous lifeboat cases, we should limit judgments of comparative social value to the specific qualities and skills that are essential to the community's immediate protection, without assessing the general social worth of persons.

It is legitimate to invoke medical utility followed by the use of chance or queuing for scarce resources when medical utility is roughly equal for eligible patients. It is also legitimate to invoke narrow considerations of social utility to give priority to individuals who fill social roles that are essential in achieving a better overall outcome. This nexus of standards should prove to be both coherent and stable, despite the mixture of appeals to egalitarian justice and utility.[102]

In certain contexts, such as allocation in a public health emergency resulting from pandemic influenza or a bioterrorist attack, and in the allocation of organs donated by the public, it is valuable, perhaps indispensable, to engage the public in setting the allocation criteria. No set of criteria is the only acceptable set, and public trust and cooperation are crucial in addressing public health crises and in securing organ donations from the public.

CONCLUSION

We have examined an array of approaches to justice, including six different theories of justice. Although we have most closely examined egalitarian and utilitarian approaches, we have maintained that no single theory of justice or system of distributing health care is sufficient for constructive reflection on health policy. Our discussions in Chapters 1, 9, and 10 expose several limitations in the use of general ethical theories, and these limitations carry over to general theories of justice as well.

The richness of our moral practices and beliefs helps explain why diverse theories of justice have received skillful defenses. Absent a social consensus about these theories of justice, we can expect that public policies will sometimes emphasize elements of one theory and at other times elements of another theory. We have done so ourselves in this chapter. However, the existence of these several theories does not justify the piecemeal approach that many countries have taken to their health care systems.

Countries lacking a comprehensive and coherent system of health care financing and delivery are destined to continue on the trail of higher costs and larger numbers of unprotected citizens. They need to improve both utility (efficiency) and justice (fairness and equality). Although justice and utility at first sight appear to be opposing values, and have often been presented as such in moral theory, both approaches are indispensable in shaping a health care system. Creating a more efficient system by cutting costs and providing appropriate incentives can conflict with the goal of universal access to health care, and justice-based goals of universal coverage also may make the system inefficient. Inevitably, trade-offs between equality and efficiency will occur.

Policies of just access to health care, strategies of efficiency in health care institutions, and global needs for the reduction of health-impairing conditions dwarf in social importance every other issue considered in this book. Global justice and just national health care systems are distant goals for millions who encounter the entrenched barriers to achieving these goals. Although every society must ration its resources, many societies can close gaps in fair rationing more conscientiously than they have to date. We have suggested a perspective from which to approach these problems. In particular, we have proposed recognition of global rights to health and enforceable rights to a decent minimum of health care within a framework for allocation that incorporates both utilitarian and egalitarian standards. This perspective recognizes the legitimacy of trade-offs between efficiency and justice, a position that mirrors our insistence throughout this book on the possibility of contingent conflicts between beneficence and justice and the need for trade-offs between them.

NOTES

1.   Jorge Luis Borges, *Labyrinths* (New York: New Directions, 1962), pp. 30–35. A lottery may, however, be a justifiable mechanism in a just system of distribution, as we propose later in this chapter.

2.   Compare the analysis in Samuel Fleishacker, *A Short History of Distributive Justice* (Cambridge, MA: Harvard University Press, 2005).

3.   See Carol Levine, "Changing Views of Justice after Belmont: AIDS and the Inclusion of 'Vulnerable' Subjects," in *The Ethics of Research Involving Human Subjects: Facing the 21st Century,*

ed. Harold Y. Vanderpool (Frederick, MD: University Publishing Group, 1996); and Leslie Meltzer and James F. Childress, "What Is Fair Subject Selection?" in *The Oxford Textbook of Clinical Research Ethics,* ed. Ezekiel J. Emanuel et al. (New York: Oxford University Press, 2008), pp. 377–85.

4.   See further Guido Calabresi and Philip Bobbitt, *Tragic Choices* (New York: Norton, 1978).

5.   *International Union… UAW v. Johnson Controls,* 499 U.S. 187 (1991), 111 S.Ct. 1196.

6.   John Stuart Mill, *Utilitarianism,* in vol. 10 of the *Collected Works of John Stuart Mill* (Toronto: University of Toronto Press, 1969), chap. 5.

7.   Locke, *Two Treatises of Government,* ed. Peter Laslett (Cambridge: Cambridge University Press, 1960), preface, bk. 1.6.67, bk. 2.7.87. On classical libertarianism generally, see Eric Mack and Gerald F. Gaus, "Classical Liberalism and Libertarianism: The Liberty Tradition," in *Handbook of Political Theory,* ed. Gaus and Chandran Kukathas (London: Sage Publications, 2004), pp. 115–30.

8.   Robert Nozick, *Anarchy, State, and Utopia* (New York: Basic Books, 1974), esp. pp. 149–82.

9.   Rawls, "Kantian Constructivism in Moral Theory" (The Dewey Lectures), *Journal of Philosophy* 77 (1980): 519.

10.   Rawls, *A Theory of Justice* (Cambridge, MA: Harvard University Press, 1971; rev. ed., 1999), pp. 60–67, 302–3 (1999: 52–58). Rawls later instructively restated, and partially reordered, these principles, giving reasons for their revision, in *Justice as Fairness: A Restatement,* ed. Erin Kelly (Cambridge, MA: Harvard University Press, 2001), pp. 42–43. This work has influenced the presentations made here.

11.   Daniels, *Just Health Care* (New York: Cambridge University Press, 1985), pp. 34–58; and *Just Health: Meeting Health Needs Fairly* (New York: Cambridge University Press, 2007).

12.   See, for example, Michael Sandel, *Democracy's Discontent: America in Search of a Public Philosophy* (Cambridge, MA: Harvard University Press, 1996); Sandel, *Public Philosophy: Essays on Morality in Politics* (Cambridge, MA: Harvard University Press, 2005); Alasdair MacIntyre, *After Virtue,* 3rd ed. (Notre Dame, IN: University of Notre Dame Press, 2007); and Michael Walzer, "The Communitarian Critique of Liberalism," *Political Theory* 18 (1990): 6–23.

13.   Charles Taylor, "Atomism," in *Powers, Possessions, and Freedom,* ed. Alkis Kontos (Toronto: University of Toronto Press, 1979): 39–62.

14.   Two instructive theories are Alasdair MacIntyre, *Whose Justice? Which Rationality?* (Notre Dame, IN: University of Notre Dame Press, 1988), esp. pp. 1, 390–403; and Michael Walzer, *Spheres of Justice: A Defense of Pluralism and Equality* (New York: Basic Books, 1983), esp. pp. 86–94. As representative of bioethics, see Daniel Callahan, "Individual Good and Common Good: A Communitarian Approach to Bioethics," *Perspectives in Biology and Medicine* 46 (2003): 496–507, esp. 500ff; and Callahan, "Principlism and Communitarianism," *Journal of Medical Ethics* 29 (2003): 287–91.

15.   See James L. Nelson, "The Rights and Responsibilities of Potential Organ Donors: A Communitarian Approach," *Communitarian Position Paper* (Washington, DC: The Communitarian Network, 1992); and James Muyskens, "Procurement and Allocation Policies," *Mount Sinai Journal of Medicine* 56 (1989): 202–6.

16.   Callahan, *What Kind of Life* (New York: Simon & Schuster, 1990), ch. 4, esp. pp. 105–13; and *Setting Limits* (New York: Simon & Schuster, 1987), esp. pp. 106–14. See also the wide-ranging "liberal communitarianism" in Ezekiel Emanuel, *The Ends of Human Life: Medical Ethics in a Liberal Polity* (Cambridge, MA: Harvard University Press, 1991).

17.   See Amartya K. Sen, "Capability and Well-Being," in *The Quality of Life,* ed. Martha C. Nussbaum and Amartya K. Sen (Oxford: Clarendon Press, 1993), pp. 30–53; "Human Rights and

Capabilities," *Journal of Human Development,* 6 (2005): 151–66; and *The Idea of Justice* (London: Allen Lane, 2009). For a recent capabilities approach, see Jennifer Prah Ruger, *Health and Social Justice* (New York: Oxford University Press, 2010).

18. Nussbaum, *Frontiers of Justice: Disability, Nationality, Species Membership* (Cambridge, MA: Harvard University Press, 2006), esp. pp. 81–95, 155–223, 281–90, 346–52, 366–79.

19. Martha Nussbaum, "Human Dignity and Political Entitlements," in President's Council on Bioethics, *Human Dignity and Bioethics: Essays Commissioned by the President's Council on Bioethics* (Washington, DC: President's Council, March 2008), p. 351, available at http://www.bioethics.gov.

20. Nussbaum, *Frontiers of Justice,* pp. 76–81, 392–401 (an extended version); and "Human Dignity and Political Entitlements," pp. 377–78 (a later, streamlined version).

21. Nussbaum, *Frontiers of Justice,* p. 175.

22. Nussbaum, "Human Dignity and Political Entitlements," pp. 357–59, 363.

23. Nussbaum, "The Capabilities Approach and Animal Entitlements," in *Oxford Handbook of Animal Ethics,* ed. Tom L. Beauchamp and R. G. Frey (New York: Oxford University Press, 2011), pp. 237–38. See also her earlier statement in *Frontiers of Justice,* chap. 6.

24. Nussbaum, *Frontiers of Justice,* pp. 2, 155, 166.

25. Powers and Faden, *Social Justice: The Moral Foundations of Public Health and Health Policy* (New York: Oxford University Press, 2006), pp. 16, 37.

26. Powers and Faden, *Social Justice,* esp. pp. 64–79.

27. Rawls, *A Theory of Justice,* pp. 73–75 (1999: 63–65) (italics added).

28. See Bernard Williams, "The Idea of Equality," in *Justice and Equality,* ed. Hugo Bedau (Englewood Cliffs, NJ: Prentice Hall, 1971), p. 135; Jeff McMahan, "Cognitive Disability, Misfortune, and Justice," *Philosophy and Public Affairs* 25 (1996): 3–35; and Janet Radcliffe Richards, "Equality of Opportunity," *Ratio* 10 (1997): 253–79.

29. H. Tristram Engelhardt, Jr., *The Foundations of Bioethics,* 2nd ed. (New York: Oxford University Press, 1996), chap. 8; and Gert Jan van der Wilt, "Health Care and the Principle of Fair Equality of Opportunity," *Bioethics* 8 (1994): 329–49.

30. See, for the United States, Brian D. Smedley, Adrienne Y. Stith, and Alan R. Nelson, eds., for the Committee on Understanding and Eliminating Racial and Ethnic Disparities in Health Care, Institute of Medicine, *Unequal Treatment: Confronting Racial and Ethnic Disparities in Health Care* (Washington, DC: National Academies Press, 2003).

31. Ivor L. Livingston, ed., *Praeger Handbook of Black American Health: Policies and Issues behind Disparities in Health* (Westport, CT: Praeger, 2004), 2 vols.; Kathryn S. Ratcliff, *Women and Health: Power, Technology, Inequality, and Conflict in a Gendered World* (Boston: Allyn & Bacon, 2002); and Nicole Lurie, "Health Disparities—Less Talk, More Action," *New England Journal of Medicine* 353 (August 18, 2005): 727–28.

32. See Edward L. Hannan et al., "Access to Coronary Artery Bypass Surgery by Race/Ethnicity and Gender among Patients Who Are Appropriate for Surgery," *Medical Care* 37 (1999): 68–77; and Ashish K. Jha et al., "Racial Trends in the Use of Major Procedures among the Elderly," *New England Journal of Medicine* 353 (August 18, 2005): 683–91.

33. Viola Vaccarino et al., "Sex and Racial Differences in the Management of Acute Myocardial Infarction, 1994 through 2002," *New England Journal of Medicine* 353 (August 18, 2005): 671–82;

Karen M. Freund et al., "Disparities by Race, Ethnicity, and Sex in Treating Acute Coronary Syndromes," *Journal of Women's Health* 21 (2012): 126–32.

34. "Cancer Screening—United States, 2010," *Morbidity and Mortality Weekly Report* 61 (January 27, 2012): 41–45.

35. See A. O. Laiyemo et al., "Race and Colorectal Cancer Disparities," *Journal of the National Cancer Institute* 102 (April 21, 2010): 538–46; John Z. Ayanian, "Racial Disparities in Outcomes of Colorectal Cancer Screening: Biology or Barriers to Optimal Care," *Journal of the National Cancer Institute* 102 (April 21, 2010): 511–13; and Amal N. Trivedi et al., "Trends in the Quality of Care and Racial Disparities in Medicare Managed Care," *New England Journal of Medicine* 353 (August 18, 2005): 692–700.

36. Salimah H. Meghani et al., "Advancing a National Agenda to Eliminate Disparities in Pain Care: Directions for Health Policy, Education, Practice, and Research," *Pain Medicine* 13 (January 2012): 5–28.

37. Nathan L. Cook, "Racial and Gender Disparities in Implantable Cardioverter-Defibrillator Placement: Are They Due to Overuse or Underuse?" *Medical Care Research and Review* 68 (April 2011): 226–46.

38. Smedley, Stith, and Nelson, eds., *Unequal Treatment.* For critical analyses of this report, see the special issue of *Perspectives in Biology and Medicine* 48, no. 1 suppl. (Winter 2005).

39. Katrina Armstrong, Chanita Hughes-Halbert, and David A. Asch, "Patient Preferences Can Be Misleading as Explanations for Racial Disparities in Health Care," *Archives of Internal Medicine* 166 (May 8, 2006): 950–54; Norman G. Levinsky, "Quality and Equity in Dialysis and Renal Transplantation," *New England Journal of Medicine* 341 (November 25, 1999): 1691–93.

40. John P. Roberts et al., "Effect of Changing the Priority for HLA Matching on the Rates and Outcomes of Kidney Transplantation in Minority Groups," *New England Journal of Medicine* 350 (February 5, 2004): 545–51, at 551. See also Jon J. van Rood, "Weighing Optimal Graft Survival through HLA Matching against the Equitable Distribution of Kidney Allografts," *New England Journal of Medicine* 350 (February 5, 2004): 535–36.

41. Eric Hall et al., "Effect of Eliminating Priority Points for HLA-B Matching on Racial Disparities in Kidney Transplant Rates," *American Journal of Kidney Diseases* 58 (2011): 813–16. See also John R. Gill, "Achieving Fairness in Access to Kidney Transplant: A Work in Progress," *American Journal of Kidney Diseases* 58 (2011): 697–99.

42. See Robert Bornholz and James J. Heckman, "Measuring Disparate Impacts and Extending Disparate Impact Doctrine to Organ Transplantation," *Perspectives in Biology and Medicine* 48, no. 1 suppl. (Winter 2005): S95–122.

43. Carl Tishler and Suzanne Bartholomae, "The Recruitment of Normal Healthy Volunteers," *Journal of Clinical Pharmacology* 42 (2002): 365–75.

44. Tom L. Beauchamp, Bruce Jennings, Eleanor Kinney, and Robert Levine, "Pharmaceutical Research Involving the Homeless," *Journal of Medicine and Philosophy* (2002), 547–64; Toby L. Schonfeld, Joseph S. Brown, Meaghann Weniger, and Bruce Gordon, "Research Involving the Homeless," *IRB* 25 (September–October 2003): 17–20.

45. For analysis of the concept of exploitation, see Alan Wertheimer, *Exploitation* (Princeton, NJ: Princeton University Press, 1996); and Jennifer S. Hawkins and Ezekiel J. Emanuel, eds., *Exploitation and Developing Countries: The Ethics of Clinical Research* (Princeton, NJ: Princeton University Press, 2008).

46. See Carol Levine, Ruth Faden, Christine Grady, et al. (for the Consortium to Examine Clinical Research Ethics), "The Limitations of 'Vulnerability' as a Protection for Human Research Participants,"

American Journal of Bioethics 4 (2004): 44–49; and Ruth Macklin, "Bioethics, Vulnerability, and Protection," *Bioethics* 17 (2003): 472–86.

47. See Debra A. DeBruin, "Looking beyond the Limitations of 'Vulnerability': Reforming Safeguards in Research," *American Journal of Bioethics* 4 (2004): 76–78; and National Bioethics Advisory Commission, *Ethical and Policy Issues in Research Involving Human Participants,* vol. 1 (Bethesda, MD: Government Printing Office, 2001).

48. See Sarah E. Hewlett, "Is Consent to Participate in Research Voluntary," *Arthritis Care and Research* 9 (1996): 400–04; and Robert M. Nelson and Jon F. Merz, "Voluntariness of Consent for Research: An Empirical and Conceptual Review," *Medical Care* 40 (2002), Suppl.: V69–80.

49. See the analysis of coercion in Jennifer S. Hawkins and Ezekiel J. Emanuel, "Clarifying Confusions about Coercion," *Hastings Center Report* 35 (September–October 2005): 16–19.

50. Common Rule for the Protection of Human Subjects, U.S. Code of Federal Regulations, 45 CFR 46.116 (as revised October 1, 2003), http://www.hhs.gov/ohrp/humansubjects/guidance/45cfr46.html (accessed July 15, 2011); and see Ezekiel Emanuel, "Ending Concerns about Undue Inducement," *Journal of Law, Medicine, & Ethics* 32 (2004): 100–5, esp. 101.

51. The justification of monetary inducement in terms of mutual benefit is defended by Martin Wilkinson and Andrew Moore, "Inducement in Research," *Bioethics* 11 (1997), 373–89; and Wilkinson and Moore, "Inducements Revisited," *Bioethics* 13 (1999): 114–30.

52. See Neal Dickert and Christine Grady, "What's the Price of a Research Subject?: Approaches to Payment for Research Participation," *New England Journal of Medicine* 341 (1999): 198–203; and David Resnick, "Research Participation and Financial Inducements," *American Journal of Bioethics* 1 (2001): 54–56.

53. See Nik Theodore, Edwin Melendez, and Ana Luz Gonzalez, "On the Corner: Day Labor in the United States" (UCLA Center for the Study of Urban Poverty, January 2006), http://www.sscnet.ucla .edu/issr/csup/uploaded_files/Natl_DayLabor-On_the_Corner1.pdf (accessed March 28, 2012).

54. For figures, see U.S. Census information on health insurance: http://www.census.gov/ prod/2011pubs/p60–239.pdf (accessed January 20, 2012), pp. 23, 75.

55. See Daniels, *Just Health Care,* chaps. 3 and 4; and *Just Health: Meeting Health Needs Fairly,* pp. 46–60.

56. Cf. Allen Buchanan, "The Right to a Decent Minimum of Health Care," *Philosophy and Public Affairs* 13 (Winter 1984): 55–78; and Buchanan, "Health-Care Delivery and Resource Allocation," in *Medical Ethics,* 2nd ed., ed. Robert M. Veatch (Boston: Jones & Bartlett, 1997), esp. pp. 337–59. Both are reprinted in Buchanan, *Justice and Health Care: Selected Essays* (New York: Oxford University Press, 2009).

57. Compare Peter A. Ubel et al., "Cost-Effectiveness Analysis in a Setting of Budget Constraints—Is It Equitable?" *New England Journal of Medicine* 334 (May 2, 1996): 1174–77; and Paul T. Menzel, "Justice and the Basic Structure of Health-Care Systems," in *Medicine and Social Justice,* ed. R. Rhodes, M. P. Battin, and A. Silvers (New York: Oxford University Press, 2002), pp. 24–37.

58. This discussion of Dworkin's position draws from his *Sovereign Virtue: The Theory and Practice of Equality* (Cambridge, MA: Harvard University Press, 2000), chap. 8.

59. Robert M. Veatch, "Voluntary Risks to Health: The Ethical Issues," *JAMA: Journal of the American Medical Association* 243 (January 4, 1980): 50–55.

60.   See the broader set of issues about fairness for noncompliant patients raised in Nir Eyal, "Why Treat Noncompliant Patients? Beyond the Decent Minimum Account," *Journal of Medicine and Philosophy* 36 (2011): 572–88.

61.   Abdou S. Gueye et al., "The Association between Recipient Alcohol Dependency and Long-Term Graft and Recipient Survival," *Nephrology Dialysis Transplantation* 22 (2007): 891–98; J. Dumortier et al., "Negative Impact of De Novo Malignancies Rather Than Alcohol Relapse on Survival after Liver Transplantation for Alcoholic Cirrhosis," *American Journal of Gastroenterology* 102 (2007): 1032–41; and Robert Pfitzmann et al., "Long-Term Survival and Predictors of Relapse after Orthotopic Liver Transplantation for Alcoholic Liver Disease," *Liver Transplantation* 13 (2007): 197–205.

62.   Alvin H. Moss and Mark Siegler, "Should Alcoholics Compete Equally for Liver Transplantation?" *JAMA: Journal of the American Medical Association* 265 (March 13, 1991): 1295–98. See also Robert M. Veatch, *Transplantation Ethics* (Washington, DC: Georgetown University Press, 2000); and Walter Glannon, "Responsibility, Alcoholism, and Liver Transplantation," *Journal of Medicine and Philosophy* 23 (1998): 31–49.

63.   On this distinction and egalitarian justice, see John E. Roemer, *Equality of Opportunity* (Cambridge, MA: Harvard University Press, 1998).

64.   An argument based on justice against the total exclusion of alcoholics from liver transplantation appears in Carl Cohen, Martin Benjamin, and the Ethics and Social Impact Committee of the [Michigan] Transplant and Health Policy Center, "Alcoholics and Liver Transplantation," *JAMA: Journal of the American Medical Association* 265 (March 13, 1991): 1299–1301.

65.   On this distinction and its importance, see the well-honed controversy in the following two articles: Thomas Nagel, "The Problem of Global Justice," *Philosophy and Public Affairs* 33 (2005): 113–47; and Joshua Cohen and Charles Sabel, "Extra Rempublicam Nulla Justitia?" *Philosophy and Public Affairs* 34 (2006): 147–75, esp. 148, 150ff on the nature of statist theories.

66.   Rawls, *A Theory of Justice,* chap. 3, § 22. See n. 3.

67.   Hume, *A Treatise of Human Nature,* ed. David Norton and Mary Norton (Oxford: Clarendon Press, 2007), 3.2.2; and *An Enquiry concerning the Principles of Morals,* ed. Tom L. Beauchamp (Oxford: Clarendon Press, 2000), sect. 3.

68.   United Nations, Office of the High Commissioner for Human Rights, "The Right of Everyone to the Enjoyment of the Highest Attainable Standard of Physical and Mental Health," United Nations Commission on Human Rights Resolution 2004/27 (New York: United Nations, 2004).

69.   See Thomas Pogge, "Severe Poverty as a Violation of Negative Duties," *Ethics & International Affairs* 19 (2005): 55–83; Pogge, ed., *Freedom from Poverty as a Human Right: Who Owes What to the Very Poor?* (Oxford: Oxford University Press, 2007); Pogge, "Human Rights and Global Health: A Research Program," *Metaphilosophy* 36 (2005): 182–209; and Pogge, *Politics as Usual: What Lies Behind the Pro-Poor Rhetoric* (Cambridge, England: Polity Press, 2010). See also Alison Jaggar, ed., *Thomas Pogge and His Critics* (Cambridge, England: Polity Press, 2010).

70.   For the precipitating history see C. R. Blagg, "The Early History of Dialysis for Chronic Renal Failure in the United States: A View from Seattle," *American Journal of Kidney Disease* 49 (2007): 482–96.

71.   See Norman Daniels and James Sabin, *Setting Limits Fairly: Can We Learn to Share Medical Resources?* (New York: Oxford University Press, 2002); and Powers and Faden, *Social Justice,* chap. 6, "Setting Limits."

72.   Oregon Senate Bill 27 (March 31, 1989). See also Lawrence Jacobs, Theodore Marmor, and Jonathan Oberlander, "The Oregon Health Plan and the Political Paradox of Rationing: What

Advocates and Critics Have Claimed and What Oregon Did," *Journal of Health Politics, Policy and Law* 24 (1999): 161–80.

73. Health Economics Research, Inc., for the Health Care Financing Administration, *Evolution of the Oregon Plan* (Washington, DC: NTIS No. PB98–135916 INZ, December 12, 1997, as updated January 19, 1999); Oregon Department of Administrative Services, *Assessment of the Oregon Health Plan Medicaid Demonstration* (Salem, OR: Office for Oregon Health Plan Policy and Research, 1999).

74. Jonathan Oberlander, "Health Reform Interrupted: The Unraveling of the Oregon Health Plan," *Health Affairs* 26 (January–February 2007): w96–105; Rachel Solotaroff et al., "Medicaid Programme Changes and the Chronically Ill: Early Results from a Prospective Cohort Study of the Oregon Health Plan," *Chronic Illness* 1 (2005): 191–205; Matthew J. Carlson, Jennifer DeVoe, and Bill J. Wright, "Short-Term Impacts of Coverage Loss in a Medicaid Population: Early Results from a Prospective Cohort Study of the Oregon Health Plan," *Annals of Family Medicine* 4 (2006): 391–98.

75. This section is indebted to Powers and Faden, *Social Justice,* chap. 6.

76. See Paul T. Menzel, *Medical Costs, Moral Choices* (New Haven, CT: Yale University Press, 1983), chap. 7; Peter J. Pronovost and Ruth R. Faden, "Setting Priorities for Patient Safety," *JAMA: Journal of the American Medical Association* 302 (August 26, 2009): 890–91; and Akc Bergmark, Marti G. Parker, and Mats Thorslund, "Priorities in Care and Service for Elderly People: A Path without Guidelines?" *Journal of Medical Ethics* 26 (2000): 312–18.

77. L. B. Russell et al., "The Role of Cost-Effectiveness Analysis in Health and Medicine," *JAMA: Journal of the American Medical Association* 276 (1996): 1172–77; Dan Brock, "Ethical Issues in the Use of Cost-Effectiveness Analysis," in *Public Health, Ethics, and Equity,* ed. Sudhir Anand, Fabienne Peter, and Amartya Sen (Oxford: Oxford University Press, 2004), pp. 201–23.

78. See Daniels and Sabin, *Setting Limits Fairly,* p. 63; Daniels and Sabin, "Last Chance Therapies and Managed Care: Pluralism, Fair Procedures, and Legitimacy," *Hastings Center Report* 28 (1998): 27–41; Dennis Thompson and Amy Gutmann, *Democracy and Disagreement* (Cambridge, MA: Belknap Press of Harvard University Press, 1996); Leonard M. Fleck, "Can a Just and Caring Society Do Health Care Rationing When Life Itself Is at Stake?" *Yale Journal of Health Policy, Law, and Ethics* 2 (2002): 255–98, esp. 270ff; Fleck, "Just Caring: Defining a Basic Benefit Package," *Journal of Medicine and Philosophy* 36 (2011): 589–611; and John D. Arras and Elizabeth M. Fenton, "Bioethics and Human Rights: Access to Health-Related Goods," *Hastings Center Report* 39 (September–October 2009): 27–38, esp. 33–34.

79. Erik Nord, *Cost-Value Analysis in Health Care: Making Sense out of QALYs* (Cambridge: Cambridge University Press, 1999); Paul Menzel, "How Should What Economists Call 'Social Values' Be Measured?" *Journal of Ethics* 3 (1999): 249–73; Christopher Murray and Arnab Acharya, "Understanding DALYs," *Journal of Health Economics* 16 (1997): 703–30.

80. On "rationing" and a defense of its broad use, see Peter A. Ubel, *Pricing Life: Why It's Time for Health Care Rationing* (Cambridge, MA: MIT Press, 2000).

81. See Peter A. Ubel and Susan D. Goold, " 'Rationing' Health Care: Not all Definitions Are Created Equal," *Archives of Internal Medicine* 158 (1998): 209–14.

82. John McKenzie et al., "Dialysis Decision Making in Canada, the United Kingdom, and the United States," *American Journal of Kidney Diseases* 31 (1998): 12–18; Adrian Furnham and Abigail Ofstein, "Ethical Ideology and the Allocation of Scarce Medical Resources," *British Journal of Medical Psychology* 70 (1997): 51–63.

83. See Peter P. Reese, Arthur L. Caplan, Roy D. Bloom, et al., "How Should We Use Age to Ration Health Care? Lessons from the Case of Kidney Transplantation," *Journal of the American Geriatric Society* 58 (2010): 1980–86; and B. E. Hippen, J. R. Thistlethwaite, Jr., and L. F. Ross, "Risk, Prognosis,

and Unintended Consequences in Kidney Allocation," *New England Journal of Medicine* 364 (2011): 1285–87.

84.   Daniels, *Just Health: Meeting Health Needs Fairly,* pp. 171–85, esp. 177–81; and *Am I My Parents' Keeper?* (New York: Oxford University Press, 1988).

85.   Alan Williams, "Intergenerational Equity: An Exploration of the 'Fair Innings' Argument," *Health Economics* 6 (1997): 117–32.

86.   For criticism, see Dan W. Brock, "Justice, Health Care, and the Elderly," *Philosophy and Public Affairs* 18 (1989): 297–312.

87.   National Kidney Foundation, "Financing a Transplant," *Transplant Living,* http://www .transplantliving.org/beforethetransplant/finance/costs.aspx (accessed January 26, 2012); Nicholas G. Smedira, "Allocating Hearts," *Journal of Thoracic and Cardiovascular Surgery* 131 (2006): 775–76.

88.   U.S. Department of Health and Human Services, *Report of Task Force on Organ Transplantation, Organ Transplantation: Issues and Recommendations* (Washington, DC: DHHS, 1986), pp. 105, 111.

89.   Contrast Norman Daniels, "Comment: Ability to Pay and Access to Transplantation," *Transplantation Proceedings* 21 (June 1989): 3434; and Frances M. Kamm, "The Report of the U.S. Task Force on Organ Transplantation: Criticisms and Alternatives," *Mount Sinai Journal of Medicine* 56 (May 1989): 207–20.

90.   Originally proposed by Nicholas Rescher, "The Allocation of Exotic Medical Lifesaving Therapy," *Ethics* 79 (1969): 173–86.

91.   Task Force, *Organ Transplantation.* On the evolution of U.S. organ transplant policies, see Jeffrey Prottas, *The Most Useful Gift: Altruism and the Public Policy of Organ Transplants* (San Francisco: Jossey-Bass, 1994).

92.   Task Force, *Organ Transplantation*, p. 95.

93.   Compare and contrast Robert M. Veatch, "The Ethics of Resource Allocation in Critical Care," *Critical Care Clinics* 2 (January 1986): 73–89; Richard Wenstone, "Resource Allocation in Critical Care," in *Ethics in Anaesthesia and Intensive Care,* ed. Heather Draper and Wendy E. Scott (New York: Butterworth-Heinemann, 2003): 145–62; Gerald Winslow, *Triage and Justice: The Ethics of Rationing Life-Saving Medical Resources* (Berkeley, CA: University of California Press, 1982); and John Kilner, *Who Lives? Who Dies? Ethical Criteria in Patient Selection* (New Haven, CT: Yale University Press, 1990).

94.   See Duff R. Waring, *Medical Benefit and the Human Lottery* (Dordrecht, Netherlands: Springer, 2004); and Barbara Goodwin, *Justice by Lottery* (Chicago: University of Chicago Press, 1992).

95.   Stone refers to the "sanitizing effect" of lotteries, which may be good or bad depending on the circumstances, in *The Luck of the Draw: The Role of Lotteries in Decision Making* (New York: Oxford University Press, 2011).

96.   The statement derives from Evan DeRenzo, as in Diane Naughton, "Drug Lotteries Raise Questions: Some Experts Say System of Distribution May Be Unfair," *Washington Post,* Health Section, September 26, 1995, pp. 14–15.

97.   In Seattle, members of a closely watched committee that selected patients for dialysis felt intense pressure and stress, often accompanied by guilt. See John Broome, "Selecting People Randomly," *Ethics* 95 (1984): 41.

98.   Robert D. Truog, "Triage in the ICU," *Hastings Center Report* 22 (May–June 1992): 13–17; see also John D. Lantos and Joel Frader, "Extracorporeal Membrane Oxygenation and the Ethics of

Clinical Research in Pediatrics," *New England Journal of Medicine* 323 (August 9, 1990): 409–13. For discussion of the development, early use, and now declining use of ECMO in neonates, see John D. Lantos, *Neonatal Bioethics: The Moral Challenges of Medical Innovation* (Baltimore: Johns Hopkins University Press, 2006), pp. 52–62.

99.   See Ramsey, *The Patient as Person* (New Haven, CT: Yale University Press, 1970), pp. 257–58. For controversy about this example, see Robert Baker and Martin Strosberg, "Triage and Equality: An Historical Reassessment of Utilitarian Analyses of Triage," *Kennedy Institute of Ethics Journal* 2 (1992): 101–23.

100.   Winslow, *Triage and Justice*; but contrast Baker and Strosberg, "Triage and Equality: An Historical Reassessment." See also Robert A. Gatter and John C. Moskop, "From Futility to Triage," *Journal of Medicine and Philosophy* 20 (1995): 191–205; Society of Critical Care Medicine—Ethics Committee, "Consensus Statement on the Triage of Critically Ill Patients," *JAMA: Journal of the American Medical Association* 271 (April 20, 1994): 1200–3.

101.   See James F. Childress, "Triage in Response to a Bioterrorist Attack," in *In the Wake of Terror: Medicine and Morality in a Time of Crisis,* ed. Jonathan D. Moreno (Cambridge, MA: MIT Press, 2003), pp. 77–93.

102.   A number of different proposals have emerged in recent years to address the allocation of scarce medical technologies and procedures. Devised for a variety of scenarios, such as the distribution of vaccines and respirators in an influenza pandemic, provision of prophylactics and treatments following a bioterrorist attack, the allocation of organs, and admission to and discharge from intensive care units, these proposals combine several of the criteria we have employed, along with others. See, for example, Govind Persad, Alan Wertheimer, and Ezekiel J. Emanuel, "Principles for Allocation of Scarce Medical Interventions," *Lancet* 373 (January 31, 2009): 423–31; Persad and colleagues argue for a "complete lives" allocation system, which gives priority to "younger people who have not yet lived a complete life." See also Douglas B. White et al., "Who Should Receive Life Support during a Public Health Emergency? Using Ethical Principles to Improve Allocation Decisions," *Annals of Internal Medicine* 150 (January 20, 2009): 132–38, which proposes an allocation strategy that builds in and balances several morally relevant considerations, including "saving the most lives, maximizing the number of 'life-years' saved, and prioritizing patients who have had the least chance to live through life's stages."

8
Professional–Patient Relationships

The previous four chapters identify moral principles that are relevant to judgments in biomedical ethics. In this chapter we put these principles to use in an interpretation and appraisal of rules of veracity, privacy, confidentiality, and fidelity, with particular attention to relationships in clinical practice, research involving human subjects, and public health.[1]

VERACITY

Codes of medical ethics have traditionally ignored obligations and virtues of veracity. The Hippocratic oath does not recommend veracity, nor does the Declaration of Geneva of the World Medical Association. The introduction to the original 1847 Code of Medical Ethics of the American Medical Association (AMA) offers flowery praise of veracity, as "a jewel of inestimable value in medical description and narrative," but the code itself does not mention an obligation or virtue of veracity, and thereby allows physicians virtually unlimited discretion about what to divulge to patients. The AMA's 1980 Principles of Medical Ethics recommends, without elaboration, that physicians "deal honestly with patients and colleagues," and the 2001 revision requires physicians to "be honest in all professional interactions."[2]

Despite this traditional neglect of veracity, the virtues of honesty, truthfulness, and candor are among deservedly praised character traits of health professionals and researchers. Nevertheless, as Annette Baier notes, honesty "is not just a hard virtue to exhibit but also a hard one to design."[3] There are definitional disputes, and the ground and weight of norms and virtues of veracity have also long been disputed. Henry Sidgwick's nineteenth-century observation still holds: "It does not seem clearly agreed whether Veracity is an absolute and independent obligation, or a special application of some higher principle."[4] More recently, G. J. Warnock claimed that veracity is an independent principle and virtue that ranks in importance with beneficence, nonmaleficence, and justice.[5]

By contrast, we view obligations of veracity as specifications of more than one of these principles.

Obligations of Veracity

Veracity in health care refers to accurate, timely, objective, and comprehensive transmission of information, as well as to the way the professional fosters the patient's or subject's understanding. In this regard, veracity is closely connected to respect for autonomy. However, three primary arguments support obligations of veracity, and they are not wholly derived from respect for autonomy. The first argument is based on the respect owed to persons in contexts beyond informed consent. The second argument connects to obligations of fidelity, promise-keeping, and contract.[6] When we communicate with others, we implicitly promise that we will speak truthfully and that we will not deceive listeners. By entering into a relationship in health care or research, the patient or subject enters into a contract that includes a right to receive truthful information regarding diagnosis, prognosis, procedures, and the like, just as the professional gains a right to truthful disclosures from patients and subjects. The third argument is based on the role of trust in relationships between health professionals and patients and subjects. Its thesis is that adherence to rules of veracity is essential to the development and maintenance of trust in these relationships.

Like all other obligations discussed in this volume, veracity is prima facie binding, not absolute. Careful management of medical information—including limited disclosure, staged disclosure, nondisclosure, deception, and even lying—is occasionally justified when veracity conflicts with other obligations such as those of medical beneficence. As contexts change, the moral weights of veracity and beneficence will be heavier or lighter, and no decision rule is available to determine that one outweighs the other when we have to determine whether to disclose or withhold information. Accordingly, the weight of various obligations of veracity is difficult to determine outside of specific contexts.

However, some generalizations may be tendered: Deception that does not involve lying is usually less difficult to justify than lying, in part because it does not threaten as deeply the relationship of trust in many contexts of health care. Deception involves intentionally leading, or attempting to lead, someone to believe what is false, while lying seeks the same aim through statements. Underdisclosure and nondisclosure of information are also, in various circumstances, less difficult to justify.[7]

The Disclosure of Bad News to Patients

An example of these problems is intentional nondisclosure to patients of a diagnosis of cancer or a similarly serious medical condition and a prognosis of imminent death. Different cultural traditions and philosophical accounts have different views of the circumstances under which nondisclosure or partial disclosure is justified.[8] From our standpoint, the physician's or nurse's fundamental obligation at the beginning of the process of disclosure is to reassure the patient while engaging sympathetically with the patient's feelings and being present as a caring, knowledgeable professional. Some information can be delayed and spread over a period of time, and some may justifiably never be mentioned. This is not to deny that the physician or nurse also has an obligation to carefully attend to proper forms of disclosure. The best approach is to balance the need for disclosure with careful attention to the patient's responses.

Poor judgments about what and to whom to disclose can result in the mishandling of complex situations. In a striking case, Mr. X, a fifty-four-year-old male patient, consented to surgery for probable malignancy in his thyroid gland. After the surgery, the physician told him that the diagnosis had been confirmed and that the tumor had been successfully removed, but did not inform him of the likelihood of lung metastases and death within a few months. The physician did inform Mr. X's wife, son, and daughter-in-law about the fuller diagnosis and about the prognosis for Mr. X. All parties agreed to conceal the diagnosis and prognosis from Mr. X. The physician told Mr. X only that he needed "preventive" treatment, and Mr. X consented to irradiation and chemotherapy. The physician did not inform Mr. X of the probable causes of his subsequent shortness of breath and back pain. Unaware of his impending death, Mr. X died three months later.[9] Here the physician and family alike made poor judgments about withholding information.

Shifts in policies of disclosure. In recent decades, a dramatic shift has occurred in many countries in physicians' stated policies of disclosure of the diagnosis of cancer to patients. In the United States, in 1961, 88% of physicians surveyed indicated that they sought to avoid disclosing a diagnosis of cancer to patients, whereas by 1979, 98% of those surveyed reported a policy of disclosure to cancer patients.[10] A notably similar, though later (1993–98) pattern of rapid change occurred in Japan.[11] In the 1979 U.S. survey, physicians indicated that they most frequently considered the following four factors in deciding what to disclose: age (56% of respondents), a relative's wishes regarding disclosure to the patient (51%), emotional stability (47%), and intelligence (44%).

Although veracity in the disclosure of bad news—and in disclosure throughout clinical practice—continued to increase, some oncologists remain reluctant to disclose bad news and choose to withhold certain types of information.[12] It is unfortunate that, as in the case of Mr. X (and as reported in the 1979 survey), familial preferences sometimes unduly influence clinicians' decisions about disclosure of diagnosis and prognosis to patients. Some physicians take the view that the family can help the physician determine whether the patient is autonomous and capable of receiving information about serious risk. Although well-intended and in some cases acceptable, this approach runs the risk of begging a critical question: By what right does a physician initially disclose information to a family without the patient's acceptance of this arrangement? Families provide important care and support for many patients, but an autonomous patient has the right to veto familial involvement altogether. Lacking careful justification, it is unethical for a physician to first disclose information to a patient's family without the patient's authorization. The best policy is to ask the patient both at the outset and as the illness progresses about the extent to which he or she wants to involve others. This generalization holds irrespective of the patient's cultural background, which often serves as a convenient, but inappropriate, excuse for going around the patient to another party.

Arguments for noncommunication and limited or staged communication of bad news. The pendulum of disclosure to nondisclosure may now have swung too far in some medical communities in the direction of interpreting physician responsibility wholly in terms of patients' rights to information and the wrongness of withholding any sort of relevant information. Especially dangerous is the model of a one-time delivery of all relevant information, by contrast to a staged delivery over time. A more precautious, and justifiable, approach balances all of the patient's relevant welfare interests and the patient's informational interests and rights. This process of balancing will sometimes lead to the judgment that the physician is morally justified in withholding certain types of information. Three arguments support some degree of nondisclosure, limited disclosure, staged disclosure, and the like in health care, especially when there is "bad news," but in other cases as well.

The first argument rests on what Sidgwick and others have called "benevolent deception." Such deception has long been a part of medical tradition and practice. Its defenders hold that disclosure, particularly of a prognosis of death, can violate obligations of beneficence or nonmaleficence by causing the patient anxiety, by destroying the patient's hope, by retarding or erasing a therapeutic outcome, by leading the patient to consider suicide, and the like. This line of argument—"What you don't know can't hurt and may help you"—is consequence-based. One objection to this argument rests largely on the uncertainty and unreliability of predicting consequences. A second objection rests on the moral wrongness of appealing to such consequences. Both objections appear in Samuel Johnson's statement: "I deny the lawfulness of telling a lie to a sick man for fear of alarming him. You have no business with consequences; you are to tell the truth. Besides, you are not sure what effects your telling him that he is in danger may have."[13]

Nonetheless, staged disclosure and cautious language about prognosis can be justified in some circumstances, despite the risk to trust between clinicians and patients. Professional norms generally support the frank and direct sharing of information about diagnosis and about therapeutic options, but they often tend to discourage these same qualities in sharing prognostic information.[14] Professional norms of disclosure should incorporate the therapeutic value of hope for patients, along with the virtues of compassion, gentleness, and sensitivity, which are often morally more important than comprehensive disclosures.

Staged disclosure and cautious language are illustrated in the following case from rehabilitation medicine.[15] For close to a month, a physician in a stroke rehabilitation unit carefully managed information in his interactions with a patient who had suffered a stroke and who asked during a first session how long it would take for his arm to improve. From the beginning the doctor knew that the patient was unlikely to recover significant use of his arm, and he offered caveats and uncertainty that did not fully match what he believed or felt. He stressed the limitations of prognostication, the unpredictability of recovery, and the need to give the brain a chance to heal. The patient received these answers well at the time, apparently preferring the physician's "ambiguous statements about the future to the alternative judgment of the permanent paralysis he fears." This indefinite, but caring and supportive, exchange continued, with the physician praising the patient's progress in walking and performing daily activities, despite residual weakness. After two weeks, the patient was enthusiastic about his progress and asked, "How about my arm?" The physician responded, "The arm may not recover as much as the leg." Although this statement confirmed his fears, the patient still focused on his overall progress. He had a strong hope that the physician might be mistaken, since he had repeatedly stressed his inability to prognosticate in accurate detail.

Commenting on this case later, the physician noted that, having been trained in the era of "patient autonomy," he had once felt that he "should share all available information [he] could provide about prognosis as early as possible," trying to temper unfavorable news, for instance, about arm recovery, with positive predictions of restored walking and independent living. However, he had found both that his patients hoped for a return to their earlier lives and that bad news at any early stage tended to overwhelm good news or signs of hope. Thus, he became convinced that most of his "patients were not ready for the cold hard facts the minute they arrived at the rehabilitation hospital. They needed time to come to terms with the reality of their disabilities, while simultaneously regaining lost function." He therefore deemed staged disclosures appropriate to sustain patients' hopes—an understandable and justified strategy under the circumstances.

The second argument is that, even if professionals know all relevant information, many patients are not able to understand and appreciate the scope and implications of the information provided. Communication can be complex, especially if the patient has limited capacity to understand, and sometimes, as in the following case, intentional verbal inaccuracy can be justified: Over the years, a ninety-year-old patient, who as a young man had been decorated for courageous actions in battle, had become fearful that he would develop cancer, which he understood to be a shameful, painful, and fatal disease that would spread inexorably. He was referred for an ulcer on his lip; a biopsy established the diagnosis of squamous cell carcinoma, which would require only a short course of radiotherapy to cure, without any need for surgery or even admission to the hospital. The elderly patient, tears in his eyes, asked, "It's not cancer, is it?" The physician emphatically denied that it was cancer.[16]

The physician justified his action on several grounds. First, he pointed to the patient's deep need for "effective reassurance." Second, he argued that it was "more truthful" to tell this patient that he did not have cancer than to tell him that he did, because it would have been impossible to inform him that he had a curable cancer "without leaving him with a false and untrue impression" because of his enduring and unchangeable beliefs. Third, addressing this patient and his concerns in his own language expressed respect rather than paternalistic arrogance. Implicit in these justifications is the conviction that, because of his apparently unalterable false beliefs, this patient lacked the capacity to adequately process the diagnosis of cancer, which, for him, entailed the prognosis of death. The physician's decision may have been warranted, given this patient's condition, the availability of effective treatment, and the depth of his false beliefs.

A third argument is that some patients, particularly the very sick and the dying, do not want to know the truth about their condition. Despite surveys in the United States that almost universally indicate that the majority of patients want to know, some physicians maintain that patients not infrequently indicate by signals, if not actual words, that they do not want the truth. This judgment may be warranted in a limited range of cases, but claims about what patients genuinely want are inherently dubious when they contradict the patients' own reports, and this third argument sets dangerous precedents for patently paternalistic actions that masquerade as respect for autonomy.

Relying heavily on the family's judgment that the patient would not want to receive "bad news" also sets dangerous precedents. An Italian oncologist reports that she tries to tell her patients "the complete truth," but sometimes the patient's family asks her not to use the word "cancer."[17] She then relies on nonverbal communication to establish truthful therapeutic relationships with patients in a manner she judges to be a traditionally accepted form of Italian medical beneficence. She tries to listen carefully and assess both the verbal and nonverbal interactions, while respecting the patients' specific needs for information. This position has its dangers, but such practices need not fail to respect individual autonomy, particularly if the patient authorizes the clinician's independent disclosure to the family. The ways in which patients exercise their autonomy will reflect their self-understandings, including sociocultural expectations and religious or other beliefs. A choice not to know can be as autonomous and as worthy of respect as a choice to know. Accordingly, a physician needs care and sensitivity to understand a particular patient's preferences and to respect that patient by managing information according to those preferences.

Nevertheless, attending to a particular patient's expressed desire for information about prognosis is often as difficult as it is delicate, and it may be unclear in the course of decision making whether a moral mistake is being made. In one case, a twenty-six-year-old woman, the mother of two young children, had an aggressive adenocarcinoma. Following radiation therapy and two different chemotherapeutic combinations, she was fragile, but stable.[18] She was on oxygen continuously and took long-acting morphine (60 mg) three times a day. Yet, she was energetic and life-affirming. She told the new hematology/oncology fellow that she had "a feeling" based on her increased hip pain and enlarged nodules that "things aren't going as well as people tell me they are" and hoped he had some new "tricks" up his sleeve. She promptly consented to a new drug after he explained its administration, its potential adverse effects, and the ways they would try to prevent those effects, as well as his "hope that we would begin to see the long-sought-for response that might begin to heal her."

However, on the way to the chemotherapy unit, she said that she had heard about a woman dying of leukemia who had written several stories for her children so that they would remember her. She continued, "My girlfriend said I should do the same thing for my kids, but I don't think I'm *that* far gone, am I, Doctor Dan?" Her physician reports his "stunned silence." Unprepared for the question, he was unsure how to respond in the hall of a busy clinic, hardly an ideal setting for breaking bad news. Faced with her radiant smile, he replied: "No, Lisa, I don't think you're at that point. I'm hopeful that this new treatment will work and that you will be able to spend a lot more time with your kids." "That's what I thought, Doctor Dan," she responded. "Thanks. Now on to round three." Fourteen days later, she died, without having written her stories for her children. Years later, the physician continued to hear the echo of his last words to her, wondering whether conveying a different message, with its depressing news, would have allowed her to pen a few words or poems or to record thoughts or messages that would provide her children a living memory of their dynamic, carefree mother.

Disclosure of medical errors. "Preventable adverse events are a leading cause of death" in U.S. hospitals, according to a report from the Institute of Medicine, which claimed that "at least 44,000, and perhaps as many as 98,000, Americans die in hospitals each year as a result of medical errors."[19] There are disputes about the classification of preventable adverse events, their numbers, their causes, and potential solutions. For instance, not all preventable adverse events—whether lethal or nonlethal, in the hospital or in other settings—are the result of medical errors or mistakes. One primary moral responsibility is to develop systems, including training programs, to reduce medical errors and other causes of preventable adverse events. A motto in the patient safety movement holds that "errors are caused by bad systems, not by bad people."[20] Nevertheless, it is important to remove professionals deficient in personal character, knowledge, or skills who make or are likely to make medical errors.

Another primary moral responsibility is to disclose specific medical errors to patients and their families. Adequate disclosure often does not occur and is rarely documented when it does.[21] Evasive formulations, including the use of the passive voice, ambiguous language, and euphemisms, frequently mark disclosures that are documented.[22] The disclosure of medical error is a subset of the provision of bad news, but it is more difficult to make these disclosures because clinicians or institutions caused the harms and now fear malpractice suits. Although these fears are understandable, nondisclosure is morally indefensible. Moreover, available evidence indicates that these fears are often overblown, and some evidence shows that disclosure may be the best policy for reducing the likelihood of malpractice suits.[23]

Other reasons for nondisclosure or limited disclosure of medical errors include concerns about harming patients and damaging patient and public trust, as well as facing staff opposition. In one case, a young boy's parents took him to a medical center for treatment of a respiratory problem. After being placed in the adult intensive care unit, he received ten times the normal dosage of muscle relaxant, and the respirator tube slipped and pumped oxygen into his stomach for several minutes. He suffered cardiac arrest and permanent brain damage. His parents accidentally overheard a conversation that mentioned the overdose. The physician involved had decided not to inform the parents of the mistake because they "had enough on [their] minds already," but the parents justifiably felt that their tragedy was compounded by the self-protective nondisclosure and duplicity of the physician, whom they had, until this point, trusted.

A basic ethical question is not only whether to disclose, but also how to disclose, how much to disclose, when to disclose, and so forth. The language of "disclosure" may inappropriately suggest a one-off provision of information, but this neglects the importance of interactive conversation between patients and clinicians. In *Talking with Patients and Families about Medical Error,* Robert Truog and colleagues focus less on specific communication skills and more on the values and attitudes that should underlie conversations between patients and clinicians following medical errors.[24] Specifically, they emphasize five core relational values in the interactions of patients and clinicians around medical errors: transparency, respect, accountability, continuity, and kindness.

For Truog and colleagues, as well as for us, balancing is required. They emphasize that in the context of medical error, and with a firm commitment to meeting patients' and families' needs while rebuilding trust, clinicians must "recognize, weigh, and balance" competing ethical considerations, such as transparency and kindness, in determining what to say about medical error. A specific apology will often be appropriate and helpful. In addition, some institutions, after medical error, provide an early offer of compensation, which sometimes may be a matter of justice, not merely compassion or generosity.

In sum, the wall of almost collusive silence that has commonly surrounded medical mistakes is an unjustified and troublesome feature of medical cultures—as is its connection to what we will later refer to as fidelity to one's professional colleagues.

Deception of Third-Party Payers

Vigorous efforts to contain the costs of health care have led some physicians to use and to justify deception to secure third-party coverage. A physician in obstetrics and gynecology presented the following example: A forty-year-old woman underwent a diagnostic laparoscopy for primary infertility. Because the woman's private insurance policy did not cover this procedure for this indication, the attending surgeon instructed the resident not to write anything about infertility in the operative notes and instead to stress the two or three fine adhesions found in the pelvic area; if these pelvic adhesions were the indication for the procedure, the patient's insurance would then cover it. When the resident refused, the attending prepared the operative note.[25]

Several studies have attempted to determine the extent to which physicians use, or would be willing to use, deception on behalf of their patients. According to one study, close to 50% of the physicians surveyed admitted that they had exaggerated the severity of their patients' medical condition so that those patients would be covered for the medical care the physicians believed they needed.[26] In another survey, 54% of the physicians surveyed acknowledged that they had deceived third-party payers in order to obtain coverage benefits for their patients' medical condition, and 39% indicated that they had exaggerated the severity of patients' conditions, altered patients' diagnoses, or reported signs or symptoms that patients did not have, with the intent to help patients obtain coverage for needed care.[27] In short, several of these studies indicate that a significant percentage of physicians lie and otherwise compromise truthfulness. In effect, for these physicians, fidelity to patients trumps veracity, but their actions are also sometimes motivated by their self-interest in reimbursement.[28]

Other studies have used vignettes to determine the extent to which physicians are willing to deceive or allow deception of a third-party payer to secure approval for procedures for patients. In one study, over half of the internists surveyed sanctioned the use of deception in cases in which the patients were at immediate risk and needed coronary bypass surgery or arterial revascularization.[29] A survey of physicians and the general public found that "the public was more than twice as likely as physicians to sanction deception (26% versus 11%) and half as likely to believe that physicians have adequate time to appeal coverage decisions (22% versus 59%)."[30]

Physicians often confront a tension between their roles as patient advocates and their roles within institutional structures related to third-party payers. As before, we do not maintain that deception can never be justified in such conflicts, but physicians should place a premium on seeking alternative, nondeceptive courses of action, such as formal appeals, and should work to alter unduly restrictive systems. The understandable temptations of deception in these systems pose threats to physician integrity, to the moral climate of organizations, and to the fair distribution of benefits in these systems. Fidelity to patients, including strong advocacy on their behalf, is noble, but it should not cross the boundary of the disclosure of truthful clinical information to which an impartial reviewer is entitled.

To conclude, we have argued in this section on veracity that rules of truthfulness and disclosure are profoundly important in health care. There is a strong presumption in favor of truthfulness and disclosure in health care. This is not merely, as one philosopher argues, "a strong moral presumption against lying and deception when they cause harm."[31] Such an approach would reduce their moral significance to the principle of nonmaleficence and would fail to address other reasons for disclosure in health care. Nevertheless, many clinical contexts call for good judgment that balances all relevant ethical considerations, rather than inflexible rules about the necessity of truthfulness and disclosure. No a priori decision rule is available to prefer instant and abrupt truth-telling over staged disclosure, limited disclosure, or even nondisclosure in all contexts. This perspective follows our framework of multiple prima facie principles and our discussion of justified paternalism in Chapter 6.

PRIVACY

Concerns about privacy and confidentiality pervade much of medical practice, health care administration, public health, and research. Privacy became a major concern more recently than confidentiality, which has a long history in medical ethics, but we will first discuss privacy because confidentiality is arguably a way to protect privacy in certain relationships.

Privacy in Law and Legal Theory

In the 1920s the U.S. Supreme Court employed an expansive "liberty" interest to protect family decision making about child rearing, education, and the like. It later adopted the term *privacy* and expanded the individual's and the family's interests in family life, child rearing, and other areas of personal choice.

Griswold v. Connecticut (1965), a contraception case, set a precedent that the right to privacy not only shields information from others, but also protects a sphere of individual and familial decision-making from governmental interference. The Court's decision overturned state legislation that prohibited the use or dissemination of contraceptives. The Court determined that the right to privacy protects liberty by exempting a zone of private life from public invasion.[32]

It may seem inappropriate to construe a right that protects individual or familial interests as one of privacy rather than liberty or autonomy. However this issue is decided, the right to privacy in American law encompasses rights of limited physical and informational access as well as rights of decisional freedom. Reducing this right to a right to be free to do something or a right to act autonomously creates confusion, for reasons we will now explore.

The Concept of Privacy

Some definitions of "privacy" focus on an agent's control over access to himself or herself, but these definitions confuse privacy, which is a state or condition of limited access, with an agent's control over privacy or a right to privacy, which involves the agent's right to control access. These definitions focus on either powers or rights rather than privacy itself,[33] but a person can have privacy without having a right or any other form of control over access by others. Privacy exists, for example, in long-term care facilities that render patients inaccessible or in settings where others are indifferent to or uninterested in persons.

Anita Allen has identified four forms of privacy that involve limited access to the person: *informational privacy,* which biomedical ethics often emphasizes; *physical privacy,* which focuses on persons and their personal spaces (the latter of which is sometimes called *locational privacy*); *decisional privacy,* which concerns personal choices; and *proprietary privacy,* which highlights property interests in the human person, for example, in a person's image.[34] We propose a fifth form of privacy—*relational* or *associational privacy.* It includes the family and similarly intimate relations, within which individuals make decisions in conjunction with others. As these different forms of privacy suggest, definitions of privacy are too narrow if they focus entirely on limited access to *information* about a person. Privacy, as limited access, extends to bodily products and objects intimately associated with the person, as well as to the person's intimate relationships with friends, lovers, spouses, physicians, and others.

In some contexts it seems desirable to provide a tighter definition of "privacy," especially when developing policies about which forms of access to which aspects of persons will constitute losses and violations of privacy. We are, however, reluctant to tinker in this way with the concept to make it more serviceable for certain types of policy. Instead, we recommend that policymakers who construct privacy policies carefully specify the conditions of access that will and will not count as a loss of privacy or a violation of the right to privacy. The policy should define the zones that are considered private and not to be invaded and should also identify interests that legitimately may be balanced against privacy interests. Often the focus will be on informational privacy, but the strategy we recommend applies to a broader range of privacy interests.

The value we place on a condition of limited access or nonaccess explains how it comes to be categorized as private. Concerns about a loss of privacy may depend not only on the kind and extent of access, but also on who has access, through which means, and to which aspect of the person. As Charles Fried notes, "We may not mind that a person knows a general fact about us, and yet feel our privacy invaded if he knows the details. For instance, a casual acquaintance may comfortably know that I am sick, but it would violate my privacy if he knew the nature of the illness."[35]

Justifications of the Right to Privacy

In their influential 1890 article "The Right to Privacy," Samuel Warren and Louis Brandeis argued that a legal right to privacy flows from fundamental rights to life, liberty, and property.[36] They derived it largely from "the right to enjoy life—the right to be let alone." But this near-vacuous right needs more content to amount to a right to privacy. In recent discussions, several justifications of the right to privacy have been proposed, three of which deserve attention here.

One approach derives the right to privacy from a cluster of other rights. Judith Thomson argues that this cluster of personal and property rights includes rights not to be looked at; not to be caused distress (e.g., by the publication of certain information); not to be harmed, hurt, or tortured (in an effort to obtain certain information, say); and so on. However, her argument relies on several allegedly foundational rights that themselves have an uncertain status, such as the right not to be looked at. We are not convinced that all of these alleged rights are rights, and some of these rights may have the right to privacy as their basis, rather than the converse.[37]

A second justification emphasizes the instrumental value of privacy and the right to privacy: Consequentialist approaches justify rules of privacy according to their instrumental value for such ends as personal development, creating and maintaining intimate social relations, and expressing personal freedom.[38] For example, privacy may be a necessary condition for intimate relationships of respect, love, friendship, and trust.[39]

Although we build and maintain various relationships by granting some persons and denying others certain kinds of access to ourselves, we question whether the instrumental value of privacy is the primary justification of rights to privacy. The primary justification seems to be closer to the domain of the principle of respect for autonomy, the third justification that is commonly offered.[40]

We owe respect in the sense of deference to persons' autonomous wishes not to be observed, touched, intruded on, and the like. The right to authorize or decline access is the basic right. On this basis, the justification of the right to privacy parallels the justification of the right to give an informed consent that we developed in Chapter 4.

Joel Feinberg has observed that, historically, the language of autonomy has functioned as a political metaphor for a domain or territory in which a state is sovereign. Personal autonomy carries over the idea of a region of sovereignty for the self and a right to protect it by restricting access.[41] Other metaphors expressing privacy in the personal domain include zones and spheres of privacy that protect autonomy.

Specifying and Balancing Rules of Privacy for Public Health Surveillance

We now consider how to specify rules and rights of privacy, while allowing for justified intrusions on privacy that balance privacy interests against other interests such as the public good and the progress of medical science. We use surveillance for public health purposes as a prime example.[42] The goal is to find the conditions under which access to a person, and to information about a person, is warranted. This question is distinguishable from questions of the uses to which information that is gained might be put, including abuses.

Surveillance is central to public health. It generates data that can be used for epidemiological purposes, for instance, to map the incidence and prevalence of disease, and for taking effective actions to protect and promote public health, for instance, to impose quarantine after exposure to communicable diseases or to notify partners that a person has a sexually transmitted disease. Epidemiological data may be anonymous, but effective actions often need personal identifiers, typically names. We will concentrate on personally identified information.

Common metaphors suggest surveillance's risk to privacy: Surveillance serves as "the eyes of public health," even the "searching or prying eyes of public health," or serves as a way to keep a "finger on the pulse of the health of a community." Each metaphor implies access to individuals and to information about them, and each indicates that surveillance entails some loss of privacy. Public health surveillance in general also infringes the right to privacy. Rarely do individuals consent to the collection, analysis, use, storage, and transfer of personal information for public health purposes. Hence, for the most part, identifier-based surveillance in public health, without individual consent, differs sharply from the collection of information in clinical care and in research, the other two domains featured in this chapter.[43]

In many cases the public health rationale—based on beneficence and justice in the prevention of harm to others—provides a sufficient justification for surveillance without consent. However, public health is not a single or monolithic goal and we need specificity to determine whether, on balance, a particular public health goal will warrant the infringement of privacy rights, as is often the case for communicable diseases such as tuberculosis and sexually transmitted diseases.[44] The justification for public health surveillance hinges on the proposed use of the data—the data by themselves will not have an impact on public health—and how effective that use is likely to be. Depending on the disease being targeted, uses of the information could include partner notification, quarantine and isolation, or case management, such as directly observed therapy for tuberculosis.

New York City's program to address uncontrolled or poorly controlled diabetes raises major questions about surveillance, in part because it targets a chronic disease rather than a communicable disease. Without doubt, diabetes is a major health problem, and it is the fourth leading cause of death in New York City, where approximately 9% of the population is affected, for a total of about half a million persons with diabetes. Public health officials call diabetes an "epidemic," a term that is technically correct but that also has the rhetorical advantage of evoking an image that can support the expansion of public health authority and actions. Inadequately controlled diabetes causes serious health problems, such as kidney disease, heart disease, and stroke. Beyond its tremendous health burdens for patients, it has major social and economic impacts, including heavy costs to the city.

In this context, the Department of Health and Mental Hygiene in New York City initiated a program in 2006 to require laboratories with electronic reporting capabilities to report to the department the blood sugar levels of persons with diabetes in order to determine how well their diabetes is being controlled. Interventions later added to the program include regularly notifying facilities and treating providers of their patients' blood sugar levels and sending letters to patients if they are overdue for a test or if their test results indicate that their blood sugar levels are too high.[45]

New York City public health officials had hoped to develop a parallel program for HIV infection but were stymied by laws protecting privacy and confidentiality. In recent years, the rationale for such a program has become even stronger in light of evidence that antiretroviral therapy not only increases the survival and improves the quality of life of infected individuals, but also significantly reduces their risk of transmitting HIV infection to others by lowering their viral load. Here therapy becomes prevention. Surveillance data about cell counts and viral loads could provide valuable information for both clinicians and patients and could have important public health effects.[46]

A major ethical and policy obstacle for either the diabetes surveillance program or the proposed HIV surveillance program is the infringement of the right to privacy because of the lack of individual consent. However, even in the absence of individual consent, the right to privacy is not absolute and must be balanced against other ethical principles and rules. Relevant factors in balancing include the importance of the goal being sought (public health or population health, along with the avoidance or reduction of social and economic burdens); whether the surveillance program would probably realize the goal; whether the infringement of privacy rights is necessary, is proportionate, and is the least intrusive consistent with realizing the goal; whether adequate security measures are in place to protect personal information (which would minimize the negative effects of overriding the right to privacy); and so forth. Cautionary notes about the diabetes program are that it does not identify persons with undiagnosed diabetes or prediabetes, and that it is solely informational—it involves report and notification without additional resources for prevention and treatment services.

Proponents of privacy rights emphasize that rules protecting privacy, at least within limits, can facilitate the cooperation needed for public health programs. In this regard, there are good reasons for vigorous public engagement, with all relevant stakeholders—both professionals and members of the public—involved in the development of surveillance policies. One concern is that public health programs such as the diabetes program, with increased scrutiny of both patients and health care providers, may wind up alienating the communities and health professionals served, reducing their motivation to seek or provide health care services.[47]

Another large concern is that the New York City diabetes program represents so-called mission creep in public health and, more dramatically, may open the way for additional and more extensive registries of sensitive data, without adequate justification, thereby further compromising rights of privacy.

CONFIDENTIALITY

We surrender some privacy when we grant others access to our personal information or our bodies, but we usually retain a significant level of control over information generated about us in diagnostic and therapeutic contexts and in research. For example, physicians are obligated not to grant an insurance company or a prospective employer access to information about patients unless the patients authorize its release. When others gain access to protected information without authorization, they infringe the right to confidentiality, the right to privacy, or both.

Confidentiality could be considered a branch or subset of informational privacy. It prevents redisclosure of information originally disclosed within a confidential relationship, that is, a relationship in which the confider has a reasonable and legitimate expectation that the confidant will not further disclose the information to anyone without the confider's authorization.[48] The basic difference between the right to privacy and the right to confidentiality is that an infringement of a person's right to confidentiality occurs only if the person or institution to whom the information was disclosed in confidence fails to protect the information or deliberately discloses it to someone without first-party consent. By contrast, a person who, without authorization, obtains a hospital record or gains access to a computer database violates rights of privacy but does not violate rights of confidentiality. Only the person or institution who obtains information in a confidential relationship can be charged with violating rights of confidentiality.

Traditional Rules and Contemporary Practices

Rules of confidentiality appear as early as the Hippocratic oath and continue today in national and international codes. They are arguably the most widespread rules in medical ethics across time and cultures. However, some commentators depict traditional confidentiality rules as little more than a convenient fiction, publicly acknowledged by health care professionals and their professional organizations, but widely ignored and violated in practice. We agree that the rules are today largely ceremonial unless an underlying medical culture values the protection of health information.

Mark Siegler has argued that confidentiality in medicine is a decrepit concept, because what both physicians and patients have traditionally understood as medical confidentiality no longer exists. It is "compromised systematically in the course of routine medical care." To make his point graphic, Siegler presents the case of a patient who became concerned about the number of people in the hospital with apparent access to his record and threatened to leave prematurely unless the hospital would guarantee confidentiality. Upon inquiry, Siegler discovered that many more people than he suspected had responsibilities to examine the patient's chart. When he informed the patient of the number—approximately seventy-five—he assured the patient that "these people were all involved in providing or supporting his health care services." The patient retorted, "I always believed that medical confidentiality was part of doctors' code of ethics. Perhaps you should tell me just what you people mean by 'confidentiality.'"[49]

This reaction is reasonable and raises questions about the seriousness of many putative institutional and professional protections. When William Behringer tested positive for HIV at the medical center in Princeton, New Jersey, where he worked as an otolaryngologist and plastic surgeon, he received numerous phone calls of sympathy within just a few hours from members of the medical staff. Within a few days, he received similar calls from his patients, and, shortly thereafter, his surgical privileges at the medical center were suspended and his practice ruined. Despite his expectation of and request for confidentiality, the medical center took no serious precautions to protect his medical records.[50]

According to one survey of patients, medical students, and house staff about expectations and practices of confidentiality, "patients expect a more rigorous standard of confidentiality than actually exists." Virtually all patients (96%) recognized the common practice of informally discussing patients' cases for second opinions. Most (69%) expected cases to be discussed openly in professional settings to receive other opinions. A majority (51%) expected cases to be discussed in professional settings simply because they were medically interesting, and half of the patients expected cases to be discussed with office nursing staff. However, they did not expect cases to be discussed in other contexts, such as in medical journals, at parties, or with spouses or friends. To take two examples, house staff and medical students reported that cases were frequently discussed with physicians' spouses (57%) and at parties (70%).[51]

Threats to confidentiality emerge in many institutions with a capacity to store and disseminate confidential medical information, such as medical records on file, drugs prescribed, medical tests administered, and reimbursement records. In occupational medicine, computer records in corporations are growing rapidly, and data in these records can be searched. If the company routinely offers medical examinations by a corporate physician, records can be computerized and merged with claims filed by an employee's private physician for reimbursement under corporate insurance policies. Many employees are concerned that this extensive, two-track medical history will be used against them if a question of continued employment arises.

It may be possible to alter current health care practices to approximate more closely the traditional ideal of confidentiality, but a gap will likely remain because of the need for efficient access to information in medicine. In this respect, confidentiality is indeed a decrepit practice in many settings and improving the security of information through technological measures will probably not be adequate to protect all of the interests traditionally protected by rules of confidentiality.

The Nature of Medical Confidentiality

Confidentiality is present when one person discloses information to another, whether through words or other means, and the person to whom the information is disclosed pledges, implicitly or explicitly, not to divulge that information to a third party without the confider's permission. Confidential information is private and voluntarily imparted in confidence and trust. If a patient or research subject authorizes release of the information to others, then no violation of rights of confidentiality occurs, although a loss of confidentiality and privacy occurs.

There exist acknowledged and justifiable exceptions or limits to the kind of information that can be considered confidential in policy and practice. For example, legal rules may set limits to confidentiality, as when they require practitioners to report gunshot wounds and venereal diseases. Some unwanted disclosures of apparently confidential information to third parties may not breach confidentiality because of the context in which the information was originally gathered. For example, IBM physician Martha Nugent informed her employer of her belief that an employee, Robert Bratt, had a problem of paranoia that affected his behavior on the job.[52] Bratt knew that Nugent had been retained by IBM to examine him, but expected conventional medical confidentiality. The company held that the facts disclosed by Nugent were necessary for evaluating Bratt's request for a job transfer and, under law, were a legitimate business communication. In our view, it is a reasonable conclusion that such information is not confidential by the standards of medical confidentiality relevant to this case and that Nugent was not bound by obligations of confidentiality in the same way a private physician would have been.

Contracts calling for such limited disclosures are legitimate as long as employees are aware of, or should be aware of, provisions in the contract. A similar point applies to military physicians who have a dual responsibility—to the soldier as patient and to the military. Nevertheless, the company and the military, along with the physicians in each context, have a moral responsibility to ensure that employees and soldiers understand, at the outset, the conditions under which rules of confidentiality and protections of privacy do and do not apply. The notably complicated institutional rules and forms of infringement of confidentiality in prisons should be no exception.[53]

The Justification of Obligations of Confidentiality

Many of the goods of medicine and research could be realized without rules of confidentiality. On what basis, then, can we justify a system of extensive, often expensive and inefficient, protections of confidentiality? Two types of argument justify (prima facie) rules to protect confidentiality: (1) consequence-based arguments and (2) arguments from autonomy and privacy rights. These arguments also help us determine legitimate exceptions to rules of confidentiality.

Consequence-based arguments. Patients would be reluctant to disclose full and forthright information or authorize a complete examination and a full battery of tests if they could not trust physicians to conceal some information from third parties. Without such information, physicians would not be able to make accurate diagnoses and prognoses or recommend the best course of treatment.

In the precedential *Tarasoff* case, a patient told his therapist about his desire to kill a young woman who had spurned his attention. The therapist alerted the university police but did not warn the intended victim. After the patient killed the young woman, the family brought a suit alleging that the therapist should have warned the intended victim. In this case, the California Supreme Court examined the basis and limits of confidentiality.[54] Both the majority opinion, which affirmed that therapists have an obligation to warn third parties of their patients' threatened violence, and the dissenting opinion, which denied such an obligation, used consequentialist arguments. Their debate hinged on different predictions and assessments of the consequences of a rule that *requires* therapists to breach confidentiality by warning intended victims of a client's threatened violence and a rule that *allows* therapists to breach confidentiality when a member of the public is endangered.

The majority opinion pointed to the victims who would be saved, such as the young woman who had been killed in this case, and contended that a professional's obligation to disclose information to third parties could be justified by the need to protect such potential victims. By contrast, the minority opinion contended that if it were common practice in such cases to override obligations of confidentiality, the fiduciary relation between the patient and the doctor would soon erode and collapse. Patients would lose confidence in psychotherapists and would refrain from disclosing information crucial to effective therapy. As a result, violent assaults would increase because dangerous persons would refuse to seek psychiatric aid or to disclose relevant information, such as their violent fantasies. Hence, the debate about different rules of confidentiality hinges, in part, on empirical claims about which rule more effectively protects the interests of other persons and the interests of patients.

We note that in cases of other legally accepted and mandated exceptions to confidentiality—such as requirements to report contagious diseases, child abuse, and gunshot wounds—no substantial evidence exists that these requirements have either reduced prospective patients' willingness to seek treatment and to cooperate with physicians or significantly impaired the physician–patient relationship.[55] However, one recent study claims that state laws that impose a mandatory duty to warn intended victims of a patient's threatened violence increase the rate of homicides by 5%.[56]

In a consequence-oriented framework, *nonabsolute* rules of confidentiality are attractive and acceptable as long as it is understood that when physicians or other health professionals breach confidentiality, they infringe their patients' rights. Such an infringement will almost always have negative effects for confiders. A physician who breaks confidence cannot ignore the potential for eroding the system of medical confidentiality, trust, and fidelity. In short, an acceptable consequentialist justification for breaching confidentiality must take into account *all* probable consequences, and policymakers must balance the probable benefits and risks of different possible *rules* of confidentiality in light of the best available evidence.

Arguments from autonomy and privacy rights. A second set of arguments to justify rules and rights of confidentiality derives from both the principle of respect for autonomy and rules of privacy. The claim is that rights to exercise autonomy and to protect privacy jointly support rights of confidentiality. Like the first argument, this second argument does not support absolute rules or absolute rights of confidentiality. When rights and rules of confidentiality are used as absolute shields, they can eventuate in outrageous and preventable injuries and harms.[57]

Justified Infringements of Rules of Confidentiality

Infringements of prima facie rules and rights of confidentiality can be justified in some circumstances in which third parties face serious harms. We here concentrate on these situations, but we note that paternalistic breaches of confidentiality in which harms may occur to the patient are also sometimes ethically justifiable.

Assessing and reducing risks to others. In assessing which risks to third parties outweigh rules or rights of confidentiality, the probability that a harm will materialize and the magnitude of that harm must be balanced against the norms of confidentiality and the possible harms that might occur by breaching those norms. The chart of risk assessment introduced on p. 233 supplies the basic categories:

		Magnitude of Harm	
		Major	*Minor*
	High	1	2
Probability of Harm			
	Low	3	4

As a health professional's reasoned assessment of a situation approaches a high probability of a major harm (category 1) to a third party, the weight of the obligation to breach confidentiality increases. As the situation approaches category 4, breaching confidentiality will likely not be justified. Many particularities of the case will determine whether the professional is justified in breaching confidentiality in categories 2 and 3. These particularities include the foreseeability of a harm's occurrence, the preventability of that harm through a health professional's intervention, the harm that will be caused to the patient, and the potential impact of disclosure on policies and laws regarding confidentiality. However, these abstractions are often difficult to operationalize and measurements of probability and magnitude of harm are often imprecise. Accordingly, we now turn to problems of practice.

Disclosure of HIV infection to third parties. Whether physicians and other health care professionals should notify at-risk persons that a patient has tested positive for HIV infection and therefore has the potential to infect others has proved controversial. In one case, after several weeks of dry, persistent coughing and night sweats, a bisexual man visited his family physician, who arranged for a test to determine whether he had antibodies to HIV. The physician informed the patient of a positive test, of the risk of infection for his wife, and of the risk that their children might lose both parents. The patient refused to tell his wife and insisted that the physician maintain strict confidentiality. The physician reluctantly agreed. Only in the last few weeks of his life did the patient allow the physician to inform his wife of the nature of her husband's illness, and a test then showed that she too was antibody-positive for HIV. When symptoms appeared a year later, she angrily—and appropriately—accused the physician of violating his moral responsibilities to her and to her children.[58] This case presents a high probability, under conditions of unprotected sexual intercourse, of a major harm to an identifiable individual, which is the paradigm case of a justified breach of confidentiality.

Many well-grounded reasons support informing spouses and sexual partners that a person has tested positive for exposure to the AIDS virus. For example, if people are at risk of serious harms, and the disclosure is necessary to prevent and probably would prevent the harms (to their spouses or lovers), then disclosure that breaks confidentiality is virtually always justified. Variations on these conditions appear in several statements of professional ethics by medical associations, but ambiguities and gaps in their statements point to the difficulties of precisely specifying the nature, scope, and strength of the clinician's ethical obligation to protect third parties. Guidelines often do not oblige the physician to determine whether the patient has, in fact, carried out a promise to terminate risky conduct or to warn those endangered, and it is not clear how far the physician should go in monitoring compliance, particularly without the patient's consent. One study concludes that it is ineffective to leave partner notification to patients.[59] The AMA's Council on Ethical and Judicial Affairs has proposed a responsible, albeit demanding, strategy: A physician who knows that "an HIV-positive individual poses a significant threat of infecting an identifiable third party...should (a) notify the public health authorities, if required by law; (b) attempt to persuade the infected patient to cease endangering the third party; and (c) if permitted by state law, notify the endangered third party without revealing the identity of the source person."[60]

Some recommendations and guidelines stress the ethical *permissibility* of the physician's disclosure, whereas others focus on its *obligatoriness*. We need not choose between these two assessments because there are circumstances in which it is obligatory to so act, centered on our category 1 in the previous chart, whereas other circumstances render it either permissible to so act or permissible not to so act. These are likely to be cases that fall in categories 2 and 3 that also border on category 1. Assessments of probability and magnitude of harm often do not clearly indicate whether an act of disclosure is obligatory even if it is obviously permitted. The justification for disclosure is the same in both sorts of cases, namely, reduction of a risk of grave injury or death; but levels of risk and the possibility of a physician's effective action will vary from case to case. These justificatory conditions reflect the requirements of constrained balancing that we introduced in Chapter 1.

In conclusion, disclosure to a third party is a morally serious act that challenges a long-standing and central professional obligation of confidentiality,[61] though historically this obligation has only rarely been viewed as absolute in the medical profession.[62] As a matter of public policy, officials need to consider both the critical need to protect innocent, endangered third parties and the impact of flexible or rigid societal rules of confidentiality—for instance, which sorts of rules of confidentiality will save more lives in the long run.

Disclosure of genetic information to third parties. Another ethical problem about notifying at-risk parties arises when physicians, genetic counselors, and others have genetic information about a particular individual that may reveal important information about other family members. Individuals who learn that they have a serious genetic condition may have a moral obligation to share that information with at-risk relatives, who may then be able to take actions to reduce risks to themselves or their offspring or to seek treatment. Health care providers should stress this obligation to their patients or clients. Genetic counselors, in particular, may have to overcome their proclivity for nondirective counseling and seek to persuade counselees to disclose the information, even though in some ways it would be preferable for the counselors to make the disclosure to ensure that adequate information is transmitted about risks and preventive or therapeutic options.

However, directive counseling is different from disclosing the information to relatives against the counselee's explicit directives. With regard to the latter, we concur with the recommendation of the Institute of Medicine Committee on Assessing Genetic Risks that "confidentiality should be breached and relatives informed about genetic risks only when (1) attempts to elicit voluntary disclosure fail, (2) there is a high probability of irreversible or fatal harm to the relative, (3) the disclosure of the information will [likely] prevent the harm, (4) the disclosure is limited to the information necessary for diagnosis or treatment of the relative, and (5) there is no other reasonable way to avert the harm."[63]

This recommendation closely matches our general approach of constrained balancing (see Chapter 1, pp. 22–24): Health care professionals have a prima facie obligation to respect the confidentiality of an individual's personal genetic information, but they also have a right and perhaps an obligation, under some circumstances, to disclose that information to protect others from harm even if the first party objects. Absent consent, the default is nondisclosure to family members at risk. Some critics of this approach propose that we take more seriously the familial nature of genetic information.[64] By analogy with a bank account, they recommend a model of genetic information as a joint account, whereas our approach views it as a personal account. The personal account model fits well with respect for autonomy, confidentiality, maintenance of trust in health care relationships, and good practice in most of health care. In the joint account model, the default is the availability of genetic information to all on the account. The default is followed unless there are good reasons not to do so, such as the probability of serious harm to the individual from whom the genetic information was generated.

The joint account is rooted in considerations of justice and reciprocity-based beneficence. Its premise is that one family member should not be able to benefit from jointly valuable information while excluding others from that information and its benefits. However, if there were to be a transition to this model, it would be morally obligatory to inform users of genetic services, at the point of entry, about the nature and limits of confidentiality, so they can choose whether to proceed. In this regard, the principle of respect for autonomy remains central to an ethically justified use of the joint account model. In our judgment, rather than changing the default regarding the sharing of information with family members, it would be better to educate individuals about their responsibilities to family members who could benefit or avoid harm by access to this genetic information.

FIDELITY

According to Paul Ramsey, the fundamental ethical question in research and health care is, "What is the meaning of the faithfulness of one human being to another?"[65] Few today would agree that fidelity is the fundamental moral norm in health care and research, but it remains a central and often underappreciated moral norm.

The Nature and Place of Fidelity

Obligations of fidelity arise whenever a physician or other health care professional establishes a significant fiduciary relationship with a patient. To establish the relationship is to give an explicit or implicit promise to faithfully carry out or abstain from carrying out an activity. Abandonment of a patient is an example of a breach of fidelity that amounts to disloyalty. Obligations of fidelity can be notably different in research ethics and in clinical ethics, but trustworthiness and loyalty are morally central virtues in both areas of biomedical ethics. Nonetheless, conflicts of fidelity sometimes emerge, creating problems of divided loyalties, and we begin with these conflicts.

Conflicts of fidelity and divided loyalties. Professional fidelity, or loyalty, has been traditionally conceived as giving the patient's interests priority in two respects: (1) the professional effaces self-interest in any situation that may conflict with the patient's interests, and (2) the professional favors the patient's interests over third-party interests. In practice, however, fidelity has never been so pristine. To take one example, caring for patients in epidemics has often been considered praiseworthy and virtuous rather than an obligatory embodiment of fidelity, and physicians have never been expected to care for a great many patients without compensation. Health care professionals also regularly use their clinical skills to serve social purposes beyond the individual patient's interests, such as protection of public health. They may, for instance, recommend vaccination when, in a context of high rates of immunization, its risks would outweigh its benefits to certain patients. Moreover, clinical skills also sometimes serve various non-health-related social activities, such as criminal justice and war, as well as religious and cultural practices, such as male circumcision. Finally, physicians sometimes serve as gatekeepers in society's assignment of certain goods and burdens. Examples include providing psychiatric evaluation as part of a criminal trial and conducting a medical review of a person's disability insurance claims.[66]

Divided loyalties typically occur when fidelity to patients, subjects, or clients conflicts with allegiance to colleagues, institutions, funding agencies, corporations, or the state. Conflicts in dual roles are often intensely felt in such fields as forensic medicine and military medicine. In these conflicts, two or more roles and their coupled loyalties and obligations become incompatible and irreconcilable, forcing a moral choice.[67]

Third-party interests. Physicians, nurses, and hospital administrators sometimes find aspects of their role obligations in conflict with obligations to patients. In some cases, they may have a therapeutic contract with a party other than the patient. When parents bring a child to a physician for treatment, for instance, the physician's primary responsibility is to serve the child's interests, even though the parents made the contract and the physician has obligations of fidelity to the parents. The latter obligations are sometimes validly overridden, as occurs when physicians go to court to oppose parents' decisions that seriously threaten their children. Courts have often allowed adult Jehovah's Witnesses, for example, to reject blood transfusions for themselves, while disallowing parental rejections of medically necessary blood transfusions for their children. Parents are also sometimes appropriately charged with child neglect when they fail to seek or permit potentially beneficial medical treatment recommended by physicians.[68]

Institutional interests. In some types of conflict, it is unclear what the health care professional owes the "patient." Often the institutions involved are not health care institutions, but, in discharging their functions, they may need medical information about individuals and may even provide some care for those individuals. Examples include a physician's contract to provide medical examinations of applicants for positions in a company or to determine whether applicants for insurance policies are safe risks. In some circumstances the health care professional may rightly not regard the person examined as his or her patient, but, even so, the professional still has certain moral responsibilities of due care, such as disclosure of serious risks ascertained through the medical examination.

In some jurisdictions the health care professional does not have a legal obligation to disclose the discovery of a risk or of a disease to the examinee. However, nondisclosure is a morally dubious practice. At a minimum, health care professionals have a moral responsibility to oppose, avoid, and withdraw from contracts that would require them to withhold vital health information from examinees. Physicians often have "due care" obligations to individuals who become their patients under a third-party contract in an institutional arrangement. Examples include industries, prisons, the armed services, and professional sports teams.[69]

Nevertheless, when care of an individual conflicts with institutional objectives and policies to which a health professional is also committed, the individual's needs do not always take precedence. For example, the military physician must accept a different set of obligations than the nonmilitary physician—in particular, to place the military's interests above both the patient's and the physician's interests. The military physician may face a genuine moral dilemma in determining whether to certify a soldier suffering from a closed-head injury, resulting from an improvised explosive device, as fit to return to the front lines. On the one hand, the soldier, while medically stable and functional, continues to experience fatigue, problems in sleeping, and daily headaches and he would be at increased risk of worse impairments and posttraumatic stress syndrome if a similar incident occurred. On the other hand, his commanding officers have indicated their strong need for his particular expertise and experience.[70] Apart from such dilemmas, some actions so grossly violate canons of medical ethics that they warrant disobedience of orders and defiance of superiors, rather than loyalty and compliance. An example is a commander's order for a physician to help torture a prisoner of war.[71]

Medical assistance in prisons also presents moral problems, in part because of the institutional mandate to punish the criminal, which limits the obligations of fidelity to the criminal as patient. Medical values are sometimes subordinated to the correctional institution's functions, and yet the physician is expected to be loyal to both. The correctional institution may expect physicians and other health care professionals to participate in the administration of justice and punishment. Examples include surgical removal of a bullet for evidence when the bullet is not a hazard to the inmate and can be safely left in place, forced examinations of inmates' body cavities for evidence of contraband drugs, and participation in corporal or capital punishment—for instance, by administering a lethal injection.[72] Moral questions also arise both about medical assessments of prisoners' physical conditions in order to determine whether they can endure punishments and about medical monitoring of prisoners during punishment. Such medical assessments and supervision can reduce the likelihood of extreme or unintended injury, but participation in the actual administration of punishment, whether corporal or capital, represents a compromise of fidelity.[73]

Nursing. Nursing may be the area of health care with the most pervasive conflicts. Codes of nursing ethics in the latter part of the twentieth century began to frame the moral responsibility of nurses in different ways than earlier codes that had discouraged nurses from making their own moral judgments. In 1950, the first code of the American Nurses' Association stressed the nurse's obligation to carry out the physician's orders, whereas the 1976 revision and subsequent revisions stress the nurse's obligation to the client and the obligation to safeguard both the client and the public from the "incompetent, unethical or illegal" practices of any person.

Moral problems can be expected wherever one group of professionals makes the decisions and orders their implementation by other professionals who have not participated in the decision making. In one study of relationships in health care, investigators examined different perceptions of ethical problems by nurses and doctors in acute care units. In structured interviews, both nurses and physicians said they frequently encountered ethical problems. Most physicians (twenty-one of twenty-four) and most nurses (twenty-five of twenty-six) recognized ethical conflicts within the health care team. In twenty-one of the twenty-five cases reported by nurses, the ethical conflict was between a nurse and a physician, whereas only one physician reported a conflict with a nurse rather than with another physician. The authors of the study conclude that it is likely that conflicts with nurses occurred, but that the physicians "were not aware of them, or did not see conflict with a nurse as forming an *ethical* problem."[74] Several features of the working relationship between physicians and nurses may explain these findings. Physicians write orders and nurses execute them. Given their close relationships with patients, nurses often experience the problems that arise from medical decisions more immediately and fully than physicians.

According to another study of physicians and registered nurses caring for dying patients in intensive care units, the nurses experienced greater moral distress, perceived their ethical environment more negatively, expressed less satisfaction with the quality of care, and experienced less collaboration than the physicians reported. As a solution, the researchers rightly propose not only improving collaboration, but also paying explicit attention to situations that generate moral distress and to differences in role perspectives.[75]

Conflicts of Interest

Over the last several years, traditional rules of fidelity have often been threatened or weakened by conflicts of interest, a fairly recent concern in medicine (and biomedical ethics) in contrast to other professions such as law. A conflict of interest exists when an impartial observer would determine that a professional's judgments, decisions, or actions are at risk of being unduly influenced by his or her personal interests, such as financial interests or friendship.[76] The risk is that the professional's personal interests will create temptations, biases, and the like that will lead to a breach of role responsibilities through judgments, decisions, and actions other than those reasonably expected in the role. The reasonable expectation is that clinicians will seek the patient's welfare and respect his or her rights, that researchers will pursue objective and valid results, and so forth. A conflict of interest poses a risk that the professional in question will compromise these expectations and thereby damage patients' interests and rights, distort research, or teach trainees in a biased way.

The analysis and assessment of the risk of different types of conflict of interest follow the risk chart introduced earlier. The degree or level of risk depends on (1) the probability that the professional's personal interests will have an undue influence on his or her judgments, decisions, or actions, and (2) the magnitude of harm that may occur as a result. Even if the circumstance of conflict does not in fact bias the individual's judgment, and even if no wrong is committed, it is still a conflict-of-interest situation that makes it reasonable to expect that tainted judgments might occur and to require that they be disclosed, mitigated, managed, or avoided altogether.

Conflicts of interest occur in medicine, health care, biomedical research, the development of clinical practice standards, and the review of grant proposals and articles submitted for publication in all of these fields. Although the medical profession has not paid adequate attention to nonfinancial conflicts, such as professional advancement or friendship, which are no less important, numerous efforts are under way to address various financial conflicts, including fee splitting, self-referring, accepting gifts, accepting fees for recruiting patients for a research protocol, outside consulting with a regulated industry by government-employed physicians, appointing industry-based physicians to government regulatory agencies, and industry-paid lecturing on an industry product.

One important issue, among others, is the referral of patients to medical facilities or services physicians own or in which they have a financial investment. Self-referral threatens fidelity to patients' interests by enlarging the temptation inherent in fee-for-service to provide unnecessary or excessively expensive care. Physicians create these financial conflicts of interest by owning or investing in medical facilities or services, such as diagnostic imaging centers, laboratories, or physical therapy services, to which they refer patients. Physician ownership of radiation therapy and physical therapy services, for instance, can substantially increase use and costs, without compensatory benefits such as increased access.[77] Self-referral is usually more problematic than fee-for-service because the patient typically cannot identify the physician's potential economic gain—unless it is explicitly disclosed—in ordering additional procedures and thus cannot proceed cautiously, perhaps by seeking a second opinion. Although disclosure is not a common practice, physicians do have an ethical obligation to disclose both economic and noneconomic conflicts of interest. Fidelity and honesty require such disclosure as an ethical minimum, even though disclosure is rarely sufficient. For instance, it is unclear how a vulnerable patient can effectively use this information in the context of self-referral. In addition, legal or professional prohibition of self-referral is warranted in many types of cases.[78]

Third-party payers and institutional providers have imposed many constraints on medical decisions about diagnostic and therapeutic procedures through mechanisms designed to control costs. These mechanisms sometimes limit and constrict the physician's fidelity to the patient through incentives and disincentives that can place the physician's self-interest in conflict with the patient's best medical interest. For example, health maintenance organizations (HMOs) often withhold a substantial part of the primary physician's income. At the end of the year, they return part or all, depending on the overall financial condition of the HMO and, in some cases, the physician's productivity and frugality. This arrangement creates an incentive for physicians to severely limit expensive procedures—a worrisome conflict of interest. The patient is in a markedly different position when the physician has a conflict because of incentives to *restrict* needed treatment than when the physician has a conflict because of incentives to provide *unnecessary* treatment. In the latter situation, patients often can obtain another opinion. In the former situation, patients may not be aware of a needed treatment.[79] Both are ethically unacceptable, at least when the incentives are likely to influence treatment decisions, and both require corrective measures.

Financial incentive structures such as those used in many diagnostic laboratories also create a motive for physicians to limit both their time and expensive procedures. Physicians are paid by measurable output and annual payments are tied to productivity (e.g., number of slides read). However, a rapid reading of data adds risk of error, substantially increasing risks of false-negative results and misdiagnosis. Pathologists who read hundreds of slides per day looking for the presence of carcinoma will substantially increase their salary, but also will increase the likelihood of failing to detect a carcinoma. Every physician will occasionally make some mistake or follow an incorrect, yet excusable, strategy, but it is not morally excusable to make mistakes where there is an inherent conflict of interest encouraging behavior that falls below an appropriate standard of due care.

Another set of conflicts of interest arises from gifts from pharmaceutical and medical device manufacturers. In contrast to a widespread assumption that only large gifts create conflicts of interest, there is evidence that even small gifts, such as pens, note pads, and lunches, intended to build and maintain relationships influence physicians' prescribing behavior.[80] Moreover, gift relationships, however small, create a variety of temptations, dependencies, friendships, and forms of indebtedness—all of which stand to create conflicts of interest with the physician's primary obligation to act in the best interest of the patients.[81] Although disclosure to patients may help to reduce the negative impact of several forms of conflict of interest, it appears to be relatively useless for conflicts of interest created by industry gifts to physicians. More stringent regulations by institutions, including academic medical centers, are needed to eliminate or modify common practices in the interactions between, for example, industries and physicians. These institutional rules could include, for example, banning gifts, not accepting funds for lunches at educational programs, and reducing the practice of accepting free samples.[82]

Conflicts of interest reach beyond practice to research. Interactions and partnerships involving industry, government, and the academy are vitally important in the development, support, and conduct of biomedical research to benefit human health, and yet they not infrequently generate conflicts of interest.[83] For instance, clinical trials of pharmaceutical products are often funded by companies willing to assume the financial risk because the returns from successful trials are the life-blood of the company. The joint financial advantages for physician-investigators and corporations promote a relationship that may ensure a steady and reliable funding stream. This relationship risks creating a motive for physician-investigators to find positive results or downplay negative results, thereby compromising scientific objectivity. It is therefore vital to control the process of interpretation and assessment through objective procedures, back-up checks, and independent controls such as data safety and monitoring boards.[84]

Journals should require researchers to provide information about sources of funds for the research. Furthermore, as an Institute of Medicine report recommended, researchers should not conduct research involving human subjects if they have a significant financial stake in the outcome of that research. For example, a researcher might hold a patent on a product being tested in a clinical trial. There can, however, be good reasons to make exceptions in rare circumstances such as when an institutional conflict-of-interest committee determines that an individual's participation is essential for the safety or validity of the research (perhaps because of the complexity of the procedure or device that the researcher developed) and that it is possible to manage the conflict and ensure the integrity of the research.[85]

Deliberative assessments need to be made regarding ways to address these various types of conflict of interest. For example, we might eliminate them, manage or mitigate them, or require disclosure of conflicts to alert parties at risk. Each strategy is justifiable in some contexts, and each is preferable to the traditional convention of relying on professional or personal character to determine whether a conflict is *actual, potential,* or *merely apparent*—a dubious set of distinctions since the potential or merely apparent conflict often constitutes a real conflict-of-interest situation. Professionals sometimes view attempts to address conflicts of interest as negative judgments on their and their colleagues' character, as though they might be corrupt and might act against the reasonable expectations of their professional roles in the pursuit of personal self-interest. However, this assessment misses the point of conflict-of-interest rules. Unconscious and unintentional distortions of professional judgments, decisions, and actions are usually the chief concern. It is impossible to do individualized assessments of the likelihood that any particular professional's conflicts of interest will lead to a breach of professional expectations; accordingly, general rules and regulations are essential.

CLINICAL ETHICS AND RESEARCH ETHICS

Now that we have completed our examination of rules of veracity, privacy, confidentiality, and fidelity, we turn to other dimensions of relationships between professionals and their patients or subjects, starting with a basic distinction between clinical research and clinical medicine and how this distinction affects our thinking about professional ethics.

Biomedical ethics has long drawn a line between clinical (medical or nursing) ethics and research ethics. This view rests on a distinction between clinical practice and clinical research, a distinction that still deeply influences how we conceptualize areas of medicine and biomedical science and how we understand ethical rules appropriate to them. The research–practice distinction also affects how we think about activities that are subject to governmental regulation. Research has been heavily regulated because it has been thought to place subjects at risk for the benefit of others and to investigate unconfirmed hypotheses about diagnoses and treatments. By contrast, medical practice is minimally regulated on grounds that it focuses on the patient's best interests and relies on interventions of proven benefit and acceptable risk.

This distinction determines which activities must undergo committee review for the protection of human subjects of research. The general rule is that if there is a component of research that introduces risk in an activity involving a human person, it must undergo review to protect subjects. Nothing comparable exists at the national level in most countries for medical practice. But is this sharp distinction between research and practice, as well as the parallel differences in ethics and regulation, truly warranted? Why, morally, should practice be treated so differently from research when it comes to the protection of patients?

The conventional assessment has been that research lacks a focus on personalized care. Its distinctive objective is scientifically designed testing of a hypothesis aimed at developing or contributing to what U.S. regulations—and the bioethics literature generally—refer to as "generalizable knowledge."[86]

By contrast, medical practice interventions are aimed at diagnosis, preventive treatment, or therapy that stands to provide optimal therapeutic benefit to each patient. Also, in clinical medicine, risks are justified by an intervention's potential benefit to the individual patient, whereas in clinical research, risks are usually justified by the potential social benefit of the research (sometimes combined with a possible benefit to the patient). Risk allocation in the clinic and in research, in this conception, sharply differ. These differences have supported the view that clinical research and clinical practice require different ethical rules, in accordance with the different objectives, roles, and relationships that characterize each. Accordingly, there are distinct particular moralities—clinical ethics and research ethics—each with its own system of moral norms.[87]

This entrenched distinction between research and practice is both puzzling and morally questionable. First, the boundaries between research and practice are often porous, especially when the two occur together in the same health care institution(s), and each one contributes to the other. A good example is pediatric oncology and its remarkable practical successes in treatment in recent decades. In this field of medicine, the research basically is the practice, and the practice is not divorced from new infusions of data from research. Second, large parts of medicine use innovative techniques or practices that have never been scientifically validated through research and lack regulatory approval for these uses. These practices are often regarded, rightly, as experimental, which suggests that patients so treated are actually subjects of research.

Innovative treatments, including off-label uses of treatments (i.e., uses of prescription drugs to treat conditions for which the drug has not been approved), fall well short of the high validation standards set by randomized clinical trials. Although the range of acceptable methods of obtaining knowledge in medicine is controversial, it is morally unsatisfactory to allow physicians to use treatments that are either new or unapproved on grounds that the patient–physician relationship is a private transaction immune from regulatory interference and unaccountable to external oversight, such as a review committee. Yet many parts of medical practice conform to this model. In general, there is no reason to think that well-designed research is riskier than forms of practice based on innovative therapies.

Accordingly, we need to ask whether we have a coherent moral conception of the ethical oversight of research and practice. The central issue is whether research projects require a higher level of scrutiny. There is an argument that if the risks are similar and the need for consent to interventions is similar, the oversight system should be relevantly similar, regardless of the conventional categorizations of research and clinical practice. The time is now ripe for a closer and more thorough examination of these categories and distinctions in biomedical ethics and public policy.

Whatever the level of scrutiny and oversight of these activities, the dual roles of clinician and investigator generate possible conflicts of obligation and of interest that require attention.

The Dual Roles of Clinician and Investigator

The Physician's Oath of the World Medical Association affirms that "the health of my patient will be my first consideration."[88] But can research involving patients and other subjects or participants consistently honor this obligation? The dual roles of research scientist and clinical practitioner pull in different directions, potentially creating significant conflicts of obligation and of interest. As an investigator, the physician acts to generate scientific knowledge to benefit individual patients and populations, usually in the future. As a clinician, the physician has the responsibility to act in the best interests of present patients. Accordingly, responsibilities to future generations may conflict with due care for current patients who become research subjects.

Research involving human subjects is a vital social enterprise, but it is morally problematic when it exposes subjects to significant risk for the advancement of science. Ethically justified research must satisfy several conditions, including (1) a goal of valuable knowledge, (2) a reasonable prospect that the research will generate the knowledge that is sought, (3) the necessity of using human subjects, (4) a favorable balance of potential benefits over risks to the subjects, (5) fair selection of subjects, and (6) measures to protect privacy and confidentiality. Only if these conditions have been met is it appropriate to invite potential subjects (or their surrogates) to give their informed consent or refusal to participate; consent can be considered a seventh condition.[89]

These conditions apply to both research that offers no prospect of direct medical benefit to the subject and research that offers some prospect of direct medical benefit to the patient-subject and that may be conducted during the course of the care of the patient. The term *therapeutic research* is potentially misleading because, when misunderstood, it draws attention away from the fact that research is being conducted. Clinical research is distinguishable from both routine therapy and experimental or innovative therapy, which are directed at particular patients. Attaching the term *therapeutic* to research may create a "therapeutic misconception," in which participants construe the protocol design as therapy directed at the individual rather than as research designed to generate generalizable knowledge.

Because society encourages and supports extensive research and because investigators and subjects are unequal in knowledge and vulnerability, public policy and review committees are responsible for ensuring that the research meets these several conditions. Some cases warrant a straightforward paternalistic decision. For example, if healthy persons free of heart disease volunteer to participate in a research protocol to test an artificial heart, as once happened,[90] an institutional review board (IRB) should declare that the risk relative to benefit for a healthy subject is too substantial to permit the research. Of course, the risk relative to benefit for a patient with a seriously diseased heart may be acceptable.

Conflicts in Clinical Trials

Controlled clinical trials are often essential to establish or confirm that an observed effect, such as reduced mortality from a disease, results from a particular intervention rather than from an unknown variable in the patient population. The evidence supporting many available treatments is tenuous, and some may have never been adequately tested for either safety or efficacy.[91] Even if adequate testing at one time occurred, the treatments may no longer be as safe or as efficacious as new treatments—a matter of comparative effectiveness. If doubt surrounds the efficacy or safety of a treatment, or its relative merits in comparison to another treatment, scientific research aimed at resolving the doubt is in order.

Controlled trials are scientific instruments intended to protect current and future patients against medical enthusiasm, hunches, and outdated procedures and products. In this research, one group receives the investigational (or experimental) therapy, while a "control group" receives either a standard therapy or a placebo (an inert preparation that resembles a drug in appearance) so that investigators can determine whether an investigational therapy is more effective and safer than a standard therapy, placebo, or no treatment. Commonly, subjects are randomly assigned to either control or investigational groups to avoid intentional or unintentional bias. Randomization is designed to keep variables other than the treatments under examination from distorting study results.

Blinding certain persons to some information about the randomized controlled trial (RCT) provides additional protection against bias. An RCT may be single-blind (the subject does not know whether he or she is in the control group or the experimental group), double-blind (neither the subject nor the investigator knows), or unblinded (all parties know). Double-blind studies are designed to reduce bias in observations and interpretations by subjects, physicians, and investigators. Blinding the physician-investigator also serves an ethical function, because it partially obviates the conflicts of obligation and of interest that arise for physicians who are simultaneously engaged in clinical practice and research with the same patient(s).

Problems of consent. By design, subjects in RCTs usually do not know which treatment or placebo they will receive. However, no justification exists for not disclosing to potential subjects the full set of methods, treatments, and placebos (if any) that will be used, their known risks and probable benefits, and any known uncertainties. Likewise, no justification exists for failing to disclose the rationale for the study, the fact of randomization, how the trial differs from clinical practice, and available alternatives to participation. Any physician-researcher with dual responsibilities also has a fiduciary obligation to inform patient-subjects of any relevant conflicts of interest.[92] With this information, potential subjects should have an adequate basis for deciding whether to participate.

In conventional RCTs, investigators screen patients for eligibility and then provide the information just noted. If a patient consents to participate, he or she is then randomized to one arm of the study. However, even in cases in which scientific evidence indicates that two proposed interventions are roughly equal in safety and efficacy, patients may have a strong preference for one over another. Consider a situation in which two surgical procedures for treating the same disease appear to have the same survival rate (say, an average of fifteen years) and we want to test their effectiveness by an RCT. A patient might have a preference if treatment A has little risk of death during the operation but a high rate of death after ten years, and treatment B has a high risk of death during the operation or postoperative recovery but a low rate of death after recovery (say, for thirty years). A patient's age, family responsibilities, and other circumstances might be factors leading to a preference for one over the other. Accordingly, some patients may choose not to enter a particular RCT even though, from the standpoint of safety and efficacy, the different arms are in clinical equipoise—our next topic of discussion.

The problem of clinical equipoise. Serving the patient's best interests intuitively is inconsistent with assigning a treatment randomly to promote social goals of accumulating knowledge and benefiting future patients. It hardly seems conceivable that optimal medical care occurs by random selection of an intervention or no intervention. No two patients are alike, and a physician should be able to select and modify the course of therapy, as needed, to promote the patient's best interests. Is this traditional axiom of medical ethics consistent with RCTs?

Proponents argue that RCTs do not violate moral obligations to patients because they are used only in circumstances in which justifiable doubt exists about the relative merits of existing, standard, and new therapies. No one knows, prior to conducting the research, whether it is more advantageous to be in the control group or in the experimental group. The community of reasonable physicians is therefore in a state of "clinical equipoise."[93] On the basis of the available evidence, members of the relevant expert medical community are uncertain about which intervention is superior and so are equally poised between the treatment strategies under examination in the RCT. That is, they are equally uncertain about, and equally comfortable with, the known advantages and disadvantages of the investigational treatment to be tested and the current treatment, placebo, or no treatment the control group will receive. No patient, then, will receive something known to be less effective or to have a higher risk than an available alternative.

When patients are not asked to forgo a superior treatment, the use of RCTs is justifiable, especially in light of the promise of benefit to future patients. In the absence of scientific grounds before the trial for preferring to be in one group rather than another, a patient may prefer one over the other on the basis of hunches or intuitions about effectiveness and safety or on the basis of factors not being studied in the trial. If two treatments for breast cancer, for example, are in veritable clinical equipoise from the standpoint of survival, a woman still may prefer the less disfiguring treatment.

Some critics of appeals to clinical equipoise as a way of establishing the moral legitimacy of clinical trials are concerned about an excessively narrow focus on the ethics of the clinical physician's role, chiefly on whether RCTs are consistent with physician duties in the physician–patient relationship. This approach, critics maintain, neglects society's considerable interest in evidence-based health policy and advances in scientific understanding needed for drug approval and coverage decisions.[94] This claim about the general justification of RCTs offers a fair warning about the need to avoid an unduly narrow focus, but it does not negate the need to investigate ethical conflicts in clinical trials, which is our focus in this section. Clinical equipoise is an important threshold condition that must be met in the conduct of RCTs, even though it is not a sufficient condition of the moral legitimacy of RCTs and is not by itself an adequate guide to social policy regarding RCTs. Whether particular RCTs do in fact satisfy this threshold condition is understandably debated, as are reasons for social policies governing research.[95]

Finally, if a cooperating physician strongly believes prior to a trial that one therapy is more beneficial or safer, he or she will have to decide whether to suspend this belief in the interests of scientific objectivity and in deference to the views of the community of experts, who find themselves in clinical equipoise. In this circumstance, the physician is obligated to disclose as part of the informed consent process both his or her personal conviction and that of the relevant community of experts to patients who are potential candidates for the trial.[96]

The problem of placebo controls. Conducting placebo-controlled and no-treatment trials is controversial, especially when an established and effective treatment exists for the condition under investigation. Some argue that the use of placebo controls is unethical because placebo-controlled trials may not be methodologically superior and patients are being denied treatment when treatment controls (a group that receives an established effective intervention, called *active controls* in the literature) could be used.[97] Opponents of this view claim that placebo-controlled trials are methodologically superior to active controlled trials and are frequently essential in the process of scientific validation.[98] Fortunately, all parties agree that use of a placebo is ethically acceptable only if there is a reasonable prospect of producing scientifically valid information by this method. As best we can determine, placebo-controlled trials are often methodologically superior to, more efficient than, and less costly than active controlled trials. They can even be necessary to distinguish treatment effects. Nonetheless, there are moral problems with their use. The best strategy in addressing this controversy is to locate the conditions under which placebo use is ethically acceptable and the conditions under which it is unacceptable.

As a start, if an established effective intervention is available for use in the population to be studied, using a placebo control is unethical if withholding the effective intervention from subjects has a significant probability of being life-threatening, of causing permanent damage, of causing irreversible disease progression, or of causing an unacceptable level of pain or suffering. Placebo use is impermissible under these conditions because the risks of the research are either too high, exceeding a threshold, or the benefits do not outweigh the risks.

By contrast, if an established effective intervention is not available for the treatment of the medical problem under study, the use of a placebo is permissible in the course of research on a new investigational therapy if the relevant expert community has significant doubts about the benefits provided by approved available treatments or if many patients cannot use the available treatment(s) because of their medical condition. Ethical acceptability may also be contingent on other conditions. For example, patients may have refused an established effective treatment when withholding that treatment will not cause serious or irreversible harm. Under these conditions, use of a placebo may be justified.

In a now classic case of a questionable use of placebo, a conflict erupted over placebo-controlled trials of AZT (azidothymidine) in the treatment of AIDS. Promising laboratory tests led to a trial (phase I) to determine the safety of AZT among patients with AIDS. Several patients showed clinical improvement. Because AIDS was then considered invariably fatal, many people argued that compassion dictated making it immediately available to all patients with AIDS and, perhaps, to those who were antibody-positive to the AIDS virus. However, the pharmaceutical company (Burroughs Wellcome Company, later GlaxoSmithKline) did not have an adequate supply of the drug to satisfy this plan, and, as required by federal regulations, it used a placebo-controlled trial of AZT to determine its effectiveness for certain groups of patients with AIDS. A computer randomly assigned some patients to AZT and others to a placebo. For several months, no major differences emerged in effectiveness, but then patients receiving the placebo began to die at a significantly higher rate. Of the 137 patients on the placebo, 16 died. Of the 145 patients on AZT, only 1 died.[99] Many moral problems surround starting such a placebo-controlled trial when a disease appears to be universally fatal and no promising alternative to the new treatment exists. There are related questions about when to stop a trial, as well as how to distribute a new treatment.

A second example comes from RCTs in surgery, which are rare (particularly when placebos are used). There are concerns that surgical procedures are too easily introduced without sufficiently rigorous evidence of their efficacy or safety. In one case, surgical researchers sought a clinical trial to determine whether transplanting fetal neural tissue into the brains of patients with Parkinson's disease (a disorder of motor function, marked by tremor, rigidity, unsteady walking, and unstable posture) would be safe and effective. Standard medical treatment consisted of levodopa, which might not restore lost motor function, might have adverse effects over a long period, and might not adequately control new manifestations of the disease. Researchers argued that surgical therapy using cells is more like the administration of pharmaceutical agents than like conventional surgical procedures. In proposing a randomized, double-blind, placebo-controlled trial, they maintained that a placebo control was scientifically preferable to the use of standard medical treatment as the control because surgery itself may have some effects, such as evoking patients' favorable subjective responses. The placebo consisted of sham surgery, that is, the administration of general anesthesia followed by bilateral surgery, a skin incision with a partial burr hole that does not penetrate the skull's inner cortex. This sham surgery was to be compared to two other procedures that differed from each other only in the amount of fetal tissue transplanted. The thirty-six subjects in this study all knew that twelve of them would undergo sham surgery and researchers promised all of them free access to the real surgery if the trial demonstrated its net benefits.

The argument against the use of sham surgery as a placebo control in this research is that risks from the procedure and the anesthesia are substantial. In this trial the best research design, from the standpoints of both the investigators involved and future patients, conflicted with investigators' obligations of beneficence and nonmaleficence to current patients invited to serve as research subjects. The ethical question that arises is whether the patient-subjects' informed consent was sufficient to justify proceeding with the research.[100] It is doubtful that informed consent is sufficient by itself in such cases; consent should be considered together with the level of risk involved, the need to reduce bias by blinding participants, the alternatives that might obviate the need for sham surgery, and the like.

Nonetheless, if we assume that other conditions for ethically justified research are met, genuinely informed consents go a long way to justify the conduct of placebo-controlled trials when prospective subjects are informed about the following: that a placebo will be used, that they could be randomized to a placebo arm, the reasons why using a placebo is part of the design, the benefits of already available treatments, the risks of refusing those treatments, the option of receiving the treatment if symptoms worsen, and the right to withdraw for any reason and at any time from the study. Disclosure of these items is a necessary condition of a truly informed consent in this context, but even an elevated informed consent does not always justify use of placebo-controlled trials.

Early Termination of and Withdrawal from Clinical Trials

Physician-researchers sometimes face difficult questions about whether to stop a clinical trial before its planned completion—particularly whether to withdraw patient-subjects from the trial before sufficient scientific data are available to support definitive conclusions. Access to data is limited during clinical trials to protect the integrity of the research. Consequently, physicians may be excluded from access to critical information about trends. If they were aware of trends prior to the point of statistical significance, they might pull their patients from the trial, and several withdrawals might invalidate the research.

However, if a physician determines that a particular patient's condition is deteriorating and that this patient's interests dictate withdrawal from the research, the physician morally must be free to act on behalf of the patient and recommend withdrawal. In an RCT, it may be agonizingly difficult to determine whether the research as a whole should be stopped, even if some physician-researchers are satisfied by what they have observed. One procedural solution is to differentiate roles, distinguishing between the responsibilities of individual physicians who must make decisions regarding their own patients and those of a data and safety monitoring board (DSMB) established to determine whether to continue or stop a trial. Unlike physicians, the DSMB is charged to consider the impact of its decision on future patients, as well as on current patient-subjects. One of its functions is to stop a trial if accumulated scientific data indicate that uncertainty has been reduced and equipoise no longer prevails,[101] as happened in the original AZT trial for AIDS. In order to ensure the integrity of the clinical trial, the DSMB needs to be independent of the investigators and sponsors and able to make objective, impartial analyses, judgments, and recommendations.[102]

This differentiation of roles by using a DSMB is procedurally sound, but it relocates, rather than resolves, some ethical questions. The DSMB must determine if it is legitimate to impose or to continue to impose risks on current patients in order to establish a higher degree of probability of the superiority of one treatment over another. It will likely decide that clinical equipoise must have been disturbed (i.e., eradicated) from the perspective of impartial observers in the expert medical community.[103] However, the individual physician and his or her patient will be primarily concerned with whether clinical uncertainty (and equipoise) has been eliminated or substantially reduced *for them.*

Many questions are relevant to a patient-subject's decision to withdraw from an RCT based on such information, including questions about interim data and early trends. Trends are often misleading and sometimes prove to be temporary aberrations. However, they might be relevant at a given point to a patient-subject's decision about whether to continue to participate, despite the fact that the evidence would not satisfy statisticians or the expert medical community. If information about trends is not to be released prior to the completion or early termination of the RCT, potential subjects need to be informed of this rule and accept it as a condition of participation.

Justifying Conditions for Randomized Clinical Trials

Despite the several problems we have identified, RCTs can be justified—including those involving placebo controls—if they satisfy the following seven substantive and procedural conditions (in addition to the general conditions of justified research previously identified):[104]

1. Clinical equipoise genuinely exists in the community of relevant and impartial medical experts.
2. The trial is designed as a crucial experiment to determine whether an investigational therapeutic alternative is superior to available alternatives and shows scientific promise of achieving this result.
3. An IRB or its functional equivalent has approved the protocol and the IRB or its functional equivalent has certified that no physician has a conflict of interest or incentive that would threaten either the patient–physician relationship or impartiality in the conduct of research.
4. Patient-subjects have given a genuinely informed consent, as we analyze this concept in Chapter 4.
5. Placebos and no-treatment options cannot be used if an effective treatment exists for the condition being studied and that condition threatens death, grave injury, or serious morbidity.
6. A data and safety monitoring board either will end the trial if statistically significant data displace clinical equipoise or will supply physicians and patients with substantive safety and therapeutic information that has emerged and is relevant to a reasonable person's decision to remain in or to withdraw from the trial.
7. Physicians have the right to recommend withdrawal and patients have the right to withdraw at any time.

CONCLUSION

In this chapter we have interpreted and specified the principles of respect for autonomy, nonmaleficence, beneficence, and justice, as analyzed in the previous four chapters. We have concentrated on obligations of veracity, privacy, confidentiality, and fidelity, and we have explored the basis, meaning, limits, and stringency of these obligations in the context of professional–patient or professional–subject relationships—and in some cases professional–professional relationships, such as those between physicians and nurses.

We now conclude our discussion, in Part II of this volume, of the four clusters of principles of biomedical ethics, the rules derivative from those principles, and their implications for professional ethics. In the final two chapters, in Part III, we turn to an examination of ethical theory and method in ethics.

NOTES

1.   We use the term *patient* in the title of this chapter although, in many of the relationships we discuss, *patient* is not the most accurate term. We make clarifications and qualifications as the chapter proceeds.

2.   *Current Opinions of the Judicial Council of the American Medical Association* (Chicago: AMA, 1981), p. ix; *Code of Medical Ethics of the American Medical Association, 2010–2011 Edition* (Chicago: AMA, 2010), p. xvii. For the original 1847 code, see American Medical Association, *Code of Medical Ethics* (Chicago: AMA, 1847), p. 88, available at http://www.ama-assn.org/resourdes/doc/ethics/1847code.pdf (accessed January 10, 2012).

3.   Annette C. Baier, "Why Honesty Is a Hard Virtue," *Reflections on How We Live* (Oxford: Oxford University Press, 2010), p. 109.

4.   Henry Sidgwick, *The Methods of Ethics,* 7th ed. (Indianapolis, IN: Hackett, 1907), pp. 315–16. Baier examines honesty from a background of Hume's thought, while Alasdair MacIntyre examines lying in reaction to Kant's and Mill's thought. See Baier, "Why Honesty Is a Hard Virtue"; and MacIntyre, *Ethics and Politics, Selected Essays,* vol. 2 (Cambridge: Cambridge University Press, 2006), chap. 6 (on Mill) and chap. 7 (on Kant).

5.   G. J. Warnock, *The Object of Morality* (London: Methuen, 1971), p. 85.

6.   See, for example, W. D. Ross, *The Right and the Good* (Oxford: Clarendon, 1930), chap. 2.

7.   Cf. Raanan Gillon, "Is There an Important Moral Distinction for Medical Ethics Between Lying and Other Forms of Deception?" *Journal of Medical Ethics* 19 (1993): 131–32; and Jennifer Jackson, *Truth, Trust, and Medicine* (London: Routledge, 2001).

8.   On different sociocultural contexts of nondisclosure and the need in health care for what is often called "cultural competence," see Antonella Surbone, "Telling the Truth to Patients with Cancer: What Is the Truth?" *Lancet Oncology* 7 (2006): 944–50. See further Loretta M. Kopelman, "Multiculturalism and Truthfulness: Negotiating Difference by Finding Similarities," *South African Journal of Philosophy* 19 (2000): 51–55.

9.   Bettina Schöne-Seifert and James F. Childress, "How Much Should the Cancer Patient Know and Decide?" *CA—A Cancer Journal for Physicians* 36 (1986): 85–94.

10.   See Donald Oken, "What to Tell Cancer Patients: A Study of Medical Attitudes," *JAMA: Journal of the American Medical Association* 175 (1961): 1120–28; and Dennis H. Novack et al., "Changes in Physicians' Attitudes Toward Telling the Cancer Patient," *JAMA: Journal of the American Medical Association* 241 (March 2, 1979): 897–900.

11.   N. Horikawa, T. Yamazaki, M. Sagawa, and T. Nagata, "Changes in Disclosure of Information to Cancer Patients in a General Hospital in Japan," *General Hospital Psychiatry* 22 (2000): 37–42; see similar results in T. S. Elwyn, M. D. Fetters, W. Gorenflo, and T. Tsuda, "Cancer Disclosure in Japan: Historical Comparisons, Current Practices," *Social Science and Medicine* 46 (May 1998): 1151–63; and a follow-up study by N. Horikawa, T. Yamazaki, M. Sagawa, and T. Nagata, "The Disclosure of Information to Cancer Patients and Its Relationship to Their Mental State in a Consultation-Liaison Psychiatry Setting in Japan," *General Hospital Psychiatry* 21 (September–October 1999): 368–73.

12.   Elisa J. Gordon and Christopher K. Daugherty, "'Hitting You over the Head': Oncologists' Disclosure of Prognosis to Advanced Cancer Patients," *Bioethics* 17 (2003): 142–68.

13.   James Boswell, *Life of Johnson,* as quoted in Alan Donagan, *The Theory of Morality* (Chicago: University of Chicago Press, 1997), p. 89.

14.   Nicholas A. Christakis, *Death Foretold: Prophecy and Prognosis in Medical Care* (Chicago: University of Chicago Press, 1999), esp. chap. 5. See also G. G. Palmboom, D. L. Willems, N. B. A. T. Janssen, and J. C. J. M. de Haes, "Doctor's Views on Disclosing or Withholding Information on Low Risks of Complication," *Journal of Medical Ethics* 33 (2007): 67–70.

15.   Joel Stein, "A Fragile Commodity," *JAMA: Journal of the American Medical Association* 283 (January 19, 2000): 305–6.

16.   Thurstan B. Brewin, "Telling the Truth" (Letter), *Lancet* 343 (June 11, 1994): 1512.

17.   Antonella Surbone, "Truth Telling to the Patient," *JAMA: Journal of the American Medical Association* 268 (October 7, 1992): 1661–62; and Surbone, Claudia Ritossa, and Antonio G. Spagnolo, "Evolution of Truth-Telling Attitudes and Practices in Italy," *Critical Reviews in Oncology-Hematology* 52 (December 2004): 165–72.

18.   Daniel Rayson, "Lisa's Stories," *JAMA: Journal of the American Medical Association* 282 (November 3, 1999): 1605–6.

19.   K. T. Kohn, J. M. Corrigan, and M. S. Donaldson, *To Err Is Human: Building a Safer Health System* (Washington, DC: National Academies Press, 1999).

20.   See Robert D. Truog, David M. Browning, Judith A. Johnson, and Thomas H. Gallagher, *Talking with Patients and Families about Medical Error* (Baltimore: Johns Hopkins University Press, 2011), p. vii. The quotation is from the Foreword by Lucian L. Leape.

21.   See Rae M. Lamb et al., "Hospital Disclosure Practices: Results of a National Survey," *Health Affairs* 22 (2003): 73–83; Lamb, "Open Disclosure: The Only Approach to Medical Error," *Quality and Safety in Health Care* 13 (2004): 3–5; and Lisa Lehmann et al., "Iatrogenic Events Resulting in Intensive Care Admission: Frequency, Cause, and Disclosure to Patients and Institutions," *American Journal of Medicine* 118 (2005): 409–13.

22.   See Thomas H. Gallagher et al., "Choosing Your Words Carefully: How Physicians Would Disclose Harmful Medical Errors to Patients," *Archives of Internal Medicine* 166 (August 14–28, 2006): 1585–93. See also David K. Chan et al., "How Surgeons Disclose Medical Errors to Patients: A Study Using Standardized Patients," *Surgery* 138 (November 2005): 851–58.

23.   See Steve S. Kraman and Ginny Hamm, "Risk Management: Extreme Honesty May Be the Best Policy," *Annals of Internal Medicine* 131 (December 21, 1999): 963–67; and A. Kachalia et al., "Does Full Disclosure of Medical Errors Affect Malpractice Liability? The Jury Is Still Out," *Joint Commission Journal on Quality and Patient Safety* 29 (October 2003): 503–11. See also Nancy Berlinger, *After Harm: Medical Error and the Ethics of Forgiveness* (Baltimore: Johns Hopkins University Press, 2005).

24.   Truog et al., *Talking with Patients and Families about Medical Error.*

25.   Joanna M. Cain, "Is Deception for Reimbursement in Obstetrics and Gynecology Justified?" *Obstetrics & Gynecology* 82 (September 1993): 475–78.

26.   Kaiser Family Foundation, "Survey of Physicians and Nurses," http://www.kff.org/1999/1503 (accessed August 20, 2007).

27.   M. K. Wynia, D. S. Cummins, J. B. VanGeest, and I. B. Wilson, "Physician Manipulation of Reimbursement Rules for Patient: Between a Rock and a Hard Place," *JAMA: Journal of the American Medical Association* 283 (April 12, 2000): 1858–65; and the editorial commentary by M. Gregg Bloche, "Fidelity and Deceit at the Bedside," in the same issue, 1881–84.

28.   The case for this assessment is made by Bloche, "Fidelity and Deceit at the Bedside," p. 1883.

29. Victor G. Freeman et al., "Lying for Patients: Physician Deception of Third-Party Payers," *Archives of Internal Medicine* 159 (October 25, 1999): 2263–70.

30. Rachel M. Werner et al., "Lying to Insurance Companies: The Desire to Deceive among Physicians and the Public," *American Journal of Bioethics* 4 (Fall 2004): 53–59, with eleven commentaries on pp. 60–80. On deception and its moral and psychological aftermath in clinical medicine, see Baback B. Gabbay, et al., "Negotiating End-of-Life Decision Making: A Comparison of Japanese and U. S. Residents' Approaches," *Academic Medicine* 80 (2005): 617–21;

31. Thomas L. Carson, *Lying and Deception: Theory and Practice* (New York: Oxford University Press, 2010), p. 2.

32. *Griswold v. Connecticut,* 381 U.S. 479 (1965), at 486.

33. See, for example, Adam D. Moore, *Privacy Rights: Moral and Legal Foundations* (University Park, PA: Pennsylvania State University Press, 2010), p. 5.

34. Anita L. Allen, "Genetic Privacy: Emerging Concepts and Values," in *Genetic Secrets: Protecting Privacy and Confidentiality in the Genetic Era,* ed. Mark A. Rothstein (New Haven, CT: Yale University Press, 1997), pp. 31–59. For a wide-ranging account of the meanings and types of "privacies" and their moral and political value, see Allen, *Unpopular Privacy: What Must We Hide* (New York: Oxford University Press, 2011), which includes a defense of "paternalistic privacy" policies. For other examinations of privacy, see Daniel J. Solove, *Understanding Privacy* (Cambridge, MA: Harvard University Press, 2008), which argues that there are multiple forms of privacy, related by virtue of family resemblances. In *Privacy in Context: Technology, Policy, and the Integrity of Social Life* (Stanford, CA: Stanford University Press, 2010), Helen Nissenbaum develops an omnibus principle of "contextual integrity" and derives context-relative rights from it on a sector-by-sector basis (see esp. p. 238).

35. Charles Fried, "Privacy: A Rational Context," *Yale Law Journal* 77 (1968): 475–93.

36. Warren and Brandeis, "The Right to Privacy," *Harvard Law Review* 4 (1890): 193–220.

37. Thomson, "The Right to Privacy," *Philosophy and Public Affairs* 4 (Summer 1975): 295–314, as reprinted in *Philosophical Dimensions of Privacy,* ed. Ferdinand David Schoeman (New York: Cambridge University Press, 1984), pp. 272–89, esp. 280–87. By contrast, Judith Wagner DeCew views privacy as "a multifaceted cluster concept" without deriving it completely from other interests. See DeCew, *In Pursuit of Privacy: Law, Ethics, and the Rise of Technology* (Ithaca, NY: Cornell University Press, 1997).

38. James Rachels, "Why Privacy Is Important," p. 292; and Edward Bloustein, "Privacy as an Aspect of Human Dignity," both in *Philosophical Dimensions of Privacy,* ed. Schoeman.

39. See Fried, "Privacy: A Rational Context."

40. Even though we consider this argument primary, the consequentialist argument also has considerable merit. These arguments are not mutually exclusive.

41. Joel Feinberg, *Harm to Self,* vol. III in *The Moral Limits of the Criminal Law* (New York: Oxford University Press, 1986), chap. 19.

42. On issues in public health ethics see James F. Childress, Ruth R. Faden, Ruth D. Gaare, et al., "Public Health Ethics: Mapping the Terrain," *Journal of Law, Medicine & Ethics* 30 (2002): 170–78; Madison Powers and Ruth Faden, *Social Justice: The Moral Foundations of Public Health and Health Policy* (New York: Oxford University Press, 2006); and Ronald Bayer, Lawrence O. Gostin, Bruce Jennings, and Bonnie Steinbock, *Public Health Ethics: Theory, Policy, and Practice* (New York: Oxford University Press, 2006).

43. See Lisa M. Lee, Charles M. Heilig, and Angela White, "Ethical Justification for Conducting Public Health Surveillance without Patient Consent," *American Journal of Public Health* 102 (January 2012): 38–44. For thorough and historically grounded analyses of and strong support for public health surveillance, see Amy L. Fairchild, Ronald Bayer, and James Colgrove, *Searching Eyes: Privacy, the State, and Disease Surveillance* (Berkeley, CA: University of California Press, 2007); Fairchild, Bayer, and Colgrove, "Privacy, Democracy and the Politics of Disease Surveillance," *Public Health Ethics* 1, no. 1 (2008): 30–38.

44. See Wendy K. Mariner, "Mission Creep: Public Health Surveillance and Medical Privacy," *Boston University Law Review* 87 (2007): 347–95.

45. The diabetes program nods to patients' autonomy by allowing them to opt out of all aspects of the program except the registry. See Shadi Chamany et al., "Tracking Diabetes: New York City's A1C Registry," *Milbank Quarterly* 87, no. 3 (2009): 547–70, with responses; and Clarissa G. Barnes, Frederick L. Brancati, and Tiffany L. Gary, "Mandatory Reporting of Noncommunicable Diseases: The Example of the New York City A1c Registry (NYCAR)," *Virtual Mentor, American Medical Association Journal of Ethics* 9 (December 2007): 827–31. For analysis and criticism, see Janlori Goldman et al., "New York City's Initiatives on Diabetes and HIV/AIDS: Implications for Patient Care, Public Health, and Medical Professionalism," *American Journal of Public Health* 98 (May 2008): 16–22.

46. See Lucian V. Torian et al., "Striving Toward Comprehensive HIV/AIDS Surveillance: The View from New York City," *Public Health Reports* 122 (2007 Supplement 1): 4–6; and Amy L. Fairchild and Ronald Bayer, "HIV Surveillance, Public Health, and Clinical Medicine: Will the Walls Come Tumbling Down?" *New England Journal of Medicine* 365 (August 25, 2011): 685–87.

47. On the latter point, see Goldman et al., "New York City's Initiatives on Diabetes and HIV/AIDS," p. 17.

48. See Mark A. Rothstein, "Genetic Secrets: A Policy Framework," in *Genetic Secrets,* ed. Rothstein, chap. 23.

49. Mark Siegler, "Confidentiality in Medicine—A Decrepit Concept," *New England Journal of Medicine* 307 (1982): 1518–21. See also Bernard Friedland, "Physician–Patient Confidentiality: Time to Re-examine a Venerable Concept in Light of Contemporary Society and Advances in Medicine," *Journal of Legal Medicine* 15 (1994): 249–77; and, on continued erosion of the concept, see Beverley Woodward, "Confidentiality, Consent and Autonomy in the Physician-Patient Relationship," *Health Care Analysis* 9 (2001): 337–51.

50. *Estate of William Behringer v. Medical Center at Princeton,* 249 N.J.Super. 597, 592 A.2d 1251 (1991).

51. Barry D. Weiss, "Confidentiality Expectations of Patients, Physicians, and Medical Students," *JAMA: Journal of the American Medical Association* 247 (1982): 2695–97.

52. *Bratt v. IBM,* 467 N.E.2d 126 (1984); *Bratt, et al. v. IBM,* 785 F.2d 352 (1986).

53. American Psychiatric Association, *Psychiatric Services in Jails and Prisons: A Task Force Report of the American Psychiatric Association* (Washington, DC: American Psychiatric Association, 2000); Emil R. Pinta, "Decisions to Breach Confidentiality When Prisoners Report Violations of Institutional Rules," *Journal of American Psychiatry and the Law* 37 (2009): 150–54.

54. *Tarasoff v. Regents of the University of California,* 17 Cal. 3d 425 (1976); 131 California Reporter 14 (1976). The majority opinion was written by Justice Tobriner; the dissenting opinion was written by Justice Clark.

55. See Kenneth Appelbaum and Paul S. Appelbaum, "The HIV Antibody-Positive Patient," in *Confidentiality Versus the Duty to Protect: Foreseeable Harm in the Practice of Psychiatry,* ed. James C. Beck (Washington, DC: American Psychiatry Press, 1990), pp. 127–28.

56. Griffin Sims Edwards, "Doing Their Duty: An Empirical Analysis of the Unintended Effect of *Tarasoff v. Regents* on Homicidal Activity," *Emory Law and Economics Research Paper No. 10–61* (January 29, 2010), available at SSRN: http://ssm.com/abstract=1544574 (accessed January 14, 2012).

57. For views to the contrary, see Michael H. Kottow, "Medical Confidentiality: An Intransigent and Absolute Obligation," *Journal of Medical Ethics* 12 (1986): 117–22; and Kenneth Kipnis, "A Defense of Unqualified Medical Confidentiality," *American Journal of Bioethics* 6 (2006): 7–18 (followed by critical commentaries, pp. 19–41).

58. Grant Gillett, "AIDS and Confidentiality," *Journal of Applied Philosophy* 4 (1987): 15–20, from which this case study has been adapted.

59. See Susanne E. Landis, Victor J. Schoenbach, David J. Weber, et al., "Results of a Randomized Trial of Partner Notification in Cases of HIV Infection in North Carolina," *New England Journal of Medicine* 326 (January 9, 1992): 101–6. See also Michael D. Stein et al., "Sexual Ethics: Disclosure of HIV-Positive Status to Partners," *Archives of Internal Medicine* 158 (February 1998): 253–57.

60. *Code of Medical Ethics 2010–2011 Edition* (adopted June 2008), 2:23, p. 127. This revision somewhat modifies guidance in earlier editions: A physician who "knows that a seropositive individual is endangering a third party...should, within the constraints of the law, (1) attempt to persuade the infected patient to cease endangering the third party; (2) if persuasion fails, notify authorities; and (3) if the authorities take no action, notify the endangered third party." *Code of Medical Ethics of the American Medical Association, 2006–2007 Edition* (Chicago: AMA, 2006), 2.23, p. 109.

61. See discussion of this problem, using an absolutist, rule-oriented solution notably different from our on-balance strategy, in Kipnis, "A Defense of Unqualified Medical Confidentiality" (and responses to his claim in the same journal issue).

62. Robert Baker, "Confidentiality in Professional Medical Ethics," *American Journal of Bioethics* 6 (2006): 39–41.

63. Lori B. Andrews et al., eds. (for the Committee on Assessing Genetic Risks, Institute of Medicine), *Assessing Genetic Risks: Implications for Health and Social Policy* (Washington, DC: National Academies Press, 1994), p. 278, and see 264–73. For an argument that medical examiners and forensic pathologists have an ethical (but not a legal) duty to warn a deceased person's relatives about genetics-related risks, such as sudden cardiac death, or about risks from environmental exposure that could affect them too, see Bernice Elger, Katarzyna Michaud, and Patrice Mangin, "When Information Can Save Lives: The Duty to Warn Relatives about Sudden Cardiac Death and Environmental Risks," *Hastings Center Report* 40 (May–June 2010): 39–45.

64. Michael Parker and Anneke Lucassen, "Genetic Information: A Joint Account?" *British Medical Journal* 329 (July 17, 2004): 165–67.

65. Paul Ramsey, *The Patient as Person* (New Haven, CT: Yale University Press, 1970), p. xii.

66. See M. Gregg Bloche, "Clinical Loyalties and the Social Purposes of Medicine," *JAMA: Journal of the American Medical Association* 281 (January 20, 1999): 268–74; and Bloche, *The Hippocratic Myth: Why Doctors Are Under Pressure to Ration Care, Practice Politics, and Compromise their Promise to Heal* (New York: Palgrave Macmillan, 2011).

67. See Stephen Toulmin, "Divided Loyalties and Ambiguous Relationships," *Social Science and Medicine* 23 (1986): 784; and Michael D. Robertson and Garry Walter, "Many Faces of the Dual-Role Dilemma in Psychiatric Ethics," *Australian and New Zealand Journal of Psychiatry* 42 (2008): 228–35.

68. *In re Sampson,* 317 N.Y.S.2d (1970).

69.   On conflicts in sports medicine, see Søren Holm, "Ethics in Sports Medicine," *BMJ: British Medical Journal* 339 (September 29, 2009): b3898, available at http://www.bmj.com/content/339/bmj .b3898 (accessed February 6, 2012).

70.   See broader questions of dual loyalties in military contexts, in comparison with sports medicine, occupational health, and health care in prisons, in Institute of Medicine, *Military Medical Ethics: Issues Regarding Dual Loyalties: Workshop Summary* (Washington, DC: National Academies Press, 2009). See also Solomon R. Benatar and Ross E. G. Upshur, "Dual Loyalty of Physicians in the Military and in Civilian Life," *American Journal of Public Health* 98 (December 2008): 2161–67; and Laura Sessums, "Ethical Practice under Fire: Deployed Physicians in the Global War on Terrorism," *Military Medicine* 174 (2009): 441–47.

71.   In *Oath Betrayed: Torture, Medical Complicity, and the War on Terror* (New York: Random House, 2006), Steven H. Miles asks, "Where were the doctors and nurses at Abu Ghraib?" and challenges medical and health professionals to recognize their responsibilities to disarmed captives and detainees. See also M. Gregg Bloche and Jonathan H. Marks, "When Doctors Go to War," *New England Journal of Medicine* 352, no. 1 (2005): 3–6; Bloche, *The Hippocratic Myth,* chaps. 7 and 8; Michael L. Gross, *Bioethics and Armed Conflict: Moral Dilemmas of Medicine and War* (Cambridge, MA: MIT Press, 2006); and Chiara Lepora and Joseph Millum, "The Tortured Patient: A Medical Dilemma," *Hastings Center* 41 (May–June 2011): 38–47.

72.   See Curtis Prout and Robert N. Ross, *Care and Punishment: The Dilemmas of Prison Medicine* (Pittsburgh, PA: University of Pittsburgh Press, 1988); Michael Puisis, ed., *Clinical Practice in Correctional Medicine,* 2nd ed. (New York: Mosby, 2006); and Kenneth Kipnis, "Ethical Conflict in Correctional Health Services," in *Conflict of Interest in the Professions,* ed. Michael Davis and Andrew Stark (Oxford: Oxford University Press, 2001), pp. 302–15.

73.   In contrast to virtually all of the developed world, the United States maintains capital punishment and has increasingly medicalized it through adoption of lethal injection. However, the AMA code bans physician participation in executions, other than to certify death after someone else has declared it. See *Code of Medical Ethics of the American Medical Association, 2010–2011 Edition,* 2.06. See also Lee Black and Robert M. Sade, "Lethal Injection and Physicians: State Law vs Medical Ethics," *JAMA: Journal of the American Medical Association* 298 (December 19, 2007). For challenges to this ban, see Lawrence Nelson and Brandon Ashby, "Rethinking the Ethics of Physician Participation in Lethal Injection Execution," *Hastings Center Report* 41 (May–June 2011): 28–37.

74.   Gregory F. Gramelspacher, Joel D. Howell, and Mark J. Young, "Perceptions of Ethical Problems by Nurses and Doctors," *Archives of Internal Medicine* 146 (March 1986): 577–78. See also R. Walker, S. Miles, C. Stocking, and M. Siegler, "Physicians' and Nurses' Perceptions of Ethics Problems on General Medical Services," *Journal of General Internal Medicine* 6 (1991): 424–29. Similar themes emerged in a recent Canadian study: Alice Gaudine, Sandra M. LeFort, Marianne Lamb, and Linda Thorne, "Clinical Ethical Conflicts of Nurses and Physicians," *Nursing Ethics* 18 (2011): 9–19.

75.   Ann B. Hamric and Leslie J. Blackhall, "Nurse-Physician Perspectives on the Care of Dying Patients in Intensive Care Units: Collaboration, Moral Distress, and Ethical Climate," *Critical Care Medicine* 35 (2007): 422–29.

76.   Compare our definition with that of a recent report from the Institute of Medicine: A conflict of interest is "a set of circumstances that create a risk that professional judgments or actions regarding a primary interest [such as patient welfare or objective research results] will be unduly influenced by a secondary interest [such as financial gain or a personal relationship]." Institute of Medicine, *Conflict of Interest in Medical Research, Education, and Practice,* ed. Bernard Lo and Marilyn J. Field (Washington DC: National Academies Press, 2009), pp. 45–46, passim.

77.   See, among other studies, Jean M. Mitchell and Jonathan Sunshine, "Consequences of Physicians' Ownership of Health Care Facilities—Joint Ventures in Radiation Therapy," *New England Journal of Medicine* 327 (November 19, 1992): 1497–1501; Jean M. Mitchell and T. R. Sass, "Physician Ownership

of Ancillary Services: Indirect Demand Inducement or Quality Assurance?" *Journal of Health Economics* 14 (August 1995): 263–89.

78. For an examination of efforts in the United States (and Japan and France) to address self-referral, see Marc A. Rodwin, *Conflicts of Interest and the Future of Medicine* (New York: Oxford University Press, 2011), esp. pp. 117–21, 145–47. See also Bruce J. Hillman, "Trying to Regulate Imaging Self-Referral Is Like Playing Whack-A-Mole," *American Journal of Roentgenology* 189 (2007): 267–68.

79. See E. Haavi Morreim, *Balancing Act: The New Medical Ethics of Medicine's New Economics* (Boston: Kluwer Academic, 1991), which has influenced our discussion.

80. Adriane Fugh-Berman and Shahram Ahiri, "Following the Script: How Drug Reps Make Friends and Influence Doctors," *PloS Medicine* 4 (April 2007): 621–25; Jason Dana and George Loewenstein, "A Social Science Perspective on Gifts to Physicians from Industry," *JAMA: Journal of the American Medical Association* 290 (July 9, 2003): 252–55; and Richard F. Adair and Leah R. Holmgren, "Do Drug Samples Influence Resident Prescribing Behavior? A Randomized Trial," *American Journal of Medicine* 118 (2005): 881–84.

81. Dana Katz et al., "All Gifts Large and Small: Toward an Understanding of the Ethics of Pharmaceutical Industry Gift-Giving," *American Journal of Bioethics* 3 (Summer 2003): 39–45, accompanied by commentaries. A summary and analysis of the relevant psychological research appears in Jason Dana, "How Psychological Research Can Inform Policies for Dealing with Conflicts of Interest in Medicine," in Institute of Medicine, *Conflicts of Interest in Medical Research, Education, and Practice,* Appendix D, pp. 358–74. The amount of money some parts of industry put into promotion in these various ways indicates their conviction that such promotional activities are effective.

82. For several proposals, see Troyen A. Brennan et al., "Health Industry Practices That Create Conflicts of Interest: A Policy Proposal for Academic Medical Centers," *JAMA: Journal of the American Medical Association* 295 (January 25, 2006): 429–33. See also Institute of Medicine, *Conflicts of Interest in Medical Research, Education, and Practice,* esp. chaps. 5 and 6.

83. See AAMC Task Force on Financial Conflicts of Interest in Clinical Research, "Protecting Subjects, Preserving Trust, Promoting Progress: Principles and Recommendations for Oversight of an Institution's Financial Interests in Human Subjects Research (I-II)," *Academic Medicine* 78 (2003): 225–45; and Teddy D. Warner and John P. Gluck, "What Do We Really Know about Conflicts of Interest in Biomedical Research," *Psychopharmacology* 171 (2003): 36–46.

84. See several chapters in part IV, "Clinical Research," in *Conflicts of Interest in Clinical Practice and Research,* ed. Roy G. Spece, Jr., David S. Shimm, and Allen E. Buchanan (New York: Oxford University Press, 1996).

85. Institute of Medicine, *Conflicts of Interest in Medical Research, Education, and Practice,* chap. 4.

86. National Commission for the Protection of Human Subjects of Biomedical and Behavioral Research, *The Belmont Report: Ethical Principles and Guidelines for the Protection of Human Subjects of Research* (Washington, DC: DHEW Publication OS 78–*0012*), pp. 2–3; Code of Federal Regulations, Title 45 (Public Welfare), Part 46 (Protection of Human Subjects), sec. 102 (2005), http://www.hhs.gov/ohrp/humansubjects/guidance/45cfr46.html (accessed July 15, 2011).

87. Cf. Franklin G. Miller, "Revisiting the *Belmont Report*: The Ethical Significance of the Distinction between Clinical Research and Medical Care," *APA Newsletter on Philosophy and Medicine* 5 (Spring 2006): 10–14; and Miller and Howard Brody, "The Clinician-Investigator: Unavoidable but Manageable Tension," *Kennedy Institute of Ethics Journal* 13 (2003): 329–46.

88. The World Medical Association, "Declaration of Geneva, Physician's Oath," adopted by the General Assembly of the World Medical Association, Geneva, Switzerland 1948 (when the wording

in this passage was slightly different) and most recently amended October 2006, http://www.cirp.org/library/ethics/geneva/ (accessed October 1, 2011).

89.   As discussed in Chapter 7, the research must not exploit populations or participants. Versions of several of these conditions appear in the Nuremberg Code and the U.S. Department of Health and Human Services, Protection of Human Subjects, 45 CFR 46. See also Ezekiel J. Emanuel, David Wendler, and Christine Grady, "What Makes Clinical Research Ethical?" *JAMA: Journal of the American Medical Association* 283 (May 24/31, 2000): 2701–11; and James F. Childress, *Priorities in Biomedical Ethics* (Philadelphia: Westminster Press, 1981), chap. 3.

90.   Disclosed by surgeon William DeVries at the University of Utah; see Denise Grady, "Summary of Discussion on Ethical Perspectives," in *After Barney Clark: Reflections on the Utah Artificial Heart Program,* ed. Margery W. Shaw (Austin, TX: University of Texas Press, 1984), p. 49.

91.   Even though we mainly use the terms *treatment* and *therapy,* the discussion also applies to diagnostic and preventive procedures, among others.

92.   See Gunnel Elander and Goran Hermeren, "Placebo Effect and Randomized Clinical Trials," *Theoretical Medicine* 16 (1995): 171–82; and Gerald Logue and Stephen Wear, "A Desperate Solution: Individual Autonomy and the Double-Blind Controlled Experiment," *Journal of Medicine and Philosophy* 20 (1995): 57–64.

93.   See Benjamin Freedman, "Equipoise and the Ethics of Clinical Research," *New England Journal of Medicine* 317 (July 16, 1987): 141–45; and Eugene Passamani, "Clinical Trials—Are They Ethical?" *New England Journal of Medicine* 324 (May 30, 1991): 1590–91.

94.   Franklin G. Miller and Steven Joffe, "Equipoise and the Dilemma of Randomized Clinical Trials," *New England Journal of Medicine* 364 (February 3, 2011): 476–80. These authors argue that "equipoise is fundamentally flawed as a criterion for determining whether a randomized clinical trial is justified," but their argument only supports the claim that equipoise is flawed if interpreted as a *sufficient condition* of the justification of RCTs; the proper claim is that equipoise is only a *necessary condition.* This latter claim is warranted and far from fundamentally flawed.

95.   Fred Gifford, "So-Called 'Clinical Equipoise' and the Argument from Design," *Journal of Medicine and Philosophy* 32 (2007): 135–50; Ezekiel Emanuel, W. Bradford Patterson, and Samuel Hellman, "Ethics of Randomized Clinical Trials," *Journal of Clinical Oncology* 16 (1998): 365–71.

96.   Don Marquis, "How to Resolve an Ethical Dilemma Concerning Randomized Clinical Trials," *New England Journal of Medicine* 341 (August 26, 1999): 691–93.

97.   Jeremy Howick, "Questioning the Methodologic Superiority of 'Placebo' Over 'Active' Controlled Trials," *American Journal of Bioethics* 9 (2009): 34–48; see also articles by his critics in this issue and his reply in "Reviewing the Unsubstantiated Claims for the Methodological Superiority of 'Placebo' Over 'Active' Controlled Trials: Reply to Open Peer Commentaries," *American Journal of Bioethics* 9 (2009): 5–7. See also Benjamin Freedman, Kathleen Glass, and Charles Weijer, "Placebo Orthodoxy in Clinical Research II: Ethical, Legal, and Regulatory Myths," *Journal of Law, Medicine & Ethics* 24 (1996): 252–59.

98.   Franklin G. Miller, "The Ethics of Placebo-Controlled Trials," in *The Oxford Textbook of Clinical Research Ethics,* ed. Ezekiel Emanuel et al. (New York: Oxford University Press, 2008), pp. 261–72. See also Robert Temple and Susan S. Ellenberg, "Placebo-Controlled Trials and Active-Control Trials in the Evaluation of New Treatments. Part 1: Ethical and Scientific Issues," *Annals of Internal Medicine* 133 (2000): 455–63; and "Placebo-Controlled Trials and Active-Control Trials in the Evaluation of New Treatments. Part 2: Practical Issues and Specific Cases," *Annals of Internal Medicine* 133 (2000): 464–70.

99.   See M. A. Fischl et al., "The Efficacy of Azidothymidine (AZT) in the Treatment of Patients with AIDS-Related Complex: A Double-Blind, Placebo-Controlled Trial," *New England Journal of*

Medicine 317 (1987): 185–91; and D. D. Richman et al., "The Toxicity of Azidothymidine (AZT) in the Treatment of Patients with AIDS and AIDS-Related Complex: A Double-Blind, Placebo-Controlled Trial," *New England Journal of Medicine* 317 (1987): 192–97.

100. For a variety of views, see Thomas B. Freeman et al., "Use of Placebo Surgery in Controlled Trials of a Cellular-Based Therapy for Parkinson's Disease," *New England Journal of Medicine* 341 (September 23, 1999): 988–92; Ruth Macklin, "The Ethical Problems with Sham Surgery in Clinical Research," *New England Journal of Medicine* 341 (September 23, 1999): 992–96; and Franklin G. Miller, "Sham Surgery: An Ethical Analysis," *American Journal of Bioethics* 3 (2003): 41–48, with several commentaries (pp. 50–71).

101. See Greg Ball, Linda B. Piller, and Michael H. Silverman, "Continuous Safety Monitoring for Randomized Controlled Clinical Trials with Blinded Treatment Information: Part 1: Ethical Considerations," *Contemporary Clinical Trials* 32, Supplement 1 (September 2011): S2–4.

102. For strong calls for the independence and integrity of the DSMB, in light of charges of recent breaches of the "wall" between DSMBs and sponsors, see Jeffrey M. Drazen and Alastair J. J. Wood, "Don't Mess with the DSMB," *New England Journal of Medicine* 363 (July 29, 2010): 477–78; and Catherine D. DeAngelis and Phil B. Fontanarosa, "Ensuring Integrity in Industry-Sponsored Research: Primum Non Nocere, Revisited," *JAMA: Journal of the American Medical Association* 303 (2010): 1196–98.

103. This was Freedman's proposal in "Equipoise and the Ethics of Clinical Research."

104. These conditions and our arguments throughout this section can profitably be compared to the following influential sources: Council for International Organizations of Medical Sciences, *International Ethical Guidelines for Biomedical Research Involving Human Subjects* (Geneva: CIOMS, 2002), available at http://www.cioms.ch (accessed July 17, 2011); National Bioethics Advisory Commission (NBAC), *Ethical and Policy Issues in International Research: Clinical Trials in Developing Countries,* vol. 1 (Bethesda, MD: National Bioethics Advisory Commission, 2001), available at http://bioethics.georgetown.edu/nbac/clinical/V0l1.pdf (accessed August 15, 2011); Nuffield Council on Bioethics, *The Ethics of Research Related to Healthcare in Developing Countries* (London: Nuffield Council, 2008), available at http://nuffieldbioethics.org/go/ourwork/developingcountries/publication_309.html (accessed July 17, 2011); U.S. Department of Health and Human Services, Food and Drug Administration, Title 21, Code of Federal Regulations, Part 314 (as revised April 1, 2011), http://www.accessdata.fda.gov/scripts/cdrh/cfdocs/cfcfr/cfrsearch.cfm (accessed October 3, 2011); World Medical Association (WMA), "Declaration of Helsinki," 2008 revision, http://www.wma.net (accessed October 2, 2011); International Conference on Harmonisation of Technical Requirements for Registration of Pharmaceuticals for Human Use, *Ero Choice of Control Group and Related Issues in Clinical Trials,* available at http://www.ich.org/ (ICH, 2000), available at http://www.ich.org/cache/compo/475-272-1.html (accessed September 11, 2011).

PART III

THEORY AND METHOD

9
Moral Theories

Several types of moral theory surfaced in earlier chapters, but we did not pursue their presuppositions and implications. In this chapter we explicate utilitarianism, Kantianism, rights theory, and virtue ethics as four influential theories. Knowledge of these theories is indispensable for reflective study in biomedical ethics because much of the field's literature presumes familiarity with them. Each theory casts light on important aspects of moral thinking in the biological sciences, medicine, and health care.

A so-called textbook approach to moral theory presents several competing theories and then proceeds to criticize them. Often the criticisms are so severe that each theory seems fatally wounded, and readers become skeptical about the value of ethical theory in general. Defects and excesses can be found in all major theories, but the theories discussed in this chapter all contain insights and arguments that deserve careful study. Our goal is to criticize what is questionable or limited in each type of theory and to appropriate what stands to make a contribution to practical ethics.

We sometimes refer to our own account of ethics in this book as a theory, but a word of caution is in order about this term. "Ethical theory" and "moral theory" are commonly used to refer to (1) abstract moral reflection and argument, (2) systematic presentation of the basic components of ethics, (3) an integrated body of moral norms, and (4) a systematic justification of basic moral norms. We attempt in this book to construct a coherent body of virtues, rights, principles, and rules for biomedical ethics. We do not claim to have developed a comprehensive ethical theory in ways suggested by the combination of (3) and (4). We engage in theory (e.g., in evaluating other ethical theories), and in doing so we engage in abstract reflection and argument (1). We also present an organized system of principles (3) and engage in systematic reflection and argument (2); but, at most, we present only elements of a general theory. Our approach to theory, method, and justification appears in Chapter 10.

Each section of this chapter, except the first and the last, is divided into subsections structured as follows: (1) an overview of the characteristic features of the theory under consideration (introduced by examining how its proponents might approach a case); (2) depiction of the salient features of the theory; (3) an examination of criticisms regarding the theory's limitations and problems; and (4) an assessment of the theory's potential or actual contribution. We accept as legitimate various aspects of all four of the theories discussed in this chapter. We do not, however, hold that the goal of philosophical ethics is to identify the single best theory and give it moral priority. There is no reason to rank one of these four theories above the others when much is to be learned from each.[1] At the same time, we reject both the hypothesis that all leading norms of the major moral theories can be assimilated into a coherent whole and the hypothesis that each theory offers an equally tenable moral framework.

CRITERIA FOR ASSESSING MORAL THEORIES

We begin with eight conditions of adequacy for a moral theory. These criteria for theory construction set forth ideal conditions for theories, but not so exacting that no theory could satisfy them. The extent to which all available theories only partially satisfy these conditions will not be our concern. In general, theories will seem most adequate if they are judged as best suited to some limited range of morality, rather than to all of it. For example, utilitarianism is a more adequate theoretical model for public policy than for clinical medical ethics, and rights theory is a better model for protecting individual interests against community interests than for evaluating close personal relationships and moral motivation.

A conflict exists between a once-popular conception of ethical theory and a newer and less settled account. In the older conception, popular roughly from the late eighteenth century to the late twentieth century, the task of moral theory is to locate and justify general moral norms as a system. In a newer and less settled conception, the task is to reflect critically on influential moral norms and practices. In this chapter and the next we discuss both conceptions, but our approach in this book is decidedly closer to the latter.

Eight conditions express a more or less traditional understanding of criteria for ethical theories:[2]

1. *Clarity.* Taken as a whole or in its parts, a theory should be as clear as possible. Although, as Aristotle suggested, we can expect only as much clarity and precision of language as is appropriate for the subject matter, more obscurity and vagueness exist in the literature of ethical theory and biomedical ethics than the subject matter warrants.

2. *Coherence.* An ethical theory should be internally coherent. There should be neither conceptual inconsistencies (e.g., "hard medical paternalism is justified only by consent of the patient") nor apparently contradictory

statements (e.g., "to be virtuous is a moral obligation, but virtuous conduct is not obligatory"). If an account contains implications that are incoherent with other parts of that account, some aspect of the theory must be changed in a way that does not produce further incoherence. As we argue in Chapter 10, a major goal of a theory should be to bring into coherence all of its normative elements (principles, virtues, rights, considered judgments, and the like).

3. *Comprehensiveness.* A theory should be as comprehensive as possible. It would be fully comprehensive if it could account for all justifiable moral norms and judgments. Although the principles presented in this book under the headings of respect for autonomy, nonmaleficence, beneficence, and justice are far from a complete system for general normative ethics, they provide a comprehensive general framework for the practical domain of biomedical ethics. We do not need additional general principles for this purpose, but we do specify these four principles to generate such rules as promise-keeping, truthfulness, privacy, and confidentiality (see Chapter 8). Specified rules increase a theory's comprehensiveness.

4. *Simplicity.* A theory that distills the demands of morality to a few basic norms is preferable to a theory with more norms but no additional content. A theory should have no more norms than are necessary (simplicity in the sense of theoretical parsimony), and also no more than people can use without confusion (a practical simplicity). However, morality is complicated both theoretically and practically, and a comprehensive moral theory is certain to be complex. If the inherent complexity of morality demands a theory too difficult for practical use, the theory cannot be faulted for this reason alone.

5. *Explanatory power.* A theory has explanatory power when it provides enough insight to help us understand morality: its purpose, its objective or subjective status, how rights are related to obligations, and the like. For the sake of clarity, we should distinguish between normative theories and metaethical theories, as we noted in Chapter 1. While a general normative theory should not be held to the task of shedding light on metaethical questions, the ideal theory is one that seamlessly constructs a normative system while addressing the relevant metaethical questions. (We do not here distinguish between theory and method; our assumption is that discussions of theory and method go hand in hand.)

6. *Justificatory power.* A theory should also provide grounds for justified belief, not merely a reformulation of beliefs we already possess. For example, the distinction between acts and omissions underlies many traditional beliefs in biomedical ethics, such as the belief that killing is impermissible and allowing to die permissible. But a moral theory would be impoverished if it only incorporated this distinction without

determining whether the distinction is justifiable. A good theory also should have the power to criticize defective beliefs, no matter how widely accepted those beliefs may be.

7. *Output power.* A theory has output power when it produces judgments that were not in the original database of considered moral judgments on which the theory was constructed. If a normative theory did no more than repeat the list of judgments thought to be sound prior to the construction of the theory, it would have accomplished nothing. For example, if the parts of a theory pertaining to obligations of beneficence do not yield new judgments about role obligations of care in medicine beyond those assumed in constructing the theory, the theory will amount to no more than a classification scheme. A theory, then, must generate more than a list of axioms already present in pretheoretic belief.

8. *Practicability.* A moral theory is unacceptable if its practical requirements are so demanding that they cannot be satisfied or could be satisfied by only a few extraordinary persons or communities. A theory that presents utopian ideals or unfeasible recommendations fails the criterion of practicability. For example, if a theory proposed such high requirements for personal autonomy (see Chapter 4) or such lofty standards of social justice (see Chapter 7) that no person could be autonomous or no society just, the proposed theory would be deeply problematic.

Other criteria of theory construction have been proposed, but the eight we have identified are the most important for our purposes. A theory can receive a high score on the basis of one or more of these criteria and a low score on the basis of other criteria. For example, utilitarianism is arguably an internally coherent, simple, and comprehensive theory with exceptional output power, but it may not be coherent with some vital considered judgments, especially with certain judgments about justice, human rights, and the importance of personal projects. By contrast, Kantian theories are consistent with many of our considered judgments, but their simplicity and output power may be limited.

UTILITARIAN THEORY

Consequentialism is a label affixed to theories holding that actions are right or wrong according to the balance of their good and bad consequences. It is a general term denoting theories that take the promotion of value to determine the rightness or wrongness of actions. The right act in any circumstance is the act that produces the best overall result as determined by the theory's account of value.

The most prominent consequentialist theory, utilitarianism, concentrates on the value of well-being, which has been analyzed in terms of pleasure, happiness, welfare, preference satisfaction, and the like. Utilitarianism accepts one, and only one, basic principle of ethics: the principle of utility. This principle asserts that we ought always to produce the maximal balance of positive value over disvalue—or the least possible disvalue, if only undesirable results can be achieved. It is often formulated as a requirement to do the greatest good for the greatest number, as determined from an impartial perspective that gives equal weight to the legitimate interests of each affected party. The classical origins of this theory are found in the writings of Jeremy Bentham (1748–1832) and John Stuart Mill (1806–73).

The model bequeathed to philosophy by these authors, principally by Mill, renders utilitarian theory consequentialist, welfarist, aggregative, maximizing, and impartial. It is consequentialist because the moral rightness and obligatoriness of actions are established by their results, and it is welfarist in that the rightness of actions is a function of goodness (good welfare outcomes). It is impersonal and aggregative because a judgment about right or obligatory action depends on an impartial appraisal of the effects of different possible actions on the welfare of all affected parties, which entails summing those positive and negative effects over all persons affected.

The Concept of Utility

Although utilitarians share the conviction that we should morally assess human actions in terms of their production of maximal value, they disagree among themselves concerning which values should be maximized. Many utilitarians maintain that we ought to produce *agent-neutral* or *intrinsic* goods, that is, goods such as happiness, freedom, and health that every rational person values.[3] These goods are valuable in themselves, without reference to their further consequences or to the particular values held by individuals.

Bentham and Mill are *hedonistic* utilitarians because they conceive utility in terms of happiness or pleasure, two broad terms that they treat as synonymous.[4] They acknowledge that many human actions do not appear to be performed for the sake of happiness. For example, when highly motivated professionals, such as research scientists, work themselves to the point of exhaustion in search of new knowledge, they do not appear to be seeking personal happiness. Mill proposes that such persons are initially motivated by success, recognition, or money, which all promise happiness. Along the way, either the pursuit of knowledge provides happiness or such persons never stop associating their hard work with the success, recognition, or money that they hope to gain.

Various recent utilitarians, by contrast to Mill, have argued that a diverse set of values other than happiness contribute to well-being. Examples are beauty, knowledge, health, success, understanding, enjoyment, and deep personal relationships.[5] Even when their lists differ, these utilitarians concur that we should assess the greatest good in terms of the total intrinsic value produced by an action. Still other utilitarians hold that the concept of utility does not refer to intrinsic goods, but to an individual's preferences; that is, we should maximize the overall satisfaction of the preferences of the individuals affected.

A Case of Risk and Truthfulness

To distinguish the major themes of each theory treated in this chapter, each of the four sections devoted to a theory explicates how its proponents might approach the same case. This case centers on a five-year-old girl who has progressive renal failure and is not responding well on chronic renal dialysis. The medical staff is considering a renal transplant, but its effectiveness is judged questionable in her case. Nevertheless, a "clear possibility" exists that a transplanted kidney will not be affected by the disease process. The parents concur with the plan to try a transplant, but an additional obstacle emerges. The tissue typing indicates that it would be difficult to find a match for the girl. The staff excludes her two siblings, ages two and four, as too young to provide a kidney. The mother is not histocompatible, but the father is compatible and has "anatomically favorable circulation for transplantation."

Meeting alone with the father, the nephrologist gives him the results and indicates that the prognosis for his daughter is "quite uncertain." After reflection, the father decides that he will not donate a kidney to his daughter. His several reasons include his fear of the surgery and his lack of "courage," the uncertain prognosis for his daughter even with a transplant, the slight prospect of a cadaver kidney, and the suffering his daughter has already sustained. The father then requests that the physician tell everyone else in the family that he is not histo-compatible. He is afraid that if family members know the truth, they will accuse him of failing to save his daughter when he could do so. He maintains that telling the truth would have the effect of wrecking the family. The physician feels "very uncomfortable" about this request but after further discussion agrees to tell the man's wife that the father should not donate a kidney "for medical reasons."[6]

Utilitarians evaluate this case in terms of the probable consequences of the different courses of action open to the father and the physician. The goal is to realize the greatest good by balancing the interests of all affected persons. This evaluation depends on judgments concerning probable outcomes. Whether the father ought to donate his kidney depends on the probability of successful trans-plantation as well as the risks and other costs to him (and indirectly to other dependent members of the family). The potential effectiveness is questionable and the prognosis uncertain, although a possibility exists that a transplanted kidney would not undergo the same disease process. There is a slight possibility that a cadaver kidney could be obtained.

The girl will probably die without a transplant from either a cadaveric or a living source, but the transplant also offers only a small chance of survival. The risk of death to the father from anesthesia during kidney removal is 1 in 10,000 to 15,000 (at the time of this case). It is difficult to put an estimate on other possible long-term health effects. Nevertheless, because the chance of success is likely greater than the probability that the father will be harmed, many utilitarians would hold that the father or anyone else similarly situated is obligated to undertake what others would consider a heroic act that surpasses obligation. Given the balance of probable benefits and risks, an uncompromising utilitarian might suggest tissue typing the patient's two siblings and then removing a kidney from one if there were a good match and parental approval. However, utilitarians disagree among themselves in these various judgments because of their different theories of value and their different predictions and assessments of probable outcomes.

Probabilistic judgments would likewise play a role in the physician's utilitarian calculation of the right action in response to the father's request. The physician would need to bear in mind a variety of sociological and psychological considerations, including whether a full disclosure would wreck the family, whether lying to the family would have serious negative effects, and whether the father would subsequently experience serious guilt from his refusal to donate. A utilitarian would argue that the physician is obligated to consider the whole range of facts and possible consequences in light of the best available information.

Act and Rule Utilitarianism

The principle of utility is the ultimate standard of right and wrong for all utilitarians.[7] Controversy has arisen, however, over whether this principle pertains to particular acts in particular circumstances or instead to general rules that determine which acts are right and wrong. The *rule utilitarian* considers the consequences of adopting certain rules, whereas the *act utilitarian* disregards the level of rules and justifies actions by direct appeal to the principle of utility, as the following chart indicates:

Rule Utilitarianism	*Act Utilitarianism*
Principle of Utility	Principle of Utility
↑	
Moral Rules	↑
↑	
Particular Judgments	Particular Judgments

The act utilitarian asks, "Which good and bad consequences will probably result from this action in this circumstance?" Although moral rules are useful in guiding human actions, they are also expendable if they do not promote utility in a particular context. For a strict rule utilitarian, by contrast, an act's conformity to a rule that is justified by utility makes the act right, and the rule is not expendable in a particular context even if following the rule does not maximize utility in that context. A weak form of rule utilitarianism holds that rules state prima facie duties that may be overridden in some circumstances. Each type of rule utilitarianism has a scope that allows it to justify not only basic moral rules, but also moral rights, professional duties, and the like.[8]

Physician Worthington Hooker, a prominent nineteenth-century figure in academic medicine and medical ethics, was an incipient rule utilitarian who attended to rules of truth-telling in medicine as follows:

> The good, which may be done by deception in a *few* cases, is almost as nothing, compared with the evil which it does in *many,* when the prospect of its doing good was just as promising as it was in those in which it succeeded. And when we add to this the evil which would result from a *general* adoption of a system of deception, the importance of a strict adherence to the truth in our intercourse with the sick, even on the ground of expediency, becomes incalculably great.[9]

Hooker argued that widespread deception and other compromises with truth-telling in medicine will have an increasingly negative effect over time and will eventually produce more harm than good.

Act utilitarians, by contrast, argue that observing a rule such as truth-telling does not always maximize the general good, and that such rules are only rough guidelines. They regard rule utilitarians as unfaithful to the fundamental demand of the principle of utility, which is to "maximize value."[10] From this perspective, physicians do not and should not always tell the truth to their patients or their families. Sometimes physicians should even lie to give hope. According to this account, selective adherence to rules does not erode either moral rules or general respect for morality.

Because of the benefits to society of the general observance of moral rules, the rule utilitarian does not abandon rules, even in such difficult situations. Abandonment threatens the integrity and existence of both the particular rules and the whole system of rules.[11] The act utilitarian's reply is that although rules such as promise-keeping usually should be kept to maintain trust, they may be set aside when doing so would maximize overall good.

An Absolute Principle with Derivative Contingent Rules

From the utilitarian's perspective, the principle of utility is the sole and absolute principle of ethics. No derivative rule, however central at present in morality, is unrevisable. For example, rules in medicine against actively ending a patient's life may be overturned or substantially revised, depending on the consequences of having or not having the rules. In Chapter 5 we assessed current debates about whether seriously suffering patients should, at their request, be actively assisted in dying rather than merely being "allowed to die." The rule utilitarian view is that we should support rules that permit physicians to hasten death if and only if those rules would produce the most utility. Likewise, there should be rules against physician-assisted death if and only if those rules would maximize utility. Utilitarians often point out that many do not currently support allowing physicians to actively bring about a patient's death because of the adverse social consequences that they believe to follow for those directly and indirectly affected. If, however, under a different set of social conditions, legalization of physician-assisted death would maximize overall social welfare, the utilitarian sees no reason to prohibit it. Utilitarians thus regard their theory as responsive in constructive ways to changing social practices.

A Critical Evaluation of Utilitarianism

Utilitarianism is an attractive moral theory, especially for the formation of public and institutional policies. However, it is not a fully adequate moral theory even for those areas, much less for all areas of the moral life, for the reasons discussed in this section.

Problems with immoral preferences and actions. Problems arise for utilitarians who are concerned about the maximization of individual preferences when some of these individuals have what our considered judgments tell us are morally unacceptable preferences. For example, if a researcher derives great satisfaction from inflicting pain on animals or on human subjects in experiments, we would condemn this preference and would seek to prevent it from being satisfied. A theory based on subjective preferences is a plausible theory only if we can formulate a range of *acceptable* preferences and determine acceptability independently of the particular preferences agents happen to have. This task seems inconsistent with a pure preference approach to utility, because there is no pure utilitarian means to elevate one set of preferences over another.[12]

A related problem concerns immoral actions. Suppose the only way to achieve the maximal utilitarian outcome is to perform an immoral act—again, as judged by the standards of the common morality—such as killing one person to distribute his organs to several others who will die without them. Act utilitarianism seems to suggest not only that such killing is permissible, but also that it is morally obligatory—assuming, of course, that the killing would in fact achieve an overall maximization of utility.

Does utilitarianism demand too much? Some forms of utilitarianism seem to demand too much in the moral life, because the principle of utility requires maximizing value. Utilitarians have a difficult time maintaining the distinction between morally obligatory actions and supererogatory actions. Alan Donagan has described a variety of situations in which utilitarian theory regards an action as obligatory even though our firm moral conviction is that the action is ideal and praiseworthy rather than obligatory.[13] For example, Donagan would regard the "voluntary" suicide of frail elderly persons who suffer from severe disabilities and are no longer useful to society as an example of acts that could never rightly be considered obligatory, regardless of the consequences. The same holds for coercive takings of bodily parts, such as kidneys and even hearts, to save another person's life. If utilitarianism makes such actions obligatory, it is a defective theory.

Bernard Williams and John Mackie have offered extensions of this thesis that utilitarianism demands too much. Williams argues that utilitarianism abrades personal integrity by making persons morally responsible for consequences that they *fail to prevent* as much as for those outcomes they *directly cause,* even when the consequences are not of their doing. Mackie argues that the utilitarian's test of right actions is so distant from our moral experience that it is "the ethics of fantasy," because it demands that people strip themselves of many goals and relationships they value in life to maximize good outcomes for others.[14]

Problems of unjust distribution. A third problem is that utilitarianism in principle permits the interests of the majority to override the rights of minorities, and does not have the resources to adequately guard against unjust social distributions. The charge is that utilitarians assign no independent weight to rights and justice and are indifferent to unjust distributions because they distribute value according to net aggregate satisfaction.[15] If an already prosperous group of persons could have more value added to their lives than could be added to the lives of the indigent in society, the utilitarian must recommend that the added value go to the prosperous group.

An example of problematic, although on balance perhaps justified, distribution appears in the following case. Two researchers wanted to determine the most cost-effective way to control hypertension in the American population. As they developed their research, they discovered that it is more cost-effective to target patients already being treated for hypertension than to identify new cases of hypertension among persons without regular access to medical care. They concluded that "a community with limited resources would probably do better to concentrate its efforts on improving adherence of known hypertensives (that is, those already identified as sufferers of hypertension), even at a sacrifice in terms of the numbers screened." No other policy would work as efficiently as targeting known hypertensives already in contact with physicians. However, this recommendation would exclude the poorest sector of the population with the most pressing need for medical attention from the benefits of publicly funded high blood pressure education and management.[16]

A Constructive Evaluation of Utilitarianism

Despite these criticisms, utilitarianism has many strengths, two of which we have appropriated in other chapters. The first is the significant role the principle of utility can play in formulating public and institutional policies. The utilitarian's requirements for an objective assessment of everyone's interests and of an impartial choice to maximize good outcomes for all affected parties are acceptable, indeed, worthy, norms of public policy, except when they might lead to unjust distributions and the like. Second, when we formulated principles of beneficence in Chapter 5, utility played an important role. We have characterized utilitarianism as primarily a consequence-based theory, but it is also beneficence-based. That is, the theory sees morality primarily in terms of the legitimate goal of promoting welfare and takes that role with appropriate seriousness. As we have argued previously, nonmaleficence and beneficence are among the most basic of moral principles, and utilitarianism is erected at its foundations on these principles.

In the end, we agree with Amartya Sen that "Consequentialist reasoning may be fruitfully used even when consequentialism as such is not accepted. To ignore consequences is to leave an ethical story half told."[17]

KANTIAN THEORY

A second type of theory denies much that utilitarian theories affirm. Often called *deontological*[18] and *nonconsequentialist*[19] (i.e., a theory of duty holding that some features of actions other than or in addition to consequences make actions right or wrong), this type of theory is now typically called *Kantian,* because the philosophy of Immanuel Kant (1724–1804) has most penetratingly shaped many of its contemporary formulations.

Consider how a Kantian might approach the previously mentioned case of the five-year-old in need of a kidney. A Kantian would insist that we should rest our moral judgments on reasons that apply to all other persons who are similarly situated. If the father has no generalizable moral obligation to his daughter, then no basis is available for morally criticizing him for not donating a kidney. The strict Kantian maintains that if the father chooses to donate out of affection, compassion, or concern for his dying daughter, his act would lack moral worth, because it would not be based on a generalizable obligation; but the donation would have moral worth if done from the duty of beneficence. Using one of the girl's younger siblings as a source of a kidney would be illegitimate because this recourse to children who are too young to consent to donation would involve using persons merely as means to others' ends. This principle would also preclude coercing the father to donate against his will.

Regarding the father's request for the physician to deceive the family, a strict Kantian views lying as an act that cannot consistently be universalized as a norm of conduct. The physician should not lie to the man's wife or to other members of the family, even if it would help keep the family intact (a consequentialist appeal). Although the physician's statement is not, strictly speaking, a lie, he still intentionally uses this formulation to conceal relevant facts from the wife, an act Kantians typically view as morally unacceptable.

A Kantian will also consider whether the rule of confidentiality has independent moral weight, whether the tests the father underwent with the nephrologist established a relationship of confidentiality, and whether the rule of confidentiality protects information about the father's histocompatibility and his reasons for not donating. If confidentiality prohibits the nephrologist from letting the family know that the father is histocompatible, then the Kantian must face an apparent conflict of obligations: truthfulness in conflict with confidentiality.

Before we can address such conflict, however, we need to have the rudiments of Kantian theory before us.

Obligation from Categorical Rules

In Kant's theory morality is grounded in reason, rather than in tradition, intuition, or attitudes such as sympathy. Human beings are creatures with rational powers that motivate them morally, that help them resist tempting desires, and that allow them to prescribe moral rules to themselves. One of Kant's most important claims is that the moral worth of an individual's action depends exclusively on the moral acceptability of the "maxim" (i.e., the general rule of conduct) on which the person is acting. True moral obligation depends on an objectively valid rule determining the individual's will; the rule provides a moral ground that justifies the action.[20]

For Kant, one must act not only in accordance with, but also for the sake of obligation. That is, to have moral worth, a person's motive for acting must come from a recognition that he or she intends that which is morally required. For example, if an employer discloses a health hazard to an employee only because the employer fears a lawsuit, and not because of the importance of truth-telling, then the employer has performed the right action but deserves no moral credit for the action. If agents do what is morally right simply because they are scared, because they derive pleasure from doing that kind of act, or because they seek recognition, they lack the requisite goodwill that derives from acting for the sake of obligation.

Kant imagines a man who desperately needs money and knows that he will not be able to borrow it unless he promises repayment in a definite time, but who also knows that he will not be able to repay it within this period. He decides to make a promise that he knows he will break. Kant asks us to examine the man's reason, that is, maxim: "When I think myself in want of money, I will borrow money and promise to pay it back, although I know that I cannot do so." Kant

maintains that this maxim cannot pass a test he calls the *cat*
This imperative tells us what must be done irrespective of ou
its major formulation, Kant states the categorical imperative
act except in such a way that I can also will that my maxir
law." Kant says that this general principle justifies all par
obligation (all "ought" statements that morally obligate).[21]

The categorical imperative is a canon of the acceptability of moral rules,
that is, a criterion for judging the acceptability of the maxims that direct actions.
This imperative adds nothing to a maxim's content. Rather, it determines which
maxims are objective and valid. The categorical imperative functions by testing
what Kant calls the "consistency of maxims": A maxim must be capable of being
conceived and willed without contradiction. When we examine the maxim of
the person who deceitfully promises, we discover, Kant says, that this maxim
is incapable of being conceived and willed universally without yielding a contradiction. It is inconsistent with what it presupposes, as if to say, "My promise can be deceitful, though promising cannot be deceitful." The universalized
maxim to the effect that a deceitful promise is permissible is inconsistent with
the institution of promising it presupposes, and this universalized maxim would
be undermined if everyone acted on it. Lying, too, works only if the person lied
to expects or presupposes that people are truthful, but, if universalized, a maxim
approving lying would make the purpose of truth-telling impossible, and no one
would believe the person who told a lie. Many examples illustrate this thesis. For
instance, maxims permitting cheating on tests are inconsistent with the practices
of honesty in taking tests that they presuppose.[22]

Kant has more than one version or formulation of the categorical imperative. His second formulation is widely cited in biomedical ethics and is more
influential in this field than the first: "One must act to treat every person as an
end and never as a means only."[23] It has often been stated that this principle categorically requires that we should never treat another as a means to our ends,
but this interpretation misrepresents Kant's views. He argues only that we must
not treat another merely or exclusively as a means to our ends. When human
research subjects volunteer to test new drugs, they are treated as a means to others' ends, but they have a choice in the matter and retain control over their lives.
Kant does not prohibit such uses of consenting persons. He insists only that they
be treated with the respect and moral dignity to which every person is entitled.

Autonomy and Heteronomy

We saw in Chapter 4 that the word *autonomy* typically refers to that which
makes judgments and actions one's own. Kant's theory of autonomy differs from
this formulation: Persons have "autonomy of the will" if and only if they knowingly act in accordance with the universally valid moral principles that pass the

ments of the categorical imperative. Kant contrasts this moral autonomy "heteronomy," which refers to any determinative influence over the will her than motivation by moral principles.[24] If, for example, people act from passion, desire, personal ambition, or self-interest, they act heteronomously. Only a rational will acting morally chooses autonomously. Kant regards acting from fear, pity, impulse, personal projects, and habit as no less heteronomous than actions manipulated or coerced by others.

To say that an individual must have "accepted" a moral principle in order to qualify as autonomous does not mean that the principle is subjective or that each individual must create (author or originate) his or her moral principles. Kant requires only that each individual will the acceptance of moral principles. If a person freely accepts objective moral principles, that person is a lawgiver unto himself or herself. Kant's account extends beyond the nature of autonomy to its value. "The principle of autonomy," he boldly proposes, is "the sole principle of morals," and it is autonomy that gives people respect, value, and proper motivation. A person's dignity—indeed, "sublimity"—comes from being morally autonomous.[25]

Kant's theory of autonomy is thus not merely about respect for the self-determination of agents who make judgments and set personal goals. Kant's theory is about *moral* self-determination. Nonetheless, Kant's second formulation of the categorical imperative is reasonably close to the normative commitments in the principle of respect for autonomy that we developed in Chapter 4.

Contemporary Kantian Ethics

Several writers in contemporary ethical theory have accepted and developed Kantian moral theories, broadly construed.

An example is *The Theory of Morality* by Alan Donagan. He seeks the "philosophical core" of the morality expressed in the Hebrew-Christian tradition, which he interprets in secular rather than religious terms. Donagan's account relies heavily on Kant's theory of persons as ends in themselves, especially the imperative that one must treat humanity as an end and never as a means only. Donagan expresses the fundamental principle of the Hebrew-Christian tradition as a Kantian principle grounded in rationality: "It is impermissible not to respect every human being, oneself or any other, as a rational creature."[26]

A second Kantian theory derives from the work of John Rawls, who challenged utilitarian theories through developing Kantian themes of reason, autonomy, individual worth, self-respect, and equality.[27] His *A Theory of Justice* uses Kant's moral theory to construct the foundation of a theory of justice (as treated in Chapter 7). For Rawls, the right to individual autonomy (as discussed in Chapter 4) of an agent does not outweigh what rational moral principles determine to be morally right. Even conscientious acts of individual autonomy do not merit respect unless they are in accord with moral principles.[28]

Several philosophers, including Bernard Williams and Thomas Nagel, have developed views about "deontological constraints" that are related to Kant's injunction never to use another person merely as a means.[29] They see that Kant is correctly maintaining that certain actions are impermissible regardless of the consequences. For example, in research involving human subjects, even if achieving great breakthroughs would have good consequences for millions of people, researchers would be treating their subjects unethically if they violated fundamental ethical constraints, such as failing to obtain subjects' voluntary, informed consent. These constraints are essentially negative duties because they specify what we cannot justifiably do to others even in the pursuit of worthy goals.

However, another influential Kantian, Christine Korsgaard, warns that we may misunderstand Kant if we interpret his moral theory through the lens of such constraints. She argues that when philosophers contrast utilitarian and Kantian theories, they often miss the fact that these two types of moral theory take strikingly different views about the subject matter of ethics. Whereas utilitarians take the subject matter to be the outcomes of actions, Kantians see the subject matter as the quality of relationships, what we owe to others, and the like. Utilitarians hold that one should be just and beneficent in relationships to others because it maximizes the good, but in Kantian theory the norm that one should produce good outcomes itself derives from norms of proper relationships. Pursuing the good of others is a duty only because of the norm that we must respect the humanity in others and help them in times of need. Korsgaard argues that it is a mistake to present Kantian theory as defending deontological constraints as if they were constraints on the goal of promoting the good. In her interpretation, Kant does not recognize that there is a general duty to promote the good that then must be constrained.[30]

Another Kantian philosopher, Onora O'Neill, has extended Kantian thought into several areas of biomedical ethics, public health, and global justice. Her themes focus heavily on "principled autonomy," public reason, a robust interpretation of universalizability, and the importance of creating conditions of trust.[31]

A Critical Evaluation of Kantian Theory

Like utilitarianism, Kant's theory and modern reformulations do not provide a fully convincing or truly comprehensive theory of the moral life, for several reasons.

The problem of conflicting obligations. Kant construes moral requirements as categorical imperatives, but this theory is inadequate to handle the problem of conflicting obligations. Suppose we have promised to take our children on a long-anticipated trip, but now find that if we do so, we cannot assist our sick mother in the hospital. A rule of promise-keeping in conflict with an obligation of care generates this conflict. Conflict can also arise from a single moral rule rather than from two different rules, as, for example, when two promises come into conflict, although the promisor could not have anticipated the conflict when making the promises. Because moral rules are *categorical* in Kant's theory, he seems to be committed to the view that we are obligated to do the impossible and perform both actions. Any ethical theory that leads to this conclusion is unsatisfactory, yet no clear way out exists for Kant or for any theory committed to categorical rules.[32]

Overemphasizing law, underemphasizing relationships. Kant's arguments concentrate on obligations from moral law, and some recent Kantian theories feature a contractual basis for obligations. But whether contract, moral law, and related staples of Kantianism deserve to occupy this central position in a moral theory is questionable. These visions of the moral life fail to capture much that is morally important in personal relationships. For example, we rarely think or act in terms of law, contract, or absolute rules in relationships among friends and family.[33] This feature of the moral life suggests that Kant's theory (like utilitarianism) is better suited for relationships among strangers than for relationships among friends or other intimates.

Virtue, emotion, and moral worth. Kant maintains that actions done from sympathy, emotion, and the like have no moral worth; only actions performed from duty (i.e., the motive of duty) have moral worth. Kant does not disallow or even discourage sympathy and moral emotions, but these motives count for nothing morally. Yet, as we argued in Chapter 2, actions done from sympathy, emotion, and the like do seem to have moral worth under some conditions. Persons with appropriate feelings and concern about their friends, for example, are morally worthier than persons who discharge obligations of friendship entirely from a sense of duty. A "friend" or a physician or a nurse who lacks appropriate attitudes of care is morally deficient. Kant's theory seems defective not because we want people to act from feelings rather than from a sense of obligation. Of course we want people to be attentive to and discharge their obligations, and there is nothing wrong with a motive of duty; but motivation from deep care and concern are also meritorious.[34]

A Constructive Evaluation of Kantian Theory

Kant argued that when good reasons support a moral judgment, those reasons are good for all relevantly similar circumstances. Most moral theories now accept roughly this claim, and Kant must be credited for a compelling and far-reaching theoretical account. For example, if we are required to obtain valid consent for all subjects of biomedical research, we cannot make exceptions of certain persons merely because we could advance science by doing so. We cannot use institutionalized populations without consent any more than we can use people who are not in institutions without their consent. Kant and many Kantians have driven home the point that persons cannot privilege or exempt themselves, their co-workers, or their favored group and still act morally.

Both Kant and contemporary Kantians have worked diligently on perhaps the single most important issue in recent moral philosophy: Are some actions wrong not because of their good or bad effects, but because of the inherent wrongness of either the actions or the rules from which the action is performed? Also, Kant's second formulation of the categorical imperative—that persons must be treated as ends and not means only—can be, and often has been, interpreted as the substantive basis of the principle of respect for autonomy. Among the most defensible implications of his philosophy is that we have a basic obligation to respect the reasoned choices of others as well as their inherent capacities of reason and choice. Kant's formulation of this claim has significantly and justifiably influenced contemporary biomedical ethics.

RIGHTS THEORY

Utilitarian and Kantian thought are committed to the language of moral obligations, but the language of moral rights is equally important. Since at least the seventeenth century[35] statements and theories of rights have been considered vital sources of the protection of life, liberty, expression, and property. They protect against oppression, unequal treatment, intolerance, arbitrary invasion of privacy, and the like. Today both human rights and animal rights are frequent topics of conversation in bioethics and have a larger presence in philosophical moral theory than at any previous time. Many philosophers, political activists, lawyers, and framers of political declarations now regard rights theory as the most important type of theory for expressing the moral point of view.

An ethical analysis of the case of the five-year-old in need of a transplant would, from the perspective of rights theory, focus on the rights of all the parties, in an effort to determine their meaning and scope as well as their weight and strength. The father could be considered to have rights of autonomy, privacy, and confidentiality that protect his bodily integrity and sphere of decision making from interference by others. In addition, he has a right to information, which he apparently received, about the risks, benefits, and alternatives of living kidney donation. The father's decision not to donate is within his rights, as long as it does not violate another's rights. No apparent grounds support a general right to assistance that could permit anyone, including his daughter, to demand a kidney. However, there are various specific rights to assistance, and it might be argued that the daughter has a right to receive a kidney from her family on the basis of either parental obligations or medical need. Even if such a right exists, which is doubtful, it would be circumscribed. For example, it is implausible to suppose that such a right could be enforced against the interests of the girl's two young siblings. Their right to noninterference, when the procedure is not for their direct benefit and carries risks, and their lack of the capacity to give a valid consent shield them from conscriptive use as sources of a kidney.

The father has exercised his rights of autonomy and privacy in allowing the physician to run some tests. He then seeks protection under his right of confidentiality, which he believes allows him to control third-party access to any information generated in his relationship with the physician. However, the precise scope and limits of his rights and the competing rights of others need to be approached cautiously. For example, does the mother herself have a right to the information generated in the relationship between the father and the nephrologist, particularly information bearing on the fate of her daughter?

Whether the physician has a right of conscientious refusal is another issue. The physician might resist becoming an instrument of the father's desire to keep others from knowing why he is not donating a kidney. But even if the physician has a right to protect his personal integrity, does this right trump either his patient's right to be treated or the father's right of confidentiality?

Rights as Justified Claims

A right gives its holder a justified claim *to* something (an entitlement) and a justified claim *against* another party. Claiming is a mode of action that appeals to moral norms that permit persons to demand, affirm, or insist upon what is due to them. "Rights," then, may be defined as justified claims to something that individuals or groups can legitimately assert against other individuals or groups. A right thereby positions one to determine by one's choices what others morally must or must not do.[36]

Rights-claiming is a rule-governed activity in each domain in which there are rights. The rules may be moral rules, legal rules, institutional rules, or rules of games. All rights exist or fail to exist because the relevant rules allow or disallow claims to be made. The rules distinguish justified from unjustified claims. Legal rights are justified by normative structures in law, and moral rights are justified by normative structures in morality.

The language of rights has served, on occasion, as a means to oppose the status quo, to demand recognition and respect, and to promote social reforms that aim to secure legal protections for individuals. The legitimate role of civil, political, and legal rights in protecting the individual from societal intrusions is undeniable, but the proposition that individual rights provide the fountainhead for moral and political theory has been strongly resisted—for example, by many utilitarians. They maintain that individual interests said to be protected by rights are often at odds with communal and institutional interests and also produce bizarre situations in which two or more rights claims are in direct conflict. In discussions of health care delivery, for example, proponents of a broad availability of medical services often appeal to the "right to health care," whereas opponents sometimes appeal to the "rights of the medical profession." Many participants in moral, political, and legal discussions presuppose that arguments cannot be persuasive unless stated in the language of rights, although other participants find this language excessively confrontational, adversarial, and unsuitable to address the moral problems that require attention. The authors of this book are not of the latter persuasion.

Are Rights Trumps?: The Debate about Absolute and Prima Facie Rights

Rights are neither as strong nor as confrontational as they have appeared to many critics. Some rights may be absolute or close to absolute[37] (e.g., the moral right to consent to surgery or to choose one's religion or to reject all religion), but, typically, rights are not absolute claims. Like principles of obligation, rights assert only prima facie claims (in the sense of "prima facie" introduced in Chapter 1).

Many in rights theory seem to dispute this claim. They use the suggestive language of Ronald Dworkin that particularly critical interests of individuals (chiefly against political states) are firmly protected by rights that have the force of trump cards.[38] However, this trump metaphor is not well-suited for situations in which one moral right conflicts with another moral right—a critical problem in many practical contexts. It is not always the case when individual rights conflict with the public interest that rights are trumps against the state. If the state needs to protect the rights of citizens—for example, the state needs to prevent the spread of a catastrophic disease—then it may legitimately override individual rights such as the right to refuse vaccination. Dworkin himself gives only a notably limited account of rights as trumps: "Rights are best understood as *trumps over some background justification for political decisions* that states a goal for the community as a whole."[39] In effect, Dworkin regards rights as stronger—much stronger—than the moral claims created by community goals and preferences. So understood, rights are instruments that function to guarantee that individuals cannot be sacrificed to government interests or mere majority interests, but they are not absolute trumps.

Interpreting rights as trumps is appealing in contexts in which individuals are vulnerable to serious harms and in which minority populations might be oppressed by majority preferences. One value of the trump metaphor is to remind us both that rights powerfully protect individuals from having their interests balanced or traded off and that proposals to override them in the public interest need the most careful inspection and justification. However, models from trumps, absolute shields, and uninfringeable deontological protections are more misleading than insightful. The reason that rights are special, and

especially cherished, is that individuals hold justified claims that they can exercise. They are not beholden to the moral beneficence of other persons.

Accordingly, all rights, like all principles and rules of obligation, are prima
facie (i.e., presumptively) valid claims that sometimes, however rarely, must yield
to other claims. In light of this need to balance claims, we should distinguish a
violation of a right from an *infringement* of a right.[40] "Violation" refers to an unjustified and wrong action against an interest that is protected by a right, whereas
"infringement" refers to an action that may or may not legitimately override a
right.

The Rights of the Incompetent and Unidentified Members of Populations

Possession of a right is independent of being in a position to assert the right or
to exercise the right. A right-holder need not be the claimant in a particular case
in order to have a justified claim. That a person does not know that he has a
right is no basis for asserting that he does not have it. For example, infants and
the severely mentally handicapped do not know, assert, or claim their rights, but
they still possess them, and claims can be made on their behalf by appropriate
representatives. Many dependent humans and dependent animals, such as animals in laboratories, have rights whether or not they have an authorized representative, such as a surrogate, who can exercise the rights.

In some circumstances there are obligations to protect rights even if no specific individuals can be identified as having rights. For example, professionals
in veterinary public health have obligations to protect both animals and people
against communicable diseases, even though no specific animal or human is
identifiable in many circumstances.[41] These right-holders are unidentified members of populations.

Positive Rights and Negative Rights

A distinction between positive rights and negative rights is generally accepted
in rights theory. A *positive* right is a right to receive a particular good or service from others, for example, a right to health care and a right to public health
protective services, whereas a *negative* right is a right to be free from some
intervention by others, for example, a right of privacy and a right to forgo a recommended surgical procedure. A person's positive right entails another's obligation to do something for that person; a negative right entails another's obligation
to refrain from doing something.[42]

Negative rights such as the right to forgo a medical procedure are arguably
grounded in the principle of respect for autonomy, and positive rights such as the
right to health care are arguably grounded in principles of beneficence and justice. Although rights theorists have generally found it easier to justify negative

rights, the modern recognition of welfare or entitlement rights has expanded the scope of positive rights in many nation-states.

The Correlativity of Rights and Obligations

How are rights related to the moral obligations that were so prominently featured in the previous two moral theories treated in this chapter?

To answer this question, consider the meaning of the abstract statement "X has a right to do or have Y." Following from the earlier analysis of the nature of a right as a valid claim, X's right entails that some party has an obligation either not to interfere if X does Y or to provide X with Y. In all contexts of rights, a system of norms imposes an obligation either to act or to refrain from acting so that X can do or have Y. The language of rights is thus translatable into the language of obligations: A right entails an obligation, and an obligation entails a right. If, for example, a physician agrees to take John Doe as a patient and commences treatment, the physician incurs an obligation to Doe, and Doe gains a correlative right to treatment. Likewise, if a state has an obligation to provide goods such as food or health care to needy citizens, then any citizen who meets the relevant criteria of need is entitled to an allotment of food or health care.

That there is a correlativity between obligations and rights is generally accepted in both philosophical ethics and in legal theory, though the precise rights and obligations involved have been difficult to pin down. Here is a brief schema, using some basic rights and obligations, to illustrate this correlativity:

Basic Obligations	**Basic Rights**
1. Do not kill.	1. The right to not be killed
2. Do not cause pain or suffering to others.	2. The right to not be caused pain or suffering by others
3. Prevent harm from occurring.	3. The right to have harms prevented from occurring
4. Rescue persons in danger.	4. The right to be rescued when in danger
5. Tell the truth.	5. The right to be told the truth
6. Nurture the young and dependent.	6. The right to be nurtured when young and dependent
7. Keep your promises.	7. The right to have promises kept
8. Do not steal.	8. The right to not have one's property stolen
9. Do not punish the innocent.	9. The right to not be punished when one is innocent
10. Obey the law.	10. The right to have others obey the law

Is the correlativity thesis flawed? The correlativity thesis has been challenged on grounds that the correlativity between obligations and rights is untidy[43] in that (1) only *some* obligations entail rights and (2) only *some* rights entail obligations.[44] We find these two challenges to correlativity unconvincing, but we will discuss only the first challenge because critics of the correlativity thesis now generally concede that all genuine rights (by contrast to merely proclaimed rights and aspirational rights) do carry correlative obligations. Also, the first challenge is the only crucial one for the theory that rights follow directly from obligations, which is the important matter under consideration.

The objection is that various appropriate uses of the term *obligation,* as well as the related terms *requirement* and *duty,* show that some obligations do not imply correlative rights. Alleged examples come from the fact that we refer to obligations of charity, and yet no person can claim another person's charity as a matter of a right. Obligations of love and obligations of conscience are also put forward as examples of obligations without correlative rights.

The problem with these objections and counterexamples is that although it is correct to say that alleged norms of "obligation" such as charity express what we "ought to do" or are "required to do" in some sense, they do not constitute genuine moral obligations. Rather, they obligate individuals committed to admirable moral ideals that exceed moral obligation. Hence, they are self-imposed rules of "obligation" that at bottom express widely admired and endorsed moral ideals rather than obligations imposed by morality. The critical point is that all genuine moral obligations have correlative rights and that all genuine moral rights have correlative obligations.[45]

The line at which an action is obligatory rather than ideal is unfortunately not always clear. Consider a circumstance in which a fire has broken out in a hospital. A child needs help to escape from a smoke-filled room. A physician sees the problem and takes the child from the room. The physician is not endangered in doing so and can easily carry the child to safety. Clearly this physician has a moral obligation to rescue the child—as would any passerby in the hall. However, if we alter the facts of this situation, it becomes questionable whether there is any such moral obligation. Suppose the walls and floor of the hospital room are ablaze all around the child and collapse of the room will almost certainly occur at any second. The original obligation of beneficence now turns into a risky rescue mission that can be described as a moral "requirement" only in the misleading sense previously mentioned. In this circumstance, the physician has no obligation of rescue and the child has no right of rescue. As risks increase in circumstances of fires, epidemics, raging rivers, and other highly risky circumstances, it becomes increasingly less likely that there is a genuine obligation, and a rescuer at some point in the risk index becomes a hero rather than a discharger of an obligation. (See further our discussion of moral ideals and moral heroes in Chapter 2.)

Are rights primary? The correlativity thesis does not determine whether rights or obligations, if either, is the more fundamental or primary category in moral theory. Proposals of a "rights-based" moral theory spring from a particular conception of the function and justification of morality.[46] If the function of morality is to protect individuals' interests (rather than communal interests), and if rights (rather than obligations) are our primary instruments to this end, then moral action guides seem to be fundamentally rights-based. Rights, on this account, precede obligations.

A theory we encountered in Chapter 7 illustrates this position: Robert Nozick maintains that "Individuals have rights, and there are things no person or group may do to them [without violating their rights]."[47] He takes the following rule to be basic in the moral life: All persons have a right to be left free to do as they choose. The obligation not to interfere with this right follows from the right, rather than the right from the obligation. That it follows in this way indicates the priority of a rule of moral right over a rule of moral obligation; the obligation is derived from a right.

Alan Gewirth has proposed a rights-based argument that recognizes *positive* or *benefit* rights (rights that Nozick does not accept):

> Rights are to obligations as benefits are to burdens. For rights are justified claims to certain benefits, the support of certain interests of the subject or right-holder. Obligations, on the other hand, are justified burdens on the part of the respondent or duty-bearer; they restrict his freedom by requiring that he conduct himself in ways that directly benefit not himself but rather the right-holder. But burdens are for the sake of benefits, and not vice versa. Hence obligations, which are burdens, are for the sake of rights, whose objects are benefits. Rights, then, are prior to obligations in the order of justifying purpose...in that respondents have correlative obligations *because* subjects have certain rights.[48]

Such rights-based accounts generally accept the correlativity of rights and obligations, but they also accept a priority thesis that obligations follow from rights, rather than the converse. Rights form the justificatory basis of obligations, proponents of these accounts maintain, because they best capture the purpose of morality, which is to secure liberties or other benefits for a rights-holder.

The specification of rights. James Griffin rightly points out that we are sometimes satisfied that a basic right exists and that there are correlative obligations, yet we are uncertain precisely what the basic right gives us a right to.[49] Basic rights are abstract moral notions that do not fix how to formulate specific policies or resolve practical moral problems. We also agree with Ronald Dworkin's assessment that "abstract rights...provide arguments for concrete rights, but the claim of a concrete right is more definitive [in political contexts] than any claim of abstract right that supports it."[50]

These important problems should be handled through what we have, in previous chapters, referred to as specification: the process of reducing the indeterminate character of abstract norms and giving them specific action-guiding content. Specifying rights to make them practical guidelines is no less important than specifying obligations.

A Critical Evaluation of Rights Theory

Problems in some areas of rights theories can now be addressed.

Problems with rights-based theories. One problem with basing ethics entirely on a grounding in rights is that the justification of the system of rules within which valid claiming occurs is not clearly rights-based. Pure rights-based accounts that aspire to be comprehensive moral theories also run the risk of truncating our understanding of morality, because rights cannot account for the moral significance of motives, supererogatory actions, virtues, and the like. A moral theory premised exclusively on rights would fare poorly under the criteria of comprehensiveness and explanatory and justificatory power proposed at the beginning of this chapter. Accordingly, it seems undesirable to limit moral theory to a rights-based model. Rights theory is best understood as a statement of minimal and enforceable rules protective of individual interests that communities and other individuals must observe.

Normative questions about the exercise of rights. Often a moral problem turns not on whether someone has a right, but whether rights-holders should or should not *exercise* their rights. If a person says, "I know you have the right to do X, but you should not do it," this moral claim goes beyond a statement of a right. One's obligation or character, not one's right, is in question. This problem shows why rights theory needs to be buttressed by theories of obligation and virtue.

The neglect of communal goods. Rights theorists sometimes write as if social morality's major concern is to protect individual rights against government or other forms of communal intrusion. This vision is too limited for a general ethical theory. It excludes not only group interests, but also communal values, such as public health, biomedical research, and the protection of animals in research. A better perspective is that social ideals, principles of obligation, and communal interests are as central to morality as rights, and that none is dispensable.

A Constructive Evaluation of Rights Theory

We have offered a sympathetic interpretation of the use of rights language to express critically important, and universally valid, moral norms. We have also offered a defense of both the correlativity of rights and obligations and the moral and social purposes served by a theory of basic rights. No part of our moral vocabulary has done more in recent years to protect the legitimate interests of citizens in political states than the language of rights. Predictably, injustice and inhumane treatment occur most frequently in political states that fail to recognize human rights in their rhetoric, documents, and actions. As much as any part of moral discourse, human rights language crosses international boundaries and enters into international law and statements by international agencies and associations. Although human rights are often presumed in public discourse to be legal rights, they are best interpreted as universally valid moral rights.

Being a rights-bearer in a society that enforces rights is both a source of personal protection and a source of dignity and self-respect. By contrast, to maintain that someone has an obligation to protect another's interest may leave the beneficiary in a passive position, dependent on the other's goodwill in fulfilling the obligation. When persons possess enforceable rights correlative to obligations, they are enabled to be independent agents, pursuing their projects and making legitimate claims.

We value rights because, when enforced, they provide protections against unscrupulous behavior, promote orderly change and cohesiveness in communities, and allow diverse communities to coexist peacefully within a single political state.[51] A major reason for giving prominence to rights in moral and political theory is that in contexts of moral practice, such as health care institutions, they have the highest respect and better shield individuals against unjust or unwarranted communal intrusion and control than does any other kind of moral category.

VIRTUE THEORY

In Chapter 2, we presented an account of moral character in terms of virtues and sketched a framework of virtues for biomedical ethics. These praiseworthy character traits are the opposite of the morally blameworthy character traits that constitute the vices. The three types of ethical theory thus far examined in this chapter recognize some important virtues and traits of character, and few would deny the importance of virtues in the moral life.

In this section we consider virtue ethics largely as a type of moral theory that is independent of utilitarian, Kantian, and rights theories. For all of their differences, utilitarians and deontologists conceive of moral philosophy and the demands of morality similarly: Ethics begins with the question, "What morally ought we to do?" and then provides general rules of obligation as guides to action. By contrast, in the classical Greek philosophy of the virtues, represented principally by Aristotle, the cultivation of virtuous traits of character is conceived as one of morality's primary functions; and in the eighteenth-century virtue theory of David Hume, even moral judgments of actions are at bottom judgments of whether certain motives and character traits are virtuous or vicious.

Some defenders of virtue ethics challenge assumptions, such as ours, that we can analyze and assess this type of theory in relation to other types of theory, as if they constituted a set of commensurate theories. They deny that virtue ethics is a theory at all, preferring to use terms such as *account* or *perspective* that can highlight virtue ethics' wide-ranging and all-embracing features. Others argue that it is incorrect to compare virtue ethics with existing theories instead of appreciating how deeply it challenges their frameworks. They charge that placing virtue ethics together with the three theories thus far examined loses sight of its radical critique of the other three approaches (and of contemporary culture).[52] Nevertheless, we contend that it is appropriate to consider virtue ethics as an alternative type of theory even though it does not address exactly the same questions as utilitarian, Kantian, or rights theories.

We begin by considering how a proponent of virtue ethics might approach the case of the father who is reluctant to donate a kidney to his dying daughter and requests physician deception of the family about his reasons. The father's confessed lack of courage to donate one of his kidneys is relevant to an evaluation of him and his refusal to donate, but he had other reasons as well, some possibly involving self-deception. He points to his daughter's "degree of suffering," which suggests that he believes she might be better off without a transplant. Hence, his motives may be partially other-directed, not purely self-centered, and may involve compassion for his very ill daughter. We could still investigate whether the father was sufficiently compassionate and caring about her welfare. His failure of courage may have overwhelmed his compassion, faithfulness, and other virtues, if they were present at all.

Several other judgments of character may be relevant in assessing this case. We lack a full description of his wife, but the father was apparently worried that she would be unforgiving in accusing him of "allowing his daughter to die." This belief underlies his request that the physician lie. In responding to the father's request, the physician apparently focused on how the act of deception might compromise his integrity, and he "felt very uncomfortable" about the request. This feeling suggests an ongoing concern not to compromise his character, especially his truthfulness and moral integrity. The physician presumably thought he could avoid a serious compromise of both truthfulness, in the sense of not directly lying, and integrity by saying that "for medical reasons" the father should not donate a kidney. However, questions arise about whether the physician here engaged in self-deception by acting on an unstable distinction between a direct lie (for instance, "he cannot donate because he is not histocompatible") and deliberately misleading statements ("for medical reasons" he should not donate).

In the remainder of this section, we will first consider the distinction between right action and virtuous action, and then turn to the special status of virtues. We will later consider how moral virtues are related to the sorts of action guides presented in the previous three theories in this chapter.

Right Action and Proper Motive

Aristotle drew an important distinction between right action and proper motive, which he analyzed in terms of the distinction between external performance and internal state. An action can be right without being virtuous, he maintained, but an action can be virtuous only if performed in the right state of mind. Both right action and right motive are present in a truly virtuous action: "The agent must...be in the right state when he does [the actions]. First, he must know [that he is performing virtuous actions]; second, he must decide on them, and decide on them for themselves; and third, he must also do them from a firm and unchanging state," including the right state of emotion and desire. "The just and temperate person is not the one who [merely] does these actions, but the one who also does them in the way in which just or temperate people do them."[53]

Aristotle has it right. In addition to being properly motivated, a virtuous person experiences appropriate feelings, such as sympathy and regret, even when the feelings are not motives and no action results from the feelings. Virtuous persons also do not act from mere inclination or for personal advantage. They act under a conception of what is morally right and worthy. However, not all virtues have a transparent link to motives, feelings, or a conception of good and worthy reasons. Moral discernment and moral integrity, two virtues treated in Chapter 2, are examples. In these two virtues, psychological properties other than feelings are paramount, and they involve morally good states of mind beyond having a conception of what is right and worthy.[54]

The terms *virtue* and *vice* have been extensively used in the history of ethical theory, even if they are today less common in our moral vocabulary than obligation, human rights, and the like. The idea behind virtue theory is both intuitive and sensible: We commend and deeply respect persons who are honest, fair, respectful, just, or caring, or have various other admirable qualities. Likewise, we condemn and disrespect persons who are dishonest, malevolent, uncaring, unjust, or dishonorable, or have other vices. A comprehensive catalogue of the virtues and the vices, as proposed in some classic moral theories and religious traditions, is a large project, because there are dozens of vices and virtues.[55] Some of them are merely proclaimed virtues that are controversial, but most have been accepted in the common morality and by the major moral theorists who have developed accounts of virtue and vice.

The Definition of "Virtue"

The definition of "virtue" was briefly addressed in Chapter 2, where we stated that "A *virtue* is a dispositional trait of character that is socially valuable and reliably present in a person, and a *moral virtue* is a dispositional trait of character that is morally valuable and reliably present." This definition builds on, but moves beyond, a prominent definition of virtue offered by Hume, who wrote that "It is the nature, and, indeed, the definition of virtue, that it is *a quality of the mind agreeable to or approved of by every one, who considers or contemplates it.*"[56] So understood, a virtue is a fusion of two components: (1) an objective mental quality in a person (a feeling, motive, or character trait), and (2) a general approval of this mental quality by all impartial persons who contemplate it. "General approval" here means that the approval focuses not only on a specific good motive—as we proposed in Chapter 2—but also on a type of mental trait. The approval of mental qualities such as benevolence, friendliness, gratitude, honesty, compassion, and public spiritedness is, in Hume's theory, universal in all impartial moral judges (hence "every one" in his definition). A mental quality is a moral virtue if and only if it evokes universal moral approval; and a mental quality is a vice if and only if the quality evokes universal condemnation in impartial persons. All morally decent persons see certain mental traits as estimable, agreeable, and amiable—to use Hume's terms.

Hume's definition provides only the skeletal beginnings of an adequate analysis of "virtue." To generalize beyond both Hume and what we said in Chapter 2, now using a more contemporary vocabulary, a virtue is a deeply entrenched, morally good and commended trait of character that makes persons morally reliable, whereas a vice is the converse. We do not always think of virtues in terms of character traits, because parts of our vocabulary include "virtuous action" and "virtuous person." This terminology is perfectly acceptable, but a virtue itself is a character trait, meaning a morally good quality that a person reliably possesses. Although such a trait disposes a person to perform right actions, virtue theory proposes that we not start with right actions as if the virtues were derivative from judgments of action. The idea is to construct a moral theory from character traits that enable and dispose a person to right actions.[57]

The Special Status of the Virtues

Some who write about virtue and character see the language of obligation as *derivative* from the more basic moral language of virtue. They think that a person disposed by character to have good motives and desires provides the model of the moral person and that this model determines our expectations of persons, which are then expressed as obligations of the persons.[58] They regard the virtue model as more important than a model of action performed from obligation, because right motives and character tell us more about the moral worth of a person than do right actions goaded by obligation.

We are often far more concerned about the character and motives of persons than about the conformity of their acts to rules. When our friends perform acts of "friendship," we expect the acts not to be motivated entirely from a sense of obligation to us, but to be motivated by a desire to be friendly accompanied by a sense of valuing our friendship. The friend who acts only from obligation lacks the virtue of friendliness, and in the absence of this virtue, the relationship lacks the moral quality of friendship.[59]

Virtue theorists argue that the attempt in obligation-oriented theories to replace the virtuous judgments of health care professionals with rules, codes, or procedures will not produce better decisions and actions.[60] Rather than relying on institutional rules and government regulations to protect human research subjects, for example, the most reliable protection is the presence of an "informed, conscientious, compassionate, responsible researcher."[61] The claim is that character is more important than conformity to rules and that a premium should be placed on inculcating and cultivating the virtues through educational interactions and guidance by role models. Persons who are respectful, benevolent, and just reliably perform right actions: The respectful person respects others; benevolent persons act beneficently; and just persons conform their behavior to the rules of justice. Even if a virtuous person makes a mistake in judgment, leading to a morally questionable act, he or she is less blameworthy than a habitual offender who performed the same act.

In his chronicle of life under the Nazi SS in the Jewish ghetto in Cracow, Poland, Thomas Keneally describes a physician faced with a moral dilemma: either inject cyanide into four immobile patients or abandon them to the SS, who were at that moment emptying the ghetto and had already demonstrated that they would torture and kill captives and patients. This physician, Keneally observes, "suffered painfully from a set of ethics as intimate to him as the organs of his own body."[62] Here is a person of the highest moral character and virtue, motivated to act rightly and even heroically, despite having no idea what the morally right action is given the traditional rules of medical ethics. Ultimately, with uncertainty and reluctance, the physician elected euthanasia (using forty drops of hydrocyanic acid) without the consent or knowledge of the four doomed patients—an act almost universally denounced by the canons of professional medical ethics. Even if one thinks that the physician's *act* was wrong and blameworthy—a judgment we reject—no reasonable person would make a judgment of blame or demerit directed at the physician's *motives* or *character*. Having already risked death by choosing to remain at his patients' beds in the hospital rather than take a prepared escape route, the physician is a moral hero who displayed an extraordinary moral character.

Although judgments of agents' praiseworthiness and blameworthiness are directly connected to their motives, which are signs of their character, the merit of actions often does not reside entirely in motive or character. Actions must be gauged to bring about desired results and must conform to relevant principles and rules. For example, the physician or nurse who is appropriately motivated to help a patient, but who acts incompetently in pursuing the desired result or violates moral rules or rights, does not act in a praiseworthy or acceptable manner.

Moral Virtues and Action Guidance

Virtues as guides to action: What do virtuous moral agents do? Some virtue theorists maintain that virtues enable persons both to discern what he or she should do and be motivated to do it in particular circumstances without need for preexisting rules. According to Rosalind Hursthouse:

> Virtue ethics provides a specification of "right actions"—as "what a virtuous agent would, characteristically, do in the circumstances"—and such a specification can be regarded as generating a number of moral rules or principles (contrary to the usual claim that virtue ethics does not come up with rules or principles). Each virtue generates an instruction—"Do what is honest," "Do what is charitable," and each vice a prohibition—"Do not...do what is dishonest, uncharitable."[63]

In this theory, what is right to do is what a virtuous agent would do, and the virtuous agent reliably does what conforms to a "virtue-rule." When moral conflicts and moral dilemmas of the sort we explored in Chapter 1 emerge, they can be handled through additional specifications. Virtue ethics therefore resembles other normative ethical theories in seeking to identify the morally relevant features of a situation that justify doing action X rather than action Y. Many proponents of virtue ethics do not lament that their approach lacks a clear and precise decision procedure for conflicts and dilemmas. They maintain that theories based on principles, rules, and rights have no advantage over virtue theory in resolving moral dilemmas; and they claim that, in irresolvable and tragic dilemmas, the virtues help direct agents to appropriate responses, including appropriate attitudes and emotions such as moral distress.[64]

Specification of the actual "instruction" or "virtue-rule" will often not be as straightforward as Hursthouse's examples suggest (e.g., consider the virtue of moral integrity), and there is no reason to think that all specifications will rely exclusively on underlying notions of virtue (e.g., rules of informed consent may rely on values of autonomy beyond the virtue of respectfulness for autonomy). Specification in virtue ethics is likely to be similar in its commitments to the theory of moral norms and specification that we proposed in Chapter 1. Virtue theory, from this perspective, does not prove that virtues have advantages over principles and rules of obligation as guides to action.

Both theories grounded in virtue and theories grounded in principles have been faulted on grounds that they fail to give adequately specific directives or instructions.[65] These theories seem to demand only that we be beneficent or that we cultivate a benevolent character, and a theory this general or vague is not practical. However, as we have suggested in our proposals about specification and balancing, it is not clear that this objection has force against either general theories or principles or virtues. It is idealistic and overdemanding to require that a general theory's norms be highly directive in contexts of practice.

Moreover, the moral life is a constant process of acquiring skills and making judgments. Over time a person gains greater understanding and becomes more skilled in specifying general guidelines, moral virtues, and moral ideals. In the case of virtues and moral ideals, one learns better how to be, for example, truthful, honest, discreet, friendly, charitable, and polite by bringing those virtues to bear in a variety of situations. This form of learning involves the acquisition of skills roughly analogous to the process of learning and using a language.[66]

The relationship between moral virtues and moral norms. There is a rough, although imperfect, correspondence between some virtues and moral principles, rules, and ideals. This relationship is less uniform and more complicated than the correlativity of rights and obligations discussed in the previous section. The following (noncomprehensive) list illustrates the correspondence between a few select virtues and norms that are prominent in our account of the common morality.

Principles	**Corresponding Virtues**
Respect for autonomy	Respectfulness for autonomy
Nonmaleficence	Nonmalevolence
Beneficence	Benevolence
Justice	Justice

Rules	**Corresponding Virtues**
Veracity	Truthfulness
Confidentiality	Respectfulness for confidentiality
Privacy	Respectfulness for privacy
Fidelity	Faithfulness

Ideals of Action	**Corresponding Ideals of Virtue**
Exceptional forgiveness	Exceptional forgivingness
Exceptional generosity	Exceptional generousness
Exceptional compassion	Exceptional compassionateness
Exceptional kindness	Exceptional kindliness

This list could be expanded to include an extensive array of additional norms and virtues, but no chart can be constructed that presents a perfect, comprehensive schema of correspondence and noncorrespondence. Many virtues do not have a direct, one-to-one correspondence to a principle. For example, caring, concern, compassion, sympathy, courage, modesty, and patience are virtues that do not correspond well to principles and rules of obligation. Other examples are cautiousness, integrity, cheerfulness, unpretentiousness, sincerity, appreciativeness, cooperativeness, and commitment.[67] Some of these virtues, including courage and integrity, are important for morality as a whole. Some of the virtues that lack corresponding norms of obligation do nonetheless (as the previous chart shows) have corresponding moral ideals.

A Critical Evaluation of Virtue Theory

Several problems merit consideration in assessing virtue theory.

How independent and comprehensive is virtue theory? Various virtues seem to be character traits compatible with the performance of morally wrong actions. For example, courage, wisdom, and loyalty can enable unethical activities. As discussed in Chapter 8, the virtues of loyalty, friendship, and solidarity can foster inadequate reporting by physicians of unethical or incompetent behavior by other physicians. In speaking of generally admirable character traits as moral virtues, virtue theory cannot speak merely of good, commendable, and useful mental traits. The scope of virtues must be limited to character traits that enable and dispose persons to morally worthy pursuits.

In the tradition descending from Aristotle (discussed in Chapter 2), a moral virtue is exclusively a moral excellence of a person. But is moral excellence or moral worthiness determined exclusively by virtue standards? It is not easy to see how the notion of a morally worthy pursuit can be adequately built into a virtue theory without reliance on at least some nonvirtue premises of what constitutes a morally good life and morally good conduct, which in turn may require reference to action guides and to the general objectives of morality. (See the late parts of Chapter 2.)

When strangers meet. Where a climate of trust prevails, virtue and character are likely to be prized and emphasized in many human relationships. Principles or rules that express the obligations of health professionals in codes of conduct and statements of patients' rights may, in these intimate contexts, seem to be intrusions rather than essential elements. However, virtue theory works less well for certain other forms of moral encounter, especially where trust, intimacy, familiarity, and the like have not been established. When strangers meet, character often plays a less significant role than principles, rules, and institutional policies. For example, when a patient first encounters a physician, the physician's conformity to moral rules may be essential in situations of obtaining consent, disclosing a conflict of interest, proposing "do not resuscitate" orders for incompetent patients, explaining surrogate mother arrangements, and so on. Likewise, physicians may welcome explicit and mutually agreed-upon rules of informed consent, advance directives, codes of ethics, and similar structures and arrangements. Here rights, rules, and guidelines are welcome and prominent parts of the moral landscape. For example, patients' rights and investigators' obligations are likely to be the most important considerations in establishing and maintaining trust and confidence in the context of a randomized clinical trial.

A Constructive Evaluation of Virtue Theory

In Chapter 2 we examined several important virtues in biomedical ethics. We argued that often we care most in moral relationships about persons who have a good and reliable character and an appropriate moral responsiveness. Virtues come to the fore in contexts in which trust, intimacy, and dependence are present. Virtue theory is well-suited to help us navigate circumstances of caregiving and the delivery of information in health care. For example, "consenting" a patient (a common expression, but an objectionable notion) by merely conforming to institutional rules of informed consent is generally less important than having a caring and discerning physician or other health professional who appreciates the importance of dialogue, reassurance, and honesty in the process of obtaining an informed consent.

Virtue theory is the most venerable type of moral theory, with a beautiful tradition descending from the ancient world to modern times, and it has also been enhanced by some impressive recent theories. Throughout the history of moral theory, leading writers on the virtues have agreed on several moral virtues and on the importance of virtue theory. Aristotle's emphasis on excellences of character and David Hume's emphasis on virtues as the basis of personal merit are jewels in the history of virtue theory and moral philosophy. Though 2,000 years separated them, their philosophies display a considerable overlap. These theories deserve a status and recognition equal to that of Mill's utilitarian views of social beneficence, Kant's deontological views about the categorical importance of respect for all persons, and celebrated writers in the history of rights theory.

CONVERGENCE OF THEORIES

Whenever competing theories, systems, or general depictions of some phenomenon are available, we usually seek out the best account. However, affiliation with a single type of ethical theory is precarious in ethical theory and even more so in biomedical ethics. If the two authors of this book were forced to rank the types of theory examined in this chapter, we would differ. Nevertheless, for both of us, the most satisfactory type of theory—if we could find *one* to be most satisfactory—would be only slightly preferable, and no theory would fully satisfy all of the criteria for assessing theories presented in the first section of this chapter.

Differences among types of theory should not be exaggerated, as these theories are not warring armies locked in combat. Many and perhaps most moral theories lead to the acceptance of the action guides we present in Chapters 1 and 10 as elements in the common morality. This thesis may work less well for act-based theories (notably for act utilitarianism), but it generally holds for theories committed to rules, rights, and virtues. These theories defend roughly the same principles, obligations, rights, responsibilities, virtues, and the like. For example, although rule utilitarianism often appears to be both starkly different from, and even hostile to, nonconsequentialist theories, utilitarian Richard Brandt rightly notes that his theory is similar, at the level of principle and obligation, to W. D. Ross's nonutilitarian theory (which was discussed in Chapter 1):

> [The best code] would contain rules giving directions for recurrent situations which involve conflicts of human interests. Presumably, then, it would contain rules rather similar to W. D. Ross's list of prima facie obligations: rules about the keeping of promises and contracts, rules about debts of gratitude such as we may owe to our parents, and, of course, rules about not injuring other persons and about promoting the welfare of others where this does not work a comparable hardship on us.[68]

That Brandt appeals to utility and Ross to deontological considerations to justify similar sets of rules is a significant difference at the level of moral theory and justification. The two authors also might interpret, specify, and balance their rules differently as a result of their theoretical commitments. Still, their lists of primary obligations display only trivial differences. This convergence on general principles is common in moral theory. Agreement derives from an initial shared database, namely, the norms of the common morality. We can say without exaggeration that the proponents of these theories all accept the principles of common morality *before* they devise their theory.

Convergence as well as consensus about norms is also common in assessing cases and framing policies, even if theoretical differences divide the discussants. In practical judgments and public policies, we usually need no more agreement than an agreement on specific action-guides—not an agreement on their theoretical foundations. Nonetheless, we should not confuse convergence to agreement on norms with questions about whether a theory adequately justifies its principles. Theoretical inquiry is worthwhile even if practical agreement can often be achieved without it.

Conclusion

Competition exists among the four types of normative theory explored in this chapter, and competing conceptions continue regarding what these theories imply for biomedical practice. Even so, each of these theories is instructive and makes a contribution to our thinking about the moral life. We have maintained that there is no reason to consider one type of theory inferior to or derivative from the other, and there is good reason to believe that these types of theory all show insights into our common moral heritage and how it can be called upon to help us develop contemporary biomedical ethics.

Every general theory risks clashing at some point with considered moral convictions, but each of the four theories examined in this chapter articulates a point of view that we should be reluctant to relinquish. This approach to theories allows us to focus on their acceptable features without being forced to choose one theory to the exclusion of the others or to judge one theory as somehow primary at the foundations.

NOTES

1. Our views on pluralism are influenced by Thomas Nagel, "The Fragmentation of Value," in *Mortal Questions* (Cambridge: Cambridge University Press, 1979), pp. 128–37; and Baruch Brody's treatment in *Life and Death Decision Making* (New York: Oxford University Press, 1988), p. 9.

2. Our discussion has profited from Shelly Kagan, *The Limits of Morality* (Oxford: Clarendon, 1989), esp. pp. 11–15, and from criticisms of our views privately presented by David DeGrazia and Avi Craimer.

3. For analysis of this utilitarian thesis, see Samuel Scheffler, *Consequentialism and Its Critics* (Oxford: Clarendon, 1988).

4. Jeremy Bentham, *An Introduction to the Principles of Morals and Legislation,* ed. J. H. Burns and H. L. A. Hart (Oxford: Clarendon, 1970), pp. 11–14, 31, 34; John Stuart Mill, *Utilitarianism,* in vol. 10 of the *Collected Works of John Stuart Mill* (Toronto: University of Toronto Press, 1969), chap. 1, p. 207; chap. 2, pp. 210, 214; chap. 4, pp. 234–35.

5. See a representative theory in James Griffin, *Well-Being: Its Meaning, Measurement and Moral Importance* (Oxford: Clarendon, 1986), especially p. 67. The most influential early twentieth-century theory of this sort was G. E. Moore, *Principia Ethica;* see the rev. ed., ed. Thomas Baldwin (Cambridge: Cambridge University Press, 1993).

6. This case is based on Melvin D. Levine, Lee Scott, and William J. Curran, "Ethics Rounds in a Children's Medical Center: Evaluation of a Hospital-Based Program for Continuing Education in Medical Ethics," *Pediatrics* 60 (August 1977): 205.

7. Writers who have been influential utilitarians in bioethics include Joseph Fletcher, *Humanhood: Essays in Biomedical Ethics* (Buffalo, NY: Prometheus Books, 1979); Peter Singer, *Practical Ethics,* 2nd ed. (Cambridge: Cambridge University Press, 1993); R. M. Hare, *Moral Thinking: Its Levels, Method, and Point* (Oxford: Oxford University Press, 1981); Hare, *Essays on Bioethics* (Oxford: Oxford University Press, 1993); Hare, "A Utilitarian Approach to Ethics," in *A Companion to Bioethics,* ed. Helga Kuhse and Peter Singer (Oxford: Blackwell, 1998), pp. 80–85; and Brad Hooker, *Ideal Code, Real World: A Rule-Consequentialist Theory of Morality* (Oxford: Oxford University Press, 2000; new edition 2002).

8. Cf. L. W. Sumner, *The Moral Foundation of Rights* (Oxford: Oxford University Press, 1987); and Hooker, *Ideal Code, Real World.*

9. Worthington Hooker, *Physician and Patient* (New York: Baker & Scribner, 1849), pp. 357ff, 375–81.

10. J. J. C. Smart, *An Outline of a System of Utilitarian Ethics* (Melbourne: University Press, 1961); and "Extreme and Restricted Utilitarianism," in *Contemporary Utilitarianism,* ed. Michael Bayles (Garden City, NY: Doubleday, 1968), esp. pp. 104–07, 113–15.

11. Richard B. Brandt, "Toward a Credible Form of Utilitarianism," in *Contemporary Utilitarianism,* ed. Bayles, pp. 143–86, and in Brandt's *Morality, Utilitarianism, and Rights* (Cambridge: Cambridge University Press, 1992). For a rule-utilitarian alternative to Brandt's rule-utilitarian formulations, see Hooker, *Ideal Code, Real World.*

12. This question is discussed in Madison Powers, "Repugnant Desires and the Two-Tier Conception of Utility," *Utilitas* 6 (1994): 171–76.

13.   Alan Donagan, "Is There a Credible Form of Utilitarianism?" in *Contemporary Utilitarianism,* ed. Bayles, pp. 187–202.

14.   Williams, "A Critique of Utilitarianism," in *Utilitarianism: For and Against,* ed. J. J. C. Smart and Bernard Williams (Cambridge: Cambridge University Press, 1973), pp. 116–17; and J. L. Mackie, *Ethics: Inventing Right and Wrong* (New York: Penguin, 1977), pp. 129, 133. For an extension, see Edward Harcourt, "Integrity, Practical Deliberation and Utilitarianism," *Philosophical Quarterly* 48 (1998): 189–98. Recent efforts to develop consequentialist theories that reduce or eliminate the "demandingness" problem include Tim Mulgan, *The Demands of Consequentialism* (Oxford: Clarendon, 2005), which offers a "moderately demanding" theory of mixed consequentialism.

15.   For a defense of utilitarianism (set against egalitarianism) in forming just policies toward people with disabilities, see Mark S. Stein, *Distributive Justice and Disability: Utilitarianism against Egalitarianism* (New Haven, CT: Yale University Press, 2006).

16.   Milton Weinstein and William B. Stason, *Hypertension* (Cambridge, MA: Harvard University Press, 1977); "Public Health Rounds at the Harvard School of Public Health: Allocating of Resources to Manage Hypertension," *New England Journal of Medicine* 296 (1977): 732–39; and "Allocation Resources: The Case of Hypertension," *Hastings Center Report* 7 (October 1977): 24–29.

17.   Amartya Sen, *On Ethics and Economics* (Oxford: Basil Blackwell, 1987), p. 75.

18.   See Stephen Darwall, ed., *Deontology* (Oxford: Blackwell, 2002), for a representative collection of works.

19.   See, for example, the writings of F. M. Kamm, including *Intricate Ethics: Rights, Responsibilities, and Permissible Harm* (New York: Oxford University Press, 2007).

20.   Kant sought to show that unaided reason can and should be a proper motive to action. What we should do morally is determined by what we would do "if reason completely determined the will." *The Critique of Practical Reason,* trans. Lewis White Beck (New York: Macmillan, 1985), pp. 18–19; Ak. 20. "Ak." designates the page-reference system of the twenty-two-volume Preussische Akademie edition conventionally cited in Kant scholarship.

21.   Kant, *Foundations of the Metaphysics of Morals,* trans. Lewis White Beck (Indianapolis, IN: Bobbs-Merrill, 1959), pp. 37–42; Ak. 421–24.

22.   For interpretations of Kant's idea of contradiction in maxims, see Christine Korsgaard, "Kant's Formula of Universal Law," *Pacific Philosophical Quarterly* 66 (1985): 24–47, and "Kant's Formula of Humanity," *Kant-Studien* 77 (1986): 183–202, both reprinted with other essays in her *Creating the Kingdom of Ends* (Cambridge: Cambridge University Press, 1996); and Barbara Herman, *The Practice of Moral Judgment* (Cambridge, MA: Harvard University Press, 1993), pp. 132–58.

23.   *Foundations,* p. 47; Ak. 429.

24.   *Foundations,* pp. 51, 58–63; Ak. 432, 439–44.

25.   *Foundations,* p. 58; Ak. 439–40.

26.   Alan Donagan, *The Theory of Morality* (Chicago: University of Chicago Press, 1977), pp. 63–66.

27.   See *A Theory of Justice* (Cambridge, MA: Harvard University Press, 1971; rev. ed., 1999), pp. 3–4, 27–31 (1999: pp. 3–4, 24–28). For an approach to Kant influenced by Rawls, see Thomas Hill, Jr., *Human Welfare and Moral Worth: Kantian Perspectives* (Oxford: Clarendon, 2002).

28.   Rawls, *A Theory of Justice,* pp. 252, 256, 515–20 (1999: pp. 221–22, 226–27, 452–56). See also "A Kantian Conception of Equality," *Cambridge Review* (February 1975): 97ff.

29. See, for example, Thomas Nagel, "Personal Rights and Public Space," *Philosophy and Public Affairs* 24 (1995): 83–107, and his *The View from Nowhere* (New York: Oxford University Press, 1986); Bernard Williams, *Ethics and the Limits of Philosophy* (Cambridge, MA: Harvard University Press, 1985), and his *Moral Luck: Philosophical Papers, 1973–1980* (Cambridge: Cambridge University Press, 1981).

30. Christine M. Korsgaard, "Interacting with Animals: A Kantian Account," in *Oxford Handbook of Animal Ethics,* ed. Tom L. Beauchamp and R. G. Frey (New York: Oxford University Press, 2011), p. 97.

31. Onora O'Neill, *Towards Justice and Virtue: A Constructive Account of Practical Reasoning* (Cambridge: Cambridge University Press, 1996), pp. 5–6. See also her *Constructions of Reason: Explorations of Kant's Practical Philosophy* (Cambridge: Cambridge University Press, 1989). Her important work in bioethics includes *Autonomy and Trust in Bioethics* (Cambridge: Cambridge University Press, 2002) and, with Neil C. Manson, *Rethinking Informed Consent in Bioethics* (Cambridge: Cambridge University Press, 2007). See our discussion in Chapter 4.

32. For innovative interpretations that respond to such an objection by giving more flexibility to Kant, see Herman, *The Practice of Moral Judgment,* pp. 132–58; Nancy Sherman, *Making a Necessity of Virtue* (Cambridge: Cambridge University Press, 1997); and Tamar Schapiro, "Kantian Rigorism and Mitigating Circumstances," *Ethics* 117 (2006): 32–57. These writings respond to forms of the third objection we mention in this section, especially regarding the place of virtue in Kant's theory.

33. Cf. Annette Baier, "The Need for More than Justice," in her *Moral Prejudices* (Cambridge, MA: Harvard University Press, 1994).

34. We are indebted to the analysis in Karen Stohr, "Virtue Ethics and Kant's Cold-Hearted Benefactor," *Journal of Value Inquiry* 36 (2002): 187–204.

35. Pioneering theories of international rights and natural rights—now often restyled as *human rights*—first prospered in philosophy through the social and political theories of Hugo Grotius, Thomas Hobbes, John Locke, and their successors. On the history of human rights, as originally expressed through the language of natural rights, see Anthony Pagden, "Human Rights, Natural Rights, and Europe's Imperial Legacy," *Political Theory* 31 (2003): 171–99.

36. Our representations on this point are indebted to the theory of rights in Joel Feinberg's *Rights, Justice, and the Bounds of Liberty* (Princeton, NJ: Princeton University Press, 1980), esp. pp. 139–41, 149–55, 159–60, 187; and *Social Philosophy* (Englewood Cliffs, NJ: Prentice-Hall, 1973), chaps. 4–6. See also Alan Gewirth, *The Community of Rights* (Chicago: University of Chicago Press, 1996), pp. 8–9; and H. L. A. Hart, "Bentham on Legal Rights," in *Oxford Essays in Jurisprudence,* 2nd series, ed. A. W. B. Simpson (Oxford: Oxford University Press, 1973), pp. 171–98.

37. A clever and atypical attempt to find an absolute right is Alan Gewirth, "Are There Any Absolute Rights?" *Philosophical Quarterly* 31 (1981): 1–16; reprinted as Chapter 9 in Gewirth's *Human Rights* (Chicago: University of Chicago Press, 1982).

38. Ronald Dworkin, *Taking Rights Seriously* (Cambridge, MA: Harvard University Press, 1977), pp. xi, xv, 92 (and, as reissued with "Appendix: A Reply to Critics," in 2002, pp. 364–66); and *Law's Empire* (Cambridge, MA: Harvard University Press, 1986), p. 160.

39. Ronald Dworkin, "Rights as Trumps," in *Theories of Rights,* ed. Jeremy Waldron (Oxford: Oxford University Press, 1984), p. 153 (italics added).

40. See Judith Jarvis Thomson, *The Realm of Rights* (Cambridge, MA: Harvard University Press, 1990), pp. 122–24, and also 106–17, 149–53, 164–75; and Joel Feinberg, *Rights, Justice, and the Bounds of Liberty,* pp. 229–32.

41. World Health Organization, "Zoonoses and Veterinary Public Health," http://www.who.int/zoonoses/vph/en/ (accessed August 1, 2010).

42.   See Feinberg, *Social Philosophy,* p. 59; and Eric Mack, ed., *Positive and Negative Duties* (New Orleans, LA: Tulane University Press, 1985).

43.   See this language in David Braybrooke, "The Firm but Untidy Correlativity of Rights and Obligations," *Canadian Journal of Philosophy* 1 (1972): 351–63; Feinberg, *Rights, Justice, and the Bounds of Liberty,* pp. 135–39, 143–44; Feinberg, *Harm to Others,* vol. 1 of *The Moral Limits of the Criminal Law* (New York: Oxford University Press, 1984), pp. 148–49; Griffin, *On Human Rights,* pp. 51, 96, 107–9; and Joseph Raz, *The Morality of Freedom* (New York: Oxford University Press, 1986), pp. 170–72. Probing discussions of correlativity are found in Gewirth's *The Community of Rights.* See also Feinberg's insightful explanation of the confusions that enter moral discourse owing to the ambiguity of the words *duty, obligation,* and *requirement,* in his *Doing and Deserving: Essays in the Theory of Responsibility* (Princeton, NJ: Princeton University Press, 1970), pp. 3–8.

44.   See the standard objections by David Lyons, "The Correlativity of Rights and Duties," *Nous* 4 (1970): 45–55; Theodore M. Benditt, *Rights* (Totowa, NJ: Rowman and Littlefield, 1982), pp. 6–7, 23–25, 77; Alan R. White, *Rights* (Oxford: Clarendon Press, 1984), pp. 60–66; and Richard Brandt, *Ethical Theory* (Englewood Cliffs, NJ: Prentice Hall, 1959), pp. 439–40.

45.   This difference is sometimes marked by saying that perfect obligations have correlative rights, whereas imperfect obligations do not. We prefer the tidier approach that only perfect obligations are moral obligations. So-called imperfect obligations are moral ideals that allow for discretion. Cf. the somewhat similar conclusions in Feinberg, *Rights, Justice, and the Bounds of Liberty,* pp. 138–39, 143–44, 148–49.

46.   Ronald Dworkin argues that political morality is rights-based in *Taking Rights Seriously,* pp. 169–77, esp. p. 171. John Mackie has applied this thesis to morality in general in "Can There Be a Right-Based Moral Theory?" *Midwest Studies in Philosophy* 3 (1978), esp. 350.

47.   Robert Nozick, *Anarchy, State, and Utopia* (New York: Basic Books, 1974), pp. ix, 149–82.

48.   Alan Gewirth, "Why Rights Are Indispensable," *Mind* 95 (1986): 333. See Gewirth's later book, *The Community of Rights* (Chicago: University of Chicago Press, 1996).

49.   James Griffin, *On Human Rights* (Oxford: Oxford University Press, 2008), pp. 97, 110.

50.   Ronald Dworkin, *Taking Rights Seriously,* pp. 93–94.

51.   See William R. Lund, "Politics, Virtue, and the Right to Do Wrong: Assessing the Communitarian Critique of Rights," *Journal of Social Philosophy* 28 (1997): 101–22; Allen Buchanan, "Assessing the Communitarian Critique of Liberalism," *Ethics* 99 (July 1989): 852–82, esp. 862–65; and William A. Galston, *Liberal Purposes* (Cambridge: Cambridge University Press, 1991).

52.   See Talbot Brewer, *The Retrieval of Ethics* (Oxford: Oxford University Press, 2009), pp. 1–11, passim.

53.   *Nicomachean Ethics,* trans. Terence Irwin (Indianapolis, IN: Hackett Publishing, 1985), 1105^a17–33, 1106^b21–23; cf. 1144^a14–20.

54.   Robert Adams distinguishes "motivational virtues" (such as benevolence) from "structural virtues" (such as courage and self-control). The latter are structural features of the agent's organization and management of his or her motives. *A Theory of Virtue: Excellence in Being for the Good* (Oxford: Clarendon, 2006), pp. 33–34, passim.

55.   Categorization has centuries of tradition behind it in ethical theory. Although there are variations in lists of virtues (and vices), much is also held common across these traditions—enough to speak of a common morality of the virtues. See David Hume's comments on the catalogue of the virtues in his *An Enquiry concerning the Principles of Morals,* ed. Tom L. Beauchamp (Oxford: Clarendon Press, 1998),

beginning at 1.10 (sect. 1, par. 10); see also 6.21, 9.3, 9.12. Hume said that he was most deeply influenced by the catalogue of virtues in *Cicero's De officiis.* For a contemporary description of positive character traits interpreted as virtues, see Christopher Peterson and Martin E. P. Seligman, eds., *Character Strengths and Virtues: A Handbook and Classification* (Washington, DC: American Psychological Association; and New York: Oxford University Press, 2004). Their chapters identify twenty-four specific character strengths under six broad virtues.

56.   Hume, *An Enquiry concerning the Principles of Morals,* sect. 8, note to the section title; and see also appendix 1, par. 10.

57.   For further analysis of the nature and definition of virtue, see Julia Annas, *Intelligent Virtue* (New York: Oxford University Press, 2011), esp. chaps. 2–5.

58.   See Philippa Foot, *Virtues and Vices* (Oxford: Basil Blackwell, 1978); Gregory Trianosky, "Supererogation, Wrongdoing, and Vice," *Journal of Philosophy* 83 (1986): 26–40; Jorge L. Garcia, "The Primacy of the Virtuous," *Philosophia* 20 (1990): 69–91; and criticisms of such a view in Lynn A. Jansen, "The Virtues in Their Place: Virtue Ethics in Medicine," *Theoretical Medicine* 21 (2000): 261–76.

59.   See Diane Jeske, "Friendship, Virtue, and Impartiality," *Philosophy and Phenomenological Research* 57 (1997): 51–72; and Michael Stocker, "The Schizophrenia of Modern Ethical Theories," *Journal of Philosophy* 73 (1976): 453–66.

60.   Cf. Gregory Pence, *Ethical Options in Medicine* (Oradell, NJ: Medical Economics, 1980), p. 177.

61.   Henry K. Beecher, "Ethics and Clinical Research," *New England Journal of Medicine* 274 (1966): 1354–60.

62.   Thomas Keneally, *Schindler's List* (New York: Penguin Books, 1983), pp. 176–80.

63.   Rosalind Hursthouse, *On Virtue Ethics* (Oxford: Oxford University Press, 2001), p. 17.

64.   See Rosalind Hursthouse, "Virtue Ethics and the Treatment of Animals," in *Oxford Handbook of Animal Ethics,* ed. Beauchamp and Frey (2011), pp. 126–27; and Hursthouse, "Virtue Ethics," *The Stanford Encyclopedia of Philosophy,* Fall 2003, http://plato.stanford.edu/archives/fall2003/entries/ethics-virtue/. See also Christine Swanton, *Virtue Ethics: A Pluralistic View* (New York: Oxford University Press, 2003), part IV; and Rebecca L. Walker and Philip J. Ivanhoe, eds., *Working Virtue: Virtue Ethics and Contemporary Moral Problems* (New York: Oxford University Press, 2009).

65.   See further our discussion in Chapter 10 of this criticism of our theory by Bernard Gert and Danner Clouser.

66.   See similar reflections about the virtues, to which we are indebted, in Annas, *Intelligent Virtue,* chap. 3, esp. pp. 32–40.

67.   For a different analysis of "the link between virtues, principles, and duties," see Edmund Pellegrino and David Thomasma, *The Virtues in Medical Practice* (New York: Oxford University Press, 1993), chap. 2.

68.   Brandt, "Toward a Credible Form of Utilitarianism," p. 166.

10
Method and Moral Justification

How can we justify moral conclusions in biomedical ethics? And which methods can we legitimately and effectively use? There is disagreement about the answers to these questions. In this chapter we step back from the first-order problems of biomedical ethics that have largely preoccupied us to this point and reflect on second-order problems of method and justification. We assess the leading methods and forms of justification, and we support a particular approach that derives in part from John Rawls's celebrated theory of reflective equilibrium.

Questions about method are intimately connected to questions about justification. The first three sections of this chapter explicate and criticize three models of method and justification and evaluate the arguments of critics of our methods and principles. Later in the chapter, we connect our account of method and justification to the common-morality theory introduced in Chapter 1 and to the account of moral character developed in Chapter 2.

JUSTIFICATION IN ETHICS

What is justification in ethics, and by which method(s) of reasoning do we achieve it?

Justification has several meanings, some specific to disciplines. In law, justification is a demonstration in court that one has a sufficient reason and evidence for one's claim or for what one has been called to answer. In ethical discourse, the objective is to establish one's case by presenting sufficient reasons for it. A mere listing of reasons will not suffice because those reasons may not adequately support the conclusion. Not all reasons are good reasons, and not all good reasons are sufficient for justification. We therefore need to distinguish a reason's *relevance* to a moral judgment from its *sufficiency* to support that judgment, and we need to distinguish an *attempted* justification from a *successful* justification. For example, chemical companies in the United States at one time argued that the presence of toxic chemicals in a work environment provides a legally and morally sound reason to exclude women of childbearing age from a hazardous workplace, but the U.S. Supreme Court overturned these policies on grounds that they discriminate against women.[1] The dangers to health and life presented by hazardous chemicals constitute a *good* reason for protecting employees from a workplace, but this reason is not a sufficient reason for a ban that impacts women alone.

Several models of method and justification operate in ethical theory and contemporary biomedical ethics. We analyze three such models. The first model approaches justification and method from a top-down perspective that emphasizes moral norms, as discussed in Chapter 1, and ethical theory, as discussed in Chapter 9. The second approaches justification and method from a bottom-up perspective that emphasizes precedent cases, moral traditions, experience, and particular circumstances. The third refuses to assign priority to either a top-down or a bottom-up strategy and instead emphasizes coherence and considered judgments. We defend a version of the third.

TOP-DOWN MODELS: THEORY AND APPLICATION

A top-down model holds that we reach justified moral judgments through a structure of normative precepts that cover the judgments. This model is inspired by disciplines such as mathematics, in which a claim follows logically (deductively) from a credible set of premises. The idea is that justification occurs if and only if general principles and rules, together with the relevant facts of a situation, support an inference to the correct or justified judgment(s). This model conforms to the way many people have been raised to think morally: It involves applying a general norm (principle, rule, ideal, right, etc.) to a clear case falling under the norms. The deductive form is sometimes considered an "application" of general precepts to particular cases. This conception originally encouraged the now widely used term *applied ethics.*

The following is the deductive form involved in "applying" a norm (here using what is obligatory, rather than what is permitted or prohibited, although the deductive model is the same for all three):

1. Every act of description A is obligatory.
2. Act b is of description A.

Therefore,

3. Act b is obligatory.

A simple example is:

1x. Every act in a patient's overall best interest is obligatory for the patient's doctor.
2x. Act of resuscitation b is in this patient's overall best interest.

Therefore,

3x. Act of resuscitation b is obligatory for this patient's doctor.

Covering precepts, such as 1 and 1x, occur at various levels of generality, and they are always universal in their logical form. The level of generality
varies according to the specificity of the description A, while the statement's
universality is ensured by the claim that "every act" of such a description is
obligatory. Particular judgments or beliefs are justified by bringing them under
the scope of one or more moral rules; and the rules may be justified by bringing
them under general principles, which in turn might be justified by appeal to a
normative ethical theory. Consider a nurse who refuses to assist in an abortion
procedure. The nurse might attempt to justify the act of refusal by the rule that
it is wrong to kill a human being intentionally. If pressed further, the nurse may
justify this moral rule by reference to a principle of the sanctity of human life.
Finally, the particular judgment, rule, and principle might all find support in an
ethical theory of the sort discussed in Chapter 9 and in a theory of moral status,
as discussed in Chapter 3.

This deductivist model functions smoothly in the simple case of a judgment brought directly and unambiguously under a rule or a principle—for
example, "You must tell Mr. Sanford that he has cancer and will probably die
soon, because a clinician must observe rules of truthfulness to properly respect
the autonomy of patients." The top-down model suggests that the judgment,
"You should not lie to Mr. Sanford," descends in its moral content directly
from the covering principle, "You should respect the autonomy of patients,"
from which we derive and justify the covering rule, "You should not lie to
patients."

Problems in the Model

This model suggests an ordering in which general theories, principles, and rules
enjoy priority over traditional practices, institutional rules, and case judgments.
Although much in the moral life conforms roughly to this covering-norm conception, much does not. Particular moral judgments in difficult cases almost always
require that we specify and balance norms (see Chapter 1), not merely that we
bring a particular instance under a preexisting covering rule or principle. The
abstract rules and principles in moral theories are extensively indeterminate. That
is, the content of these rules and principles is too abstract to determine the specific acts that we should and should not perform. In the process of specifying and
balancing norms and in making particular judgments, we often must take into
account factual beliefs about the world, cultural expectations, judgments of likely
outcome, and precedents to help assign relative weights to rules, principles, and
theories.

The moral life often requires even more than specified general norms. A
situation may be such that no general norm (principle or rule) clearly applies.

The facts of cases are usually complex, and the different moral norms that can be brought to bear on the facts may yield inconclusive, or even contradictory, results. For example, in the controversy over whether it is permissible to destroy a human embryo for purposes of scientific research, embryo destruction does not clearly violate rules against killing or murder, nor does the rule that a person has a right to protect his or her bodily integrity and property clearly apply to the destruction of human embryos. Even if all relevant facts are available, our selection of pertinent facts and pertinent rules may generate a judgment that is incompatible with another person's selection of facts and rules. Selecting the right set of facts and bringing the right set of rules to bear on these facts are not reducible to a deductive form of judgment.

The top-down model also creates a potentially infinite regress of justification—a never-ending demand for final justification—because each level of appeal to a covering precept requires some further general level to justify that precept. Theoretically, we could handle this problem by presenting a principle that is self-justifying or that is irrational not to hold, but proof that some principles occupy this status and that they justify all other principles or rules is an arduous demand that current ethical theory cannot meet. Yet, if all standards are unjustified until brought under a justified covering precept, it would appear, on the assumptions of this approach, that there are no justified principles or judgments.

A Theory of "Morality as a Public System"

One important version of top-down theory, and the most developed theory in biomedical ethics (though it is not a pure deductivism), has been developed by Bernard Gert and his coauthors Danner Clouser and Charles Culver. Gert, the primary author of the basic ethical theory, refers to it as a theory of "morality as a public system." The moral system is the institution of morality at work in our daily lives—lived, pretheoretical morality—whereas the moral theory that describes and defends the norms of morality is a philosophical account. This theory can be thought of as top down in the sense that the major elements of the theory are set forth as general moral rules, moral ideals, the morally relevant features of situations, and procedures for dealing with conflicts and assessing whether certain moral rule violations are justified. Morality is envisaged in this theory as a public system of norms that are applicable to all persons in all places and times.[2]

When challenges arose to our framework of principles in the 1980s, these authors emerged as our most unsparing critics and wrote several articles and part of a book to express concerns about our prima facie principles. They coined the label "principlism" to refer to any account of ethics comprising a plurality of potentially conflicting prima facie principles. Gert and colleagues are in several respects not distant from the views we defend in this book. Like us, they understand the common morality as universal morality that is not relative to cultures, individuals, religions, or professional associations. However, Gert and colleagues reject both the language and the substance of our account of principles, while putting forward their own impartial rules and moral ideals as a superior and alternative framework in biomedical ethics.

We will concentrate in this section more on their criticisms of our principles and methods than on their general theory and its limits.[3] First, they charge that principles function as little more than names, checklists, or headings for values worth remembering, but lack deep moral substance and capacity to guide action. That is, principles point to moral themes that merit consideration by grouping those themes under broad headings, but do little more. A second criticism is that, because moral agents confronted with bioethical problems receive no specific, directive guidance from principles, they are left free to deal with the problems in their own way. They may give a principle whatever weight they wish, or even no weight at all. From this perspective, our account is insubstantial, permissive, and lacking a controlling, comprehensive theory. A third criticism is that the prima facie principles and other action guides in our framework often conflict, and our account is too indeterminate to provide a decision procedure to adjudicate the conflicts.

Clouser and Gert are particularly fond of pointing to these deficiencies in the principles of justice discussed in Chapter 7 of this book. They maintain that no specific guide to action derives from these principles. All of the principles of justice we mention, they say, merely instruct persons to attend to matters of justice and think about justice, but they give no specific normative guidance. Because such vagueness and generality underdetermine solutions to problems of justice, agents are free to decide what is just and unjust as they see fit.

Gert and Clouser also criticize our theory for giving status to both nonmaleficence and beneficence as principles of obligation. They maintain that there are no moral rules of beneficence, although they agree that we should encourage moral ideals of beneficence. The only obligations in the moral life, apart from duties encountered in professional roles and other specific stations of duty, are captured by moral rules that prohibit causing harm or evil. For Gert and colleagues, the general goal of morality is to minimize evil or harm, not to promote good. Rational persons can act impartially at all times in regard to all persons with the aim of not causing evil, they say, but rational persons cannot impartially promote the good for all persons at all times.[4]

The Limitations of "Morality as a Public System"

We agree that the problems Gert, Clouser, and Culver present deserve sustained reflection. We reject, however, the key criticisms they direct at our account, some of which can be turned back on their own theory. In particular, their criticism that our principles lack directive moral substance (being unspecified principles) applies to their rules in a near-identical way, one level down in the order of abstraction. Any norm, principle, or rule will have this problem if it is underspecified for the task at hand. A basic norm of any sort is intrinsically general, designed to cover a broad range of circumstances. If general rules are not specified in biomedical ethics, they are almost always too general and will fail to provide adequate normative guidance. Clouser and Gert's rules (e.g., "Don't cheat," "Don't deceive," and "Do your duty") are comparable to our principles in that they lack specificity in their original general form. One tier less abstract than principles, their rules are at the level of *specified* principles, which explains why their rules do, we agree, have a more directive and specific content than our abstract principles. Our full account of principles and rules, however, includes a set of moral rules similar to the rules embraced by Gert and his colleagues.[5]

Regarding their criticism that our principles are checklists or headings without deep moral substance, we agree that principles order, classify, and group moral norms that require additional content and specificity. However, until we analyze and interpret the principles (as we do in every first section of Chapters 4–7) and then specify and connect them to other norms (as we do in later sections of each of these chapters), it is unreasonable to expect much more than a classification scheme that organizes the normative content and provides general moral guidance.[6]

Regarding the criticism that principles compete with other principles in ways that our account cannot handle, we have acknowledged that moral frameworks of principles do not themselves resolve conflicts among principles and derivative rules. No framework of guidelines could reasonably anticipate the full range of conflicts, but the Gert and Clouser system does no more to settle this problem than our framework does. It does not follow that our principles are inconsistent or that we encounter incompatible moral commitments in embracing them. Our theory calls for balancing and specification, whereas their account assumes that its "more concrete" rules escape the need for specification. Only a theory that could put enough content in its norms to escape conflicts and dilemmas in all contexts could live up to the Clouser–Gert demand. In our judgment, no general theory does so.[7]

Experience and sound judgment are indispensable allies in resolving these problems. No one has produced or ever will produce a fully specified system of norms for health care ethics. Thomas Nagel has forcefully argued that an unconnected heap of obligations and values is an ineradicable feature of morality, and W. D. Ross has rightly argued that many philosophers have forced an architectonic of unwarranted simplicity on ethics.[8] Whereas some critics of Ross's account, and ours, rely on an ideal of systematic unity in moral theory, we regard disunity, conflict, and moral ambiguity as pervasive features of the moral life that are unlikely to be eliminated by a moral theory. Moral theory offers methods such as specification, balancing, and ways of adjusting norms to achieve consistency, but theories will not eliminate all untidiness, complexity, and conflict.

Regarding the criticism that our principle-based analysis fails to provide a general ethical theory, the criticism is correct, but not a telling objection. We do not attempt to construct either a general ethical theory or a comprehensive theory of the common morality and do not claim that our principles and methods are analogous to or substitute for the principles and methods of justification in leading classical theories, such as utilitarianism, with its principle of utility, and Kantianism, with its categorical imperative. We expressed some skepticism about such theories in Chapter 9 on grounds that the goal of a unified foundation for ethics is likely to misrepresent some aspects of the moral life.[9]

In response to the criticism that the principle of beneficence expresses an ideal, not a moral obligation, we contend that this thesis distorts the common morality. The claim implies that one is never morally required (except by role and professional or community duties) to prevent or remove harm or evil, but only to avoid causing harm or evil. They recognize no requirement to *do* anything that confers a benefit or prevents a harm—only to *avoid* causing harmful events.[10] Their thesis makes beneficence merely a moral ideal, and thereby misreads the commitments of the common morality. Moreover, the claim that beneficence is never morally required is not supported even within Gert's own account of moral obligations. In his book *Morality: Its Nature and Justification,* Gert relies on the premise that one is morally obligated to act beneficently under many conditions. He interprets one of his basic rules, "Do your duty," to incorporate many obligations of beneficence. Gert explains his system and its commitments as follows:

> Although duties, in general, go with offices, jobs, roles, etc., there are some duties that seem more general....A person has a duty...because of some special circumstances, for example, his job or his relationships....In any civilized society, if a child collapses in your arms, you have a duty to seek help. You cannot simply lay him out on the ground and walk away. In most civilized societies one has a duty to help when (1) one is in physical proximity to someone in need of help to avoid a serious evil, usually death or serious injury, (2) one is in a unique or close to unique position to provide that help, and (3) it would be relatively cost-free for one to provide that help.[11]

Gert maintains that all such requirements are supported by the moral rule "Do your duty," but these norms often appear to be effectively identical to the obligations that follow from what we call beneficence, a term in wide use in ethical theory since at least the eighteenth century. It therefore is not the case that Gert's system lacks obligations of beneficence in our sense of the term (although possibly his theory might be reconstructed to mean only that there is no general principle of beneficence, only specific duties of beneficence).[12] To generalize, much in principlism that Clouser and Gert appear to reject is presupposed by Gert's final rule, "Do your duty." It is therefore hard to see how their theory of the moral system provides an alternative to our substantive claims regarding the nature and scope of obligations.

A further reason favoring our theory is that some substantive requirements of the common morality are better expressed in the language of principles than in the language of rules. Consider respect for autonomy, which Gert and his colleagues find as problematic as principles of justice and beneficence. Their disregard of this principle renders their assessments of some cases convoluted and puzzling. Here is such a case: Following a serious accident, a patient, while still conscious, refuses a blood transfusion on religious grounds; he then falls unconscious, and his physicians believe that he will die unless he receives a transfusion. Gert and Culver argue that the provision of a blood transfusion under these circumstances is paternalistic and wrong because, after the patient regains consciousness following the transfusion, the physicians must then violate either the moral rule against deception or the moral rule against causing pain: If they did not tell the patient about the transfusion, they would violate the rule against deception; if they did tell him, they would cause him pain.[13]

Gert and Culver's rejection of the principle of respect for autonomy leads to this conclusion. They lack the normative resources to argue that the transfusion, in this case, is paternalistic and prima facie wrong because it violates the patient's expressed wishes and choices. Paradoxically, their analysis implies that if the patient had died after the transfusion and without regaining consciousness, the physicians would not have acted wrongly because they would have violated no moral rules. Gert's moral rule "Do not deprive of freedom" was originally construed to prohibit blocking a person's opportunities to take action. To address problems that arise from the blood transfusion case, and similar cases, Gert and his colleagues later interpreted this moral rule to include the "freedom from being acted upon."[14] This expanded interpretation is reasonable, but their rule, so interpreted, now approximates the principle of respect for autonomy.

BOTTOM-UP MODELS: CASES AND ANALOGICAL REASONING

Many writers in biomedical ethics concentrate on practical decision making rather than on principles or theories. They believe that moral justification proceeds bottom up (inductively) by contrast to top down (deductively). Inductivists, as we will refer to them, argue that we reason from particular instances to general statements or positions. For example, we use existing social practices, insight-producing novel cases, and comparative case analysis as the starting points from which to make decisions in particular cases and to generalize to norms. Inductivists emphasize an evolving moral life that reflects experience with difficult cases, analogy from prior practice, and exemplary lives and narratives. From this perspective, "inductivism" and "bottom-up models" are broad categories that contain several methodologies that are wary of top-down theories. Pragmatism,[15] particularism,[16] and narrative approaches,[17] as well as some forms of feminism and virtue theory, qualify as such accounts.

Inductivists propose that cases and particular judgments provide warrants to accept moral conclusions independently of general norms. They usually see rules and principles as derivative, rather than primary, in the order of knowledge. That is, the meaning, function, and weight of a principle derive from previous moral struggles and reflection in particular circumstances. For example, physicians once regarded withdrawing lifesaving medical technologies from patients as an act of impermissible killing. After confronting agonizing cases, they and society came to frame many of these acts as cases of permissible allowing to die and sometimes as morally required acts of acknowledging treatment refusals by patients. This change resulted from extensive experience with cases of both withdrawing and not withdrawing treatment. From this perspective, all specific moral norms arise and are refined over time; they never become more than provisionally secure points in a cultural matrix of guidelines. A society's moral views find their warrant through an embedded moral tradition and a set of procedures that permit and foster new insights and judgments.

Consider an example from the explosion of interest that has occurred in surrogate decision making in the last quarter of the twentieth century. A series of cases, beginning with the case of Karen Ann Quinlan (1976),[18] challenged medical ethics and the courts to develop a new framework of substantive rules for responsible surrogate decision making about life-sustaining treatments, as well as authority rules regarding who should make those decisions. This framework was created by working through cases analogically, and testing new hypotheses against preexisting norms. Subsequent cases were addressed by appealing to similarities and dissimilarities to *Quinlan* and related cases. A string of cases with some similar features established the terms of the ethics of surrogate decision making. Even if a rule was not entirely novel in a proposed framework, its content was shaped by problems needing resolution in the cases at hand. A consensus gradually emerged in the courts and in ethics about a framework for such decision making.

Casuistry: Case-Based Reasoning

Casuistry, an influential version of bottom-up thinking, has revived a model that enjoyed an impressive influence in medieval and early modern philosophy and has refashioned it for modern biomedical ethics.[19] The term *casuistry* refers to the use of case comparison and analogy to reach moral conclusions.[20] Albert Jonsen and Stephen Toulmin, the spearheads of this approach in recent biomedical ethics, are critics of our framework of principles.[21] In general, casuists are skeptical of rules, rights, and general theories that are divorced from cases, history, precedents, and circumstances. Appropriate moral judgments occur, they argue, through an intimate acquaintance with particular situations and the historical record of similar cases. Casuists dispute, in particular, the goal of a tidy, unified theory containing inflexible universal principles.[22] Although a foundational and even an absolute principle is conceivable, casuists maintain that moral beliefs and reasoning do not assume or stand in need of unbending principles.

Casuists do not entirely exclude rules and principles from moral thinking, and they even welcome them when they are consistent with case analysis. However, casuists insist that moral judgments are often made when no appeal to principles is available. For example, we make moral judgments when principles, rules, or rights conflict and no further recourse to a higher principle, rule, or right is available. Furthermore, when principles are interpreted inflexibly, irrespective of the nuances of the case, casuists see a "tyranny of principles"[23] in which attempts to resolve moral problems suffer from a gridlock of conflicting principles and moral debate becomes intemperate and interminable.

This impasse can often be avoided, Jonsen and Toulmin argue, by focusing on points of shared agreement about cases rather than on principles. The following is their prime example, drawn from their personal experiences with the National Commission for the Protection of Human Subjects of Biomedical and Behavioral Research:

> The one thing [individual commissioners] could not agree on was *why* they agreed....Instead of securely established universal principles,...giving them intellectual grounding for particular judgments about specific kinds of cases, it was the other way around.
>
> The *locus of certitude* in the commissioners' discussions...lay in a shared perception of what was specifically at stake in particular kinds of human situations....That could never have been derived from the supposed theoretical certainty of the principles to which individual commissioners appealed in their personal accounts.[24]

In this account casuistical reasoning rather than universal principles forged agreement. The commission functioned successfully by appeal to paradigms and families of cases, despite the diverse principles and theoretical perspectives held by individual commissioners. Although commissioners often cited moral principles to justify their collective conclusions—and unanimously endorsed several general principles late in the commission's existence[25]—Jonsen and Toulmin argue that these principles were less important in the commission's moral deliberation than were judgments about cases.[26]

A simple example illustrates the claim that moral certitude resides in case judgments rather than (or at least more relevantly for moral reasoning than) principles or theory: We know that it is generally morally wrong to introduce significant risks to children in biomedical research that does not offer them the prospect of direct medical benefit. We are confident in the statement, "We should not give this healthy baby the flu in order to test a new decongestant," even though we may be unsure which principle controls this judgment or whether some viable theory sanctions the judgment. The casuist assessment is that we are almost always more secure in particular moral conclusions than we are about *why* they are correct. In this respect, practical knowledge about cases takes priority over theoretical knowledge. For example, if a principle or a theory instructed us to give the flu to children in order to test drugs, as some versions of utilitarianism seem to propose, this instruction would provide us with a good reason for rejecting that principle or theory. Moral certitude, then, is found at the bottom—in precedent cases and traditions of practical judgment—not at the top in a principle or theoretical judgment.

Casuists decide about new cases by comparing them to paradigmatically right and wrong actions and to similar and acceptable cases, as well as similar and unacceptable cases. Thus, precedent cases and analogical reasoning are paramount in this method. For example, if a new case arises involving a problem of medical confidentiality, casuists consider analogous cases in which breaches of confidentiality were justified or unjustified to see whether such a breach is justified in the new case. So-called paradigm cases become the enduring and authoritative sources of appeal. For example, the literature of biomedical ethics frequently invokes cases such as *Quinlan* and the Tuskegee syphilis experiments as sources of authority for new judgments. Decisions reached about moral rights and wrongs in seminal cases become authoritative for new cases and they profoundly affect prevailing standards of fairness, negligence, paternalism, and the like.[27]

A similar method appears in case law through the doctrine of precedent. When an appellate court decides a particular case, its judgment is positioned to become authoritative for other courts hearing cases with relevantly similar facts. Casuists argue that moral authority likewise develops from a social consensus about proper conduct that has been formed around cases. This consensus is then extended to new cases by analogy to the past cases around which the consensus was formed. As similar cases and similar conclusions evolve, a society becomes increasingly confident in its moral conclusions and acknowledges secure generalizations in the form of principles, rules, and rights in its evolving tradition of ethical reflection. These generalizations are interpreted as summary statements of a society's developed moral insights about cases.

The Limits of Casuistry

Casuists have tended to overstate the power of their account and understate the value of competing accounts, but a balanced assessment of the role of cases in moral reasoning can remedy these problems. We note, however, that some major casuistical writers have recently qualified their positions in ways that make them no longer clear competitors to an approach that features general principles. These accounts are free of various problems we bring forward in this section.[28]

Casuists sometimes write as if paradigm cases speak for themselves or inform moral judgment by their facts alone, an implausible thesis. For the casuist to move constructively from case to case, a recognized and morally relevant norm must connect the cases. The norm is not part of the facts or narrative of the cases involved; it is a way of interpreting, evaluating, and linking cases. All analogical reasoning in casuistry requires a connecting norm to indicate that one sequence of events is morally like or unlike another sequence in relevant respects. The creation or discovery of these norms cannot be achieved merely by analogy. It is insufficient to appeal to the fact that one case is similar to another to reach a moral conclusion. It must be shown that the two cases are similar in morally relevant respects.

Jonsen addresses this problem by distinguishing descriptive elements in a case from moral maxims embedded in the case: "These maxims provide the 'morals' of the story. For most cases of interest, there are several morals, because several maxims seem to conflict. The work of casuistry is to determine *which maxim* should *rule the case* and to what extent."[29] We accept this thesis, which conforms to our views about prima facie principles and rules, as well as analogy. So understood, casuistry presupposes principles, rules, or maxims as essential moral elements in paradigm cases and in the assessment of new cases. As Jonsen puts it, "The principles are, in the casuist's view, embedded in the case."[30]

The casuists' "paradigm cases" combine both *facts* that can be generalized to other cases (e.g., "The patient refused the recommended treatment") and *settled values* that are generalized (e.g., "Competent patients have a right to refuse treatment"). These settled values are analytically distinct from the facts of particular cases. In casuistical appeals, values and facts are bound together and the central values are preserved from one case to the next. The more general the central values—the connecting norms—the closer they come in status to prima facie principles.

Casuists maintain that cases point beyond themselves and evolve into generalizations, but a key problem is that they can evolve in the wrong way if improperly handled from the outset. This problem of justification is worrisome: Casuists have no methodological resource to prevent a biased development of case-based judgments or an ignoring of morally relevant features of cases. There can be a tyranny of the paradigm case just as there can be a tyranny of unyielding principles.

How, for casuists, are cases to be identified and labeled? How does the casuist determine what kind of a case is on hand—a necessary first step in taxonomic analysis? The system of identifying and labeling cases often seems to be less than explicit and more intuitive than reasoned, with insufficient attention to the process of evaluative description. Narrative analysts who have investigated cases as mini-narratives have directed attention to the evaluative and other assumptions that can structure cases and lead to both classifications and conclusions that may not be adequately examined or warranted.[31]

Consider two evaluative descriptions of cases, the first relatively uncontroversial and the second quite controversial. First, several years ago, the *Journal of the American Medical Association* reported a case under the title "It's Over, Debbie."[32] In this case, a medical resident injects a terminally ill woman with enough morphine to end her life in response to her request, uttered in their first encounter, "Let's get this over with." Jonsen classifies this case as one of killing—bringing it under a taxonomy of cases of killing, governed by various maxims—and then reasons analogically from paradigm cases in this taxonomy.[33]

Jonsen's case description, classification, and analysis appear to be straightforward, but conflicts arise about the evaluative judgments that are reached about cases because of the type and classification chosen, as is evident in another example, which we introduced in Chapter 5: A clinical case involving the disconnection of a ventilator maintaining the life of a patient with amyotrophic lateral sclerosis (Lou Gehrig's disease) was presented and described as an end-of-life case, in which the "patient" decided to discontinue the ventilator.[34] However, members of the audience, many of whom were experienced in the long-term use of ventilators, challenged this classification. For them this was a "disability" case in which the patient needed better care, more complete information, and increased options, particularly to help him deal with the isolation he felt following his wife's recent death. This dispute shows the importance of examining the assumptions, perspectives, and evaluations that enter into the description of cases. Although the clinicians presenting this case thought it was a "textbook case" of decision making at the end of life, their audience considered it to be "a story in which a life was ended as a result of failures of information and assistance by the presenters themselves."[35]

Accordingly, careful attention must be paid to "moral diagnosis"[36] and to how we describe and frame cases. It is particularly important to recognize and reduce bias in the "describing, framing, selecting and comparing of cases and paradigms."[37] Bias-reduction strategies should include richer, fuller descriptions of cases and the incorporation of a wide range of possible descriptions from a variety of perspectives.

These several problems lead to questions about the justificatory power of casuistry. How does the justification of a moral judgment in a paradigm case or the choice of a paradigm case occur? The casuists' answer seems to rest on tradition, social convention, and analogy. However, different analogies and novel cases still might generate competing "right" answers on any given occasion. Without a stable framework of norms, we lack both controls on judgment and ways to prevent prejudiced or poorly formulated social conventions.

This criticism is a variant of another problem with casuistry: Insofar as this theory works only from the bottom up, it lacks critical distance from cultural blindness, rash analogy, and tyrannical popular opinion.[38] How is the casuist to identify unjust practices, predisposing bias, and prejudicial use of analogy to avoid one-sided judgments? In casuistry, identification of the morally relevant features of a particular case depends on those who make judgments about cases, and these individuals may operate from unduly partial perspectives. In this respect, the ethics of casuistry contrasts sharply with a stable system of impartial principles and human rights, although, even in the case of these impartial norms, there are problems of partial perspectives entering in specification and balancing. Even if we are confident that morally mature cultures usually have built-in resources for critical distancing and self-evaluation, these resources do not emerge from the methods of casuistry. The root of this problem is that casuistry is a method that fails to provide content. It provides a vital instrument of thought that displays the fundamental importance of case comparison and analogy in moral thinking, but it lacks initial moral premises, tools of criticism, and adequate forms of justification. It also lacks a substantive ground of "certitude," in Jonsen and Toulmin's language.

Casuistry is at its best in emphasizing that we regularly reason by analogy and are often confident in the conclusions we reach. For example, if we feel better after using a certain medicine, then we feel comfortable in recommending it to other persons, in the expectation that they too will feel better. A logical form is present in all uses of analogy: If some person or thing has one property associated with a second property, and another person or thing also has the first property, it is justified to infer that the second person or thing also has the second property. However, such analogies often fail: Our friends may not feel better after they take our favored medicine. Analogies never warrant a claim of truth, and we often do not know something by analogy that we think we know. The method of casuistry leaves us with this problem: No matter how many properties one case and a similar case share, our inference to yet another property in the second case may mislead or produce false statements.

These concerns do not amount to sufficient reasons for rejecting either the casuistical method or the use of analogy in moral reasoning. Both are helpful as long as we have a solid knowledge base that allows us to use them. However, to obtain that knowledge, the casuistical method must be supplemented by norms of moral relevance that incorporate prior judgments of right and wrong conduct.[39] We will return to this problem of a proper knowledge base when we come to the subject of "considered judgments" later in this chapter.

Casuists sometimes seem to confuse the fact that we may have no need for a general ethical theory for purposes of practical ethics with the lack of a need for practical principles and their specification. They also sometimes conflate certitude about universal principles with certitude about matters of theory. One of our most important claims in this chapter is that the general public and the mainstream of moral philosophy have found a "locus of certitude" in considered judgments about universal moral norms, although not in a particular moral theory about the foundation of these principles. We agree with casuists that in practical deliberation we often have a higher level of confidence in our judgments about particular cases than we have in appeals to moral theories, but the principles, rules, and practices that are central to the common morality enjoy the highest level of certitude.

In a later methodological statement, Jonsen describes connections between principles and casuistry:

> Principles, such as respect, beneficence, veracity, and so forth, are invoked necessarily and spontaneously in any serious moral discourse.... Moral terms and arguments are imbedded in every case, usually in the form of maxims or enthymemes. The more general principles are never far from these maxims and enthymemes and are often explicitly invoked. Thus, casuistry is not an alternative to principles, in the sense that one might be able to perform good casuistry without principles. In another sense, casuistry is an alternative to principles: they are alternative scholarly activities.[40]

We agree that the two are complementary, but we think it is unlikely that *alternative* scholarly activities are at work. Prima facie principles of the sort we propose are not vulnerable to the casuists' critique of rigid principles and are not excluded by their methodology. The movement from principles to specified rules is similar to Jonsen's account of casuistical method, which involves tailoring maxims to fit a case through progressive interactions with other relevant cases that are governed by maxims. Casuists and principlists should be able to agree that when they reflect on cases and policies, they rarely, if ever, have in hand principles that were formulated without reference to experience with cases, or paradigm cases that lack embedded general norms.

REFLECTIVE EQUILIBRIUM AS AN INTEGRATED MODEL

Accounts from "the top" (principles, rules) and "the bottom" (cases, particular judgments) both need supplementation. Neither general principles nor paradigm cases adequately guide the formation of justified moral beliefs in some circumstances. Instead of a top-down or bottom-up model, we support a version of a third model, usually referred to as "reflective equilibrium." This account of method, justification, and theory construction is sometimes characterized as a form of coherence theory, or coherentism. However, coherentists hold that there is no body of central initial norms that are justified beliefs, and we reject this view.

John Rawls coined the term *reflective equilibrium* to depict a way of bringing principles, judgments, and background theories into a state of equilibrium or harmony. The thesis is that justification in ethics and political philosophy occurs through a reflective testing of moral beliefs, moral principles, judgments, and theoretical postulates with the goal of making them coherent.[41] Proponents argue that a theory or a set of moral beliefs is justified if it maximizes the coherence of the overall set of beliefs that are accepted upon reflective examination.

Method in ethics, in this account, properly begins with a body of beliefs that are acceptable initially without argumentative support. Rawls calls these starting points "considered judgments," that is, the moral convictions in which we have the highest confidence and believe to have the least bias. They are "judgments in which our moral capacities are most likely to be displayed without distortion." Examples are judgments about the wrongness of racial discrimination, religious intolerance, and political repression. "Without distortion" does not merely refer to correct judgments, which would run the risk of circular argument. It refers to the conditions under which the judgments are formed. These considered judgments occur at all levels of moral thinking, "from those about particular situations and institutions through broad standards and first principles to formal and abstract conditions on moral conceptions."[42]

Whenever some feature in a person's or a group's prevailing structure of moral views conflicts with one or more of their considered judgments (a contingent conflict), they must modify something in their viewpoint in order to achieve equilibrium. Even the considered judgments that we accept as central in the web of moral beliefs are, Rawls argues, subject to revision once we detect a conflict. The goal of reflective equilibrium is to match, prune, and adjust considered judgments, their specifications, and other beliefs to render them coherent. We then test the resultant guides to action to see if they yield incoherent results. If so, we must further readjust the guides.

Consider again the place of the traditional moral axiom, "Put the patient's interests first." We seek in biomedical ethics to make this rule as coherent as possible with other considered judgments about responsibilities in clinical teaching, to subjects in the conduct of research, to patients' families, to sponsors in clinical trials, to health care institutions such as hospitals, in public health, and so forth. The requirement to bring these diverse moral responsibilities into coherence and then test the results against all other moral commitments is demanding and daunting. Even such an intuitively attractive rule as "Put the patient's interests first" is not absolute when we consider possible conflicts with other commitments in a variety of circumstances. The rule is an acceptable starting premise—a considered judgment—but not acceptable as an absolute principle. We are left with a range of options about how to specify this rule and check and balance it against other norms, but no matter which option we select, the coherence of our norms will always be a primary objective in the process of specification.[43]

Here is an example from the ethics of the distribution of organs for transplantation. Policymakers may be attracted to each of the following options: (1) distribute organs by expected number of years of survival, to maximize the beneficial outcome of the procedure, and (2) distribute organs by using a waiting list to give every candidate an equal opportunity. As they stand, these two distributive principles are inconsistent. We can retain elements of both in a coherent policy, but to do so we must introduce limits on these principles that specify them into consistency. The outcome of this process must then be made coherent with other principles and rules, such as norms of nondiscrimination against the elderly and the role of ability to pay in the allocation of expensive medical procedures. We can never assume a completely and permanently stable equilibrium in our moral beliefs. The pruning and adjusting of beliefs occur continually.

The overall set of relevant beliefs to be brought into maximal coherence includes moral norms such as initial considered judgments and relevant empirical beliefs. This position is a version of what has been called "wide reflective equilibrium,"[44] in which equilibrium occurs after assessment of the strengths and weaknesses of the full body of all relevant and impartially formulated judgments, principles, theories, and facts (hence the "wide" scope of the account). Moral views to be included are beliefs about particular cases, about rules and principles, about virtue and character, about consequentialist and nonconsequentialist forms of justification, about the moral status of fetuses and experimental animals, about the role of moral sentiments, and so forth.

Achieving a state of reflective equilibrium in which all beliefs fit together coherently, with no residual conflicts or incoherence, is an ideal that will not be comprehensively realized. The trimming, repair, and reshaping of beliefs will occur again and again in response to new situations of conflicting norms. However, this ideal is not a utopian vision toward which no progress can be made. For instance, particular moralities (those of individuals and groups) are works continuously in progress, rather than finished products. Moreover, moral projects such as developing the most suitable system for organ distribution inevitably stand in need of adjustment by specification and balancing in the ongoing search for reflective equilibrium.[45]

Consider, as an example of the threat of incoherence in the search for reflective equilibrium, our limited support in Chapter 5 of physician-assisted death at a patient's request. We there take seriously slippery-slope arguments in opposition to physician-assisted dying, yet we support various forms of physician assistance in choosing to die. David DeGrazia has questioned our assertion that these two claims can be rendered consistent. He views our position as a "compromise [that] apparently leads to contradiction."[46] To see how the two views are consistent, we return to the distinction that we introduced in Chapter 1 between the justification of policies and the justification of acts. Public rules or laws sometimes justifiably prohibit conduct that is morally justified in individual cases. Two moral questions about physician-assisted hastening of death need to be distinguished: (1) Are physicians ever morally justified in complying with patients' requests for assistance in *acts* of hastened death? (2) Is there an adequate moral basis to justify the *legalization* of physician-assisted hastening of death? We argue in Chapter 5 that there are morally justified *acts* of assisting patients in hastening their deaths, but that once public considerations and consequences external to the private relationship between a physician and a patient are the issue—including the implications of legalized physician-assisted hastening of death for medical education and medical practice in hospitals and nursing homes—these external considerations may (but also may not) provide sufficient moral reasons for prohibiting physicians from engaging in such actions as a matter of public law. We argue that some policies that legalize physician assistance would be morally unacceptable under some circumstances. There is no inconsistency in this position on physician-assisted hastening of death.

Although justification is a matter of reflective equilibrium in our model, bare coherence never provides a sufficient basis for justification, because the body of substantive judgments and principles that cohere could themselves be morally unsatisfactory. Bare coherence could be nothing more than a system of prejudices and therefore needs constraint by substantive norms. An example of this problem is the "Pirates' Creed of Ethics or Custom of the Brothers of the Coast."[47] Formed as a contract between marauders circa 1640, this creed is a coherent set of rules governing mutual assistance in emergencies, penalties for prohibited acts, the distribution of spoils, modes of communication, compensation for injury, and "courts of honour" that resolve disputes. All crew members had to swear an oath of allegiance, commonly taken on a Bible. This body of substantive rules and principles, although coherent, is a moral outrage. Its requirement to bear arms for purpose of theft, acceptance of a distributive scheme of spoils, and provision of slaves as compensation for injury involve immoral practices. But what justifies us in saying that such a code, if coherent, is an unacceptable code of ethics?

This question points to the importance of starting with considered judgments that are the most well-established moral beliefs, which we take to be those in the common morality. Once this collection is assembled, we must cast the net more broadly in interpreting, specifying, and generalizing those convictions. Certain normative views are unacceptable not merely because of incoherence. They are wrong because there is no way, when starting from considered moral judgments in the common morality, that, through reflective equilibrium, we could wind up with anything approximating the provisions in the Pirates' Creed.

The thesis is that reflective equilibrium needs the common morality to supply initial norms, and then appropriate development of the common morality requires specification, balancing, and reflective equilibrium, a method of coherence. A warranted approach using reflective equilibrium does not involve the relentless reduction to coherence of any set of preferred beliefs. We start in ethics with a particular set of beliefs—namely, the set of considered judgments that are acceptable initially without argumentative support. We cannot justify every moral judgment in terms of another moral judgment without generating an infinite regress or vicious circle of justification in which no judgment is justified. The way to escape this regress is to accept some judgments as justified without dependence on other judgments.

Such claims are commonly associated with foundationalist moral theories, rather than coherence theories, whereas we have given a central role to coherence achieved through the process of reflective equilibrium. Coherence theory is widely considered antifoundationalist, whereas common-morality theory appears to be foundationalist. This is one reason why we do not speak of our account as coherentism or as a coherence theory, but present our work as reaching for coherence after starting with considered judgments as basic building blocks. We cannot here work through tangled issues about whether coherentism is philosophically preferable to foundationalism and whether a common-morality approach is compatible with traditional understandings of a pure coherence theory of justification. The easiest path around these problems, and the one we take, is to accept a version of reflective equilibrium as our primary methodology and to join it with our common-morality approach to considered judgments. In this way, coherence serves as a basic constraint on the specification and balancing of the norms that guide actions. This constraint cannot be compromised or avoided in the attempt to achieve justification. This proposal is fundamentally Rawlsian, though with some departures from Rawls, and it avoids categorization by labels such as foundationalism and coherentism.

A moral belief that is used initially and without argumentative support can only serve as an anchor of moral reflection if it survives subsequent testing for coherence. This outlook may seem to introduce an unwarranted conservative bias into the account, but the method actually encourages constant improvement and advances through innovative reformulations that foster improved coherence. Almost all justified criticisms of social practices proceed by appeal to considered moral judgments that are extended in fresh ways into new territory. It is not conservative to suggest, as we did in Chapter 3, that the principle of nonmaleficence needs to be extended to increase current protections of animals in biomedical and behavioral research. This extension would significantly modify social practices, but would not modify the norms of nonmaleficence on which the criticism is based.

To avoid an unduly conservative or parochial basis of belief, a wide body of moral experience should be consulted to collect points of convergence. Consider an analogy to eyewitnesses in a courtroom. If sufficient numbers of independent witnesses converge to agreement in recounting the facts of a story, the story gains credibility beyond the credibility of any one individual who tells it. This process helps eliminate biases found in some accounts and helps eradicate stories that do not converge and cannot be made consistent with the main lines of testimony. The greater the coherence in a story that descends from initially credible premises and convergent testimony, the more likely we are to believe it and accept the story as correct. As we increase the number of accounts, establish convergence, eliminate biased observers, and increase coherence, we become increasingly confident that our beliefs are justified and should be accepted. When we find wider and wider confirmation of hypotheses about what should be believed morally, the best explanation of this confirmation is that these hypotheses are the right ones, though several factors will be at work in determining whether moral beliefs held by others actually have epistemic legitimacy.

Rawls had relatively little to say about the conditions under which considered judgments are formed, an important matter because the selection of considered judgments can be influenced by bias or other distorting factors. Reflective equilibrium does not itself justify considered judgments, and therefore other justifying conditions are required for initial judgments and beliefs. These conditions should sort out unduly parochial sets of judgments. Mere coherence is an inadequate criterion, so on what basis can we be confident that considered judgments are sufficiently free of bias and constitute justified beliefs?

This problem is best handled by a delineation of the epistemic qualities of persons that should be present in the selection of considered judgments. Moral judges are entitled to claims to have reached considered judgments only if those judgments have been framed from an impartial perspective that reins in conflicts of interest and other temptations of self-interest; the evaluator exhibits attitudes of sympathy and compassion for the welfare of others; the evaluator possesses pertinent information about the relevant matters; the evaluator is able to display these attitudes in a consistent and sustained way; and the like. The point of appealing to these epistemic virtues is not to generate considered judgments but to explain the conditions under which it is justified to claim that a judgment qualifies as "considered." It is not mere commonness of moral beliefs that provides normative force, but commonness of viewpoint reached by individuals who are qualified to reach considered judgments.

In the context of using reflective equilibrium in theory construction, a theorist will need to formulate considered judgments about the theory itself during the process of its development. The criteria of a good theory of authoritative beliefs in the model we are defending correspond roughly to the criteria of good theories developed in Chapter 9. The following, then, are basic criteria of a justified set of ethical beliefs: consistency (noncontradiction), coherence with warranted nonmoral beliefs (empirical evidence, well-established scientific theories, and inference from both), comprehensiveness (covering the appropriate territory in the moral domain), absence of bias, argumentative support, and restriction of starting premises to considered judgments (those worthy of belief independent of whether they can be supported by reasons). Any theory or body of beliefs about morality is justified if it satisfies these conditions in the ways we have proposed in this section.

In conclusion, we note several unresolved problems about the method of reflective equilibrium that we are not able to address here.[48] First, ambiguity often surrounds the precise aim of the method. It might be used in reflecting on communal policies, constructing a moral philosophy, or strengthening an individual's set of moral beliefs. The focus might be on judgments, on policies, on cases, or on finding moral truth. Second, it is not entirely clear how to know when our effort to achieve reflective equilibrium is going well, or how to know when we have succeeded. Explicit uses of the method (by contrast to claims to be using it) are difficult to find in the ethics literature. Most discussions are heavily theoretical and distant from contexts of practice. We are still learning how well or poorly the method has served or can serve practical ethics. Third, the wide-ranging objectives of even a weak wide reflective equilibrium are at minimum intimidating and may be unattainable ideals of both comprehensiveness and coherence. For instance, the goal of bringing into coherence widely divergent sets of beliefs drawn from diverse traditions has not yet been achieved.

COMMON-MORALITY THEORY[49]

We have argued that justification requires considered judgments drawn from the common morality. We now return to the section of Chapter 1 where we began to develop our account of the common morality as the source of considered judgments. One of our assumptions is that no more central moral content exists as a starting point for biomedical ethics than the kinds of norms from which we have formulated our four clusters of principles presented in Chapters 4 through 7. "No more central" should not be understood here as an assertion that the principles provide the sole moral content. We do not claim that principles and derivative rules, as we have formulated them, establish the basic content of the common morality—as we discuss in Chapters 1, 2, and 9 in our account of virtues in the common morality. We do not understand the principles—or the principles together with the focal virtues and the human rights that we discuss—as alone constituting the common morality; rather, these principles are *drawn from* the territory of common morality, however small or large it may be, a matter we do not try to resolve in this book. Our thesis is merely that the principles and rules are a reasonable formulation of some vital norms of the common morality and that the principles we analyze are particularly suited to biomedical ethics. Our focus in this book is not on the common morality per se, but on its pertinence for biomedical contexts. We would agree with critics[50] of our claims that there is much more to the common morality than we are able to capture in this book. In this section we develop the idea that the common morality supplies considered judgments, and we connect this idea to the prior sections of this chapter.

All common-morality theories share several features: First, they rely on ordinary, shared moral beliefs for their starting content. Second, all common-morality theories hold that an ethical theory that cannot be made consistent with these pretheoretical moral values falls under suspicion. Third, all common-morality theories are pluralistic: They contain two or more nonabsolute (prima facie) moral principles.

Our common-morality theory does not view *customary* moralities as part of the common morality even though they may embody elements of the common morality. That there are customary codes of conduct and that they can differ in beliefs and practices are indisputable facts, but the general norms in the common morality provide a basis for evaluating and criticizing customary moral viewpoints that are in some respects deficient. Our account unites the common morality with the method of reflective equilibrium delineated earlier. This strategy gives authority to the norms in the common morality while incorporating tools to refine and correct unclarities and to allow for additional specification of principles, rules, and rights. As ethical reasoning progresses, a body of more specific moral guidelines is formed (the set of specifications of the principles and rules).

The reason why norms in particular moralities, including customary moralities, often differ is that the abstract starting points in the common morality—the considered judgments, including initial norms—can be developed in different ways to create practical guidelines and procedures with varying degrees of coherence. Crucial questions arise about how to justify particular specifications when competing specifications emerge. As we maintained in Chapter 1, different resolutions by specification and balancing are often possible, and nothing in our method ensures that only one specification or only one line of coherent specification will be justifiable.

The Limitations of General Ethical Theories

We now consider why the common morality is better suited to play a vital role in biomedical ethics—more suited, we think, than the ethical theories examined in Chapter 9.

Some writers in ethical theory and applied ethics seem to think that we would rightly have more confidence in our principles and considered judgments if only we could justify them on the basis of a comprehensive ethical theory. However, this outlook has the cart pulling the donkey: We should have more confidence in an ethical theory if it could be shown coherent in a comprehensive way with the considered judgments and norms comprising the common morality. If an ethical theory were to reject the various central principles and virtues we have discussed in this book—as examples of norms derived from the common morality—we would have a sound reason for skepticism about the theory more than skepticism about these principles and virtues. Our presentation of principles, virtues, and rights, together with our attempts to show their consistency with other aspects of the moral life such as moral emotions, constitutes *the nor-mative account* in this volume. In this theory (if it is truly a "theory," a question we do not here consider), there is no single unifying norm or concept. We do not mean to imply, of course, that some other common-morality theory cannot be superior to our account.[51]

Any moral theory should attempt to capture the pretheoretical moral point of view, and in this regard the common morality is the anchor of theory. If we could be confident that some abstract moral theory was a better source for codes and policies than the common morality, we could work constructively on prac-tical and policy questions by progressively specifying the norms of that theory. However, at present, we have no such theory. Advocates of systematic theory may have aspirations of decisively settling applied questions, but they are no better positioned to do so than pluralistic accounts. Proponents of the same type of general theory commonly disagree about its commitments, how to apply it, and how to address specific issues (for which we do not fault them, given our earlier arguments that such disagreement is ineliminable). The general norms and schemes of justification found in philosophical ethical theories are invar-iably more contestable than the norms in the common morality. We cannot reasonably expect that an inherently contestable moral theory will be better for practical decision making and policy development than the morality that serves as our common heritage.

Moral Change

Because the common morality can and should be progressively made more specific, specified moral norms are certain to be altered over time. It is simply a fact that particular moralities, customary practices, and so-called consensus moralities can and do change. They may even change by a complete reversal of position on some issues. For example, a code of research ethics might at one time endorse placebo-controlled trials only to condemn such trials at a later time. When relevant circumstances change or new insights emerge, revisions are war-ranted and to be welcomed. Change in particular moralities therefore occurs and can be justified.

Earlier in this chapter we defended a form of the method of reflective equi-librium that invites questions about moral change. Although considered judg-ments occupy a central position and are the root of many other inferred beliefs, even considered judgments are, in principle, revisable. It follows that no norm can, in the method we have defended, claim a privileged status as immune to revision even though considered judgments are the central starting norms.

However, both the method of reflective equilibrium and the fact of change in particular moralities leave unresolved whether *the common morality* itself changes by a process of either subtraction or addition. Can a universal morality be subject to change? Such moral change entails that what was morally required (or prohibited) in the common morality at a later time morally required (or prohibited). Could it come to be the case, morally, that we no longer have to keep our promises, that we can lie and deceive, or that a vice is now a virtue? If such norms are not fixed, then they could evolve into different norms and alter the normative content of the concept of morality. In Gert's theory change cannot occur in the norms of the common morality because the basic moral rules are both essential and timeless: "A *general* moral rule concerns actions open to all rational persons in all societies at all times. . . . A general moral rule is unchanging and unchangeable; discovered rather than invented. . . . Since general moral rules apply to all rational persons at all times, obviously they cannot be invented, or changed, or subject to the will of anyone."[52] But is Gert right in this assessment?

To the extent that we can envisage circumstances in which human society is better served by substantively changing or abandoning a norm in the common morality, change could occur and could conceivably be justified. For example, it is conceivable, however unlikely, that the rule that we are obligated to tell the truth could become so severely dangerous that we might therefore abandon the rule altogether. The very possibility of such change seems to weaken the claim that there is a common morality with essential conditions and normative authority for all moral agents in all times and places.

It would be dogmatic to assert without argument that the basic norms of morality cannot change, but it is difficult to construct a historical example of a central moral norm that has been or might be valid for a limited duration and was abandoned because some good moral reason was found for its displacement. No evidence known to us suggests that societies have handled moral problems by either rejecting or altering basic norms in the common morality. As circumstances change, we find moral reasons for saying that a norm has new specifications or valid exceptions or can be outweighed by other norms. These adjustments are not reasons to discard the norm; indeed, they show the lengths we go to in order to retain certain norms.

Clear-cut exceptions exist to even the most indispensable rules, such as the rule against killing. Particular moralities have carefully constructed exceptions in cases of war, self-defense, criminal punishment, martyrdom, misadventure, and the like. There is no reason to think that we cannot continue to handle social change through allowing exceptions to one or more stable norms in the common morality. These exceptions are often made explicit through new specifications.

In at least one notable respect moral change in the way we use norms in the common morality has occurred and will continue to occur. Even if abstract norms do not change, the *scope* of their application does change. That is, to whom many or all of these principles are deemed to apply has changed and we may anticipate still further change. Our arguments in Chapter 3 regarding moral

·Who qualifies as belonging to the moral com-
question as, "Who qualifies for moral status?" It is
.tically alter our understanding of who or what qualifies

envision a situation in which corresponding rules would be
.mon morality, by contrast to rules being abandoned or swapped
.ple, the common morality could be expanded to include a rule of
 .l consideration of persons, a rule of nondiscrimination. Depending
on the .ormulation of this rule, it could prohibit, for example, the various forms
of sexual discrimination that are now widely regarded in many customary
moralities as at least morally tolerable, and perhaps even thoroughly justified.
Examples are found in contexts that disallow women from being religious lead-
ers, that allow discrimination against gay and lesbian individuals, that allow
small businesses to discriminate in hiring by choosing only persons who are of
a preferred sex (e.g., an ethnic restaurant that uses only male waiters and kitchen
help), and so forth. Inclusion of a rule of equal consideration of persons that
challenged such practices would constitute a substantial change in the common
morality.

Even though these changes currently seem unlikely to occur, we can conceive of the conditions under which such changes could occur. Some might argue
that the common morality has already been refined in a conspicuously similar
manner by changes in the way slaves, women, people of differing ethnicities,
and persons from many groups who were once denied basic human rights have
come to be acknowledged as owed equal moral consideration. These changes
in the scope of the application of norms constitute major, and actual rather than
hypothetical or merely conceivable, changes in moral beliefs and practices. But
are such historical changes, which have upgraded the moral status of various
classes of individuals, changes in the common morality?

Changes in the way slaves, women, and so forth are regarded seem more
to be changes in either particular moralities or in ethical and political theories
than in the common morality. The most defensible view, we suggest, is that the
common morality does not now, and has never, included a provision of equal
moral consideration for all individuals, whatever such a provision might entail.
We are confident that empirical investigation of rules determining who should
receive equal consideration would reveal pervasive differences across individuals and societies that could reasonably be said to be firmly committed to proper
moral conduct. A theory of the common morality therefore should remain open
to the possibility that the common morality could and should include rules of
equal moral consideration for groups such as women, people of every ethnicity,
the great apes, and other parties now excluded. Where we are in the common
morality is not necessarily where we should be, for reasons we will make clear
in the following section.[53]

Finally, can we confi[dent]
slave-owning are justifie[d]
cannot be said to be then[?]
that the common moralit[y]
common morality does h[ave]
commitments of the com[mon]
and the like contain impl[icit]
as slave-owning. Slave-o[wning]
omy and nonmaleficenc[e]
common morality in a st[ate]
societies recognize this f[act]
ing the causation of har[m]
conclusion might not lea[d]
significant change in the
unnecessary harm.

We will not further p[ursue]
tance. Changes in the sc[ope]
morality are among the
moral practices. A *theor[y]*
criticize and even cond[emn]
morally unacceptable wo[uld]

actices such as
[throu]gh these norms
[safe]ty (in the sense
[...]? We think the
that the explicit
nonmaleficence,
it practices such
[re]spect for auton-
would leave the
[n]ot slave-owning
[...]e reached regard-
[...] in this case the
[rese]arch but only to a
[s]afeguards against

mark their impor-
[...]ns of the common
[...]r in the history of
[...]ies our capacity to
[...]ose viewpoints are
[...]le theory.

Three Types of Jus[tification for the] Universal Common Morality

There are three different[ly]
common morality migh[t]
theoretical justification,
justification, and their o[verlap]
to keep them distinct. E[ach]
set of conclusions about
a justification that uses
the case of each of the t[hree]
available types of justifi[cation]

Empirical justification[:]
mon morality might be
about the prospects for a
us as holding (in previ[ous]
in nature and requires e[mpirical]
diversity of approaches
common morality, some
an empirical investigati[on]

of claims about the
[...]ation, (2) normative
These three types of
[...]d, and it is essential
[di]fferent conclusion or
[...]claim to produce here
[...]es—a large project in
[...]on is to identify three
[...]ify.

existence of the com-
[thou]gh many are skeptical
[commen]tators have interpreted
[moral]ity theory is empirical
[in]terpretation misses the
[...]ion of claims about the
We start with the idea of
[co]mmon morality.

[emp]irical inquiry, but the goal is
[...]arget (namely, the most gen-
[...]l to morality and to impartial
[s]tudying only persons known
[...]morality. The question could
[...] the only persons tested are
[...]s the investigator is testing
[...]ing the study so that all per-
[...]moral norms and impartial
[...]in favor of the hypothesis
[...]s biasing the study against

[...]e, but not insurmountable.
[...]he set of norms shared by
[...]re committed to morality
[...]commitments; other per-
[...]ho are not committed to
[...]ould not appropriately be
[...]t conclude that we have
[...]y might say that we are
[...]al commitment and then
[...]e identified to qualify as
[...]osition risks stipulating
[...]ageable through careful
[...]tline of one design that
[...]support or to falsify our

[...]ould include only per-
[...]are committed to *some*
[...]lly committed persons
[...] nonmaleficence, as it
[...]uld reject this general
[...]nclusion criterion, and
[...] single general moral
[...]ct study subjects for
[...]imed to be central to
[...]ould not be screened
[...]rsons not committed
[...]purpose of the study
[...]rences emerge in the
[...]ned with respect for

autonomy, beneficence, justice, and other hypothesized norms in the common morality including promise-keeping, truth-telling, helping incompetent persons, respecting confidentiality, and so forth. The research design could also test whether various norms are universally held that we have not presented as universal.

Should it turn out that the persons studied do not share the norms that we hypothesize to have their roots in the common morality (we claim to present only norms pertinent for biomedical ethics), then the research would have shown that there is no common morality of the sort we have envisioned, and our hypothesis would be falsified.[57] If norms other than the ones we have mentioned were demonstrated to be shared across the subjects tested, as we anticipate would be the case, this finding would presumably yield insights about the breadth of the common morality. Only if no moral norms were found in common across cultures would the general hypothesis that a common morality exists be rejected. It is clearly a possibility that the study, as we have outlined its design, might demonstrate that there is no common morality.

We have not claimed in this section that empirical confirmation of the hypothesis that there exists a common morality constitutes a normative justification of the norms of the common morality. A strictly empirical finding by itself cannot do so. However, empirical findings can assist us in using the method of reflective equilibrium defended earlier in this chapter—in particular, "wide reflective equilibrium." We were there concerned with how to control for bias and lack of objectivity in the choice of considered judgments. One way to control for bias is to use information about what is widely, preferably universally, agreed to be correct. This kind of information can then be employed in the process of reflective equilibrium. Disputed or unshared judgments are not well-positioned to qualify as considered judgments, whereas shared agreement is a relevant consideration. Shared agreement helps sustain claims about considered judgments, and these judgments have priority. Universally shared agreement is, in this respect, integral to the justificatory process. Although empirical information about commonness is not normatively determinative, it does in this way stand to contribute to the process of normative justification. With this caveat, we turn now to nonempirical methods of theoretical justification that may have this capacity.

Normative theoretical justification.   Whatever might be established empirically about the existence of universal norms of a shared common morality, nothing normative would follow directly from this finding. Neither historical facts, such as facts about the history and traditions of medical ethics, nor social science facts of the sort envisaged in the previous section serve to justify moral norms. In Chapter 9 we discussed criteria of normative theories and the approach to justification taken by four different types of theory. Utilitarian theories, Kantian theories, rights theories, and virtue theories, among others, could be employed

Finally, can we confidently assert that norms that prohibit practices such as slave-owning are justified by the common morality, even though these norms cannot be said to be themselves included in the common morality (in the sense that the common morality has no explicit standards of this sort)? We think the common morality does have this capacity. The justification is that the explicit commitments of the common morality to respect for autonomy, nonmaleficence, and the like contain implicit commitments to norms that prohibit practices such as slave-owning. Slave-owning involves clear violations of respect for autonomy and nonmaleficence, and a rule allowing this practice would leave the common morality in a state of moral incoherence, whether or not slave-owning societies recognize this fact. Much the same conclusion can be reached regarding the causation of harm to experimental animals, although in this case the conclusion might not lead to a prohibition of biomedical research but only to a significant change in the thresholds of acceptable harm and safeguards against unnecessary harm.

We will not further pursue these lines of argument, but we mark their importance. Changes in the scope of persons protected by the norms of the common morality are among the most momentous changes to occur in the history of moral practices. A *theory* of the common morality that denies our capacity to criticize and even condemn traditions or communities whose viewpoints are morally unacceptable would be an ineffectual and indefensible theory.

Three Types of Justification of Claims about a Universal Common Morality

There are three different methods by which different types of claims about the common morality might be justified: (1) empirical justification, (2) normative theoretical justification, and (3) conceptual justification. These three types of justification, and their objectives, have often been confused, and it is essential to keep them distinct. Each type of strategy justifies a different conclusion or set of conclusions about the common morality. We do not claim to produce here a justification that uses one or more of the three strategies—a large project in the case of each of the three. Our limited aim in this section is to identify three available types of justification and what they stand to justify.

Empirical justification.   In Chapter 1 we stated that the existence of the common morality might be demonstrated empirically, although many are skeptical about the prospects for achieving this goal. Some commentators have interpreted us as holding (in previous editions) that common-morality theory is empirical in nature and requires empirical proof.[54] However, this interpretation misses the diversity of approaches we recommend for the justification of claims about the common morality, some empirical and some normative. We start with the idea of an empirical investigation into whether there exists a common morality.

If an empirical investigation were to show that a universal content is found in moral belief, the claim that a common morality exists would be empirically justified. In several previous chapters we have noted that there are multiple particular moralities and that similarities and differences between them are empirically confirmable. This view is noncontroversial. In addition to these particular moralities, we have proposed that certain central norms of morality are held universally in common among morally committed persons. As best we can determine, no empirical studies throw into question whether some particular moralities accept, whereas others reject, the norms of the common morality. Existing empirical data descend from studies of particular moralities that were never designed to determine whether a universal morality exists. These empirical investigations have usually studied cultural differences in the way rules have become embedded and applied in cultures and organizations, but they have not investigated whether there is a common morality. These studies succeed in showing cultural differences in the *interpretation* and *specification* of moral norms, but they do not show that cultures accept, ignore, abandon, or reject the standards of the common morality. For example, empirical studies do not test whether a cultural morality rejects rules against theft, promise-breaking, or killing. Rather, investigators study what particular societies consider to be theft, promise-breaking, and killing; how they handle exceptive cases; and the like.

Some critics of our common-morality thesis claim that anthropological and historical evidence already speaks against the empirical hypothesis that is assumed in the claim that a universal morality exists.[55] However, these critics seem not to appreciate the nuances that surround the design of empirical research that would test specific hypotheses about the common morality. In principle, scientific research could either confirm or falsify the hypothesis that there exists a universal common morality, but such research must state which hypotheses are to be tested, how to formulate inclusion/exclusion criteria for study subjects, and why these hypotheses and criteria were selected. To date, critics who argue that available empirical studies falsify common-morality claims have not attended to any of the specific issues that must be addressed in the scientific investigation of hypotheses about the common morality.

The primary hypothesis that we propose for empirical testing is this: All persons committed to morality and to impartial moral judgment in their moral assessments accept at least the norms that we have proposed as central to the common morality. The persons to be included in a study that investigates this hypothesis are (1) persons who pass a rigorous test of whether their beliefs conform to some critical considered judgment, to use Rawls's term (this judgment to be designated in the study design), and (2) persons who qualify as having the ability to take an impartial moral point of view.

It would be difficult to design such an empirical inquiry, but the goal is achievable despite problems of either missing the target (namely, the most general beliefs of all and only those who are committed to morality and to impartial judgment) or begging the question by insisting on studying only persons known to accept what we have declared to be the common morality. The question could be begged either by (1) designing the study so that the only persons tested are those who already have the commitments and beliefs the investigator is testing for (e.g., our four clusters of principles) or (2) designing the study so that all persons are tested whether or not they are committed to moral norms and impartial assessment. The first design risks biasing the study in favor of the hypothesis that a common morality exists. The second design risks biasing the study against the hypothesis.

These problems in research design are formidable, but not insurmountable. We have defined the *common morality* in terms of "the set of norms shared by all persons committed to morality." Some persons are committed to morality but do not always behave in accordance with their commitments; other persons are not committed to morality at all.[56] Persons who are not committed to morality are not within the scope of our claims and could not appropriately be included as subjects in an empirical study. Some might conclude that we have constructed a circular and self-justifying position. They might say that we are defining the common morality in terms of a certain moral commitment and then allowing only those who accept the norms that we have identified to qualify as persons committed to morality. We appreciate that our position risks stipulating the content of "morality." Nonetheless, this risk is manageable through careful research design. Here we can provide only a basic outline of one design that would manage this risk and would allow the research to support or to falsify our hypothesis.

In the methodology we propose, an investigation would include only persons who have already been screened to ensure that they are committed to *some* norm of morality that is reasonable to expect all morally committed persons to accept. We suggest that a reasonable such principle is nonmaleficence, as it is unimaginable that any morally committed person would reject this general principle. Acceptance of this principle could serve as an inclusion criterion, and nonacceptance as an exclusion criterion. This choice of a single general moral norm does not bias the study because it does not preselect study subjects for their beliefs in any of the several other norms we have claimed to be central to the common morality. The group of persons to be tested would not be screened by presupposing any norm other than nonmaleficence. Persons not committed to the principle of nonmaleficence would be excluded. The purpose of the study would be to determine whether cultural or individual differences emerge in the included group over the acceptance of moral norms concerned with respect for autonomy, beneficence, justice, and other hypothesized norms in the common morality including promise-keeping, truth-telling, helping incompetent persons, respecting confidentiality, and so forth. The research design could also test whether various norms are universally held that we have not presented as universal.

Should it turn out that the persons studied do not share the norms that we hypothesize to have their roots in the common morality (we claim to present only norms pertinent for biomedical ethics), then the research would have shown that there is no common morality of the sort we have envisioned, and our hypothesis would be falsified.[57] If norms other than the ones we have mentioned were demonstrated to be shared across the subjects tested, as we anticipate would be the case, this finding would presumably yield insights about the breadth of the common morality. Only if no moral norms were found in common across cultures would the general hypothesis that a common morality exists be rejected. It is clearly a possibility that the study, as we have outlined its design, might demonstrate that there is no common morality.

We have not claimed in this section that empirical confirmation of the hypothesis that there exists a common morality constitutes a normative justification of the norms of the common morality. A strictly empirical finding by itself cannot do so. However, empirical findings can assist us in using the method of reflective equilibrium defended earlier in this chapter—in particular, "wide reflective equilibrium." We were there concerned with how to control for bias and lack of objectivity in the choice of considered judgments. One way to control for bias is to use information about what is widely, preferably universally, agreed to be correct. This kind of information can then be employed in the process of reflective equilibrium. Disputed or unshared judgments are not well-positioned to qualify as considered judgments, whereas shared agreement is a relevant consideration. Shared agreement helps sustain claims about considered judgments, and these judgments have priority. Universally shared agreement is, in this respect, integral to the justificatory process. Although empirical information about commonness is not normatively determinative, it does in this way stand to contribute to the process of normative justification. With this caveat, we turn now to nonempirical methods of theoretical justification that may have this capacity.

Normative theoretical justification. Whatever might be established empirically about the existence of universal norms of a shared common morality, nothing normative would follow directly from this finding. Neither historical facts, such as facts about the history and traditions of medical ethics, nor social science facts of the sort envisaged in the previous section serve to justify moral norms. In Chapter 9 we discussed criteria of normative theories and the approach to justification taken by four different types of theory. Utilitarian theories, Kantian theories, rights theories, and virtue theories, among others, could be employed to provide a theoretical justification of the norms of the common morality. We argued that the norms supported in these theories tend to converge to the acceptance of the norms of the common morality, but establishing such convergence is also not a moral justification.

Earlier in the present chapter we discussed Bernard Gert's attempts to justify the common morality in his books *Morality: Its Nature and Justification* and *Common Morality: Deciding What to Do*. Gert has effectively shown that there is no reason why the norms in the common morality cannot be justified by a general ethical theory. We do not mean that he has conclusively shown the correctness of his particular form of theoretical justification—only that he has convincingly shown that a normative ethical theory can be put to the work of justifying the norms of the common morality. Gert rightly says that his account of ethics does not make "*empirical* claims about morality," but rather provides justification of the substantive norms that constitute the common morality.[58]

In his theory, common morality is justified on the basis of rationality. He regards it as clear to all rational persons that we should not act irrationally because irrational actions are those that should not be performed:

> Rational persons want to avoid death, pain, disability, loss of freedom, and loss of pleasure, and they know not only that they are fallible and vulnerable but that they can be deceived and harmed by other people. They know that if people do not act morally with regard to them, they will be at significantly increased risk of suffering some harm. If they use only rationally required beliefs, it would be irrational not to endorse common morality as the system to be adopted to govern the behavior of all moral agents.[59]

Acting irrationally has a close relationship to acting in ways that will increase the likelihood of certain basic harms, and Gert argues that the moral rules have the goal of prohibiting the causing of these harms or contributing to conditions that may cause them.[60]

Ethical theories other than Gert's, and other than the four types discussed in Chapter 9, might be employed to justify the common morality. Pragmatism nicely illustrates a type of theory that could be adapted to this purpose.[61] Pragmatic justification holds that moral norms are justified by their effectiveness in achieving the object of morality. Once an operative purpose or objective of an institution or system of thought has been identified, a set of standards is vindicated if it is better for reaching the identified objectives than any alternative set of standards. For example, a pragmatist can conceive the goal or object of morality as that of promoting human flourishing by counteracting conditions that cause the quality of people's lives to worsen and can argue that the norms of the common morality are the best instrument to combat these conditions. A set of standards is pragmatically justified if and only if it is the best means to the end identified when all factors—including human limitations, shortcomings, and vulnerabilities—are taken into consideration.

We will not here attempt an actual justification of the pertinent moral norms by appeal to a particular type of general ethical theory, though we encourage such theoretical endeavors. Our conclusion in this section is merely that such theories have been and can be constructed and, if they are successful, they would justify the norms of the common morality.

Conceptual justification.[62] In Chapter 1 we discussed the importance in metaethics of conceptual analyses of normative notions such as *right, obligation, virtue, justification,* and *responsibility.* The concept of morality is clearly connected to normative notions. It is less clear but still a plausible hypothesis, and one that we accept, that the concept of morality contains normativity not only in the sense that morality inherently contains *some* action guiding norms, but also in the sense that it contains *certain specific* moral norms—that is, a body of norms in morality in the normative sense. No system of belief lacking these norms counts as morality, and if someone claimed that a system without these common-morality norms is a moral system, the claim should be rejected as conceptually mistaken. Philippa Foot defends such a claim in a celebrated essay:

> A moral system seems necessarily to be one aimed at removing particular dangers and securing certain benefits, and it would follow that some things do and some do not count as objections to a line of conduct from a moral point of view.... [T]here are starting-points...fixed by the concept of morality. We might call them "definitional criteria" of moral good and evil, so long as it is clear that they belong to the concept of morality—to *the* definition and not to some definition which a man can choose for himself. What we say about such definitional criteria will be objectively true or false....
>
> [I]t does not follow that we can settle all moral questions in this [definitional] way.... [T]he concept of morality while it fixes a great deal also leaves quite a lot open.[63]

We agree with Foot that certain norms are essential to morality, whether they be principles, virtues, or rights. These norms are also essential to any acceptable system of norms in what we have called particular moralities. By contrast, some norms that are referred to as "moral," such as norms that reject human rights, are external to, and their content excluded by, the normative concept of morality, even though morality in a descriptive sense—the sense of "morality" commonly used in the social and behavioral sciences—allows inclusion of such norms. In this descriptive sense, "morality" refers to a group's code of conduct, or to individuals' important beliefs and attitudes about their own conduct. There are plural descriptive "moralities," and they can differ extensively in the content of beliefs and in standards of practice. However, reports of morality in the descriptive sense have no implications for how persons should behave, whereas in a normative sense of "morality" some actions are immoral and others morally required.[64]

The norms internal to morality in the normative sense are indispensable points of reference without which we could not get our moral bearings. As we have occasionally said about the four clusters of principles that provide the framework of norms in this book, they are starting points that have a secure place in the common morality. One way of understanding this claim is that these anchoring norms are crucial elements of the concept of morality, whereas the distinctive norms in particular moralities are not essential even though they may be entirely coherent with the common morality. By contrast, some "moralities" depicted in historical and social scientific literature may contain practices that contradict norms of morality in the normative sense—for example, a so-called "medical morality" of not reporting harmful medical mistakes to hospital administrators or patients, which amounts to a body of indefensible customs.

We do not claim that our four clusters of principles form the conceptual heart of the common morality in a way that other principles, rules, rights, and virtues do not. Our claim is merely that we *draw from* the common morality to formulate the principles *of biomedical ethics* in our book. The two italicized parts of this sentence are critical: Unlike Gert, we do not claim to have removed the veil from the full set of norms that constitute the common morality. The norms in the common morality undoubtedly reach out beyond the principles on which we concentrate. Put another way, we do not claim that our principles exhaust the norms in the common morality; and what we said in Chapters 1 and 2 about the virtues as having a secure place in the common morality illustrates one domain of the larger territory of the common morality.[65] Second, we claim for our framework of four clusters of principles only that these principles are well-suited as a general framework for biomedical ethics. We do not claim more.

If this line of argument is correct, it is a conceptual mistake, when using "morality" in the normative sense, to assert that morality allows persons to trade in slaves, coerce persons to be subjects in high-risk biomedical experimentation, or conceal harmful medical mistakes. The proposition that such practices are permissible might correctly characterize the beliefs of certain groups when "morality" is used in the descriptive sense, but it is conceptually incorrect of "morality" in the normative sense. Likewise, the proposition that "lying is morally permissible" is an unacceptable general norm in morality, even though "lying is not permissible" is only a prima facie rule that can sometimes be justifiably overridden. The fact that lying is sometimes justified does not entail that the rule "Lying is not permissible" is not a conceptually central norm in "morality" in the normative sense.

A good example of these problems is found in the moral vices that we mentioned in Chapters 1, 2, and 9—vices such as malevolence, dishonesty, lack of integrity, and cruelty. In morality in the normative sense these character traits are excluded from the domain of the morally acceptable, even though they too lack an absolute status. There may be rare circumstances in which dishonesty is appropriate, as with lying. Similarly, rules that allow causing suffering to others and punishing the innocent are excluded from the domain of the morally acceptable (as prima facie wrong).

Adequate defense of these claims would require more extensive analysis of the concept of morality than we can undertake here. It would not be enough to argue that morality is the social institution that functions to ameliorate or counteract the tendency for things to go badly in human relationships. Morality would also have to be shown to be more than taking what some philosophers have called "the moral point of view"—that is, taking a view with a certain moral attitude such as compassion and adopting an impartial perspective that sets aside self-interest. No such approach would adequately capture morality in the normative sense.[66]

Moral pluralists claim that there are multiple concepts of morality in the normative sense, but moral pluralism is a group-relative notion best interpreted as a version of "morality" in the descriptive sense. It would be incoherent to formulate the normative meaning of the term *morality* as consisting of the norms of multiple moralities, because contradictory advice would be given. One could deny that the term is univocal and then formulate two or more normative senses of "morality" (ns_1, ns_2, etc.), each with a different set of substantive norms, just as we can distinguish descriptive and normative senses. However, this maneuver is the functional equivalent of analyzing "morality" descriptively rather than normatively. Accordingly, we see no promise in conceptual pluralism.

In line with our arguments in Chapter 9 about convergence in moral theory, we caution against an undue emphasis on differences among moral theories that seem to amount to a pluralism of theory. These disagreements are usually about the theoretical foundations of morality. Hence, they may mask an underlying and abiding agreement about central considered moral judgments. Theoreticians tend to assume, rather than disagree about, these moral norms (e.g., prohibiting the breaking of promises, requiring that we not cause harm to others, requiring respect for autonomous choice, etc.).[67] Put another way, many philosophers with different conceptions of the theoretical justification of universal morality do not significantly disagree on the substantive norms that comprise morality in the normative sense, even though they may significantly disagree on both theoretical foundations.

Problems for Common-Morality Theory

We acknowledge that our theory of the common morality leaves unsettled problems that we would have to address in a more complete account. Three problems deserve more attention than they can receive here.

Specification and judgment. Do specified principles enable us to reach practical judgments, or are they still too general and indeterminate to generate such judgments? Our theory requires that we specify to escape abstract indeterminateness and to provide action-guiding content, but there is also a danger of over-specifying a principle or rule, thereby leaving insufficient room for deliberation, judgment, and balancing of norms in some circumstances. Balancing judgments in concrete circumstances can be as important as specification for moral thinking. However, without tighter controls on both permissible balancing and permissible specification, critics will reasonably insist that too much room remains for judgments that are unprincipled and yet sanctioned or permitted by the theory. Questions that remain include, "Can the conditions intended to structure and constrain balancing presented in Chapter 1 reduce intuition to an acceptable level?" and "Can the constraints of our proposals about justification be tightened to respond to these concerns?"

Coherence in the common morality?   We have linked reflective equilibrium to a common-morality theory of normative ethics and have attempted to integrate them as an approach to method and justification. However, is it reasonable to expect that the common morality itself is coherent? If one argues, as we do, that a heap of obligations and values unconnected by a first principle comprises the common morality, is it possible to show that there is a coherent moral system (or a way of revising it into coherence) without radically reconstructing norms so that they only vaguely resemble the norms that we claim to be those of the common morality?

Theory construction.   The language of "common-morality theory" suggests that an ethical *theory* can be constructed that is based only on norms drawn from the common morality. Is there good reason to believe that a theory—not merely an unconnected collection of principles and rules—is possible? Perhaps general principles, analyses of the moral virtues, and statements of human rights are all that we should aspire to, rather than a *theory* that conforms to the criteria delineated at the beginning of Chapter 9. Perhaps "ethical theory" has been so diluted in meaning in the case of "common-morality theories" that we should abandon the goal of a theory altogether.

In part, these problems turn on different expectations for a "theory." Gert and Clouser expect a strong measure of unity and systematic connection among rules and moral ideals, a clear pattern of justification, and a practical decision procedure that flows from a theory, whereas other philosophers are skeptical of one or more of these conditions, and even of the language of "theory."[68] We have encouraged theory in this chapter, as in Chapters 1, 2, and 9; but we have also cautioned against expecting too much from ethical theories in the way of systematic tidiness and action guidance. Moreover, no available ethical theory will eliminate the importance of specification, balancing, and reaching for reflective equilibrium as aids in practical ethics.

CONCLUSION

The model of working "down" by applying theories or principles to cases has attracted many who work in biomedical ethics, but we have argued that this model needs to be replaced by the method of reflective equilibrium. We have also maintained that we have reason to trust norms in the common morality more than norms found in general theories. Ethical theories should not be expected to yield concrete rules or judgments capable of resolving all contingent moral conflicts. No theory has such power. Nonetheless, we have not defended a so-called antitheoretical position. We have encouraged moral reflection of several types, including the development of moral theories, especially as ways to discover and explicate the common morality and to determine the place of principles, virtues, and rights in biomedical ethics.

NOTES

1. U.S. Supreme Court, *United Automobile Workers v. Johnson Controls, Inc.,* 499 U.S. 187 (1991) (Argued October 10, 1990. Decided March 20, 1991).

2. K. Danner Clouser and Bernard Gert, "A Critique of Principlism," *Journal of Medicine and Philosophy* 15 (April 1990): 219–36. This article, and others that followed it, defend Gert's ethical theory in his book *Morality: Its Nature and Justification,* now in its 2nd rev. ed. (New York: Oxford University Press, 2005). See also *Common Morality: Deciding What to Do* (New York: Oxford University Press, 2007). Gert and Clouser published, with Charles M. Culver, *Bioethics: A Return to Fundamentals* (New York: Oxford University Press, 1997), and the second edition, retitled as *Bioethics: A Systematic Approach* (New York: Oxford University Press, 2006); both contain sustained criticisms of our views. Gert, Culver, and Clouser accept both the language of the common morality and a conception of it not dissimilar to ours. The first publication on the subject was Clouser, "Common Morality as an Alternative to Principlism," *Kennedy Institute of Ethics Journal* 5 (1995): 219–36. See also Gert, Culver, and Clouser, "Common Morality versus Specified Principlism: Reply to Richardson," *Journal of Medicine and Philosophy* 25 (2000): 308–22. For critical essays on Gert's moral theory, see Robert Audi and Walter Sinnott-Armstrong, eds., *Rationality, Rules, and Ideals: Critical Essays on Bernard Gert's Moral Theory* (Lanham, MD: Rowman & Littlefield, 2003).

3. Clouser and Gert, "A Critique of Principlism"; Gert and Clouser, "Morality vs. Principlism," in *Principles of Health Care Ethics,* ed. Raanan Gillon and Ann Lloyd (Chichester, England: Wiley, 1994), pp. 251–66; Gert, Culver, and Clouser, *Bioethics: A Systematic Approach,* chap. 5.

4. Gert, Culver, and Clouser, *Bioethics: A Systematic Approach,* pp. 11–14, 32ff, passim.

5. Gert and associates, like us, appeal to a relatively small number of norms drawn from the common morality. See Gert, Culver, and Clouser, *Bioethics: A Systematic Approach,* pp. 22–23, 34–36.

6. Gert has maintained in private conversation that once principles are interpreted as normative headings under which rules fall, they become unobjectionable, but they also become expendable. His published view is that "if specified principlism develops properly, it will become our account." See Gert, Culver, and Clouser, *Bioethics: A Return to Fundamentals,* p. 90. See also a clarification and partial retraction of their earlier criticism in Gert and Clouser, "Concerning Principlism and Its Defenders: Reply to Beauchamp and Veatch," pp. 190–91.

7. For a proposed method to handle this problem, see Gert, Culver, and Clouser, *Bioethics: A Systematic Approach,* pp. 27–32, 38–42, 83–87; and "Morality vs. Principlism," pp. 261–63. For relevant criticism of their claims, see Henry Richardson, "Specifying, Balancing, and Interpreting Bioethical Principles," *Journal of Medicine and Philosophy* 25 (2000): 285–307, esp. 293–97.

8. Thomas Nagel, *Mortal Questions* (Cambridge: Cambridge University Press, 1979), pp. 128–37; W. D. Ross, *The Right and the Good* (Oxford: Clarendon, 1930; reprinted Indianapolis, IN: Hackett, 1988).

9. See, further, Michael Quante and Andreas Vieth, "Defending Principlism Well Understood," *Journal of Medicine and Philosophy* 27 (2002): 621–49.

10. Gert, Culver, and Clouser, *Bioethics: A Systematic Approach,* pp. 11–13.

11. Gert, *Morality: A New Justification of the Moral Rules* (New York: Oxford University Press, 1988), pp. 154–55.

12. Cf. Gert, Culver, and Clouser, *Bioethics: A Systematic Approach,* pp. 89–93; and the formulation in Gert and Clouser, "Concerning Principlism and Its Defenders: Reply to Beauchamp and Veatch," pp. 190–91.

13. See Gert and Culver, "The Justification of Paternalism," *Ethics* 89 (1979): 199–210; for a critique, see James F. Childress, *Who Should Decide? Paternalism in Health Care* (New York: Oxford University Press, 1982), pp. 237–41.

14. See Gert, Culver, and Clouser, *Bioethics: A Systematic Approach,* p. 36.

15. See the comments, formulations, and frameworks in John D. Arras, "Pragmatism in Bioethics: Been There, Done That," *Social Philosophy and Policy* 19 (2002): 29–58; Heike Schmidt-Felzmann, "Pragmatic Principles—Methodological Pragmatism in the Principle-Based Approach to Bioethics," *Journal of Medicine and Philosophy* 28 (2003): 581–96; Henry Richardson, "Beyond Good and Right: Toward a Constructive Ethical Pragmatism," *Philosophy and Public Affairs* 24 (1995): 108–41; Joseph J. Fins, Franklin G. Miller, and Matthew D. Bacchetta, "Clinical Pragmatism: A Method of Moral Problem Solving," *Kennedy Institute of Ethics Journal* 7 (1997): 129–45; and Lynn A. Jansen, "Assessing Clinical Pragmatism," *Kennedy Institute of Ethics Journal* 8 (1998): 23–36.

16. See Alisa L. Carse, "Impartial Principle and Moral Context: Securing a Place for the Particular in Ethical Theory," *Journal of Medicine and Philosophy* 23 (1998): 153–69; Daniel Callahan, "Universalism & Particularism: Fighting to a Draw," *Hastings Center Report* 30 (2000): 37–44; and Earl Winkler, "Moral Philosophy and Bioethics: Contextualism vs. the Paradigm Theory," in *Philosophical Perspectives on Bioethics,* ed. L. W. Sumner and Joseph Boyle (Toronto: University of Toronto Press, 1996), pp. 50–78.

17. For interpretations, defenses, and critiques of narrative approaches to bioethics, see Hilde Lindemann Nelson, ed., *Stories and Their Limits: Narrative Approaches to Bioethics* (New York: Routledge, 1997); and Anne Hudson Jones, "Narrative in Medical Ethics," *British Medical Journal* 318 (January 23, 1999): 253–56.

18. *In the matter of Quinlan,* 70 N.J. 10, 355 A.2d 647, cert. denied, 429 U.S. 922 (1976).

19. See Albert R. Jonsen and Stephen Toulmin, *The Abuse of Casuistry: A History of Moral Reasoning* (Berkeley, CA: University of California Press, 1988); Carson Strong, "Specified Principlism: What Is It, and Does It Really Resolve Cases Better than Casuistry?" *Journal of Medicine and Philosophy* 25 (2000): 323–41; and Strong, "Critiques of Casuistry and Why They Are Mistaken," *Theoretical Medicine and Bioethics* 20 (1999): 395–411.

20. Casuists have had relatively little to say about the nature or definition of a "case," or about the meaning of the term *casuistry,* but see Albert R. Jonsen, "Casuistry and Clinical Ethics," in *Methods in Medical Ethics,* ed. Jeremy Sugarman and Daniel P. Sulmasy (Washington, DC: Georgetown University Press, 2010), pp. 110–11, 119; and Albert R. Jonsen, Mark Siegler, and William J. Winslade, *Clinical Ethics,* 6th ed. (New York: McGraw-Hill, 2006).

21. See, for example, Albert R. Jonsen, "Casuistry: An Alternative or Complement to Principles?" *Journal of the Kennedy Institute of Ethics* 5 (1995), esp. 246–47; "Strong on Specification," *Journal of Medicine and Philosophy* 25 (2000): 348–60; and "Morally Appreciated Circumstances: A Theoretical Problem for Casuistry," in *Philosophical Perspectives on Bioethics,* ed. Sumner and Boyle, pp. 37–49.

22.   Here are two kinds of claims of a unified theory of the sort casuists presumably would disparage (these examples are ours, not one specifically selected by casuists): (1) Jeremy Bentham: "From utility then we may denominate a principle, that may serve to preside over and govern...several institutions or combinations of institutions that compose the matter of this science." *A Fragment on Government,* ed. J. H. Burns and H. L. A. Hart (London: Athlone Press, 1977), p. 416. (2) Henry Sidgwick: "Utilitarianism may be presented as [a] scientifically complete and systematically reflective form of th[e] regulation of conduct." *Methods of Ethics* (Indianapolis, IN: Hackett, 1981), bk. 4, chap. 3, § 1, p. 425.

23.   Stephen Toulmin, "The Tyranny of Principles," *Hastings Center Report* 11 (December 1981): 31–39.

24.   Jonsen and Toulmin, *Abuse of Casuistry,* pp. 16–19.

25.   National Commission for the Protection of Human Subjects of Biomedical and Behavioral Research, *The Belmont Report: Ethical Principles and Guidelines for the Protection of Human Subjects of Research* (Washington, DC: DHEW Publication OS 78–0012, 1978); James F. Childress, Eric M. Meslin, and Harold T. Shapiro, eds., *Belmont Revisited: Ethical Principles for Research with Human Subjects* (Washington, DC: Georgetown University Press, 2005); Tom L. Beauchamp, *Standing on Principles: Collected Essays* (New York: Oxford University Press, 2010), chaps. 1–2.

26.   In addition to *Abuse of Casuistry,* see Jonsen's latest views on principles in "Casuistry and Clinical Ethics," pp. 112–18, and Toulmin, "The National Commission on Human Experimentation: Procedures and Outcomes," in *Scientific Controversies: Case Studies in the Resolution and Closure of Disputes in Science and Technology,* ed. H. Tristram Engelhardt, Jr., and Arthur Caplan (New York: Cambridge University Press, 1987), pp. 599–613.

27.   See Arras, "Getting Down to Cases: The Revival of Casuistry in Bioethics," *Journal of Medicine and Philosophy* 16 (1991): 29–51, at 31–33; Jonsen and Toulmin, *Abuse of Casuistry,* pp. 16–19, 66–67.

28.   Carson Strong is a particularly striking example, beginning with his "Specified Principlism" in 2000, esp. p. 337. His most recent theses incorporate both principles and common morality; see especially "Theoretical and Practical Problems with Wide Reflective Equilibrium in Bioethics," *Theoretical Medicine and Bioethics* 31 (2010): 123–40. Also notably accommodating to principles is Jonsen's "Casuistry and Clinical Ethics," esp. p. 120 (where it is said that casuistry "does not deny that certain methodological moves in moral theory might be quite relevant to casuistic thinking, such as the reflective equilibrium and specification methods"). This accommodating, sometimes integrative, approach perhaps began as early as Arras's 1991 article "Getting Down to Cases: The Revival of Casuistry in Bioethics," and Jonsen's 1995 article, "Casuistry: An Alternative or Complement to Principles?" esp. pp. 248–49.

29.   Jonsen, "Casuistry as Methodology in Clinical Ethics," p. 298.

30.   Jonsen, "Casuistry and Clinical Ethics," p. 119.

31.   Tod Chambers, *The Fiction of Bioethics: Cases as Literary Texts* (New York and London: Routledge, 1999); see also James F. Childress, "Narratives versus Norms: A Misplaced Debate in Bioethics?" in *Stories and Their Limits: Narrative Approaches to Bioethics,* ed. Hilde Lindemann Nelson (New York: Routledge, 1997). For related problems of paradigm cases and of making casuistry effective in practice, see Annette Braunack-Meyer, "Casuistry as Bioethical Method: An Alternative Perspective," *Social Science and Medicine* 53 (2001): 71–81.

32.   Anonymous, "It's Over, Debbie," *Journal of the American Medical Association* 259, no. 2 (1988): 272.

33.   Jonsen, "Casuistry as Methodology in Clinical Ethics."

34.   J. K. Kaufert and T. Koch, "Disability or End-of-Life: Competing Narratives in Bioethics," *Theoretical Medicine* 24 (2003): 459–69.

35. Kaufert and Koch, "Disability or End-of-Life," p. 462.

36. Arras, "Getting Down to Cases."

37. Loretta M. Kopelman, "Case Method and Casuistry: The Problem of Bias," *Theoretical Medicine* 15 (1994): 21–37, at 21.

38. See Cass Sunstein, "On Analogical Reasoning," *Harvard Law Review* 106 (1993): 741–91, esp. 767–78; Kopelman, "Case Method and Casuistry"; Arras, "Getting Down to Cases"; Kevin Wildes, *Moral Acquaintances: Methodology in Bioethics* (Notre Dame, IN: University of Notre Dame, 2000), chaps. 3–4; and Mark G. Kuczewski, *Fragmentation and Consensus: Communitarian and Casuistic Bioethics* (Washington, DC: Georgetown University Press, 1997).

39. See John Arras, "A Case Approach," in *A Companion to Bioethics,* ed. Helga Kuhse and Peter Singer (Oxford: Blackwell, 1998), pp. 106–13, esp. 112–13.

40. Jonsen, "Casuistry: An Alternative or Complement to Principles?" pp. 246–47.

41. John Rawls, *A Theory of Justice* (Cambridge, MA: Harvard University Press, 1971; rev. ed., 1999), esp. pp. 20ff, 46–50, 579–80 (1999: 17ff, 40–45, 508–9). See also Rawls's comments on reflective equilibrium in his later book, *Political Liberalism* (New York: Columbia University Press, 1996), esp. pp. 8, 381, 384, and 399.

42. Rawls, "The Independence of Moral Theory," *Proceedings and Addresses of the American Philosophical Association* 48 (1974–75): 8; and, more generally, Rawls, "Outline of a Decision Procedure for Ethics," *Philosophical Review* 60 (1951): 177–97.

43. Cf. the conclusions reached in Richardson, "Specifying, Balancing, and Interpreting Bioethical Principles," p. 302.

44. Norman Daniels, "Wide Reflective Equilibrium in Practice," in *Philosophical Perspectives on Bioethics,* ed. L. W. Sumner and J. Boyle (Toronto: University of Toronto Press, 1996), pp. 96–114; *Justice and Justification: Reflective Equilibrium in Theory and Practice* (New York: Cambridge University Press, 1996); "Reflective Equilibrium," *Stanford Encyclopedia of Philosophy* (online, first published April 28, 2003; accessed August 24, 2007).

45. Rawls, *A Theory of Justice,* pp. 195–201 (1999: 171–76).

46. DeGrazia, "Common Morality, Coherence, and the Principles of Biomedical Ethics," *Kennedy Institute of Ethics Journal* 13 (2003): 219–30, esp. p. 226.

47. Circa 1640. Published 1974 by Historical Documents Co., available at http://www.jollyrogercayman .com/web%20pages/pirates_creed.htm (accessed August 17, 2007).

48. For these and related problems, see John D. Arras, "The Way We Reason Now: Reflective Equilibrium in Bioethics," in *The Oxford Handbook of Bioethics,* ed. Bonnie Steinbock (Oxford: Oxford University Press, 2007), pp. 46–71; Strong, "Theoretical and Practical Problems with Wide Reflective Equilibrium in Bioethics"; Michael R. DePaul, *Balance and Refinement: Beyond Coherence Models of Moral Inquiry* (London: Routledge, 1993); and Kai Nielsen, "Relativism and Wide Reflective Equilibrium," *Monist* 76 (1993): 316–32.

49. Revisions of our theory over the different editions of this book have benefited from the criticisms of Ruth Faden, Oliver Rauprich, John Arras, Norman Daniels, Bernard Gert, Dan Clouser, Rebecca Kukla, Carson Strong, Albert Jonsen, Earl Winkler, Frank Chessa, Robert Veatch, David DeGrazia, Ronald Lindsay, Avi Craimer, and others.

50. See especially Rebecca Kukla, "Living with Pirates: Common Morality and Embodied Practice," *Cambridge Quarterly of Healthcare Ethics,* forthcoming. Gert and Clouser have long presented this thesis.

51.   We have been criticized for an incautious formulation of this point in our sixth edition by Jan Reinert Karlsen and Jan Helge Solbakk, "A Waste of Time: The Problem of Common Morality in Principles of Biomedical Ethics," *Journal of Medical Ethics* 37 (2011): 588–91.

52.   Gert, *Morality: Its Nature and Justification,* pp. 114–15; and Gert, Culver, and Clouser, *Bioethics: A Systematic Approach,* p. 104. See also the gloss in Gert, Culver, and Clouser, "Common Morality versus Specified Principlism: Reply to Richardson," pp. 310, 316.

53.   We are indebted in this formulation to Ronald A. Lindsay, "Slaves, Embryos, and Nonhuman Animals: Moral Status and the Limitations of Common Morality Theory," *Kennedy Institute of Ethics Journal* 15 (December 2005): 323–46.

54.   For sources that make such a claim, and the unlikely character of the claim, see Peter Herissone-Kelly, "The Principlist Approach to Bioethics, and Its Stormy Journey Overseas," in *Scratching the Surface of Bioethics,* ed. Matti Häyry and Tuija Takala (Amsterdam: Rodopi, 2003), pp. 65–77, esp. 66. See also Ronald A. Lindsay, "Bioethics Policies and the Compass of Common Morality," *Theoretical Medicine and Bioethics* 30 (2009), first section; Rebecca Kukla, "Living with Pirates"; and William T. Branch, "Is Rorty's Neopragmatism the 'Real' Foundation of Medical Ethics: A Search for Foundations," *Transactions of the American Clinical and Climatological Association* 117 (2006): 257–71. We profited from these criticisms and have attempted to remove some of the unclarities to which they point.

55.   See Leigh Turner, "Zones of Consensus and Zones of Conflict: Questioning the 'Common Morality' Presumption in Bioethics," *Kennedy Institute of Ethics Journal* 13 (2003), 193–218; Donald C. Ainslie, "Bioethics and the Problem of Pluralism," *Social Philosophy and Policy* 19 (2002): 1–28; Carson Strong, "Exploring Questions about Common Morality," *Theoretical Medicine and Bioethics* 30 (2009): 1–9; and DeGrazia, "Common Morality, Coherence, and the Principles of Biomedical Ethics."

56.   When we say that some persons are not committed to morality, we do not mean that they are not dedicated to a way of life that they consider a moral way of life or that anthropologists would say they are not committed to morality. Religious fanatics and political zealots have this self-conception even as they act against or neglect the demands of the common morality.

57.   If the selected group shares the norms, this supports the idea of a common morality, but it is not conclusive. For a conclusive confirmation one would need to investigate all persons committed to a moral way of life, which is not feasible. Thus, there remains an issue of what would constitute sufficient evidence.

58.   Gert, "The Definition of Morality" (italics added).

59.   Gert, *Common Morality: Deciding What to Do,* p. 84.

60.   Gert, Morality: Its Nature and Justification, pp. 29–33, 39–41, 181.

61.   Tom L. Beauchamp, "A Defense of the Common Morality," *Kennedy Institute of Ethics Journal* 13 (2003): 259–74; Oliver Rauprich, "Common Morality: Comment on Beauchamp and Childress," *Theoretical Medicine and Bioethics* 29 (2008): 43–71, at 68; and K. A. Wallace, "Common Morality and Moral Reform," *Theoretical Medicine and Bioethics* 30 (2009): 55–68.

62.   Revision of the account in this section has benefited from published criticisms by and private conversations with Peter Herissone-Kelly, Bernard Gert, and Rebecca Kukla. Herissone-Kelly appropriately, and constructively, criticized us in his original work on the subject, "The Principlist Approach to Bioethics."

63.   Foot, *Moral Dilemmas* (Oxford: Oxford University Press, 2002), pp. 6–7. Peter Herissone-Kelly directed us to this passage; see his use of it in "Determining the Common Morality's Norms in the

Sixth Edition of *Principles of Biomedical Ethics*," *Journal of Medical Ethics* 37 (2011): 584–87, at 584.

64.   For a defense of this distinction between the descriptive and the normative, see Gert's "The Definition of Morality."

65.   See Chapter 1, p. 3, on central virtues ("ten examples of *moral character traits,* or virtues, recognized in the common morality").

66.   Philosophers who attempt to analyze the concept of morality exhaustively in terms of formal (nonsubstantive) conditions miss what is morally most important in the concept. Examples of these approaches are theories that analyze morality as composed of (1) norms that are regarded as supremely authoritative and of overriding social importance, (2) norms that are prescriptive in form (i.e., action-guiding imperatives that do not describe states of affairs), or (3) norms that harmonize pro and con interests. By design, these accounts do not address whether there is a specific normative content that is privileged and constitutive of morality.

67.   Cf. Gert's similar view in "The Definition of Morality."

68.   See Annette Baier, *Postures of the Mind* (Minneapolis: University of Minnesota Press, 1985), pp. 139–41, 206–17, 223–26, 232–37.

INDEX